FUNDAMENTAL ISSUES IN STRATEGY

12

FUNDAMENTAL ISSUES IN STRATEGY

A Research Agenda

Edited by
Richard P. Rumelt
Dan E. Schendel
David J. Teece

HARVARD BUSINESS SCHOOL PRESS
Boston, Massachusetts

Published by the Harvard Business
School Press in hardcover, 1994;
in paperback, 1995

02 01 00 99 98   13 12 11 10 9 8 7 6 (pbk)

Library of Congress Cataloging-in-Publication Data

Fundamental issues in strategy : a research agenda / edited
by Richard P. Rumelt, Dan E. Schendel, David J. Teece.
    p. cm.
    Includes bibliographical references and index.
    ISBN 0-87584-343-3 (acid-free paper) (hc)
    ISBN 0-87584-645-9 (pbk)
    1. Strategic planning. I. Rumelt, Richard P.
II. Schendel, Dan E. III. Teece, David J.
HD30.28.F86 1994
658.4'012—dc20   93-38541
                                                  CIP

The paper used in this publication meets the requirements of the
American National Standard for Permanence of Paper for Printed
Library Materials Z39.49-1984.

Contents

Acknowledgments

No book is possible without the help of many contributors, those in proximity to and in direct support of the immediate work, and those whose contributions preceded the work and provided its foundations. For a book with as many direct contributors as this one has, those in proximity are many, and those whose work provided the foundations are even more numerous.

The authors, who responded to our invitation to address fundamental questions we had defined, came to the challenge with a perspective of disciplines other than strategic management. We owe them a considerable debt for their work and for their willingness to respond so constructively to what must have seemed to them unreasonable requests on their professional life and unwarranted inroads upon their discretionary time. Of course, we always needed it "tomorrow" and asked to receive it "yesterday." Truly, their hard work and contributions have made this book possible. Without them, the perspectives offered would not be as varied, as interesting, or as challenging as we believe them to be. We hope you will agree with our assessment, and that you will express your appreciation when you have the chance, either directly by a note or in person, or by accepting the many invitations embedded in their work to contribute to our accumulating knowledge. Only through your further work will we find more complete answers to the fundamental questions posed here.

The disciplines from which the authors proceeded are worth noting, not by repeating their nomenclature, but by recognizing the contributions they have made possible. There is no thanking something as impersonal as a discipline perhaps, but there is a need to recognize the many scholars whose work accumulates over many years to build the foundations on which such disciplines rest. As you will discover, we don't always see the basic discipline making direct or even positive contributions to addressing the fundamental questions we pose. But we have found that varied discipline perspectives offer invaluable insight in answering questions as fundamental as ours. To those in economics, sociology, political science, and the other disciplines represented in this volume, we express our appreciation for their contributions. Without them, this volume would be much less rich in content than it is.

Those who supported this work need to be recognized as well. The interaction of the authors and special participants at a conference held in Napa, California, November 29–December 1, 1990, made a strong contribution to this volume. This conference was special because of the opportunity and ambience it provided for the exchange of views among more than 60 participants interested in the field and its development.

Institutions that supported the conference and commissioned works that appear include the John M. Olin Foundation, the UCLA Center for International Business Education and Research (CIBER), and the Anderson Graduate School of Management, all of the University of California, Los Angeles. The Sloan Foundation, through its "Consortium on Competitiveness and Cooperation," provided substantial help, as did the University of California, Berkeley, particularly its Haas School of Business. The Strategic Management Society provided support, as did the Krannert Graduate School of Management at Purdue University.

Individuals who supported this volume are many. The work of Kendall Artz especially, and Sam Florance, Michael Leiblein, and other doctoral students at the Krannert Graduate School of Management, who helped in checking references and proofreading, all have our thanks. To our editors at the Harvard Business School Press also go our thanks for the many improvements made in the presentation you read here. And finally, to all our colleagues working in the field of strategic management, our thanks for your encouragement and our appreciation for your patience.

It is customary to end acknowledgments absolving all but the editors for any errors. We are no different and no more original in asking for this necessary absolution. We all make errors—in fact, in judgment, in omissions, and in many other ways. We are certain we commit these transgressions here, but we do hope that the collective contributions offered far outweigh the errors. Ultimately you are the judge. We rely on your kindness.

RICHARD P. RUMELT
DAN E. SCHENDEL
DAVID J. TEECE

Preface

We believe strategic management is one of the most exciting areas of inquiry within the social sciences. Its subject matter—the purposeful direction and natural evolution of enterprises—is central to the working of our civilization. Its audience—general managers, consultants, and students in professional schools of management—is alert, demanding, and appreciative of useful contributions. Its intellectual foundations—drawn from microeconomics, cognitive psychology, organizational sociology, and political science—are in fields that are themselves in fascinating ferment. Its strong pragmatic bias—management practice continues to rely chiefly on a base of experience rather than on causal and predictive theory—provides freshness and some protection against the retreat into tautology that infects so much of the academy.

This book is about strategic management's intellectual backbone. It grew out of the editors' shared interest in examining strategic management's intellectual roots and in extending and strengthening its theoretical foundations. In particular, we believe the time is ripe for strategy scholars to redefine the field in terms of fundamental questions rather than in terms of techniques, empirical methods, "conceptual schemes," or even the perspective of purely discipline-based theories. We believe that by centering on the right substantive questions, we can build a place to stand that will allow a strategy scholar to borrow the power of underlying base disciplines without being defined as being in that discipline, or vice versa. We also hope these questions and perspectives will appeal to discipline-based scholars, especially those who are uncomfortable with their discipline's blinders and conventional wisdom, and encourage them to cross over and see themselves as members of the strategy field.

Our specific goals are to affect the field by: (1) encouraging a focus on the fundamental questions that lie at its center; (2) calling for a significant increase in the sophistication, rigor, and scholarly quality of policy or strategy research; (3) demonstrating a fruitful interaction between strategy researchers and discipline-based scholars; and (4) showing the potential of the intersection of basic disciplines and strategy for gaining new insights that will ultimately pay off in improving management practice and organizational performance.

Acting on our convictions and goals, we designed a conference that would bring scholars from the basic social science disciplines together with strategy researchers. Twenty-five scholars were invited to present their thinking on individual questions assigned to them. Another 35 scholars attended the conference and participated in the commentary and discussion. Most of the material in this volume was presented at the conference or developed in response to it.

Some will argue that our interest in theory and foundations is misplaced, noting that management is an art, resists systematic analysis, and involves a great deal of luck. We are very sympathetic to this view. Indeed, it is now understood that under conditions of ambiguity, uncertainty, complexity, opportunism, and change, it is to be expected that much knowledge will be tacit, that decisions will not be based on deductive logic but will instead derive from hard-won rules of thumb and skilled routines, and that excellence will resist analysis and imitation. However, these same conditions also encourage superstitious learning, the acceptance of fads, and resistance to change. Thus, the conditions that make analysis difficult also act to undermine one's confidence in using current practice as a guide. The normal response to ambiguity may be retreat to the use of metaphor and displaced routine, but the scholar's duty should be to attack the ambiguity and attempt to reduce it. The book's premise is that there is nothing (ultimately) so practical as good theory in solving managerial problems.

We are fully aware that this book will distress some colleagues who see our expedition into different disciplines as unwise and, perhaps, disloyal. And we know that other readers will not find any direct relevance to practice. We also understand that what we have assembled here is not easy to comprehend without appropriate background and experience. Bear with us and we hope to convince you that fundamental questions are worth pursuing, even though they may not yield definitive answers.

Los Angeles, California	Richard P. Rumelt
West Lafayette, Indiana	Dan E. Schendel
Berkeley, California	David J. Teece

Introduction: Structure of the Book

At any given moment a field of inquiry's frontier can be defined by a set of fundamental issues or questions. The relatively young field of strategic management is no different, and so this book is, as its title suggests, about a set of fundamental issues presently facing the field. If the issues raised here could be resolved, or if substantial progress toward their resolution were shown, the field would reach a new level; the understanding of practice would be improved, and even deeper issues would undoubtedly be raised for research. Our objective is to give focus to these crucial issues and increase the attention they receive.

Kuhn (1962), in his well-known treatise on how science progresses, offered the notion that fields develop through paradigm shifts, intermixed with periods of "normal science," during which the implications of the paradigm are explored. Indeed, announcements of new paradigms and calls for agreement on a paradigm have been frequent in this field, but the reality is that no such agreement exists. In Kuhnian terms, perhaps strategic management is pre-paradigmatic. However, our message here is that the Kuhnian model of science may not be the best way to think about the state of strategic management, or to assess its progress. As an interdisciplinary subject, strategic management may never enter an era of "normal science," but will probably always offer shifting perspectives and relatively incommensurable research approaches.

What will most benefit strategic management, we suggest, is not a unifying paradigm, but the articulation of the fundamental issues underlying the field and a refocusing of research to confront them. These issues have implications for practice, teaching, and research, and, if resolved, could contribute enormously to the effort to manage complex organizations more efficiently and effectively.

1

The Four Questions

This book develops four fundamental issues posed in the form of questions we have about business firms and other organizations. The four questions help define the field of strategic management—its boundaries as they exist today, its concerns, and how it can make contributions to the practice of management. These same questions helped us to structure a conference of scholars working with theory relevant to the field. The questions are:

- How do firms behave?
- Why are firms different?
- What is the function of, or value added by, the headquarters unit in a multibusiness firm?
- What determines the success or failure of the firm in international competition?

Although these questions will be developed in greater detail in later chapters, some words about their significance are warranted here.

How Do Firms Behave?

The most basic differences among discipline-based views of the firm, and of management, stem from assumptions about behavior. Indeed, much of the modern stream of thinking about management has its origins in the Carnegie School's "behavioral" model of the firm, a bold rejection of economists' deeply held presumption of individual and collective rationality. Yet, with new models of strategic behavior under conditions of asymmetric information and uncertainty, economics has reasserted its claim to be able to model virtually all important phenomena as outcomes of rational action. Do we need a nonrational model of the firm? What phenomena cannot be adequately dealt with by rational models? Can we find or develop models of nonrational behavior that can make useful predictions?

Why Are Firms Different?

In the neoclassical theory of the firm, competition acts to homogenize firms. Opportunities that produce profit are sought by others, and inputs and skills that are used to advantage are bid up in price or imitated. Thus, the classical picture of an industry was that of a group of firms, homogeneous except for scale. Following a different road, organizational theorists, seeking to break away from the "one best way" of the classical management writers, linked structure to environment. Thus, neither discipline had any place for the existence of sustained heterogeneity within an industry. But "strategy" as a teaching concept first developed from the observation that firms within the same industry often competed in very different ways. What sustains this heterogeneity? Is it imperfect factor markets? Is it causal ambiguity? Is it a fine-structure of niches? Is it groups that enact the same environment in different ways? Is it differential learning, or organizational culture? Is it the embodiment of alternative purposes? This question places strategy at the forefront and sharpens its clash with many of its associated disciplines. Progress in answering this question will not only clarify theory, it may help firms create and sustain valuable differences and provide clues as to how management practice and structure should vary with differences in strategy.

What Is the Function of, or Value Added by, the Headquarters Unit in a Multibusiness Firm?

The development of multidivisional, multibusiness firms has been a central research subject within strategic management, "belonging" more to it than to any allied discipline. In such organizations there is a level of management activity that deals with integrating the various divisions or businesses that make up the firm. We call that level of responsibility the headquarters unit and ask what its role is and what value it contributes. Some complain no value is contributed, and yet in competitive systems that cannot be so. How then is value contributed? What is its nature? What can headquarters-level management do to create such value?

What Determines the Success or Failure of the Firm in International Competition?

One of the strongest trends in business today is that toward the globalization of markets and industries. In addition, one of the most striking events of the past two decades has been the rise of enormously successful, globally oriented, technology-based firms in Japan. If a field is to be driven by phenomena, rather than by theory, these phenomena are clearly of paramount importance. We suggest that the fundamental question that needs to be asked is whether success and survival at the global level is a different matter than at the national or some lesser geographic level. Are successful global firms simply more "efficient" than their competitors, or are there other mechanisms at work? This question forces us to look beyond the competitiveness of an enterprise and ask where competitive enterprises themselves come from. And, how do they sustain themselves over time? Competitiveness is at the heart of strategic management, so this final question in many respects overarches the others.

Structure of the Book

Much of the work appearing in this volume derives from a conference held in late 1990.[1] To enlist the aid of underlying social science disciplines, scholars from strategic management and its allied disciplines were invited to prepare papers and discuss the fundamental questions. This book is not a proceedings, or a record of the conference itself, although the conference was an important contributor to this book's contents. The book is rather the result of a process intended to explore the issues reflected in the questions we posed. The process involved paper preparation, discussion of the papers, revision, and the preparation of the editors' remarks.

To accomplish its purpose the book is divided into six major sections. The first is the editors' introduction, which contains three subsections: (1) a history of the strategic management field, which is intended to illustrate the fundamental nature of the questions posed; (2) developments in allied or related social science disciplines which have made, and will continue to make, contributions to answering the questions; and (3) the role of fundamental questions in the development of the strategy field.

The next four sections of the book deal with the fundamental questions themselves. Each section will contain an editor's brief

---

[1] "Fundamental Issues in Strategy: A Research Agenda for the 1990s," Silverado, Napa Valley, California, November 29–December 1, 1990. Organized by Richard P. Rumelt, Dan E. Schendel, and David J. Teece.

guide to the authors and their papers, the papers themselves, all as they were revised, some substantially, following the conference.

The final section of the book contains two subsections. The first treats potentially fundamental questions not otherwise addressed in the book. One of these is the "policy process" question, which was part of the conference but which we chose not to include in the book. Another is the central problem of organizational inertia. The second subsection focuses on the role of economics in strategic management. This subject was singled out for attention because economic theory has rapidly become a major contributor to the field, and to some, represents a tradition that is hostile to alternative viewpoints.

Two appendices are included. Appendix A contains a statement prepared by the editors and the hosts of the conference for the attendees. This statement catalyzed the arguments and insights we gather in this volume. The value of reproducing the statement is that it represents something of a "Before" and the book the "After." Appendix B contains a listing of the attendees at the conference and to them must go credit for whatever contributions are made in this book.

What Will Be Gained from Reading This Book?

Why should anyone read this book? What can be gained from it? We expect that readers who bring a sufficient background to the book—practicing executives, professional managers, public policy makers, students beyond the first course in strategy, and certainly research workers in the field—will find the questions that provide the central architecture for the book are relevant to problems they face in their work. The questions can be related to many practical details of managing the firm, and to most substantive aspects of research in the field.

The book offers readers a broader perspective on very practical problems. Suppose you are responsible for managing a firm. Your first charge is to keep the firm alive and economically healthy, and to make a profit. How do firms make profit? Is it through luck or skill? And if skill is involved, what skills? There are many books available that provide lists of proper skills and even attitudes; consultants are constantly coming up with "the answer" and the case du jour that tells just how to do it. But do they really? Do they provide convincing, enduring evidence, anything more than an anecdote, or an example carefully chosen? This book seeks to identify differences that matter, differences that persist, and to explain why these differences matter from a theoretical perspective capable of empirical verification.

In this book we offer no cases for emulation, no lists of things to do, no recipes for success. None appear to exist. What is offered are high-quality theories capable of explaining some phenomena central to strategic management practice and research interests. Not all the theories have been formally tested, but all are capable of scientific investigation and of being tested in ways that can be replicated.

Those who see the search for truth as a clash of views, constrained by the discipline of logic based on premises and identifiable assumptions, can gain much from this book. The authors here are not singing a hymn in unison, or even in harmony, but each is a skillful and practiced singer. You will find attacks on conventional wisdom, intellectual turf claimed, defended, and, perhaps, lost. At the center of the contest is the rationale for strategic management and its appropriate scope. According to many well-developed doctrines, strategic management as a field should not exist, it should not even be necessary. The problems with which it deals are not real, or should not be real. Yet the problems are there and the field exists. If you would like to know more about why this is so, you will benefit from reading this book.

This will not be an easy book to read. It assumes certain levels of preparation and experience. In fact, for understanding it requires such background. We make no apologies for that and direct those in search of *The One-Minute Guide to the Intellectual Foundations of Strategy* to look elsewhere. Questions to which there are ready answers are never fundamental.

Who Can Benefit from Reading This Book?

The readers we seek, then, include curious professionals with an inclination to question conventional answers, with the experience and insight to know that the latest executive alphabet soup provides no lasting answers to their challenges. Professional managers and consultants know there are no easy answers, researchers know there are no easy pickings left if there ever were any. Those who are prepared by experience and training to understand the underlying disciplines discussed here, who understand the controversies that exist within those disciplines, and who realize that the challenges facing business firms are complex will find help in this volume. For those who realize that science is not a field but a way of thinking about problems, evidence, and solutions, there is much to ponder in this book. Readers will realize that management scientists, in the broad sense of that term, are offering their work. The reader who is trained and inclined to think like a scientist will benefit.

We also look to students and scholars in the field. Some are teachers, some are researchers, and some are in training to be one or the other, or to be practitioners. To teachers this volume is a call to transmit honestly what we know and what we don't know about the field of strategic management. We know less than we try to teach, and many teachers contribute to myths of management, and consequently, to the economic and managerial failures that are induced by the false sense of security given by unproven but easy answers, unsupported assertions, and ideas that are just plain wrong.

We beg the students to be skeptical, to always ask the deeper question, to always pursue the logic contained in the answer. If you can do that, you will understand the spirit of this volume and gain whatever substance it has to offer. The book should take you to the frontiers of the field and show you the issues that are under examination and why they are important.

In the end we are all students. Our attention should focus on what we don't know, and we should be concerned that we don't know enough. What we don't know restricts our opportunities to build and prosper. What we think we understand but really don't, leads us to mistakes, to uncompensated risk, and to failure, for our firms, for ourselves, and in the end, for society.

1
Fundamental Issues in Strategy

Richard P. Rumelt, Dan E. Schendel and David J. Teece

History of Strategic Management

Strategic management, often called "policy" or nowadays simply "strategy," is about the direction of organizations, and most often, business firms. It includes those subjects of primary concern to senior management, or to anyone seeking reasons for success and failure among organizations. Firms, if not all organizations, are in competition—competition for factor inputs, competition for customers, and ultimately, competition for revenues that cover the costs of their chosen manner of surviving. Because of competition, firms have choices to make if they are to survive. Those that are *strategic* include: the selection of goals; the choice of products and services to offer; the design and configuration of policies determining how the firm positions itself to compete in product markets (e.g., competitive strategy); the choice of an appropriate level of scope and diversity; and the design of organization structure, administrative systems, and policies used to define and coordinate work. It is a basic proposition of the strategy field that these choices have critical influence on the success or failure of the enterprise, and that they must be integrated. It is the integration (or reinforcing pattern) among these choices that makes the set a strategy.

Strategic management as a field of inquiry is firmly grounded in practice and exists because of the importance of its subject. The strategic direction of business organizations is at the heart of wealth creation in modern industrial society. The field has not, like political science, grown from ancient roots in philosophy, nor does it, like parts of economics, attract scholars because of the elegance of its theoretical underpinnings. Rather, like medicine or engineering, it exists because it is worthwhile to codify, teach, and expand what is known about the skilled performance of roles and tasks that are a necessary part of our civilization. While its origins lie in practice and codification, its advancement as a field increasingly depends upon building theory that helps explain and predict organizational success and failure.

Strategic management as an academic field is much younger than its actual practice. While its date of conception (not to mention parentage) is somewhat uncertain, the academic field of strategic management is certainly a child of the 1960s. As such, it is now entering upon its "thirty-something" decade, a time of self-examination and of coming into its own. The premise of this book, and of the conference which preceded it, is that academic strategic management is indeed ready to come into its own, through the identification and clarification of the fundamental issues of scientific interest that distinguish it as a field of scholarly inquiry.

As an introduction to those fundamental issues, we briefly review the history of the academic field. If the child is indeed father to the man, a look back will help put the fundamental issues we identify into perspective, provide context, and clarify terms.

The Business Policy Course and Faculty

Strategic management, as a field of study, originated as a teaching area in business schools. The first business school, The Wharton School, was established at the University of Pennsylvania over 100 years ago. Harvard established its school some years later, but soon assumed a leadership role in business education. As far as can be determined, it was at Harvard that the first business policy course was taught.

The Harvard curriculum was built out of so-called functional courses, corresponding to business functions like accounting, marketing, and manufacturing. The policy course "integrated" what the student had learned in the functional courses, serving as a capstone to the core curriculum. True to Harvard tradition, the case method was employed. The course was not burdened with teaching substantive mechanisms of achieving integration—it simply presented administrative problems faced by senior executives that naturally required a multifunctional perspective.

Harvard served as an important model for other business and management schools, leading many to imitate its design. Business policy as a capstone course became a standard part of the curriculum across the United States. Indeed, today, the Association of American Collegiate Schools of Business (AACSB) includes instruction in business policy among its guideline requirements for accreditation. Tellingly, though, the AACSB has left "business policy" open to very broad interpretation.

As an integrative capstone course, business policy may have had some measure of prestige, but it had no prescribed content. No received theory grounded in the professional norms of a business function, or in the basic disciplines of the social sciences, needed to be taught. Historically, the course was often staffed by full professors, experienced teachers thought to have developed a broad view of business, or by adjunct professors, often former general managers with the wisdom of experience to transmit. With no theory to teach, any discipline or experience base seemed satisfactory, and indeed, eclecticism and a holistic view were valued.

Relegation of strategic management to a capstone course in business policy had serious structural consequences for the development of strategic management as a scholarly field of inquiry, however, and probably stifled its emergence for many years. A single, capstone course permitted no development of follow-on courses, and in turn limited the scope for expanding consideration of the subject. Since the teachers used to staff the course were either already full professors or were adjunct teachers without hope of tenure or interest in full rank, there was no evolutionary career path from assistant to full professor. The career paths to tenure and advanced rank remained in functional areas of business (e.g., marketing, finance) or in the traditional social science disciplines (e.g., economics, organization theory).

Faculty for the business policy course made their intellectual homes elsewhere. If serious research was done, it was done for the basic disciplines in which faculty members were trained. Moreover, the acceptability of using senior faculty members from a variety of disciplines often meant, as a practical matter, that the business policy course became something of a burying ground for academic white elephants long in the tusk but short on remaining research potential.

Some work had to be done, of course, to support course development. This scholarship tended to result in cases and notes of value to teaching, not articles and books of interest to other researchers, and it generated little theory or academic debate. One of the positive legacies of this practice, however, was extensive institutional knowledge and rich general descriptions of practice as observed from case writing and consulting.

In important respects, the field of strategic management only began to develop in terms of research accumulation in the early 1970s. It was then that the first faculty were hired as "policy" teachers, as pioneers expected to find their way up the promotion system to gain tenure in their own field, that of strategic management, by developing research records. Then the questioning of constructs and attention to tools and techniques of scientific research began in earnest. Then, too, professional associations and journals began to be needed.

Journals and Professional Societies

Any field develops around an infrastructure of journals and professional meetings, through which results are argued and disseminated. Initially, strategic management took advantage of the infrastructure built in the 1950s and 1960s to accommodate the increased interest in business and administrative organization. Before 1970, there were no distinct professional societies or publications devoted to the field.

The early history of strategic management showed remarkable interest in "planning," and although it proved short-lived, enthusiasm for planning dominated strategic management in the late 1960s and early 1970s. Consequently, some of the earliest efforts to organize societies and publications centered on planning per se. The Institute of Management Sciences developed a College on Planning, which attracted a small band of workers interested in formal models of the firm useful for planning long-range operation of organizations. The college did not flourish and was ultimately abandoned. The Planning Executives Institute (PEI) devoted its energy to budgeting and short-term financial planning, and was not truly interested in strategy concepts. PEI later was to combine with a practitioner group, the North American Society of Corporate Planners, to form The Planning Forum, which continues to operate throughout North America. Planning societies devoted to improving the state of practice for professional planners formed in various countries in Europe and elsewhere. Some, such as the Strategic Planning Society of the United Kingdom, are quite large.

Publications like *Long Range Planning* and *The Planning Review* were among the early outlets for work in strategy. Early work in strategy also found its way into general management journals such as the *Harvard Business Review, Sloan Management Review, Journal of Business, Business Horizons,* and *California Management Review.* Academic journals devoted to management topics, such as *Administrative Science Quarterly, Academy of Management Journal,* and *Management Science,* also provided important opportunities to publish scholarly research.

About 1969, the Academy of Management elected to form professional divisions to better reflect the specialized interests of its members. One of the first divisions formed, in 1971, was the Business Policy and Planning Division, since renamed the Business Policy and Strategy Division to reflect the ascendance of strategy concepts and the decline of planning. The division became an important base of support for the establishment of tenure-track strategy faculty.

Although interest in planning per se fell off, the number of practitioners and academics interested in topics of strategic management grew steadily through the 1970s. The growth of interest and support was reflected in the 1980s in the formation of societies and publications specialized to strategic management. In 1980, two journals devoted exclusively to strategy commenced publication: the *Strategic Management Journal (SMJ)* and the *Journal of Business Strategy,* the former oriented to academic research and the latter to practice. Both flourished, and *SMJ* rapidly became the leading research journal in the field, as reported in the Social Science Citation Index.

Also in the early 1980s, the Strategic Management Society was formed as an organization of practitioners, consultants, and academics interested in developing the field. Unlike predecessor organizations, it held international meetings and tried to attract members from all over the world. With members from about 50 countries, it sponsors meetings around the world and a publication (*SMJ*) devoted to advancing scholarship in the field.

The Development of Strategy Theory and Research

Precursors. The prehistory of strategic management as an academic field lies in studies of economic organization and bureaucracy. The vigorous interaction with economics and the study of organization, which characterizes the field today, reflects its origins in these disciplines. Work in a wide variety of areas contributed to a single task vital to the emergence of strategic management: preparing the ground for concepts of strategy.

Mainstream economic theory—price theory—has traditionally ignored the role of managers and left little scope for strategic choice in economic affairs. From the time of Adam Smith down to the present day, economists have sought to show that a completely decentralized economic system, coordinated only through market prices, could and would be efficient. Little attention has been given to why private firms might make use of managerial hierarchies to plan and coordinate. Institutional settings and arrangements have been largely abstracted away. The varied character and capabilities of actual business organizations have not been considered. The firm of economic theory observes market prices and then makes an efficient choice of output quantities; all firms are essentially alike, having the same access to information and technology, and the decisions they make are essentially rational and predictable, virtually compelled by cost and demand conditions.

While conventional economic theory did not recognize most of the choices open to managers of firms, work in a wide variety of areas—more than can be cited here—served to establish a basis for studying the role of management and the possibilities for strategic choices, before strategic management began to emerge as a field of study.

In the mid-twentieth century Taylor (1947) initiated a "science of work" in an organizational setting, beginning the effort to understand what economists might call "technical efficiency" or "x-efficiency." Taylor's enduring contribution was the conviction, and demonstration, that "natural" practices could be improved through careful observation and analysis.

Barnard (1938) elevated the analysis of organizational work from Taylor's shop floor to the executive ranks in his classic work, *Functions of the Executive.* He stressed the difference between managerial work directed at making the organization efficient, and work that made the organization effective, a distinction critical to the concept of strategy. Simon (1947) extended Barnard's ideas in his attempt to build a framework for analyzing administration. Selznick (1957) explored the roles of institutional commitment and introduced the idea of an organization's "distinctive competence."

The difficult economic conditions of the 1930s raised many questions about capitalism and the real efficiency of business. During this period, theories of imperfect competition were developed by Robinson ([1933] 1959) and Chamberlin (1933). Schumpeter's (1934) innovative entrepreneur and agent of creative destruction provided an alternative to the static concept of competitive efficiency favored by most economists. Later, Frank Knight's (1965) work on the risk-bearing function of entrepreneurs laid an early foundation for much of what we now call organizational economics.

Despite the increasing interest in business organization from the turn of the century on, there was no sustained debate about business strategy and its role in the success of firms. The founder of McKinsey & Co. evidently wrote about strategy in the 1930s. Newman (1951) used the concept of strategy to differentiate certain important work of the manager from the day-to-day work of running an organization. However, it was not until the 1960s that a field of interest could be seen forming.

1960s: Birth. The birth of strategic management in the 1960s took place against a background of tremendous ferment in organization theory. Universalistic principles and maxims of administration were being overthrown in favor of concepts of contingent design. March and Simon (1958) had developed the cybernetic or information-processing metaphor for management structure. Cyert and March (1963) had laid out a behavioral theory of the firm. Open systems theories and approaches, which tended to suggest that organizations were somewhat akin to organisms in a natural environment, had a major influence. Burns and Stalker (1961) contrasted organic and mechanistic types of management organization. Woodward (1965) showed how production process technology influenced organizational structure. Thompson (1967), in a bold, propositional inventory, and Lawrence and Lorsch (1967), in a more empirical work, proposed that managerial organization was contingent on "environmental uncertainty." The 1960s were a propitious time to introduce concepts of strategic adaptation by organizations.

The birth of the field of strategic management can be traced to three works of the 1960s: Alfred Chandler's *Strategy and Structure* (1962); Igor Ansoff's *Corporate Strategy* (1965); and the Harvard textbook, *Business Policy: Text and Cases* (Learned et al., 1965), the declarative text of which is attributed to Kenneth Andrews.

The foundation of strategic management as a field may very well be traced to the 1962 publication of Chandler's *Strategy and Structure*. Chandler's seminal book, subtitled "Chapters in the History of the Industrial Enterprise," was about the growth of large businesses and explored how their administrative structures had been adapted to accommodate that growth. In the process of telling the story of growth and administrative change at General Motors, Sears, Standard Oil of New Jersey (Exxon), and DuPont, Chandler showed how executives at these companies discovered and developed roles for themselves in making long-term decisions about the direction of their enterprises and then made investments and modified organizational structure to make those strategies work. A compelling and fascinating story of economic innovation, organizational behavior, and managerial achievement, it naturally attracted much interest and attention. Most important for the field, Chandler showed executives doing strategic management work and achieving remarkable performance outcomes. Moreover, he showed a process of administrative change within organizations that involved shifts in strategic direction, rather than adjustments for simple efficiency.

In formulating a thesis to summarize his findings, Chandler found it convenient to define two terms, strategy and structure:

> The thesis that different organization forms result from different types of growth can be stated more precisely if the planning and carrying out of such growth is considered a strategy, and the organization devised to administer these enlarged activities and resources, a structure. Strategy can be defined as the determination of the basic long-term goals and objectives of an enterprise, and the adoption of courses of action and the allocation of resources necessary for carrying out these goals. (pp. 15–16)

The concept of strategy used by Chandler was a handy way of characterizing the relationship among a set of managerial purposes and choices, and was explicitly distinct from a structure.

Andrews, in his text for Business Policy, accepted the strategy idea from Chandler, but added Selznick's "distinctive competence" and the notion of an uncertain environment to which management and the firm had to adapt. In Andrews's view, the environment, through constant change, gave rise to opportunities and threats, and the organization's strengths and weaknesses were adapted to avoid the threats and take advantage of the opportunities. An internal appraisal of strengths and weaknesses led to identification of distinctive competencies; an external appraisal of environmental threats and opportunities led to identification of potential success factors. These twin appraisals were the foundation for strategy formulation, a process analytically (if not practically) distinct from strategy implementation. Andrews conceived of strategy as akin to identity, defining it as "the pattern of objectives, purposes, or goals and major policies and plans for achieving these goals, stated in such a way as to define what business the company is in or is to be in and the kind of company it is or is to be" (p. 15). Andrews considered it a "matter of indifference" whether to include selection of goals as well as the deployment of resources in pursuit of goals as part of strategy. He regarded strategy formulation as "analytically objective," while implementation was "primarily administrative."

H. Igor Ansoff was general manager of the Lockheed Electronics Company (New Jersey) and developed his strategy concepts out of frustration with planning as the naive extrapolation of past trends. Ansoff was more explicitly interested in understanding what was meant by "strategy" and took some care to develop his ideas. He accepted that the objective for the firm ought to be to maximize economic return, which he distinguished from accounting return. For Ansoff, strategy provided a "common thread" for five component choices: (1) product-market scope; (2) growth vector (the direction in which scope was changing, e.g., the emphasis on old versus new products or markets); (3) competitive advantage (unique opportunities in terms of product or market attributes); (4) synergy internally generated by a combination of capabilities or competencies; and (5) the make or buy decision. In tracing this common thread of strategy through its components, Ansoff emphasized the potential for success arising from mutual reinforcement among the components.

In retrospect, it seems that Ansoff was more interested in what we would today call *corporate* strategy, while Andrews was more focused on *business* strategy. Ansoff's more elaborate analysis of the *concept* of strategy was also reflected in a more elaborate view of the *process* of creating strategy, a difference in emphasis that promoted the cause of strategic planning. Both Ansoff and Andrews, however, had gone beyond the traditional Business Policy course metaphor of functional integration.

These three authors—Chandler, Andrews, and Ansoff—gave first form to the basic concepts of strategic management. Nearly all of the ideas and issues that concern us today can be found in at least embryonic form in these key writings of the 1960s. It should be acknowledged, though, that their audience was primarily students and professors. None of these three authors directly and immediately influenced practice. Many of the changes in practice that occurred by the late 1960s can instead be traced to the influence of consulting firms. Leadership in this arena was provided by the exemplar of strategy consulting firms, The Boston Consulting Group.

Founded by Bruce Henderson in the mid-1960s, The Boston Consulting Group (BCG) had a major impact on the strategy field. Although a great deal of BCG's practice consisted of "segmentation studies" which simply reanalyzed cost and profit data using economic concepts rather than accounting measures, BCG became best known for its two related conceptual inventions: the experience curve, and the growth-share matrix. In brief, experience curve theory maintained that whoever captured market share early, whoever gained the most experience in production would end up with the lowest cost (assuming efficient operational management practice), and whoever had the lowest cost would have the highest margin. With the highest margin came cash flow and an ability to withstand competition and whatever actions it required. Within a few years, such reasoning led to the growth-share matrix, whose terminology of cash cows, dogs, stars, and question marks became famous and widely used.

The rapid expansion of the firm, successful spin-offs like Bain, and imitation by old-line rivals like McKinsey, attests to the influence that BCG had on practice. In contrast to many other consultants to top management, who emphasized long-term planning without much attention to strategy, BCG made strategic conception central. The experience curve and growth-share matrix drew a sharp, clear line between operational decision making and corporate strategy, highlighting the latter. The corporate strategist was encouraged to assume that efficient operations management would achieve the cost reductions projected along the experience curve and to make corporate investment decisions and plans accordingly. Moreover, the dynamic aspect of competition implied by the experience curve clearly called for strategic behavior: preemption of rivals with commitment today was necessary for success tomorrow.

Together with the work of Chandler, Andrews, and Ansoff, the developments at The Boston Consulting Group gave a powerful new thrust to managerial work and responsibility during the 1960s. The entrepreneurial responsibility of management was recognized—not just an act performed at birth—but as a continuing, pervasive responsibility to consider the long-run, dynamic direction of the firm, even while maintaining routine and efficient operations.

1970s: Transition toward a research orientation.   While the work of Andrews and Ansoff, and of others who aimed to provide material for the policy course, expanded consideration of strategy concepts, there was no early reflection on the normative character of the statements made. Experiential, case-based evidence lay behind the writing, but there was little analysis, and no evidence was offered to satisfy a critical reader. Chandler's work, supported by historical methods, was much less aggressively normative and prescriptive, of course, but was still essentially inductive in character. At best, these first works offered a set of constructs and propositions about how strategies formed and how they affected the performance of business enterprises. Systematic observation, deductive analysis and modeling, and careful empirical testing had to wait for the 1970s.

As strategic management began to advance in the direction of positive science in the 1970s, a dichotomy developed between those pursuing essentially descriptive studies of how strategies were formed and implemented (process) and those seeking to understand the relationship between strategic choice and performance (content). It is not clear that the work of Chandler, Andrews, or Ansoff fits easily into either category. The work of all three appears to have implications for both content and process. The seeds of division between process and content may have been sown by distinctions made for rhetorical or expository reasons. Andrews, for example, wrote: "Corporate strategy has two equally important aspects, interrelated in life but separated to the extent practicable in our study of the concept. The first of these is formulation; the second is implementation" (p. 17).

The convenience of analytically isolating strategic choice remains difficult to reconcile with the reality of organizational, strategy-making processes. However, today we are seeing signs of a reconciliation that promises new gains. The developments yielded by recent research efforts suggest that processes to formulate strategy themselves have asset-generating capability.

Late in the 1960s and early in the 1970s, concepts of strategic and long-term planning played important roles in the field. This movement owed much to the diffusion of war-based planning experience in the corporate world. For example, George Steiner had learned planning by working on materials allocation in Washington during World War II, by serving as director of policy in the Office of Defense Mobilization during the Korean War, and then as chief economist at Lockheed (1953–1954). Later, as an academic, he wrote extensively on formal long-range planning processes. Much of this literature was descriptive of selected industry practices and was strongly prescriptive, never attempting to be analytical or empirical.

The prominence of long-range planning, and then strategic planning, failed to survive the economic turmoil that began with the oil embargo of 1973 and continued with the advent of floating exchange rates, high inflation, and increasing international competition; organizations learned from practical experience that simple extrapolations of history and cadres of professional planners failed to lead to innovation, adaptation to change, or even survival. Planning processes too easily degenerated into goal-setting exercises, failing to embody any real understanding of competitive advantage. Moreover, when more sophisticated planning process designs were advanced, problems of execution or implementation increased. An organizational process to both create and execute strategy proved to be poor at conception and not influential enough to make a substantial difference in implementation.

Careful observation of actual organizational decision making gave rise to more subtle conceptions of process, in which strategies were arrived at indirectly and, to some degree, unintentionally. Uncertainty ex ante led to tentativeness, search and serial trial, and some learning—a somewhat chaotic process—which, with a certain amount of luck, might accumulate to a strategy, which could be named and described as coherent only ex post. Lindblom's (1959) "muddling through," Quinn's (1980) "logical incrementalism," and Mintzberg and Waters's (1978) "emergent strategy" all attempted to gain insight into organizational processes which produced strategy as a somewhat unintended outcome.

Attempts to understand and test the connection between strategy and performance also began in the 1970s. In this work, three streams ought to be highlighted. One, centered at Harvard and following on Chandler, generated and tested propositions about corporate growth and diversification strategies. A second, focusing on business strategies, began with the so-called brewing studies at Purdue. The third, also at Harvard, used an industrial organization economics perspective to study business strategy, and culminated in Michael Porter's work on analyzing competitive strategy and competitive advantage.

The brewing studies done in the early 1970s at Purdue examined the strategies and performance of major U.S. brewers over time. Their goal was to explore the proposition that performance was a function of strategy and environment. The brewers were chosen because they represented a group of mostly undiversified firms, and because, due to product taxation and heavy regulation, good data were available for representing the constructs (i.e., strategy and environment) and functional form of the relationship.

The brewing study results (Hatten and Schendel, 1977; Hatten, Schendel, and Cooper, 1978), were generally consistent with the notion that strategy, in addition to "environment," mattered, so that a "better" strategy, relative to competitors, was associated with better performance. The studies also revealed the considerable heterogeneity in strategy and performance that can exist within a single industry; the differences were far greater than was generally presumed in industrial organization economics and, indeed, in most management and strategy thinking. These differences led to very interesting research on strategic groups and to further explanations of performance differences based on concepts of competitive advantage.

The brewing studies demonstrated that the strategy construct could be represented by measurable variables, and that empirical evidence supported the usefulness of the strategy construct itself. What had been derived on the basis of experiential, inductive methods had been supported by more objective, deductive methods of research. This represented a new departure in research philosophy for the field, and changed the direction of research in the field in ways that were more significant than the findings themselves.

At about the same time as the brewing studies, enthusiasm for Chandler's historical work had inspired further interest in empirically demonstrating a relationship between growth strategy, organization form, and the expected performance of the enterprise. This work led ultimately to important findings concerning the forms of diversification that improved performance and those that did not. Wrigley (1970), working under Bruce Scott, did the first work in trying to classify diversification strategies. Other dissertation work followed, conducted in a variety of national economies: Channon (1973) studied the United Kingdom; Pavan (1972) studied Italy; Thanheiser (1972) studied Germany; and Pooley-Dias (1972) studied France. Rumelt (1974) pushed this stream of work even further, contributing more discriminating measures of diversification and testing the impact of diversification strategy and organizational structure on performance. Like the brewing studies, this work was at least as significant for introducing new methodological approaches to the field as for its findings.

In a third major departure for studies of the relationship of performance and strategy, Porter (1980) imported into the strategy field the concepts developed over the years in industrial organization (IO) economics. Using a large number of case studies as a factual base, Porter employed IO concepts concerning market power and profitability to build a general, cross-sectional framework for explaining individual firm performance. Until Porter, firms in strategic management had been seen as adapting to general, even rather vague environments.

Porter's "Five Forces" framework substituted a structured, competitive economic environment, in which the ability to bargain effectively in the face of an "extended rivalry" of competing firms, customers, and suppliers determined profit performance. By making managerial choice in an explicitly economic environment the focal point of analysis, Porter succeeded in turning IO economics on its head. Its traditional role was to identify socially wasteful sources of "monopoly" profits, but Porter instead used the framework to define and explain the strategies available to firms in their quest for survival and profit. Drawing on his extensive case study research, he catalogued, described, and discussed a wide range of phenomena that interfered with free competition and thus allowed abnormal returns, and he suggested how their interaction and relative importance varied across contexts.

Porter's work opened an important bridge to IO economics across which traveled more than the Structure-Conduct-Performance paradigm he employed himself. The "Chicago" critique of traditional entry barrier theory, which supported the alternative view that high profits were returns to specialized, high-quality resources or capabilities, became an important inspiration for the resource-based theory of the firm. Game theory modeling in industrial organization found applications in strategic management, too.

In addition to these broad perspectives developed *within* the field during the 1980s, strategy scholars dramatically increased their use of economic theory and their sophistication in doing so, as the examples that follow indicate. The event-study methods of financial economics were used to investigate strategic and organizational change as well as the strategic fit of acquisitions. New security-market performance measures were applied to old questions of diversification and performance, market share and performance, as well as other new areas of inquiry. Transaction cost viewpoints on scope and integration were adopted and new theories of the efficiency of social bonding were advanced. Studies of innovation began to use the language and logic of economic rents and appropriability, and research in venture capital responded to the agency and adverse selection problems characteristic of that activity. Agency theory perspectives have been used in the study of firm size, diversification, top management compensation, and growth. The new game-theoretic approach to industrial organization has informed studies of producer reputations, entry and exit, technological change, and the adoption of standards.

At the same time, research on the strategy process continued apace. Interestingly, the most vital new ideas were generated by those studying global firms. In the 1980s, the increasing globalization of the world's economy was leading students of general management to look ever more carefully at how large multinational corporations directed and coordinated their myriad resources and activities. An important early work was Stopford and Wells (1972). The new framework is first seen in the dissertations of the key authors: Prahalad (1975), Doz (1976), Bartlett (1979), and Ghoshal (1986). Their insights began to challenge the received wisdom about structure and process. In particular, the need to consider functional, product, and geographical bases for specialization forced thinking beyond the increasingly stale product-function dichotomy. The emerging framework represents management as needing to maintain "differentiation" in some activities to achieve gains from specialization or administrative isolation, and tight integration in other areas to achieve economies of scale and focus.[1] In addition, management is seen as actively managing a complex system of linkages among activities, which enables critical coordination and facilitates organizational learning.

In looking back over these three decades, what comes into focus is the search, sometimes in vain, for theoretical explanations of very complex phenomena. The purpose has been to understand real-world phenomena and establish a base for making useful prescriptions. For the first time, basic disciplines of the social sciences, especially economics, have been linked with practical issues involved in managing the firm. What began in the 1960s as rather simple concepts of strategy intended to give insight into the phenomena described in cases has evolved into a serious search for intellectual foundations with explanatory and predictive power.

Developments and Trends in Allied Disciplines

During the past decade strategic management research has increasingly relied on the theories and methods of economics

---

[1]   See Chapter 17 of this volume.

and organizational sociology, as well as (but to a lesser extent) on political science and psychology. As a consequence, the boundaries that mark the strategy field have been blurred. Not so long ago there was no doubt about what "policy" or "strategy" research was, and certainly there was no difficulty in separating it from work in economics or other disciplines. Now those distinctions are less clear.

Given these trends, it is important to understand the fundamental questions being asked in the allied disciplines and to be aware of the changes sweeping these fields. This understanding will serve two purposes. First, it will help us to place strategic management's fundamental questions in context, and to see how strategic management is related to, yet differentiated from, its allied disciplines. Second, the blurring of boundaries makes it important to examine the interrelationships between strategy and its allied disciplines. As the strategy field begins to adopt the language and tools of agency theory, population ecology, behavioral decision theory, political science, and so on, and as scholars in those fields realize that the strategy field addresses truly important and significant questions and issues, how should the relationship between strategy and its allied disciplines be viewed, and in particular, what does it mean for a research agenda for strategy? Indeed, does strategy have an independent research future, or should it merely wait for research developments to occur and then give attention to their application? Even more pointedly, does strategy have a future as a field at top research universities, or will its subject matter be taught and researched by economists, sociologists, political scientists, and psychologists?

Economics

In the beginning, economics was centrally concerned with understanding what governed the efficient generation of goods and services and what determined the distribution of wealth in society. However, in this century classical economics, now called microeconomics, has been driven more by its internal logic than by external phenomena in need of explanation. The overriding fundamental question has been, What phenomena can be explained by models that assume that human action is rational? And even in cases where no human agent has made a coherent choice, economists ask, Which institutions can be explained by assuming they were designed and stuctured by a rational actor? This program of research, begun by the Enlightenment thinkers of the eighteenth century, has reached its full flower in the economics departments of U.S. universities during the last 30 years. Indeed, Gary Becker's recent Nobel Prize was awarded for his work on extending economic reasoning to the family and beyond—his boldest work asserts that drug addiction can be explained as a rational choice.

Although the central quest of economics, the explication of phenomena as the products of rational action, is unchanged, the context within which action is envisioned has undergone a dramatic evolution. During the first half of this century the great task before economics was the mathematization of Marshall's theories to produce the "neoclassical" theory of the firm. The economist's neoclassical model of the firm, still enshrined in textbooks, is a smoothly running machine in a world without secrets, without frictions or uncertainty, and without a temporal dimension. That such a theory, so obviously divorced from the most elementary conditions of real firms, should continue to be taught in most business schools as the "theory of the firm" is a truly amazing victory of doctrine over reality. This era may, however, finally be coming to an end as the cumulative impact of new insights takes its toll.

During the past 30 years, and especially during the last 20, at least five conceptual monkey wrenches have been thrown into what was once a smoothly running machine. These five are: *uncertainty, information asymmetry, bounded rationality, opportunism,* and *asset specificity.* Each of these phenomena, taken alone, violates crucial axioms in the neoclassical model. In various combinations they are the essential ingredients of new subfields within economics. For example, transaction cost economics rests primarily on the conjunction of bounded rationality, asset specificity, and opportunism. Agency theory rests on the combination of opportunism and information asymmetry. The new game-theoretic industrial organization derives much of its punch from asymmetries in information and/or in the timing of irreversible expenditures (asset specificity). The evolutionary theory of the firm and of technological change rests chiefly on uncertainty and bounded rationality. Each of these new subfields has generated insights and research themes that are important to strategic management. Here each is briefly treated in turn.

Transaction cost economics.   Of all the new subfields of economics, the transaction cost branch of organizational economics has the greatest affinity with strategic management. The links derive, in part, from common interests in organizational form, including a shared concern with the Chandler-Williamson M-form hypothesis. They also derive from a common intellectual style, which legitimizes inquiry into the reasons for specific institutional details. The clinical studies conducted by strategy researchers and business historians are grist for the transaction cost mill. A theory that seeks to explain why one particular clause appears in a contract is clearly of great interest to strategic management scholars, who have a definite taste for disaggregation. For an example of such detail, see Joskow's (1988) study of price-adjustment clauses in long-term coal contracts.

For many economists, the assumption of unlimitedly rational actors is the defining characteristic of their field. Consequently, transaction cost economics, which follows Simon in positing bounded rationality, has had an uphill struggle for recognition and acceptance. The subfield got its start in the mid-1970s as some economists, building on Coase's (1937) seminal work, began to systematically probe questions of firm boundaries and internal organization. Williamson (1975) was the chief architect of a framework that explored the limits or boundaries of both markets and business firms as arrangements for conducting economic activity. His basic point was that transactions should take place in the regime which best economizes on the costs imposed by bounded rationality and opportunism. This framework was explicitly comparative (the relative efficiencies of markets and hierarchies were exposed) and enabled economists for the first time to say something about the *efficiency* properties of different organizational forms. (Previously economists had commonly sought and found monopoly explanations for complex forms of business organization; efficiency explanations were ignored or denigrated.) In addition to comparing markets and hierarchies, transaction cost researchers also began to look at questions of internal structure and the manner in which specific decisions and actions were taken. In particular, the Chandler-Williamson M-form hypothesis raised important issues relating to corporate control. These ideas began to achieve wider acceptance after being supported in a number of empirical studies (Armour and Teece, 1978; Monteverde and Teece, 1982).

Within strategic management, transaction cost economics is

the ground where economic thinking, strategy, and organizational theory meet. Because of its focus on institutional detail rather than mathematical display, it has a broader audience among noneconomists than other branches of organizational economics. During the 1980s, a considerable amount of work was done in applying the transaction cost framework to issues in organizational structure. In particular, research has been carried out on vertical supply arrangements in a number of industries,[2] the structure of multinational firms (Buckley and Casson, 1976; Teece, 1985; Kogut, 1988), sales force organization (Anderson and Schmittlein, 1984), joint ventures (Hennart, 1988; Pisano, 1990), and franchising. Williamson (Chapter 13, this volume) provides a useful review of additional applications of interest to strategic management.

Agency theory. Agency theory concerns the design of incentive agreements and the allocation of decision rights among individuals with conflicting preferences or interests. Although it deals with the employment transaction, agency theory is not compatible with transaction cost theory. Whereas transaction cost economics begins with the assertion that one cannot write enforceable contracts that cover all contingencies, agency theorists make no such presumption, and instead seek the optimal form of such a contract.

Agency theory has developed in two branches. The *principal-agent* literature is chiefly concerned with the design of optimal incentive contracts between principals and their employees or agents. Principal-agent economics is largely mathematical in form and is relatively inaccessible to those who have not made investments in its special technology. The standard problem has the agent shirking unless rewards can be properly conditioned on informative signals about effort. The interesting aspect of the problem is that both parties suffer if good measures are not available. A version of the problem that links with strategic management concerns project selection and the design of incentives so that agents will not distort the capital budgeting process.

The second, *corporate control* branch of the agency literature is less technical and is concerned with the design of the financial

---

[2] Early contributions were Monteverde and Teece's (1982) study of auto components and Masten's (1988) study of aerospace.

claims and overall governance structure of the firm. It is this branch which is most significant to strategic management. The corporate control hypothesis most familiar to strategic management is Jensen's (1986) "free cash flow" theory of leverage and takeovers. According to Jensen, in many firms, managers have inappropriately directed free cash flow toward wasteful investments or uses. Two cures for this problem have been proposed: use of high levels of debt to commit managements to payouts, and hostile takeovers, which put new management teams in place. What should strike strategic management scholars is that BCG offered precisely this diagnosis for many diversified firms in the early 1970s. According to BCG, most firms mismanaged their portfolios, misusing the funds generated by mature cash-rich businesses ("cows"), usually by continuing to reinvest long after growth opportunities had evaporated.

The corporate control perspective provides a valuable framework for strategic management research. By recognizing the existence of "bad" management, identifying remedial instruments, and emphasizing the importance of proper incentive arrangements, it takes a more normative stand than most other subfields of economics. However, scholars working in this area of agency theory also have the tendency to see all managerial problems as due to incorrect incentives—a tautology for a perspective that assumes away any other sources of dysfunction (e.g., capital markets problems like those discussed by Shleifer and Vishny later in this book, managerial beliefs about cause and effect, management skills in coordination, and the presence or lack of character and self-control).

Game theory and the new IO. Three of the papers in this book deal with implications of game theory for strategic management, so our remarks here will be brief. Mathematical game theory was invented by von Neumann and Morgenstern (1944) and Nash (1950). However, little progress was made in developing economic applications until the late 1970s. It was probably Spence's (1974) work on market signaling that sparked the modern interest of economists, and it was Stanford's "gang of four," Kreps, Milgrom, Roberts, and Wilson (1982), who codified the treatment of sequential games with imperfect information.[3]

---

[3]   Much of the technical foundation they used had been laid by Selten (1965) and Harsanyi (1967).

Modern game theory raises deep questions about the nature of rational behavior. The idea that a rational individual is one who maximizes utility in the face of available information is simply not sufficient to generate "sensible" equilibria in many noncooperative games with asymmetric information. To obtain "sensible" equilibria, actors must be assigned beliefs about what others' beliefs will be in the event of irrational acts. Research into the technical and philosophical foundations of game theory has, at present, little to do directly with strategic management, but much to do with the future of economics as the science of "rational" behavior.

Game theory as applied to industrial organization has two basic themes of particular interest to strategic management: commitment strategies and reputations. Commitment, as Ghemawat (1991) emphasizes, can be seen as central to strategy. Among the commitment games that have been analyzed are those involving investment in specific assets and excess capacity, research and development with and without spillovers, horizontal mergers, and financial structure.

Reputations arise in games where firms or actors may belong to various "types" and others must form beliefs about which type is the true one. Thus, for example, a customer's belief (probability) that a seller is of the "honest" type constitutes the seller's reputation, and that reputation can be lost if the seller behaves in a way that changes the customer's beliefs. Reputations can also describe relationships within the firm, and the collection of employee beliefs and reputations can be called its "culture." Given the competitive importance of external reputations, the efficiency properties of internal reputations, and the relative silence of game theorists about how various equilibria are actually achieved, there is clearly much room for contributions, including those from strategic management research.

Evolutionary economics. There has been a long-standing analogy drawn between biological competition (and resulting evolution) and economic competition, and students of both phenomena often ground ideas by pointing to the parallel. Making the analogy concrete, however, has largely been the work of Nelson and Winter (1982), who married the concepts of tacit knowledge and routines to the dynamics of Schumpeterian competition. In their framework, firms compete primarily through a struggle to improve or innovate. In this struggle, firms grope toward better methods with only a partial understanding of the causal structure of their own capabilities and of the technological opportunity set. Key to their view is the idea that organizational capacities are based on routines which are not explicitly comprehended, but which are developed and bettered with repetition and practice. This micro-link to learning-by-doing means that the current capability of the firm is a function of history, and implies that it is impossible to simply copy best practice even when it is observed.

Because evolutionary economics posits a firm that cannot change its strategy or its structure easily or quickly, the field has a very close affinity to population ecology views in organization theory. Researchers interested in the evolution of populations tend to work in the sociology tradition, while those more interested in the evolution of firm capabilities and technical progress tend to work in the economics tradition. Both frameworks challenge the naive view that firms can change strategies easily, or that such changes will even matter when attempted and made.

Organizational Sociology

The fundamental issue addressed by sociology is the structure and subjective meaning of social interaction. The center of the puzzle was and continues to be the stability of social structures and the amazingly strong controlling forces they exert on their members' actions. Although economists are also interested in patterns of exchange, two concerns distinguish the sociologists' approach: an interest in authority and a real concern with the subjective experience of social interaction. Whereas economists almost always study voluntary exchange, sociologists normally begin with the presumption that authority is a key source of social order. Equally distinctive and crucial is the sociologist's concern with the subjective. To an economist, exchange is a means to an end. When an employee exchanges labor for pay, for example, the economist sees two gains: the employee values the pay more than the discomfort of work, and the employer values the labor received at least as greatly as the cost of employment. To a sociologist, the exchange itself, and the system of exchanges within which it is embedded, generate value and meaning apart from their instrumental worth.

Organizational sociology grew from two important traditions. The "main line" flows from the work of Durkheim ([1893] 1984) and Weber (1947) through Parsons (1937), Merton (1940), and Homans (1950), to Selznick (1949, 1957) and Blau and Scott (1962). In general, this tradition has been concerned with the processes whereby authority is legitimized (accepted), with the general problem of social structure in society, and with the limits and dysfunctions of bureaucracy. The second tradition is more normative and practice-oriented, and springs from the early management theorists and from the "human relations" movement inaugurated by industrial psychologists.

From the mid-1960s through the 1970s, the contingency theory synthesis emerged and was widely disseminated. Contingency theory built on a variety of earlier insights: Woodward (1965) and Burns and Stalker (1961) showed that high-performing organizations did not have the same structure, but matched structure to the technological demands of production; the Aston studies established that there is no single factor with which organizational characteristics covary; Emery and Trist (1965) stressed the importance of the environment in determining structure; and Lawrence and Lorsch (1967) drew from their empirical work the picture of an organization with subunits adapted to differing local environments and with integrative mechanisms that assert the interests of the whole. Contingency theory hypothesized that organizations which contain subsystems "matched" to their environments perform better than those with a less perfect fit. Under competition, this implies that structure follows environment and must be able to cope with uncertainty, the most important variable in the environment. If strategy is taken to include the choice of environment, this hypothesis is consistent with Chandler's (and now strategic management's) dictum that structure follows strategy.

But contingency theory's apparent success at solving the puzzle of formal structure did not ensure its longevity. Carroll (1988: 1) gives a vivid explanation of what happened in the mid-1970s:

> Although its adherents continue working at a feverish pace, the once hegemonic contingency theory of organization has been deposed by a paradigmatic revolution. The beginnings of the revolution can be dated sometime around 1975, a period marked by the appearance of four new seminal theoretical statements about organizations: (1) the book on transaction

cost economics by Oliver Williamson (1975), *Markets and Hierarchies;* (2) the article on the population ecology of organizations by Michael T. Hannan and John Freeman (1977); (3) the article on institutionalized organizations by John Meyer and Brian Rowen (1977); and (4) the book on resource dependence theory by Jeffrey Pfeffer and Gerald Salancik (1978), *The External Control of Organizations.*

Each of these subfields of organizational sociology is relevant to strategic management (we have already viewed transaction cost economics in the previous section).

Resource dependence. Who or what determines what organizations do? The resource dependence model argues that much of what organizations do is determined by outsiders—by those parties who control the flow of critical resources upon which the organization depends. The strategic activities of management, according to this perspective, are those of accommodating or finding ways to insulate the organization from the demands of those who control critical resources. Resource dependence explains mergers, joint ventures, diversification, and board memberships in this way, and scholars working in this tradition have provided empirical support for these claims. Note that there is an affinity between resource dependence theory and transaction cost theory. Both are concerned with the governance of critical transactions, and both are concerned with the power of one party to damage the other.

Resource dependence theory also speaks to the distribution of power within organizations. Power, it is argued, is possessed by those who can influence the flow of critical resources from external sources and by those who have influence over the flow of discretionary resources. Thus, power in a consulting firm resides in those who can generate new business or influence clients, and great power in universities can be wielded by those who control relatively small discretionary funds.

Organization ecology. Economics and, to a large extent, strategic management view the firm as actively adapting to changed conditions. Organization ecology makes the opposite presumption—that firms do not adapt. Instead of the adaptive firm, organization ecology sees a population of firms that changes in composition over time as some flourish, others perish, and new organizations are born. The metaphor of biology has been frequently used by economists and strategy researchers, but Hannan and Freeman (1977) were the first to complete the metaphor, placing firms in the position of individuals with fixed genetic endowments and advocating the study of a population of firms (i.e., a species) over time, rather than the idiosyncratic features of individuals.

Although it assumes that firms do not adapt, organization ecology is much more receptive to the concept that firms have strategies than traditional organization theory. The critical difference is that organization ecology sees the strategy of a firm as fixed at its inception and as unchanging over time.[4] Once it is fixed, of course no further room is left for the strategic manager. This view is obviously at odds with much of the literature in strategic management, especially that which emphasizes strategic change, organization renewal and transformation, and flexibility. Nevertheless, it may be that strategic management scholars need to reexamine their assumptions—strategic change may well be the exception rather than the rule. Given the large number of case studies that feature companies unable to perceive or cope with a changing environment, it may be that the ecologist's assumption of strategic inertia is more realistic than the economist's assumption of rapid, rational response to change.

Much of the research in organization ecology has been directed at measuring the birth and death rates of organizations and, therefore, the rate of expansion or decline of the population under study. More recently, interest has focused on *density dependence:* the degree to which birth and/or death rates vary with the size of the population. In addition, interest attaches to niching, niche-overlap, and measures of competition across subpopulations. By keeping the economist's notion that the environment changes and selects the most efficient organizations, but abandoning rational adaptation, organization ecologists are able to measure "niche-width," competition, and similar concepts using straightforward data. This is in marked contrast to the difficulty in developing proper empirical measures of economic concepts, such as cross-elasticity of demand, or strategic management concepts such as "mobility barriers."

Of course, the fact that some organizations do adapt creates a natural tension within organization ecology. A natural response is to shift the locus of selection from the firm as a whole

---

[4]   More precisely, organization ecologists assume strategic change is infrequent and independent of immediate environmental demands.

to some part of the firm, say its policies or its organizational subunits, and to see these subunits as unchanging but also subject to birth, proliferation, and extinction (Burgelman, 1990). It remains to be seen whether an empirical demography of policies or subunit forms can be created.

New institutionalism. The basic tenet of economics, much of strategic management, and a great deal of sociology and organization theory is rationality or functionalism—that the structures, concepts, and social arrangements which evolve are the "rational" or "efficient" solutions to the problems of production, coordination, and change. These functional structures are either designed, selected, or otherwise evolve. It is this view that motivates case studies of successful firms and that lies behind the economic analysis of institutions.

The new institutionalism[5] provides a contrary view. It claims that whereas some organizations survive through technical efficiency, there are others that survive through legitimacy—by acting in socially expected ways. Put differently, whereas an economist might see a joint venture as an arrangement for efficiently dealing with certain forms of co-specialized assets in a context of opportunism, the (new) institutionalist would see it as a currently accepted (or rationalized) activity. Joint ventures are undertaken, it might be argued, because other firms have done them and because academics have rationalized them. Hence, more firms undertake them. From this point of view, joint ventures may be something like a virus, multiplying in the social, cognitive, and economic context of modern corporate life. They proliferate not because they are efficient, but because they have become *institutionalized* (and are not obviously dysfunctional). As DiMaggio and Powell (1988: 3) put it, "The distinguishing contribution of institutional theory rests in the identification of causal mechanisms leading to organizational change and stability on the basis of preconscious understandings that organizational actors share, independent of their interests."

The new institutionalism is an intellectual descendant of the old, which was best represented by Selznick (1957). But Selznick used the word to denote the way value and meaning attached to a specific organization and its mission. To the new writers,

---

5   The best survey is Powell and DiMaggio (1991), especially their introductory essay.

society at large is the source of concepts, professional roles, rules, standards, expectations, policies, strategies, and standard organizational arrangements. Organizations institutionalize (adopt) these things and thereby gain legitimacy. Thus, business schools teach business policy because it is "the thing to do" rather than because it is technically necessary. This form of nonrational behavior draws on new work in cognitive psychology that identifies behavior derived from unconscious scripts, rules, and routines. It is also akin to that studied by Elster (1988), who distinguishes between consequentialist and nonconsequentialist behavior: the first is action impelled by a consideration of consequences or payoffs; the second is action chosen according to a rule or according to its "appropriateness" in the context. Finally, and perhaps most simply, it should be recognizable as the logic of the legal system—procedural rationality.

Institutional theory is at its strongest in explaining those aspects of organizational life that are taken for granted. For example, the fact that superiors judge the performance of subordinates but not vice versa, the annual planning cycle, and the general use of financial measures of subunit performance are "institutions" which are accepted virtually without question. This viewpoint has obvious bite with regard to the diffusion of many new management concepts and fads (e.g., quality circles, value-based strategy, and TQM).

Another developing stream of thought that intersects organizational sociology in many areas is concerned with organization culture.[6] The study of organization culture derives from functional anthropology, semiotics, and phenomenology. It tends to reject reductionism, seeing culture as something that must be comprehended as a whole, and perhaps only by direct participation. It is a nonrational view to the extent that social behavior cannot be expressed as the outcome of individual rational optimizing behavior. Some scholars, however, do view the culture as a whole as the functional solution to problems of communication, cooperation, and intertemporal opportunism. Culture is sometimes seen as the impediment to change and at other times as the source of unusual excellence; in either case, the technology of changing, protecting, or creating culture is at a very primitive state of development.

---

[6] See Ouchi and Wilkins (1985) for an insightful review.

Political Science

The systematic investigation of political structures and processes has a tradition extending back to the Greek philosophers. And most political science has been within the classical form: the discussion of ideal states, the histories of particular political conflicts or events, descriptions of political structures and the rules governing their operation, and framers' expectations as to the value and functioning of various political structures. Like strategic management, political science lacks a central, generally accepted paradigm, and its many streams are not tied together in any coherent way.

However, two dramatic shifts in paradigm have occurred in American political science in the last 50 years. The first was the "behavioral revolution" that commenced in the 1950s. Just as the Carnegie School's views on behavioral, rather than "rational," models of human behavior influenced research and thinking in management schools, they also had an impact on political science. The new mode saw researchers looking at what political actors actually did rather than at descriptions of rules and structure or at a framer's expectations. For example, see Kaufman (1960) for a fascinating account of the Forest Service.

The second paradigm shift was political science's own "new institutionalism." Among its antecedents were the many empirical studies of voting that had been carried out over the years. These studies examined the effects of blocs, splinter groups, rules, and so forth, on voting behavior and outcomes. New institutionalism in political science also included abstract and rigorous analysis of how individual preferences combine through voting to produce political outcomes. This avenue of study had its origins in Arrow's (1951) Impossibility Theorem, which showed that literally centuries of talk about "the public interest" was vacuous—that one cannot aggregate preferences and treat a collection like an individual. The early attempts to model democratic processes took their structure from economics; voters were likened to consumers, policy makers to producers, and politics and voting to market competition. Of the many important contributions to this literature, two that stand out are Black's (1958) analysis of bloc voting and Buchanan and Tullock's (1962) analysis of when collective democratic action is individually preferred.

One might expect an economic metaphor applied to politics to produce the same conclusion—that competitive markets maximize welfare—but political scientists discovered substantial difficulties. When preferences were modeled as differing in only one dimension, everything worked well, with the policy outcome being the preferences of the median voter. But with two or more dimensions to preferences, outcomes were indeterminate. McKelvey (1976) is credited with the first "chaos theorem," proving that if there is no clearly dominating policy, any policy can be made the outcome through some adjustment of the agenda. That is, given majority-rule voting, a sufficiently clever chairperson can obtain any result he or she desires.

Although analysis showed chaos, real political institutions demonstrated substantial stability and predictability. Thus, the actual outcome of democratic processes, or at least their stability, it was argued, must be at least as greatly determined by the structure of institutions as by the preferences of voters. This insight generated a renewed interest in the structure of institutions, and a great deal of research has been done on the committee structures of the U.S. Congress and on its voting rules (Shepsle, 1979; Weingast, 1989).

A final stream of political science research of interest to strategic management is the study of bureaucratic biases or failures. The studies in this stream most familiar to strategic management are Selznick's (1949) study of the TVA and Allison's (1971) analysis of the Cuban missile crisis. Other important works in this genre are Downs's (1967) study of bureaucracy and Wilson's (1989) analysis of the properties and behavior of government agencies.

Summary

Each of the allied disciplines speaks to a unique metaphor. Economics is concerned with public welfare and wealth distribution in society. Sociology is concerned with groups of individuals and their activities as groups. Political science is concerned with choices made by groups where the objective function is diffuse and specified by the group itself. Psychology is concerned with individuals, the mind, and individual behavior. That all of these have something to do with individuals in combination with group choices and welfare is evident. But what of strategic management? What is its metaphor, and what is its domain? And how does it relate to these basic disciplines?

Strategic management has to do with groups, their birth and their continuing success. It does not assume that the group's purpose is beneficial, but simply that the group forms and tries to exist because it has purpose. Moreover, the group exists within a context, and the context governs conditions of success. It is management's responsibility to see that the group adapts to its context, and survival in the end is an objective definition of success. So the perspective is that of the management team assigned the responsibility of ensuring success, with success defined as either the entrepreneurial act of starting an organization, or those acts that condition survival.

The fundamental issues addressed by strategic management then are different from those addressed by the allied disciplines themselves. Related they are to be sure, but different perspectives separate their domains of inquiry, and one must expect different fundamental questions to be addressed by each discipline.

We turn now to an examination of what we see as fundamental questions of interest to strategic management. In so doing, we define the field as we see it today, and further, we separate the field from the allied disciplines with which it overlaps and with which it has common interests. Perhaps most important, by posing fundamental questions, we outline what we believe to be the boundaries of the field and its current and ongoing agenda for research.

The Fundamental Questions in Strategy

The Value of Fundamental Questions

A fundamental question acts to define a field of inquiry and to orient the efforts of researchers who work in that domain. Ronald Coase, for example, defined the field of institutional economics by asking, Why are there firms? Despite its apparent simplicity, this question has great power. When it was posed, the neoclassical theory of the firm was well advanced, but that theory sought to characterize the behavior of the firm, taking its existence as a given. Thus, Coase's question was a subtle critique of the state of microeconomics, and it proved to be an extremely fruitful impetus to new thinking. The value of the question is undiminished by the fact that it has not yet been answered entirely satisfactorily.

Fundamental questions are not necessarily the most often stated or the most fashionable; nevertheless, they serve to highlight the issues and presumptions that differentiate a field of inquiry, making its axioms, its methods, and the phenomena it studies different from those of other related fields. Thus, one of the fundamental questions for the strategy field is, Why are firms different?—a question that echoes Coase's but that directs attention away from common properties of all firms and focuses instead on the phenomena which produce and sustain continuing heterogeneity among firms.

For a fundamental question to energize research it must not only address a critical issue, it must also offer at least one clear path to follow in seeking answers. Thus, the power of Coase's question derives not only from its focus on the basics, but also from its association with a method for seeking its answer— comparative institutional analysis. Adam Smith invented economics by coupling the question, What determines the wealth of nations? with a new method of analyzing the collective results of individual self-seeking behavior. Durkheim virtually invented sociology by asking, What binds individuals into societies? and advocating the statistical comparison of behavior and social structure in various settings.

There are many questions addressing important issues that cannot motivate useful research. Some are too general; others lack connection to any usable theoretical structure or research methodology. For example, the question, What is good management? is too general, given our current knowledge, to be fundamental. We know that managerial work depends sharply on the task, the role, and the organization. In business research there is also the problem of asking questions that are too close to the entrepreneurial heart of the matter. In a competitive world, there can be no general answer to the query, How can a firm increase its market share? because if it were really general, it would also apply to the firm's competitors.

What questions energize research around a critical issue in the strategy field? And which of these provide a clear path to follow in seeking answers? Clearly, we need to understand how firms and organizations in general make assumptions and decisions about context. In other words, we need to learn more about just how organizations reach conclusions about action, and whether they can in fact be more rational than the individuals that comprise them. Certainly none of the basic and allied disciplines we have examined tells us how firms behave. All seem either to be passively descriptive or to postulate behavior from the outset.

We can also wonder how competition among organizations influences their nature. Among competitive business firms, we see a variety of successful firms with very different natures. Yet theory would suggest this should not be true. No good explanations exist for the difference.

There are concerns about the role of senior management that span several strategically distinctive business firms. Why are they needed and what do they do? All theory available suggests they add costs without corresponding value. Yet they persist, and though we know much about their activities, which are typically strategic in character, we don't know enough about the value they create.

As the world shrinks, competition intensifies, environments grow more complex, and it becomes increasingly difficult to survive. We know too little about these complex processes on an international scale, and we know too little about competitiveness. Nothing in theory much helps to explain this dynamic process of birth, survival, and death.

These kinds of concerns lead us to four fundamental questions that we believe characterize major concerns of the strategic management field. We now turn to their specific development.

The four questions addressed in this volume represent some of the most crucial puzzles in the strategy field, and emphasize the links between strategy and its allied disciplines. While other questions can be posed, almost all relate in one way or another to the four developed here. To satisfy the curious, we include a brief summary of some of the "also-ran" questions in the Afterword.

How Do Firms Behave?

Or, do firms really behave like rational actors, and, if not, what models of their behavior should be used by researchers and policy makers?

Strategy is about the choice of direction for the firm.[7] But what assumptions should the strategist entertain about the choices made by competitive firms, choices that inevitably are interdependent? Is it even reasonable to think of the behavior of a firm as reflecting "choices," or should a much less rational model be used? Thus, the question of how firms behave has two components: (1) the empirical issue of the actual patterns of behavior observed among firms, and (2) the more abstract question of what modeling assumptions are most fruitful in explaining observed patterns or guiding competitive strategy.

The dominant assumption used by economists is that the firm behaves like a rational individual. Therefore, the question, How do firms behave? directs attention toward situations in which the dominant assumption is unwise. Since there is good empirical evidence that individual behavior does not meet strict norms of rationality, even when it is intendedly rational, and since most firm behavior reflects organizational outcomes rather than individual action, it is a reasonable conjecture that the standard rational model of firm behavior is rarely accurate.

The subquestions that appear appropriate to this fundamental question are these:

- What are the foundation assumptions that differentiate among various models of firm behavior (e.g., resource dependence, "garbage can" models, Nelson and Winter's routines, and population ecology models)?
- According to behavioral decision scientists, there are predictable biases in human decision making. Are there predictable biases in firm or organizational behavior? What do we know about the relationships between organizational size (or other stable characteristics) and behavior?
- "Rational" models of competitive interaction posit players who engage in very subtle and complex reasoning. Yet our common experience is that decision makers are far less analytic and perform far less comprehensive analyses than these models posit. If one is a player, is it really "rational" to posit such complex behavior in others?
- Can game theorists deal with biased behavior or with the

---

[7] Clearly, the organization does not have to be a business firm. Any type of organization could be substituted in the remarks made here and those that follow.

nonrational aspects of firm behavior? Can analytic models of nonrational or extrarational behavior move beyond their present ad hoc status?

Why Are Firms Different?

Or, what sustains the heterogeneity in resources and performance among close competitors despite competition and imitative attempts?

One of the key empirical observations made by strategy researchers, an observation as well as a perspective that sets the strategy field apart from industrial organization economics, is that firms within the same industry differ from one another, often dramatically. In a recent study, Rumelt (1991:179) found that among businesses in the FTC Line of Business sample, the variance in return on capital could be apportioned as follows: 0.8% due to corporate effects, 8.3% due to stable industry effects, and 46.4% due to stable business-unit effects. Thus, the differences among business units within the same industry were eight times as great as the differences among industries. The source of this heterogeneity lies at the root of competitive advantage, and understanding *why* it arises and translating that into *how* it can be achieved is of central concern to the field.

For those who do not accept the idea of equilibrium, there is, of course, no puzzle in heterogeneity—people differ and so must firms. But competition, it is normally thought, should eliminate differences among competitors; good practices and successful techniques will be imitated, and firms that cannot or will not adopt good practices will be driven from the field. Therefore, the challenge is to retain the power of equilibrium thinking and still correctly explain the observed differences among competitors.

Differences among firms may arise from intention, or stochastically, and they may be created and sustained through property rights, active prevention of imitation, or through natural impediments of limitation and resource flows. In addition, these differences may also arise and be sustained through differing conceptual views, theories, or causal maps, differing organizational processes within firms, different levels of organizational learning and team skills, and/or through the action of ambiguity.

There are many different theories that can be used to deal with this question. The following subsidiary questions suggest the range of these theories and the underlying disciplines that may have something to offer:

- To what extent are the differences among firms the results of purposeful differentiation rather than unavoidable heterogeneity in resources and their combinations? That is, should strategy be thought of as the exploitation of existing asymmetry, or the search for and creation of unique resources or market positions?
- Are the most important impediments to equilibration rooted in market phenomena (e.g., first-mover advantages), or are they chiefly rooted in internal organizational phenomena (e.g., cultural differences or learning)?
- Is the search for rents based on resource heterogeneity contrary to public welfare, or does it act in the public's welfare?

What Is the Function of or Value Added by the Headquarters Unit in a Diversified Firm?

Or, what limits the scope of the firm?

The diversified corporation is the dominant form of business firm in the industrialized world. The creation and management of these enterprises has been heavily researched by strategy scholars. Nevertheless, the relative strengths and weaknesses of this organizational form remain poorly understood. In particular, the question of what is, or should be, the value added by the headquarters unit of such firms is of central concern to the strategy field.

There appear to be two general points of view with regard to the role of the headquarters unit in multibusiness firms: the first emphasizes value creation, and the second emphasizes loss prevention. According to the first viewpoint, the headquarters unit formulates the overall strategy for the corporation, including its degree of diversification and organizational form. Also, it manages the process of resource allocation among constituent businesses, apparently better than would the unaided capital markets. Finally, the headquarters unit maintains the existence of key shared resources and manages the processes by which business units share these resources.

By contrast, the loss prevention school of thought sees management as reviewing the strategies of the business units (strategic management), apparently to make sure that egregious logical errors are not made. Second, the headquarters unit monitors the operations of the subunits, providing surer supervision of the agents operating the businesses than would independent boards of directors or the competitive marketplace. Finally, the headquarters unit can extract free cash flow from a mature business unit at much lower cost than can the unaided capital markets or the market for corporate control.

There are, of course, perspectives beyond these two. Financial economics suggests gains from corporate diversification if bankruptcy is costly, and transaction cost economics suggests gains from internalizing businesses sharing co-specialized assets. Finally, there is a skeptical perspective that sees these complex firms as the result of agency problems—as long as managers prefer to invest excess cash rather than pay it back to stockholders, and as long as they can do so, maturing profitable businesses will spawn diversified firms.

The persistence of multibusiness firms cannot be ignored. However, it is no trivial task to isolate the forces that generate and sustain these firms. The subsidiary questions that may aid inquiry into these considerations include:

- Which is primary, strategy or structure? That is, is the multidivisional form (M-form) the administrative solution to the problems created by product-market diversification and/or the need to internalize transactions, or is it itself the innovation that permits efficiencies from the assembly of various business units in a common hierarchy?
- Which is primary, the entrepreneurial (value-creating) role of the headquarters unit, or the administrative (loss-preventing) role? Can a headquarters unit simultaneously perform both roles?
- What, if any, are the limits to the amalgamation of business units in multibusiness firms? Relatedly, how can the value now being created by the breakup of diversified firms be reconciled with the value created by their formation in the past?
- Strategic management is normally taken to mean the explicit oversight and review of the strategy formulation pro-

cess together with systems for allocating resources among businesses. Do firms that impose "strategic management" on portfolios of businesses add value, and if so, what is the mechanism?

- Are there corollaries to headquarters units in nonbusiness organizations and, if so, what are the comparative lessons to be learned?

What Determines Success or Failure in International Competition?

Or, what are the origins of success and what are their particular manifestations in international settings or global competition?

This question has two parts of interest. One part is the more fundamental issue of why some firms enjoy more success than others. What is the dynamic competitive process that leads to the relative success of some firms, and what causes some to decline and some to fail (or, more commonly, to be sold to other firms that more efficiently employ their assets)? This issue is at the heart of competitive dynamics and the workings of capitalism and needs to be understood better in its own right.

Another part of the question deals with international competition and the competitiveness of firms, and indeed, of nations and cultures. At stake is not just firm survival or success, but the quality of life in economies and their respective cultures.

There are a number of disciplines that can shed light on these fundamental issues, including international trade theory, political science, and organizational theory. Subsidiary questions that need to be addressed include these:

- To what extent do firms from different countries (cultures) possess inherent competitive advantages in certain arenas? The issue at stake is not simply the economists' comparative advantage, which would not operate when a domestic firm invests abroad, but a subtler set of management skills, technologies, and norms of work.
- Are there "strategic" industries and, if so, what makes them strategic? That is, are there significant positive externalities associated with the presence of a particular industry within a nation? Note that the often postulated efficacy of

Japan's MITI or an "industrial policy" in the United States rests on the presumption that there are strategic industries.
- Are there rules for global competition that are not simply the extension of rules for competition within a large nation-state or continent?

Summary

These four questions help define the field of strategic management. In our view they are fundamental to understanding the matter of managing groups, their formation or birth, their relative success, and ultimately their adaptation and survival. These questions relate to allied disciplines, but they are not central to them, and their perspectives differ.

The next four sections of the book present the papers that deal with each of the four questions, and the papers in turn present the perspectives of authors whose disciplines are not necessarily those of strategic management. Collectively, the perspectives offered raise research questions and practice issues we believe can help set important research and practice agendas within the strategic management field.

Part I

How Do Firms Behave?

The only well-worked-out, crisply predictive, and internally consistent theory of firm behavior is that of rational maximizing behavior—the economist's model. Unfortunately, most students of strategy and organization believe it is wrong. The dominant view outside economics is that although organizational actions can usually be individually rationalized by various interested parties, the actions are not consistent, nor can they be expressed, taken as a whole, as the consequences of maximizing choices. It is this split that has generated most of the heat and friction between the perspectives of economics and organizational studies.

This split in perspective has taken on a new shape in the last six or seven years because of two phenomena: the takeover boom of the mid-1980s, and the rise of game theory. To rationalize the takeover boom with theories of market efficiency, financial economists have been forced to argue that many managements may not be acting to maximize the value of the firms they control. As a consequence, the market for corporate control, working via takeovers, acts to replace such inefficient managements (see Shleifer and Vishny, Chapter 14, this volume). The intriguing result of this line of argument is that large numbers of firms may not be acting to maximize wealth and, therefore, do not act like rational "individuals." At the same time, another branch of economics has made great strides in applying game theory to competitive situations. As a consequence, there is a rapidly expanding literature on strategy in which firms are presumed to act with great rationality in complex competitive situations. Thus, economics no longer speaks with one voice on the question of how to describe the behavior of firms.

In this section, a group of researchers tackles the problem of describing firm behavior. Jay Barney ("Beyond Individual Metaphors in Understanding How Firms Behave: A Comment on Game Theory and Prospect Theory Models of Firm Behavior") leads off by criticizing the general tendency to use "individual metaphors" in modeling or simply in thinking about firm behavior. In particular, Barney challenges the practice of modeling firm behavior "as if" the firm were a rational individual, or "as if" it were an individual described by prospect theory. Barney argues that such models miss the essential point that firms are collections of individuals. As Freud recognized, the simplest model of irrational and inconsistent behavior is a "committee" of three rational individuals: superego, ego, and id. Larger "committees" are no more rational, and Barney argues that a realistic theory of firm behavior must confront the inconsistencies inherent in the behavior of collectives. In addition, Barney offers the argument that the individual metaphor may incorrectly focus attention on the "big" or strategic decisions. Real competitive success, he notes, may derive from a myriad of "small" decisions which would more appropriately be described collectively as culture or process.

In the next paper, "Timid Choices and Bold Forecasts: A Cognitive Perspective on Risk Taking," Daniel Kahneman and Dan Lovallo provide a model that, at first glance, appears to be exactly the type Barney attacks: an extension of individual cognitive models to the firm as a whole. Kahneman and Lavallo offer the fascinating proposition that individual and social psychological phenomena lead firms to produce optimistic forecasts of the future and to simultaneously avoid making choices and commitments. The cleverness in this argument, one that defuses most of the Barney critique, is that it joins a theory of expectations with a theory of action, and the combination predicts inconsistent behavior.

In the third paper, "Structure, Strategy, and the Agenda of the Firm," Thomas Hammond offers a theory of firm behavior drawn from political science. In particular, Hammond argues that organizations act to shape the information and choices that managers see; thus, structure has a strong influence on the types of decisions that are made. Hammond's model is clear and offers testable propositions about firm behavior, propositions that differ substantially from those produced by strictly rational models.

The next three papers address the connections between modern game theory and strategic management. Garth Saloner, in his paper, "Game Theory and Strategic Management: Contributions, Applications, and Limitations," provides a viewpoint on the usefulness of game-theoretic modeling in strategic management. His basically positive view is conditioned by two major cautions: there is no evidence of any real-world use of game theory by companies, and game-theoretic approaches are "too hard" to be applied to anything but very simple "boiled-down" models of reality. The second issue may, of course, be the reason for the first, and it is interesting to speculate on what consequences would flow from the invention of a game theory "engine" that quickly and clearly yielded the equilibria of very complex models.

Saloner's enthusiasm for game-theoretic models survives these two considerations and is based on their necessity, the "audit trail" they provide, their metaphorical value, and their growing importance in empirical research. Saloner dismisses the use of game theory to calculate actual behavior, stressing instead the value of understanding why certain results obtain in certain situations and the possibility of gaining novel insights. As work progresses, he argues, research will build up a mosaic of models, each providing insights about a particular aspect of strategic interaction. Game theory's contribution to strategic management will be the sum total of the insights this mosaic provides.

One of the most challenging questions Saloner tackles is the reasonableness of the rationality imputed to players in game theory. There is no escape, he suggests, from using judgment on this matter, and he notes that your own play in a game might be affected by whether your opponent was David Kreps, a fourth grader, an average undergraduate, or the CEO of a typical U.S. firm.

Colin Camerer ("Does Strategy Research Need Game Theory?") also addresses the utility of game theory to strategic management. Like Saloner, Camerer is concerned with the sparseness of modern analysis, termed "no-fat" modeling, and with the fact that game analysis is hard. If neoclassical analysis is like eating with a fork, he analogizes, game theory is like using chopsticks. Game theory is not only hard, Camerer stresses, it is also too easy. That is, it is too easy to generate explanations for all sorts of behavior. This happens because behavior is not just determined by preferences, but also by the presence of hidden information.

The heart of Camerer's essay addresses the rationality assumption—is it too demanding to be reasonable? His own laboratory work on games shows tl•at people do not arrive at strategies using the cognitive methods of the theorist. Consequently, theoretical equilibria are usually approached only after repeated play. Nonetheless, through processes of adaptation and/or evolution, theoretical equilibria are approached. Camerer also points out that the strict rationality assumptions of the theorist are sometimes only an analytical convenience; the same equilibria can often be justified with weaker assumptions, though the analysis is more difficult.

Despite these and other difficulties in living with game theory, Camerer favors welcoming it into the strategic management family. Like Saloner, he feels that it is the best way to look at interactions among alert rivals. In addition, Camerer sees opportunities to inform areas of interest to strategic management, such as the properties of collective resources (reputations and capabilities). Finally, he argues that the problem of too many explanations and too many equilibria provides opportunities for good empirical work to point the way.

Steven Postrel's paper, "Burning Your Britches Behind You: Can Policy Scholars Bank on Game Theory?" is a comment on Saloner's and Camerer's discussions of game theory and strategy, especially the "Pandora's Box" problem that the theory has too few constraints for generating explanations of behavior. Postrel uses humor to show how a game theorist could build a model to rationalize unreasonable behavior. His point is that game theory is not really a theory of strategy, but is only a methodology for analyzing games structures. Other than rationality, the substantive theory present in a model is in the assumptions, not in the mechanics of the solution.

A significant goal of this section is to question what assumptions managers are willing to make about behavior—not merely individual, but also group behavior—and the influence these assumptions have on resulting choices. Clearly, there is much yet to be understood about group behavior and how we can think about the basis for the choices that organizations make. If there is any message at all in the recent interest in worldwide competitive behavior, and particularly the recent success of Japanese firms, it is that (often implicit) assumptions made (or not made) about organization behavior have a powerful impact on ultimate success. This section attacks this matter at a fundamental level and should lead all of us to rethink how we approach management of organizations.

2
Beyond Individual Metaphors in Understanding How Firms Behave: A Comment on Game Theory and Prospect Theory Models of Firm Behavior

Jay B. Barney

Metaphors have long been an important analytical tool for understanding how firms behave. Metaphors help organize and communicate complex descriptions of organizations and organizational phenomena, and can suggest important insights about those phenomena that may not be accessible through more traditional analytical means (Pepper, 1942; Kuhn, 1962). In organization theory, for example, the "garbage can" metaphor has had an important influence on the study of decision making in firms (March and Olsen, 1976). In finance, the "nexus of contracts" metaphor enabled theorists to begin to examine intra-organizational phenomena using agency theory (Jensen and Meckling, 1976). Recently, Morgan (1986a) has suggested a wide range of metaphors for organizations, and has traced many of the interesting implications that these metaphors have for our understanding of organizations and organizational phenomena.

Though not strict examples of metaphorical reasoning (Morgan, 1986a), the papers in this section are nevertheless grounded in two different metaphors of organizations. The game theory papers suggest that organizations can be analyzed as if they were rational (perhaps even hyperrational) utility-maximizing individuals. For game theorists, the question of how firms behave in competitive situations becomes, How would hyperrational individuals behave in these situations? The prospect theory paper adopts a different metaphor when it suggests that organizations can be analyzed as if they were systematically nonrational individuals. For prospect theorists, the question of how firms behave in competitive situations becomes, How would biased decision makers behave in these situations?

Each of these metaphors for strategic analysis has a long tradition, and each has been shown to be fruitful in certain theoretical and empirical contexts. The rational individual metaphor has been at the core of most (but not all) economic analysis of organizations (see Simon, 1947, for a discussion of alternative rationality assumptions). It helps focus theoretical attention on the relationship between a firm (as a utility-maximizing entity) and its competitive environment, and thus enables the application of the powerful analytical tools of game theory and price theory in strategic analysis.

While a somewhat more recent development, the biased individual metaphor of prospect theory has also been shown to have important implications for strategic analysis. This metaphor goes beyond suggesting that perfect rationality can be costly and that individual decision makers have limited information processing capabilities (Simon, 1947) to suggest that there are some very strong psychological biases built into the decision-making process that make purely rational decision making virtually impossible (Kahneman and Tversky, 1979a). The growing body of experimental evidence in this area is impressive (Kahneman, Slovic, and Tversky, 1987).

Though separate groups of scholars have continued to research the implications of these two metaphors for strategic management for at least several decades, it would be incorrect to suggest that these views have not come into conflict. Indeed, the entire development of the biased individual metaphor in prospect theory can be thought of as an elaborate criticism of the hyperrationality metaphor (Kahneman and Tversky, 1979a). Adherents to these different metaphors continue to argue for the importance of simplicity and parsimony (for the rational individual metaphor) versus the importance of empirical validity and richness (for the biased individual metaphor).

While there is little doubt that at one level of analysis these two metaphors for how firms behave come into direct conflict, at another level they are in fundamental agreement. The agreement concerns the appropriateness of studying the strategic behavior of organizations as if organizations were individual decision makers. Each of these metaphors discounts differences in the decision-making calculus (rational or biased) used by different individuals within an organization. Since all individuals within an organization are assumed to be homogeneous in their decision making (homogeneously rational or homogeneously biased), it becomes a reasonable simplification to analyze organizations as if they were individuals, and to use logics originally designed to study individual decision making to study strategic actions of firms, e.g., game theory and prospect theory.

There is, beyond convenience, some justification for adopting the "as if" assumption in these two metaphors. In the case of the rational decision-making metaphor, there was until recently no theoretical or empirical alternative to the rational decision-making model that was sufficiently specific and rigorous to allow the kind of analytical work that was the objective of game theorists and other economists (Hirshliefer, 1988). While theories of organizational behavior provided alternative views on motivation (e.g., equity theory [Adams, 1963]; expectancy theory [Vroom, 1964], most economists would argue that these theories were either not sufficiently specific to allow rigorous theoretical work, or were special cases of utility-maximizing approaches. In the case of the biased individual decision-making metaphor, empirical work suggests that the biases that have been discovered are so pervasive, that the assumption that all decision makers are systematically biased in the same ways, and to the same extent, seems a justifiable simplification (Kahneman, Slovic, and Tversky, 1987). In both cases, concluding that individual differences in decision making within a firm are either uninteresting or unimportant has made it possible to use the metaphors to analyze strategic actions taken by firms as if they were individual phenomena.

Although the as if approach to organizational analysis has numerous benefits, it has liabilities as well. Metaphors enlighten certain aspects of organizations by darkening others. While the as if assumption enables game theorists and prospect theorists to make strong statements about the strategies firms will pursue in different situations, it also eliminates several phenomena that may be important for understanding the competitive actions and reactions of "real" organizations. This paper examines three important limitations of analyzing the strategic actions of firms as if firms were individuals. First, I discuss how the as if metaphor focuses attention on "big decisions" in organizations as sources of competitive advantage. Next, I examine how this individualistic metaphor assumes away intraorganizational contradictions that can have an important impact on strategic behavior. Finally, I discuss how the use of this metaphor eliminates broad classes of intraorganizational phenomena as possible sources of competitive advantage.

Big Decisions and Competitive Advantage

Analyzing firm strategic actions as if firms were individuals tends to focus on big decisions made by organizations as sources of competitive advantage. Big decisions in organizations are decisions that define an entire organization's relationship with its competitive environment. Game theorists focus on these big decisions when they discuss how one organization (taken as a whole) responds to the competitive actions of another organization (taken as a whole). Prospect theorists focus on big decisions when they suggest that the strategic decisions made by firms (taken as a whole) will be systematically biased.

In focusing on big decisions as strategy, both game theory and prospect theory reinforce a long tradition of research in strategic management. The tradition began at the Harvard Business School, with research on the role of general managers in large organizations (Learned, Christensen, Andrews, and Guth, 1965). This research adopted the same kind of as if assumption used in game theory and prospect theory. However, instead of firms being analyzed as if they were hyperrational individuals or biased individuals, firms were analyzed as if they were general managers, and the decisions made by general managers were assumed to determine the long-term success of a firm. While general managers might rely on other line and staff managers, ultimately general managers themselves held the future of their corporation in their hands. In this framework, understanding how firms behave becomes understanding how general managers behave.

This emphasis on general managers has had important pedagogical implications. In many of the cases used in capstone business policy courses, the task is to analyze how a particular general manager came to make the big decisions he (they usually are men) did, and what implications these big decisions had for a firm's performance. The case is an attempt to force students to ask the question, If I had been in this person's place, what decisions would I have made, and what impact would they have had on this firm's competitive position? Whether it is Howard Head at Head Ski (Christensen, Andrews, Bower, Hamermesh, and Porter, 1987), John Connelly at Crown, Cork, & Seal (Christensen et al., 1987), or Marcel Bich at BIC Pen Company (Christensen et al., 1987), the emphasis in much of traditional strategic management research has been on the big decisions made by "important general managers." The message of these cases has been clear: if you want to positively affect the competitive position of the organization you work for, you too must become a general manager.[1]

One reaction to this almost exclusive emphasis on the importance of the general manager for understanding how firms behave is Porter's (1980, 1985) work on the impact of a firm's environment on its competitive position. Porter suggests that the strategic options facing an organization are significantly constrained by the structure of the industry within which the firm conducts business. The competitive environment places constraints on the impact of general managers in a firm, and thus on how firms behave.

However, even incorporating the Porter framework into strategic analysis has not led to the complete abandonment of studying organizations as if they were general managers. General managers, in Porter's framework, are still assigned the responsibility of analyzing their firm's competitive situation and choosing a strategy to steer a course through that competitive environment. The strategic decisions these managers make, whether they concern product differentiation, cost leadership, or focus, define an entire organization's relationship to its competitive environment, and are still the big decisions of classic strategic

---

[1] This emphasis on general managers in case analysis is perhaps most completely revealed in the series of cases on International Harvester (Christensen et al., 1987). The first case describes problems requiring the attention of a "strong" general manager. The second case identifies this general manager, Archie McCardell. Accompanying this case is a video recording of McCardell giving a speech at the Harvard Business School, where he receives a 15-minute standing ovation from the students. The third case chronicles the steady deterioration of International Harvester and McCardell's role in that deterioration. In all the cases on International Harvester, the general manager, whether hero or villain, is represented as the person whose decisions ultimately determine the fate of the firm.

management research. If a general manager chooses wisely, the firm can gain competitive advantage. If a general manager chooses less wisely, no competitive advantage is forthcoming.

There is little doubt that big decisions made by general managers can sometimes have an enormous impact on the performance of a firm. Bich's decision to invest in low-cost pens, despite five years of losses, had a huge impact on BIC. Connelly's emphasis on customer service had a similar impact on Crown, Cork, & Seal. Head Ski's inability to exploit Howard Head's inventive genius significantly hurt that organization's performance.

However, big decisions made by general managers may not be the only source of competitive advantage for a firm. Indeed, such big decisions may not even be the most important sources of sustained competitive advantage. Consider, for example, a firm like Wal-Mart. It is obvious to everyone that Wal-Mart follows a low-cost leadership strategy. Thus, the big decision made by Sam Walton to be a low-cost leader is not, by itself, proprietary, nor is it a source of competitive advantage. To the extent that Wal-Mart enjoys a competitive advantage, that advantage does not reflect just the big decision to be a low-cost firm, but rather the hundreds of thousands of "small decisions" that operationalize a big decision on a daily basis. Other discount retailers can easily duplicate Wal-Mart's big decision to be a low-cost firm, but still fail to duplicate the hundreds of thousands of smaller decisions that make the big decision real.

From a competitive point of view, small decisions have at least two advantages as potential sources of competitive advantage. First, these kinds of decisions, because they are so "small" and so numerous, are virtually invisible to those outside a firm (Itami and Roehl, 1987; Barney, 1992). Even managers inside a firm may not be fully aware of the cumulative impact of these kinds of decisions (Polanyi, 1962). When competing firms are unable to describe the basis of a particular firm's competitive advantage, because that advantage is based on thousands of small decisions, that competitive advantage may be immune to competitive duplication and imitation (Reed and DeFillippi, 1990) and thus may be sustained over time (Lippman and Rumelt, 1982).

Second, it may be the case that competitive advantage depends not on any one, or any subset, of these small decisions, but rather on the interrelated set of these decisions. Other firms may be able to imitate one or two, or even a majority of these small decisions, but may find it more difficult to imitate the entire set of interrelated decisions. Because this system of small decisions works as a whole, it may be less subject to imitation and duplication, and thus a source of sustained competitive advantage (Barney, 1991; Dierickx and Cool, 1989).

Consider, for example, attempts by U.S. auto manufacturers to duplicate the quality and cost positions of Japanese auto manufacturers. Firms like GM have invested billions of dollars based on a series of hypotheses about what makes the Japanese plants so effective. One hypothesis was that Japanese robots were the source of the advantage. After several billions of dollars of investment there was some improvement, but GM found itself using world-class robot technology to manufacture mediocre cars. Another hypothesis was that it was the Japanese just-in-time inventory system. GM rearranged its supplier relationships and inventory management systems. Again, there was some improvement, but the Japanese were still ahead. Several other hypotheses were used as a basis for additional investment (e.g., quality circles, labor-management relations, and the location of plants in rural areas). While each one of these changes in manufacturing improved the situation, what became clear was that the source of advantage was not in any one of these attributes of Japanese automobile plants, but in the simultaneous implementation of all of them.

Recent work on lean manufacturing suggests that it is the simultaneous combination of several factors that enables a manufacturing facility to be both very high quality and very low cost (MacDuffie, 1989; MacDuffie and Krafcik, 1990). This complicated system of numerous interrelated, mutually supporting small decisions is difficult to describe, and even more difficult to imitate, and thus a source of sustained competitive advantage (Barney, 1992).

Another way to think about the emphasis on big decisions in strategic management research is to observe that this kind of research tends to focus on strategy formulation and ignore strategy implementation. The emphasis on strategy formulation implies a belief that the decisions made about which strategies a firm should pursue will have a definitive impact on a firm's competitive advantage. Recognizing that small decisions may be more important for understanding competitive advantages than big decisions suggests that the study of strategy implementation—the process by which big decisions are translated into operational reality—may be more important for understanding competitive advantage than the study of strategy formulation.

Harold Demsetz (1973) once observed that sometimes it is very difficult to know why some firms do better than others. Competitive advantage can often be found in this causal ambiguity (Reed and DeFillippi, 1990). To the extent that the as if metaphors of game theory and prospect theory simply perpetuate the field's historical emphasis on big decisions made by general managers, the impact that numerous small decisions can have on competitive advantage will be lost.

Intraorganizational Contradictions and Firm Behavior

Another limitation of as if assumptions in game theory and prospect theory models of how firms behave is the simple model of individuals used in these metaphors. In game theory, individuals (and thus organizations) are assumed to rigorously and unerringly apply precisely the same decision calculus (utility maximization) in making decisions. There is no doubt, no hesitancy, no internal conflict and disagreement, only unalterable application of an established decision calculus. The decision calculus in prospect theory (biased rationality) is perhaps more complicated than the rationality assumption of game theory. However, the application of that biased rationality decision-making process is assumed to be just as unerring, just as internally consistent, just as predictable. In its application to organizations, internal contradictions (e.g., those that occur when different parts of the same organization are biased in different ways) are not emphasized. The individuals described in game theory and prospect theory are less like the individuals described by Freud (1953) and more like those described by Skinner (1953). These simple models of individual decision making are translated, by the as if metaphor, into rather simple models of how organizations behave.

If one desires to maintain an individualistic metaphor in analyzing firm behavior and decisions, perhaps an additional metaphor (beyond "firms as rational decision makers" or "firms as biased decision makers") could be "firms as individuals with multiple personality disorder." This metaphor admits the possibility that, within a single organization (individual), several distinct, often conflicting "personalities" might exist, that the content of decisions and actions taken by firms depends upon which personality happens to dominate at a particular time, that who will be dominant in decision making is essentially unpredictable, and that different personalities within an organization may be more or less skilled and able to make quality decisions (Kluft, 1987). Like individuals afflicted with multiple personalities, organizations with multiple personalities may sometimes appear to be perfectly rational, at other times to be biased rational decision makers, and at other times to be nonrational decision makers, and they may be continuously contradicting themselves over time (Ross and Gahan, 1988; Spanos, Weekes, and Bertrand, 1985).

The organization imagined by such a metaphor is not nearly as neat and easy to analyze as the organizations imagined by game theory and prospect theory. However, the multiple personality metaphor may be more appropriate in some situations, and it certainly raises a broad set of issues that are relevant in the study of how firms behave and that are not easily accessible to analysis using more traditional metaphors.

Of course, just as there are some individuals who are internally consistent and single-minded, there may be some organizations that behave as if they had no internal conflicts or contradictions. However, research in organization theory suggests that these organizations are the exception rather than the rule (Morgan, 1986b; Simon, 1947). More typically, different individuals and groups within an organization vary in their commitment to courses of action (Staw and Ross, 1988; Bowen, 1987). Some of this variance in commitment reflects the allocation of resources and rewards implied by a particular decision. Marketing and sales managers, for example, will often be very supportive of implementing a product differentiation strategy because such a strategy puts a premium on the skills they possess. Manufacturing managers may be less enthusiastic about product differentiation strategies, but strong supporters of a cost leader strategy. Other conflicts within an organization may reflect individual differences in experience, intelligence, and taste, and be independent of traditional organizational categories. Certain decisions may be preferred by some managers while contradictory decisions may be preferred by other managers.

Analyzing firms that contain numerous subgroups pursuing a variety of potentially contradictory agendas certainly complicates the study of how firms behave. Instead of firms behaving as if they were rational, or biased, or irrational, and so forth, researchers face the difficult problem of studying firm behavior as if it were simultaneously rational and biased and irrational.

One solution to this problem has been proposed by several organizational theorists (Pfeffer and Salancik, 1978). These theorists recognize the multiple, conflicting groups within an organization, and then focus on the political processes that unfold within firms and that enable firms to make decisions. And, once again, these researchers apply the as if assumption. In this case, however, firm decisions are analyzed as if they were the decisions of the "dominant coalition." Studying how firms behave thus involves (1) understanding how a particular group becomes part of the dominant coalition, and (2) examining how that dominant coalition makes decisions.

This solution to the multiple personality metaphor of organizations has many attractive properties. For example, it recognizes intraorganizational processes without losing the parsimony associated with as if kinds of analyses. However, this approach also makes some strong assumptions about the impact on firm behavior of groups that are not part of a firm's dominant coalition. Much of this work assumes that if a group is not part of the dominant coalition, it no longer has a significant impact on firm behavior. When researchers study firms as if they were a dominant coalition, they are implicitly assuming that those groups and individuals outside the coalition are not important for understanding how firms behave.

This simplification is inconsistent with the multiple personality disorder metaphor of organizations. The metaphor suggests that "losing" groups or individuals (i.e., those not in a firm's dominant coalition) continue to have an impact on firm behavior. These "other personalities" resist change and continue to pursue their own agendas, quite independent of the wishes of the dominant coalition (Staw and Ross, 1988). In other words, dominant coalitions are rarely as dominant as our simplified models would suggest. From the outside, firms do not appear to be implementing a single consistent strategy over time; rather they appear to be implementing several strategies, each of which may be internally consistent but which contradict one another. Sales managers may be trying to pursue a low-price, high-volume strategy, while marketing managers may be trying to pursue a low-volume product differentiation strategy, while accounting managers are focusing their efforts on reducing a firm's tax liability, while human resource managers are most concerned with meeting EEO requirements. How does this firm behave? Like a person with multiple personality disorder.

At first, it might appear that this kind of schizophrenic organization will be at best a temporary phenomenon, since more focused firms—even if they are biased in their rational decision making—will generally have a better chance of surviving over the long run (Friedman, 1953). And this may be true in industries characterized by little uncertainty, where optimal strategic paths can be chosen and implemented (Alchian, 1950). However, in a highly uncertain context, a multiple personality disorder may be a source of creativity, innovation, and random variation (Woodman and Schoenfeldt, 1990), which may enable this type of firm to survive where a more focused, less creative organization may be selected against by the environment (Hannan and Freeman, 1977). When a firm cannot know for sure what the "best" thing to do is, doing lots of different things at the same time can increase the chance of stumbling onto a good strategy (Kogut, 1991). Peters's (1987) description of a chaotic, playful organization includes many of the characteristics of multiple personality disorder described here—and he suggests that this structure is essential for success in highly turbulent environments.

Moreover, even in industries characterized by low levels of uncertainty, the time period needed to generate an equilibrium of all focused, single-personality firms can be substantial (Nelson and Winter, 1982). If we are to understand how firms behave, we must at least admit the possibility that some firms simultaneously pursue multiple contradictory strategies. To the extent that game theory and prospect theory models of strategy adopt relatively simple models of individuals as metaphors for the firm, this kind of behavior will remain inaccessible to systematic analysis.

As If Assumptions and Firm Heterogeneity

A final limitation of as if assumptions in game theory and prospect theory models of strategy focuses on the assumption of firm homogeneity implicit in these models. In game theory models, firms (as individuals) are assumed to accurately perceive the actions of competing firms, and then to calculate a response based on some well-defined objective function. In prospect theory models, firms (as individuals) are assumed to perceive the actions of competing firms in a biased manner, and then to calculate a response based on some well-defined, but not fully rational, objective function. Differences across firms in these models are limited to differences in their position in the competitive environment and differences in objective functions.

Models of firm behavior that assume high levels of interfirm homogeneity have recently become popular in strategy research. Most of this work is derived from industrial organization economics (Conner, 1991). The original objective of industrial organization (IO) economics was the identification of the structural attributes of industries that either facilitated or prevented the development of perfect competition (Porter, 1981). Thus, the level of analysis in IO economics was the industry, and firm differences within an industry were not a primary concern (Rumelt, 1984; Barney, 1991). As applied in strategy research, this emphasis on the impact of industry structure on average firm performance has continued (Porter, 1985). Models of the impact of industry structure on firm performance either assume that firms within an industry are homogeneous, or that firms within the same "strategic group" within an industry are homogeneous (Barney, 1991). When these models attempt to make statements about firm heterogeneity within an industry, they largely abandon their IO economic theoretical roots (Porter, 1985).

While models that assume firm homogeneity within an industry (or group) have grown in popularity, they are not fully consistent with the strategy formulation problem as it has been traditionally posed in the field (Christensen et al., 1987). Historically, strategy researchers have looked both to a firm's competitive environment and to its internal strengths and weaknesses in order to understand strategic actions. In the traditional framework, how firms behave was seen as depending both on the firm's competitive environment and on the unique resources and capabilities it possessed. By adopting the assumption that competing firms are relatively homogeneous, game theory and prospect theory models fail to acknowledge the importance of firm heterogeneity in determining behavior.

Recently, there has been a resurgence of interest in understanding the sources and competitive implications of firm heterogeneity. The models developed to analyze firm heterogeneity are collectively referred to as the resource-based view of the firm (Barney, 1991). This view generally adopts two assumptions about firms: first, that firms within an industry may possess different strategically relevant skills and capabilities and, second, that these differences can last over time. Skills and capabilities that enable an organization to conceive of, choose, and implement strategies that exploit environmental opportunities or neutralize environmental threats are strategically valuable. If few competing firms possess these resources, exploiting them can give a firm a competitive advantage. If firms without these resources face a cost disadvantage in obtaining them, and if there are no substitutes for these resources, they can be sources of sustained competitive advantage.

Applications of this resource-based logic are growing. It is even possible to apply this logic to game theory and prospect theory models of strategic behavior. For example, a resource-based game theory model would begin with the assumption that firms are fundamentally heterogeneous, in terms of the objective functions they pursue, the skills and abilities they bring to bear in maximizing their objective functions, and the strategies they can conceive of and implement in response to their competition. Indeed, several game theory models have been developed where firms are presumed to be heterogeneous in terms of some underlying key attribute (e.g., some firms are more "honest" than other firms [Axelrod, 1984], some firms are able to act more quickly than other firms [Leiberman and Montgomery, 1988], and so forth).

Prospect theory models that adopt a more resource-based view would also reflect firm heterogeneity. Thus, some firms might be dominated by one kind of cognitive bias, while other competing firms might be dominated by another type of cognitive bias. There is, for example, some recent research that suggests that entrepreneurs are systematically subject to some kinds of biases to a greater extent than managers in large organizations

(Busentiz, 1992). Thus, the behavior of firms dominated by entrepreneurs might be systematically different from the behavior of firms dominated by managers in large organizations. How these different kinds of firms would interact in a competitive setting is an interesting question.

It is not true, then, that game theory and prospect theory approaches to understanding how firms behave are incapable of being generalized to include firm heterogeneity. The models are probably general enough to include such work. However, to capture firm heterogeneity, these models will have to be extended in directions where they have traditionally not been extended.

To accomplish this generalization, both game theory and prospect theory will have to adopt an even more microanalytic perspective. This call for more microanalytic research may seem ironic, since game theory is a microeconomic technique, and prospect theory is grounded in cognitive psychology. However, the micro kind of analysis that is required would recognize that individuals (and by analogy, firms) can be fundamentally different, and that theories of how firms behave must include this heterogeneity in the analysis. Thus, future research will not only have to examine the implications of different decision-making calculi on individual and firm behavior, but also how different individuals and firms have different decision-making calculi.

Conclusion

There is little doubt that both game theory and prospect theory have a great deal to add to our understanding of how firms behave. The metaphors that firms behave as if they were rational individuals and as if they were biased individuals have obviously generated numerous important insights in strategy and related fields. However, additional progress in understanding how firms behave may depend at least in part on abandoning the comfort and convenience of these as if assumptions. Once abandoned, they are replaced by different kinds of game theory and prospect theory models of firm behavior. Some possible models have been examined here, including models of firms that focus on the cumulative impact of thousands of small decisions, models of firms that adopt a multiple personality metaphor, and models of firms that recognize firm heterogeneity and its impact on competitive advantage.

There are obviously many other ways that the as if assumptions of game theory and prospect theory can be modified. There is also a great deal of work to be done in tracing the implications of retaining these two metaphors. The next decade of research on how firms behave will depend, in large part, on how these metaphors are both extended into new areas and abandoned in favor of alternative metaphors.

3
Timid Choices and Bold Forecasts: A Cognitive Perspective on Risk Taking

Daniel Kahneman and Dan Lovallo

The thesis of this paper is that decision makers are excessively prone to treat problems as unique, neglecting both the statistics of the past and the multiple opportunities of the future. In part as a result, they are susceptible to two biases, which we label isolation errors: their forecasts of future outcomes are often anchored on plans and scenarios of success rather than on past results, and are therefore overly optimistic; their evaluations of single risky prospects neglect the possibilities of pooling risks and are therefore overly timid. We argue that the balance of the two isolation errors affects the risk-taking propensities of individuals and organizations.

The cognitive analysis of risk taking that we sketch differs from the standard rational model of economics and also from managers' view of their own activities. The rational model describes business decisions as choices among gambles with financial outcomes, and assumes that managers' judgments of the odds are Bayesian, and that their choices maximize expected utility. In this model, uncontrollable risks are acknowledged and accepted because they are compensated by chances of gain. As March and Shapira (1987) reported in a well-known essay, managers reject this interpretation of their role, preferring to view risk as a challenge to be overcome by the exercise of skill,

Acknowledgments: The preparation of this article was supported by the Center for Management Research at the University of California, Berkeley, by the Russell Sage Foundation, and by grants from the Sloan Foundation and from AFOSR, under grant number 88-0206. The ideas presented here developed over years of collaboration with Amos Tversky, but he should not be held responsible for our errors. We thank Philip Bromiley, Colin Camerer, George Loewenstein, Richard Thaler, and Amos Tversky for their many helpful comments.

and choice as a commitment to a goal. Although managers do not deny the possibility of failure, their idealized self-image is not that of a gambler, but of a prudent and determined agent, who is in control of both people and events.

The cognitive analysis accepts choices between gambles as a model of decision making, but does not adopt rationality as a maintained hypothesis. The gambling metaphor is apt because the consequences of most decisions are uncertain, and because each option could in principle be described as a probability distribution over outcomes. However, rather than suppose that decision makers are Bayesian forecasters and optimal gamblers, we shall describe them as being subject to the conflicting biases of unjustified optimism and unreasonable risk aversion. It is the optimistic denial of uncontrollable uncertainty that accounts for managers' views of themselves as prudent risk takers, and for their rejection of gambling as a model of what they do.

Our essay develops this analysis of forecasting and choice and explores its implications for organizational decisions. The target domain for applications includes choices about potentially attractive options that decision makers consider significant and to which they are willing to devote forecasting and planning resources. Examples may be capital investment projects, new products, or acquisitions. For reasons that will become obvious, our critique of excessive risk aversion is most likely to apply to decisions of intermediate size: large enough to matter for the organization, but not so large as to be truly unique, or potentially fatal. (Of course, such decisions could be perceived as both unique and potentially fatal by the executive who makes them.) Two other restrictions on the present treatment should be mentioned at the outset. First, we do not deal with decisions that the organization explicitly treats as routinely repeated. Opportunities for learning and for statistical aggregation exist when closely similar problems are frequently encountered, especially if the outcomes of decisions are quickly known and provide unequivocal feedback; competent management will ensure that these opportunities are exploited. Second, we do not deal with decisions made under severely adverse conditions, when all options are undesirable. These are situations in which high-risk gambles are often preferred to the acceptance of sure losses (Kahneman and Tversky, 1979a), and in which commitments often escalate and sunk costs dominate decisions (Staw and

Ross, 1989). We restrict the treatment to choices among options that can be considered attractive, although risky. For this class of projects, we predict that there will be a general tendency to underestimate actual risks, and a general reluctance to accept significant risks once they are acknowledged.

Timid Choices

We begin by reviewing three hypotheses about individual preferences for risky prospects.

Risk aversion. The first hypothesis is a commonplace: most people are generally risk averse, normally preferring a sure thing to a gamble of equal expected value, and a gamble of low variance over a riskier prospect. There are two important exceptions to risk aversion. First, many people are willing to pay more for lottery tickets than their expected value. Second, studies of individual choice have shown that managers, like other people, are risk-seeking in the domain of losses (Bateman and Zeithaml, 1989; Fishburn and Kochenberger, 1979; Laughhunn et al., 1980).[1] Except for these cases, and for the behavior of addicted gamblers, risk aversion is prevalent in choices between favorable prospects with known probabilities. This result has been confirmed in numerous studies, including some in which the subjects were executives (MacCrimmon and Wehrung, 1986; Swalm, 1966).[2]

The standard interpretation of risk aversion is decreasing marginal utility of gains. Prospect theory (Kahneman and Tversky, 1979a; Tversky and Kahneman, 1986, 1992) introduced two other causes: the certainty effect and loss aversion. The certainty effect is a sharp discrepancy between the weights that are attached to sure gains and to highly probable gains in the evaluation of prospects. In a recent study of preferences for gambles, the decision weight for a probability of 0.95 was approximately 0.80 (Tversky and Kahneman, 1992). Loss aversion refers to the observation that losses and disadvantages are

---

[1]   Observed correlations between accounting variability and mean return have also been interpreted as evidence of risk seeking by unsuccessful firms (Bowman, 1982; Fiegenbaum, 1990; Fiegenbaum and Thomas, 1988), but this interpretation is controversial (Ruefli, 1990).

[2]   A possible exception is a study by Wehrung (1989), which reported risk-neutral preferences for favorable prospects in a sample of executives in oil companies.

weighted more than gains and advantages. Loss aversion affects decision making in numerous ways, in riskless as well as in risky contexts. It favors inaction over action and the status quo over any alternatives, because the disadvantages of these alternatives are evaluated as losses and are therefore weighted more than their advantages (Kahneman et al., 1991; Samuelson and Zeckhauser, 1988; Tversky and Kahneman, 1991). Loss aversion strongly favors the avoidance of risks. The coefficient of loss aversion was estimated as about 2 in the Tversky-Kahneman experiment, and coefficients in the range of 2 to 2.5 have been observed in several studies, with both risky and riskless prospects (for reviews, see Kahneman, Knetsch, and Thaler, 1991; Tversky and Kahneman, 1991).

Near-proportionality. A second important generalization about risk attitudes is that, to a good first approximation, people are proportionately risk averse: cash equivalents for gambles of increasing size are (not quite) proportional to the stakes. Readers may find it instructive to work out their cash equivalent for a 0.50 chance to win $100, then $1,000, and up to $100,000. Most readers will find that their cash equivalent increases by a factor of less than 1,000 over that range, but most will also find that the factor is more than 700. Exact proportionality for wholly positive prospects would imply that value is a power function, $u(x) = x^a$, where x is the amount of gain (Keeney and Raiffa, 1976). In a recent study of preferences for gambles (Tversky and Kahneman, 1992), a power function provided a good approximation to the data over almost two orders of magnitude, and the deviations were systematic: cash equivalents increased slightly more slowly than prizes.

Much earlier, Swalm (1966) had compared executives whose planning horizons, defined as twice the maximum amount they might recommend be spent in one year, ranged from $50,000 to $24,000,000. He measured their utility functions by testing the acceptability of mixed gambles, and observed that the functions of managers at different levels were quite similar when expressed relative to their planning horizons. The point on which we focus in this paper is that there is almost as much risk aversion when stakes are small as when they are large. This is unreasonable on two grounds: (1) small gambles do not raise issues of survival or ruin, which provide a rationale for aversion to large risks; (2) small gambles are usually more common, offering more opportunities for the risk-reducing effects of statistical aggregation.

Narrow decision frames. The third generalization is that people tend to consider decision problems one at a time, often isolating the current problem from other choices that may be pending, as well as from future opportunities to make similar decisions. The following example (from Tversky and Kahneman, 1986) illustrates an extreme form of narrow framing:

> Imagine that you face the following pair of concurrent decisions. First examine both decisions, then indicate the options you prefer.
>
> Decision (i) Choose between:
> (A) a sure gain of $240 (84%)
> (B) 25% chance to gain $1000 and 75% chance to gain nothing (16%)
>
> Decision (ii) Choose between:
> (C) a sure loss of $750 (13%)
> (D) 75% chance to lose $1000 and 25% chance to lose nothing (87%)

The percentage of respondents choosing each option is shown in parentheses. As many readers may have discovered for themselves, the suggestion that the two problems should be considered concurrently has no effect on preferences, which exhibit the common pattern of risk aversion when options are favorable, and risk seeking when options are aversive. Most respondents prefer the conjunction of options A & D over other combinations of options. These preferences are intuitively compelling, and there is no obvious reason to suspect that they could lead to trouble. However, simple arithmetic shows that the conjunction of preferred options A & D is dominated by the conjunction of rejected options B & C. The combined options are as follows:

> A & D: 25% chance to win $240 and 75% chance to lose $760,
> B & C: 25% chance to win $250 and 75% chance to lose $750.

A decision maker who is risk averse in some situations and risk seeking in others ends up paying a premium to avoid some risks and a premium to obtain others. Because the outcomes are ultimately combined, these payments may be unsound. For a more realistic example, consider two divisions of a company that face separate decision problems.[3] One is in bad posture and faces a choice between a sure loss and a high probability of a larger loss; the other division faces a favorable choice. The natural

---

[3]   We are indebted to Amos Tversky for this example.

bent of intuition will favor a risk-seeking solution for one and a risk-averse choice for the other, but the conjunction could be poor policy. The overall interests of the company are better served by aggregating the problems than by segregating them, and by a policy that is generally more risk-neutral than intuitive preferences.

People often express different preferences when considering a single play or multiple plays of the same gamble. In a well-known problem devised by Samuelson (1963), many respondents state that they would reject a single play of a gamble in which they have equal chances to win $200 or to lose $100, but would accept multiple plays of that gamble, especially when the compound distribution of outcomes is made explicit (Redelmeier and Tversky, 1992). The question of whether this pattern of preferences is consistent with utility theory and with particular utility functions for wealth has been discussed on several occasions (e.g., Lopes, 1981; Tversky and Bar-Hillel, 1983). The argument that emerges from these discussions can be summarized as, "If you wish to obey the axioms of utility theory and would accept multiple plays, then it is logically inconsistent for you to turn down a single play." We focus on another observation: the near-certainty that the individual who is now offered a single play of the Samuelson gamble is not really facing her last opportunity to accept or reject a gamble of positive expected value. This suggests a slightly different argument: "If you would accept multiple plays, then you should accept the single one that is offered now, because it is very probable that other bets of the same kind will be offered to you later." A frame that includes future opportunities reduces the difference between the two versions of Samuelson's problem, because a rational individual who is offered a single gamble will adopt a policy for $m + 1$ such gambles, where m is the number of similar opportunities expected within the planning horizon. Will people spontaneously adopt such a broad frame? A plausible hypothesis, supported by the evidence for narrow framing in concurrent decisions and by the pattern of answers to Samuelson's problems, is that expectations about risky opportunities of the future are simply ignored when decisions are made.

It is generally recognized that a broad view of decision problems is an essential requirement of rational decision making. There are several ways of broadening the decision frame. Thus, decision analysts commonly prescribe that concurrent choices should be aggregated before a decision is made, and that outcomes should be evaluated in terms of final assets (wealth), rather than in terms of the gains and losses associated with each move. The recommended practice is to include estimates of future earnings in the assessment of wealth. Although this point has attracted little attention in the decision literature, the wealth of an agent or organization therefore includes future risky choices, and depends on the decisions that the decision maker anticipates making when these choices arise.[4] The decision frame should be broadened to include these uncertainties: neglect of future risky opportunities will lead to decisions that are not optimal, as evaluated by the agent's own utility function. As we show next, the costs of neglecting future opportunities are especially severe when options are evaluated in terms of gains and losses, which is what people usually do.

The Costs of Isolation

The present section explores some consequences of incorporating future choice opportunities into current decisions. We start from an idealized utility function which explains people's proportional risk preferences for single gambles. We then compute the preferences that this function implies when the horizon expands to include a portfolio of gambles.

Consider an individual who evaluates outcomes as gains and losses, and who maximizes expected utility in these terms. This decision maker is risk averse in the domain of gains, risk-seeking in the domain of losses, loss averse, and her risky choices exhibit perfect proportionality. She is indifferent between a 0.50 chance to win $1,000 and a sure gain of $300 (also between a 0.50 chance to win $10,000 and $3,000 for sure) and she is also indifferent between the status quo and a gamble that offers equal chances to win $250 or to lose $100. The aversion to risk exhibited by this individual is above the median of respondents in laboratory studies, but well within the range of

---

[4] Two agents that have the same current holdings and face the same series of risky choices do not have the same wealth if they have different attitudes to risk and expect to make different decisions. For formal discussions of choice in the presence of unresolved uncertainty, see Kreps (1988) and Spence and Zeckhauser (1972).

observed values. For the sake of simple exposition we ignore all probability distortions and attribute the risk preferences of the individual entirely to the shape of her utility function for gains and losses. The preferences we have assumed imply that the individual's utility for gains is described by a power function with an exponent of 0.575 and that the function in the domain of losses is the mirror image of the function for gains, after expansion of the X-axis by a factor of 2.5 (Tversky and Kahneman, 1991). The illustrative function was chosen to highlight our main conclusion: with proportional risk attitudes, even the most extreme risk aversion on individual problems quickly vanishes when gambles are considered part of a portfolio.

The power utility function is decreasingly risk averse, and the decrease is quite rapid. Thus, a proportionately risk-averse individual who values a 0.50 chance to win $100 at $30 will value a gamble that offers equal chances to win either $1,000 or $1,100 at $1,049. This preference is intuitively acceptable, indicating again that the power function is a good description of the utility of outcomes for single gambles considered in isolation. The power function fits the psychophysical relation of subjective magnitude to physical magnitude in many other contexts (Stevens, 1975).

To appreciate the effects of even modest aggregation with this utility function, assume that the individual owns three independent gambles:

one gamble with a 0.50 chance to win $500.
two gambles, each with a 0.50 chance to win $250.

Simple arithmetic yields the compound gamble:

0.125 chance to win $1,000, and 0.25 to win $750, $500, and $250.

If this individual applies the correct probabilities to her utility function, this portfolio will be worth $433 to her. This should be her minimum selling price if she owns the gamble, her cash equivalent if she has to choose between the portfolio of gambles and cash. In contrast, the sum of the cash equivalents of the gambles considered one at a time is only $300. The certainty premium the individual would pay has dropped from 40% to 13% of expected value. By the individual's own utility function, the cost of considering these gambles in isolation is 27% of their expected value, surely more than any rational decision maker should be willing to pay for whatever mental economy this isolation achieves.

The power of aggregation to overcome loss aversion is equally impressive. As already noted, our decision maker is indifferent between accepting or rejecting a gamble that offers a 0.50 chance to win $250 and a 0.50 chance to lose $100. However, she would value the opportunity to play two of these gambles at $45, and six gambles at $304. Note that the average incremental value of adding the third to the sixth gamble is $65, quite close to the EV of $75, although each gamble is worth nothing on its own.

Finally, we note that decisions about single gambles will no longer appear risk-proportional when gambles are evaluated in the context of a portfolio, even if the utility function has that property. Suppose the individual now owns a set of eleven gambles:

one gamble with a 0.50 chance to win $1,000,
ten gambles, each with a 0.50 chance to win $100.

The expected value of the set is $1,000. If the gambles were considered one at a time, the sum of their cash equivalents would be only $600. With proper aggregation, however, the selling price for the package should be $934. Now suppose the decision maker considers trading only one of the gambles. After selling a gamble for an amount X, she retains a reduced compound gamble in which the constant X is added to each outcome. The decision maker, of course, will only sell if the value of the new gamble is at least equal to the value of the original portfolio. The computed selling price for the larger gamble is $440, and the selling price for one of the smaller gambles is $49. Note that the premium given up to avoid the risk is 12% of expected value for the large gamble, but only 2% for the small one. A rational decision maker who applies a proportionately risk-averse utility function to aggregate outcomes will set cash equivalents closer to risk-neutrality for smaller gambles than for larger ones.

As these elementary examples illustrate, the common attitude of a strong (and proportional) aversion to risk and to losses entails a risk policy that quickly approaches neutrality as the portfolio is extended.[5] Because possibilities of aggregation over future decisions always exist for an ongoing concern, and because the chances for aggregation are likely to be inversely correlated with the size of the problem, the near-proportionality of risk attitudes for gambles of varying sizes is logically incoherent, and the extreme risk aversion observed for prospects that are small relative to assets is unreasonable. To rationalize observed preferences one must assume that the decision maker approaches each choice problem as if it were her last—there seems to be no relevant tomorrow. It is somewhat surprising that the debate on the rationality of risky decisions has focused almost exclusively on the curiosities of the Allais and Ellsberg paradoxes, instead of on simpler observations, such as the extraordinary myopia implied by extreme and nearly proportional risk aversion.

Risk Taking in Organizations: Implications and Speculations

The preceding sections discussed evidence that people, when faced with explicitly probabilistic prospects in experimental situations, tend to frame their decision problem narrowly, have near-proportional risk attitudes, and are, as a consequence, excessively risk averse in small decisions, where they ignore the effects of aggregation. Extending these ideas to business decisions is necessarily speculative, because the attitudes to risk that are implicit in such decisions are not easily measured. One way to approach this problem is by asking whether the organizational context in which many business decisions are made is more likely to enhance or to inhibit risk aversion, narrow framing, and near-proportionality. We examine this question in the present section.

Risk aversion. There is little reason to believe that the fac-

---

[5] The conclusions of the present section do not critically depend on the assumption of expected utility theory, that the decision maker weights outcomes by their probabilities. All the calculations reported above were repeated using cumulative prospect theory (Tversky and Kahneman, 1992) with plausible parameters (a = 0.73; b = c = 0.6 and a loss aversion coefficient of 2.5). Because extreme outcomes are assigned greater weight in prospect theory than in the expected utility model, the mitigation of risk aversion as the portfolio expands is somewhat slower. Additionally, the risk seeking that prospect theory predicts for single low-probability positive gambles is replaced by risk aversion for repeated gambles.

tors that produce risk aversion in the personal evaluation of explicit gambles are neutralized in the context of managerial decisions. For example, attempts to measure the utility that executives attach to gains and losses of their firm suggest that the principle of decreasing marginal values applies to these outcomes (MacCrimmon and Wehrung, 1986; Swalm, 1966). The underweighting of probable gains in comparisons with sure ones, known as the certainty effect, is also unlikely to vanish in managerial decisions. The experimental evidence indicates that the certainty effect is not eliminated when probabilities are vague or ambiguous, as they are in most real-life situations, and the effect may even be enhanced (Curley et al., 1986; Hogarth and Einhorn, 1990). We suspect that the effect may become even stronger when a choice becomes a subject of debate, as is commonly the case in managerial decisions: the rhetoric of prudent decision making favors the certainty effect, because an argument that rests on mere probability is always open to doubt.

Perhaps the most important cause of risk aversion is loss aversion, the discrepancy between the weights that are attached to losses and to gains in evaluating prospects. Loss aversion is not mitigated when decisions are made in an organizational context. On the contrary, the asymmetry between credit and blame may enhance the asymmetry between gains and losses in the decision maker's utilities. The evidence indicates that the pressures of accountability and personal responsibility increase the status quo bias and other manifestations of loss aversion. Decision makers become more risk averse when they expect their choices to be reviewed by others (Tetlock and Boettger, 1992) and they are extremely reluctant to accept responsibility for even a small increase in the probability of a disaster (Viscusi et al., 1987). Swalm (1966) noted that managers appear to have an excessive aversion to any outcome that could yield a net loss, citing the example of a manager in a firm described as "an industrial giant," who would decline to pursue a project that has a 50–50 chance of either making for his company a gain of $300,000 or losing $60,000. Swalm hypothesized that the steep slopes of utility functions in the domain of losses may be due to control procedures that bias managers against choices that might lead to losses. This interpretation seems appropriate since "several respondents stated quite clearly that they were aware that their choices were not in the best interests of the company, but that they felt them to be in their own best interests as aspiring executives."

We conclude that the forces that produce risk aversion in experimental studies of individual choice may be even stronger in the managerial context. Note, however, that we do not claim that an objective observer would describe managerial decisions as generally risk averse. The second part of this essay will argue that decisions are often based on optimistic assessments of the chances of success, and are therefore objectively riskier than the decision makers perceive them to be. Our hypotheses about risk in managerial decisions are: (1) in a generally favorable context, the threshold for accepting risk will be high, and acceptable options will be *subjectively* perceived as carrying low risk; (2) for problems viewed in isolation the willingness to take risks is likely to be approximately constant for decisions that vary greatly in size; and (3) decisions will be narrowly framed even when they could be viewed as instances of a category of similar decisions. As a consequence, we predict (4) an imbalance in the risks that the organization accepts in large and in small problems, such that relative risk aversion is lower for the aggregate of small decisions than for the aggregate of large decisions. These hypotheses are restricted to essentially favorable situations, which often yield risk aversion in laboratory studies. We specifically exclude situations in which risk seeking is common, such as choices between essentially negative options, or choices that involve small chances of large gain.

Narrow framing. We have suggested that people tend to make decisions one at a time, and in particular that they are prone to neglect the relevance of future decision opportunities. For both individuals and organizations, the adoption of a broader frame and of a consistent risk policy depends on two conditions: (1) an ability to group together problems that are superficially different, and (2) an appropriate procedure for evaluating outcomes and the quality of performance.

A consistent risk policy can only be maintained if the recurrent problems to which the policy applies are recognized as such. This is sometimes easy: competent organizations will identify obvious recurring questions—for example, whether or not to purchase insurance for a company vehicle—and will adopt policies for such questions. The task is more complex when each decision problem has many unique features, as might be the case for acquisitions or new product development. The explicit adoption of a broad frame will then require the use of an abstract language that highlights the important common dimensions of diverse decision problems. Formal decision analysis provides such a language, in which outcomes are expressed in money and uncertainty is quantified as probability. Other abstract languages could be used for the same purpose. As practitioners of decision analysis well know, however, the use of an abstract language conflicts with a natural tendency to describe each problem in its own terms. Abstraction necessarily involves a loss of subtlety and specificity, and the summary of descriptions that permit projects to be compared almost always appear superficial and inadequate.

In the case of the individual executive who faces a succession of decisions, the maintenance of a broad decision frame also depends on how her performance will be evaluated, and on the frequency of performance reviews. For a schematic illustration, assume that reviews occur at predictable points in the sequence of decisions and outcomes, and that the executive's outcomes are determined by the *value* of the firm's outcomes since the last review. Suppose the evaluation function is identical to the utility function introduced in the preceding numerical examples: the credit for gaining 2.5 units and the blame for losing 1 unit just cancel out. With this utility function, a single gamble that offers equal probabilities to win 2 units or to lose 1 unit will not be acceptable if performance is evaluated on that gamble by itself. The decision will not change even if the manager knows that there will be a second opportunity to play the same gamble. However, if the evaluation of outcomes and the assignment of credit and blame can be deferred until the gamble has been played twice, the probability that the review will be negative drops from 0.50 to 0.25 and the compound gamble will be accepted. As this example illustrates, reducing the frequency of evaluations can mitigate the inhibiting effects of loss aversion on risk taking, as well as other manifestations of myopic discounting.

The attitude that "you win a few and you lose a few" could be recommended as an antidote to narrow framing, because it suggests that the outcomes of a set of separable decisions should be aggregated before evaluation. However, the implied tolerance for "losing a few" may conflict with other managerial imperatives, including the setting of high standards and the maintenance of tight supervision. By the same token, of course, narrow framing and excessive risk aversion may be unintended consequences of excessive insistence on measurable short-term successes. A plausible hypothesis is that the adoption of a broad frame of evaluation is most natural when the expected rate of success is low for each attempt, as in drilling for oil or in pharmaceutical development.[6] The procedures of performance evaluation that have evolved in these industries could provide a useful model for other attempts to maintain consistent risk policies.

Near-proportionality of risk attitudes. Many executives in a hierarchical organization have two distinct decision tasks: they make risky choices on behalf of the organization, and they supervise several subordinates who also make decisions. For analytical purposes, the options chosen by subordinates can be treated as independent (or imperfectly correlated) gambles, which usually involve smaller stakes than the decisions made personally by the superior. A problem of risk aggregation inevitably arises, and we conjecture that solving it efficiently may be quite difficult.

To begin, ignore the supervisory function and assume that all decisions are made independently, with narrow framing. If all decision makers apply the same nearly proportional risk attitudes (as suggested by Swalm, 1966), an unbalanced set of choices will be made: the aggregate of the subordinates' decisions will be more risk averse than the supervisor's own decisions on larger problems—which in turn are more risk averse than her global utility for the portfolio, rationally evaluated. As we saw in an earlier section, the costs of such inconsistencies in risk attitudes can be quite high.

Clearly, one of the goals of the executive should be to avoid the potential inefficiency, by applying a consistent policy to risky choices and to those she supervises—and the consistent policy is *not* one of proportional risk aversion. As was seen earlier, a rational executive who considers a portfolio consisting of one large gamble (which she chose herself) and ten smaller gambles (presumably chosen by subordinates) should be considerably more risk averse in valuing the large gamble than in valuing any one of the smaller gambles. The counter-intuitive

---

[6] We owe this hypothesis to Richard Thaler.

implication of this analysis is that, in a generally favorable context, an executive should encourage subordinates to adopt a higher level of risk acceptance than the level with which she feels comfortable. This is necessary to overcome the costly effects of the (probable) insensitivity of her intuitive preferences to recurrence and aggregation. We suspect that many executives will resist this recommendation, which contradicts the common belief that accepting risks is both the duty and the prerogative of higher management.

For several reasons, narrow framing and near-proportionality could be difficult to avoid in a hierarchical organization. First, many decisions are both unique and large at the level at which they are initially made. The usual aversion to risk is likely to prevail in such decisions, even if from the point of view of the firm they could be categorized as recurrent and moderately small. Second, it appears unfair for a supervisor to urge acceptance of a risk that a subordinate is inclined to reject— especially because the consequences of failure are likely to be more severe for the subordinate.

In summary, we have drawn on three psychological principles to derive the prediction that the risk attitudes that govern decisions of different sizes may not be coherent. The analysis suggests that there may be too much aversion to risk in problems of small or moderate size. However, the conclusion that greater risk taking should be encouraged could be premature at this point, because of the suspicion that the agents' view of prospects may be systematically biased in an optimistic direction. The combination of a risk-neutral attitude and an optimistic bias could be worse than the combination of unreasonable risk aversion and unjustified optimism. As the next sections show, there is good reason to believe that such a dilemma indeed exists.

Bold Forecasts

Our review of research on individual risk attitudes suggests that the substantial degree of risk to which individuals and organizations willingly expose themselves is unlikely to reflect true acceptance of these risks. The alternative is that people and organizations often expose themselves to risk because they misjudge the odds. We next consider some of the mechanisms that produce the "bold forecasts" that enable cautious decision makers to take large risks.

Inside and Outside Views

We introduce this discussion by a true story, which illustrates an important cognitive quirk that tends to produce extreme optimism in planning.

> In 1976 one of us (Daniel Kahneman) was involved in a project designed to develop a curriculum for the study of judgment and decision making under uncertainty for high schools in Israel. The project was conducted by a small team of academics and teachers. When the team had been in operation for about a year, with some significant achievements already to its credit, the discussion at one of the team meetings turned to the question of how long the project would take. To make the debate more useful, I asked everyone to indicate on a slip of paper their best estimate of the number of months that would be needed to bring the project to a well-defined stage of completion: a complete draft ready for submission to the ministry of education. The estimates, including my own, ranged from 18 to 30 months. At this point I had the idea of turning to one of our members, a distinguished expert in curriculum development, asking him a question phrased about as follows: "We are surely not the only team to have tried to develop a curriculum where none existed before. Please try to recall as many such cases as you can. Think of them as they were in a stage comparable to ours at present. How long did it take them, from that point, to complete their projects?" After a long silence, something much like the following answer was given, with obvious signs of discomfort: "First, I should say that not all teams that I can think of in a comparable stage ever did complete their task. About 40% of them eventually gave up. Of the remaining, I cannot think of any that was completed in less than seven years, nor of any that took more than ten." In response to a further question, he answered: "No, I cannot think of any relevant factor that distinguishes us favorably from the teams I have been thinking about. Indeed, my impression is that we are slightly below average in terms of our resources and potential."

This story illustrates several of the themes that will be developed in this section.

Two distinct modes of forecasting were applied to the same problem in this incident. The *inside view* of the problem is the one that all participants in the meeting spontaneously adopted. An inside view forecast is generated by focusing on the case at hand, by considering the plan and the obstacles to its completion, by constructing scenarios of future progress, and by extrapolating current trends. The *outside view* is the one that the curriculum expert was encouraged to adopt. It essentially ignores the details of the case at hand, and involves no attempt at detailed forecasting of the future history of the project. Instead, it focuses on the statistics of a class of cases chosen to be similar in relevant respects to the present one. The case at hand is also compared to other members of the class, in an attempt to assess its position in the distribution of outcomes for the class (Kahneman and Tversky, 1979b). The distinction between inside and outside views in forecasting is closely related to the distinction drawn earlier between narrow and broad framing of decision problems. The critical question in both contexts is whether a particular problem of forecast or decision is treated as unique, or as an instance of an ensemble of similar problems.

The application of the outside view was particularly simple in this example, because the relevant class for the problem was easy to find and to define. Other cases are more ambiguous. What class should be considered, for example, when a firm considers the probable costs of an investment in a new technology in an unfamiliar domain? Is it the class of ventures in new technologies in the recent history of this firm, or the class of developments most similar to the proposed one, carried out in other firms? Neither is perfect, and the recommendation would be to try both (Kahneman and Tversky, 1979b). It may also be necessary to choose units of measurement that permit comparisons. The ratio of actual spending to planned expenditure is an example of a convenient unit that permits meaningful comparisons across diverse projects.

The inside and outside views draw on different sources of information, and apply different rules to its use. An inside view forecast draws on knowledge of the specifics of the case, the details of the plan that exists, some ideas about likely obstacles and how they might be overcome. In an extreme form, the inside view involves an attempt to sketch a representative scenario that captures the essential elements of the history of the future. In contrast, the outside view is essentially statistical and comparative, and involves no attempt to divine future history at any level of detail.

It should be obvious that when both methods are applied with equal intelligence and skill, the outside view is much more likely to yield a realistic estimate. In general, the future of a long and complex undertaking is simply not foreseeable in detail. The ensemble of possible future histories cannot be defined. Even if this could be done, the ensemble would in most cases be huge, and the probability of any particular scenario negligible.[7]

---

[7] For the purposes of this exposition we assume that probabilities exist as a fact about the world. Readers who find this position shocking should transpose the formulation to a more complex one, according to their philosophical taste.

Although some scenarios are more likely or plausible than others, it is a serious error to assume that the outcomes of the most likely scenarios are also the most likely, and that outcomes for which no plausible scenarios come to mind are impossible. In particular, the scenario of flawless execution of the current plan may be much more probable a priori than any scenario for a specific sequence of events that would cause the project to take four times longer than planned. Nevertheless, the less favorable outcome could be more likely overall, because there are so many different ways for things to go wrong. The main advantage of the outside approach to forecasting is that it avoids the snares of scenario thinking (Dawes, 1988). The outside view provides some protection against forecasts that are not even in the ball-park of reasonable possibilities. It is a conservative approach, which will fail to predict extreme and exceptional events, but will do well with common ones. Furthermore, giving up the attempt to predict extraordinary events is not a great sacrifice when uncertainty is high, because the only way to score "hits" on such events is to predict large numbers of other extraordinary events that do not materialize.

This discussion of the statistical merits of the outside view sets the stage for our main observation, which is psychological: the inside view is overwhelmingly preferred in intuitive forecasting. The natural way to think about a problem is to bring to bear all one knows about it, with special attention to its unique features. The intellectual detour into the statistics of related cases is seldom chosen spontaneously. Indeed, the relevance of the outside view is sometimes explicitly denied: physicians and lawyers often argue against the application of statistical reasoning to particular cases. In these instances, the preference for the inside view almost bears a moral character. The inside view is valued as a serious attempt to come to grips with the complexities of the unique case at hand, and the outside view is rejected for relying on crude analogy from superficially similar instances. This attitude can be costly in the coin of predictive accuracy.

Three other features of the curriculum story should be mentioned. First, the example illustrates the general rule that consensus on a forecast is not necessarily an indication of its validity: a shared deficiency of reasoning will also yield consensus. Second, we note that the initial intuitive assessment of our curriculum expert was similar to that of other members of the team. This illustrates a more general observation: statistical knowledge that is known to the forecaster will not necessarily be used, or indeed retrieved, when a forecast is made by the inside approach. The literature on the impact of the base rates of outcomes on intuitive predictions supports this conclusion. Many studies have dealt with the task of predicting the profession or the training of an individual on the basis of some personal information and relevant statistical knowledge. For example, most people have some knowledge of the relative sizes of different departments, and could use that knowledge in guessing the field of a student seen at a graduation ceremony. The experimental evidence indicates that base-rate information that is explicitly mentioned in the problem has some effect on predictions, though usually not as much as it should have (Griffin and Tversky, 1992; Lynch and Ofir, 1989; for an alternative view see Gigerenzer et al., 1988). When only personal information is explicitly offered, relevant statistical information that is known to the respondent is largely ignored (Kahneman and Tversky, 1973; Tversky and Kahneman, 1983).

The sequel to the story illustrates a third general observation: facing the facts can be intolerably demoralizing. The participants in the meeting had professional expertise in the logic of forecasting, and none even ventured to question the relevance of the forecast implied by our expert's statistics: an even chance of failure, and a completion time of seven to ten years in case of success. Neither of these outcomes was an acceptable basis for continuing the project, but no one was willing to draw the embarrassing conclusion that it should be scrapped. So, the forecast was quietly dropped from active debate, along with any pretense of long-term planning, and the project went on along its predictably unforeseeable path to eventual completion some eight years later.

The contrast between the inside and outside views has been confirmed in systematic research. One relevant set of studies was concerned with the phenomenon of overconfidence. There is massive evidence for the conclusion that people are generally overconfident in their assignments of probability to their beliefs. Overconfidence is measured by recording the proportion of cases in which statements to which an individual assigned a probability p were actually true. In many studies this proportion has been found to be far lower than p (see Lichtenstein et al., 1982; for a more recent discussion and some instructive exceptions see Griffin and Tversky, 1992). Overconfidence is often assessed by presenting general information questions in a multiple-choice format, where the participant chooses the most likely answer and assigns a probability to it. A typical result is that respondents are only correct on about 80% of cases when they describe themselves as "99% sure." People are overconfident in evaluating the accuracy of their beliefs one at a time. It is interesting, however, that there is no evidence of overconfidence bias when respondents are asked after the session to estimate the number of questions for which they picked the correct answer. These global estimates are accurate, or somewhat pessimistic (Gigerenzer et al., 1991; Griffin and Tversky, 1992). It is evident that people's assessments of their overall accuracy does not control their confidence in particular beliefs. Academics are familiar with a related example: finishing our papers almost always takes us longer than we expected. We all know this and often say so. Why then do we continue to make the same error? Here again, the outside view does not inform judgments of particular cases.

In a compelling example of the contrast between inside and outside views, Cooper et al. (1988) interviewed new entrepreneurs about their chances of success, and also elicited from them estimates of the base rate of success for enterprises of the same kind. Self-assessed chances of success were uncorrelated to objective predictors of success such as college education, prior supervisory experience, and initial capital. They were also wildly off the mark on average. Over 80% of entrepreneurs perceived their chances of success as 70% or better. Fully one-third of them described their success as certain. On the other hand, the mean chance of success that these entrepreneurs attributed to a business like theirs was 59%. Even this estimate is optimistic, though it is closer to the truth: the five-year survival rate for new firms is around 33% (Dun & Bradstreet, 1967).

The inside view does not invariably yield optimistic forecasts. Many parents of rebellious teenagers cannot imagine how their offspring would ever become a reasonable adult, and are consequently more worried than they should be, since they also know that almost all teenagers do eventually grow up. The general point is that the inside view is susceptible to the fallacies of scenario thinking and to anchoring of estimates on present values or on extrapolations of current trends. The inside view burdens the worried parents with statistically unjustified premonitions of doom. To decision makers with a goal and a plan, the same way of thinking offers absurdly optimistic forecasts.

The cognitive mechanism we have discussed is not the only source of optimistic errors. Unrealistic optimism also has deep motivational roots (Tiger, 1979). A recent literature review (Taylor and Brown, 1988) listed three main forms of a pervasive optimistic bias: (1) unrealistically positive self-evaluations, (2) unrealistic optimism about future events and plans, and (3) an illusion of control. Thus, for almost every positive trait—including safe driving, a sense of humor, and managerial risk taking (MacCrimmon and Wehrung, 1986)—there is a large majority of individuals who believe themselves to be above the median. People also exaggerate their control over events, and the importance of the skills and resources they possess in ensuring desirable outcomes. Most of us underestimate the likelihood of hazards affecting us personally, and entertain the unlikely belief that Taylor and Brown summarize as "The future will be great, especially for me."

Organizational Optimism

There is no reason to believe that entrepreneurs and executives are immune to optimistic bias. The prevalence of delusions of control among managers has been recognized by many authors (among others, Duhaime and Schwenk, 1985; March and Shapira, 1987; Salancik and Meindl, 1984). As we noted earlier, managers commonly view risk as a challenge to be overcome, and believe that risk can be modified by "managerial wisdom and skill" (Donaldson and Lorsch, 1983). The common refusal of managers to refuse risk estimates provided to them as "given" (Shapira, 1986) is a clear illustration of illusion of control.

Do organizations provide effective controls against the optimistic bias of individual executives? Are organizational decisions founded on impartial and unbiased forecasts of consequences? In answering these questions, we must again distinguish problems that are treated as recurrent, such as forecasts of the sales of existing product lines, from others that are considered unique. We have no reason to doubt the ability of organizations to impose forecasting discipline and to reduce or eliminate obvious biases in recurrent problems. As in the case of risk, however, all significant forecasting problems have features that make them appear unique. It is in these unique problems that biases of judgment and choice are most likely to have their effects, for organizations as well as for individuals. We next discuss some likely causes of optimistic bias in organizational judgments, some observations of this bias, and the costs and benefits of unrealistic optimism.

Causes. Forecasts often develop as part of a case that is made by an individual or group that already has, or is developing, a vested interest in the plan, in a context of competition for the control of organizational resources. The debate is often adversarial. The only projects that have a good chance of surviving in this competition are those for which highly favorable outcomes are forecast, and this produces a powerful incentive for would-be promoters to present optimistic numbers. The statistical logic that produces the winner's curse in other contexts (Capen, Clapp, and Campbell, 1971; Bazerman and Samuelson, 1983; Kagel and Levin, 1986) applies here as well: the winning project is more likely than others to be associated with optimistic errors (Harrison and March, 1984). This is an effect of regression to the mean. Thus, the student who did best in an initial test is also the one for whom the most regression is expected on a subsequent test. Similarly, the projects that are forecast to have the highest returns are the ones most likely to fall short of expectations.

Officially adopted forecasts are also likely to be biased by their secondary functions as demands, commands, and commitments (Lowe and Shaw, 1968; Lawler and Rhode, 1976; Lawler, 1986; Larkey and Smith, 1984). A forecast readily becomes a target, which induces loss aversion for performance that does not match expectations, and can also induce satisficing indolence when the target is exceeded. The obvious advantage of setting high goals is an incentive for higher management to adopt and disseminate optimistic assessments of future accomplishments—and possibly to deceive themselves in the process.

In his analysis of "groupthink," Janis (1982) identified other factors that favor organizational optimism. Pessimism about what the organization can do is readily interpreted as disloyalty, and consistent bearers of bad news tend to be shunned. Bad news can be demoralizing. When pessimistic opinions are suppressed in this manner, exchanges of views will fail to perform a critical function. The optimistic biases of individual group members can become mutually reinforcing, as unrealistic views are validated by group approval.

The conclusion of this sketchy analysis is that there is little reason to believe organizations will avoid the optimistic bias— except perhaps when the problems are considered recurrent and subjected to statistical quality control. On the contrary, there are reasons to suspect that many significant decisions made in organizations are guided by unrealistic forecasts of their consequences.

Observations. The optimistic bias of capital investment projects is a familiar fact of life: the typical project finishes late, comes in over budget when it is finally completed, and fails to achieve its initial goals. Grossly optimistic errors appear to be especially likely if the project involves new technology or otherwise places the firm in unfamiliar territory. A Rand Corporation study on pioneer process plants in the energy field demonstrates the magnitude of the problem (Merrow et al., 1981). Almost all project construction costs exceeded initial estimates by over 20%. The norm was for actual construction costs to more than double first estimates. These conclusions are corroborated by PIMS data on start-up ventures in a wide range of industries (cited by Davis, 1985). More than 80% of the projects studied fell short of planned market share.

In an interesting discussion of the causes of failure in capital investment projects, Arnold (1986) states:

> Most companies support large capital expenditure programs with a worst case analysis that examines the project's loss potential. But the worst case forecast is almost always too optimistic. . . . When managers look at the downside they generally describe a mildly pessimistic future rather than the worst possible future.

As an antidote against rosy predictions Arnold recommends staying power analysis, a method used by lenders to determine if organizations under severe strain can make payments. In effect, the advice is for managers to adopt an outside view of their own problem.

Mergers and acquisitions provide another illustration of optimism and of illusions of control. On average, bidding firms do not make a significantly positive return. This striking observation raises the question of why so many takeovers and mergers are initiated. Roll (1986) offers a "hubris hypothesis" to explain why decision makers acquiring firms tend to pay too much for their targets. Roll cites optimistic estimates of "economies due to synergy and (any) assessments of weak management" as the primary causes of managerial hubris. The bidding firms are prone to overestimate the control they will have over the merged organization, and to underestimate the "weak" managers who are currently in charge.

Costs and benefits. Optimism and the illusion of control increase risk taking in several ways. In a discussion of the Challenger disaster, Landau and Chisholm (1990) introduced a "law of increasing optimism" as a form of Russian roulette. Drawing on the same case, Starbuck and Milliken (1988) noted how quickly vigilance dissipates with repeated successes. Optimism in a competitive context may take the form of contempt for the capabilities of opponents (Roll, 1986). In a bargaining situation, it will support a hard line that raises the risk of conflict. Neale and Bazerman (1983) observed a related effect in a final-offer arbitration setup, where the arbiter is constrained to choose between the final offers made by the contestants. The participants were asked to state their subjective probability that the final offer they presented would be preferred by the arbiter. The average of these probabilities was approximately 0.70; with a less sanguine view of the strength of their case the contestants would surely have made more concessions. In the context of capital investment decisions, optimism and the illusion of control manifest themselves in unrealistic forecasts and unrealizable plans (Arnold, 1986).

Given the high cost of mistakes, it might appear obvious that a rational organization should want to base its decisions on unbiased odds, rather than on predictions painted in shades of rose. However, realism has its costs. In their review of the consequences of optimism and pessimism, Taylor and Brown (1988) reached the deeply disturbing conclusion that optimistic self-delusion is both a diagnostic indication of mental health and well-being, and a positive causal factor that contributes to successful coping with the challenges of life. The benefits of unrealistic optimism in increasing persistence in the face of difficulty have been documented by other investigators (Seligman, 1991).

The observation that realism can be pathological and self-defeating raises troubling questions for the management of information and risk in organizations. Surely, no one would want to be governed entirely by wishful fantasies, but is there a point at which truth becomes destructive and doubt self-fulfilling? Should executives allow or even encourage unrealistic optimism among their subordinates? Should they willingly allow themselves to be caught up in productive enthusiasm, and to ignore discouraging portents? Should there be someone in the organization whose function it is to achieve forecasts free of optimistic bias, although such forecasts, if disseminated, would be demoralizing? Should the organization maintain two sets of forecasting books (as some do, see Bromiley, 1986)? Some authors in the field of strategy have questioned the value of realism, at least implicitly. Weick's famous story of the lost platoon that finds its way in the Alps by consulting a map of the Pyrenees indicates more respect for confidence and morale than for realistic appraisal. On the other hand, Landau and Chisholm (1990) pour withering scorn on the "arrogance of optimism" in organizations, and recommend a pessimistic failure-avoiding management strategy to control risk. Before further progress can be made on this difficult issue, it is important to recognize the existence of a genuine dilemma that will not yield to any simple rule.

Concluding Remarks

Our analysis has suggested that many failures originate in the highly optimistic judgments of risks and opportunities that we label bold forecasts. In the words of March and Shapira (1987), "managers accept risks, in part, because they do not expect that they will have to bear them." March and Shapira emphasized the role of illusions of control in this bias. We have focused on another mechanism—the adoption of an inside view of problems, which leads to anchoring on plans and on the most available scenarios. We suggest that errors of intuitive prediction can sometimes be reduced by adopting an outside view, which forecasts the outcome without attempting to forecast its history (Kahneman and Tversky, 1979b). This analysis identifies the strong intuitive preference for the inside view as a source of difficulties that are both grave and avoidable.

On the issue of risk we presented evidence that decision makers tend to deal with choices one at a time, and that their attitudes to risk exhibit risk aversion and near-proportionality. The reluctance to take explicit responsibility for possible losses is powerful, and can be very costly in the aggregate (for a discussion of its social costs see Wildavsky, 1988). We claimed further that when the stakes are small or moderate relative to assets the aversion to risk is incoherent and substantively unjustified. Here again, the preference for treating decision problems as unique causes errors that could be avoided by a broader view.

Our analysis implies that the adoption of an outside view, in which the problem at hand is treated as an instance of a broader category, will generally reduce the optimistic bias and may facilitate the application of a consistent risk policy. This happens as a matter of course in problems of forecasting or decision that the organization recognizes as obviously recurrent or repetitive. However, we have suggested that people are strongly biased in favor of the inside view, and that they will normally treat significant decision problems as unique even when information that could support an outside view is available. The adoption of an outside view in such cases violates strong intuitions about the relevance of information. Indeed, the deliberate neglect of the features that make the current problem unique can appear irresponsible. A deliberate effort will therefore be required to foster the optimal use of outside and inside views in forecasting, and the maintenance of globally consistent risk attitudes in distributed decision systems.

Bold forecasts and timid attitudes to risk tend to have opposite effects. It would be fortunate if they canceled out precisely to yield optimal behavior in every situation, but there is little reason to expect such a perfect outcome. The conjunction of biases is less disastrous than either one would have been on its own, but there ought to be a better way to control choice under risk than pitting two mistakes against each other. The prescriptive implications of the relation between the biases in forecast and in risk taking is that corrective attempts should deal with these biases simultaneously. Increasing risk taking could easily go too far in the presence of optimistic forecasts, and a successful effort to improve the realism of assessments could do more harm than good in an organization that relies on unfounded optimism to ward off paralysis.

4
Structure, Strategy, and the Agenda of the Firm

Thomas H. Hammond

Introduction

A central argument of Alfred Chandler's classic study, *Strategy and Structure* (1962), is that the chief executives of a firm choose a structure that enables them to pursue the strategy they have chosen for the firm; in Chandler's well-known phrase (p. 14), "structure follows strategy." Illustrated by case studies of strategy formulation and structural innovation in DuPont, Sears, General Motors, and Standard Oil of New Jersey and buttressed by other empirical evidence, this argument proved enormously stimulating to students of strategic management over the next decades. Numerous studies have been conducted in Chandler's terms, and even now, 30 years later, his approach

Acknowledgments: The earliest version of this paper, "Corporate Structure and Corporate Organization," was presented at the Conference on Adaptive Institutions, Stanford University, November 8–9, 1984. A later version, titled "Notes on the Theory of Corporate Organization," was written at Washington University in St. Louis in the spring of 1988 and presented at an Industrial Organization seminar there. The next version was presented at the Fundamental Issues in Strategy Conference, Napa, California, November 29–December 1, 1990. Research was supported at various times by NSF grant SES-8207904, by the Department of Political Science at Michigan State University, and by the Center in Political Economy and the Olin School of Business at Washington University. Conversations with Richard Cook, Krishna Ladha, Gary Miller, Richard Peck, Andy Rutten, Paul Thomas, and Julie Withers have been very helpful, as were written comments by Lee Benham, Ken Koford, Steven Maser, Annette Milford, Mathew McCubbins, and Rowena Pecchenino. The encouragement of Lee Benham and Gary Miller was especially appreciated. Richard Rumelt offered useful editorial suggestions on how to shorten the final draft. Despite my criticisms of the work of Alfred Chandler and Oliver Williamson, both participants at the "Fundamental Issues in Strategy" conference, I want to acknowledge the great influence their work has had on my own; they have set my own agenda to a very substantial degree.

remains a dominant one in the study of strategic management in the firm.

In recent years, however, a careful rereading of Chandler's case studies, combined with detailed empirical studies of the process by which strategies were developed in other firms, has raised questions about the adequacy of the "structure follows strategy" argument. One major criticism is that Chandler gave undue emphasis in *Strategy and Structure* to the role of top managers in the development of the strategies of his four firms. For example, Burgelman (1983: 63) charged that Chandler adopted a "heroic view" of strategy formulation: "[Chandler's] theoretical generalizations . . . collapse this strategic process into a top management activity. Even though the influence of lower levels in the determination of the content of the strategy is recognized, the major emphasis is on the role of top management."

While Chandler's "structure follows strategy" argument takes a top-down view of strategy formulation, studies of decision making and policy making in large organizations have long suggested a much more diffuse kind of process. Over 50 years ago, for example, Chester Barnard (1938: 187) argued, "The formulation of organizational purposes or objectives and the more general decisions involved in this process and in those of action to carry them into effect are distributed in organizations, and are not, nor can they be, concentrated or specialized to individuals except in minor degree." In the initial flurry of enthusiasm over Chandler's book, Barnard's view was neglected, but within a few years dissents to the "structure follows strategy" argument which were compatible with Barnard began to be voiced by students of strategic management; see Christensen, Andrews, and Bower (1973), Bower (1974), Bower and Doz (1979), Burton and Kuhn (1979), Bourgeois and Astley (1979), Hall and Saias (1980), Fahey (1981), Burgelman (1983), and Fredrickson (1986).

These critics advanced an alternative view: because top-level executives are generally unable, by themselves, to formulate a sensible strategy for their firm, strategy formulation necessarily becomes a much more *organizational* process, involving many people spread out among multiple levels in the firm. Chandler's own case studies were cited as supporting this alternative view. It appeared to Burgelman (1983: 62), for example, that "multiple layers of management were involved in the strategic initiatives that produced the extensive diversification, and in response to which the new strategy and the new structure eventually emerged."

Several of Chandler's critics went so far as to suggest that a contrary empirical proposition—"strategy follows structure"—was as reasonable as "structure follows strategy." To Burton and Kuhn (1979), for example, Chandler's book contained substantial evidence for this alternative generalization: in Chandler's four case studies even recognizing that there was a problem took time, and diagnosing what the problem was often proved difficult. For these reasons, Burton and Kuhn (1979: 4) felt it reasonable to conclude that

> a structure eliminates or discourages search for alternative strategies among the environment's complete set of possibilities. . . . The corporate structure encasing the firm focuses its attention, creates its unique view of the environment, limits its search and investigation; and from this, there emerges a corporate strategy, or the lack of one. Corporate structure again establishes corporate strategy.

Some scholars even began to argue that *both* assertions—that structure follows strategy, and that strategy follows structure— find empirical support. For example, Burgelman (1983: 61) wrote, "Previous research has, indeed, produced apparently conflicting propositions regarding the directionality of these relationships. Depending on which body of empirical evidence is used to bolster the argument, 'structure follows strategy' and 'strategy follows structure' both seem to be valid propositions." Galbraith and Nathanson (1979: 283) and Hall and Saias (1980: 161–162) make similar observations.

In sum, there is growing agreement that "structure follows strategy" is an oversimplified description of how strategies are actually formulated in firms. But while the critics have established plausible grounds for believing that a firm's structure can be expected to shape, constrain, and otherwise influence the development and content of the firm's strategy, there is a striking absence of any positive theory of how particular structures actually affect or bias policy decisions or strategies. The primary purpose of this paper, then, is to develop the "strategy follows structure" argument in greater depth. By examining the problem of how a firm's organizational structure can affect the choices made via the structure, it is hoped that our understanding of the structural design of the firm, and of the structure's impact on the choice of the firm's strategy, can be advanced.

Chandler and Williamson on the Hierarchies of Business Firms

In the past two decades, the literature on the theory of the firm has expanded enormously. Several comprehensive surveys of this literature are available (Leibenstein, 1979; Galbraith and Nathanson, 1979; Caves, 1980; Marris and Mueller, 1980; Jennergren, 1981; Williamson, 1981a; Levinthal, 1988; Eisenhardt, 1989a), and so no attempt will be made at a summary. However, because the work of Alfred Chandler and Oliver Williamson occupies such a prominent place in much of this literature, it will be useful to examine their arguments and evidence about structural design and strategy formulation in the firm.

Functional Departments and Product-Line Divisions in Chandler's Firms

In *Strategy and Structure* Chandler described the transformation of the structures of four large corporations—DuPont, General Motors, Standard Oil of New Jersey, and Sears, Roebuck—in the first decades of this century. In the case of DuPont, for example, the original structure was based on functional departments (purchasing, production, sales, and so forth), but when the firm began making a large and heterogeneous range of products, this functional structure proved inadequate in a variety of ways. Eventually DuPont adopted a structure based on product-line divisions (explosives, dyestuffs, paints, and chemicals).

Chandler's explanation for the adoption and retention of this product-line divisional structure is rich and multifaceted, but his arguments might be summarized in the following way. For firms with a large and heterogeneous range of products, matters of product design, production, and sales were initially handled by different functional departments. But organizing by function eventually caused severe coordination problems: to coordinate the functional activities for each product, central office managers were required to gather and process large amounts of information. Since this was a very time-consuming activity, it left them little time for addressing the larger issues of corporate strategy. Reorganization into product-line divisions placed most product-related coordination decisions in the hands of division managers, who were better able to coordinate the various activities involving each of the products. Relieved of day-to-day operational responsibilities, central office managers were left free to address the larger issues of the firm's overall strategy.

Chandler's general insights about these matters had a remarkable impact on students of the modern corporation. But while a great many studies of the structures of large firms have been conducted in Chandler's terms (see especially the review by Galbraith and Nathanson, 1979), and while these studies have been fruitful and informative, there are limits to their utility. They make a strong case *that* structure matters, but it is not always clear just *why* structure matters. Chandler's original study is a case in point. In Chandler's view, interdependencies among the functional departments in DuPont, for example, required central office managers to coordinate the functional activities for each product. The product-line structure was presumably chosen because it required less coordination among divisions, thereby placing less of a burden on central office managers.

If there were few interdependencies among the divisions, the superiority of the product-line division form over the functional department form might be easy to understand. However, careful examination of Chandler's case studies reveals that his firms' product-line divisions were characterized by substantial interdependencies. Sears retained a centralized purchasing department (i.e., a functionally defined unit) from which all its retail stores obtained their goods. While the geographically based divisions were independent of each other, they were nonetheless all dependent on central purchasing.[1] The General Motors automotive divisions (Chevrolet, Pontiac, Buick, Oldsmobile, Cadillac) were dependent to a considerable extent on the parts and accessories divisions, and there were important functional departments and interdivisional committees for purchasing, standardization of parts, technical engineering problems, and many other such matters; see Chandler and Salsbury (1971: 546–549), Sloan (1964: ch. 7), and Kuhn (1986: ch. 6–9). Interdependencies

---

[1] Stinchcombe (1990: 126–135) presents a rather critical account of Chandler's discussion of Sears, focusing in large part on Chandler's relative neglect of the very important, and functionally defined, purchasing department.

in Standard Oil were even greater, since the different grades of crude oil pumped from the wells required different kinds of refining, and since all of the products sold on the market had to come from a handful of large refineries. Even DuPont, which probably had the least interdependence among divisions, organized a number of important activities, such as purchasing and some aspects of development and engineering, in separate functional departments.

If there are interdependencies like these among a firm's product-line divisions, or among the product-line divisions and other branches of the firm, it is not obvious why one structure for a firm will be superior to some other structure: these extensive divisional interdependencies would be as likely to require central office intervention, with all its attendant costs (cognitive as well as financial), as the interdependencies among functional departments. Given the extensive cross-divisional interdependencies in Chandler's firms, it is not clear what accounted for the (apparent) superiority of the product-line divisional form.

The important functional units in both General Motors and Sears (and, to a lesser extent, in DuPont), the geographically based retailing units in Sears, and the important interdivisional and interdepartmental dependencies in GM and Standard Oil all lead one to the conclusion that these firms should be referred to as product-line/functional or geographical/functional *hybrids*. In each case, the hybrid form was apparently chosen because it appeared that economies of scale (or scope) for some activities would be lost if each product-line division had its own subunit for these activities. Chandler's explanation for the superiority of the product-line form, so convincing on first reading, seems somewhat less complete on closer analysis.[2]

Williamson's Transaction Cost Analysis

Probably the most sustained effort to build a unified theory of the existence, organization, and operation of the modern cor-

---

[2] It may be argued that much of the success of Standard Oil and General Motors stemmed from more "traditional" economic factors involving the economies of scale and the internal rationalization achieved early in the histories of these two firms. Note that Chandler's more recent study, *Scale and Scope* (1990a), places great stress on the importance of economies of scale (and scope) and internal rationalization in accounting for the differential success of various firms in the United States, England, and Germany.

poration has been conducted by Oliver Williamson; see Williamson (1970; 1975: ch. 8; 1981a; 1981b; 1985: ch. 10). Williamson has been a major developer of the Coase (1937) argument that *transaction costs* account both for why the hierarchically organized firm even exists, and for why particular kinds of hierarchies have evolved in particular kinds of economic environments.

In Williamson's account, transaction costs arise due to two fundamental factors. One is that individual actors are self-interested and thus are prone to strategic behavior, or *opportunism,* as Williamson calls it; the other is that individual actors are *boundedly rational.* These two factors interact to make a particular transaction more costly in some institutional contexts (such as markets) than in others (such as hierarchies). Williamson's general argument is that, in the pursuit of efficiency, the structures which are adopted are those which minimize these transaction costs in the firm. For our purposes here, the key question is whether transaction cost analysis provides a useful guide to the benefits and costs of different kinds of structures for a hierarchically organized firm.[3]

Using a transaction cost perspective, Williamson attempts to explain why a functional structure might be inferior to a product-line structure. His central argument comes directly from Chandler: the functional structure creates an information overload problem for central office managers. Chandler's arguments about the functional structure began with these observations (1962: 291) about the duties of the central office in a functional structure:

> One critical role became the coordination and integration of the output of the several functional departments to changing market demands, needs, and tastes. This included the coordination of product flow from one functional department to another. . . . It also required the maintenance of cooperation between the manufacturing, sales, and development or engineering departments regarding the improvement or redesign of products. Second, expansion and vertical integration encouraged the growth of auxiliary or service departments in the central office which could relieve the administrative load on the functional departments by taking

---

[3] Alchian and Woodward (1988) provide a useful exposition of the meaning of "transaction costs" in a highly favorable review of Williamson (1985). More critical views of transaction cost analysis are available in Barzel (1985), Buchanan (1986), and Dow (1987). My own thoughts on transaction cost analysis (as well as on several other bodies of relevant theory) were presented at greater length in the conference draft of this paper.

over more specialized activities. Finally, besides coordinating activities with the market and providing specialized services, the central office, of course, allocated the future use as well as appraised the present performance of the resources of the enterprise.

For each product, then, the central office had to ensure that the development department created a product that the manufacturing department could make, that manufacturing built a product that the sales department could sell, and that sales sold the product for enough money to keep the accounting department (and shareholders) satisfied. These all imposed heavy coordination responsibilities on the central office. As Chandler remarked, in a passage quoted by Williamson (1985: 280):

> The inherent weakness in the centralized, functionally departmentalized operating company . . . became critical only when the administrative load on the senior executive officers increased to such an extent that they were unable to handle their entrepreneurial responsibilities efficiently. This situation arose when the operations of the enterprise became too complex and the problems of coordination, appraisal, and policy formulation too intricate for a small number of top officers to handle both long-run, entrepreneurial, and short-run, operational administrative activities. To meet these new needs, the [organizational] innovators built the multidivisional structure with a general office whose executives would concentrate on entrepreneurial activities and with autonomous, fairly self-contained operating divisions whose managers would handle operational ones. (*Strategy and Structure:* 299)

Williamson (1985: 281) considers these coordination problems the result of an information overload: "Bounds on rationality were reached as the U-form [functional] structure labored under a communication overload. . . ."

It is clear that these central office managers did face some difficult problems. But to pin the blame on the functional structure in the way Williamson does (and as Chandler did) mischaracterizes the essential point. Consider one possible organizational reform of one of Chandler's functionally organized firms. Instead of having the heads of the functional departments (who, in the case of DuPont, served on the firm's executive committee of the board of directors) doing the coordination, a separate interdepartmental coordinating committee could be created to handle these cross-functional matters.[4] This committee need not include the functional department heads, and without them it could avoid the problem of subgoal pursuit that concerned Chan-

---

[4]   Indeed, this seems to be what General Motors did to a considerable extent.

dler and Williamson.[5] And by taking over these operational responsibilities, the committee would give top-level executives the time to engage in long-range strategic planning. Thus it would appear that the problems of information overload (as well as subgoal pursuit) could be alleviated while retaining the functional structure.

So one might conclude that information overload for top-level executives was not necessarily a generic feature of the functional organization. But if information overload was not a generic problem, why did DuPont, for example, completely abandon its functional structure and switch to a product-line structure? When judged from the viewpoint of what the central office needed to know to coordinate the functional departments, the problem could be diagnosed as a *lack* of information about how to coordinate the activities of the functional departments: central office managers could not possibly know what the functional managers and their subordinates knew. While lack of information is also an aspect of bounded rationality (in Williamson's terms), and thus might be considered a transaction cost problem, it is a rather different problem from that of too much information.

However, even this argument about lack of information is not completely satisfactory. The problem with the functional structure was neither too much information for central office managers nor too little information. Instead, the problem was that the *wrong kind* of information was being produced by the functional structure for use by the central office. The virtue of the product-line structure was that it produced information that made possible a comparison of the relative profitabilities of each of the products or product lines. As central as this information about product-line profitability is in a firm operating in a market, getting such information from a functional structure was extraordinarily difficult; Chandler's account of the DuPont transformation provides a striking illustration of this point.

---

[5]   Unfortunately, there is not space for a discussion of subgoal pursuit in different kinds of structures. Suffice it to say that the pursuit of subgoals should be expected in *every* kind of structure; that is, we should find it not only in functionally organized firms but in product-line firms as well. When there are substantial interdependencies among the divisions (as in several of Chandler's firms), divisional subgoal pursuit may be as much of a problem as the functional subgoal pursuit that concerns Williamson.

It should be acknowledged that Williamson elsewhere argues that the product-line structure eases profitability comparisons among divisions (see, for example, 1985: 281). But his strong emphasis on the information overload problem draws attention away from this perhaps more critical point. Being overloaded with the wrong kind of information is a different problem from not having enough access to the right kind of information. One could even be "overloaded" with the right kind of information, but this is certainly less worrisome than being overloaded with the wrong kind of information.

Summary

Chandler's views on structure and the more analytical transaction cost theory raise a host of important questions about how particular institutional forms actually work, or can be expected to work. But they do not comprise a theory of institutional form. Williamson himself provides some support for this view. In his own critique of the transaction cost approach in his conclusion to *The Economic Institutions of Capitalism* (1985: 392), for example, he observes:

> Another aspect of incompleteness [of transaction cost economics] to which I would call special attention is the underdeveloped state of the theory of bureaucracy. As compared with the market failure literature, the study of bureaucratic failure is very primitive. What are the biases and distortions to which internal organization is given? Why do they arise? How do they vary with organizational form? An adequate understanding of economic organization plainly requires more attention to those issues.

But given Williamson's 20 years of concern for explaining the existence and structure of the hierarchically organized firm, from Williamson (1970) to Williamson (1985) and beyond, a reasonable inference is that the transaction cost approach has not yet provided the needed theory.

If transaction cost analysis needs a better theory of bureaucracy, the goal here will be to attempt to supply some elements of one. Hence, it is to the nature of a firm's hierarchy, and to the question of how the hierarchy affects the strategy formulation process, that we now turn.

Overview of the Structure-As-Agenda Approach

The past four decades have seen the development of what has come to be called the "neo-institutional" literature in economics and political science. The central theme of the neo-institutional literature, represented by such works as Arrow (1963), Downs (1957, 1967), Black (1958), Buchanan and Tullock (1962), Olson (1965), McKelvey (1976, 1979), Plott and Levine (1978), Shepsle (1979), and Riker (1962, 1980, 1982), is that the rules by which institutions are governed affect institutional choices. As North (1986: 230) put it, in his essay "The New Institutional Economics,"

> Modern institutional economics begins with two premises: 1) that the theoretical framework should be capable of integrating neo-classical theory with an analysis of the way institutions modify the choice set available to human beings; and 2) that this framework must build upon the basic determinants of institutions, so that we can not only define the choice set really available to people at any time, but also analyze the way in which institutions change and therefore alter the available choice set over time.

One important strand of the neo-institutional literature focuses on how the *agenda* of a committee meeting shapes the choice set available to the committee, and thus shapes the choices that the committee ultimately makes. An agenda governs which option is compared to which other option, and in what order these comparisons are to be made. An increasingly sophisticated literature (Plott and Levine, 1978; McKelvey, 1981; Miller, 1980; Bjurulf and Niemi, 1982; Shepsle and Weingast, 1984; Ordeshook and Schwartz, 1987) has demonstrated that whoever controls the agenda can have a great impact on outcomes. For example, consider a majority rule committee with three people who are to choose one option from the set {x,y,z}. Assume the three actors have the following preferences, a configuration generating a majority rule cycle:

Person 1's Preference Ordering	Person 2's Preference Ordering	Person 3's Preference Ordering	Committee's Preference Ordering
x	y	z	x
y	z	x	y
z	x	y	z
			x

Three different binary agendas are possible for {x,y,z}:

1. Compare y and z, and then pit the majority winner against x;

2. Compare **x** and **z,** and then pit the majority winner against **y;** and
3. Compare **x** and **y,** and then pit the majority winner against **z.**

Diagrammatically, we have:

Agenda 1	Agenda 2	Agenda 3

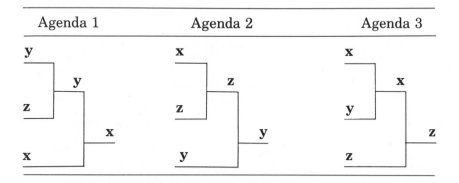

As the diagrams demonstrate, each agenda yields a different winner. In fact, whoever controls the agenda here *completely* determines the outcome. If person 1 controls the agenda, he would choose agenda 1 since this agenda produces **x,** his preferred outcome. For person 2, agenda 2 produces **y,** his preferred outcome. And for person 3, agenda 3 produces **z,** his preferred outcome.

While this simple example illustrates agenda influence on the smallest of scales, the entire body of an institution's rules can be seen as setting the decision-making agenda for the institution. Indeed, the central argument of this paper is that the hierarchical structure of a firm sets the decision-making agenda for the firm. More concisely, *the firm's structure is its agenda.* Note that if we rotate the three diagrams counterclockwise 90°, each agenda looks something like the traditional pyramidal bureaucracy of a hierarchically organized firm. Changing the firm's structure is thus equivalent to changing its decision-making agenda, and so can be expected to change outcomes.[6]

There is something of a tradition of treating business firms

---

[5] Considering the "agenda" of a firm is not entirely novel; for example, Chapter 3 in Arrow's *The Limits of Organization* (1974) is titled "The Agenda of Organizations." The present paper pushes the agenda metaphor considerably further in the neo-institutional direction.

as quasi-political institutions in this fashion; see Dalton (1959), March (1962), Bower (1970), Marglin (1974), and Pfeffer (1981). Bower (1970: 2) expresses the general point nicely:

> [T]here is a growing awareness that the firm, in many respects, is a political organism, and that the analysis of rules of choice undertaken in the study of voting or the committee problem provides insights into the problem of decentralized choice in the firm. For example, it has tentatively been suggested that the job of top management in the large firm may be something quite analogous to constitution writing.

Nonetheless, this approach, while often suggested, has never been developed in any systematic degree. The remainder of this paper will attempt to do so, by studying one essential component of a general theory of the firm, the firm's formal hierarchical structure.[7]

Chandler's historical studies of DuPont, General Motors, Sears, and Standard Oil will figure prominently as illustrations of the arguments. Williamson's transaction cost questions about individual self-interest, uncertainty, and informational asymmetry will also be a part of the story. Moreover, while the neo-institutional literature, especially in political science, has tended to focus on the impact of an institution's rules on some decision maker's choices, central to the making of intelligent choices is the gathering and processing of information for the reduction of uncertainty. Several previous studies have urged an "information processing approach" to the study of the hierarchies of firms (Galbraith, 1973: ch. 2; Tushman and Nadler, 1978; Egelhoff, 1982; Williamson, 1985: 281), and this paper focuses considerable attention on the relationship between formal structure and uncertainty, information, and learning.

Three Organizational Tasks

The goals of the chief executive of a firm presumably have something to do with profit maximization, rate of growth, market share, and so forth. But whatever the chief executive's goals, he will not necessarily know whether there are current problems in achieving these goals, nor will it be clear just how to

---

[7] This paper can be seen as one element in the author's long-standing enterprise of attempting to understand the political nature of hierarchies. For some other studies in this project see Hammond (1986, 1993), Hammond and Thomas (1989, 1990), Hammond and Horn (1983, 1985), and Hammond and Miller (1985).

solve any of these problems. Much of the needed data and information is either in the hands and minds of his subordinates or lies out in the economic environment somewhere and has not yet been collected by his firm. Even to design an incentive system to elicit information from subordinates, or induce them to gather the proper information, requires the chief executive to have considerable knowledge about what he is looking for. To understand decision making by the chief executive thus requires that we know what information flows up to the chief executive and, most critically for our purposes, how the firm's structure influences this flow.

It is obvious that information can flow to the chief executive in a wide variety of ways, but this paper will focus only on information that comes to him via subordinates. The approach presented here thus follows the Burgelman (1983: 63) recommendation of an approach to strategy formulation that allows for a "bottom-up conception of strategy formulation in which top management's role is not necessarily critical. . . ."

There are three different reasons why information will flow to the chief executive from subordinates. Each is related to one of the chief executive's various responsibilities. As I noted earlier, one responsibility is to ensure that he and his subordinates maintain a general awareness of, and orientation toward, what is happening in current and potential markets for the firm's products; for subordinates this is the *orientation task*. While the chief executive may become aware of some problem that needs to be faced, he may not know how to solve the problem. It is only when he receives information and advice from subordinates on what to do that he is able to engage in the necessary policy making. This is the *policy-making task*. And once the chief executive has recognized that a problem exists (orientation), and has decided what policy to adopt (policy making), he still needs to see that the chosen policy is implemented by subordinates; this is the *implementation task*.

The next three sections discuss these three tasks in detail. Describing the three tasks in this "bottom-up" fashion, and implying a temporal sequence among them, undoubtedly oversimplifies the processes of individual decision making and organizational policy making. The distinctions are made primarily for analytical and presentational tractability. The larger argument about the influence of structure on organizational policy making would still hold even with a richer, and less sequential, model of policy making.

The Conduct of Orientation Tasks

Much of the information that a firm's chief executive needs to know about his organization and about the outside world must come to him from subordinates. Since the amount of information flowing into the firm is far in excess of what any one chief executive can absorb, it is necessary for subordinates to assess, condense, and summarize the information for him. This is not necessarily a bad thing; as Arrow (1974: 53–54) notes,

> The economies of information in the organization occur because in fact much of the information received is irrelevant. The terminal acts within the competence of the organization do not require for assessment the entire probability distribution of states of the world but only some marginal distributions derived from it. Hence, in general, the information received by a member of the organization can be transformed into a much smaller volume for retransmission without losing value for choice of terminal acts.

The organizational literature has long suggested that the nature of information transmission has implications for power in the organization. For example, March and Simon (1958: 165) coined the term "uncertainty absorption" to refer to the process that occurs "when inferences are drawn from a body of evidence and the inferences, instead of the evidence itself, are then communicated." The person who makes these inferences can have great power since he becomes "an important source of informational premises for organizational action." The impact on policy making is clear.

> Through the process of uncertainty absorption, the recipient of a communication is severely limited in his ability to judge its correctness. Although there may be various tests of apparent validity, internal consistency, and consistency with other communications, the recipient must, by and large, repose his confidence in the editing process that has taken place, and, if he accepts the communication at all, accept it pretty much as it stands.

The literature on strategic management further suggests that the information channels can bias what flows through them. Bower (1970: 287), for example, argues that the structure of the firm shapes and biases the information from subordinates that ultimately reaches the top. See also Bourgeois and Astley (1979: 46) and Hall and Saias (1980). Monsen and Downs (1965: 229) even developed a simple model of the process by which information is modified and distorted when it is transmitted via a hierarchy. In their model each level suppresses some fraction of the information it receives. In a five-level hierarchy with 10% suppression at each level, the top would receive only 66% ($.9^4 = .656$) of the data passed up from the bottom.

For Williamson (1975: 122–124), this vulnerability of information transmission to distortion (and even deliberate manipulation) has a profound impact on the size and nature of the firm:

> [M]embers of the organization may seek to promote personal goals by diverting the communication system to their own uses. . . . Communication distortions can take either assertive or defensive forms. Defensively, subordinates may tell their supervisor what he wants to hear; assertively, they will report those things they want him to know. . . . Distortion to please the receiver is especially likely where the recipient has access to extensive rewards and sanctions in his relations with the transmitter, as in up-the-line communication in an administrative hierarchy. . . . The cumulative effects across successive hierarchical levels of these real and related adjustments to the data easily result in gross image distortions . . . and contribute to a limitation of firm size. . . .

While this literature on information distortion in a hierarchy makes an important point, it has a serious limitation: almost invariably it emphasizes merely *that* distortion takes place. But if some sort of bias is unavoidable—and no one even hints that bias can be completely avoided—then it is essential to know *what kind* of distortion can be expected to occur. After all, given the inevitability of bias, organizational design necessarily becomes a question of choosing among different kinds of biases. Strangely enough, though, the literature on information distortion is virtually silent on this matter.

Different Inferences from the Same Messages

To explore this problem, let us begin with a simple model of how a shift from a functional structure to a product-line structure can affect what kind of inference the chief executive might draw from the information he receives. The model will focus on the question of what the chief executive infers from messages subordinates send upward as to whether or not there are opportunities for increased profits by the firm.

Assume the following four messages are sent upward from the bottom in each structure. The production supervisor for product 1 always sends the message "There are opportunities for cost reduction of product 1," and the production supervisor for product 2 always sends the message "There are no opportunities for cost reduction of product 2." The salesman for product 1 sends the message "There are opportunities for sales and revenue increases for product 1," while the salesman for product 2 sends the message "There are no opportunities for sales and revenue increases for product 2."

Now consider the structures in Figure 4-1. In the functional structure the two production supervisors are grouped in a Production Department under the production manager, while the two salespeople are grouped in a Sales Department under the sales manager. Assume that department managers must aggregate information before passing it up the hierarchy. Thus, when the production manager receives divergent messages—"There are opportunities for cost reduction of product 1" and "There are no opportunities for cost reduction of product 2"—he summarizes them for the chief executive as "There is mixed evidence as to whether there are cost-reduction opportunities in the Production Department." Similarly, when the sales manager receives divergent messages—"There are opportunities for sales and revenue increases for product 1" and "There are no opportunities for sales and revenue increases for product 2"—he summarizes them for the chief executive as "There is mixed evidence as to whether there are revenue-increase opportunities in the Sales Department." In the functional structure, then, the chief executive receives the messages "There is mixed evidence on cost-reduction opportunities in production" and "There is mixed evidence on revenue-increase opportunities in sales." One conclusion he might draw from these ambiguous messages is that "there is mixed evidence on whether there are opportunities for increased profits." He might then simply decide to do nothing and just monitor the situation until something more definite appears.

The product-line structure would organize these same messages differently, and might lead the chief executive to draw different inferences. The product 1 division manager would receive the message "There are opportunities for cost reduction of product 1" from the production supervisor for product 1 and "There are opportunities for sales and revenue increases for product 1" from the salesperson for product 1. He might plausibly summarize these in a message to the chief executive that

Figure 4-1
Different Structures Can Lead the Chief Executive to Draw Different Inferences from the Same Messages

Functional Structure

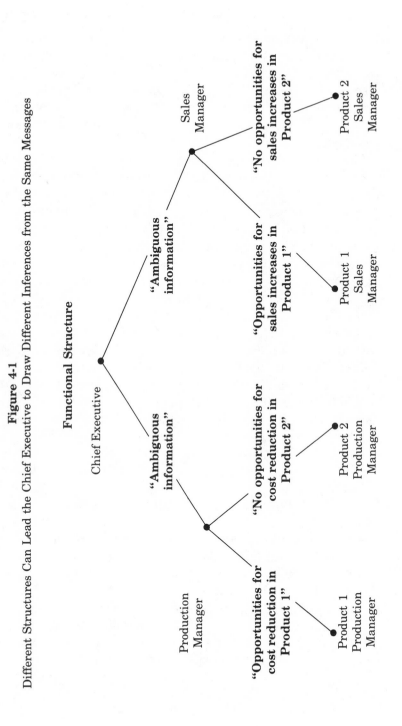

Product-Line Structure

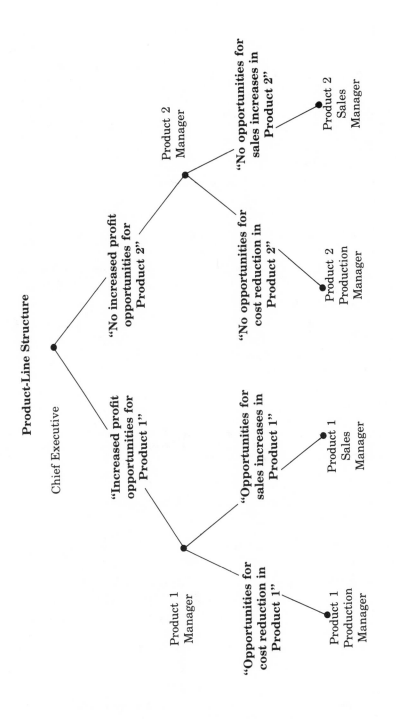

states, "There are opportunities for increased profits from product 1." The product 2 division manager would receive the messages "There are no opportunities for cost reduction of product 2" and "There are no opportunities for sales and revenue increases of product 2." He might reasonably summarize these in a message to the chief executive that states, "There are no opportunities for increased profits from product 2." One conclusion the chief executive might draw from these two messages is that "there is good reason to think that by devoting time and energy to product 1 we can increase profits; however, there are no improvements possible for product 2, so let's not pay any attention to it." It seems plausible, then, that a chief executive would draw different inferences from these two different sets of messages.

If a chief executive is dependent on others to summarize and transmit information to him, the structure will affect what information he receives, what inferences he draws about the state of his organization and of the outside world, and thus how the organization's problems are framed and defined (Tversky and Kahneman, 1981). In fact, even if precisely the same raw data come up from the bottom, different structures will process and summarize these data in different ways for the chief executive.[8] We can summarize this as:

> **Proposition 1:** Since different organizational structures will process the same raw data in different ways, the chief executive will draw different inferences from the messages initially received by the firm.

Functional versus Product-Line Information in DuPont: An Illustration

Proposition 1 can be illustrated by Chandler's discussion of DuPont's transformation from a functional structure to a product-line structure. According to Chandler's account, DuPont was exclusively a producer of explosives in its first century of business, starting in 1802. Its organization was based simply on the physical plants where the explosives were produced. In the late 1800s it gradually began adding product lines based on dyna-

---

[8]   Kim (1992) presents a model of organizational information processing under uncertainty, with Bayesian decision makers, which formally demonstrates how different structures can lead to different inferences from the same raw data.

mite (from nitroglycerin) and on smokeless powder (guncotton), but its business was still largely based on its original product, black powder.

Following 1902, when cousins Alfred, Coleman, and Pierre du Pont bought a controlling interest in the company from an older generation of du Ponts, the company's formal structure was changed a number of times, but the general organizing principle remained one of functional specialization. For example, from 1919 to 1921 (see Chandler, 1962: 74–77) there were separate departments for Development, Engineering, Purchasing, Production, and Sales (and a couple of others). Included within Production was an Explosives Manufacturing Department (with divisions for high explosives, black powder, and blasting supplies), a Cellulose Products Manufacturing Department (with divisions for Pyralin [celluloid], Fabrikoid [artificial leather], and smokeless powder [a propellant for ammunition]), and a Dyestuffs Department (with sales and manufacturing divisions). The other functional departments, especially Sales, had their own subunits based on products.

The diversity of the DuPont product line steadily increased after 1902. The greatest increases came during World War I, when the company was flush with profits from the sale of explosives and ammunition to England and France. Expecting the demand for explosives and ammunition to drop when the war ended, the du Ponts began to consider alternative uses of the company's plants and products. They purchased a number of other companies, each representing a possible outlet for DuPont's chemical products or chemical expertise. With the increasingly diverse range of products, the central office came to have responsibility for coordinating development, production, and sales of this wide range of products.

During the severe recession that followed the end of the war, DuPont's revenues plummeted. Everyone in the firm had predicted the drop in sales of explosives. But what was confusing was that losses were occurring in the newer product lines, such as paints and varnishes, despite the fact that other companies were apparently making profits on the same kinds of products. What was causing these losses was not clear, and there were disagreements within the firm about what should be done. Some of the more senior managers thought that the problems occurred in part because the central office lacked information about various aspects of these new product lines. Their view was that better information for the central office would solve the problems, just as better information had solved many other problems in the previous two decades.

One informational problem in particular stood out. The Purchasing Department made its own estimate of the quantities and costs of materials it thought the Production Department would need over the next months, Production made its own prediction of how much it would make, and Sales made its own prediction of what sales were likely to be. However, there was no point at which these forecasts were all brought together. One result was that the company often carried excessive and costly inventories of materials. The solution proposed by these senior managers was simply to provide some means whereby better-quality and agreed-upon forecasts would be produced. Much of the improvement in the management of the firm since 1902 had come from precisely this kind of improved information.

In 1921 a committee of junior managers who had been asked to investigate reasons for DuPont's losses suggested that the problem was one of organization and not one of information and coordination of forecasts. Regarding the losses in paints and celluloid articles in 1919 and 1920, they noted that despite "an excellent line of responsibility for carrying on each of the functions of the business," they were "unable to find the exact responsibility for profits" (Chandler, 1962: 95–96). "In other words," Chandler continued (p. 96), "the activities of each line within each functional department were effectively managed, but no one was responsible for administering them so as to assure a profit on each individual line of products. . . ."

Tabulation of the losses in the paint and celluloid product lines depended on statistics that apparently were available in the functional departments. For example, Chandler (p. 92) cited statistics on the extent of losses in the paint and varnish business, and while (somewhat surprisingly) he did not say where these data came from, it would seem that DuPont's functional departments were producing data that could, in fact, be compiled into information on production costs and sales revenues for particular products. If the existence of raw data was not the problem, this would suggest that the problem was instead how the structure aggregated these data, where this aggregated information went, and what happened to it when it got there. In

Chandler's words (p. 101), senior managers saw this simply as a problem of bringing the right information together in one place: "The current data were adequate enough, but were not properly utilized." The junior managers, on the other hand, thought that the proper way to aggregate and utilize this information was to reorganize the firm.

The junior managers had recommended a product-line structure, but the senior managers hesitated; they were reluctant to abandon the practice of management by functional specialists which had served the firm so well for so long. But continued losses in 1921 finally convinced the senior managers that drastic action was necessary, and so the functional departments were reorganized into divisions based on responsibility for products or lines of related products such as explosives, dyestuffs, Pyralin, paints and chemicals, Fabrikoid, and photographic film.

Each product-line division now contained subunits with responsibility for the various functional activities—such as development, production, and sales—necessary to produce and sell its particular products. The managers of each division were given the task of integrating and coordinating information on most aspects of a product, from invention and development through to the ultimate accounting for profits and losses. Overseeing these product-line divisions was a central office with accounting and finance staffs, which could assess the divisions' profitability prospects and allocate the firm's financial resources accordingly. Thus, central office personnel were now handed information highlighting differences and distinctions among product-line divisions rather than differences and distinctions among functional departments.

In sum, while essentially the same initial data were created as in the functional structure, the product-line structure *aggregated it in different ways* and routed the result to different levels, which meant that different inferences were drawn from it by top-level officials.

Biased Information from Functional and from Product-Line Structures

Because it is difficult for the chief executive of a functionally organized firm to learn the costs and revenues for each product or product line, the functional structure would appear to have a bias against the creation of product-related data for the chief executive. Accounting information collected by the functional departments and forwarded to the central office may not even be collected and recorded in product or product-line categories. In fact, if different products are produced in the same physical plant, and if management desires to allocate all of the plant's costs to the products, it may be very difficult to allocate overhead costs to products in a meaningful manner; see Thomas (1969, 1974, 1977, 1980) and Groves (1985). Similarly, it may be difficult for the firm's sales representatives to determine how much of their costs can be attributed to each of their products. If a single sales call on a customer, for example, results in orders for a wide range of products, how should the cost of the sales call be allocated to the various products? By dividing the firm into product-line divisions, this bias against the production of meaningful product-related information might be overcome.

However, the product-related data produced by a product-line structure should be seen as having their own kind of bias. If the product-line divisions aggregate information before it is sent to the chief executive, what the chief executive receives—in its most aggregated form, it is simply the profit-and-loss statement from each division—may make it difficult for him to discover the reasons behind any particular profit or loss. If there is a loss, is too little research being conducted in the division, and are the division's product lines then stagnating? Are costs too high? Are prices too low or too high? The chief executive cannot tell from a simple profit-and-loss statement what the reasons are for the numbers. Thus, as far as the chief executive is concerned, the product-line structure can be said to have a bias against the revelation of function-related data.[9]

The fact that the structure of an organization can lead the chief executive to make different inferences from the same initial messages can be seen as an example of the kinds of "bias"

---

[9] Jacquemin (1987: 150) suggests another potential bias of the product-line structure: "In order to supervise and direct the various operational divisions engaged in different activities, financial control, which is based on the common denominator of monetary return, has taken a dominant position in the organization, whereas the importance of managers specialized in marketing, technology, and human resources has declined. This evolution has resulted in an excessive weight being given to financial criteria. . . ."

and "distortion" that were discussed at the beginning of this section. However, if the initial perceptions of "reality" by workers are partial and fragmentary (which is inevitable), and if information aggregation and condensation have to go on (which they do), perhaps all that should be said is that there are several reasonable ways to interpret the information. If there is not any obvious reason, at least a priori, to think that one inference is necessarily "more accurate" or "more reasonable" than another, perhaps the terms "bias" and "distortion" should be avoided because of their unjustifiably negative connotations. Without knowing more about the ultimate implications of each inference, we cannot necessarily say that one inference is *better* than the other; it may be that all we can say is that the inferences are simply *different*.

What Role for Opportunism?

One noteworthy feature of the preceding analysis is that structure appears to affect information processing, and thus what the chief executive learns, even in the absence of self-interested or opportunistic behavior by subordinates. Of course, one can imagine a version of the Figure 4-1 example in which subordinates try to influence what the chief executive learns by deliberately distorting the information they send him. And one might reasonably guess that the particular kinds of distortions imparted would differ between a functional structure and a product-line structure. But even with completely "honest" subordinates who are interested only in what is good for the firm and who thus attempt to "tell the truth" as they know it, the discussion suggests that biases can be expected in hierarchical information processing.[10]

Williamson does acknowledge (1985: 281–282) that "organi-

---

[10] Even here, of course, it is possible that a subordinate interested only in what is good for the firm might distort information because he thinks this will lead the chief executive to make a better decision for the firm. This might happen especially if our subordinate believes that others are sending distorted information for self-interested reasons. Our subordinate might then believe that he has to distort his own information in order to counteract the (illegitimate) actions of the others. Since the other subordinates might fear the same thing about our first subordinate, there may be a Nash equilibrium in which everyone lies, even though everyone prefers to tell the truth and prefers that everyone else tell the truth too.

zation form matters even in a firm in which incentive problems attributable to opportunism are missing." But to Williamson self-interest and opportunism constitute a central part of transaction cost analysis, and it is not yet clear whether this central role can be justified.

The Conduct of Policy-making Tasks

Even when a chief executive does clearly perceive a problem, how to solve it may remain unclear. He may realize that he needs to decrease losses, for example, but he may not have a more specific goal in mind. For this reason he may solicit advice from subordinates on what specific goals the firm should pursue—e.g., Should we cut these particular costs? or, Should we drop this old product line?—and how to pursue them. With their recommendations in hand, he can then make his choices.

The structure of the firm can be expected to influence this policy-making process in four different ways. First, the advice that ultimately reaches the chief executive will be a function of the firm's structure: different structures will provide different sets of options—or *choice sets,* to use the North (1986) term— from which he may choose. Given different choice sets, we can expect the chief executive to make different choices.

Second, the structure of the firm influences the basic characteristics of the options themselves. That is, *what kinds of options* end up in the chief executive's choice set will be influenced by the structure.

Third, the structure influences what *criteria* the chief executive uses to evaluate and compare the options in the choice set. The kinds of options coming to him in one type of structure will suggest particular kinds of criteria by which the options might be evaluated and compared, while the different kinds of options produced by a different structure will suggest other kinds of criteria.

Fourth, the structure will affect what the chief executive *learns about how to choose* among these options. Since a particular structure will routinely present a chief executive with particular kinds of options, the chief executive will, over time, learn more about what is involved in making these particular kinds of choices rather than what is involved in making other kinds of choices.

This section will address each of these matters in turn.

Bottom-Up Planning and the Structure of the Firm

One of Chandler's major arguments on behalf of the product-line divisional structure was that it frees top-level executives from involvement in operational activities, thus providing time to address the larger questions of corporate strategy. To plan intelligently requires understanding what opportunities for profit there are in current and potential product lines. Each chief executive with experience in the firm will have accumulated a considerable store of knowledge about these profit opportunities. But since each chief executive necessarily follows some particular career path, he thereby gains less experience in some aspects of the business than in others. Thus a chief executive will be at least somewhat dependent on other employees for advice about what specific goals to adopt and about how these goals should be put into effect.

Much of this information and advice will come from low-ranking subordinates since it is often these subordinates—the scientists in the laboratories, the engineers in the manufacturing plants, the salespeople in the customers' offices—who will discover new opportunities for products, manufacturing techniques, and sales. The subordinates' contribution to strategic planning will then take the form of advice to superiors on how to pursue these newly discovered opportunities.

So when top-level managers adopt a new goal for the firm, or decide to pursue some goal in a new way, it is often because a subordinate has urged this new goal upon them. It was precisely this kind of bottom-up process that Bower (1970) discovered in his study of the capital budget planning process in the pseudonymous "National Products Corporation." He notes (1970: 42–43), for example, that

> in all cases, planning begins at some low level and moves up toward division management. Generally speaking, there is a review of all plans and once accepted they are both abstracted and collected for inclusion in the division plan. . . . Planning is "bottom-up"; there is no division planning staff that prepares a plan that the sub-units must then meet.

Bower also suggests that the structure of the firm and its reward system can affect how managers view their jobs, and thus can affect what particular proposals for investment emerge from lower organizational levels:

> [T]he organization, measures, and rewards—what we will call the corporate structure—indicate to a manager what "the corporation wants of me," and hence play a critical role in shaping the decision rules a manager uses to organize the demands of his job. If management wants to change those decision rules, it only has to change the structure within which a manager works. . . . (1970: 54)
>
> Instead of the traditional top-down view of planning . . . , what emerges from the argument above is a more complex process. It is subject to top management influence but indirectly through changes in the structural context of the planning process. (1970: 296)

Bower (1970: 300) then provides a hypothetical example of a study by National Products' management of how to improve the profitability of its plastics division. What emerges from this example is a clear statement of the impact of structure on the choices made available to management:

> At best, the result of such a study is a set of alternative recommendations. In the end, management must make a choice. The discussion of how the planning process works indicates that top management's *only* real choice is whether it will accept the recommendation of those managers who performed the integrating phase tasks. The last true discretion of the corporate officers was exercised in establishing the context and choosing personnel for the study. The corporate officers can send the study back, but they cannot change it substantively without reorganizing the company.

The Impact of Structure on Choice Sets

Bower's study suggests, then, that the firm's structure will influence the set of options made available to the top levels of management. Two examples of how this might happen will be presented. In the first, the jurisdictions of subordinates will be defined in terms of sets of discrete options. In the second, no jurisdictions will be imposed: for the problem at hand, subordinates are all considered to be "generalists," whose contributions are, in principle, granted equal consideration.[11]

---

[11] For reasons of space a third kind of example has been eliminated, in which the jurisdictions of subunits are defined in terms of dimensions, each subunit having responsibility for one dimension. Each subunit contributes to policy making by fixing a point on a dimension. The final policy that results is thus a vector consisting

Jurisdiction over discrete options.   In our first example, the jurisdictions of workers are defined in terms of discrete sets of options. In the top diagram in Figure 4-2A, the firm is organized into functional departments, while in the bottom diagram the firm is organized into product-line divisions. Assume each bottom-level employee can propose just one project related to his responsibilities (i.e., to his jurisdiction). Each employee forwards a proposal to his immediate superior for consideration. Each of these managers receives a proposal from each of his two subordinates, and will recommend just one of these two proposals to the chief executive. The chief executive thus receives two proposals, one from each of the two managers. The managers and the chief executive are able to make judgments about the relative value of options in this set. For simplicity, let us assume that the subordinates do not know what their superiors' choices would be. This inhibits their ability to engage in strategic behavior, and it will be taken to mean that they always recommend the option that is, in their judgment, the "best" by whatever criteria they happen to use. Each employee's judgments about the relative values of the options are listed in Figure 4-2B.

In the functional structure in Figure 4-2A, employee 1 in the Production Department handles production of product 1 and can recommend that either **s** or **t** be funded. He thinks **s**, upgrading the assembly line for product 1, will have a higher payoff than **t**, building an entirely new manufacturing facility for product 1. So he recommends **s** to his superior. Employee 2, who handles production of product 2, predicts that **v**, building a new facility for product 2, will have a higher payoff than **u**, which involves merely upgrading the current assembly line for product 2. So he recommends **v** to his superior. The production manager thus receives proposals for allocating resources either to **s** or **v**. Believing that **s** is likely to have the higher payoff, he recommends **s** to the chief executive.

In similar fashion, employee 3 in the Sales Department recommends **w** and employee 4 recommends **y**. The sales manager judges **y** to be the better project, and so recommends **y** to the

---

of a list of points, one on each of the dimensions. Changing the jurisdiction of a subunit from one dimension to another, and changing the sequence in which choices are made on the various dimensions, can be expected to change the outcomes. For an example see Hammond (1986, 388–391).

Figure 4-2A
How Structures Can Affect Outcomes: Jurisdictions with Discrete Options

Functional Structure

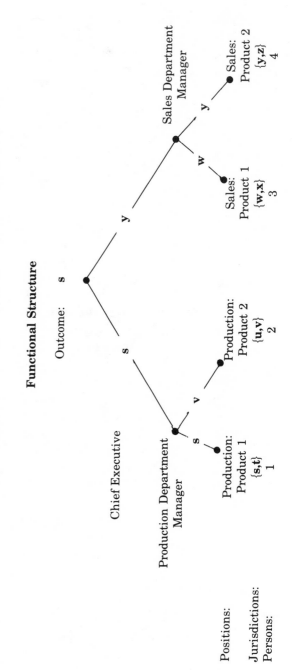

Outcome: **s**

Positions:

Jurisdictions:
Persons:

Product-Line Structure

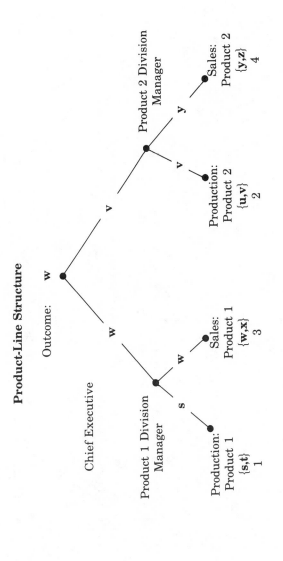

Outcome: **w**

Chief Executive

Product 1 Division Manager

Product 2 Division Manager

Positions:
Jurisdictions:
Persons:

Production: Product 1
{**s,t**}
1

Sales: Product 1
{**w,x**}
3

Production: Product 2
{**u,v**}
2

Sales: Product 2
{**y,z**}
4

Figure 4-2B

Options under Consideration

s = Attempt to decrease costs of producing product 1 by upgrading current assembly line
t = Attempt to decrease costs of producing product 1 by building new manufacturing facility

u = Attempt to decrease costs of producing product 2 by upgrading current assembly line
v = Attempt to decrease costs of producing product 2 by building new manufacturing facility

w = Attempt to increase sales of product 1 by hiring new salespeople
x = Attempt to increase sales of product 1 by increasing advertising budget

y = Attempt to increase sales of product 2 by hiring new salespeople
z = Attempt to increase sales of product 2 by increasing advertising budget

Employees' Judgments about the Relative Value of Each Option

An option ranked above another means the employee judges the higher option more likely to be profitable than lower option

--------Partial Rankings--------

	Employees			Manager Production Department/ Product 1 Division	Manager Sales Department/ Product 2 Division	Chief Executive
1	2	3	4			
s	v	w	y	w	v	s w
t	u	x	z	s	y	y v
				v	w	

--------Complete Rankings--------

	Employees			Manager Production Department/ Product 1 Division	Manager Sales Department/ Product 2 Division	Chief Executive
1	2	3	4			
u	z	y	x	u	v	u
x	v	t	u	x	x	s
v	u	z	s	w	y	w
s	y	u	w	s	t	y
t	t	v	y	t	u	z
w	x	s	z	v	w	v
y	s	w	t	z	s	x
z	w	x	v	y	z	t

129

chief executive. The chief executive thus receives proposals **s** and **y**—these constitute his choice set—from the Production and Sales Departments, respectively. Since he judges **s** to be a better project than **y,** he decides to allocate resources to project **s.**[12]

Now assume the firm is reorganized into product-line divisions: responsibility for both production and sales of product 1 are grouped in one division, and responsibility for production and sales of product 2 are grouped in another division. Thus employee 3, with jurisdiction over product 1 sales, now joins employee 1 in the product 1 division, while employee 2, with jurisdiction over product 2 production, joins employee 4 in the product 2 division. Assume the person who is the Production Department manager now becomes the product 1 division manager, and the person who is the Sales Department manager now becomes the product 2 division manager. The chief executive remains the same. Following the same procedures as before, **s** and **w** are now recommended to the product 1 division manager, and he in turn recommends **w** to the chief executive. The product 2 division manager now receives recommendations of **v** and **y** from his subordinates, and he recommends **v** to the chief executive. Thus the chief executive receives **w** and **v** and, judging **w** to be the better of the two projects, allocates resources to it.

In this case, then, *the reorganization completely changes the choice set*—from {**s,y**} to {**w,v**}—that is presented to the chief executive, and thus unavoidably affects the ultimate choice that is made.

There is also a remarkable, though distressing, aspect of the choice of **s** and **w** in these two structures. Assume that employees, managers, and the chief executive are able to make a judgment about the likely profitability of all eight options (see the complete rankings in Figure 4-2B). In the functional structure, *all* officials prefer option **u** to the final choice of **s**, while in the product-line structure *all* officials prefer option **u** to the final choice of **w**. The reason this happens in the functional structure, for example, is that only employee 2 can recommend option **u**,

---

[12] The preferences of the managers and chief executive are to be treated here as latent, in the sense that when presented with a pair of options, each official will spend time and energy deciding which is the better option; the choices that each would make, if forced to, are summarized in Figure 4-2B. What is listed for the managers and chief executive here should not be taken as clear-cut preferences that they have at the outset. If they had such clear-cut preferences at the outset, they would have no reason to consult their respective subordinates.

and he ranks option **u** below option **v,** thus eliminating **u** from further consideration. Option **v** itself is eliminated from further consideration by the Production Department manager.

Thus it is quite possible for the option ultimately selected to be judged *worse* than some other particular option by *all* officials in the firm. Subject matter jurisdictions, though integral to specialization and decentralization in a firm, nonetheless can have some undesirable side-effects. Individual specialization and organizational efficiency do not always go hand in hand.[13]

No jurisdictions.   Jurisdictions are not the only reason that structure affects outcomes. In our next example we see that structures can affect outcomes even when no jurisdictions at all are imposed on subordinates. In this case, the chief executive treats his subordinates as "generalists" rather than "specialists." Instead of restricting each subordinate to advice about a particular set of options or aspect of the plans, as in the previous examples, each subordinate is simply asked which of *all* possible plans he thinks is best. If subordinates give the same advice, assume their manager rubber-stamps this consensus advice and simply forwards it to the chief executive; for a manager or chief executive to disregard consensus would require him to spend his own scarce time and energy deciding what to do. For our example, let us assume that managers and the chief executive will accept unanimous advice from subordinates, and that only if there is any disagreement will they resort to making up their own minds.[14]

When there are no jurisdictions, what is critical is how subordinates with particular preferences are grouped into subunits. Consider the structures in Figure 4-3. Assume that when faced with a choice between **x** and **y,** one sales and one production employee would each choose **x,** the other sales employee and the other production employee would choose **y,** the middle-level

---

[13]   For an extensive examination of this general point see Hammond and Miller (1985) and Miller (1992, ch. 4).

[14]   In previous work—see, for example, Hammond and Horn (1985)—this decision rule has been called "management by exception" (MBE), a term that captures some of the flavor of the meaning of the identical term occasionally used in the management literature. While MBE economizes on a manager's time and energy, it has the potential for concentrating effective decision-making power in the hands of subordinates. Hammond and Thomas (1990) demonstrate that in relatively large hierarchies, widespread use of an MBE decision rule has the potential for giving decision-making power to a very small number of low-level subordinates.

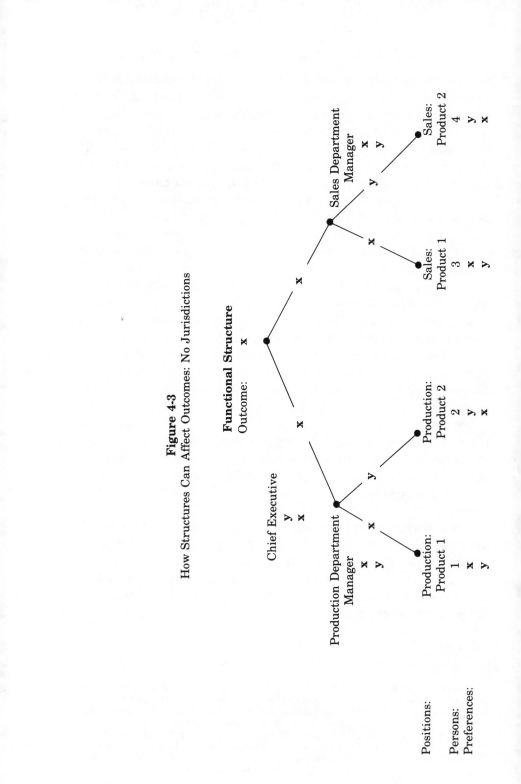

Figure 4-3

How Structures Can Affect Outcomes: No Jurisdictions

Functional Structure

Product-Line Structure

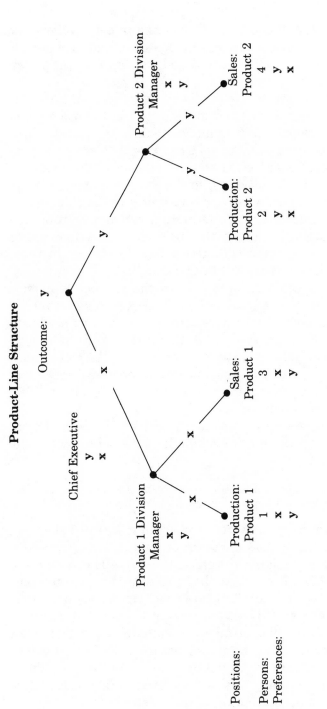

Outcome: y

Chief Executive
y
x

Product 1 Division
Manager
x
y

Product 2 Division
Manager
x
y

Sales:
Product 1
3
x
y

Production:
Product 1
1
x
y

Production:
Product 2
2
y
x

Sales:
Product 2
4
y
x

Positions:

Persons:

Preferences:

133

managers would both choose **x** (if they had to get involved and develop their own preferences), and the chief executive would choose **y** (if he had to get involved and develop his own preferences).

In the functional structure, the two production employees disagree with each other (one recommends **x** and the other **y**), so the Production Department manager makes up his own mind and forwards option **x** to the chief executive. The same happens in the Sales Department: the two sales employees disagree (one recommends **x** and the other **y**), so the Sales Department manager makes up his own mind and forwards **x** to the chief executive. Since the chief executive receives a recommendation of **x** from each manager, he rubber-stamps their agreed-upon option and so anoints **x** as organizational policy. In the product-line structure, employees 2 and 3 have traded places. The two product 1 employees agree on option **x,** so the product 1 division manager accepts their advice and forwards **x** as his own recommendation to the chief executive. Similarly, the two product 2 employees agree on option **y** and so the product 2 division manager forwards this advice to the chief executive. The chief executive is now getting conflicting advice from the managers and so makes his own judgment that **y** is the better policy. Recall that the first structure produced **x**.

In sum, whether we are considering discrete jurisdictions or no jurisdictions at all, our two examples both point toward the same general conclusion:

> **Proposition 2:** Different organizational structures can produce different sets of options for consideration by the chief executive.

Moreover, while this proposition is phrased in a relatively weak manner, it is actually possible to prove a much stronger result: it is *impossible* to design an organization—see Hammond and Thomas (1989)—so that when the structure changes, the outcome is guaranteed not to change. In other words, "neutral hierarchies" cannot exist. It is also important to note that the proof of this result does not depend on any assumptions of self-interest or opportunism. It is the formal structure alone which drives the result, not the characteristics or behavior of the individuals in the structure. Even if the individual actors are complete automatons, with no conception of self-interest whatsoever, the structure will still affect outcomes.

The Strategic Provision of Advice

The structure will affect outcomes even if subordinates are not self-interested. Nonetheless, when the chief executive is dependent on subordinates for advice, this does give subordinates an opportunity to manipulate his choices by providing advice different from what they "truly" think is "best." As already noted, Williamson has emphasized the importance of opportunism in hierarchies, and Jennergren (1981) and Burton and Obel (1984: ch. 6) have demonstrated that strategic behavior by subordinates can indeed affect outcomes. In general, we can state:

> **Proposition 3:** Each subordinate may be able to improve organization outcomes for himself by recommending an option different from what he most prefers.

Hammond (1986: 393–398) and Hammond and Horn (1983, 1985) illustrate several ways in which a subordinate in a multilevel hierarchy can improve outcomes for himself by misrepresenting his own views.

While no method of choosing policies is completely immune to manipulation (see Gibbard, 1973; Satterthwaite, 1975; Walker, 1980), a question can be raised as to how significant this problem is. One reason is that not all situations are "ripe" for manipulation by subordinates. How often situations are ripe for manipulation depends both on the details of the firm's advisory process and on the preferences of employees in the firm. Sometimes there is nothing a subordinate can do to improve outcomes for himself by misrepresenting his views. For example, assuming no jurisdictions, Hammond and Horn (1985) calculate the frequency with which a subordinate in a two-level hierarchy might find it profitable to engage in strategic behavior. The general lesson from this particular model is that strategic behavior is beneficial mostly when there are relatively few subordinates and relatively few options under consideration. In richer and more complex organizational contexts, strategic behavior by any one individual is less likely to be profitable.[15]

Even when a situation is ripe for manipulation, this does not

---

[15] Other models might produce very different patterns of benefit of strategic behavior to subordinates; see Burton and Obel (1984: ch. 6) for a review of a number of studies.

mean that an individual will be able to figure out a good strategy. One difficulty is that strategizing requires accurate information about the likely choices of other actors. This information may not be easy to get, and without it attempts at strategizing may be as likely to hurt as help the manipulator.

A second difficulty is that even when the necessary information is in hand, the calculations needed to use the information can be very complex. This is especially true if many subordinates are simultaneously attempting to behave strategically. Each subordinate may have to make some very subtle calculations of precisely how he should modify his advice, given that the advice of others may depend on what he does. This is a much more difficult computational problem than if only one subordinate is acting strategically.[16] Others have reached similar conclusions about the difficulty of calculating strategies. From a laboratory study of manipulation, for example, Burton and Obel (1984: 174) concluded that "it is not obvious how to misrepresent advantageously even if one so desires. That is, an adequate procedural understanding of the process does not necessarily imply that one can game it."

There is one final point to make about strategic behavior. Williamson generally depicts strategic behavior as having negative consequences for the firm. But this may not always be the case. In the example of jurisdictions with discrete options in Figure 4-2, it was observed that the outcomes, s and w, were inferior in everyone's eyes to option u. These inferior outcomes can be avoided if at least one official behaves strategically. In the functional structure in Figure 4-2A, for example, if employee 2 forwards not v (which he prefers to u), but u, then the production manager receives s and u. Since this manager prefers u to s, he forwards u to the chief executive. The chief executive's choice set is now {u,y} and he would choose u over y. Since the Pareto inferior choice, s, is avoided here if employee 2 behaves strategically, we can conclude that strategic behavior can have virtues, not only for an individual but for the whole firm as well.

---

[16] The strategizing required in two-level hierarchies is described in Hammond and Horn (1985), while Hammond and Horn (1983) discusses the far greater complexities of strategizing in three-level hierarchies.

What Kinds of Options?

The structure of the firm has a second kind of impact on the advisory process: the structure not only affects *which* options are in the choice set but also *what kinds* of options they are.

Consider a resource allocation problem that is handled via the routines of the firm's capital-budgeting process. Low-level units begin by submitting requests for resources to their immediate superiors. Each superior adjusts these requests in some fashion, aggregates them into a single package, and forwards this package to his superior. What finally arrive at the chief executive's office are large, aggregated request packages from each subunit.

Changes in the structure of the firm can lead to changes in the fundamental characteristics of these requests. For example, given the nature of the responsibilities assigned to the subunits of a functionally organized firm, the aggregate requests forwarded to the chief executive will tend to focus on improvements (e.g., increased efficiency) in the performance of the subunits' functional activities. It will not necessarily be obvious from these functional requests how any one particular product will benefit. In a product-line structure, on the other hand, subunit responsibilities will lead to the generation of proposals focusing on improvements (e.g., increased profits) in performance of the subunits' products or product lines. It will not necessarily be obvious from these product-line requests what particular functions will benefit. Thus, functional structures will tend to produce choice sets containing proposals about functions, while product-line structures will tend to produce choice sets containing proposals about products. More generally, we can state:

Proposition 4: Different organizational structures produce different kinds of options for consideration by the chief executive.

Learning and the Suggestion of Criteria for Choice

Whatever the nature of the choice set given to the chief executive (which options? what kind of options?), a further aspect of policy making—how he goes about deciding what advice to accept—is also influenced by the structure. Choosing among options involves the selection of criteria by which to evaluate and compare the options. The nature of the options in the choice set will suggest *which particular criteria* will be most useful and appropriate for evaluating and comparing the options.

For example, if requests from different functional departments are to be compared by the chief executive, the proposals will tend to have one common denominator—the variable of function. Consideration of proposals in the choice set will thus tend to be conducted in terms of which function the chief executive is most concerned about, e.g., Are production costs too high? or, Are revenues from sales too low? If the requests are from different product-line divisions, the competing requests will have a different common denominator—the product line—that suggests comparison. In this case, consideration of proposals in the choice set will tend to be conducted in terms of which product or product line the chief executive is especially concerned about. In either case, only with extra work will the chief executive be able to analyze a set of proposals in terms of criteria for comparison different from those implied by the organization's structure. This yields:

> **Proposition 5:** The organizational structure, and thus the characteristics of the chief executive's choice set, suggests some kinds of criteria rather than other kinds of criteria on which to base comparisons of options.

Finally, since a structure exposes the chief executive to some kinds of proposals rather than others, and since some kinds of criteria for comparing proposals are more available than others, it seems reasonable to argue that what he *learns* about proposals and how to compare them will also be influenced by the structure. In different structures he will learn different things as he works at making his decisions. A chief executive at the head of a functional structure will, over time, become expert at making comparisons and choices among functional options; he will learn less about making choices among product or product-line options. At the head of a product-line structure, on the other hand, he will become expert at making comparisons and choices among product or product-line options, but will learn less about making choices among functional options. So we can state:

> **Proposition 6:** To the extent that a manager learns about different kinds of issues by making comparisons among different sets of options, the organizational structure will influence what is learned.[17]

---

[17] Hammond (1993) offers a more extensive discussion of how structures affect the nature of the comparisons that lie at the heart of learning and decision making.

The Conduct of Implementation Tasks

Even if a chief executive has been able to identify the key problems facing his firm, and even if he has been able to make a satisfactory choice of what the firm's response should be, there still remains the problem of implementing his chosen policy. It is difficult, however, for the chief executive to describe how to implement his policy in such a way that *all* possible contingencies are covered by his instructions. Even if subordinates try in good faith to do what they are told, unforeseen contingencies will arise for which the chief executive's initial instructions will prove unclear.

Without clear instructions, subordinates with different responsibilities and concerns will often develop different views on how to solve these unanticipated problems. Since different solutions to these problems will affect how each subordinate does his work and, in the long run, will also affect what happens to each subordinate's career, a subordinate may be inclined to press for one kind of solution rather than another.

If subordinates cannot settle differences of opinion among themselves, higher-level managers may be called upon to resolve them. Economists have occasionally remarked on the conflict-resolution role that managers play in a firm. For example, Boulding (1964: 48–49) once suggested:

> The hierarchical structure of organizations can largely be interpreted as a device for the resolution of conflicts, with each grade of the hierarchy specializing in resolving the conflicts of the grade beneath it. The very structure of an organization can be regarded as a "constitution," a constitution being defined as a previously agreed method of resolving conflicts which have not yet arisen. We can go even further and argue that virtually all organizational decisions are the end product of a process of conflict resolution between the points of view of various sections and departments.

Williamson's stress on the importance of the "governance structure" of a firm (1981a: 1539) finds clear expression in observations like these (see also Leibenstein [1979: 480]).

Every manager has responsibility for settling conflicts among his subordinates. For each manager, the contents of this class of conflicts will be influenced by the structure: some kinds of conflicts will be routed to the manager in one type of structure while other kinds of conflicts will be routed to him in another type of structure. How the chief executive's policies are ultimately implemented will thus depend on the structure, and what the managers and chief executive learn from this conflict-resolution process will also be influenced by the structure.

Structure and the Routing of Conflicts

To analyze the impact of the structure on the distribution and resolution of conflicts, we assume that there is substantial interdependence among the bottom-level employees: in effect, how one bottom-level employee does his job is presumed to affect how most other bottom-level employees do their jobs. For example, some kind of joint production might require two or more employees to carry out a task, and they might disagree about how to do this. Or some common resource might be in short supply, and the employees might be divided over who gets to use how much. Or it might be that one employee's activities impose costs (i.e., negative externalities) on another employee, and the second employee may object to bearing these costs.

When differences of opinion about how to carry out a task cannot be resolved "horizontally" by the employees directly involved, they may consider referring their conflict upward to superiors for resolution. Several different factors affect this decision. For example, employees may sometimes find it in their mutual interest to resolve the dispute themselves. The reason is that the superior who settles the dispute may impose a decision that neither employee likes. In this case, the employees would be better off settling their differences and never letting superiors get involved.

However, horizontal settlement must appeal to *both* employees. If one employee prefers the solution likely to be imposed from above to what could be agreed on horizontally, he will be less likely to agree to a horizontal compromise. In general, then, we can state:

> **Proposition 7:** For each employee involved in a conflict, the greater the value of the policy that would be imposed by a superior or superiors, compared to the value of the policy that could be agreed on horizontally, the more desirable it is to refer the conflict upward.

This kind of sophisticated behavior requires, of course, that subordinates be able to guess how their superior or superiors might resolve the dispute.

For his own part, the superior may not want to be drawn into subordinates' disputes. For example, he may feel that to take a position on the dispute would be time-consuming, that it might irritate one or both subordinates, and that it might be politically costly for his career. In general, taking no position at all is sometimes the safest thing to do. So the superior may threaten to impose penalties on subordinates who force him to get involved in their conflicts. Rational subordinates would then be more inclined to settle their own differences. Hence:

> **Proposition 8:** The greater the penalties associated with referring a conflict upward, the more likely it is employees will reach a horizontal agreement.

Also affecting the subordinates' decision to send a conflict upward is the severity of the dispute. An employee who feels especially strongly about some issue may find it worthwhile to risk the possibility of a penalty for bothering his superiors; he may also find it worthwhile to risk an adverse decision from some superior. So we can state:

> **Proposition 9:** The greater the severity of conflict between two employees, the greater the probability they will refer their conflict upward for resolution.

If employees have perfect knowledge of each other's preferences as well as how a superior would resolve a dispute, no conflict will ever be referred upward. If both parties to the conflict prefer a horizontal settlement to what the superior would impose, the conflict will be settled horizontally. If at least one employee prefers what the superior would impose to what might be agreed on horizontally, the other employee will be in a weak strategic position and will agree to a compromise. In either case, a horizontal settlement should be expected. So if a conflict is in fact sent upward, the reason must be factors like subordinate misperception of, or uncertainty about, what solution a superior would be likely to impose, or to the fact that the subordinate is playing a richer, multiperiod game in which a short-term loss on the current dispute will lead to longer-term gains on other issues. In what follows, the assumption is made that the latter conditions generally prevail, and that conflicts are generally sent upward for resolution.

If a conflict is sent upward, it will normally rise no higher than the lowest common superior of the employees involved; a subordinate relatively infrequently "appeals" a decision over the head of his superior. For every pair of subordinates, then, the structure determines who their lowest common superior is.

It follows that the grouping of employees in a structure affects how high in the structure the conflict might rise before resolution. Hence:

> **Proposition 10:** For a conflict that is not horizontally resolved, the structure determines how high the conflict may have to rise before it is resolved by the lowest common superior of the employees involved.

This proposition can be illustrated by examining conflicts in a firm in terms of their treatment in functional and product-line structures. Consider the structure in Figure 4-4. Each structure here has the same number of officials, and the bottom two levels contain the same positions and people. The bottom-level employees are labeled (1) through (8) and the managers are labeled (9) through (12).

We begin by acknowledging that the two structures might route a given conflict to the same person. Consider a conflict between (1) and (2) over design and manufacturing aspects of product 1: the product 1 production manager (9) would resolve the dispute in both the functional and product-line structures. In each case, the conflict rises only one level, and for this conflict these two structures behave in an identical fashion. Thus the structure does not *necessarily* affect how conflicts are handled.

But now consider a dispute between employee (1), who designs product 1, and employee (6), who sells product 1 to customers in the field; the dispute might concern what features product 1 should have. In the functional structure this dispute between (1) and (6) might be referred upward to the product 1 production manager and the product 1 sales manager. If they cannot settle the matter, the general production and sales managers might get involved. If they cannot work things out, the conflict might go all the way to the chief executive. In the product-line structure, on the other hand, this same dispute between (1) and (6) would rise no further than the product 1 manager; the chief executive would never get involved.

The latter example can be put in more general terms. In the functional structure every conflict between anyone in Production (employees [1], [2], [3], and [4]) and anyone in Sales (employees [5], [6], [7], and [8]) might conceivably rise all the way to the chief executive. In the product-line structure, however, conflicts involving any one product would be resolved by either the product 1 manager or the product 2 manager and would never rise to the chief executive. In this structure, only conflicts *between* products would have the potential for rising to the chief executive.

Proposition 10 and the examples above characterize in more abstract terms an observation about functional and product-line structures that has already been discussed by several analysts. For example, Sherman (1966: 34) once observed:

> A common problem in industry when profits decline under the functional type of organization is for the sales people to complain that no one could sell the poor quality product being turned out by the manufacturing people, whereas the latter maintain that the product is fine but the salesmen are incompetent. Such conflicts are less apt to reach the chief executive under the product type organization, though a vice president for a product division that is losing money will face the same problem among those reporting to him.

Similarly, Williamson (1985: 296) remarked that in a change to a product-line divisional structure, "operating decisions were no longer forced to the top but were resolved at the divisional level, which relieved the communication load."

Walker and Lorsch (1970) studied manufacturers of corrugated containers which were organized either functionally or by product line. The authors observed (1970: 47) that in the functional structure in "Plant F" interfunction conflicts increased the burden of coordination for upper-level managers: "While use of the management hierarchy is one acceptable way to resolve conflict, so many disagreements at Plant F were pushed upstairs that the hierarchy became overloaded and could not handle all the problems facing it. So it responded by dealing with only the more immediate and pressing ones." Another manufacturer of corrugated containers shifted from a product basis to a functional basis in the hope that it would lead to efficiencies in production and marketing. Walker and Lorsch (1970: 39) described the consequences of this shift:

> While the organization did accomplish these aims, it found itself less able to obtain coordination among its local sales and production units. The functional specialists now reported to the top officers in charge of production and sales, and there was no mechanism for one person to coordinate their work below the level of divisional management. As a result, the company encountered numerous problems and unresolved conflicts among functions and later returned to the product form.

It should be clear, though, that changing from a functional structure to a product-line structure will cause some conflicts

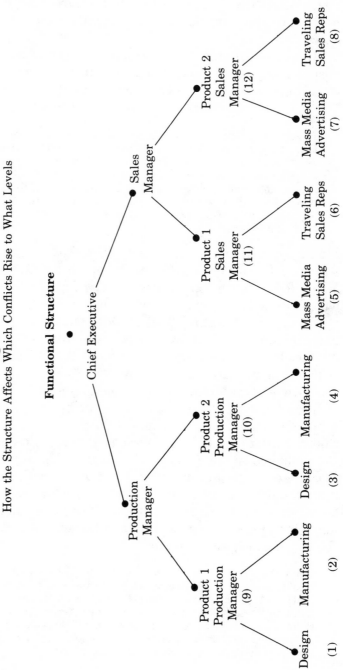

Figure 4-4
How the Structure Affects Which Conflicts Rise to What Levels

Functional Structure

144

Product-Line Structure

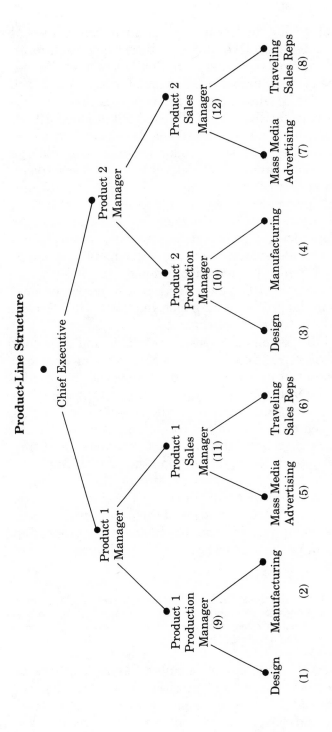

previously resolved low in the functional structure to rise all the way to the chief executive in the product-line structure. In Figure 4-4, for example, consider a conflict between employees (2) and (4) involved in manufacturing products 1 and 2; the dispute might arise because each employee wants exclusive use of a manufacturing facility currently used for producing both products. In the functional structure the dispute would be referred upward to the product 1 production manager and the product 2 production manager, labeled (9) and (10) respectively, both located in the Production Department. If (9) and (10) are unable to work out these differences, the overall production manager might have to resolve the dispute, but it would go no higher. In the product-line structure, however, the same dispute between (2) and (4) over use of the manufacturing facility might rise first to the product 1 production manager (9) and product 2 production manager (10), who are now in different product divisions, then to the product 1 manager and the product 2 manager, and finally to the chief executive.

The general implication of Propositions 7, 8, 9, and 10 is that how the employees are grouped into departments or divisions can have a substantial impact on which conflicts rise to the chief executive. For the interfunctional conflicts regarding a particular product in a functional structure, the conflict may rise all the way to the chief executive for resolution, whereas in the divisional structure these interfunctional conflicts involving just one product would rise no higher than the product-line division manager. In the product-line structure, on the other hand, interproduct conflicts may rise all the way to the chief executive, while in the functional structure some of these interproduct conflicts would rise no higher than the sales manager or production manager. In sum, then, we can pose the following corollary to Proposition 10:

> **Proposition 11:** For a conflict that is not horizontally resolved, structures based on some methods of grouping will resolve the conflict at low levels, while structures based on other methods of grouping may route the conflict to higher levels for resolution.

Proposition 11 links questions about different methods of grouping to questions about "centralization" and "decentralization" in a firm. A move from a functional to a product-line structure is sometimes described as "decentralizing" in nature; see

Ansoff and Brandenburg (1971), for example. But this is an oversimplification. Each structure will resolve some conflicts at low levels and other conflicts higher up. A change in structure, as with a shift from the functional to the divisional structure, means that some conflicts previously resolved lower down will now be resolved higher up, and vice versa. That is,

> **Proposition 12:** To structure an organization so that some kinds of conflicts rise to the top for resolution implies that other kinds of conflicts will be resolved at lower levels.

This proposition has implications for an accurate characterization of the shift from the functional to the product-line structure. There is general agreement that the functional structure *centralizes* cross-function "operational" questions, in the sense that cross-functional issues (involving a particular product, for example) often end up being handled by central office managers. At the same time, however, it might be said that cross-product "strategic" questions are thereby *decentralized* to the functional departments: it is left to each department to figure out what goals to pursue for each product and how to pursue them. A shift to the product-line structure reverses this pattern: the product-line structure *decentralizes* to each of the divisions the cross-functional coordination problems for each product at the same time that it *centralizes* cross-product strategic planning in the central office. Caves (1980: 69) puts the issue in something close to its proper form: the product-line divisional form "serves to decentralize operating authority while centralizing the planning and coordinating roles. . . ."

It seems reasonable to think that conflicts resolved at low levels will be resolved in terms of the beliefs and preferences of the low-level employees or managers, while conflicts resolved at higher levels will be resolved in terms of the beliefs and preferences of the higher-level managers or chief executive. In other words, to the extent that the resolution of conflicts involves policy making (i.e., decisions about precisely how the firm's operational tasks are to be carried out), the structure can be expected to influence the firm's policies. Hence:

> **Proposition 13:** If the beliefs and preferences of the officials at the lower levels are different from those of officials at the middle and top, the structure will affect how conflicts are resolved and thus will affect what policies the employees in conflict at the bottom are ultimately told to implement.

Since what a chief executive learns stems, in part, from involvement in subordinates' conflicts, the way conflicts are processed in different kinds of structures has implications for what the chief executive learns. We begin by noting the following:

> **Proposition 14:** For each manager and the chief executive, the structure determines which kinds of conflicts come to him for resolution and which do not.

In Figure 4-4, for example, by getting involved in conflicts between the Production and Sales Departments in a functional structure, the chief executive will learn much about the differing virtues and perspectives of these two departments. He will not learn as much about the details and nuances of different kinds of production strategies (many conflicts over these issues are resolved solely within the Production Department) or of different kinds of marketing strategies (many conflicts over these issues are resolved solely within Sales). In the product-line structure, on the other hand, the chief executive will learn much about the differing virtues and perspectives of the product-line divisions but little about functional disputes among officials within each division.

From this perspective, then, the structure will have a systematic effect on what the chief executive learns and what he does not learn:

> **Proposition 15:** Because a chief executive learns about different kinds of issues in part by resolving conflicts among subordinates, the organizational structure will influence what he learns.

Propositions 14 and 15 place in more abstract terms an observation that Chandler made in *Strategy and Structure* (1962: 312) about the training of managers in functional versus product-line structures. Chandler describes the functional structure as training "specialist" managers and the product-line structure as training "generalist" managers:

> Besides allocating decision making more effectively and assuring more precise communication and control, the new structure proved to have another advantage over the functionally departmentalized organization. It provided a place to train and test general executives. Under the earlier structure, no one but a president or chairman of the board ever had a continuing, over-all view of the company's affairs. The departmental vice-presidents, as members of an Executive Committee or other senior central office group, might have some experience in over-all coordination, appraisal, and policymaking, but even here they tended to be primarily

concerned with their own particular functional activity. Now all the division managers had to be generalists rather than specialists, and thus they gained experience in running a complex business.

While insightful, Chandler's observation about training and experience can be phrased in a somewhat more precise manner. On the one hand, a functional structure trains a department manager to become a *specialist in function* and a *generalist in products:* each functional manager deals with the entire range of products but only with a particular functional aspect of each. On the other hand, a product-line structure trains a manager to become a *specialist in product* and a *generalist in functions:* each product-line manager deals with the entire range of functions but only for a given product or product line.

Chandler argues, in effect, that the multifunctional perspective instilled in product-line division managers is more valuable for a firm than the multiproduct perspective instilled in functional department managers. Chandler's reasoning appears to be that a functional department manager who becomes the chief executive (or rises to some other central office position) will approach his new job in terms of his old functional responsibilities and perspectives. If we accept this logic, we should also expect that the product-line division manager who becomes chief executive will approach his new job in terms of the responsibilities and perspectives of his old product-line responsibilities and perspectives.

But when phrased in this manner, it is not immediately obvious why one malady is necessarily worse for the firm than the other. Even if Chandler's overall conclusion is correct, the reason cannot lie in his assertion that one kind of manager is a broadly trained "generalist" and the other a narrowly trained "specialist": after all, *each* kind of manager has become a specialist in some kinds of matters and a generalist in others.

It may be that learning how to maximize profits (only product-line division managers learn fully how to do this) is particularly appropriate for a firm that sells its products in a competitive market. Learning how to minimize costs (in a functional structure's production department) or maximize sales (in a functional structure's sales department) will not necessarily be the most useful or appropriate type of learning here. Nonetheless, if a firm is selling its product in an environment in which price is limited (owing, for example, to a government-mandated price ceiling), it may be to the firm's advantage to have a chief executive particularly experienced at cutting costs since this is where profits will have to come from.

Prescription and Contradiction in Structural Design

The structure of the firm affects what information the chief executive sees, and so it affects how he defines strategic problems facing the firm. It affects what options are made available to him, and it affects the criteria he might use in choosing among the options. Finally, it affects what implementation disputes come to him for resolution. But just as Chandler was criticized for presenting an overly executive-centered, top-down view of strategic management, this bottom-up "structure-as-agenda" perspective on structure and strategy formulation might be criticized for treating the chief executive as an entirely passive recipient of whatever the structure brings to him. Rounding out this bottom-up picture, then, requires some attention to the role the chief executive might play; rarely is he such an innocent victim of structural arrangements.

From the bottom-up perspective, the obvious role for the chief executive is to design the structure in the first place. But even if structure does affect policy making, and even if it is the chief executive's role to select the structure, it is still not clear what structure he should choose. The literature on organizational design and strategic management does, of course, contain some prescriptions. However, the bottom-up approach to organizational structure leads us to the conclusion that two of the major prescriptions are mutually incompatible. More important, it also clarifies the nature of the structural choices and trade-offs which this contradiction poses for the chief executive.

At the heart of strategy formulation is the matter of what the chief executive and his managers *learn* about problems facing the firm, about proposals for solving these problems, and about disputes over implementation of the solutions. Several of the propositions advanced in this paper highlight the impact of the structure on this learning process. Each person's location in the structure means that he will learn some things and not other things; indeed, learning about some things *implies* not learning about other things. Whatever conceptual categories the chief executive uses to define his firm's structure, what he learns from the structure can be summarized in the following way:

> **Proposition 16:** The orientation, policy-making, and implementation tasks all produce information for the chief executive relevant to *intercategory* perspectives, comparisons, and conflicts. The chief executive's choice of structural categories is thus equivalent to a decision that he will be ignorant about *intracategory* perspectives, comparisons, and conflicts.

If structure systematically affects what the chief executive learns and what he does not learn, the structural design question then becomes something like this: *What should the chief executive learn and what should he remain ignorant about?*

The strategic management literature advances a prescription directly relevant to this question: since the chief executive's primary responsibility is to address the key strategic issues facing his firm, it follows that the chief executive should design a structure that keeps him well informed about key strategic issues. If the chief executive believes that some decisions for his firm are more critical than others, and if he wants to be the person who makes the critical decisions, then each possible structure should be evaluated in terms of the extent to which it brings him what he needs to know—the information, advice, and conflicts—for making these critical decisions. How should he carry out this evaluation?

In thinking about strategic issues in his firm's environment, the chief executive will presumably create a set of categories for classifying elements of the environment. For example, these categories might correspond to separate markets for the firm's products, to particular suppliers of inputs and buyers of outputs, or to different governmental bodies that are important to the firm (e.g., an executive agency such as the Defense Department, or a regulatory body such as the Environmental Protection Agency). One of the most prominent prescriptions advanced by the organization design literature is to "match" the structure to the categories used to classify the objects or activities in the firm's environment: each important category should be assigned its own division or department, presumably headed by its own manager. A good "fit" between structure and environment, it is argued, will enhance the firm's performance in the market.

Now assume that one category contains objects or activities that are more important for the firm's survival than the objects or activities in the other categories. It would thus seem that the chief executive's strategic management responsibilities require him to be exposed to information regarding these objects or activities. But a problem with the matching prescription now becomes clear: a structure whose subunits match those of the firm's environment will cut the chief executive off from crucial sources of information *within* this category of greatest interest. If there is a single buyer for the firm's products, or a single supplier for some critical input, or some key government agency that regulates the price, quality, or quantity of the firm's service, then the chief executive's *subordinate* dealing with this critical contingency will end up making some of the most critical decisions, not the chief executive. That is, the chief executive will not be able to perform the major role that the strategic management literature assigns to him, which is to make the critical strategic decisions.

Ironically, then, it is only if the chief executive wants *someone else* in his firm to become most knowledgeable about the critical category of the environment that he should select an organizational structure whose categories "match" those of the environment. If the categories embodied in the firm's structure correspond to the categories of the environment, this means that the chief executive will remain relatively ignorant about what is going on within each environmental category, including the most critical one. So it turns out that the proper structural design advice goes directly contrary to the matching prescription:

> **Proposition 17:** If the chief executive is to be well informed about the most critical category in his firm's environment, the categories on which the firm is structured should *cut across* the categories used for classifying elements of the firm's environment.

It is only in this fashion that the chief executive can design a structure that enables him to fulfill his strategic management responsibilities.

This argument also suggests that the prescriptions of transaction cost minimization and the creation of product-line divisions advanced by Williamson and Chandler may be incompatible with the continuing involvement of the chief executive in what he considers the firm's most critical issues. In a product-line structure, for example, the chief executive might be able to play a strategic role in deciding *that* his firm would produce a given product, and thus that there should be a division which produces that product. However, he would be unable to have much say in determining the particular features of the product that is ultimately produced; the trade-offs among features would largely be determined *within* the division. But if it is the particular mix of trade-offs that will determine the product's ultimate success in the market, then that decision has, in effect, been delegated to others. In other words, for all the undoubted costs of the functional structure—e.g., the heavy burden of coordination imposed on central office managers, as stressed by Chandler and Williamson—this structure does provide a chief executive with an institutionalized opportunity to learn a great deal about the nature of each of his firm's products or product lines, and thereby play a role in their definition and ultimate success. To choose a product-line divisional structure is equivalent to cutting the chief executive off from intradivisional debates about what should be the characteristics of each of his company's products.

Moreover, while the product-line structure may enhance the chief executive's ability to judge the relative profitabilities of the various divisions (as Williamson and Chandler noted), this structural form does not necessarily provide information or understanding for the chief executive as to *why* divisional profitabilities differ, nor does it necessarily put the chief executive in a position to learn what to do about poorly performing divisions. The product-line structure may be able to tell the chief executive *that* a product line is not profitable. But it can't tell him *why* the product line is not profitable. The functional structure, on the other hand, can tell him *why* the product line might not be profitable. But it can't tell him *whether* the product line is profitable or not.

In fact, from this perspective, one might even argue that the product-line structure, while decreasing the subordinates' transaction costs in performing their duties, actually serves to *increase* the transaction costs that the chief executive incurs in determining why his subordinates happen to perform as they do. The functional structure, on the other hand, while increasing the subordinates' transaction costs in performing their duties, may actually *decrease* the transaction costs that the chief executive incurs in determining why they happen to perform as they do. Thus it may be misleading to assert that the product-line structure minimizes the firm's transaction costs. Instead, it is more accurate to say that each structure reduces some employees' transaction costs while increasing the transaction costs of other employees. It follows that structural design hinges on the question of whether the chief executive's transaction costs are more important, or less important, than those of the subordinates. Unfortunately, transaction cost analysis to date provides little insight into whose transaction costs it is most important for the firm to minimize.

These arguments, along with the propositions, make it clear that the structural design of a firm involves choices among imperfect, and often unpalatable, alternatives. Thus, choosing among structural alternatives ultimately entails making trade-offs. The bottom-up, structure-as-agenda approach advanced here cannot, by itself, tell a chief executive how to make the trade-offs; it does no more here than the other bodies of literature that were criticized. But the bottom-up approach to the structure of the firm does suggest some ways of clarifying what the costs and benefits of each kind of structure might be. The approach thus goes some distance in clarifying our understanding of the nature of the structural choices that a chief executive faces. Only when the nature of the alternatives is understood can an adequate theory of structural choice, and its impact on strategy formulation, be developed.

5

Game Theory and Strategic Management: Contributions, Applications, and Limitations

Garth Saloner

1. Introduction

During the 1970s and 1980s considerable effort was devoted to applying game-theoretic techniques to the analytic modeling of issues in industrial economics. The sophistication and breadth of the models described in *The Handbook of Industrial Organization* or in Jean Tirole's *The Theory of Industrial Organization* bear witness to the extent of that effort.

Many of the issues examined in that body of work are of direct relevance to competitive strategy, the branch of strategic management concerned with what one might call "external" strategy issues, i.e., the firm's strategy vis-à-vis its rivals. These include issues such as the importance of first-mover advantages and the role of commitment in staking out a market position[1]; reputation formation and exploitation[2]; signaling[3]; and the strategic control of information more generally.[4]

Acknowledgments: I thank Robert Burgelman, J. Michael Harrison, Jeffrey Pfeffer, John Roberts, Julio Rotemberg, Richard Rumelt, Dan Schendel, Birger Wernerfelt, and the Silverado conference participants for comments and suggestions.

[1]   See Lieberman and Montgomery (1988) for an overview of first-mover advantages and Schmalensee (1978, 1982) and Spence (1977, 1981) for specific examples. Dixit (1980), discussed in Section 3 below, and Judd (1985) contain analyses of the importance of the ability to make commitments.

[2]   See Camerer and Weigelt (1988) and Kreps and Spence (1984) for overviews, and Kreps (1990a), Rotemberg and Saloner (1986, 1990a), Green and Porter (1984) for examples. The work of Kreps and Wilson (1982), Milgrom and Roberts (1982b), and Kreps, Milgrom, Roberts, and Wilson (1982) is discussed in Section 5 below.

[3]   See Spence (1974) for the development of the theory and Milgrom and Roberts (1982a) discussed in Section 3 for an application to entry deterrence.

[4]   See Fudenberg and Tirole (1986), for example.

While most of the models have focused on external strategy issues, recently these tools have been turned increasingly to other questions of direct relevance to strategic management having to do with the internal organization of the firm and the appropriate scope of its activities. These include questions relating to the vertical scope of the firm's activities[5]; the effect of incentives on the optimal horizontal scope of the firm[6]; and the appropriate breadth of the firm's business and corporate strategies.[7,8]

Finally, issues at the intersection of these "internal" and "external" orientations constitute a growth area within economics. The issues here include the effect of incentive schemes within the firm on product-market competition[9]; the ability to use vertical integration to achieve competitive advantage[10]; and the effect of distribution channel design on competition.[11]

Despite the relevance of these issues to strategic management, the impact on that field has mainly been through "importing" relevant implications from economics. The question arises, however, whether there isn't a more direct role for game-theoretic modeling within strategic management—whether it might not provide a useful tool to scholars who regard strategic management as their primary field.

This question is complicated by the difficulty that once a model has the trappings of microeconomics[12] there is a tendency to define it as being about economics rather than strategic management. If strategic management is defined by a set of research questions or by the subject matter of the field, however, this problem does not arise. Models of strategic groups, generic strategies, or how organizational structure influences strategy all fall within the domain of strategic management whether they have the trappings of microeconomic models or not. It is the

---

[5]   See Grossman and Hart (1986), for example.
[6]   See Jensen (1986), for example.
[7]   See Rotemberg and Saloner (1990b).
[8]   In their book, *Economic Organization and Management,* Milgrom and Roberts (1992) provide a detailed analysis of many of these issues and describe numerous implications for strategic management.
[9]   See Fershtman and Judd (1987), discussed later, for example.
[10]   Ordover, Saloner, and Salop (1990), Hart and Tirole (1990), and Bolton and Whinston (1989).
[11]   Coughlin and Wernerfelt (1988), Moorthy (forthcoming), and Bonanno and Vickers (1988).
[12]   Rational decision makers with well-defined objective functions and possible actions.

prospect of the development of such models that we have in mind below.

The question of whether there is a role for game-theoretic modeling within strategic management has two components. The first is whether there is a role in strategic management for *modeling of the microeconomic variety* at all, whether game theoretic or not. The second, which arises only if the first is answered in the affirmative, is whether such modeling should be game theoretic. Most of the attention among strategic management scholars seems to be focused on the latter question. This is probably, at least in part, a spillover from the debate within the economics profession itself about the relative merits of the more recent game-theoretic modeling and the "older" standard neoclassical methods.[13]

However, it is probably also because some observers within strategic management are troubled by the complexity of the reasoning of which the agents whose behavior is being analyzed are assumed to be capable. For example, Rumelt, Schendel, and Teece (1990: 9) write:

> Rational models of competitive interaction posit players who engage in very subtle and complex reasoning. Yet our common experience is that decision-makers are far less analytic and perform far less comprehensive analyses than these models posit. If one is a player, is it really 'rational' to posit such complex behavior in others?

The degree of rationality assumed in game-theoretic models is often much greater than in other economic models. In game-theoretic models each firm's optimal action depends on what it believes its rivals will do. In order to decide what to do itself, the firm must put itself in its rival's shoes and analyze the situation from its rival's perspective. The analysis therefore requires assumptions about the rival's rationality, as well as the assessment of the rival's belief about one's own rationality, and so on. These assumptions are particularly striking in a field like strategic management, which tolerates a wide variety of behavioral assumptions.

The increased burden the assumption of rationality is asked to bear in game-theoretic models can be seen by contrasting duopoly theory with the theories of perfect competition and of

---

[13] See, for example, the debate between Fisher (1989) and Shapiro (1989) in the *Rand Journal of Economics*.

monopoly. In the case of monopoly the firm faces a "simple" optimization problem. The situation is even more straightforward for a perfectly competitive firm, which, as a price taker, only has to ascertain whether it can profitably produce *any* quantity at the equilibrium price. The duopolist's optimal decision, on the other hand, depends on what its rival will do.

In order to make the critique of the rationality assumption in game-theoretic models even more concrete, consider the following game. In this game you choose "top" or "bottom" while your opponent simultaneously chooses "left" or "right." Your actions lead to the payoffs in Table 5-1, where, as usual, the first number in each cell is the "row player's" (your) payoff and the second is the "column player's":

Table 5-1
The "Rationality" Game

		Opponent	
		Left	Right
You	Top	1,0	1,1
	Bottom	−1,000,0	2,1

Thus, for example, if you choose "top" and your opponent chooses "left," you receive 1 and your opponent receives 0 (where higher numbers denote more desirable outcomes; perhaps the numbers represent dollars or a measure of utility).

To the casual observer the most striking feature of these payoffs is the "−1,000" that you receive if the "bottom left" outcome occurs. From a game-theoretic point of view, however, the most striking feature is the fact that choosing "right" is the best strategy for your opponent regardless of what you do: he earns 1 if he chooses "right" and 0 if he chooses "left."[14]

Given the "compelling logic" that your rival should play "right," your own choice boils down to choosing "top" and receiving 1 (the "top right" outcome) or choosing "bottom" and receiv-

---

[14] In the language of game theory, playing "right" is a *dominant strategy*.

ing 2 ("bottom right"). Clearly you "should" choose "bottom." Game theory predicts the "bottom right" outcome.

Notice, however, that you stand to lose a great deal (1,000) if you behave as game theory predicts you will and your opponent does not. A "mistake" by your opponent would not be very costly to him or her, but it would be extremely costly to you. Indeed, the cost to your opponent of making a mistake could be arbitrarily small without changing the structure of the argument.[15]

Given the degree of rationality assumed in game-theoretic models, can they usefully be employed in strategic management? The answer to this question must depend on the role these models are expected to play. One role is a rather literal one in which the model is supposed to mirror an actual managerial situation and the desired output is an exact prescription of what action to take: how much capacity to install, how much to produce, how to position one's product, and so forth. In such settings, as in the rationality game, the burden on the rationality assumption may be quite severe.

I argue in Section 2, however, that there are numerous games, including many of the kind that arise in strategic management, where the degree of rationality required does not strain the limits of plausibility. We illustrate this by an examination of the popular Cournot model, which in many respects provides the best case for the plausibility of a literal model.

In Section 3, however, I argue that literal interpretations of game-theoretic models are largely irrelevant and that the debate about whether firms would play the Cournot game as game theorists would is largely academic. Rather I argue that the appropriate role in strategic management for microeconomic-style modeling generally, and for game-theoretic modeling in

---

[15]   To demonstrate this, imagine replacing the zeroes in Table 5-1 by $1 - \varepsilon$ and consider ε to be as small as you like. Now imagine what you would in fact choose to do if you were "playing" this game against a variety of opponents: David Kreps, a fourth grader, an average undergraduate, and the CEO of a typical U.S. firm.

A somewhat cautious player might choose to play "top" in these circumstances, in which case she is assured of earning at least 1. A conservative strategy of this kind is called a "maximin strategy" since it asks the question, What is the minimum I can earn with this action? and selects the action that results in the largest of these minima. In the present case, if both players used maximin strategies, the outcome "top right" would result. A maximin strategy is conservative but not maximizing and therefore not "rational." If you knew your opponent was using a maximin strategy, you would prefer to play "bottom" to using your own maximin strategy.

particular, is not literal but metaphorical. The nature and role of metaphorical modeling, its potential for contributing to strategic management, and the lower burden placed on the rationality assumption in such settings is discussed there.

In Section 4 I discuss the distinction between the profit maximization and rationality assumptions. The profit maximization hypothesis has two parts: that firms maximize "something," and that the "something" is profits. The rationality assumption is only concerned with the first of these, i.e., with the proposition that firms attempt to maximize something, though not necessarily profits.[16] Indeed, I show in Section 4 that it may sometimes be in a profit-maximizing firm's interests to convince its rivals or employees that it (or its managers) are interested in maximizing something other than profits.

In Section 5 I discuss settings where, unlike the Cournot setting in Section 2, the degree of rationality the players possess has a significant impact on the prediction of the models. We discuss and evaluate attempts to deal with this issue by modeling irrationality within game-theoretic models.

Finally, in Section 6 I examine the role that game-theoretic modeling can play in providing advice to managers and in conducting empirical work. Section 7 contains concluding remarks.

2. A Literal Interpretation of Game-Theoretic Modeling: Rationality in the Cournot Model

In this section I take a literal approach to game-theoretic modeling. I examine the role that the rationality assumption plays in a game that is beloved of many industrial organization economists: Cournot duopoly, perhaps the most frequently applied game in industrial organization. My interest is not in the Cournot game per se, however. I look at it because it illustrates the nature and role of rationality in a fairly broad class of the applications of game theory of interest to strategic management.

In the game first considered by Augustin Cournot more than 150 years ago, two firms simultaneously choose how much of a homogeneous good to produce, and each firm must make its output decision in ignorance of the other's. The firms' chosen pro-

---

[16] The question of whether firms maximize profits has received considerable attention elsewhere (see Kreps [1990a] for a discussion).

duction is "sent to the market," where it fetches the highest price at which the combined output of the firms can be sold.

In many respects the Cournot model represents the "best case" for literal game-theoretic modeling. It is a one-shot game (i.e., the firms meet in this way only once), so that "repeated play" considerations do not arise; there is no asymmetric information, and, as discussed below, there is a unique equilibrium outcome which does not involve mixed strategies.

To be concrete let's assume a particular form of the demand function, that is, the highest price at which a combined output of the two firms of Q units can be sold is represented by $P = a - Q$. Let's suppose further that it costs a firm cq_i to produce q_i units, so that c is the (constant) per unit cost of production.

How "should" a firm that wants to maximize profits play this game? The firm's optimization problem and its "solution" are deceptively easy to write down. Denoting the firm's own output by q_i and its belief about what its rival will produce by q_j, firm i's profit can be written as:

$$\pi_i = (a - q_i - q_j - c)q_i \tag{1}$$

Differentiating with respect to q_i, the solution is:

$$q_i = [a - q_j - c]/2 \tag{2}$$

Equation (2) and the corresponding equation for firm 2 are depicted in Figure 5-1.

Predicting Outcomes

To obtain a prediction as to what each firm will in fact produce in the Cournot setting, one must go considerably further than equation (2). Each firm must predict what its rival will do. But how should it do this? The standard solution offered by game theory, the Nash equilibrium, does not specify the logic by which a firm should decide what to do, but rather leaps directly to the solution by specifying desirable properties that strategies should possess in order to be equilibrium strategies.[17] In particu-

---

[17] Note that the notion of equilibrium in game-theoretic models is somewhat different from that used elsewhere (even in other economic applications). Here equilibrium does not mean that, after a long period of adjustment, the system has come to rest. Rather, it simply means that given the strategy each player is using, no single agent has an incentive to deviate unilaterally from its proposed strategy.

Figure 5-1
Best-Response Functions in the Cournot Game

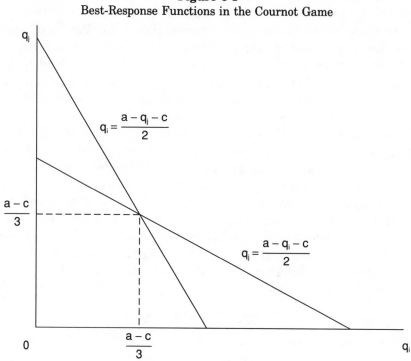

lar, each player's strategy must be optimal given the other's strategy.

In this setting this means that for $\{q_1^*, q_2^*\}$ to be a solution to the game it must be the case that $q_1^* = [a - q_2^* - c]/2$, i.e., firm 1's strategy is optimal given q_2^*, and $q_2^* = [a - q_1^* - c]/2$, i.e., firm 2's strategy is optimal given q_1^*. The only way both of these conditions can hold is if $q_1^* = q_2^* = (a - c)/3$.

Because of the way in which it is defined, the Nash equilibrium has the attractive property that if, ex post, one observes that the Nash strategies have been played, it is very easy to rationalize the firms' behavior. Given what firm 2 did, firm 1 behaved optimally and vice versa. Put differently, each firm's belief about what its rival would produce turned out to be correct. Moreover, this could only be said about strategies that formed a Nash equilibrium, since if the firms did not both play their Nash strategies, ex post both would regret not having taken a different course of action.

As pointed out above, however, the Nash equilibrium does not describe how the firms come to have the "correct" beliefs in the first place. In the case of the Cournot game, given profit-maximizing objectives and rationality on the part of the players, it turns out that logic alone is enough to derive the solution. To see this, note from (2) that firm i's optimal output is decreasing in q_j, the amount that it believes its rival will produce. Therefore, the most that firm i should ever produce can be derived from (2) by setting $q_j = 0$, i.e., firm i should never produce more than $(a - c)/2$, the amount it would produce if its rival stayed out of the market. But if firm j knows that firm i won't produce more than $(a - c)/2$, then it should produce at least $[a - \{(a - c)/2\} - c]/2 = (a - c)/4$. Knowing this, firm i should produce at least $[a - \{(a - c)/4\} - c]/2 = 3(a - c)/8$. This reasoning converges (with infinitely many iterations) to the conclusion that each firm should produce $(a - c)/3$.[18] At each stage of the reasoning, a dominance argument is applied.[19]

The fact that the Cournot game can be "solved" through the pure logic of iterated dominance in this way should not give one enormous comfort. Recall, for example, that the rationality game discussed at the beginning of this section was solved there in the identical manner.[20] Even though iterated dominance is a strong argument by game-theoretic standards, the fact that the argument must be repeated infinitely often may make one skeptical about the ability of the "typical" player to apply it successfully.

Robustness

There is, however, a sense in which one should feel much more confident in playing the Cournot-Nash strategy than in playing "bottom" in the rationality game—Cournot is more robust when "small mistakes" occur. Suppose, for example, that the firm believes the rival is "trying" to behave as game theory suggests a "rational" opponent should, but that the rival is not

---

[18] The nth term in the sequence is given by $t_n = [(a - c)/2] - [t_{n-1}/2]$, with $t_0 = 0$.
[19] Milgrom and Roberts (1990b) show that a large class of important games with unique equilibria can be "solved" in this way.
[20] It does, however, distinguish it from many other games. In this sense the Cournot game has a "more obvious" way to play than many other games. See Kreps (1990a) for a detailed discussion of games with "less obvious" solutions.

very good at it and so is likely to make a small mistake in its calculations. What are the consequences for the firm? Since the firm's profits are continuous in the decision of the rival, a small mistake leads to a small loss of profits. For this particular example, if the rival produces $(1 + \varepsilon)(a - c)/3$ instead of just $(a - c)/3$, the firm's profits fall to $(1 - \varepsilon)(a - c)^2/9$, i.e., if the rival's output is 1% higher than the Cournot-Nash level, the firm's profits are 1% lower than at the Cournot equilibrium.[21]

Communication and Learning

So far we have given the rationality assumption its harshest test by assuming that the firm must make its own output decision in complete ignorance of what its rival will do. In practice the firm will often have some information about its rival's intentions. In particular, there are at least two settings where the firms might feel more confident playing their Cournot-Nash strategies.

The first of these is a setting in which the firms have had an opportunity (whether through the media or in person) to discuss their planned actions ahead of time. By this I do not mean that the firms are able to enter into discussions leading up to a binding contractual agreement. Communication of that kind would more likely lead to a collusive agreement than to Cournot behavior. Rather I have in mind that the final output decisions are still made independently.

There is a sense in which such pre-play communication (known as "cheap talk" in the literature) should have no effect on the outcome since the payoffs and strategic options that the firms face aren't altered at all.[22] However, pre-play communication can remove the doubts that each firm has about the reasoning process its rival is going through. Thus, for example, if firm 2 claimed it was going to produce $(a - c)/2$,[23] firm 1 might make the following speech: "You're only saying that to try to fool me into playing $(a - c)/4$, my best response to $(a - c)/2$. However,

---

[21] The loss of profits to the firm is, however, larger than a corresponding mistake by the firm itself. If the firm produces $(1 + \varepsilon)(a - c)/3$ by mistake, its profits only fall to $(1 - \varepsilon)(a - c)^2/9$. Thus the loss is of second-order importance.

[22] See Farrell (1987) for a discussion of cheap talk.

[23] As we shall see later, firm 2 would like to be able to be able to commit to producing $(a - c)/2$ if that commitment could credibly be communicated to firm 1.

if you believed you had fooled me into doing that you would produce $3(a - c)/8$, your best response to $(a - c)/4$ and not $(a - c)/2$, so why should I believe you?" The only claim that either firm could make that would not be challenged by its rival would be the claim that the firm intended to produce its Cournot-Nash output! And if both firms have made such claims, each will feel quite confident in going ahead and producing its Cournot-Nash output.[24,25] Indeed, in this sense, a Nash equilibrium can be viewed as a self-enforcing agreement. If the players have agreed to play their Nash strategies and then go off and make their decisions independently, no individual would have an incentive to deviate from the agreement.

Another setting in which a firm might feel more comfortable playing its Cournot-Nash strategy is when its competitor is drawn from a pool of firms with experience at the game. With enough experience, the strategies used by the players should not remain biased away from the Cournot-Nash prediction. Suppose, for example, that each firm has developed a strategy it uses in playing the one-shot Cournot game and that the average of the strategies of the players in the pool is an output of $(a - c)/3 + \varepsilon$ rather than $(a - c)/3$. If this fact were common knowledge among the players, each would soon figure out that it could do better by producing $(a - c)/3 - \varepsilon/2$, the best response to $(a - c)/3 + \varepsilon$. But if they all behaved this way, of course, *this* would become the average production of the pool. The learning process would lead them to $(a - c)/3$, the only "average" production level that would not induce a change in behavior by a rational opponent.

Some Experimental Evidence

In experimental settings, the Cournot-Nash predictions are fairly strongly borne out. Moreover, learning of the kind described above does appear to be important in practice. Holt (1985), for example, conducted experiments on undergraduates at Minnesota taking introductory and intermediate economics

---

[24]   In contrast to how it would feel in the "rationality" game at the beginning of Section 2.

[25]   Cooper et al. (1989) provide some experimental evidence that suggests that cheap talk can in fact make a difference.

classes (in which the instructors had not discussed the Cournot game). Twelve students participated in 11 one-shot plays of the Cournot game, of which the first was a "trial run." Half of the monopoly output (the collusive outcome) was 6 units, the symmetric Cournot-Nash was 8, and if each produced 12 units, profits would be zero.[26]

Unfortunately, Holt's experiment is not as clean as it might be because with the payoff structure he used, there are also asymmetric Cournot-Nash equilibria: one in which one firm produces 6 and the other 10, and another in which one produces 7 and the other 9. In all cases, however, the predicted total is the same: 16. Another shortcoming is that if one's rival produced its symmetric Cournot-Nash output of 8, the firm would only earn one penny more by producing 8 rather than 9.

Despite these shortcomings, the results, presented in Table 5-2 below, are quite striking:

Table 5-2
Outcomes of Ten Plays of the Cournot Game in an Experiment

Subject Period	1	2	3	4	5	6	7	8	9	10	11	12
Trial	7	8	22	10	5	7	13	7	6	8	10	5
1	5	8	9	10	8	6	11	6	9	8	7	7
2	6	8	9	10	8	10	10	7	9	8	7	8
3	6	8	9	9	8	8	10	7	9	8	8	9
4	6	9	9	8	8	8	9	6	9	8	8	9
5	6	9	9	9	9	8	9	8	9	8	8	9
6	7	8	9	9	9	9	8	8	9	8	8	9
7	7	9	9	9	9	9	9	8	9	8	8	9
8	7	9	9	9	9	8	8	8	9	8	8	9
9	7	9	9	9	9	8	8	8	8	8	8	9
10	7	9	9	8	9	8	8	8	8	8	8	10

---

[26] Forty-five cents was added to all profit numbers to give subjects a reasonable return on their time.

By the final round the outputs were on average very close to the Cournot-Nash levels. After the fifth round all the players except player 1 (and player 12 in round 10 only) chose to produce either 8 or 9 units. Notice, however, that almost all of the players started out some distance away from Cournot-Nash, illustrating the role that learning played.

Evaluation of "Literal" Models

In this section I take a rather literal view of the Cournot model in order to explore the role and limitations of the rationality assumption. What does this exploration suggest about how well we would do predicting behavior in "real-world" settings using a game-theoretic analysis, assuming the model accurately captured the setting of interest?

Several general qualitative conclusions seem uncontroversial. First, the burden on the rationality assumption is clearly much higher in some circumstances, such as the rationality game, than in others, such as Cournot. This is due in large part to the robustness of the latter to small mistakes by the players. Second, one's confidence in the predictive power of the models is likely to be significantly greater if the players have had the opportunity for pre-play communication or, as suggested by the experimental evidence, if they have some experience with the decisions being analyzed.

Despite the rather sanguine view of the ability of the Cournot game to predict behavior in experimental settings, game-theoretic models have failed the market test abysmally. For example, I know of no instance in which the Cournot model, or even a sophisticated variant of it, has been used in practice by the management of a real-world enterprise to guide it in making its output decisions. Moreover, much the same can be said for most of the vast accumulation of models cited with approval in the Introduction. Not only are these models not used in their "purest" form to predict what rivals "should" do and hence what one's own best response should be, they are not even used in modified form to predict what rivals *will* do (even if the firm believes they will not behave as the model says they should) and therefore what the firm should do in that case.[27]

---

[27] There are some exceptions. For example, auction theory has proven useful for competitive bidding.

Perhaps game-theoretic models will become more useful for these purposes over time as the techniques improve. I am skeptical, however.[28] Game-theoretic models tend to be so complicated that they defy analysis unless they are boiled down to their essence. For example, a model designed to study capacity choices must typically ignore other issues. However, the world does not present itself in such a convenient format. For managers, capacity decisions come bundled with product-line decisions, quality decisions, advertising decisions, and so on. The complexity of those situations easily overwhelms the ability of simple models to cope with them.[29]

Overwhelming complexity also typically arises in "chess-like" situations; those involving long sequences of moves and counter-moves where analysis revolves around questions like, What should firm 1 do if firm 2 does this? and, How, in turn, should firm 2 respond? The Kodak-Polaroid and Coke-Pepsi battles, both of which are the subjects of Harvard Business School teaching cases, are examples of situations of this type. In the game of chess itself, for example, while game theory yields the information that there is a solution, it has virtually nothing to say about how one should play the game. And yet chess is a remarkably simple game by comparison with, say, the Polaroid-Kodak battle. At least in chess there is no asymmetric situation, and the potential actions are always well defined; it is clear whose chance it is to move, and, after a player moves, what his move was, and so on.

3. The Role for Game-Theoretic Modeling in Strategic Management: A Metaphorical Approach

Microeconomic Mathematical Modeling as Metaphor

The rather negative view of the usefulness of game-theoretic modeling in strategic management reflected in the previous sec-

---

[28] For a somewhat contrary view, see Camerer (1991).

[29] As an exact predictive model of duopoly, Cournot has many shortcomings. The quantity-setting assumption does not mirror most actual settings, in which price rather than quantity tends to be the variable on which firms compete. (Although Kreps and Scheinkman [1983] have shown that in some cases the Cournot model can be interpreted as a two-stage model in which the firms first choose capacities and then choose prices.) Moreover, the model lacks the temporal nature of actual competition.

tion results from attempting to give game-theoretic models a literal interpretation such as mathematical modeling plays in management science (or engineering) applications. It is important to note, however, that while those models are similar in form to models of the microeconomic variety, they are quite different in their objectives.

In most models in management science the goal is to provide an algorithm which, when data are fed in as inputs, will produce the answer to some management problem (how to schedule production, how much inventory to hold, and so forth). When that is achieved, how the algorithm "works" is of secondary interest.

By contrast, the aim in the kind of microeconomic modeling contemplated here is metaphorical. The model captures and formalizes only selected features of interest; the objective is to create a model that qualitatively simulates the type of environment being studied. Thus, there is no attempt to calibrate the model so that it is quantitatively true to a particular setting. Once the formalism is established it is used to derive new qualitative results from the assumptions by a process of deduction. Overall, the model provides well-reasoned arguments by which one can proceed from the assumptions to the conclusions. Understanding why the results obtain, i.e., how the model works, is of primary interest. That understanding is what provides the "insights" which are the final outputs of the endeavor.

The Cournot model provides a good example of the insights that can be gained from metaphorical models. For example, the model demonstrates two important features of noncooperative duopoly behavior: why firms are unable to collude perfectly in a one-period setting, and why they are able to earn higher profits than if there were many symmetric firms in the industry.[30]

The model also illustrates why a first-mover advantage might be important. In particular, if firm 1 moves first, it produces

---

[30] If the firms "agreed" in pre-play communication to each produce $(a - c)/4$, half of the monopoly outcome, each would have an incentive to renege on the agreement when it actually came to choosing its production level, since from (2) a firm's best response to $(a - c)/4$ is $3(a - c)/8$. The same reasoning explains why profits fall as the number of firms in the industry rises. Consider breaking firm 2 into firms 2 and 3. If firm 1 produced its Cournot output of $(a - c)/3$ as before, firms 2 and 3, instead of behaving as a monopolist on the "piece" of demand remaining for them and producing $(a - c)/3$, they would compete like duopolists and would produce more in total than firm 2 alone would have.

more and earns higher profits than in the simultaneous move version.[31] The reason is that firm 1 can credibly commit to a larger output than in the simultaneous move game when it physically makes its production decision before firm 2 does.

The Case for Mathematical Modeling of the Microeconomic Variety

Despite the potential for "insight-oriented" mathematical modeling in strategic management, almost all development of theory has been via broad conceptual frameworks, verbally reasoned arguments, or models of the boxes-and-arrows kind. Some of this, such as the conceptual framework captured in Porter's five-forces model, has been both influential and useful.

However, as Montgomery, Wernerfelt, and Balakrishnan (1989) argue, "many strategy content publications suffer from serious shortcomings" on the theory development side. Those authors make an appeal for "well-reasoned theory" but stop short of calling for mathematical modeling. Indeed the examples they cite with satisfaction do not utilize mathematical modeling but instead proceed by verbal argument.

Of course, mathematical modeling is not *necessary* for careful reasoning, and the central arguments in mathematically derived propositions can generally be verbally explained in "well-reasoned" prose. Moreover, formal modeling is very costly to both authors and readers in terms of the overhead it imposes.

However, formal modeling has three very powerful attributes. The first of these is that it provides an "audit trail"[32] that allows one to distinguish between groundless assertions and logical propositions. By laying out a set of assumptions and deriving the qualitative proposition of interest from them, the author

---

[31] Suppose, for example, that we modify the timing of the original game and assume instead that firm 1 gets to produce its output and send it to market before firm 2 does (and that firm 2 observes how much firm 1 has produced before it must make its own output decision). Since firm 2 knows firm 1's output choice when it makes its output decision, its output choice requires no conjecture about what firm 1 "will do." Its optimization problem is to choose q_2 to maximize $\pi_2 = (a - q_1 - q_2 - c)q_2$, where now q_1 is firm 1's *actual* output. The solution to this problem is that firm 2 produces its best response to q_1, i.e., $q_2 = (a - q_1 - c)/2$. For its part, knowing that firm 2 will respond according to its best-response function, firm 1 chooses q_1 to maximize $\pi_1 = [a - (a - q_1 - c)/2 - c]q_1$. This maximization problem has the solution $q_1 = (a - c)/2$.

[32] I am grateful to Mark Wolfson for the accountant's terminology.

provides the detailed logic that underlies the assertions. There is no ambiguity in such a setting about what it means to be "well-reasoned," and both the reader and the author can probe the robustness of the results with respect to changes in the assumptions.

Perhaps more important, by laying out the underlying assumptions carefully and explicitly, the author makes it easier for the reader to pinpoint what he or she likes *or dislikes* about the model. If the assumptions are unpalatable, so are the propositions that flow from them. And if the proposition is unpalatable or unintuitive, the model provides an audit trail to help point out what unreasonable assumption or assumptions are responsible. This constant external auditing of the inner workings of the model and its underlying premises provides strong incentives for authors to build their models on solid (and palatable) foundations.

The second important attribute of formal modeling is that it is a methodology that is capable of *creating novel insights*. These insights are often unforeseen and sometimes surprising. They may even seem unintuitive. However, the audit trail that the methodology creates enables one to trace the logic of the argument and reveal whether the surprise is due to an implausible assumption (or assumptions interacting in implausible ways) or to a feature of the "story" being woven which the author did not realize was there. This virtue of formal modeling stands in contrast to "models" of the boxes-and-arrows variety, which have no built-in capacity for going beyond a mere description of the model itself.

A third major advantage of formal modeling is that it provides a common language that allows related results to be compared and new results to be built on the foundations laid by earlier models. It thus provides a basis for cumulative learning.

For these reasons modeling has proved very effective in advancing microeconomic theory (including many fields closely related to strategic management) and holds considerable promise for development of theory in strategic management as well.

Game-Theoretic Modeling

If one accepts the virtues of mathematical modeling of the microeconomics variety, it does not follow that one should embrace game-theoretic modeling. Yet in strategic management, game-theoretic modeling is likely to constitute a very high fraction of all "microeconomic-style" modeling.

The reason has to do with the nature of the beast. Game-theoretic modeling is the appropriate tool for studying strategic interactions between agents with differing goals. This kind of interaction is, of course, precisely what characterizes many interesting strategic management issues.[33]

Two examples illustrate the necessity of strategic thinking in situations where strategic interactions are of the essence. The first, again, is the Cournot model. In order to act sensibly a firm *must* think about what its rival is going to do. Whether or not one accepts the "solution" to the problem that game theory offers, if one concedes that the duopolists are attempting to maximize profits, one *must* accept the "strategic thinking" that characterizes game-theoretic analyses.

The second example is a case often taught in MBA strategic management classes, *General Electric Versus Westinghouse in Large Turbine Generators*.[34] That case examines the sharp price discounting that plagued the highly concentrated large turbine generator market in the early 1960s. The difficulty that GE, as the dominant firm, had in stabilizing prices could be attributed to a number of market-specific factors.[35] The result in a very price-sensitive market was that it was difficult for the firms to achieve a "mutual understanding" as to what prices should prevail and to ascertain whether their rivals had "cheated" by undercutting those prices. The firms gave in to the unilateral

---

[33] A second reason why most microeconomic-style modeling in strategic management is likely to be game theoretic is that game-theoretic modeling has proven useful in a very broad class of settings, including many for which game theory is not essential to the analysis. An example is the well-known signaling model put forward by Spence (1974). In Spence's original analysis there is a competitive labor market and the analysis is carried out without any of the trappings of game theory. Now, however, models of that type tend to be framed in the language of game theory: game theory is emerging as the lingua franca of microeconomic modeling. The reason for this is probably related to the appealing audit trail properties of explicitly game-theoretic models. As a result, game theory is approaching the status of calculus in the curricula of graduate departments of economics, being required of all students, with courses in elementary game theory often being offered in the first semester of study.

[34] Part A of the case is presented in Porter (1983).

[35] These include the fact that, at least for sales to private utilities, sales were made through confidential negotiations, and that the product sold was not standard but rather bids were made to satisfy the idiosyncratic specifications set by buyers.

temptation to give discounts off list prices in order to win sales, leading to a steady erosion in prices.

GE's response to this problem was, inter alia, to produce a pricing book with simplified pricing formulas that made it possible to map consumer specifications into list prices, to announce that it would sell to all customers at a specified discount off those list prices, and to commit to a most-favored-customer policy through which any customer who after purchasing from GE learned that GE had later sold similar equipment at a lower price, would be reimbursed the difference.[36] This new pricing policy had the effect, within about a year, of ending the deep discounting that had characterized the market previously.

To effectively formulate a new pricing policy GE had to take into account how Westinghouse would respond. They thus had to put themselves in Westinghouse's shoes and predict how Westinghouse would read the signals contained in any change in GE's policy. The policy GE adopted was successful because Westinghouse (ultimately) understood, as GE correctly predicted they would, that the standardized pricing book and commitment to a fixed discount provided an opportunity to coordinate pricing.[37] The issues that GE had to consider have to do with the essence of game-theoretic models.

The Rationality Assumption in Metaphorical Models

In the previous subsection I stressed the fact that many of the situations of interest in strategic management involve strategic interactions among rivals and therefore require game-theoretic modeling if microeconomic modeling is to be used at all. Just because it is the appropriate tool doesn't mean that one has to like it, however, and those who are skeptical about the degree of rationality required to reach the proffered "insights" might balk at employing microeconomic modeling at all.

Happily, many of the insights that one obtains from game-theoretic models do not require an extreme degree of rationality. For example, while the implications of the Cournot model do require logical reasoning, the logical reasoning required is far

[36] The details of GE's pricing policy are discussed in part B of the case, Harvard Business School, 1-380-129.
[37] The logic behind the GE pricing policy was not lost on the Justice Department, which concluded that it violated the antitrust laws. (See part C of the case.)

more elementary than the infinite regress of the "If I believe that you believe that I believe . . ." type of reasoning that is often suggested is required. In order to demonstrate that the collusive equilibrium is not sustainable in a one-shot game, for example, all that one has to accept is that either firm will perceive that it can profit by unilaterally deviating. To appreciate that there is a first-mover advantage in the Stackelberg game, one simply has to realize that a firm can obtain an advantage by committing itself to a course of action and thereby forcing its rival to respond to a fact of life.

There is a broad class of useful models for which the degree of rationality is not very extreme. These are "two-stage" models where the primary focus is on just one action. Examples of this type include how much capacity a firm facing potential entry should install and how it should price its product, how many products a first mover should have in its product line, whether firms should make their products compatible or incompatible, how firms should position their products, and so on. In the first stage of these models, the action of primary interest is taken, and in the second, the firms compete. The issue of interest is typically how the actions taken in the first stage affect competition in the second.

Often the Cournot model is used as the model of second-stage competition. However, only very broad qualitative features of the Cournot model are drawn upon. Thus, in these models, whether firms would replicate the Cournot outcome in the Cournot setting (the question of Section 2) is virtually irrelevant.

To see how these models work and to describe the role of the Cournot model in them, I illustrate the role that the Cournot model plays when embedded in models that address questions of broader interest. The two related examples discussed briefly below were also selected because they help illustrate some of the advantages of formal modeling mentioned above.

The examples concern entry into an industry that can accommodate only a small number of firms. Since entry into new markets often requires a major commitment of the firm's resources, these issues are directly relevant to strategic management.

Excess Capacity and Entry Deterrence

According to received theory in the early 1970s, an incumbent monopolist could deter entry into its market by producing more than its monopoly output or, equivalently, charging a price below the monopoly price (for which the term "limit price" was coined). This theory was based on the "maintained output hypothesis," which held that potential entrants would believe that the incumbent would maintain its pre-entry output after entry occurred. The reasoning in the Cournot model discussed above makes it clear how the maintained output hypothesis led to the conclusions it did.

The statement that the entrant believes the incumbent will maintain its pre-entry output if entry occurs is tantamount to the assertion that the incumbent is able to commit, before entry occurs, to the level of output it will produce if entry does occur. As we saw in the previous section, the ability to commit to a level of output before your rival makes its output decision endows the incumbent with a Stackelberg leadership position. Once entry occurs, however, the incumbent's past actions are water under the bridge. Simply producing at a higher rate pre-entry does not commit the firm to do the same post-entry. The potential entrant's entry decision should therefore be based on its assessment of its profits when the incumbent reacts optimally to the fact of entry. The flaw in the maintained output hypothesis is that there is no logical connection between the incumbent's pre-entry and post-entry output choices.

There may, however, be a connection between the incumbent's pre-entry capacity choice and its post-entry output. Dixit (1980) develops a model in which the incumbent chooses capacity before the potential entrant makes its entry decision. If entry occurs, the firms compete as in the Cournot model. Dixit shows that an incumbent firm facing a potential entrant might have an incentive to install more capacity than it otherwise would in the hope of deterring entry.

Dixit's argument relies on an intuitive qualitative feature of the Cournot model—that firm 2's profits are lower the lower are firm 1's production costs. To see why, consider the Cournot model discussed in the previous section and suppose that firm 1's (but not firm 2's) costs of production fall to c'. The "new" solution is that firm 1 produces more and firm 2 produces less than with the original parameters. This is illustrated in Figure 5-2, which shows that firm 1's best-response function shifts "outwards" when its costs fall, i.e., whatever firm 1 believes that firm 2 is going to produce, it will produce more if its costs are

Figure 5-2
Effect of Lower Costs for Firm 1

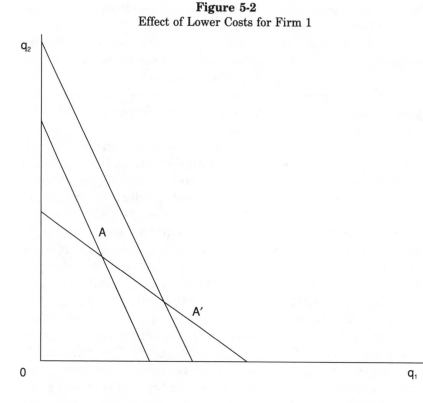

c′ than it would have if they were c. Since it rationally anticipates that firm 1 will produce more, firm 2 curtails its own
output in equilibrium. Diagrammatically, the predicted "solution" shifts from A to A′.

It is possible that firm 2 earns positive profits at A where its
share of output is high but not at A′. Then if firm 1 is the
bent and it is able to lower its marginal production costs before
entry occurs, it will be able to deter the potential entrant (firm
2) from entering. The incumbent can in fact do that by installing
more capacity before entry takes place than it needs in order to
produce its monopoly output. With its monopoly capacity in
place the firm does not have a credible threat that it will act
aggressively in response to entry since that would require installing costly additional capacity. If the incumbent installs the
capacity in advance, however, its marginal production costs are
low and the entrant may be deterred from entering.

Note that the Cournot model plays a relatively minor role in this story. The only attribute of that model that is relied upon is the qualitative feature that firm 2's profits are lower the lower its rival's costs. The same conclusions would apply if any duopoly model were used which had the commonsense property that the Cournot model possesses.

Moreover, if one accepts this qualitative feature of the Cournot model, the remaining reasoning in Dixit's model is relatively straightforward. The incumbent merely has to recognize that it is a less attractive rival if its post-entry costs are low and that it can achieve that position by installing additional capacity before the potential entrant makes its entry decision. For its part, the potential entrant need only understand the relationship between the incumbent's capacity and post-entry costs of production, and the ramifications of those costs for its own profitability.

Limit Pricing

Dixit's model shows that since there is a connection between pre-entry capacity and post-entry output, a pre-entry capacity expansion can deter entry. Similarly, in order for pre-entry pricing or output decisions to deter entry, there must be some logical connection between pre- and post-entry pricing. Milgrom and Roberts (1982a) show that if there is asymmetric information between the incumbent and the potential entrant, there may be such a logical connection.

In their model, as in Dixit's, a potential entrant is considering entering against an incumbent monopolist. If entry does occur, the Cournot game ensues. The critical element in the model is that the potential entrant is unsure of the incumbent's production costs. In the Cournot model, the potential entrant's profits are higher the higher the incumbent's costs. Therefore it may be profitable to enter only if the incumbent's costs are relatively high.

In that setting, the incumbent's pre-entry pricing can serve as a signal of its costs, and thus influence the entry decision. The reason for this is that low prices (which involve higher outputs) are relatively more costly for high-cost firms than low-cost firms. Thus, while the incumbent would like to convince the potential entrant that its costs are low (whether they are or not), it may be too costly for high-cost firms to do the requisite signaling. Then low-cost firms will signal through lower prices, and the potential entrant will be deterred from entering by those low prices.

Milgrom and Roberts's model, like Dixit's, relies on a simple qualitative feature of the Cournot model that any well-behaved oligopoly model should exhibit—namely, that the potential entrant's profits are lower if it faces a low-cost rather than a high-cost incumbent.

There is a sense in which game-theoretic analyses have taken us full circle in the past 20 years. Theory now, as 20 years ago, suggests that low pre-entry pricing can deter entry. The difference, however, is that the current theory rests on solid foundations. Moreover, being explicit about the nature of the interaction between the firms lays a clear audit trail which has been followed, extended, and clarified several times.[38]

The Explanatory Power of Metaphorical Models

As in the above two examples of entry deterrence, game-theoretic models have the ability to explain a wide variety of observed behavior. Unfortunately, they may be capable of generating too broad an array of predictions. There are two different ways in which this problem arises.

The first is what researchers (somewhat glumly) refer to as the "fundamental theorem of industrial organization." This is the assertion that since the assumptions in metaphorical models are selected by the modeler rather than strictly being dictated by a physical setting, and since there is such a rich set of assumptions from which to choose, the degree of modeling discretion is so significant that a model can be devised to explain almost any fact.

---

[38] For example, Harrington (1986) has shown that the implications for pricing are different if the potential entrant's costs are the same as the incumbent's and the asymmetry of information concerns that level of costs. (That is, the potential entrant is unsure about the level of common costs rather than relative costs.) In that case the incumbent may want to convince the entrant that its costs (and therefore the entrant's too) are high, and may therefore charge higher prices than it normally would. In other extensions Matthews and Mirman (1983) show that the results continue to hold even if price is a noisy signal of output, Saloner (1982) shows that if there is noise, the equilibrium outcome may involve delayed entry, and Bagwell and Ramey (1989) raise questions about the applicability of the methodology in the case of incumbent oligopolists (although they do not consider the case of noisy signals).

The second way in which the problem of diffuse predictions arises is via multiple equilibria. A wide range of equilibrium behavior may be consistent with the same underlying set of basic assumptions. This is especially true of supergames, which consider infinitely repeated interactions, where multiplicity of equilibria is the focus of the folk theorem. I briefly consider each of these issues below.

Multiple Equilibria

The issue of multiple equilibria is of some importance since I shall argue that one of the criteria for choosing among competing models is to consider their predictions about how a particular variable changes as others change (comparative statics). For example, the Cournot model predicts that if firm 1's costs go up, firm 1's output will fall, and by more than firm 2's output will rise. In a model in which there are multiple equilibria, however, such a thought experiment is impossible without also specifying which equilibrium to look at as the variable of interest changes.

Recently game theory itself has been of some help in models with asymmetric information by providing refinements to the Nash equilibrium concept that help the modeler in selecting among equilibria.[39] In supergames, however, selection among equilibria is often ad hoc. For example, sometimes an equilibrium seems particularly "focal." At other times, pre-play communication would significantly reduce the number of equilibria.

In many of the supergame applications of interest to strategic management, however, the supergame format is selected because it enables consideration of such issues as cooperation and reputation. In such cases—for instance, where one is attempting to examine the ability of firms to collude over time—one is interested in the extent to which the environment limits the ability of the firms to cooperate. In order to determine the maximal amount of cooperation that can be sustained without explicit cooperation, it makes sense to look at the equilibrium in which the firms do as well as possible. When, in addition, the firms are symmetric or are able to make monetary transfers, this narrows the plethora of possible equilibria to just one and renders the comparative statics exercise sensible.

---

[39]   See Kreps (1990a) for details.

In cases where some of the equilibria are implausible and others are not, it may be that the model is incomplete. Examination of what gives rise to the implausible equilibria may enable the model to be refined by incorporating some important element of the institutions being modeled, eliminating the implausible equilibria, and improving the model overall.

In some settings, however, none of the above mechanisms can be called upon to reduce the set of equilibria, and one is left with an embarrassment of riches. Yet for some games there just is no obvious way that the game "should" be played. If game theory were somehow to provide unique predictions in every setting, it would be too powerful for its own good.

The Fundamental Theorem

The complaint against the "fundamental theorem" is that it is somehow "too easy" to come up with explanations for phenomena using the tools of game theory. This is a curious complaint. It is the role of theory to come up with explanations. Some of these are likely to be good explanations and others not. And the means for telling them apart are similar, whether the theory is generated by game-theoretic modeling or by other means. However, the fact that the explanation has been formally modeled at least ensures that it is internally consistent.

Moreover, modeling provides additional means for telling good explanations from bad ones. First, the audit trail makes it easier to assess the argument. Second, and more important, in addition to explaining the phenomenon of interest, the model typically generates a number of other implications, especially of a comparative statics nature. This provides a means to put the model to the test, whether on its surface plausibility or via formal empirical or experimental techniques. If the corollary implications of the model fail to hold, the model must be rejected or at least modified.

4. Rationality and Profit Maximization

Rationality is sometimes taken to be synonymous with profit maximization in microeconomic models. Accordingly, to the extent that firms do not seek to maximize profits, this is taken to be a limitation of microeconomic modeling. However, game-theoretic reasoning can be applied even if the objective of the firm, or its management, is not that of profit maximization. Indeed, a profit-maximizing firm may be better off if its management is not profit maximizing!

In the discussion of the Cournot model we repeatedly encountered the fact that either firm would value the ability to commit to producing a larger output than it "rationally" would in the simultaneous move game. I particularly noted that a firm would like to be able to credibly tell its rival that it was committed to producing $(a - c)/2$ (its Stackelberg output).

In such a setting it would be valuable to the firm's shareholders if the manager responsible for the output decision were "irrational" in that he had a preference for producing more than he would if he were a profit maximizer. For example, the manager might want to maximize sales revenue. Supposing that the manager is the decision maker in firm 1, he would seek to maximize:

$$R = (a - q_1 - q_2)q_1,$$

yielding the best-response function:

$$q_1 = (a - q_2)/2. \tag{3}$$

Comparing (2) and (3) it is evident that this manager behaves more aggressively than his profit-maximizing counterpart. But as discussed previously, having a manager who behaves in this way may be advantageous to the firm because it effectively commits it to higher outputs, which in turn induces the rival to curtail its own output. As illustrated in Figure 5-3, the outcome shifts from B to B' when the manager's goal shifts from profit to sales maximization. It is easy to show that firm 1's profits may be higher at B' than at B.

Profit-maximizing shareholders might therefore have reason to deliberately select a decision maker who is not profit maximizing.[40] Alternatively, the shareholders might have reason to provide the manager with incentives that have the same effect. Thus, a firm that can credibly commit to rewarding its manager based on some combination of profits and sales (instead of simply

---

[40] Sales-maximizing managers are not the only ones who might enhance the firm's performance. A manager with a passion for market share or for operating near capacity (provided capacity is not too large) can have similar results.

Figure 5-3
Firm 1 as a Sales Maximizer

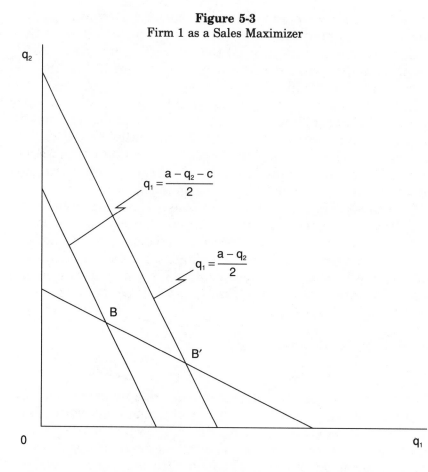

profits) might induce more aggressive behavior in the manager and, consequently, higher profits.[41]

Similarly, a firm may have reason to install senior management that is not profit maximizing in order to improve incentives within the organization. For example, suppose that it is desirable for employees to innovate and that they have the opportunity to generate proposals for projects that will enhance profitability. If it is not possible to compensate those workers for the effort that they expend in researching these proposals (because such effort is not observable and hence not contractible), and if the "quality" of a proposal is too subjective to base compensation on, the only monetary incentive the management

---

[41] See Fershtman and Judd (1987) for a model along these lines.

can provide is to reward employees when they generate profitable proposals that are in fact implemented.

However, the implementation decision itself is typically in the hands of the senior management. Given the ex post compensation they must make to the worker if they choose to implement the proposal, the management will be reluctant to implement proposals that are profitable if the profits cannot be used to cover the additional compensation they must pay the worker. That is, profit-maximizing senior management will be too reluctant to implement projects.

Rotemberg and Saloner (1991) show that this problem can be overcome by installing senior management that cares not only about maximizing profits, but also about the welfare of their employees. Such managers will be more likely to implement their employees' projects and hence will earn higher profits than profit-maximizing managers would! In essence, having non-profit-maximizing management commits the organization to implementing the innovative ideas that employees generate and discourages acting opportunistically to squelch such ideas in order to save on incentive compensation.

5. Rationality in More Complicated Models

So far I have concentrated on examples in which game-theoretic modeling puts its best foot forward. The Cournot model, which has been the focus of much of the analysis, is extremely well behaved in a variety of ways, and the two-stage games, which it was argued hold a great deal of promise for strategic management, have a very simple set of moves and an equilibrium that involves straightforward logic. I argued that in those settings the results were fairly robust to the degree of rationality assumed. However, I also pointed out that confidence in the predictions of the models, even when the models are interpreted metaphorically, wanes considerably when one moves to more "chess-like" settings. In this section I discuss such a setting and illustrate why the degree of rationality of the firms has a large impact on the predicted outcome.

A question that has received a great deal of attention from industrial organization economists and that is of considerable importance for antitrust policy is whether an incumbent firm can protect its monopoly position by driving new entrants out of the markets it serves. One issue of particular interest is whether a firm might be willing to incur the costs of driving rivals out of some markets even if the expected future gains in those markets cannot possibly compensate the incumbent for those costs, simply in order to develop a reputation for such behavior which will serve it well later by discouraging other firms from entering markets in which it is an incumbent.

This issue is studied in a game that has become known as the "chain-store paradox" because of its counterintuitive conclusions.[42] An incumbent monopolist in N geographically separated markets is assumed to face a different potential entrant into each of its markets. The potential entrants are assumed to make their entry decisions sequentially, one potential entrant making its decision each "period." If entry does occur, the incumbent can engage in "predatory pricing" against the entrant, which is sure to lead to a loss for the latter. Alternatively the incumbent can behave in a more accommodating manner. For example, the firms could behave as Cournot duopolists. We can summarize the post-entry payoffs in any particular market as in Table 5-3:

Table 5-3
Payoffs in the Chain-Store Paradox

	Payoffs Incumbent	Entrant
Incumbent predatory prices	P^I	P^E
Incumbent accommodates entry	A^I	A^E

If an entrant chooses not to enter the market, its payoff is 0, and the monopolist earns M, its monopoly payoff.

It is assumed that $M > A^I > P^I$ so that the incumbent prefers monopoly to accommodating entry which in turn it prefers to predation. For the entrant it is assumed that $A^E > 0 > P^E$ so

<hr>

[42] This discussion draws heavily on the treatment of the chain-store paradox in Ordover and Saloner (1989).

that an entrant desires to enter if and only if it will not meet a predatory response.

The intuition that many people have about this game (especially if N is large) is that even though it is costly for the monopolist to predatory price against any single entrant, it ought to drive the first few entrants out in order to deter later potential entrants, i.e., the incumbent should develop a reputation for being tough.

For example, suppose that $N = 2$ and that $P^I + M > 2A^I$. If by predatory pricing in the first period the incumbent can scare off a second-period potential entrant who would otherwise have entered, the incumbent is better off overall.

Applying game-theoretic reasoning to the problem, however, establishes that it is impossible for the incumbent to effectively develop a reputation no matter how large N is (as long as it is finite). To see why, consider the very last potential entrant. That entrant should always enter. Since there are no later entrants to consider, if the Nth potential entrant does enter, the monopolist faces the choice of predatory pricing (and earning P^I) or accommodating the entry (and earning P^E). Since $P^I > P^E$ the monopolist will accommodate the entry. Knowing this, the potential entrant should enter and earn $A^E > 0$.

Thus, *regardless of what has happened before*, the Nth potential entrant will enter. In light of this fact, the monopolist knows that nothing it does before the Nth period will have any bearing on what happens then. In particular, what it does in the N − 1st period will not affect the Nth period. Accordingly, if the N − 1st potential entrant enters, the monopolist should accommodate the entry. The same argument that leads to this conclusion in the Nth period holds in the N − 1st. Knowing this, the N − 1st potential entrant will enter. But now, of course, the monopolist knows that the Nth and N − 1st potential entrant will enter, regardless of what has happened before. This logic can be extended by backward induction all the way to the first period. Game theory has a clear prediction: entry should occur and be accommodated at every period.

It is worth noting that if N is not finite, there do exist equilibria in which the monopolist can deter entry by building a reputation for toughness.[43] The above argument depends critically

---

[43] Providing the monopolist does not discount the future too heavily.

on having a last period (no matter how distant) from which to begin the backward induction argument.

The backward induction argument is troubling, aside from its reliance on the finite horizon, because it attributes an extreme degree of rationality to the players. To see how much weight that assumption is asked to bear here, suppose that, contrary to what is *supposed* to happen, the monopolist predatory prices against the first entrant. What should later entrants believe? Since the same logic that applied to the N period game still applies to the remaining N − 1 period game, they could simply write it off as a mistake and continue as though nothing had happened. But suppose that the monopolist then predatory prices against the second, third, and fourth potential entrants. Should those occurrences be written off as mistakes too?

In contrast to the Cournot model, small changes in the incumbent's ability to "think like a game theorist" can have profound effects on what happens. If, for example, the monopolist "naively" believes that it can influence later behavior, it may choose to predatory price early on. Then if potential entrants see prior episodes of predatory pricing, rather than simply dismissing them as mistakes, they may instead infer that the monopolist is "naive." If they reach that conclusion, they may in fact be deterred from entering. But, paradoxically, if that is the case, even a monopolist that is "fully rational" might try to convince later entrants that it is "naive" by predatory pricing against early entrants!

Arguments of this kind were first made precise by Kreps, Milgrom, Roberts, and Wilson.[44] Interestingly from our point of view, even though they can be interpreted as dealing with irrationality, they do so within the context of a fully rational game-theoretic model. They model the chain-store paradox as above, with one seemingly minor alteration. Instead of assuming that the payoffs the monopolist faces are necessarily as outlined above, they admit a small probability that for the monopolist $P^I > P^E$, i.e., that the monopolist prefers predatory pricing to accommodating entry.

It is of no consequence to their theory *why* this possibility exists. One attractive interpretation is simply that there is no

[44] Kreps, Wilson, Milgrom, and Roberts (1982), Milgrom and Roberts (1982b), and Kreps and Wilson (1982).

good explanation for the behavior! That is, for reasons that defy logic, the monopolist prefers to predatory price or somehow believes that it is in its interest to do so. In other words, there may simply be a small probability that the monopolist is "irrational."

Having modified the game slightly in this way, the authors are then able to analyze it in formal game-theoretic fashion.[45] The questions that can be asked are, as before, How should the entrants behave? and, How should the monopolist behave if in fact it is rational? (If it is irrational, it will simply predatory price against any entrant.)

The answer is that even a very small probability that the monopolist is irrational can have profound implications for the behavior of all the players. Roughly speaking, if there is even a tiny probability that the monopolist is irrational, then for sufficiently large N even the rational monopolist will predatory price against any entrant foolish enough to enter in the early periods. As a consequence, potential early entrants will in fact stay out, and only later might they challenge the monopolist.

The intuition for this is that if the monopolist predatory prices early on, this will reinforce the possibility (in the minds of the later potential entrants) that the monopolist is "irrational." If, in contrast, the monopolist accommodates entry, it reveals to the later potential entrants that it is rational and thereby invites a steady sequence of entrants. Early on, the monopolist almost welcomes the opportunity to demonstrate that it enjoys predatory behavior. Knowing that the monopolist will relish the opportunity to demonstrate its willingness to predatory price early on, wise potential entrants stay out of its way. Later on, however, the monopolist has less incentive to maintain its reputation for toughness (since there are fewer periods in which to reap the benefits of that reputation), and so it may accommodate entry. Knowing this, a potential entrant may take the chance and enter.

Similar reasoning can be applied to games, such as Cournot, in which cooperation is desirable but where the incentives to deviate in a one-period setting result in uncooperative outcomes. If such games are repeated a finite number of times, the backward induction argument again leads to the conclusion that

---

[45] Since the potential entrant is unsure about the exact "type" of monopolist it is facing, the game is now one of incomplete information.

players should play uncooperatively from the start. In practice, however, many players do attempt to cooperate. As a result, optimal strategies may involve cooperation (in the early rounds) even by rational players.[46]

The chain-store "paradox" and its "resolution" by explicitly modeling irrationality both illustrate the limitations to game-theoretic modeling. The "answer" provided by a fully rational game-theoretic model is implausible and in fact not borne out in experiments. Thus, as a metaphor for finitely repeated interaction it seems "unreasonable."

However, the resolution achieved by invoking irrationality is itself unsatisfying since it leaves open the question of what kind of irrationality one should invoke. Unfortunately, the predictions one obtains may be very sensitive to how one models irrationality and hence much of the predictive power of the modeling approach is lost.

Nonetheless, the fact that the chain-store problem has been labeled a "paradox" illustrates the ability of the community of consumers of these models to distinguish among models with differing degrees of plausibility. If one adopts the metaphorical view of modeling, making choices among models on the basis of plausibility and how well they capture what they are designed to is part and parcel of the process. There is no point in becoming the slave of any particular model. There are "good" and "bad" models and if the "answers" seem paradoxical, there is probably something wrong with the model. Over time those models that prove useful in understanding the world or that provide enduring insights will themselves endure, while others will slowly fade away.

6. From Theory to Practice

The preceding has focused on the role of game-theoretic modeling in producing theoretical insights for strategic management. However, strategic management has historically had very strong normative and empirical orientations. Can game-theoretic modeling contribute in those areas?

---

[46] See Milgrom, Kreps, Roberts, and Wilson (1982) for the theoretical treatment of this case. For evidence on how such games are played in practice, see the description of the contests run by Axelrod and Hamilton (1981).

Normative Role

It was argued above that the prospects are slim for using game-theoretic models as mechanisms for simulating a managerial situation and providing precise prescriptions for managerial action as in a "management science" type model.

This critique of the direct applicability of game-theoretic models does not mean that they are normatively irrelevant, however. Only by having a good understanding of how its world works can a firm's management understand the repercussions of its own actions and hence how it should behave. The powerful descriptive features of models and their normative relevance are closely related. The normative role for strategic management here is to provide management with a broad qualitative understanding of the effects of their actions and to ensure that the broad qualitative prescriptions can be given firm foundations.

Empirical Role

Significant difficulties arise in directly testing many of the game-theoretic models that have been developed in industrial organization. One reason is that the models tend to be rather specific; the behavior that emerges in equilibrium depends on the precise state of the environment that obtains. In empirical work it is difficult to find large samples of firms that face exactly the kinds of environments envisaged by the models. A second reason pertains to models with asymmetric information, such as the Milgrom-Roberts limit pricing model. The chief implication of that model is that low-cost incumbents will charge less than high-cost ones and thereby successfully deter entry. Unfortunately, the cost structure of the firm must be unobservable to the researcher, since if it were observable by the researcher it would be observable by the potential entrant and the model would not apply.

Despite the difficulty that is often encountered in directly testing game-theoretic models, they have had a tremendous impact on empirical research in industrial organization, and hold out similar prospects for strategic management. As Bresnahan and Schmalensee write in "The Empirical Renaissance in Industrial Organization" (p. 374): "The theoretical developments that began in the 1970s produced a rich set of hypotheses, along with a powerful set of modeling techniques. . . ."

This quote is suggestive of two different roles that game-theoretic modeling plays in empirical work. The first is in developing and refining hypotheses for reduced-form empirical models. Here the specific structural characteristics of the models are not used, but instead the empirical investigation examines whether the data are consistent with the broad qualitative features.

As an example, consider the issue of predatory pricing discussed in the previous section. The models discussed there suggest that a firm that has developed a reputation for predatory behavior should find it easier to drive out rivals than firms with no such reputation. Furthermore, Saloner (1987) shows that a firm may have an incentive to predatory price against a rival in anticipation of a merger with that rival to enable it to purchase the rival on better terms. Both of these qualitative features are examined in Burns's (1986) empirical investigation of the acquisitions by the American Tobacco Company. He finds that "alleged predation significantly lowered the acquisition costs of the tobacco trust both for asserted victims and, through reputation effects, for competitors that sold out peacefully" (p. 266). Moreover, the effects were significant in magnitude: "The estimated direct savings range up to 60 percent of what some targets would have cost if they had not been preyed on, and the trust's reputation produced an additional discount averaging 25 percent" (p. 269).

In addition to directly examining the central qualitative predictions of models as in these examples, hypotheses are, as discussed above, often generated from the comparative statics of the model. For example, in a supergame-theoretic model Rotemberg and Saloner (1986) show that an implicitly colluding oligopoly might find it most difficult to collude when demand is at its strongest because the incentive for a firm to cheat is greatest then. A corollary of that analysis is that price-cost margins should be lower for such firms when demand is high, so that measured price-cost margins should be countercyclical. Empirical evidence, much of it supportive of this hypothesis, has been produced by Rotemberg and Saloner (1986), Domowitz, Hubbard, and Petersen (1987), and Rotemberg and Woodford (1989, 1991).

The second role that game-theoretic modeling plays in empirical work is in generating and testing structural models. These empirical investigations focus on a particular industry over time. Typically demand, costs, and behavior are estimated simultaneously, and the relationships between the various parameters to be estimated are dictated by oligopoly theory.[47] While detailed game-theoretic models underlie these structural models, the estimation relies on the broad qualitative features, especially the relationships among the degree of collusion, price-cost margins, and demand elasticities, which hold at equilibrium, and the comparative static properties of those relationships.

Two of the best examples of this style of work are the papers by Porter (1983) and Bresnahan (1987). Porter (1983) uses a switching regression model to estimate periods of cooperation and reversion in the railroad cartel of the 1880s. The pattern of behavior estimated by the model is consistent with that predicted by the Green and Porter (1984) model, and the estimated price-cost margins during periods of collusion are consistent with the exercise of considerable market power. Bresnahan (1987) uses a model of product differentiation to estimate the degree of collusion among U.S. auto manufacturers from 1954 to 1956. He finds that the years 1954 and 1956 were collusive, while 1955 was competitive. His structural estimation allows him to estimate price-cost margins during periods of collusion and competition for different car models.

There has been a tendency among some observers to stress the difficulties in directly testing some game-theoretic models. However, the renaissance in empirical work that has followed the theoretical developments has been remarkable, and while the pace of development of theory within industrial organization seems to be slowing, "the new empirical industrial organization" continues apace.[48]

7. Conclusions

When small numbers of rivals compete, a sensible analysis of what a firm should do involves a careful assessment of what its

---

[47]   A detailed discussion of this methodology is contained in Bresnahan (1989).
[48]   See Bresnahan (1989) for a detailed discussion of the "new empirical industrial organization."

rivals' actions are likely to be. A formal analysis of such situations therefore requires assumptions about how rivals behave. Game theory proceeds, for the most part, by assuming that all the rivals behave rationally.

I have argued that in order to evaluate game-theoretic modeling it is important to consider the goals of the analysis. I have argued that one's appraisal of the rationality assumption and of the usefulness of the models depends on whether one takes a literal or metaphorical view of microeconomic-style modeling.

When one takes the literal view, comparing the role of the rationality assumption in the Cournot game and in the chain-store paradox leads to quite different impressions. The degree of rationality assumed in the latter is clearly much greater than in the former. Reasonable people might reach different conclusions about whether the degree of rationality assumed in each is within the realm of plausibility. That judgment must, however, be made on a case-by-case basis. Thus, one might well be willing to accept the conclusions of game-theoretic reasoning in some settings and not in others.

I have argued that one ought to be relatively more comfortable with the predictions of game-theoretic analyses in literal models, all else equal, when the prediction is robust to small mistakes by the players, when the players have some experience with the decisions being analyzed, or when the players have some basis on which to form beliefs about what their rivals will do (whether because there has been pre-play communication or because they have had opportunities to observe each other's behavior in the past).

However, I have argued that literal game-theoretic models are likely to have only a limited role. In particular, game-theoretic models have not proven very useful, nor are they likely to, for providing *precise* prescriptions for managerial behavior. Rather, the role of game-theoretic modeling is to produce insights from well-reasoned models. That is, the virtues of game-theoretic modeling have as much to do with the virtues of modeling as with the virtues of the game-theoretic approach.

The virtues of formal modeling are, inter alia, that it provides an "audit trail" documenting that a coherent explanation for the phenomenon under study can be given; that it provides a system of logic to root out the flaw in the reasoning in incorrect analyses (as in the case of the maintained output hypothesis);

that it is a methodology capable of generating new insights (including "surprises"), and that it provides a common language which allows related results to be compared, and new results to be built on the foundations laid by earlier models.

What does the field have to look forward to if there is indeed a large increase in the "domestic" production of game-theoretic modeling in strategic management? If experience in industrial organization is any indicator, the cumulative output is more likely to resemble a mosaic in which each paper contributes a small piece of the picture than it is to make up a broad generalizing theory. That is, results are more apt to describe what happens in particular circumstances than to describe behavior that will occur in all, or even in a very broad variety of, situations. As theory develops, more and more is learned about the limits of particular models and the circumstances under which their results hold. Pieces of the mosaic are replaced by others, and empty spots are filled in. Some, such as Fisher (1989), lament the scale of the mosaic. However the large scale is due to the enormous variability of the settings and decisions that senior management must confront. The enormous scope of those settings requires richly textured theory.

It is the task of the scholars in the field to develop and maintain this richly textured mosaic, to contribute the pieces to it, and to haggle over which ones belong and how they fit. While it is time-consuming, this approach is also cumulative. Rather than haphazardly generating a myriad of disconnected and conflicting theories, each starting from scratch, in this approach each contribution builds upon those of its predecessors. This task is both theoretical and empirical. Theory provides both hypotheses to test and specific structural models in which to test them. Empirical results, in turn, provide evidence on the limits, applicability, and failures of the theory, pointing to deficiencies in the mosaic and presenting new challenges to theory.

As it develops, each part of the mosaic provides understanding of some aspect of the business environment, which, in turn, enables managers to make sensible decisions. Thus, while not narrowly prescriptive, as in literal models, metaphorical models nonetheless are normatively useful.

The program being called for in this paper is not the continued development of game-theoretic modeling in industrial organization for export to strategic management. Rather, it is the development, within strategic management, of its own mosaic: the rigorous development of theory on topics central to strategic management by scholars in strategic management.

As far as subject matter is concerned, there are topics to be addressed in both the internal and external parts of strategic management. On the external side, for example, a topic that has received a huge amount of attention in the strategy literature but little formal modeling is the issue of strategic groups (see Porter, 1980).

On the internal side, many issues are related to the growing body of work in "contract theory." In particular, questions relating to the appropriate boundaries of the firm, which are central to strategic management, may be amenable to analysis using these tools. These include the study of joint ventures and strategic alliances as well as issues relating to the scope of the firm. The latter include optimal diversification policy as well as questions such as why firms often set narrow strategic objectives for themselves (see Mintzberg, 1987b).

A related set of issues are raised by the resource-based view of the firm (Penrose, 1959; Wernerfelt, 1984). Which resources and core competencies are worth developing depends, in part, on the extent to which the firm is able to capture the rents from them. It also depends on the firm's ability to commit itself to adequately rewarding those individuals in the firm who must put forth the effort to develop these resources and competencies. How the implicit and explicit contractual relationships that the firm can enter into with its employees and the nature of rent sharing within the firm influence the development of the resource base of the firm are important topics that may be amenable to contract-theoretic modeling.

In the final analysis, the proof of the pudding is in the eating. Only by applying game-theoretic modeling to issues in strategic management will we be able to assess its usefulness to the field. Perhaps the next time a conference of this nature is convened the debate over the virtues of game-theoretic modeling in strategic management will be concrete rather than merely philosophical.

6

Does Strategy Research Need Game Theory?

Colin F. Camerer

This is a paper about the tools and inspiration that game theory may lend to strategy research, and vice versa. My purpose is to address some criticisms of game theory commonly voiced by strategy researchers, offer some new ones, and suggest a few areas of productive complementarity. It helps to start with some rough boundaries for the two fields.

I take strategy to be the study of the sources (and creation) of the efficiencies that make firms successful. Popular strategy topics include: innovation, new product introduction, diversification, entry, corporate governance, acquisitions, joint ventures and strategic alliances, executive compensation, influence of top-management teams, and managerial cognition.

Game theory is the analysis of rational behavior in situations involving interdependence of outcomes (when my payoff depends on what you do). Its greatest impact has been in economics, especially in the last 15 years in industrial organization, but application in other disciplines and functional areas is active too.[1]

Most of the research in business strategy is empirical. The typical approach is to form several hypotheses based on results from some theoretical literature (but usually not from a formal

Acknowledgments: Thanks to Rebecca Henderson, Marc Knez, Jacqueline Meszaros, Laura Poppo, Dick Rumelt, Dan Schendel, Keith Weigelt, and participants at the Silverado conference and an MIT seminar, for helpful conversations and comments.

[1] Including accounting (Wilson, 1983); biology (Smith, 1982); finance (Myers and Majluf, 1984); law (Ayres, 1990); marketing (Moorthy, 1985); and political science (Ordeshook, 1986).

model). Then hypotheses are tested using cross-sectional data on firm- or business-unit-level measures of profitability, diversification, advertising, and so forth. Of course, there has been some shift in the style of strategy research over the last two decades. Early strategy research (in the 1960s and 1970s) set out to discover empirical "laws of business," working roughly within the structure-conduct-performance paradigm popular in industrial organization. More recent work focuses on sources of efficiencies, beginning with several premises that are opposite to those in neoclassical economics: markets may be in disequilibrium; there is imperfection in markets for factors of production (labor, know-how, and so forth); and internal organization of firms matters.[2]

Since many business strategy decisions involve interdependent outcomes, game theory would seem to apply to business strategy. Indeed, the only setting in which game theory should *not* apply is perfect competition, the limiting case in which firms are too small (or know too little) to measure their impact on others and the impact of others on them. Some business strategy decisions might fit the limiting case, but most fit within the broader scope of game theory. Why have strategy researchers hesitated to pick up the tools of game theory and apply them? There are at least three reasons.

One reason is sheer ignorance. Many researchers reject a brand of game theory that is long outdated. Recent work on the "noncooperative" approach to games focuses mostly on repeated games, with asymmetric information, in which players can sometimes discuss their strategies beforehand (but cannot make binding agreements about what to do). The new focus completely invalidates stale criticisms that game theory is static, requires all players to perceive the game in the same way, and rules out communication. Strategy scholars who know about recent developments in game theory often lack the training to apply them. But the mathematics of game theory is no more sophisti-

---

[2] These premises lead in different research directions than the laws-of-business approach. For example, a popular topic in the laws-of-business approach is measuring whether diversification into related or unrelated products is more profitable. The sources-of-efficiencies approach seeks to understand why related diversification might be profitable: Are benefits due to disequilibrium in markets for acquisitions? To scope economies in using know-how or customer reputation? To superior organizational forms for managing related products? I suspect game theory might be more useful in the sources-of-efficiency approach than in the earlier approach.

cated than the econometrics or psychometrics routinely used in strategy research; game theory is mostly logic and algebra. And now there are more good books to learn from,[3] and more to learn, than ever before.

A second reason for not applying game theory is that the "theory" is actually a set of methods. The methods are generally applicable, but applying them does not usually lead to predicted general regularities of the sort strategy researchers like to test using firm-level cross-sectional data.[4]

A third reason for hesitance in application of game theory—a better reason than ignorance or a craving for generality—is that analysis of games often assumes more rationality than players may be capable of (e.g., Zajac and Bazerman, 1991).

My argument in this paper is that all three are poor reasons not to use game theory to do strategy research, but that there are other reasons to proceed carefully. Ignorance is easily cured by reading recent books; good research does not have to result in general theorems or widespread regularities; and there are several good defenses to the charge that game theory assumes too much rationality. One defense is that in some games (though not all), less rationality is needed for equilibrium calculations than has been commonly assumed. Another defense is that communication, adaptation, and evolution could produce equilibration even if players are not rational enough to reason game-theoretically.

The paper has four sections. In the next section I distinguish between games, game-theoretic reasoning, and equilibrium analysis. The study of games and equilibria might be useful, even if game-theoretic reasoning is too difficult for players, be-

---

3   Rasmusen (1989) is a great intermediate-level book with just the right amount of math. McMillan (1992) is aimed at MBAs, with less math and lots of examples and insight. Kreps's (1990a) book covers intermediate microeconomics using much game theory. Tirole (1988) summarizes applications in industrial organization (more technically than in the other books above).

4   Entry deterrence is an example. In one popular model, potential entrants and incumbents have costs that are uncorrelated (and privately known). Then monopolist incumbents will set prices *lower* than the monopoly price to signal that their costs are low and deter entrants (Milgrom and Roberts, 1982a). In a different model, the incumbents and entrants have the same costs, which are known by experienced incumbents but not by entrants. These incumbents will set prices *above* the monopoly price, to signal to entrants that their costs would be high and their profits would be low if they entered (Harrington, 1985). The two models predict that behavior depends on the correlation between firms' costs. (The models predict an interaction, not a main effect.)

cause games provide a helpful taxonomy, and reasoning is not required for equilibration.

The second section describes the popular "no-fat" modeling approach used in many game theory applications—the search for lean sets of assumptions which predict an observed regularity—and mentions several problems with the approach.

In the third section I ask whether game theory provides sound advice for managers. It does not, but it answers questions managers should want to know the answers to, and it should be part of a sensible package of advice. The best advice will come from an empirically grounded "behavioral game theory" that tells managers how others are likely to play during the process of convergence to equilibrium.

The fourth section is a conclusion.

Games, Game-Theoretic Reasoning, and Equilibrium Analysis

A brief introduction to game theory is necessary to establish a vocabulary. A game consists of a set of players who choose strategies.[5] Their choice of strategies determines consequences, which yield payoffs to each player (possibly random). (The payoffs need not be financial, but players are assumed to have preferences among the different payoffs which obey some of the axioms of utility theory.) A repeated game consists of several different choice stages, perhaps a "single-stage game" played repeatedly. An "equilibrium" is an outcome of the game (or a set of outcomes) picked out by some theory.

It is important to distinguish among three elements of game theory: games, game-theoretic reasoning, and equilibrium points (which are determined by game-theoretic reasoning). I argue the value of each in turn. The main point is that games and equilibrium analysis can be useful even if game-theoretic reasoning is too complicated for individual or collective minds.

I will use two examples in this section. One is the well-known Cournot quantity-setting game in which two firms simultaneously decide how much of a good to produce (denoted q_1 and

---

[5] In game theory, the term "strategy" refers to actions of players. This use should not be confused with the way the word "strategy" is used in strategy research or practice.

Figure 6-1
The Centipede Game (Rosenthal, 1981)

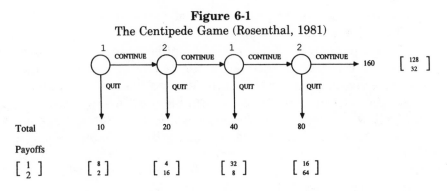

$$\begin{bmatrix} 1 \\ 2 \end{bmatrix} \quad \begin{bmatrix} 8 \\ 2 \end{bmatrix} \quad \begin{bmatrix} 4 \\ 16 \end{bmatrix} \quad \begin{bmatrix} 32 \\ 8 \end{bmatrix} \quad \begin{bmatrix} 16 \\ 64 \end{bmatrix}$$

q_2). Each unit costs c. The market price is determined by some unspecified price-setting process given the firms' production decisions (e.g., spot-market competition for OPEC oil), and yields a price of $P = a - (q_1 + q_2)$.

The second example is the "centipede game" (Rosenthal, 1981), shown in Figure 6-1. Player 1 goes first. She either "quits" a productive relationship or "continues" it. If she continues it, then player 2 can either quit or continue, and so forth. Eventually there is a final stage at which player 1 either quits or the relationship ends. At each stage of the game, the total payoff doubles (from 10, to 20, to 40 . . .). When one player quits the relationship (a downward arrow) she takes 80% of the payoff at that stage; the other player gets 20%.

Consider player 1's initial choice. If she quits, she gets 80% of 10, or 8. If she continues and player 2 quits, then player 1 gets 20% of twice as large a total payoff, or 4. But if both player 1 and player 2 continue, player 1 gets *at least* 16, and maybe much more. Thus, player 1 should continue unless she is fairly certain player 2 will quit at the next stage.

The centipede game captures elements of trust and reciprocity. (It is a close relative of the repeated prisoner's dilemma and the "chain-store paradox" [Selten, 1978].) Consider a strategic relationship between firms (or more likely, within a firm)—say, a buyer-supplier relationship. There are many times when a supplier is forced to make some sort of sacrifice for the sake of the relationship (absorbing a price increase rather than passing it on, or rushing a delivery). The supplier makes such sacrifices because it expects the relationship will continue long enough for it to be paid back. If the supplier thought the buyer would quit doing business the first time *it* had to sacrifice, the supplier would make no sacrifices either.

The existence of a final period implies that neither player should ever choose "continue" in the centipede game; quitting immediately is the unique equilibrium outcome. The argument is simple; it works by backward induction. In the last stage, player 1 will choose "quit" because it gives 128 rather than 64. Anticipating that final choice, player 2 will quit in his last stage (earning 64) rather than continuing (and earning 32, when player 1 quit). The logic works all the way back to the first stage, when player 1 quits right away.

Games

Even without equilibrium analysis, game theory provides a taxonomy of interactive situations, like biological classification of species or the periodic table of chemical elements (Aumann, 1985). I think some of the building blocks of modern game theory should take their place in the strategy dictionary (and in the conversation of strategy research) because they classify strategic formulation situations which share important features. Some useful terms are defined in the Appendix: equilibrium, pooling versus separating, battle of the sexes, rationalizability, reputation, the folk theorem, coordination games, and trigger strategies. These ideas could prove useful in the vocabulary of strategy, like more familiar ideas: learning curve, strategic groups, muddling through, entry barriers, and scope and scale economies.

Game-Theoretic Reasoning

Game-theoretic reasoning is expressed in a decision rule or algorithm which selects an equilibrium strategy. In the quantity-setting game, Cournot-Nash equilibrium reasoning poses the question, What quantity should I pick to respond best to her quantity choice, if she is doing the same? and answers it. The answer may come from intersecting two reaction functions,[6] listing all possible quantity pairs and checking them for mutual

---

[6] A reaction function prescribes an optimal choice given the choice the other player is expected to make.

best-response consistency, using a "tracing procedure" (Harsanyi, 1975) or some other algorithm.

In the centipede game, equilibrium analysis poses the question, How should I move, given rational anticipation of my opponent's future moves (which includes her rational anticipation of *my* moves, and so on)? The answer comes from an algorithm that starts at the last possible move and works backward.

Many people, game theorists included, have expressed doubts that game-theoretic reasoning of any sort is a good description of how people or institutions decide which strategies to play. There are several reasons for doubt about its descriptive accuracy: rules for game-theoretic reasoning are computationally difficult;[7] some rules require players to believe *others* are using the same rule (which players may doubt); and some rules require players to maintain the assumption that players are rational, even after they make irrational choices ("off the equilibrium path"), which seems nonsensical (Binmore, 1987, 1988).

Equilibrium Analysis

Equilibrium analysis is the discovery and analysis of equilibrium points. Various rules for game-theoretic reasoning (or "equilibrium concepts") pick out different points. The focus on equilibrium could be justified by the presumption that players discover equilibria by introspection, except that game-theoretic reasoning is unnatural and difficult. In the Cournot game, for instance, players are presumed to introspect by mentally simulating the results of various quantity choices in their heads (or meeting rooms), eliminating quantities that are not best responses or adjusting them until a set of quantities that are mutual best responses are found. In the centipede game, players are presumed to anticipate the entire path of play by working backward from the end to the beginning.

I would like to dispel two widely held myths about equilibrium analysis. One myth is that players who do not reason game-theoretically will never converge to an equilibrium. This

---

[7] For example, Gilboa and Zemel (1989) and Gilboa, Kalai, and Zemel (1989) proved that even simple decision rules like the iterative elimination of dominated strategies are "NP-complete," in optimization jargon. That means the time a computer would need to pick the best of N strategies increases with N more swiftly than a polynomial (N^k) does.

is a myth because game-theoretic reasoning is only one of several kinds of equilibrating forces (and is perhaps the least likely kind, empirically). Another myth is that players must think others are rational, and think others think they are rational, ad infinitum, to reach an equilibrium. Not always; in some classes of games much less rationality suffices. (Brandenburger, 1991, gives an elegant taxonomy of how much rationality is required for what kinds of equilibriums in what sorts of games.)

How Much Rationality Is Necessary for Equilibrium?

Even among sophisticated game theorists, there is a common confusion about the amount of rationality that is required for players to find an equilibrium strategy and play it. (The actual requirements were not known until quite recently, and are still not completely understood.) Much of the confusion revolves around "common knowledge." A fact is common knowledge if everyone knows it, everyone knows that everyone knows it, and so on ad infinitum. If players have common knowledge of a game's payoffs, and common knowledge that all players are rational, players will converge to an equilibrium by introspection. (Common knowledge is *sufficient* for justifying an equilibrium.) But often common knowledge is more than enough for justifying an equilibrium; it is not *necessary*. In many games, players can make equilibrium choices just by being rational, or thinking others are rational.

The prisoner's dilemma is a familiar example. (For strategy scholars, the problem of firms deciding whether to maintain high prices or low production amounts in a cartel may spring to mind; it is a prisoner's dilemma.) In a single play of the prisoner's dilemma, rational, self-interested players should defect. They do *not* need to know anything about the rationality of the other player; they do not even need to know the other player's payoffs. Since defecting is a dominant strategy (it is better for *any* choice by the other player), it makes no difference whether the other player is rational or not.

In the Cournot quantity-setting game with two firms, simple rationality is not enough to produce equilibrium play, but two kinds of "mutual knowledge" are enough. (A fact is *mutual* knowledge if everyone knows it and everyone knows that others know it.[8]) Equilibrium occurs in the Cournot game and the centipede game if players have mutual knowledge of the *beliefs* players have about what others will choose—i.e., if firms know how their competitors think about them—and if each player knows the other is rational. It does not matter whether players know that others know they are rational, and so forth.

The assumptions of mutual knowledge of rationality, and even plain rationality, may still be empirically unrealistic. But mutual knowledge is certainly much weaker, and much more likely to be satisfied in strategic settings, than strong assumptions of *common* knowledge.

It is also worth mentioning that there are many alternatives to Nash equilibrium reasoning in game theory.[9] For example, "justifiable" strategies are choices that are optimal for *some* belief about what the other player will do; the belief need not come from difficult introspection about the other player's thinking (as in Nash equilibrium). In the Cournot game, quantities between 0 and $(a - c)/2$ are justifiable. In the centipede game, *any* behavior is justifiable, except continuing at the very last stage. (The only strategies that are *not* justifiable are those that are dominated, or inferior, regardless of what others do, to another strategy.)

"Rationalizable" strategies are justifiable strategies in which players believe others will use justifiable strategies. In the Cournot game, quantities between $(a - c)/4$ and $(a - c)/2$ are rationalizable. In the centipede game, any choice except continuing at the last available stage is rationalizable.

Rules like justifiability and rationalizability are not as precise as Nash equilibrium (which predicts exactly $(a - c)/3$ in Cour-

---

8   A fact that is *mutual* knowledge may not be common knowledge. For example, suppose Keith transmits a message to Marlene, and Marlene sends back an acknowledgment that she received the message. Then the information in the messages is mutual knowledge, but not common knowledge: Keith and Marlene both know it, and both know that the other person knows it, but Marlene may be unsure whether Keith knows she got the message (since her acknowledgment might have got lost). In a high-risk situation requiring coordination of their activities—like shipping goods to a foreign country, or unveiling a new product in many cities or countries simultaneously—mutual knowledge may be insufficient for players to invest confidently.

9   "Refinements" of Nash equilibrium impose further rationality requirements to reduce the set of predicted strategies (if there are many) to those that seem especially rational. "Coarsenings" of Nash equilibrium, like justifiability and rationalizability, relax the rationality requirements and expand the set of predicted strategies.

not and immediate quitting in the centipede game), but they do exclude some choices. And these simpler rules are likely to apply in many business strategy situations, when firms make choices in unique situations where payoffs (and even the set of competitors) are highly uncertain and firms have no experience to learn from (Milgrom and Roberts, 1990: 1275).

Four Kinds of Equilibrating Forces

Walrasian tatonnement is a fictional substitute, in the economic theory of competitive equilibrium, for a detailed model of price adjustment. Game-theoretic reasoning is a kind of cognitive tatonnement:[10] sensible game theorists think of convergence to an equilibrium by introspection as a theoretical fiction which substitutes for a more detailed account of the forces that actually produce equilibration.[11]

Besides introspection, there are at least three other kinds of forces that might produce equilibration in games. The three forces, ranked from most cognitively demanding to least, are communication, adaptation, and evolution. Absent evidence, sheer faith in the power of these equilibrating forces is what sustains the belief that equilibrium predictions will prove true even when game-theoretic reasoning is too difficult.

Communication. One defense of the idea that an equilibrium will actually be chosen is the possibility that players can announce their intentions. Pre-play announcements that are nonbinding, and impose no direct penalty if they are not followed, are called "cheap talk" (Farrell, 1987). Cheap talk makes it possible to include the pre-play communication that is typical in business strategy (such as pre-announcements of new computers or airline fare changes) in game-theoretic models.

Cheap talk could encourage equilibration by sharpening players' beliefs about what others will actually do. Experiments

---

[10] That is, the prediction of Nash equilibrium is derived "as if" players do game-theoretic reasoning in their heads. Replacing parts of a model with as if asssumptions is common throughout science, and absolutely necessary. Theories of atoms, organizations, and nations all abstract from the specific behavior of the quarks, people, and states which make them up. Otherwise models would be crowded with too much detail to be useful, just as listing every house on a map of Chicago would defeat the purpose of making a map.

[11] For example, Aumann (1991), Binmore (1987, 1988, 1990), Brandenburger (1991), Fudenberg and Kreps (1988), Milgrom and Roberts (1991), and Selten (1991).

show that cheap talk is helpful in some kinds of coordination games, but not in others (Cooper et al., 1992). For example, cheap talk did not help in experimental games with first-mover advantages (like battle of the sexes, or product standardization); both subjects announced their intention to move first, which did not help them coordinate.

In the duopoly game, the intention to choose the Cournot quantity (a − c)/3 is the only announcement worth carrying out if others believe it and respond appropriately. But there are two reasons to be skeptical that communication is an equilibrating force in duopoly games. First, players must figure out the equilibrium before they can announce it. (Communication therefore *complements* introspection as an equilibrating force, rather than *substituting* for it.) Second, imaginative players will use communication to establish advantages or convey information about their utilities. In the Cournot game, I bet that if intentions are announced sequentially the first player will announce the "Stackelberg" output[12] (a − c)/2 to gain a first-mover advantage; if announcements are simultaneous, they will declare collusive output levels ((a − c)/4) which maximize *joint* profits. Why should players squander a valuable chance to communicate by reassuring each other that they will play the Cournot equilibrium, rather than trying to engineer better-than-Cournot profits for one of them (Stackelberg) or both (collusion)?

In the centipede game, communication would likely be used to establish trust and encourage the opponent to continue rather than quit. (Indeed, experiments on multiperson prisoners' dilemmas show that cheap talk does boost cooperative action even when cooperation is *not* an equilibrium, e.g., Dawes and Thaler, 1988.)

Adaptation. Adaptation is defined here as learning *which* strategy to play in a particular game. Adaptation is perhaps the most effective and common equilibrating force. Since it requires only some memory of past experience, and minimal computational ability, adaptation is less demanding than introspection or communication. Recent theory also suggests that convergence

---

[12] This output level, often called the "Stackelberg" equilibrium, is the level that maximizes the first mover's profits, anticipating that firm 2 will choose its profit-maximizing level after observing 1's choice. It is computed by putting 2's optimal quantity choice, $q_2^* = (a - c - q_1)/2$, into 1's profit function $(a - q_1 - q_2^* - c)q_1$ and choosing the value of q_1, which maximizes 1's profits.

under adaptation will occur under remarkably general conditions (e.g., Kalai and Lehrer, 1990; Milgrom and Roberts, 1991).

Adaptation has a long history in game theory. Brown (1951) suggested finding equilibria with a "fictitious play" algorithm: each player makes a choice and observes the other player's choice. She then makes her next choice by choosing a best response to the empirical distribution of actual choices by her opponent. Robinson (1951) proved that for two-player zero-sum games the algorithm converges to an equilibrium. Theorists lost interest when Shapley (1964) gave an example showing that the algorithm *doesn't* always converge in two-player games. But Milgrom and Roberts (1990b) showed that *any* adaptive rule—including fictitious play—leads to convergence in the broad class of games with "strategic complementarities"[13] (see also Binmore, 1990b, ch. 9).

Experimental evidence suggests adaptation *is* common (e.g., Van Huyck et al., 1991). Of course, adaptation of this sort will only converge if the same game is played repeatedly and players act myopically (thinking only one round ahead). When a game is first played, or when a game changes every day, or month, we might observe firms in chronic disequilibrium, continually converging to an equilibrium point that is always out of grasp. An important empirical question for game theory, which strategy empiricists could help answer, is whether the pace of environmental change outstrips the pace of adaptation.

Experiments indicate that adaptation does coax subjects toward the Nash equilibrium in duopoly (Plott, 1989: 1154–1155) and, very slowly, in the centipede game. For example, in centipede games with four moves studied by McKelvey and Palfrey (1990), the percentage of players choosing to quit at each stage were 5%, 32%, 57%, and 75% in the first five repetitions of the entire game. (The equilibrium is 100% quitting throughout.) In the next five repetitions, quitting happened earlier: the percentages choosing to continue were 8%, 49%, 75%, and 82%. Subjects seemed to learn that when their opponent quit at stage k, they

---

[13] A game exhibits strategic complementarities if the strategies can be ordered from low to high (perhaps by relabeling them) and the optimal strategy for each player is an increasing function of the choice by the other player. (That is, the reaction functions have positive slopes.) The Cournot game exhibits strategic complementarities if player 2's choice variable is labeled $(a - c)/2 - q_2$, rather than q_2. Milgrom and Roberts (1990b) give details and many examples.

should quit at stage k − 1 in the next play of the entire four-round game. However, even ten repetitions of concentrated experience did not produce convergence to the Nash equilibrium.

Evolution. Biologists use game theory to predict the mixture of behavior by animals in a steady-state population. Equilibration occurs because animals that use equilibrium strategies are more likely to survive and produce more offspring than others. Equilibrium strategies are selected naturally (much as game-theoretic reasoning selects them mentally). While useful in biology, evolutionary equilibration seems like an inappropriate justification for equilibrium analysis of business strategies, because the process of evolution is probably far too slow to produce convergence before a game's equilibrium changes.

Evolutionary arguments can have surprising results, too. For instance, Nash equilibrium play is *not* the inevitable outcome of evolution in the centipede game. Simulations show that immediate-quitters come to dominate a population of organisms, but then get "invaded" by a small number of continuers. The continuers grow in numbers until they are invaded (and vanquished) by immediate-quitters, and so on, in a chronic cycle of disequilibrium ebb and flow (Ho, 1991). This surprising result from centipede games should caution those who assume that evolutionary forces naturally impel a population toward an equilibrium (even when that equilibrium is unique).

To summarize this section:

1. Game theory provides a useful taxonomy of interactive situations, even if the analysis of equilibrium choices is too complicated to predict choices well.

2. It is clear that game-theoretic reasoning may be too difficult for players (even including firms). Even if players are smart enough, game-theoretic reasoning requires answers to equations that are fundamentally empirical—how rational are others?—rather than logical. At the same time, recent work shows that the knowledge required for players to find equilibria is not always as great as was previously thought.

3. Even if game-theoretic reasoning is too hard (point 2), equilibrium play may result from equilibrating forces other than reasoning.

4. Of other equilibrating forces, communication and evolution (natural selection) seem to be too weak to produce convergence in business strategy games. Adaptation to observed

choices is probably the strongest equilibrating force. Game-theoretic reasoning can be defended as a mathematical shortcut that is used by theorists to figure out where adaptive players will end up. But the shortcut only works if adaptation is fast enough to outrun environmental change.

Four Problems with No-Fat Game Theory

In the last section I tried to rebut some criticisms of game theory, criticisms that may account for why it has rarely been applied in a domain where it could naturally be (business strategy decisions). In this section I offer four other criticisms, a mild warning to users of some potential hazards.

Game-theoretic modeling in economics generally follows a style Rasmusen (1989) calls "no-fat modeling." (There are other approaches, too, most of which omit the first step below.) No-fat modeling works as follows:

1. Observe a stylized fact;

2. Find a series of premises which mathematically imply behavior that resembles the stylized fact. (Keep the premises as simple and appealing as possible; tell a story.)

Here are four examples of no-fat game-theoretic modeling:

Fact: strikes occur. Premise: suppose there is asymmetric information about how cheaply workers will work (or how much profit a firm makes), and unions ask for wage hikes but have no credible way to convey how little they will accept. Explanation of fact: since workers who will accept a low wage are forgoing more surplus by being on strike, the length of a strike signals how high their acceptable wage is. Strikes occur because they signal high acceptable wages (e.g., Kennen and Wilson, 1990).

Fact: warranties exist. Premise: suppose consumers do not know how sturdy toasters are. Explanation of fact: only firms that make sturdy toasters will sell warranties. Firms that make unreliable toasters cannot afford the repair cost of servicing the warranties. Warranties exist because they signal toaster quality (Grossman, 1981).

Fact: law firms have "up-or-out" policies in which lawyers become partners, or are fired, after a fixed number of years. Premise: suppose the ability of lawyers and the effort they expend is difficult to evaluate. Explanation of fact: partnership is a "tournament" in which the lawyers with the highest output become partners. Tournaments exist because they elicit maximum effort from lawyers and help firms identify the most able, hardworking ones (Lazear and Rosen, 1981).

(Potential) fact: managers underinvest. Premise: suppose capital markets do not know the true earnings of firms, but take high current earnings as a sign of high future earnings. Explanation of fact: farsighted managers are forced to underinvest and behave myopically (their myopia is strategic, not irrational) because underinvestment inflates current earnings and keeps stock prices high (Stein, 1989).

In each case mathematical reasoning shows how the premises can explain the fact. No-fat models are appealing because they are simple. They also leave an open "audit trail" of logic that can be criticized and extended (Chapter 5, this volume); but most other styles of research leave audit trails too (or permit replication of one sort or another).

No-fat modeling with game theory has swept the economics profession and some allied disciplines, but has had relatively little impact on strategy research. Perhaps there is a mismatch between the spare, customized, storytelling style of the models and the traditional strategy emphasis on comprehensive empirical studies.

I think a dash of no-fat modeling would be very useful in strategy, but the approach has many shortcomings. The models provide a *sufficient* explanation for an observed fact, but the explanation may not be necessary. For example, many sets of premises other than those given above can explain why there are strikes, warranties, legal partnerships, and underinvestment. The firm mathematical footing underlying no-fat explanations may be a poor reason to prefer them to competing explanations which are hard to express formally.

At the risk of spoiling the reader's appetite for the no-fat approach (which I genuinely admire), let me point out four of its shortcomings, which may be of special concern to strategy researchers.

The Chopstick Problem: Game Theory Is Too Hard

Game theory is hard to do. It is especially hard for economists trained in the neoclassical tradition, and for strategy scholars trained in various ways (perhaps in disciplines emphasizing little economics of any kind). Is the hard work worthwhile? I think it could be, for modeling those situations in which one firm's action has a large impact on another firm, because no other modeling language is well suited to such situations.

In most economic models, the key tool in the analysis is competition. A modeler figures out where the rents are, and then figures out the implications of competition for rents by the firms in the model. Game-theoretic models work similarly, except the key tool is the presumption that firms best respond to each other (rather than seek rents). The best-response tool is like a pair of chopsticks because it requires a delicate balance between simultaneous best responses by two (or more) firms. Neoclassical competitive analysis is much simpler, like using a fork. I claim that part of the difficulty with game theory is simply generational. Students who grow up using chopsticks—learning game theory from Rasmusen (1989), economics from Kreps (1990a), and industrial organization from Tirole (1988)—will struggle less with game theory than the fork-users before them. So encourage your students to practice using chopsticks (without ignoring forks).

Another difficulty is that outcomes in games can depend subtly on structural parameters. In the study of competitive equilibria, most of the work is in construction of demand and supply curves. Once demand and supply are built up, finding competitive equilibrium is simple: set the two equal and solve for price and quantity. Game-theoretic analysis is harder because equilibria may depend delicately on the order of play, number of players, information known at each node in the game tree, and so forth. (Merely drawing a game tree of any complexity can take a lot of paper and brainpower.) And games often have many equilibria. Multiplicity is awkward for some purposes—like testing models or drawing comparative static conclusions about how variables affect outcomes—but also provides valuable freedom to capture various kinds of path dependence and complexity.

Labor-saving technology may help with some of the hard parts of doing game theory. Some theorists use computer programs to search for equilibria in specific games with numerical payoffs. Coupling such programs with other programs that do algebraic manipulation (e.g., Mathematica) might lead to computerized research assistants that find equilibria for games with symbolic payoffs.

The Pandora's Box Problem: Explaining Is Too Easy

In no-fat game models, introducing asymmetric information opens Pandora's box by making it almost *too easy* to explain stylized facts: bad explanations are as easy to construct as good ones (and may be difficult to distinguish empirically). Some may question whether this approach is something like the Pandora's box problem and is worth the possibly bad side effects that may accompany it.

Economic models generally rely on three assumptions: stable preferences, maximizing behavior, and competition. From these assumptions, implications can be deduced and tested. Models based on maximizing and competition usually predict a clear link between preferences and predicted behavior, which provides a simple reality check. For example, if firms prefer higher profits, and if they maximize profits and compete, prices should equal marginal cost. A formal model that predicts prices above or below marginal cost probably contains a mistake.

The revolution in information economics added a fourth assumption to economic models: information is costly, and often asymmetrically distributed among agents (or "hidden"). Adding costly information is sensible; it makes models more realistic. The problem is that hidden-information models sever the intuitive link between preferences and behavior. When information is asymmetric, behavior that seems to be foolish (given assumed preferences) might actually be rational because it conveys information. As a result, hidden-information models threaten to explain *too much;* any kind of behavior that goes contrary to preferences can be explained by the information the behavior conveys.

For example, in the no-fat model of strikes, nobody likes strikes but they occur because strikes convey information. The case of underinvestment is similar. In Scharfstein and Stein (1990) it pays for rational managers to mimic the actions of others, exhibiting inefficient "herd behavior," because of hidden information about their abilities.

Hidden-information models of strikes, underinvestment, and

herd behavior all predict behavior that goes against preferences (creating inefficiencies). The models depict "a world of intelligent men and ludicrous outcomes" (Rasmusen, 1989: 14). But unintelligent men can cause ludicrous outcomes too. The empirical challenge is to separate the predictions of no-fat models of intelligent managers from competing models in which managers are hotheaded, myopic, or eager to conform. Put differently, how do we judge the quality of models if ludicrousness of outcomes is a modeling achievement rather than a mistake? The answer is obvious: data!

The Testing Problem: How to Test No-Fat Models Efficiently

While empirical tests are the obvious way to distinguish among game-theoretic models, tests are especially difficult because the results of many models depend so delicately on structure. Empirical tests would require measures of many subtle variables—which firm moved first, what announcements were made (and how widely they were known), how many players were involved (including potential entrants), and so on.

Strategy research could test game theories, if studies were done differently in a few simple ways. First, testing game theory requires finer-grained observation—about timing, information (including meta-information about information of others), and horizons—than is available from most archival sources. Researchers might have to focus on smaller samples of firms and study each firm more carefully. Longitudinal tests are much more useful than cross-sectional ones. Ironically, the implication is that focused case studies of firm behavior and industry evolution, which have been largely replaced in strategy by large empirical studies of archival data, might be an excellent source of data if the case researchers are sensitive to game-theoretic variables.

Second, dependent variables in game theories, like first-mover advantage, will generally be affected in complicated ways by industry variables (because of the strategic interdependence game theory captures). For example, being the first mover in an industry with network externalities or customer lock-in is good; being the first mover and generating technological spillovers that later entrants can exploit more easily can be bad. A regression of profitability against first-mover advantage would therefore turn up no "main effect" of a first-mover variable; instead, the first-mover variable interacts with variables measuring lock-in and spillover. Studies would have to be designed with special sensitivity to such interactions (which, of course, use up degrees of freedom rapidly).

The Collage Problem: Local Models versus General Principles

A final concern is that the no-fat search for sufficient premises to explain facts discourages the search for unifying *general* principles. The result is a collage or mosaic of simple "local" models which do not form a coherent whole (cf. Fisher, 1989; Shapiro, 1989). If neoclassical economics is like Lotus 1-2-3 (just press "competitive equilibrium" and wait), game theory is a catalogue of very specialized computer software.

The collage problem is only a problem if one's scientific ideal is nineteenth-century physics, which embodies knowledge in broadly applicable laws. If the ideal is biology or chemistry, which embody knowledge in classification systems constructed by careful observation, then the collage approach is better. For strategy scholars searching for "laws of business," the collage problem is disheartening. For those searching for idiosyncratic guidance for why some firms succeed (and a basis for advising other firms how to succeed), the collage problem is not a problem at all.

Research Complementarities

Some productive complementarities between game theory and strategy research can come from the reciprocal guidance that game theory and empirical work give each other. Game-theoretic no-fat models usually begin with a stylized fact about managerial practice, and strategy studies are a rich source of such stylized facts. (A good no-fat explanation repays the debt by making new predictions empiricists can test.) For example, Eccles and White (1988) discovered that product buyers generally liked buying from outside suppliers because intrafirm suppliers made lower-quality goods. Rotemberg (1991) noticed this fact and invented a simple no-fat explanation: long-term intrafirm contracts reduce quality because they reduce the threat to quit buying, which disciplines a bad supplier.[14]

Besides providing grist for the theory mill, strategy research could inform game theory by tackling the important question of how firms perceive the games they play: When do games begin, what strategies are permitted, and who are the competitors? (From a game-theoretic view, a strategic group is a cluster of competitors who see themselves in a game with each other; cf. Porac and Thomas, 1991.) If games exist only in the mind of a player (as Rubinstein, 1991, suggests), the minds of players are a useful place for an empiricist to be.

Game theory (and recent economic theory) suggests a wide range of new variables which might be important for strategy research (like the ability to precommit to the choice of a strategy, the anticipated horizon of exchange, asymmetric information, players' beliefs); evidence can test whether such variables are important. As mentioned above, suitable tests might require more fine-grained, longitudinal studies of interactions among structural variables than is common. Experiments might be useful too, since the premises underlying a formal model can be artificially created in an experiment (at the expense of generalizability; see Weigelt, Camerer, and Hanna, forthcoming).

Examples of suitable empirical work are hard to think of. Over a decade after it was written, the classic study of corn wet milling by Porter and Spence (1979), is still as good an example as any. Wolfson's (1985) study of the reputations of oil-and-gas tax-shelter partners and Lambert, Larcker, and Weigelt's (1990) study of tournament effects in managerial compensation are other examples that were inspired by game-theoretic predictions.

Game theory might have another benefit to offer strategy research: defining games as situations of economic interdependence erases the distinction between strategy formulation and implementation, promising some unification (or at least communication) between the two subfields. Roughly speaking, formulating a strategy is a game *among* firms and implementing a strategy has features of a game *within* a firm. Effective imple-

---

[14] Intrafirm contracts are profitable in Rotemberg's model, despite the weak discipline they exert on suppliers, because the alternative—ensuring quality of outside suppliers—requires a price premium (Klein and Leffler, 1981) which dissipates rents the firm can recapture by internalizing the transaction.

mentation requires workers' incentives and motivation to be properly aligned with the strategy (which is the focus of game-theoretic models of agency relations and incentives; e.g., Holmstrom and Tirole, 1989) and requires agents to coordinate their activities (the focus of research on coordination games).

Along similar lines, game theory might play a special role in explicating the fashionable "resource-based view" (which has emerged as a candidate for a unifying paradigm in strategy research). Compared to earlier approaches, the resource-based view shifts attention away from external competition among firms (which is naturally modeled game-theoretically), toward internal management of a firm's resources (which does not seem to be game-theoretic). But why are resources tied to a firm? Game theory suggests answers by tracing immobility of resources to informational asymmetries, participation externalities[15] within firms, existence of untradeable cultural capital which solves coordination problems (Kreps, 1990b), and so forth.

Does Game Theory Give Good Advice?

Business strategy is a practical field. As a byproduct of their research, scholars in a practical field should be able to give good advice to people in practice, through teaching, consulting, and publications (like this one). It is useful to ask how good the advice based on game theory is.

Most of game theory is not meant to be either normative (describing the ideal choices people *should* make) or descriptive (describing actual choices). It is not purely normative because an equilibrium strategy is only an ideal choice if other players behave in certain ways, which requires the theory to be descriptive of others in order to be normative for the advisee. Game theory is probably not purely descriptive either (except perhaps after adaptation in a stable environment).

Aumann (1989) suggests that game theory belongs to a third category of theories that are "analytic": game theorists analyze

---

[15] A participation externality is created when participation by one agent in an activity affects the desirability of the activity to another agent. Computer users, phone customers, or traders create a positive participation externality, because more users make participation more attractive. Positive participation externalities might tie valuable workers to a firm if the workers are productive together, but could not collectively agree to move to a better-paying firm.

the formal implications of various levels of mutual rationality in strategic situations. The analysis tells players what they should do when certain assumptions are met—when others are rational, for instance. There is no guarantee that the assumptions are met; game theory just tells you what to do if they are. It is *part* of a package of sensible advice, but it is not the whole package.

Many people (like Raiffa, 1982) argue for a practical brand of game theory which is "asymmetrically normative": it tells players what they should do (normatively) if their opponents behave in typical ways (descriptively). For example, Raiffa auctions off a $10 bill in his MBA classes. Bidders submit written bids; the highest bidder gets the $10 and pays her bid. What should you bid?

Game theory points out that the equilibrium bid is $9.99. The asymmetrically normative approach chooses the best bid using data on previous bids, or a guess based on a descriptive theory, to predict how others will bid. If you are one of two bidders, the profit-maximizing bid is around $7.60 (given observed bids, according to Raiffa, private communication). With three bidders, you should bid $8.40; with four, bid $9.20. Note that bids do converge to the $9.99 benchmark if the number of bidders is large (and they converge if the auction is repeated). But taking game theory too seriously and bidding $9.99 immediately is a mistake during the *process* of convergence.

Obviously, having a good descriptive theory is crucial to the asymmetrically normative approach. (The $10 bidding example is helped by having a large sample of past bids.) Analytic game theory is useful because it gives us an idea of how to behave in the limiting case when we suspect other players are rational or have learned to be. While we are far from having a good descriptive theory on which to base symmetrically normative advice, experimental evidence suggests three behavioral principles that give some guidance on how others will play during the process of convergence.

One principle is that players will initially try cooperative strategies, which make everyone better off than under equilibrium strategies if everyone uses them. For example, in Raiffa's $10 auction players start by bidding less than the $9.99 equilibrium, trying to collectively squeeze more profit from the seller than the penny they would get in an equilibrium. In a repeated series of prisoner's dilemmas, cooperation is usually sustained until the end is clearly in sight (e.g., Andreoni and Miller, 1991). In duopoly experiments, subjects often start by restricting supply or fixing high prices to signal cooperation (Plott, 1989). In all three cases, cooperation usually crumbles after a while and play converges to an equilibrium. But cooperating along the convergence path is more profitable than choosing the equilibrium strategy immediately.

A second behavioral principle is that players won't bet confidently on the rationality of others, at first.[16] Ironically, in many settings where players aren't sure others are rational, their doubts are unfounded—others *are* fairly rational. A smart player *should* bet on others being rational, but should not expect others to do the same.

A third behavioral principle is that players don't look very far forward or backward in games. Some colleagues and I have studied subjects' thinking patterns in games using a unique software system. The system hides all the numerical payoffs in a game behind separate boxes, which can be opened using a mouse. Subjects who reason game-theoretically must open certain boxes in a certain order. By observing the boxes they open, we can test whether subjects look forward and backward in the game. They usually don't, but can be taught to (Cachon et al., 1991; Johnson et al., 1991).

Natural illustrations of failures to think ahead are easy to find (see Zajac and Bazerman, 1991). Several years ago, one major airline announced triple-mileage awards to frequent flyers, hoping to grab market share. But their move was quickly matched by the other major airlines. In the end, the first mover got little permanent advantage, overall air travel rose only a little, and the airlines are now stuck with billions of miles pay-

---

[16] In Beard and Beil (1990) subjects play the following game:

		player 2	
		l	r
player 1	L	7,3	7,3
	R	3,4.75	10,5

The first (second) payoff in each pair is player 1's (2's). Note that r is a dominant strategy for player 2 (it always pays at least as much as l). In fact, player 2 actually plays the dominant strategy r 97% of the time. But about 20% of the subjects in the role of player 1 play L, earning a sure $7, because they are unwilling to risk earning only $3, for a chance at earning $10, by choosing R and betting that their opponent is rational enough to play r.

able. If the first mover had looked further ahead in the game, and anticipated the competitive reaction, the mileage war might never have occurred. (The war might still have occurred, if all players anticipated it but overestimated their own chances of winning.) Apparently the airlines haven't learned much: a few years later several of them became embroiled in a 2-for-1 fare war very similar to the triple-mileage war (*Philadelphia Inquirer*, 1990).

Conclusion

The answer to my title question is: it wouldn't hurt. Game theory is best used to work out the logical implications of the decision process in which rational players think hard about what they can expect each other to do. Those logical implications should certainly be of interest to strategy researchers, since many aspects of strategy formulation (*and* implementation) fit the game-theoretic template. But they are not the only strategic thought processes of interest.

My main point in this paper is that common criticisms of game theory are not the deepest criticisms. Recent game theory (post-1970) does not, as critics have charged, neglect dynamics, require all players to see the world in the same way, or exclude pre-game communication. The criticism that game-theoretic analyses assume too much rationality of players is often misguided since strong rationality assumptions are not always needed, and equilibrium analysis may be worth doing since even boundedly rational players can reach an equilibrium through adaptation or other mechanisms. (Whether adaptation is likely to occur in unique encounters between firms, or in repeated encounters where learning tries to outrun environmental change, are important empirical questions strategy researchers could help answer.)

Other criticisms are deeper. I distinguished four problems to make strategy researchers tread carefully in their use of game theory: a chopstick problem (game-theoretic models are too hard to use); a collage problem (the models form an incoherent collage, suggesting no general principles); a testing problem (the models are hard to test); and a Pandora's box problem (the models can explain anything). The chopstick problem can be overcome by education, practice, and (possibly) by software. The collage problem and the testing problem present opportunities for empirical strategy research to test game theories in a unique way, but only if researchers turn from broad cross-sectional tests to more specialized longitudinal studies with finer-grained observation. The Pandora's box problem will take theoretical discipline and empirical constraint—supplied, perhaps, by strategy research.

Appendix: A Brief Glossary of Game Theory Terms

Here is an imprecise glossary of game-theoretic terms which could prove useful for strategy research. See Rasmusen (1989) and other sources in note 3 for more detailed discussions.

A (Nash) *equilibrium* occurs when each player's action is rational, given the other players' (equilibrium) actions. A *pooling* equilibrium occurs when players with different privately known information or utilities (different "types") choose the same action; a *separating* equilibrium occurs when they choose different actions. The *battle of the sexes* is a particular game in which there are two equilibria, one of which is better for each player. (By moving first, a player can reach the equilibrium, which is better for her.) *Rationalizable* strategies are those which are optimal, for some beliefs about the choices others are likely to make, provided one does not expect others to choose a *dominated* strategy (i.e., a strategy which is never better, and sometimes worse, than another strategy). *Coordination* games are those with multiple equilibria—the battle of the sexes is an example—in which players strive to agree on one equilibrium because out-of-equilibrium responses hurt everyone. *Reputation*, in game theory, is the common perception of another player's privately known type. A *trigger strategy* in a repeated game is a strategy which chooses an action that punishes another player for breaking an unspoken agreement; tit-for-tat is one well-known example. The *folk theorem* is a group of theorems showing that in repeated games, virtually any outcome can be sustained as an equilibrium.

7

Burning Your Britches Behind You: Can Policy Scholars Bank on Game Theory?

Steven Postrel

> The trouble with game theory is that it can explain anything. If a bank president was standing in the street and lighting his pants on fire, some game theorist would explain it as rational.
>
> —Richard Rumelt, discussion
> comment, at the Fundamental
> Issues in Strategy: A Research
> Conference, Napa, California, 1990.

Is game theory too adaptable for its own good? Researchers have already proved a "folk theorem" stating that any outcome in the range from total cooperation to total defection is possible in the repeated prisoner's dilemma. Now Rumelt has proposed what might be called the Flaming Trousers Conjecture: that there exists a reasonable game-theoretic model in which it is optimal for bank presidents to set their pants on fire in public. This is a special case of what Colin Camerer (Chapter 6, this volume) has called the Pandora's box problem, and certainly would qualify as a case of "intelligent men and ludicrous outcomes" (Rasmusen, 1989:14). In the interests of science, I will now attempt to verify Rumelt's conjecture.

Suppose that depositor services are experience goods, the quality of which (e.g., accuracy, helpfulness, and speed) can be ascertained only after putting one's money into a bank. Quality is exogenous and unchangeable by managers (say, for example, that it is determined by employee ability which is not observable at the time of hiring, or by unalterable organizational "culture"). Word of mouth among consumers is assumed not to be an effective transmitter of reputation, either because talking about your bank is too boring for polite company or because consumers don't trust one another's judgment. Bank presidents know their own bank's quality, and they are paid a share of profits. Interest rates and other nonquality dimensions of banking are assumed to be common and fixed across all banks.

For simplicity, let there be two periods and let the service quality Q be either high, H, or low, L; consumer utility follows the relation $u(H) > u(L)$, where $u(Q)$ is the one-period utility of having an account with a bank of quality Q, so that consumers will always want to switch from a low-quality bank before the second period. There are M consumers. It is common prior knowledge that half of the 2N banks that exist at the beginning of the game are high-quality. Bank president utility is given by $sR(Q)(x_1 + x_2) - Jz$, where s is the president's share of profits (common across all banks), $R(Q)$ is the one-period profit on a depositor's account conditional on the level of service quality, x_i is the number of depositors attracted in period i, J is an indicator variable that takes the value one if the president sets his pants on fire in public and zero otherwise, and z is the private disutility to the president of burning his trousers (including pants replacement cost).

At the outset of the first period, bank presidents either do or do not set their pants aflame publicly. Consumers then choose where to open accounts; if a consumer is indifferent to the entire set of banks, he is equally likely to go to any of them. Appropriate profits and utilities are then earned, and each consumer learns the quality of his bank. At the outset of the second period, each consumer can costlessly switch to another bank. Profits and utility are again accrued.

We look for a "separating equilibrium": a situation in which all high-quality banks have smoldering presidents and get customers for two periods, while the presidents of low-quality banks do not burn and never have any customers. For a customer, the proposed equilibrium strategy is, "Deposit in the first period in a bank whose president has burned his pants. If the bank is low-quality, switch in the second period to another bank with a president who burned his pants." For such an equilibrium to hold, it must not pay for any president of a low-quality bank to burn his pants and fool customers for one period: $sR(L)(M/N) - z < 0$. Conversely, the president of each high-quality bank must find flaming trousers to be an acceptable price to pay for getting two periods worth of business: sR(H)(2M/N) − z > 0. Both conditions hold if and only if 2sR(H) > zN/M > sR(L), so that the one-period profit margin from serving a customer is at least half as big for a high-quality bank as for a low-quality one, and the disutility of burning one's pants in public multiplied by N/M is intermediate between these two quantities. Thus, there exists a subgame perfect Bayesian Nash equilibrium of this game in which bank presidents publicly set their pants on fire. QED.

The Flaming Trousers equilibrium is similar to the "burning money" story of advertising in Nelson (1974), which has been elaborated by Schmalensee (1978b) and further explored by Milgrom and Roberts (1986).[1] More generally, what I have done here has been done in hundreds of papers: start with a phenomenon one wishes to explain, then specify a game in which the phenomenon emerges in equilibrium. Try to make the rules of the game resemble, in a stylized way, the conditions surrounding the phenomenon, while keeping things simple enough for easy solution. Look for an intelligible story that provides "intuition" for the equilibrium (e.g., "The presidents of high-quality banks wish to distinguish themselves from low-quality banks, so they send out a costly signal that is profitable only for a bank that can get repeat business"). Finally, add whatever texture is needed to keep the results from being too extreme. In this case, one could add (by assumption) some customers who are unresponsive to quality (they want nearness) so that the low-quality banks have some business in equilibrium.

The only deviation from accepted practice here is that I have started with a counterfactual phenomenon. Okay, make that an *intendedly* counterfactual phenomenon; I can't vouch for the existence of a number of unlikely things that have been "explained" in the literature, such as predatory pricing. *The point is that game theory does not, of itself, contain a substantive account of behavior.* Game models are extremely sensitive to assumptions about information, the order of moves, constraints on action, and players' beliefs. Yet these assumptions, not game logic itself, are the real substance of a theory of business compe-

---

[1] For a discussion of such models, see Tirole (1988:118–121). This is by no means the unique rational model of burning pants; were the phenomenon actually observed, the creative imaginations of economists would generate many more explanatory stories, not to mention amendments and generalizations to the signaling tale described above.

tition. Game theory is no more a theory of business behavior than calculus is a theory of consumer behavior.

What game theory does provide is a set of tools and components for the construction of logically consistent models of rational human action. These enable the theorist to rule out explanations of behavior in which people act against their own objectives, neglect opportunities, or ignore the strategic behavior of other parties. The discipline exercised by game theory upon the theorist's speculations is quite real, but it is not a discipline that leads to particular empirical conclusions; rather, it is a constraint on stories and explanations. This constraint has real value: the theorist is often surprised to discover that a favorite story does not work as originally imagined. Once the order of moves and strategy spaces has been clearly specified, it may become apparent that a different mechanism will be needed. A good example was the discovery that limit pricing to deter entry makes little sense unless there is asymmetric information about industry demand or cost conditions. Loose discussions of limit pricing as a means to exploit "market power" were thereby completely transformed.

Scholars of strategic management have something to gain from a knowledge of game theory, partly because our theories and prescriptions too often fail to ask questions like What will happen if all firms act sensibly? or Why do we believe that some particular asymmetry between firms constitutes an entry barrier? Some of our most popular stories may have to be modified in the light of game-theoretic scrutiny. But the imaginary spectacle of bank presidents igniting their pants should serve as a reminder that game theory, by itself, is not a theory of business strategy; it is only a set of logical tools that constrain and shape our arguments.

Part II

Why Are Firms Different?

Interest in this question tends to be a litmus test for interest in the economic perspective. It is economics that sees competition, not as a struggle for influence or as a type of warfare, but rather as a process through which societies discover and disseminate efficient ways of doing things. In addition, it is economics that views the firm, not as the shadow of an individual or as a miniature society, with all the idiosyncratic features that individuals and societies possess, but rather as a mechanism for hiring factors of production and combining them to generate outputs. In this perspective, some factors of production (e.g., purchased inputs) may be both rare and especially productive, but it is the factors, not the firm, that receive rents. Can this perspective be reconciled with the obvious empirical facts that firms in the same line of business differ from one another, that these differences persist over long periods of time, that significant differences in efficiency are rarely attributable to identifiable purchased inputs, and that these differences in efficiency generate substantial and sustained rents?

The first theory offered to address this question was that of the experience curve. According to Henderson (1979), firms differed in efficiency because their histories of production differed. Firms with more useful experience in producing a product (or portion of a product) would have, Henderson argued, lower average unit costs. Thus, efficiency is related to an intangible asset which cannot be purchased or easily replicated, and differences in efficiency are reconciled with competitive equilibrium. The argument that fundamental strategic advantage arises out of what has been *done* rather than out of what is *known* remains a cornerstone in a great deal of strategic thinking. Whether the context is core competence or product development, current thinkers stress the fact that sustained differences in performance derive from different histories of activity, and not simply from differences in the allocation combination of resources.

A second popular theoretical explanation for sustained differences in performance relates them to market positions and timing. Thus, if the relationships between market size, scale economies, and the durability of specialized investment are suitable, the first firm to commit specialized resources to a submarket may continue to dominate that niche for a considerable time. Somewhat more subtle, but logically identical, stories can be told about the creation of reputations for quality or integrity. In these cases the firm's efficiency is a result of its position rather than vice versa. This line of reasoning is at the heart of industrial organization explanations for heterogeneity within industries, the classic paper being that by Caves and Porter (1977).

A third explanation for sustained heterogeneity is causal ambiguity or uncertain imitability (Lippman and Rumelt, 1982). According to this theory, the reasons for many important differences in efficiency or performance are not well understood, even by those who possess them. This fundamental ambiguity sharply limits any firm's ability to emulate best practice. Thus, one of the key processes generating variety also acts to limit its equilibration through imitation.

Once we abandon rational maximizing assumptions, the range of explanation for heterogeneity dramatically expands. Firms faced with the same situation may act differently due to differences in beliefs, differences in aspirations, or differences in the administrative processes producing decisions. Similarly, firms (or their managers) may fail to adopt best practice because they do not perceive it, because they do not like it, or because of internal organizational impediments to change.

It should be clear by now that there is no shortage of explanations for why firms are different. What is needed is wisdom regarding which explanations are likely to be the most important, views that synthesize and integrate, and, finally, empirical work that shows which phenomena are most important in various contexts. Happily, our three papers on this subject each make a substantial contribution. In the first paper, "Strategy and the Search for Rents: The Evolution of Diversity among Firms," Williams combines the behavioral theory of the firm with more modern perspectives. He defines a firm as an evolving collection of capabilities and paints a picture of the firm as searching for rents rather than as making decisions. Whereas the search paradigm in economics concentrates on the cost of search (or the cost of becoming informed about an option), Williams emphasizes the importance of heterogeneity in beliefs. Firms search in different areas with different strategies, he argues, because managers have differing beliefs about how the world works and about what actions are prudent in any given situation.

In Williams's view, heterogeneity in beliefs is a key ingredient in explaining differences in strategy, but the conditions of sustainability are equally important. Here he makes a useful distinction between slow-, medium-, and fast-cycle environments, arguing that different capabilities and different isolating mechanisms are critical in each. In slow-cycle environments, individual skills are a key source of firm differences, whereas in medium-cycle environments team-coordination skills are central. In fast-cycle environments it is the ability to innovate and adapt that differentiates firms.

In the second paper, "Why Do Firms Differ, and How Does It Matter?" Nelson provides an economist's view, although his view is admittedly that of one of the foremost critics of the neoclassical paradigm. He reviews the basic approach taken by most economists in studying industry, emphasizing the centrality of resource allocation. Nelson sees innovation as central to the social and private performance of firms, and he is led, therefore, to ask an intriguing question: Why are the many studies of innovation in modern economics ultimately so unrevealing? He suggests that the problem derives from the assumption that the choice set facing the firm is obvious. Once this assumption is removed, firms must be seen as groping forward with imperfect views of their situations and their options. Without perfect vision, competition should be seen, he argues, as evolution.

Nelson's paper provides a number of nuggets that should be of great interest to students of strategic management. He defines strategy as a set of commitments that define objectives and that serve to rationalize future decisions. He defines capabilities as a hierarchy of practiced organizational routines. He makes a forceful argument that firms must innovate over time or die. Indeed, he argues that a firm's ability to imitate the innovation of another is limited by its practice at the steps leading up to the innovation; hence, many will be led to build their own innovative paths rather than follow the leader. Finally, Nelson argues that the organizational capabilities that matter, the ones that make a difference in the long run, are those that enhance the firm's ability to innovate.

In the third paper, "A Sociological View on Why Firms Differ," Carroll provides a perspective shaped by his home discipline: organizational ecology. To begin, he makes an important distinction. There are unsurprising differences, he reminds us, among failing firms and between failing firms and successful firms. The interesting question is: Why are *successful* firms different? Carroll cites empirical studies that show that CEOs differ in their beliefs, expectations, and basic personality profiles. Not only are these differences expressed in decisions, they also affect the organizational forms that are adopted. Thus, especially in entrepreneurial firms, differences in both strategy and structure reflect differences in personality and belief.

In the longer run, Carroll argues, heterogeneity is supported by impediments to adaptation. Among the most important are: (1) differing expectations, (2) uncertain imitability, (3) physical, legal, or financial constraints, (4) organizational or bureaucratic opposition, and (5) the large failure risk associated with any significant change in strategy or structure.

Thus, though the question of why firms in the same industry differ seems simple, its answer proves complex. The question is interesting because differences among competing firms are so obvious and yet, under the assumptions of conventional economic theory, so impossible. By taking different perspectives, and making different assumptions, we see that there are a number of promising avenues for research and further theoretical development which can help explain why differences exist among successful competitive firms.

8
Strategy and the Search for Rents: The Evolution of Diversity among Firms

Jeffrey R. Williams

Introduction

Why are firms different? The question, an extension of Coase's (1937) challenge, "Why do firms exist?," is increasingly at the heart of business strategy. In what follows I have been asked to give my view on how our understanding about the distinctive nature of the firm is evolving—in particular, how it is becoming focused on fine-grained questions of a dynamic nature. What follows is a view on how firms create and destroy rents according to principles that are making business strategy more of a science than it was in the past.

Firms exist as collections of evolving capabilities that are managed dynamically for the purpose of earning rents. Differences among firms arise from the interplay of capabilities, search behavior, and sustainability conditions. As firms attempt to attain their ends, robust differences arise, are nullified, and arise again. An understanding of this dynamic process has great scientific potential; moreover, it can guide the actual practice of business strategy. Considering the firm as a rent-seeking mechanism brings together the interests of the strategy researcher and the manager. Both seek to identify the distinctive character of the firm.

Sidney Winter pointed out at the ninth annual (1989) Strategic Management Society Conference that there is a factor of 100,000 in size between the largest and smallest firms in our economy and that this and other measures of diversity are growing. Economic growth in a free economy, it is argued, leads to greater and greater division of capital and labor. Indeed, specialization, the complex mosaic of market imperfections associated with economic advance, is the foundation of wealth creation.[1]

Still, if we succeed too well in seeking to emphasize diversity, we discover that every firm is ultimately distinct. We end up with an unwieldy structure that is of limited use for advancing theory or practice. In the physical sciences, Harre (1985: 102) describes a similar challenge: "Diversity of materials is explained by treating the diversity as due to differences in structure among a small number of more basic materials. . . . Each is composed of molecules which are different combinations of atoms of a smaller number of basic materials. . . . [By probing deeper into these basic materials, perhaps scientists] hope in the end to reduce all diversity to structural diversity of combinations of only one kind of ultimate stuff."

What is the "ultimate stuff" of strategy? The argument put forth here is that the basic material is the idiosyncratic character of the firm. Yet, as Nelson and Winter (1982) have argued, the firm's production set and its decision rules are interdependent. Further, capabilities operate in time; that is, they are created and destroyed, and perhaps in ways not unlike processes in the physical sciences. But in contrast to the physical sciences, the competitive systems in which firms operate are continually reshaped by purposeful, adaptive search behavior.

Rents arise through purposeful action, but rents also arise through chance and uncertainty. Search behavior is the process of discovering and exploiting rent-earning opportunities from any source, including uncertainty. As I will suggest, rent-earning capabilities (the idiosyncratic character of the firm), rent-search behavior, and sustainability conditions (rent appropriability) are interdependent; they derive their distinctive character from one another. By studying how organizations and markets are dynamically interdependent, we can improve our

---

[1]   Although often associated with market failures, market imperfections are market failures only in the sense that they are departures from the model of perfect competition. As Yao (1988) argues, market imperfections are at the root of many unanswered questions in strategy, and arguably, economics. Scitovsky (1990: 148) puts it this way: "General equilibrium theory, which deals with an imaginary economy modeled on commodity exchanges, had good reason to ignore the social benefits of non-price competition. But for those who seek to understand the real economy in all its depth and complexity, the benefits of monopolistic, asymmetric, non-price competition cannot be ignored."

Figure 8-1
Capability Formation, Search Behavior, and Sustainability Conditions
Determining Diversity among Firms

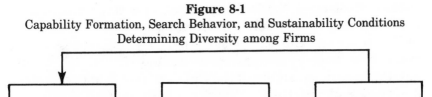

knowledge of organizational processes, market outcomes, and differences among firms (see Figure 8-1).

Capability Formation

The neoclassical view sees firms as identical and information as costless, and it relies on opportunity sets that can be specified. The theory of perfect competition, which yields an equilibrium of zero profits, gave way early on to modeling the firm as a mechanism to restrain output through monopoly or collusion. Under the Mason/Bain structure-conduct-performance paradigm (Mason, 1939; Bain, 1956), firm differences are few; they are limited to differences in size, product differentiation, and vertical integration. Competitive behavior is more or less limited to pricing and advertising. Differences that matter are market share and industry concentration.

Schumpeter (1934, 1942) emphasized that the better questions are of a dynamic nature. Firms are different because of "new methods of production . . . new markets . . . [and] new forms of organization" (1934: 82). Firms are seekers and destroyers of continually evolving sources of advantage. However, because "the gale of creative destruction," as Schumpeter wrote, is inherently unknowable, firms need a guaranteed source of rents. Monopoly power serves a socially useful good where it encourages innovation.

The Chicago school's view (Stigler, 1968b) is that differentiated firms yield beneficial effects to society. Collusion is possible, but monitoring and enforcement costs limit it. Market outcomes, size, and profit differences result from efficiency differences in capabilities. Differences among firms arise where costs of acquiring and processing information are high. The purpose of advertising, for example, is not to extract rents, but to provide a way for customers to learn about quality differences. Still, within the Chicago school, efficiency differences mainly result from scale economies. As Teece and Winter (1984) point out, this limits the ability of the Chicago view to uncover robust differences among firms.

The major advance in examining the question of why firms are different came through Coase's (1937) original proposition that firms exist where they can lower the costs of production and market exchange. Differences among and within firms arise where and when the benefits of internal market exchange are realized, i.e., the point at which internal exchange equals the benefits provided by the open market, or the costs of organizing another firm.

Williamson (1975, 1989) identifies three types of market exchange in which this will happen: (1) where assets are uniquely dependent upon each other for their value, (2) where the market between assets is thin, and (3) where knowledge about performance is costly to obtain. According to Williamson, differences among firms arise where combinations of asset specificity, small numbers, or imperfect information prevail. Briefly then, the main contributions toward determining why firms are different derive from the Coase/Williamson and Schumpeterian views, with a lesser contribution from the Chicago school (Conner, 1991).

Still, the argument about whether industry structure or firm capability matters more in explaining performance is far from resolved. Schmalensee (1985) and Wernerfelt and Montgomery (1988) have shown that industry structure is important to performance. However, by looking at data with a methodology designed to reveal firm differences, Rumelt (1991) found that profit levels are highly sensitive to the idiosyncratic character of firms. He concludes that fundamental sources of rent are business specific.

In support of the latter view, Jacobson (1988) and Jacobson and Aaker (1985) find that return on investment is only weakly correlated with market share, and that a predominance of unobservable, firm-specific factors are present. Hansen and Wernerfelt (1989) argue that important differences can be organizational in nature. Research on the insurance industry (Fiegenbaum and Thomas, 1990) and in pharmaceuticals (Cool and Schendel, 1987) supports the distinctive character of the firm. Early on, Hatten and Schendel (1977) pointed the way in their studies of the brewing industry.

The evidence can be seen as illustrating the tenet that you find what you are looking for. Two-thirds of the U.S. economy now relies on service- and information-based firms, but only one-third of the Standard Industrial Classification (SIC) codes recognize this. (SIC codes do not even exist for business units with complex market imperfections, such as those in the computer and telecommunications industries.) The Commerce Department has recently concluded that traditional methods used to categorize companies are woefully out of date, including the SIC, which downplays firm differences. Ravenscraft and Wagner (1991) have rethought the role of the FTC's line-of-business data. Foremost among their conclusions is the need for more fine-grained research. They cite Coase in support of their conclusion (1991: 717).

> What is wanted in industrial organization is a direct approach to the problem. This would concentrate on what activities firms undertake, and it would endeavor to discover the characteristics of the groupings of activities within firms. Which activities tend to be associated and which do not? The answer may well differ for different kinds of firms; for example, for firms of different size, or for those with a different corporate structure, or for firms in different industries. It is not possible to forecast what will prove to be of importance before such an investigation is carried out; which is, of course, why it is needed.

Early strategy writers like Learned, Christensen, Andrews, and Guth (1965), Selznik (1957), and Ansoff (1965) stressed the distinctive character of firms. Wernerfelt (1984) revitalized this view by arguing that analysis of competition in product markets must be augmented with analysis of competition in resource markets. Resources may be intangible, and include property rights (Alchian and Demsetz, 1972), but they also include firm reputation (Klein and Leffler, 1981; Kreps and Wilson, 1982) and firm-specific knowledge of buyers and sellers, or employee capabilities (Prescott and Visscher, 1980).

Firms may also combine otherwise nondistinct resources in unique ways. Penrose (1959) was among the first to stress corporatewide capabilities. The idea was expanded into Nelson and Winter's (1982) concept of firm routines, or team-embodied (rather than individual) capabilities. Variations on this theme have been worked out by Huff (1982), Prahalad and Bettis

(1986), Aaker (1989), and Spender (1989). Implicit in these writings is the role of corporate culture (Camerer and Vepsalainen, 1988)—where it occurs inadvertently (Arrow, 1974; Hayek, 1978) or where it is exceedingly complex or invisible (Itami, 1987). Most recently, attention has turned to the role of co-specialized assets (Teece, 1987) and core competencies (Prahalad and Hamel, 1990) in making the firm more than the arithmetic sum of individual elements.

Williamson (1985) suggests that the character of the firm is linked to the process of "fundamental transformation," whereby ex ante large numbers and competitive, non-rent-generating assets are transformed into ex post small numbers, which are more imperfect and are well suited to generating rents in a firm's specific environment. Henderson (1989) has long stressed the dynamic, Darwinian nature of distinctive processes: no two competing organizations can earn rents in exactly the same way.

Barney (1986) argues that if we think of the firm's input markets as strategic factors (to be purchased at low prices), superior rents can only be earned when firms hold different expectations about the value of such resources (or where luck dominates). Dierickx and Cool (1989) take the argument deeper within firms. They argue that rents are created through "flows," difficult-to-imitate internal processes that augment spot purchases of "stocks" in otherwise competitive strategic factor markets.

Most writers agree that the most fundamental, and inherently unknowable, source of capabilities is entrepreneurial activities (Guth and Ginsberg, 1990). These are distinguished from important, but "knowably innovative" activities, such as the learning curve, by a predominance of uncertainty (Knight, 1965). Central for strategy is the question, Is it possible to sustain rents through purely entrepreneurial activities?

Schumpeter argued that it was not possible. Barney argues that it is impossible as well; any logically formulated set of rules that can systematically create advantage is inherently self-destructive, i.e., they will be copied and become part of expectations used in strategic factor market pricing. Dierickx and Cool leave us more room to explore this question; by turning their focus on the innermost dynamic processes of firms (time compression diseconomies, asset mass efficiencies, interconnectedness), they suggest that rents may be sustained where asset accumulation and regeneration processes are private but knowable within the firm.

Can the success of firms like Intel and Sony in Schumpeterian-like industries be seen as evidence that entrepreneurial activities sustain advantage? Or do entrepreneurial firms survive, as Schumpeter said, only if they have access to other, more stable sources of rent? Perhaps such environments are not as creatively destructive as generally assumed, or maybe some firms are lucky. The possibility that intrigues me, and one that I will explore next, is that firms can sustain rents in uncertain environments through superior search behavior.

Search Behavior

As the firm searches for rents from unique capabilities, a second source of diversity is that no two managers make decisions in quite the same way. This has been shown to be true in controlled experiments, even when managers possess similar endowments and are presented with nearly the same information. After studying 500 managers, MacCrimmon and Wehrung (1990) conclude that managers vary greatly in their disposition toward uncertainty. Search behavior can be thought of as arising whenever project value: (1) is not understood; (2) is misrepresented, as occurs when the discount rate employed in evaluation is higher or lower than the project's actual cost of capital; or (3) cannot be justified by traditional financial analysis.

On the occasion of his Nobel award, Simon (1978) noted that to the extent that bounds to rational behavior are present—and he argued that they are present in many cases—search cannot be conducted in a systematic way. Often, the problem-solving domain cannot even be specified. This is a principle in the behavioral theory of the firm (Cyert and March, 1963). As search behavior begins to influence decision making, the probability increases that otherwise identical outcomes will diverge.

That search behavior and environment are strongly interdependent is increasingly recognized. Alchian and Woodward (1988) propose that in idiosyncratic environments it is transaction-specific labor that hires capital, not the other way around. Demsetz and Lehn (1985) suggest that noisier environments give rise to more concentrated governance structures. Morone and Paulson (1991) believe that cost-of-capital use differs widely, even within capital-intensive industries. Where projects contain many real-asset options, as for rapid innovation, traditional search heuristics can bias managers toward disinvestment. In these settings, traditional investment criteria may destroy the very sources of value they are intended to identify (Kaplan, 1986).

Ghemawat (1991) argues that in extended rivalry, rents accrue to firms that excel at making decisions that require long-run, irreversible commitments. By contrast, in Schumpeterian-like markets, Eisenhardt (1990) has found that the ability to make decisions that are compressed in time is more critical to sustaining advantage. Bourgeois and Eisenhardt (1988) have discovered the value of processing a greater number of alternatives in these settings, rather than fewer. In all cases it seems the ecological character of the firm's environment dictates the heuristics used to conduct search, a theme that underlies work by Shoemaker (1990) and by Pfeffer and Salancik (1978) in their seminal book on resource dependency.

Even game theory, that repository of rational behavior, has made advances in modeling decision making based on beliefs (Fisher, 1989; Shapiro, 1989). In all cases, equilibrium is achieved within models that are well specified; beliefs and actions of decision makers are known and converge, with limiting values depending upon the particular problem and path providing the equilibrium. But what if the model is misspecified? Nyarko (1990) points out that when decision makers' parameters lie outside their expectations, the solution to the game is characterized by endless search cycles, in which the actions and beliefs of the decision maker move back and forth forever. Lippman and Rumelt (1982) show how, by introducing ambiguity into the manager's knowledge of how a firm replicates itself, even identical firms can coexist in an otherwise perfectly competitive equilibrium, with both earning above-normal rates of return.

Mintzberg and Waters (1978) and Mintzberg (1987a) point out that to understand strategy we must recognize that strategy is a process of crafting, based on attitudes and perceptions. Beliefs are not readily observed and not easily monitored. Their very existence remains submerged in the specification of the search process unless special efforts are undertaken to reveal them (Sterman, 1989; Gioia and Chittipeddi, 1991). Work that characterizes beliefs as resulting from a cumulative Bayesian process

(Howard, 1989) serves to reinforce the message; beliefs, like capabilities, are path-dependent, contingent on the life experiences of the manager.

Beliefs generate entrepreneurial activities, and thus, leadership. Hambrick (1989: 5) puts it this way: "In the face of the complex, multitudinous and ambiguous information that typifies the top management task, no two strategists will identify the same array of options for the firm. They will rarely prefer the same options. If, by remote chance, they were to pick the same options, they almost certainly would not implement them identically. Biases, blinders, egos, aptitudes, experiences, fatigue and other human factors in the executive ranks greatly affect what happens to companies." In uncertain environments, managers may achieve the distinction of "leader" through chance. In these cases, does leadership not matter? Even in a purely random game, leadership can also be defined as the ability to recognize and act quickly upon opportunities as they arise.

A universal theme in search behavior is expressed by Cyert and Simon (1983: 236): "Substantially all assumptions of market imperfections and 'sticky' adjustments are assumptions of behavioral rules attuned to imperfections of rationality." The job of the social scientist "is to demonstrate through the use of all the knowledge available why the firm stops its search process when it does; to explain how all of the forces within the organization as well as the market have combined to make the level of investment in the plant what it is." Robert Hayes (1985: 118) affirms that "real strategic advantage comes from changing the way a company behaves, a task far more difficult and time-consuming than simply making a few structural decisions. . . . Do not develop plans and then seek capabilities; instead, build capabilities and then encourage the development of plans for exploiting them."

Sustainability Conditions

Organizations and markets evolve according to a central law of competition—the expectation of profits attracts imitators. Observation of the world around us reveals that many ingredients of rivalry are linked to universal processes of convergence. The idea, of course, is centrally Schumpeterian, as Nelson and Winter stress in their evolutionary theory. But here we can ask:

Are Schumpeterian processes uniform across firms—or do firms differ for reasons of imitation? As McGee and Thomas (1989: 106) put it, "Are firms more or less competitive because their assets are different? . . . [Or are] patterns of rivalry and oligopolistic reaction functions . . . a function of underlying asset structures?"

A primary component of dynamic rivalry is learning. Spence (1981) suggested that different market structures might result from different rates of learning and appropriability. But we also know that organizations "forget"; knowledge has a tendency to depreciate unless it is reinforced through practice (Argote, Beckman, and Epple, 1990). Learning also leaks out, is adopted, and "sticks" at different rates in firms. Winter's (1987) study of R&D executives shows considerable variation in this regard. In commercial banking, response lags also vary greatly, from six to 36 months, for innovations that otherwise ought to disperse at the same rate (MacMillan et al., 1985). Cohen and Levinthal (1990) have formalized a link between imitative learning and capabilities in terms they describe as the firms' "absorptive capacity."

Consider a hypothetical case in which three firms introduce a product—a software program for tracking customer orders—that is broadly similar except for factors associated with speed and appropriability of learning. In the first firm, a systems software house, the program is interwoven with a customized order-entry and tracking system for a long-standing customer. The relationship with the customer is complex, with systems requirements and firm-specific capabilities to be uncovered and coded. Programmers working on the project in both firms come to know and trust each other. In the second case, the firm distributes its software to the mass market, as part of its larger product line of company-branded software distributed through nationwide retailers. In the third case, the firm places advertisements in trade catalogues, sells by phone, and offers discounts on demonstration copies to encourage sales.

In the case of the catalogue company, sales grow fast. However, the catalogue firm soon finds that competitors are offering knockoff software that replicates the features of the original program at deep discounts. Margin pressure becomes severe as sales decline. As time passes, the second company, the mass market distributor, comes under price pressure, but because its software is bundled with other programs it can use its bargaining power with retailers to mitigate that pressure. In the case of the first company, the systems software house, as time passes its software becomes tightly interwoven, part of a complex, bilateral relationship with its client company that evolves into a quasi-vertical relationship. The systems software house experiences fewest competitive pressures.

Rumelt (1987) suggests that differences in sustainability conditions such as those I have characterized here can be classified according to the relative influence of "isolating mechanisms"— factors that retard imitation. A few of the categories include information impactedness, response lags, economies of scale, producer learning, buyer switching costs, reputation, communication effects, buyer evaluation costs, advertising, and channel crowding. Teece (1987) adds that, depending on the complementary relationship between the innovation and firm capabilities (general, specialized, or co-specialized), imitative effects will differ for firms that commercialize an otherwise similar innovation.

If isolating mechanisms are the firm-level equivalent of entry barriers, they must be a constituent of firm diversity. But unlike entry barriers, isolating mechanisms operate in time. To expand on the implications, I have found it useful to characterize firms in terms of their place along a competitive imitability spectrum. Here, depending on appropriability conditions, we can imagine appropriability and rivalry ranging from static (slow cycle), through traditional (standard cycle), to dynamic (fast cycle).

In slow-cycle rivalry, firms rely on the creative talents of individuals to produce idiosyncratic, one-of-a-kind products and services. These firms have inherently isolated capabilities. Because rents do not depend on high-volume replication, i.e., economies of scale, slow-cycle markets are fragmented; but, in contrast to the traditional view of low-profit fragmentation, slow-cycle firms can earn significant rents.[2] For example, the structure of the defense industry in the United States has remained fragmented since World War II, but with hundreds of profitable firms. Consistent with the "no free lunch" maxim, growth barri-

---

[2] It can be argued that slow-cycle settings benefit from localized scale economies, as in the case of hub-controlling airlines and defense contractors. For my purposes, the distinction turns on the ease with which the routines internalized by slow-cycle firms can be transferred to standard-cycle organizations and conversely. I believe transference to be quite difficult.

ers created by idiosyncratic capabilities are strong, even when such firms may wish to grow, and duplication of their capabilities can be difficult. Thus, in ecological terms—in an argument similar to the one made by Carroll (1985)—firms in slow-cycle environments are different because they must be. Resource dependence is high. Durability of rents, and fragmented industry structure, is a direct function of irreproducibility of capabilities.

In standard-cycle rivalry, firms pursue distinctive capabilities that are shaped by extended rivalry. Here, coordination of large teams of workers and complex, volume-based production processes are required to serve mass markets, as in the production of automobiles, or the mass-market activities associated with financial services and the consumer products industries. Firms employ classical search procedures of the kind documented in Porter's (1979, 1980) influential treatment of oligopolistic rivalry and Chandler's (1990a) comprehensive history of scale and scope in American industry. These studies show that market leaders must maneuver carefully. Even the slightest deviation from market standards, misalignments between internal requirements and customer needs, can lead to losses. Holiday Corporation found it necessary to drop some 300 nonconforming hotels from its chain in order to strengthen customer brand perceptions of its 1,400 remaining hotels. Mobility is limited (Caves and Porter, 1977). This is especially so because long-run commitment is required to sustain scale advantage (Caves, 1980; Porter, 1985; Ghemawat 1991).

In fast-cycle rivalry, firms seek rents in Schumpeterian-like environments. Innovations are freestanding, that is, they do not benefit from strong isolating mechanisms, or complementary assets (like personal relationships, economies of scale), which can slow down the ability of rivals to duplicate innovation. Examples include semiconductor memory devices, electronic chemicals, and consumer products like cellular telephones, facsimile machines, and compact disk players. Initially, firms compete based on their capabilities at R&D or marketing. Next comes a follower stage, where the idea is copied and firms dominate through manufacturing and distribution. Finally, at a third stage, an adopter stage, firms earn rents by adding ideas from outside the original industry to what have become zero-rent technologies (such as Reebok molding the once-pioneering computer chip into the soles of its running shoes to give runners information on distance, elapsed effort, and so forth). Because market evolution is so quick, fast-cycle products "pass through" firms quickly; rents are earned by focusing on the stage of a product's life cycle—innovator, follower, or adopter—that matches the more stable capabilities of the firm.

The Evolution of Diversity among Firms

A higher-order source of diversity is change in sustainability conditions. Tushman, Newman, and Romanelli (1986) have compared the organizational challenges created by a shift from change that is continuous to change that is frame-breaking. Second-order sustainability conditions, or frame-breaking change, arise through shocks in the political environment (AT&T under deregulation), changes in technology (RCA in vacuum tubes and IBM in computers), or management innovation (McDonald's in the lunchcounter industry). In a study of discontinuities in financial services, Sipple (1989) found that some firms changed their organization and culture easily while others exhibited extreme resistance to change. Firms can break away from their histories, but only at great risk and with great effort, as Miles and Snow (1984) point out. As firms evolve, strategy is responsible for what amounts to an exceedingly complex problem of dynamic investment and control (Bower, 1970; Schendel and Patton, 1978; Hidding, 1992).

In the airline industry under deregulation (Bailey and Williams, 1988), some carriers entered the deregulatory period with a slow-cycle capability honed in thin monopoly routes. One carrier, USAir, increased its control of gates in Pittsburgh from 60% to 82%, allowing it to price high with little concern for quality or competitive entry. Carriers like American and United, with large routes in place at the time of deregulation, sought to extend their long-haul endowments to enhance economies of scale. The latter class of firms would, for example, be the first to pursue innovations tied to economies of scale, e.g., reservations systems and frequent flyer programs, as a means of strengthening standard-cycle barriers to entry. A new entrant, People Express, offered a "cheap seat" strategy. In response, incumbents innovated their own cheap seats; low-cost excess capacity made available through forward pricing (Super Saver seats). The capability of People Express was, for a time, unique, but it was readily imitated and People's advantage was not sustainable. Within a few years of deregulation, the airline industry evolved into a rich dispersion of cost and differentiation (Karnani, 1984), with varying levels of sustainability.

Search behavior plays a role in explaining divergent outcomes where firms face similar opportunities. Otherwise, how could we explain why Frontier Airlines chose to abandon its strong hub control in Denver (a position similar to USAir's control in Pittsburgh) in pursuit of nationwide dominance? (An inability to achieve efficiencies in nationwide operations led Frontier to bankruptcy.) The answer lies in the search behavior of Frontier's management—perhaps they had been schooled only in the virtues of traditional oligopolistic rivalry.

Discussions with thoughtful executives make clear that they act as though the emergence of even the slightest differences among them and their rivals can change outcomes dramatically. This is especially true for successful businesses. The evidence is overwhelming in this regard: when a firm strays into a new environment without successfully changing its practices, the odds increase that the firm and its environment will become severely mismatched and performance will suffer. Practices of successful firms are often the most difficult to change.

We might have predicted that when General Mills, which had traditionally operated in standard-cycle consumer foods, entered the fast-cycle fashion business (by purchasing Izod sportswear) and the toy business (Parker Bros. and Kenner Toys), the potential for mismatch would increase.[3] Industry analysts have subsequently found that a chronic problem for General Mills was management's inability to break away from its slower, more analytical upbringing in the food business. One of United Technologies' worst-performing groups in recent years has been its Mostek division, the only fast-cycle business held by an otherwise more stable slow- and standard-cycle corporation.

General Motors' acquisition of Hughes Aircraft provides another illustration; it was argued that as the role of electronics in automobiles grows, there would be an opportunity to transfer technology more efficiently, through internal ownership, from aerospace to automobiles. However, the success of Hughes in

---

[3]   On this and other questions of organizational coherence I have benefited considerably from discussions with Dan Levinthal.

satellites and defense contracting is based on mastery of guild-like, idiosyncratic, slow-cycle routines, with little focus on cost or speed of production. Merging Hughes with General Motors' volume-based, standard-cycle automotive businesses may prove challenging.

The strategic evolution of Westinghouse shows a methodical turn away from standard-cycle businesses, such as appliances and light bulbs. These businesses were replaced with slow-cycle, idiosyncratic businesses (defense electronics, nuclear power, cable TV). Dosi, Teece, and Winter (1990) point out that standard-cycle firms like Mercedes do well in manufacturing automobiles and trucks, but not in slow-cycle markets like aerospace. Similarly, aerospace companies seem to face entry barriers in commercial markets that cannot be explained by technological barriers alone, as in the case of Grumman Aerospace's disastrous expedition into the commercial bus market.

Examples like these are stylized, but they suggest that capability, search, and sustainability are interlocked. As capabilities are formed, dynamic lock-in occurs, both purposefully and by chance, that distinguishes the character of firms and the structure of markets (Williams, 1992). As Teece (1990: 63) points out, historically there has been "a failure of the strategic management literature to partition industry environments according to the nature of the intellectual property regime. This is a critical factor for all industries." Do we have a promising new area of inquiry?

Summary

My purpose has been to say something about "why firms are different" that ties together the thinking of many. I have tried to do this in a way that suggests the dynamic, interlocking character of organizations and markets. However by any measure and in any perspective, interest in the firm, relative to the industry, is growing. Hints of the emerging landscape were contained in Schendel and Hofer's *Strategic Management: A New View of Business Policy and Planning* (1979). Since then, certain core themes have taken on greater clarity. I summarize five of them here.

1. Firms are becoming more, rather than less, distinct. Firms are, after all, structured the way they are only as long as it pays their rent-seeking owners to keep them that way. Thus, it would seem natural that as economies evolve and market imperfections proliferate, so do differences among firms. Current trends toward narrowing of scope, "downsizing," and "corporate unbundling" (Williams, Paez, and Sanders, 1988) are evidence of this. But these trends are especially notable alongside the prevalence of increasingly sophisticated control systems; these should have empowered managers to expand the scope of the firm. Managers certainly don't lack incentives to do so. I think we must conclude that the firm is becoming increasingly specialized.

2. *Firms are different because of the actions of managers.* It seems time to argue that firms do not exist because of markets— rather, markets exist because of firms. In spite of its formidable intellectual underpinnings, neoclassical economic theory did not predict, and cannot now explain, how otherwise late, disadvantaged entrants, the Japanese in particular, could come to challenge and overtake dominant American firms in such a short time, or for that matter, in any time frame. If industry structure (size, advertising, signaling, and collusion) was the stuff of strategy, General Motors would still command 60% of the North American market for automobiles and Texas Instruments would still lead the world in semiconductor innovation. Simon (1991: 41) puts it clearly: "Modern industrial societies are better understood not as market economies, but as organizational economies."

3. *Firms are different because of the effects of time.* We simply cannot understand important, robust differences in firms unless we model the fundamental questions within a dynamic calculus.[4] Questions in strategy—why firms are different, how firms behave, how the strategy process affects strategy outcomes, how the headquarters unit functions—are influenced by the effects of time. Mahoney (1991: 39) has found that Alfred Marshall (1890) emphasized this a century ago: "Time is the center of the chief difficulty of almost every strategic problem. . . . Time is the important mechanism that keeps everything from happening at once." We can employ the power of

---

[4] Dierickx and Cool (1989) emphasize that the firm's financial statements mirror only a sampling of the stocks versus flows in the firm's inventory. Momentum accounting (triple-entry bookkeeping) may provide a method for evaluating relationships between stocks and flows. See Ijiri (1989).

equilibrium thinking, but as a calculus of complex trajectories, to explain important differences among firms.

4. The search for rents is consistent with long-run welfare. In financial services and telecommunications, the switch to a competitive, rent-seeking environment has led to more choices, higher quality, and lower prices. Similar benefits have been gained in airlines and financial services, and in nearly every industrialized sector where rent-seeking behavior has been allowed to go forward.[5] One need only compare the robust diversity of Western economies to the barren Eastern European sectors to affirm the benefits of rent-seeking behavior. Strategies may not have welfare as their concern—but acting through the firm they achieve it.

5. Placing the firm on center stage bridges theory and practice. Functioning through imperfect markets for physical, human, and financial capital, managers seek rents under uncertainty. By studying the rich mosaic of imperfections in real-asset markets, business scholars are gaining fundamental scientific insights into how economies work. But the search for rents bridges theory and application. The strategy scholar and the business manager both validate the distinctive character of the firm as the unit of analysis through which economic gain is achieved.

Conclusion

It has been argued that strategies are inherently self-destructive and thus cannot yield sustainable rents. As the argument goes, any useful strategy attracts imitators, which destroy the rent-earning power of that strategy. Thus, strategy (or more precisely, any given strategy) cannot matter, at least not for long. As I suggested earlier, this proposition yields powerful insights into strategy. I have also suggested how erosion differs. But in any case, the self-destructive view is incomplete. The reason, as Rumelt continually reminds us, is uncertainty. As I have attempted to underscore, the opportunity set in which firms operate is continually being shaped by the economics of search. Organizational characteristics establish market outcomes. Behavior changes structure. The Schumpeterian engine

---

[5]   Benefits of competition may vary by appropriability conditions. Health care, because of slow-cycle conditions, is particularly resistant to the benefits of competition.

of competition ensures that this must be true. Through search, uncertainty is created, then reduced, and then created again. In parallel with this creative competitive process, we advance our knowledge of the unfolding global economic structure.

Firm differences are greater today than they were yesterday. New capabilities, new Coasian boundary conditions, and the character of advanced economies are evolving. Only in the final equilibrium—where no asymmetries existed in capabilities and search—would strategy yield zero rents. In the interim, strategy, although it shares interests with many disciplines, may be distinguished by its interest in rent-seeking behavior. For some time yet, opportunities await us.

9

Why Do Firms Differ, and How Does It Matter?

Richard R. Nelson

Introduction

This paper is concerned with the sources and significance of interfirm differences, from the viewpoint of an economist. How might an economist's perspective on this issue differ, say, from that of a student of business management? I would argue that the most important difference is that economists tend to see firms as players in a multiactor economic game, and their interest is in the game and its outcomes, rather than in the particular play or performance of individual firms. That is, economists are interested in how the automobile industry works, and its performance in various dimensions, and not in General Motors or Toyota per se, except insofar as the particularities of these firms influence the industry more broadly. This perspective is quite different, it seems to me, from that of a student of management who is concerned with the behavior and performance of individual firms in their own right.

My objective is to make a strong case for the economic significance, in the above sense, of discretionary firm differences. My position certainly has been influenced by the work of scholars of firm management who have persuasively documented significant differences among firms in an industry in behavior and performance, and proposed that these differences largely reflect different choices made by firms. However, because the interests of those authors have differed from the interests of economists, almost no attention has been paid to the industrywide or economywide implications of such different choices. Thus while the management literature provides a start for my argument, there is much that I need to build myself, in cooperation with like-minded friends.

It should be recognized that, in trying to make a case for the economic significance of discretionary firm differences, I and my co-arguers are fighting against a strong tide in economics, particularly in theoretical economics, that downplays or even denies the importance of such differences. The argument in economics is not that all firms are alike; economists recognize that computer firms differ from textile firms, and in both industries, German firms almost certainly differ from Taiwanese firms. Rather, the position is that the differences aren't discretionary, but instead reflect differences in the contexts in which firms operate: computer design and production technology and the computer market differ from the situation in textiles. Factor prices and availabilities and product markets in Germany differ from those in Taiwan. Thus, firms are forced to be different.

The tendency to ignore discretionary firm differences in part reflects the fact that economists are not interested in behavior and performance at the level of firms, but rather in broader aggregates—industrywide or economywide performance. It also reflects strong theoretical views held by most mainline economists about what economic activity is all about, and about the role and nature of firms in economic activity. My argument that discretionary firm differences within an industry exist and do matter significantly is part and parcel of my broader argument that neoclassical economic theory is badly limited.

Let me flag here, for future elaboration, what I do and don't mean by the term "discretionary." I do mean to imply a certain looseness of constraints, both in the short and long run, which allows firms that differ in certain important respects to be viable in the same economic environment. I do mean that to some extent these differences are the result of different strategies that are used to guide decision making at various levels in firms. On the other hand, I do not mean that what a firm is and does is tightly controlled by high-level decision makers. And I certainly do not mean that what makes a firm strong or weak at any time is well understood, even within the firms themselves, although there well may be an articulated point of view on this. More on these matters later.

The remainder of this paper is structured as follows. In the following section I shall flesh out my above remarks on the very significant differences in perspective between scholars trained or inclined to see discretionary firm-level variables as important and economists who see firm differences as determined largely by more aggregative economic forces. Then I focus on the basic theoretical preconceptions of neoclassical economic theory that lead to this position, and that make it very difficult to move any distance from it. I follow with an exploration of evolutionary economic theory, which provides a very different view of what economic activity is all about and within which firm differences are central, and I go on to consider the role of firm differences in the evolution of technology and modes of organizing economic activity. Finally, a reprise.

The Divergent Literatures on "Competitiveness"

The differences in perspective can be seen clearly in the divergent literatures concerned with what now popularly is called the "competitiveness" issue—the recent weakness of American firms, particularly vis-à-vis Japanese ones, in industries where not so long ago U.S. firms were doing very well. There is a sharp split between studies that focus on the differences between American and Japanese firms, and studies by economists that are focused on more aggregated variables.

Made in America, a publication issued in the summer of 1989 by the MIT Commission on Industrial Productivity, is a good example, and summary, of the former line of research. While the staff of the commission undertook considerable research on its own, the multifaceted diagnosis it presents is quite consistent with that presented in a number of prior studies concerned with why American firms have been losing out.

American firms are hooked on old-style mass-production methods, in an era when flexible manufacturing has become a more effective mode of operation. Similarly, our hierarchical mode of organization and custom of specifying job assignments narrowly, while perhaps appropriate in an earlier era, now are sources of weakness. Research and product design and development stand too distant from manufacturing and production engineering. It thus takes American companies much longer than the Japanese to go from conception to production; often our production costs are higher and our quality is inferior. American firms are myopic, both in the sense of their failure to look at world rather than national markets, and in the sense that their time horizons are short. The latter partly has to do with the high cost of capital in the United States, but also with the way our managers think and the tools of analysis they are taught in business schools. Compared with the Japanese and Germans, our blue-collar work force comes to the workplace poorly trained by the public education system. This is compounded by a weakness of in-company training and retraining programs. Together, this puts American firms at a significant disadvantage regarding labor skills. American firms are less willing to cooperate with each other on matters where cooperation would yield payoff, partly because of the attitudes of managers, but also partly because government looks on cooperation with suspicion or hostility. More generally, business and government seldom work together and often are at odds.

Others might summarize the central arguments somewhat differently, but I believe the above does represent fairly the kinds of propositions about firm differences made in the report. The arguments are plausible and provocative, and may provide important guidance to American management, and for public policy.

However, there are two important issues one can raise about the conclusions of the study. First, one can question how much confidence should be placed in the causal connections asserted in studies like *Made in America*. Second, one also can question whether the variables treated there as basic really are so, or whether they are determined by broader forces.

At this stage I want only to take note of the former issue. However, there really is a big question about just what Japanese firms in the automobile industry, or the semiconductor industry, are doing that allows them to perform better in various dimensions than American or European firms. Later in this paper I shall focus on this uncertainty and explore some of its implications.

For the present I want to focus on the latter question, because it brings sharply into view the contrast between analyses like *Made in America* and the standard views of economists about the determinants of "competitiveness." There is some discussion in *Made in America* of macro or national-level variables like the exchange rate, the cost of capital, or, more generally, the system of corporate finance, the effectiveness of the public education system, government policies, and so forth. However, this is not where the focus is. It is firm-level variables that receive the top billing, and it is presumed that these are discretionary to a considerable degree. In contrast, the inclination of economists is to focus on macro or environmental-level variables, and to play down or ignore the role of firm discretion.

The same year that *Made in America* was published, three economists, Baumol, Blackman, and Wolff, published their interpretation and diagnosis of lagging American productivity growth rates, and the convergence of productivity and living standards among the major industrial nations. The focus of *Productivity and American Leadership: The Long View* (1989) is usually at the level of the national economy, and sometimes at the level of the sector or industry. The variables considered are national savings and investment rates, investments in education, processes through which technology flows from creators to followers, and the like. There is scarcely a word about discretionary behavior at the level of firms.

It is strongly tempting, and I think justifiable, to propose that each of the studies has described part of the elephant. The argument in the MIT study, that many of the difficulties American firms are having are self-inflicted, is quite persuasive. At the same time the economist's proposition, that to a considerable extent firms are molded by the broader economic conditions surrounding them, is compelling. What seems sorely needed is an analysis that links both of these arguments in a coherent way.

While the authors of *Made in America* didn't seriously analyze environmental variables, it does not seem difficult to take an analysis that starts at the firm level and augment it with a consideration of firm environments. Two new books are exemplary in that they do just this. Both recognize explicitly that national or environmental variables strongly influence firm strategy and structure, and that firms have considerable range of choice about these variables. Chandler's *Scale and Scope* (1990a) describes in some depth how the different economic conditions, institutions, and cultures of the United States, Great Britain, and Germany molded the nature of modern manufacturing firms in the first decade of the twentieth century and influenced the industries in which these nations developed special strength. However, there is nothing deterministic about Chandler's description of how the environment shapes firms and influences their performance.

Porter's *The Competitive Advantage of Nations* (1990) presents a similar perspective, in which environmental influences matter greatly, but the firms have a considerable range of freedom regarding whether, or just how, they will take advantage of the opportunities the environment affords. Indeed both authors see the firms as to some extent molding their own environment, as, for example, in calling forth significant public investments in education in the United States and Germany.

Chandler is a historian by training. Porter's formal training is in economics, but his career has been at a business school and his research focus has been on management. It should be recognized that the orientation of these authors to firms is quite different from that of most economists. Indeed it is apparent that for both authors the center of attention is the firms, and the central questions are, How are they doing? and, What makes them strong or weak? They are drawn to wider economic mechanisms and institutions in the search for answers to these questions. And firm performance clearly is related to broader economic performance, but I have argued above they are not the same thing. Since neither Chandler nor Porter presents a coherent statement of the economywide problem, their analyses stop considerably short of providing an answer that would satisfy economists to the question, Why do firms differ, and how does it matter?

Firms in Neoclassical Economic Theory

To get at that question from an economist's perspective, one needs to start with a broad understanding of what economic activity is all about, and what constitutes good economic performance or poor. For several reasons, neoclassical theory, which provides the current conventional wisdom on these matters for economists, militates against paying attention to firm differences as an important variable affecting economic performance.

The first reason is the perception of what economic activity is all about. Since the formulation of general equilibrium theory almost a century ago, the focus has largely been on how well an economy allocates resources, given preferences and technologies. This position is far from universal. Empirically oriented economists have been interested in things like technical change, and recently there has been a rash of work on economic institutions and how and why these change over time. Some time ago Schumpeter put forth a strong general theoretical challenge to the effect that innovation ought to be the center of economic analysis. But it is hard to overestimate the degree to which economists continue to see the central economic problem as that of meeting preferences as well as possible, given existing resources, technologies, and institutions. This perspective implies a rather limited view of what firms are about.

The second reason reflects this general orientation, though it is not the only possible formulation of firms' decision processes that is consistent with such a view. Many economists have been wedded to a theory of firm behavior that posits that firms face given and known choice sets (constrained for example by available technologies) and have no difficulty in choosing the action within those sets that is the best for them, given their objectives (generally assumed to be as much profit as possible). Thus the "economic problem" is basically about getting private incentives right, not about identifying the best things to be doing, which is assumed to be no problem.

The perspective on the economic problem and the theory of firm behavior described above do not invite a careful inquiry into what goes on in firms. However, the tradition in economics of treating firms as "black boxes" was not inevitable either. The fact that, at least until recently, this has been the norm deserves recognition in its own right.

The overall result is a view that what firms do is determined by the conditions they face, and (possibly) by certain unique attributes (say a choice location, or a proprietary technology) they possess. Firms facing different markets will behave and perform differently, but if the market conditions were reversed, firm behaviors would be too. Where the theory admits product differentiation, different firms will produce different products, but in the theoretical literature any firm can choose any niche. Thus there are firm differences, but there is no essential autonomous quality to them.

The theoretical orientation in economics thus leans sharply away from the proposition that discretionary firm differences matter. Of course economists studying empirical or policy questions have a proclivity to wander away from the tethers of theory when the facts of the matter compel them to do so. Thus in doing industry studies, economists often have been forced to recognize, even highlight, firm differences, and differences that matter. One cannot study the computer industry sensitively without paying attention to the peculiarities of IBM. The recent history of the automobile industry cannot be understood without understanding Toyota and GM. But as the Baumol, Blackman, and Wolff book testifies, the theoretical preconceptions shared by most economists lead them to ignore firm differences, unless they are compelled to attend to them.

Several recent developments in theoretical economics would appear to be changing this somewhat. The same summer that *Made in America* and *Productivity and American Leadership* were published, the long-awaited *Handbook of Industrial Organization* (1989) came out. It included several chapters surveying theoretical work that does recognize firm differences.

There are, first of all, the essays by Ordover and Saloner, and by Gilbert, which are expressly concerned with theoretical work that aims to explain firm differences, or at least some consequences of firm differences. In the models reported, there usually is an incumbent in the industry, or in the production of a particular product, which has certain advantages over firms that might think of joining the action. The presence of these advantages, or threats of action should a newcomer try to encroach, is enough to make the advantages durable. Gilbert deals more generally with models in which firms incur costs if they change their market positions. However, with few exceptions the models surveyed in these chapters do not consider the original sources of firm differences in much depth or detail.

Reinganum's chapter, which surveys modern neoclassical models of technological innovation, is focused on what certainly is an important source of such differences—industrial R&D and the innovation R&D makes possible. In the models she surveys, a firm's technology may differ from a rival's because of the luck of an R&D draw, with the advantages made durable by patent protection or subsequent learning curve advantages. Given an initial difference, firms may face different incentives and thus find different courses of action most profitable. However, while these models may rationalize the observation that firms possess different technologies, the explanations offered certainly aren't very deep. And one comes away from them, or at least I do, with very little theoretical insight into why IBM is different, or Toyota, and what their differences mean.

Recently, economists have provided some theoretical work that looks inside firms, at their structure; this work seems to give promise of a theoretical window for a deeper look into why firms differ. The chapters by Holmstrom and Tirole, and by Williamson, report on such contributions. The questions explored in the surveyed work include what determines, through make or buy decisions, the boundaries of a firm, how firms are organized, the relative bargaining power of owners, managers, and workers, and so on. But, again, the ultimate reason for why firms differ is rather superficial. Implicitly they differ because some chance event, or some initial condition, made different choices profitable.

In my view, recent theoretical developments in neoclassical theory have loosened two of the theoretical constraints making it difficult if not impossible to see firm differences as important. Economists are getting away from the theoretical tethers of static general equilibrium theory and are treating technology as a variable, not a given. And they are trying to look inside the black box of the firm. However, for the most part they have failed to get away from the third tether—considering that a firm's choice sets will be obvious to the firm and that the best choice will be similarly clear. And because of that, the reasons for firm differences, in technology or organization, are ultimately driven back to differences in initial conditions, or to the luck of a draw, which may make choice sets different. Given the same conditions, all firms will do the same thing.

As I indicated above, I certainly do not want to play down the role of environment in constraining and molding what firms do. And I do not want to play down the role of chance in causing large and durable subsequent differences among firms. But in my view the models most economists keep playing with do not effectively come to grips with what lies behind the firm differences highlighted in *Made in America*, or the implications of those differences.

The reason, I want to argue, is that while the surveyed work purports to be concerned with "innovation," with the introduction of something new to the economy in the form of new technology or a new way of organizing a firm, the models in question completely miss what is involved in innovation. Thus, nowhere in the models Reinganum describes are the fundamental uncertainty, the differences of opinion, the differences in perceptions about feasible paths (which tend to stand out in any detailed study of technical advance) even recognized, much less analyzed in any detail. Williamson's own work on the determinants of firm organization has been much influenced by Chandler, and he dedicates part of his chapter to a transactions cost interpretation of Chandler's account of the rise of the modern corporation. But nowhere does he recognize explicitly the halting, trial-and-error process—often reactive rather than thought through—which led to the new ways of organizing that Chandler describes.

Put compactly, the treatment of technological and organizational "innovation" described in these chapters simply takes the given "choice set" and the presumptions of standard neoclassical theory that call for "maximizing over it" and applies them to "innovation." That is, innovation is treated as being basically like any other choice. Investment costs may need to be incurred before the new product or organizational design is ready to be employed, but in neoclassical theory this is true of other capital goods like bridges or machines. There may be high risks involved in doing something new, in a formal sense of that term, but this is treated as statistical uncertainty with the correct probability distribution known to all, as is standard in microeconomic theory. The innovation may yield a new latent or manifest public good, which raises theoretical problems of "market failure," but this is no different than investment in, say, public health.

But what if effective treatment of innovation (and perhaps other activities) requires breaking away from the assumptions of clear and obvious choice sets and correct understanding of the consequences of making various choices? Does it really make sense to work with a model that presumes that the transistor, or the M-form of organization, were always possible choices known to all relevant parties, and that they simply were chosen and thus came into existence and use when conditions made profitable the relevant investments? Does the assumption that "actors maximize" help one to analyze situations where some actors are not even aware of a possibility being considered by others?

If one reflects on these issues, one may be moved to adopt a very different view of the economic problem. Within this view, which I will call evolutionary, firm differences play an essential role.

Innovation and Firms in Evolutionary Theory

The models of technological innovation surveyed by Reinganum show economists interested in the theory of the firm struggling to break away from the orientation of general equilibrium theory, which sees the economic problem as allocating resources efficiently, given technologies. So too the new literature on organizational innovation. Here economists seem to be basically interested in how new ways of doing things—technologies, and ways of organizing and governing work—are introduced, winnowed, and where proven useful, spread, as contrasted with how familiar technologies and organizational modes are employed. Many years ago Schumpeter insisted that the focus of general equilibrium theory was on questions that, over the long run, were of minor importance compared with the question of how capitalist economies develop, screen, and selectively adopt new and better ways of doing things. Many of the writers surveyed by Reinganum call themselves "neo-Schumpeterians."

However, the dynamic processes Schumpeter described are not captured by the new neoclassical models. As he put it, "In dealing with Capitalism, you are dealing with an evolutionary process." He clearly had in mind a context in which people, and organizations, had quite different views about what kinds of innovations would be possible, and desirable, and would lay their bets differently. There are winners and losers in Schumpeter's "process of creative destruction," and these are not determined mainly in ex ante calculation, but largely in ex post actual contest.

In his 1911 *Theory of Economic Development*, Schumpeter saw the key innovative actors as "entrepreneurs." His "firms" were the vessels used by entrepreneurs, and by other decision makers forced to adapt to the changes wrought by entrepreneurial innovators or to go under. By the time (1942) he wrote *Capitalism, Socialism, and Democracy*, Schumpeter's view of the sources of innovation had changed, or rather it might be better to say that there had been a transformation of the principal sources of innovation from an earlier era, and Schumpeter's views reflected this transformation. Modern firms, equipped with research and development laboratories, became the central innovative actors in Schumpeter's theory. The chapter by Cohen and Levin in the *Handbook* admirably surveys the wide range of empirical research that has been inspired by Schumpeter, particularly the research concerned with the relationships among innovation, firm size and other firm characteristics, and market structure.

In our book, *An Evolutionary Theory of Economic Change* (1982), Winter and I spent quite a bit of space presenting a "theory of the firm" which is consistent with, and motivates, a Schumpeterian or evolutionary theoretic view of economic process and economic change. Our formulation drew significantly on Simon (1947), on Cyert and March (1963), and on Penrose (1959), as well as on Schumpeter. With hindsight it is clear that our writing then was handicapped by insufficient study of the writings of Chandler, particularly his *Scale and Scope* (1990b).

Since the time we wrote, there have been a number of theoretical papers on firm capabilities and behavior that draw both on Chandler and on our early formulation, and that add significantly to the picture. Papers by Teece (1980, 1982), Rumelt (1984), Cohen and Levinthal (1989), Dosi, Teece, and Winter (1989), Prahalad and Hamel (1990), Pavitt (1987, 1990), Cantwell (1989, 1990), Kogut (1987), Henderson (1990), Burgelman and Rosenbloom (1989), Langlois (1991), and Lazonick (1990) all present a similar or at least a conformable theoretical view, although with differences in stress. The paper by Teece, Pisano, and Shuen (1990) provides an overview of many of these works, and I believe correctly states that the common element is a focus on firm-specific dynamic capabilities.

This emerging theory of dynamic firm capabilities can be presented in different ways. Here it is convenient to focus on three different, if strongly related, features of a firm that must be recognized if one is to describe it adequately: its strategy, its structure, and its core capabilities. While each has a certain malleability, major changes in at least the latter two involve considerable cost. Thus, they define a relatively stable firm character.

The concept of strategy in this theory of the firm follows the definition of business historians and scholars of management, as contrasted with game theorists. It connotes a set of broad commitments made by a firm that define and rationalize its objectives and how it intends to pursue them. Some of this may be written down; some may not be but is in the management culture of the firm. Many economists would be inclined to propose that the strategy represents a firm's solution to its profit maximization problem, but this seems misconceived to me. In the first place, the commitments contained in a strategy often are as much a matter of faith (coming from top management and company tradition) as they are of calculation. Second, firm strategies seldom determine the details of firm actions, but usually at most the broad contours. Third, and of vital importance, there is no reason to argue a priori that these commitments are in fact optimal or even not self-destructive. If it is proposed that competition and selection force surviving strategies to be relatively profitable, this should be a theorem, not an assumption.

The concept of firm structure in this literature also is in the spirit of Chandler, as is the presumption that strategy tends to define a desired firm structure in a general way, without giving the details. Structure involves how a firm is organized and governed, and how decisions are made and carried out, and thus largely determines what the firm actually does, given the broad strategy. If a firm's strategy calls for it to be a technological leader, and if it lacks a sizeable R&D operation or an R&D director with strong input into firm decision making, it clearly has a structure out of tune with its strategy. However, the high-level strategy may be mute about such matters as links between its R&D lab and universities, whether to have a special biotech group, and so forth.

Change in strategy may require a change in management as well as a change in articulation; indeed, for the latter to be serious may require the former. However, within this theory of the firm, structure is far more difficult to change effectively than is strategy. While changing formal organization, or at least the organization chart, is easy, and sell-offs and buy-ups are possible, significantly changing the way a firm actually goes about making operating-level decisions and carries them out is time-consuming and costly to do. Or rather, while it may not be too difficult to destroy an old structure or its effectiveness, it is a major task to get a new structure in shape and operating smoothly. Thus, to the extent that a major change in strategy calls for a major change in structure, effecting the needed changes may take a long time.

The reason for changing structure, of course, is to change, and possibly to augment, the things a firm is capable of doing well. Which brings the discussion to the concept of core capabilities. Strategy and structure call forth and mold organizational capabilities, but what an organization can do well has something of a life of its own.

Winter and I have proposed that successful firms can be understood in terms of a hierarchy of practiced organizational routines, which define lower-order organizational skills and how these are coordinated, and higher-order decision procedures for choosing what is to be done at lower levels. The notion of a hierarchy of organizational routines is the key building block under our concept of core organizational capabilities. At any time the practiced routines that are built into an organization define a set of things the organization is capable of doing confidently. If the lower-order routines for doing various tasks are absent, or if they exist but there is no practiced higher-order routine for invoking them in the particular combination needed to accomplish a particular job, then the capability to do that job lies outside the organization's extant core capabilities.

The developing theory of dynamic firm capabilities I am discussing here starts from the premise that, in the industries of interest to the authors, firms are in a Schumpeterian or evolutionary context. Simply producing a given set of products with a given set of processes in a competent way will not enable a firm to survive for long. To be successful for any length of time a firm must innovate. The capabilities on which this group of scholars focus are capabilities for innovation and for taking economic advantage of innovation.

In industries where technological innovation is important, a firm needs a set of core capabilities in R&D. These capabilities will be defined and constrained by the skills, experience, and knowledge of the personnel in the R&D department, the nature of the extant teams and procedures for forming new ones, the character of the decision-making processes, the links between R&D and production and marketing, and so forth. This means that at any time there will be certain kinds of R&D projects that a firm can carry out with some confidence and success, and a wide range of other projects that, while other firms might be able to do them, this particular firm cannot with any real confidence.

R&D capabilities may be the lead ones in defining the dynamic capabilities of a firm. However, in a well-tuned firm, the production, procurement, marketing, and legal organizations must have built into them the capabilities to support and complement the new product and process technologies emanating from R&D. In Teece's terms, the firm's capabilities must include control over, or access to, the complementary assets and activities needed to enable it to profit from innovation. And in an environment of Schumpeterian competition, this means the capability to innovate, and to make that innovation profitable, again and again.

The concept of organizational capabilities, and the theory that Winter and I proposed as to what determines and limits them, does not directly imply any coherency to the set of things a firm can do. However, Dosi, Teece, and Winter (1989) argue that, in effective firms, there is a certain coherency. There would appear to be several reasons. The ones stressed by Dosi, Teece, and Winter are associated with localized learning in a dynamic context, and follow on the arguments Winter and I made some time ago that, to be under control, a routine needs to be practiced. Firms need to learn to get good at certain kinds of innovation, and to develop the skills and resources needed to take advantage of these innovations, and this requires concentration or at least coherency, rather than random spreading of efforts. Further, in many technologies one innovation points more or less directly to a set of following ones, and the learning and complementary strengths developed in the former effort provide a base for the next round.

But I think it also is the case that to be effective a firm needs a reasonably coherent strategy, which defines and legitimizes, at least loosely, the way the firm is organized and governed, enables it to see organizational gaps or anomalies given the strategy, and prepares the ground for bargaining over the resource needs for the core capabilities a firm must have to take its next step forward. Absent a reasonably coherent and accepted strategy, decision making about rival claims on resources has no legitimate basis. Decisions from above have no supportive rationale, and there is no way to hold back log-rolling bargaining among claimants other than arbitrary high-level decisions. There is no real guidance regarding the capabilities a firm needs to protect, enhance, or acquire in order to be effective in the next round of innovative competition.

But I think I am simply restating what Chandler, Lazonick, Williamson, and other scholars of the modern corporation have been saying for some time. To be successful in a world that requires firms to innovate and change, a firm must have a coherent strategy that enables it to decide what new ventures to go into and what to stay out of. And it needs a structure, in the sense of a mode of organization and governance, that guides and supports the building and sustaining of the core capabilities needed to carry out that strategy effectively.

If one thinks within the frame of evolutionary theory, it is nonsense to presume that a firm can calculate an actual "best" strategy. A basic premise of evolutionary theory is that the world is too complicated for a firm to comprehend, in the sense that a firm understands its world in neoclassical theory. There are certain characteristics of a firm's strategy, and of its associated structure, that management can have confidence will enhance the chances that it will develop the capabilities it needs to succeed. There are other characteristics that seem a prescription for failure. However, there is a lot of room in between, where a firm (or its management) simply has to lay its bets knowing that it does not know how they will turn out.

Thus, diversity of firms is just what one would expect under evolutionary theory. It is virtually inevitable that firms will choose somewhat different strategies. These, in turn, will lead firms to develop different structures and different core capabilities, including their R&D capabilities. Inevitably firms will pursue somewhat different paths. Some will prove profitable, given what other firms are doing and the way markets evolve, others not. Firms that systematically lose money will have to change their strategy and structure and develop new core capabilities, or make more effective use of the ones they have, or drop out of the contest.

The Evolution of Technology

In real capitalist economies, in contrast with the neoclassical models, technical advance proceeds through an evolutionary process, with new products and processes competing with each other and with prevailing technology in real time, rather than solely in ex ante calculation. Some of the innovations will be winners, others losers. With the advantage of hindsight the whole process looks messy and wasteful, and a more coherent planning approach to technological advance appears attractive.

However, it is striking how inefficient and misguided efforts to plan and control significant technical advance have been. Where, for one reason or another, society has been denied the advantages of multiple independent approaches to advanced technology, which flow naturally from a basis of independent rivalrous firms, the approach chosen has almost always turned out, after the fact, to have major limitations. And since alternatives had not been developed to a point where they could be tried in comparison, there has been lock-in. A number of U.S. military R&D efforts since 1960 are striking examples. Nuclear power programs are another. The fact is that in virtually every field where we have had rapid technical advance that has met a market test or its equivalent, we have had multiple rivalrous sources of new technology.

While Winter and I formally modeled company R&D programs as generating results through a random draw, in fact in the industries that I know well there has tended to be a certain consistency in the R&D efforts of particular companies. This consistency reflects a basically stable company "strategy," and the core R&D and other dynamic capabilities it has put in place to carry it out. Where company strategies and associated capabilities differ significantly, their patterns of innovation are likely to differ significantly as well.

This has an important consequence often overlooked in the literature on technological imitation. When one firm comes up with a successful innovation, its competitors may differ significantly among themselves in their ability to imitate it effectively or to develop something comparable. Contrary to many economic models, effective technological imitation very often requires the imitating firm to go through many of the same design and development activities as did the innovator, and to implement similar production and other supporting activities. Thus, firms with similar strategies and core capabilities are in a much better position to imitate or learn and build from each other's work than firms with different strategies and capabilities.

To an extent, then, the market is selecting on strategies and companies, as well as new technologies. This suggests that in some circumstances strategic diversity may be extinguished.

There is something to this argument. A number of analysts, some working in the tradition of economic research, some in a business school research tradition, have suggested that there is a natural industry life cycle. When an industry or a broad technology is new, a wide variety of approaches to technological innovation—strategies—is taken by different firms. As experience grows, certain of the approaches begin to look significantly better than others. Firms that have made the right bets do well. Those that have not need to switch over or drop out. A number of studies have shown that, as an industry or technology matures, there is a significant reduction in the number of firms, and in some cases the emergence of a "dominant design" with all surviving firms producing some variety of that tuned to the niche they have found.

One fascinating question is what happens in a relatively mature industry when a new and potentially superior technology comes into existence. The evidence suggests that it matters whether the new technology is conformable with the core capabilities of extant firms, or requires very different kinds of capabilities. Tushman and Anderson (1986) call these two kinds of developments "competence enhancing" and "competence destroying." Under the latter circumstances, new firms are likely to be the innovators, and old firms often are unable to respond effectively. Tushman and Anderson note that a change in management, and presumably a major change in strategy, often is necessary if the old firm is to survive in the new environment. But it may not be sufficient. Structure and core capabilities are far more difficult to change than management and articulated strategies.

For a student of business management the question of what enables a firm to change direction effectively and be a viable competitor in the new regime is of great interest in its own right. For an economist what matters is that pharmaceutical R&D take advantage of the new possibilities opened by new biotechnology; as long as new pharmaceutical firms take up the torch, it matters little whether old firms do it or whether they fail.

However, the fact that the leading-edge companies in a field often change is a fascinating matter. It is consistent with the theory of focused and constrained core capabilities presented above. And it is a central reason why, for an economist interested in technological advance, firm differences matter considerably.

The Evolution of Firm Organization

There has been far more study of the way technology advances than there has been of the way firm organization changes. By organization I mean what I think Chandler (1966) means by strategy and structure, those aspects of a firm that are wider and more durable than the particular technologies and other routines it employs at any moment, or even its extant core capabilities, and which in effect guide the internal evolution of these core capabilities and organizational routines. It is apparent that change in organization in this broad sense, as well as advance in technology, has been an essential feature of the enormous economic progress that has characterized the last century and a half.

Some writers clearly would like to give organizational change separate and equal billing with technical advance as a source of economic progress. I argue here, however, that organizational change is usually a handmaiden to technological advance, and not a separate force behind economic progress.

If I understand him correctly, this would be Chandler's position. The new technology of the railroads required, for its effective implementation, the development of organizational capabilities far beyond that possessed by traditional owner-managed firms. Line and staff organizational form, along with the development of the position of hired manager, enabled the railroads to be effectively "governed," to use Williamson's term. Later, new technologies that promised economies of scale and scope in manufacturing called for large firms operating in several different product fields, or market areas. The M-form of managerial structure evolved to govern effectively this kind of business operation.

Over the long run what has mattered most has been the organizational changes needed to enhance dynamic innovative capabilities. Reich (1985), Hounshell and Smith (1988), and other writers have described how the organizational device of the industrial R&D laboratory came into existence, to permit firms to shield a portion of their scientific and technical personnel from the pressures of day-to-day problem solving so that they could work on the development of new products and processes. This development was preconditioned by the rise of a new "technology" for product and process development, one employing the understandings and techniques of the sciences and engineering disciplines in a systematic way. One can read Chandler's and Lazonick's account of the rise of other aspects of the modern corporation in terms of Teece's arguments about needed complementary assets or capabilities.

As I read the case-study evidence, devising and learning to use effectively a significantly new organizational form involves much the same kind of uncertainty, experimentation, and learning by making mistakes and correcting them, that marks technological invention and innovation. New modes of organization aren't simply "chosen" when circumstances make them appropriate. They, like technologies, evolve in a manner that is foreseen only dimly. And even when a firm makes a conscious decision to reorganize, it may take a long time before it is comfortable and effective in its new suit of clothes.

I want to return here to a point I made at the start. I suspect that the uncertainties about new organizations are even greater than those surrounding technological innovations. Students of the field are especially uncertain about what kind of organization is needed to mold effective dynamic innovative capabilities and the ability to profit from innovation. At present there is little in the way of tested and proved theory (let me use the less pretentious word "knowledge") that would enable us to predict confidently the best way of organizing a particular activity or the consequences of adopting a different mode of organization. If the "rationally choosing" view of technological advance is misguided, the "rationally choosing" view of organizational change is even more so.

Just as important, it not infrequently happens that a particular mode of organization put in place for one reason turns out to have advantages—or disadvantages—in arenas that were not considered at the time it was originated. It is also not infrequent for there to be considerable dispute about just what features of a firm's organization are responsible for certain successes or failures.

Thus, as I understand it, large Japanese firms adopted "life-time employment" for their skilled workers in the early postwar era to try to deal with a problem of skill shortages and labor unrest. It is quite unclear how many Japanese managers foresaw advantages associated with worker loyalty, or with the ability of a firm to do in-house training without fear of losing the investment through worker defection. Just-in-time was, I understand, largely a response to scarce space, high inventory costs, and input shortages. It is not clear how many saw that it would facilitate quality control.

American companies looking at their Japanese competitors often have been uncertain about just why the Japanese are better in some respects, and just what they can effectively transplant. They will only be able to learn by trying some things, seeing what happens, and having the good luck to judge what they see correctly.

The evidence is very limited, but there is reason to believe that firms have greater ability to replicate themselves in another setting in a way that preserves their strength, than to comprehend and adopt what gives their rivals strength. Thus as Womack, Jones, and Roos (1991) and Clark and Fujimoto (1991) document convincingly, American automobile manufacturers are still struggling to catch up with the Japanese in terms of productivity and quality of production. Where they are coming close seems to be in cases where the Japanese are serving as partners. This does not look accidental. Florida and Kenney (1991) report that Japanese-owned automobile assembly plants in the United States have rather quickly been able to establish practices—strategies and structures—similar to their home operations, and with comparable outcomes.

I want to put forth the argument that it is organizational differences, especially differences in abilities to generate and gain from innovation, rather than differences in command over particular technologies, that are the source of durable, not easily imitable, differences among firms. Particular technologies are much easier to understand and imitate than broader firm dynamic capabilities.

From one point of view it is technological advance that has been the key force driving economic growth over the past two centuries, with organizational change acting as a handmaiden. But from another perspective, we would not have gotten that technological advance without development of new modes of organization that can guide and support R&D and enable firms to profit from these investments.

I have concentrated on firm organization. However, it is clear that the organizational changes that have enabled nations to support the modern R&D system and the technological advance it generates go far beyond those of firm organization. Universities had to change. New scientific disciplines and societies had to come into being. In many cases new bodies of law were needed. Some technologies required major new public infrastructure for their effective development.

The coevolution of technology and institutions is a fascinating subject. Chandler and a few other scholars such as Hughes (1983) and Freeman (1989) have begun to address it. There clearly have been major national differences in how the institutions needed to support particular evolving technologies themselves evolved. Perhaps in the study of the coevolution of technology and institutions we will begin to develop a serious theory of how national comparative advantage comes into being, or is lost. But I now am far beyond the scope of this paper.

Reprise

Students of firm management, in particular those working in the strategy field, treat discretionary firm differences as their bread and butter. Economists have tended to play down these differences, or to argue that they are the result, not the cause, of general economic differences. In good part the difference in viewpoints is due to differences in basic interests—the student of firm management is concerned with the fate of individual firms, and the economist is interested in the general economic performance of an industry or nation. But I have argued that the lack of interest by economists in discretionary firm differences also stems from a particular theoretical view of economic activity and the role and behavior of firms.

If one takes an evolutionary rather than a neoclassical view of what economic activity is about, firm differences matter greatly with regard to issues that traditionally have been the central concern of economists. Competition is then not merely about incentives and pressures to keep prices in line with minimal feasible costs, and to keep firms operating at low costs;

much more important, it is about exploring new and potentially better ways of doing things. Long ago Schumpeter remarked that the former function was trivial compared with the latter, if the measure was contribution to the economic well-being of humankind.

From the perspective of evolutionary theory, firm diversity is an essential aspect of the processes that create economic progress. Monopoly, or tight oligopoly with strong barriers to entry, can be seen as serious economic problems not so much because they permit a large gap between price and cost, but because such market structures are unlikely to generate the variety of approaches, and the shifts in allocation warranted when a new approach proves workable, that economic progress depends upon. One is suspicious of arguments to "rationalize" production and innovation for the same reasons, particularly when the winds of change are blowing from unpredictable directions.

Thus, the "dynamic capabilities" view of firms being developed by scholars in the strategy field may be important not only as a guide to management, but also as the basis for a serious theory of the firm in economics. When imbedded in an evolutionary theory of economic change, it helps provide an answer to the question, Why do firms differ, and how does it matter?

10

A Sociological View on Why Firms Differ

Glenn R. Carroll

In modern economies, firms do differ. That fact is so obvious it rarely generates debate. But consensus about organizational heterogeneity pretty much starts and ends with that simple empirical observation. Questions concerning both the nature and sources of differences among firms engender a wide variety of answers.

The diversity of thought arising in this context reflects not so much disagreement among social scientists as it does the complexity of the issue. Heterogeneity can crop up at any stage of the organizational life cycle of an individual firm and as the result of many possible forces internal or external to the firm. Within a population of established firms, evolutionary processes such as selection may either winnow heterogeneity or cause it to proliferate. The matter is complicated further by how close the competitive system is to its equilibrium since this state usually implies the elimination of diverse but relatively inefficient competitor firms. As all this serves to show, the seemingly straightforward query, Why do firms differ? actually encompasses a broad range of other questions.

In order to make headway in identifying the sources of firm differences, we need to impose some structure on our thinking.

Acknowledgments: Much of the work for this paper was done while I was a Fellow at the Netherlands Institute for Advanced Study in Wassenaar. I am grateful to that Institute as well as to the Institute of Industrial Relations at Berkeley for financial support. I wish to thank the following friends and colleagues for critical comments on earlier drafts: J. Richard Harrison, Heather Haveman, Charles O'Reilly, Jeffrey Pfeffer, Hein Schreuder, Anand Swaminathan, Jeffrey Williams, and Oliver Williamson. I also appreciate the advice and encouragement of the editors.

Toward this end, I believe it is useful to distinguish between the sources of firm differences and questions about expected firm differences at equilibrium. By equilibrium, I mean temporal equilibrium of the competitive system within which organizations operate and compete. Because most analysts assume that the system functions in ways that favor efficient firms, this distinction is virtually equivalent to that between questions of why firms differ and why successful (that is, efficient) firms differ.[1] The answers to the two questions are very different, and although the difference is often noted in passing, I do not believe that the implications of this distinction are well appreciated. Consequently, I shall attempt to draw them out as I discuss pertinent theory and evidence.

Why Firms Differ

If one examines a representative cross section of firms from a modern economy, one finds a mixture of various types of firms, including many that are inefficient in a technical sense and that will eventually fail.[2] Most theories of organization and virtually all normative theories of strategic management are constructed in ways that either ignore these inefficient firms or pretend they do not exist. Yet they are always there, in every modern society and at every point in time. Usually they are present in large numbers and most of the time they probably constitute a sizeable majority. Without these firms there would be no need for normative theory since all existing firms would be doing the right things.

Any theory that purports to explain why firms differ can ill afford to ignore the largest proportion of those units to which it is alleged to apply. So at its most fundamental level, the question of why firms differ must ignore the question of success (or efficiency, if the competitive system operates on that basis) and

[1]   I shall use the term "equilibrium" throughout the paper to refer to temporal equilibrium of the competitive system. Other conceptualizations of equilibrium may or may not yield different problems and conclusions. Also, in much of the discussion I shall presume efficiency is the equilibrium target because this is by far the most commonly accepted view in the strategy realm. Using other equilibrium criteria does not change the logic or implications of my arguments, although some readers may object to the use of the word "success" in this context.

[2]   Caves and Barton (1990) review and present evidence regarding the prevalence of technical inefficiency, which appears to be fairly common.

deal with what is out there—the complete heterogeneity of all firms *in existence*. Normative questions about why successful firms differ represent a second step, perhaps one more relevant to strategy, but nonetheless secondary.[3]

Scholars from a variety of social science disciplines have identified and documented sources of firm heterogeneity at the individual, organizational, and environmental levels of analysis. Some of these are thought to be present from the time of founding, while others are seen as the result of processes experienced by ongoing organizations. I review here briefly some of the relevant theories and studies, focusing my efforts on those with at least some minimal empirical support.

Individual sources—dispositional. The best-known theories of entrepreneurship are not merely psychological: they are also dispositional in that they attribute important stable characteristics to individuals. The notion of an entrepreneurial personality has long been linked both to particular types of individuals and to their organizations. The classic entrepreneurial firm is free from bureaucracy, has little role formalization, and operates via a highly centralized command structure emanating directly from the entrepreneur (see Mintzberg, 1979). While it is too much to say that the entrepreneur is the organization, it is fair to say that in this characterization the organization is the social embodiment of his or her personality.

The systematic and careful empirical study by Miller and Dröge (1986) shows that dispositional explanations of organizational structure should not be lightly dismissed. Using a sample of 93 firms in Quebec, these investigators show that a CEO's score on the need for achievement scale (nAch) is strongly associated with organizational structure measures of formalization, centralization, and integration. These effects persist even when organizational size, technology, and environmental uncertainty are controlled. Furthermore, nAch shows its strongest effects in

---

3   Considering the full range of firms in existence is not nearly as "anormative" as it seems at first glance. Suppose that the supply of new firms could be turned off abruptly. Even with intense efficiency-based selection pressures it would take several years for the inefficient enterprises to get weeded out. In the interim some of these firms might figure out how to become efficient. (And, conversely, some of the efficient ones might "forget" how they do it or make some major mistake.) Furthermore, if environmental conditions change during this period, the organizational arrangements that were efficient earlier might no longer be so and vice versa. It does not take much imagination to devise a scenario where momentary inefficiency may be necessary for long-term survival.

smaller and in relatively new organizations, suggesting that the initial sources of heterogeneity in firms reflect at least this personality characteristic of the founder.

Individual sources—situational. Much earlier research on entrepreneurship and self-employment is plagued by sample selection bias: samples consisting only of entrepreneurs were used in attempts to detect the causes of entrepreneurship. Besides the usual problems of sample selection (see Heckman, 1979) these data are contaminated by the tendency of entrepreneurs to overestimate their chances of success and to overrationalize their initial motivations (Cooper et al., 1989). The result reinforces the classic portrait: an entrepreneur is an economically rational profit-seeking person who, because of a good idea or the intention to work harder than any competitors, made the conscious decision to go into self-employment after weighing his or her other employment options.

Recent research using sounder methods and designs yields a different image. These studies use representative samples of all persons and attempt to predict prospectively who will become self-employed (for examples, see Fuchs, 1982; Borjas, 1986; Carroll and Mosakowski, 1987). Although it is difficult to find any consistently strong single determinant, the findings are consistent in uncovering situational factors that push individuals into self-employment, usually because their other options are diminished. For example, unemployment frequently shows a strong positive effect on becoming self-employed. So do retirement and forced resignation. Other factors associated with self-employment, such as parental self-employment and marital status, may or may not involve such an explicit push. But they are situational in a sociological sense, and together they strongly suggest that the "decision to enter" is conditioned by social structure. Presumably, such social structures have a lot to do with the types of organizations that get founded by these persons, but the evidence here is virtually nonexistent.

Organizational sources—spin-offs. Because a focal organization does not exist prior to the event of interest, theories of entrepreneurship have generally not considered organizational sources (Delacroix and Carroll, 1983). However, the high visibility of so-called spin-offs in areas such as Silicon Valley has increased awareness of the potential for existing firms to beget new firms (Cooper, 1971). Sometimes this process may occur by the explicit design of "incubator firms." But often it is the result of structural features of existing organizations.

The rate at which firms spawn new firms varies tremendously. What might account for this variation? Brittain and Freeman (1986) focus on the probable political consequences of particular structural arrangements and events. They argue that when prized and highly knowledgeable employees perceive their internal career prospects as jeopardized, they will be prompted to start new firms. In the context of the semiconductor manufacturing industry of northern California, Brittain and Freeman specify that CEO succession from the outside, corporate takeover by a firm in another industry, and demographic bulges of older workers each operate in this way. In a unique empirical study of all firms in this industry from 1958 to 1982, they present evidence showing that firms characterized by these factors did indeed have higher rates of spin-off.

Organizational sources—internal change. Most strategic theory posits that firms differ because managers figure out ways to distinguish their firms from others. Usually this is assumed to be the result of a rational planning exercise or at least to involve procedures that might be so codified. Sophisticated versions of such theory (e.g., Alchian 1950; Nelson and Winter, 1982) specify an intendedly rational search and planning process but do not claim that an optimal or even effective outcome will emerge.

More generally, we can say that firm heterogeneity often comes about through the transformation of existing firms. Undoubtedly these changes may be enacted as the result of a rational planning process by managers. But internal organizational change may also be undirected and unintentional (March, 1978, 1982). Moreover, intended change often carries with it unintended consequences.

Theories of organizational change abound, and they go straight to the heart of fundamental differences among the various major theoretical perspectives in organizational sociology (i.e., institutional theory, organizational ecology, resource dependence theory, transaction cost economics). Perhaps because organizational change is so closely bound up with these paradigmatic constructions, we know much less about it than we might. Most theories currently popular embrace a model of environmentally driven change whereby external changes produce organizational changes (more on this below). But we do not have a basic systematic accounting of the rates of change by organizational form, nor the prevalence of different types of changes, let alone good general studies of the determinants of either.

Despite these serious problems of evidence, there seems to be some agreement about several organizational characteristics thought to be associated with change. The distinction between change in the core features (e.g., mission, function, technology) and the peripheral features (e.g., products, location, subunits) is critical (Scott, 1987a; Hannan and Freeman, 1984). Changes in peripheral structure are, of course, more frequent. I also venture to suggest that organizational theorists would expect rates of peripheral change to be higher in new organizations, in less formalized organizations, and in those organizations operating in changing and uncertain environments. In addition, changes in the more fundamental core structures would be expected to be higher in more turbulent environments. It would also be likely to be greater in organizations with a "soft" technological core, such as many service organizations.

Environmental sources. Most organizational theorists would ultimately trace the differences among firms to the diversity of environments or resources on which they depend (Hannan and Freeman, 1977; Scott, 1987a). But there are two problems with such a general claim. First, it is essentially an equilibrium claim—the argument is about the types of firms favored by the environment and the maximum level of sustainable diversity, not the level possible in disequilibrium.

The second and more difficult problem with the argument is that it simply recasts the problem at a higher level of analysis: it does not tell us what the important dimensions of environmental diversity are. Indeed, the major debates within organizational theory are over exactly this question. Some perspectives, such as organizational ecology, seem to argue mainly on behalf of material differences in resources and technology (Hannan and Freeman, 1989). Others, such as sociological institutional theory, see rules and normative constraints as defining separate environments (Meyer and Rowan, 1977). The structuralist view of White (1981, 1988) envisions consumer tastes and the dispersion in their valuation relative to costs as setting the range of possible resource bases. As currently stated by Williamson (1985, 1991), transaction cost economics views legal and political environments as dominant, although a more general rendering might view any factor (physical, technological, political, and so forth) that creates significant transaction costs as differentiating the environment.

In exploring these issues in the current context, it is helpful to come down a level or two of abstraction and ask the rather simple question, What types of environmental changes shift the equilibrium criteria or "target" of the system, thereby exacerbating disequilibrium and producing new types of organizations? That is, which environmental changes produce market or other disjunctures that some entrepreneurs will perceive as opportunities and thereby be prompted to found new organizations? Substantively oriented researchers, often combining a variety of theoretical perspectives, have given us a number of solid clues.

One broad class of important environmental changes involves *technological discontinuities*. Often arising from the isolated work of an individual genius, these major breakthroughs in technology typically substitute for and eventually supplant an existing technology (see Tushman and Anderson, 1986). The initial discovery is often called paradigmatic (or "frame breaking" or "competence destroying") because it renders obsolete previous ways of doing things. Subsequent technological progress proceeds incrementally down an uncertain but directed trajectory according to an accepted regime (Dosi, 1982). The organizational structures associated with the new technology differ from those associated with the old technology.

A good example of technological change affecting organizational change is found in the world watch industry. Until about 1950, mechanical watches using pin lever and jewel lever technologies dominated the industry. The firms producing these watches were overwhelmingly Swiss firms, relatively small operations consisting of highly trained craftsmen who were not involved in the distribution of their products. Between 1950 and 1970 new types of watches using electric and tuning fork technologies appeared. These watches were produced primarily by large American firms that often had their own distribution and retail networks. The biggest technological change occurred in the 1970s, however, with the introduction of quartz watch technology. This technology virtually eliminated the old Swiss watchmaking companies whose products suddenly seemed less reliable and much more expensive than the new electronic watches. The quartz technology regime in the world watch industry is dominated by large vertically integrated Japanese firms such as Hattori Seiko. Hong Kong also maintains a strong presence in this industry.

Another type of broad environmental change with pervasive organizational implications involves *political discontinuities in government*. National revolutions, in particular, often espouse ideologies—for example, egalitarianism, communism, democracy—that prescribe new or different types of organizational forms (see Stinchcombe, 1965; Aldrich, 1979; Carroll et al., 1988). A similar but far less profound process occurs with regime change. Once in power, new governments frequently provide the authority and funds to proliferate their preferred organizational forms. Similarly, taxes, laws, and other incentive mechanisms may be changed with this end in mind.

The establishment of state socialist governments has historically produced some of the most dramatic changes in the organizational panorama. The East German case illustrates this well. Between 1971 and 1987, the state directed its nationalization efforts toward the abundant Mittelstand (small companies). The result was a decrease in the numbers of small companies: while in 1971 over 8,000 firms with fewer than 100 employees operated, by 1987 there were fewer than 1,000. Average firm size increased dramatically, as it often does under state socialism (even when the guiding ideology favors small producers—see Colburn [1986] for an account of the economic changes in Nicaragua between 1979 and 1983). There seems little doubt that after reunification a rapid reversal of this process is under way in the former East Germany.

Finally, we know that *changes in the distributions of ethnic groups* constitute important environmental changes. Most of the time these changes occur as the result of large-scale immigration of minority groups into advanced economies, but they can also involve the activation of new or latent identities (e.g., the black power movement). Both blocked upward mobility channels (due to discrimination against the minority) and ethnic solidarity by ethnic consumers (reinforced by geographic settlement patterns and caused in part by discrimination) create new ethnic-based forms of organization, which are often situated in ethnic enclaves and provide numerous alternative sources of opportunity (Evans, 1989; Olzak and West, 1991).

An obvious example of how organizational change follows from ethnic change can be found in the history of the U.S. newspaper industry. Waves of ethnic papers were generated by waves of immigration (see Park, 1922). The ethnic press peaked at the start of World War I, then dropped off during the war as many German papers went out of business. Evidence of a less obvious link of this kind comes from Russell and Hanneman's (1991) study of cooperative organizations in Israel. They show a strong association between immigration and cooperative founding rates and mortality rates.

Explanations for these types of changes are sometimes embedded in the logic of general models of industrial evolution. For instance, the well-known technology model of Utterback and Abernathy (1975) posits that as product-market sectors unfold over time, the associated technological advances and economic changes may foster the success of different types of entrepreneurs and organizations. Early on, product innovators are attracted; later, it is process innovators. A similar though more general statement of this kind can be found in Porter's (1980) discussion of industry evolution. Although both models contain some equilibrium (success) logic, they also realistically depict profit-seeking entrepreneurs responding to changing industry structure.

Organizational blueprints. Some of the theories and research that bear on firm differences make no specific predictions about what sort of difference is expected (e.g., the study of spin-offs among semiconductor producers). Others seem to imply some specific difference, but making it explicit usually requires invoking an assumption or two (e.g., the structure of ethnic-based firms). Yet others seem to make specific predictions about firm differences (e.g., centralization in decision making varies with nAch of CEO). Even when combined, however, these predictions are unable to account for the actual complexity of new firms. So a more general question underlies the one about firm differences—namely, Where do specific organizational blueprints come from? It makes most sense to address the question by considering the initial structure put in place during the establishment period.

At one extreme we can imagine the all-knowing industrious rational entrepreneur. He or she plans every detail of his or her new firm and manages to implement the design as intended except, of course, for some fine-tuning in midstream (perhaps to take care of unexpected developments). At the other extreme we have the imitative entrepreneur who borrows an organizational design from a successful firm or perhaps buys one from a franchise vendor complete with an instruction kit and occasional visits from a quality control monitor, who might also provide technical assistance.

Another possibility is that the entrepreneur's organizational blueprint is less conscious or controllable. The initial design for the organization may reflect the culturally defined building blocks that the entrepreneur takes for granted and makes use of. Or, the design may merely set the initial conditions for an emergent social process that determines the eventual persisting organizational structure.

Unfortunately, we know very little about how the entrepreneur develops this organizational blueprint (Spender, 1989). Stinchcombe's (1965) famous analysis of organizational forms shows that the general characteristics of the blueprint are history dependent (see Kimberly, 1975, for a more fine-grained illustration of this process). Boeker's (1988) study shows that the founder's prior work experience often gets reflected in the initial structure and strategy. And it is hard to imagine any entrepreneur planning and thinking through every detail, especially with the time pressures usually involved. Entrepreneurs, then, are likely to be consciously rational in only very limited ways in designing their organizations. The domain of the rationality is apt to be set by their prior educational and work experience and, perhaps, by the constraints imposed by involved outsiders such as investors. A few features of an entrepreneur's organization may represent attempts to solve the problems that he or she considers salient based on this experience. But the list of such features is probably not very long and surely does not cover many aspects of a firm. Most features adopted are likely copied or put into place without any thought, perhaps coming from observation, reading, or consultation. The result is a semi-planned venture where the planned elements represent the entrepreneur's priorities for perceived success of the firm.

Why Successful Firms Differ

Claiming that disequilibrium is common does not imply that the world is not driven by a process that would reach equilibrium if left unperturbed. The relevant question at any point in time concerns the *general* criteria driving the process producing success in disequilibrium and ensuring existence at equilibrium. (Random and idiosyncratic factors may, of course, be very important in accounting for the success of specific firms but need not concern us here.) For the issue of firm heterogeneity, the extent to which individual organizational change is adaptive or selective in moving the system toward equilibrium is an important but secondary question.

Most theories of strategic management and organization hold (sometimes implicitly) that the dominating equilibrium criterion is efficiency, although definitions of this concept vary (again often implicitly). These theories also differ markedly, first, in their specifications of the factors upon which efficiency depends and, second, in their assessments of the relative efficiency of various organizational configurations. Each element in turn contains a theory's answer to the question of firm differences at equilibrium. Consider the following examples of the wide range of theories about strategic success and their implications for organizational heterogeneity at equilibrium.

Porter's economic model.   According to Porter (1980), organizational efficiency is indicated by profitability in the short term and survival in the long term. Porter's influential normative theory of strategy implies that a firm's market position is the key factor in determining success. As is well known, his major thesis is that in the long run only three generic market positions are viable: (1) low-cost production, (2) product differentiation, and (3) segmented focus. Although different industries may be especially favorable for one or the other at any point in time, the equilibrium apparently has room for all three types simultaneously.

Contingency theory.   Found in every textbook on organizational design, the so-called contingency theory of organizations specifies that size, technology, and environment are the relevant conditional factors determining efficient organizational structure. Although many variants of this theory exist (see Scott, 1987a, for a review), the logic of most remains faithful to the seminal contributions of Woodward (1965), Blau (1970), and Lawrence and Lorsch (1967). More specifically, for technology, Woodward (1965) argued that there are three basic types of technological systems (unit and small batch, large batch, and process), each requiring a different organizational configuration for effective functioning. Blau (1970) rigorously defined the relationship between efficient administrative overhead and organizational size. Lawrence and Lorsch (1967) showed that organizational subunits adapt separately to their specific environments, thus leading to the overall design statement that organizations facing heterogeneous environments require greater structural differentiation and integrative effort to be successful.

Resource dependence models. Theories of resource dependence emphasize the ways in which organizations reduce or overcome environmental uncertainty. Thus, the equilibrium criterion is uncertainty reduction (Pfeffer, 1982). Depending on the form and level of uncertainty, a hierarchically ordered set of appropriate organizational responses are posited as enhancing the chances of success (Thompson, 1967). These include both internal organizational "buffering" strategies (e.g., coding, stockpiling, differentiation) and external interorganizational "bridging" strategies (e.g., co-optation, alliance, joint venture, merger). Some versions of resource dependence theory look at structural environmental constraints and strategies for overcoming them more generally (see Burt, 1983; Pfeffer, 1987). Firm differences expected at equilibrium by resource dependence theory thus reflect both the variety of structural constraints and the number of effective organizational responses for reducing uncertainty.

Process models. Another common line of thought about successful strategy harks back to classical management theory. This view emphasizes the importance of internal organization and process. Early versions of process-oriented strategy theory stressed the role of cooperation (Barnard, 1938). A radical process model of firm success is given by Weick (1987), who argues that what is important is not the content of a firm's strategy but its existence in the first place and the form of its enactment in the second. In other words, firm success is primarily the result of differences in process (possibly including formulation, articulation, and implementation) rather than differences in content. Less extreme models of this kind are conditional on the type of externally oriented competitive posture the firm has adopted. For instance, Miles and Snow (1978) emphasize consistency between strategy and organizational structure as the key to success. More recently, Hambrick (1987) trumpets the role and composition of top management teams. O'Reilly (1989) advances logically similar arguments about the role of organizational culture.

Dispositional models. A different but overlapping tradition of management theory focuses on the CEO and his or her personal characteristics. Many theories of this kind maintain that leadership on the part of the CEO is the single most important criterion determining success. Such ideas help explain the fascination of organizational behavior researchers with executive succession processes. More complex versions of dispositional theory make conditional arguments about the executive's leadership style or personality and the firm's market strategy or technological base. The best known of these is McClelland's (1961) theory of entrepreneurship wherein he argues that an achievement motive (or need) will dominate in entrepreneurial settings. Miner et al. (1989) have developed a similar but more elaborate role motivation theory that specifies five different leadership roles. Yet another type of CEO-based model focuses on entrepreneurial human capital (see Preisendoerfer and Voss, 1990).

Transaction cost economics. Many theories of firm success are derivable from the more abstract transaction cost perspective of Williamson (1985). In its most general formulation, transaction cost theory holds that activities are organized optimally when they minimize the production costs and economize the transaction costs involved in producing the desired outcome. In other words, the equilibrium criterion of this theory is efficiency as indicated by cost minimization. The factors associated with transaction costs (and thus determining the optimal level and shape of formal organization) include asset specificity, uncertainty, and frequency of transaction. Sometimes this general theory leads to specific predictions about when a particular activity, say production of a component, will be done in-house and when it will be purchased in the market (Monteverde and Teece, 1982). Recent efforts by Williamson (1991) and Teece (1989) specify in much greater detail the range of specific factors affecting transaction costs and the myriad hybrid organizational forms associated with varying levels of cost.

Organizational ecology. Another general theory is that of organizational ecology. This perspective uses organizational survival itself as the outcome variable of primary interest but accepts a very broad range of equilibrium criteria. Some models of organizational ecology, such as Hannan and Freeman's (1984) fitness set theory of specialism and generalism, or Carroll's (1985) model of resource partitioning, clearly have efficiency interpretations. In these models, environmental and market conditions set the stage for some organizational forms to outperform others (usually by virtue of market compatibility rather than by internal efficiency). Other ecological models depend on noneconomic or nonefficiency-based equilibrium criteria. For instance, Singh et al. (1986a) argue that institutional legitimacy is an important success factor for voluntary social service organizations. They measure legitimacy by looking at whether the organization is listed in the charitable registry and endorsed by the local chamber of commerce. They find that such endorsement by institutional authorities lowers the organizational death rate. A more general model of institutionally driven organizational evolution is embodied in Hannan's (1986) powerful theory of density-dependent legitimation and competition (see Hannan and Carroll, 1992). Other ecological analyses of this kind focus on political environments and related turmoil (see Carroll et al., 1988).

Institutional theory. Sociological institutional theory also differs markedly from the efficiency-based models. This view holds that although the pretense of rationality and efficiency is usually maintained, the actual equilibrium criterion is normative (Meyer and Rowan, 1977). That is, institutional theory posits that normatively defined models of formal organization drive the system. These models are socially constructed definitions of appropriate ways to organize, which are usually rationalized in terms of efficiency. For any specific organizational population or industry sector, the state and other professional bodies endorse and sanction morally the diffusion of particular models or blueprints for organizing. Research conducted within this perspective identifies these models, describes the processes by which they emerge, and documents their diffusion through sectors of the economy (see Rowan, 1982). The most fascinating studies of this kind examine organizational contexts where normative rationality does not coincide with technical rationality or efficiency (e.g., Meyer and Scott, 1983).

The state. What other equilibrium criteria drive organizational evolution? Analyses of nonmarket contexts such as state socialism help in identifying these phenomena (see, for example, Kornai, 1986). These studies show a normative process somewhat different from that depicted by institutional theory.[4] Whereas in institutional theory the impression is often given that models of organizing are adopted without cognition or even awareness on the part of the participants (through a sort of cultural enactment process), under state socialism conformity to an externally defined model of organizing is consciously undertaken. Indeed, the whole process is much more direct and explicit in that authorities specify and sanction what is wanted while organizations below attempt at least to give the appearance of conformity. The equilibrium criteria also typically have a heavy ideological flavor in these types of processes.[5] These studies often show that the success and survival of individual firms rests more with their interorganizational relations than with internal efficiency. Knowing state officials, building relationships with them, and using the firm's status to bargain all work to the advantage of the firm under state socialism (see Carroll et al., 1990). To a lesser degree, the same processes can be seen in capitalist economies, of course. While resource dependence theorists might claim that little is distinctive about these phenomena, they do seem to have greater salience in these contexts, sometimes growing to absurd dimensions and frequently having little to do with technical efficiency. The state is also endowed with unique authority that makes it different from other external organizations controlling resources.

Adaptation versus selection. Most of the theories of why successful firms differ embrace (or at least imply) an adaptation model of organizational change. Although the difference between an adaptation and a selection model may not matter in terms of which types of organizations are expected at equilibrium (provided the two processes are driven by the same crite-

---

4   In some renditions, these arguments are considered part of sociological institutional theory (see Scott, 1987b). Note also that at some point arguments of this kind become indistinguishable from resource dependence theory.
5   Carroll et al. (1988) provide some examples.

ria), it does matter greatly for a theory of strategic management. The point is not that selection-based theories such as organizational ecology are irrelevant, as some strategists would argue, or that adaptation-based theories are unrealistic, as some organizational theorists hold. Rather, strategic management is inherently concerned with both—and theoretical analyses conducted within this field should reflect that fact. Strategy theory should be concerned not only with the likely success of particular actions once implemented, but also with the risks entailed by undertaking such actions in the first place. In other words, what are the risks of adaptation? How do they differ by type of action and by organizational context?

Since organizational ecology challenges the adaptation model most directly, researchers working within this perspective have begun studying such questions. While still very tentative, the results to date seem generally consistent with Hannan and Freeman's (1984) conjecture that "core" organizational features (i.e., mission, technology, resource base) generate greater risks when changed.[6] For instance, the study by Singh et al. (1986b) of mortality among voluntary social service organizations in Toronto shows that changes in goals, service area, and organizational structure (each of which is argued to be a core feature of this type of organization) all increase the death rate, while changes in chief executive and location (peripheral features) lower it. In an empirical study of semiconductor manufacturers, Freeman and Hannan (1990) demonstrate that reorganizations accompanying product changes in this industry have a strong initially positive effect on the exit rate, even though such changes enhance long-term survival. Studies by Amburgey et al. (1990) of newspapers in Finland and by Haveman (1990) of the California savings and loan industry show consistent preliminary findings. So it looks as though major adaptations involve great survival risks, even when the intended change would increase survival probabilities if successfully effected.

Organizational theorists often assume that selection processes operate only on individual firms or organizations. Thus the observation that each organization is embedded in a network of organizations, and that some are able to exert great influ-

[6] It is interesting to note that Teece et al. (1990) claim to derive a similar argument from the so-called resource-based approach to strategy.

ence over other members of the network, is taken as evidence of the absence (or implausibility) of selection (Perrow, 1986). But this assumption is mistaken—frequently the fates of firms are tightly interconnected with those of other firms (Porter, 1980; White, 1981). In the context of early American telephone companies, Barnett and Carroll (1987) show that such interdependencies can be determined empirically. Other studies of higher-order selection processes rely on known differences in technology (Barnett, 1990a) or strategic groups (Carroll and Swaminathan, 1991; Barnett, 1990b). In general, selection processes might operate on firms, groups of firms (by, say, technological type or strategy), populations of firms, or communities of populations of firms.

One plausible interpretation of systems apparently driven by equilibrium criteria other than efficiency (by, say, political conformity in a statist system or by co-optive ability in a capitalist system) is that they create interdependencies among organizations that force efficiency-driven selection processes to operate on higher-order groupings of organizations (Hannan and Freeman, 1977). This view implies that although selection is always efficiency based, the best strategy for any given individual firm may be to act otherwise (e.g., build interorganizational bridges with the state rather than economize internal operations). Moreover, it appears that when many individual firms manage to get their fates tied to those of many other organizations, especially governmental organizations, the disequilibrium can be maintained for a long period (witness the long survival of East European state socialism). So, for instance, firms under state socialism manage to survive and even prosper by creating resource dependencies with the state. However, in this interpretation the entire system eventually experiences the selection pressures of efficiency, and if changes are not made, it collapses. Presumably, resource dependencies in market contexts can have similar effects, no matter how wise they may be as courses of action for the managers of individual firms. This suggests that analysis of interorganizational relations and alliances needs to be conducted from other than just the focal organization perspective commonly used in strategic management.[7]

---

[7] Please note, however, that some analyses of interorganizational groupings and alliances actually make arguments about the efficiency of the entire interdependent group (e.g., Gerlach, 1987). Here the logic used above obviously does not apply.

In the abstract, the appropriate level of analysis for studying firm success is determined by the strength of interdependencies among firms relative to the strength of selection processes. While mixed indications about the appropriate level appear when firm survival is the outcome variable, the evidence for profitability favors the business unit level. In the most thorough study to date (to my knowledge), Rumelt (1991) shows that approximately 45% of firm profitability is accounted for by differences in business units (meaning firm-specific differences in organizational form and environment for a particular line of business). This important finding suggests that selection may apply with greatest force to business units rather than to larger divisional or corporate units, as some strategy theories imply.

On the Persistence of Heterogeneity

As characterized by the above theories, organizational evolution usually proceeds down a systematic path, no matter how much noise and disequilibrium the system contains. At some point the evolutionary process likely becomes calculable in that successful firms are readily recognizable and managers can formulate pretty good guesses as to what equilibrium criterion is being favored and what organizational factors might produce it. This situation raises the crucial question of why firms pursuing unsuccessful strategies do not change to more successful strategies, including possibly imitating the winners. Another way of stating this question is in terms of firm heterogeneity: Why do firm differences persist once strategic and organizational recipes for success become known?

The first point to recognize is that heterogeneity does not always persist. In some industries, imitation is relatively easy and firms simply follow the leaders. In others, selection processes are so severe and rapid that unsuccessful firms are eliminated before their managers can figure out what is going on. This appears to be the case especially in industries driven by strong economies of scale, such as beer brewing, where thousands of firms have gone under in a relatively short period, reducing heterogeneity enormously.

In many instances, however, firm heterogeneity persists for long periods. For the current issue, the least interesting case is when this heterogeneity is simply the result of multiple organizational forms being the equilibrium targets of evolution, as with Porter's three generic strategies. The more interesting situation involves the persistence of heterogeneity that falls outside the equilibrium range. The precondition for such a situation, of course, is a selection environment loose enough to allow such firms to operate for nontrivial periods of time. If we then ask why these firms do not switch to more successful strategies,[8] a variety of answers seem plausible in one context or another.

1. Environmental expectations. Although management may recognize that their firm's strategy is currently unsuccessful, they may believe that the environment will soon shift to a condition more favorable to their position. That is, staying the course may be the intention despite hard times at the moment.

2. Ambiguity excellence. Industry leaders may be easily recognizable and the general features of their activities known, but there may still be ambiguity regarding exactly which features generate success. This situation is especially common when the leaders themselves exhibit differences, thus introducing many factors that might plausibly account for success. The plethora of books and articles about Japanese management suggests that this kind of ambiguity surrounds the success of Japanese firms.

3. Imitation inability. Despite a known recipe for success and a decision to pursue it, firms may be unable to implement the strategy. This problem is especially common when large firms attempt to pursue specialist strategies. Despite apparently having all the necessary technical and other resources, imitation is often an impossible feat.

4. Structural constraints. As detailed by Hannan and Freeman (1977, 1989) a variety of political, social, and economic forces act to constrain change and keep inertia strong. Organizational culture is also highly inertial, even in the midst of great demographic change (Harrison and Carroll, 1991).

5. Precariousness of change. The transition period surrounding a major strategic change is fraught with inherent difficulties and risks independent of the content of the change. Rational managers may decide to forgo such risks even if undertaking change would enhance the firm's prospects of success.

---

[8] That many such firms do not successfully adapt is obvious given the extremely large number of organizational failures seen continuously in modern economies.

Conclusion

Organizational heterogeneity is a very complex issue involving questions about where variation comes from, how it is winnowed by selection and other evolutionary processes, and why it persists in firms performing poorly. Although research conducted on any of these questions might benefit the strategy field, the evolutionary process is, I contend, the most germane for strategic management because strategy researchers have been interested primarily in firm performance. I suggest that the fundamental question for strategic management is not why firms differ but why successful firms differ.

Part III

What Are the Functions of the Headquarters Unit in a Multibusiness Firm?

The study of *business* strategy has been principally concerned with product-market competition. By contrast, the study of *corporate* strategy addresses a different set of issues: the scope of the firm and the administrative systems that span that scope. In each of these subjects, the comparison of an existing or proposed arrangement and competing alternatives can yield insights. In the case of business strategy, the useful comparison is between a product-market offering and those offered, or potentially offered, by competitors. In the case of corporate strategy, the useful comparison is normally between a business operating within a corporation's governance system and the same business operating as a freestanding entity. In such a comparison we ask, What is the function of or value added by the headquarters unit's governance?

In the 1970s this question was usually answered by reference to Chandler's (1962) developmental view or to various portfolio concepts. According to Chandler, in certain industries the underlying technologies and market conditions permitted growth through diversification. In these cases, a competent headquarters unit removed itself from operating responsibility, created a set of relatively autonomous divisions to manage the businesses, and devoted itself to strategy. That is, the headquarters unit made key decisions about the sharing of resources, allocation of capital, and entry into and exit from areas of activity. Portfolio views emphasized the role of the headquarters unit in creating a "balanced" portfolio of businesses and in channeling cash from slow-growing into faster-growing activities.

During the 1980s scholars in the field began to focus less attention on the gains yielded by diversification and instead to examine its limits. This shift in focus was engendered by both theory and practice. On the theoretical side, an increasingly rich set of ideas was developing in the new field of organizational economics. This perspective placed primary emphasis on the comparison of organizations and markets; it asked for a justification of the multibusiness firm in terms of gains that could not be obtained through market transactions or simple contracts. On the practical side, the conglomeration movement followed by the restructuring wave gave strong impetus to the idea that many firms were "too" diversified and that the market for corporate control, while present, was a costly, blunt instrument for correcting administrative error. As a consequence, the issue of the multibusiness firm is one of the most interesting and instructive in strategic management today. It is clearly informed by economic perspectives, but there is also ample evidence—hard market evidence—that many observed structures are not efficient.

Each of the four papers on multibusiness structure approaches the question of the headquarters role from a different point of view, and each produces valuable insights. In the first paper, "Diversification and Economic Performance: Bringing Structure and Corporate Management Back into the Picture," Hill argues that there are two main avenues for creating value open to multibusiness firms: economies of scope and economies of allocation. The first—economies of scope—requires that divisions share resources, transfer information, and act cooperatively. The second—economies of allocation—flows from a system of governance for the internal capital market that emphasizes clear measures and competition among divisions for capital. Because these approaches are incommensurate, Hill argues, firms cannot blend, but must choose between, systems emphasizing coordination and those emphasizing competition. With regard to the ultimate scope of the firm, Hill suggests interdependencies among divisions generate the need for nuanced central control, which can only be effective when the informational load, and hence scope, is limited.

Alfred Chandler's original study of the rise of multibusiness firms was a key stimulus for the development of a scholarly research tradition in strategic management. In the second paper of this section, "The Functions of the HQ Unit in the Multibusiness Firm," Chandler revisits the question, using the events of the last 25 years to inform a new view of the administrative limits of corporate headquarters units. In particular, he examines how continued growth forced the standard M-form organizations of the immediate post–World War II era to adopt a three-tiered structure, and how prosperity (and hubris) led to diversification strategies that overtaxed these structures.

The basic conceptual scheme Chandler brings to this paper is that developed in *Scale and Scope* (1990a). Heavy and technologically complex industries are characterized by inexhaustible technical economies of scale and scope, but the ability of firms to exploit these economies is limited by their entrepreneurial skill in guiding complementary investments and their administrative skill in coordinating the resultant operations. Thus, in Chandler's view, it is the managerial capabilities of the corporate office that ultimately determines the size, scope, and success of the enterprise. In this paper, Chandler borrows Goold and Campbell's (1987) typology of headquarters styles, identifying those using purely financial controls as essentially administrative and those using strategic planning or strategic control methods as performing some entrepreneurial functions. He analyzes the recent histories of British and U.S. firms and concludes that multibusiness companies employing financial controls have been successful only when they have restricted their ownership to firms in services and in simple mature industries. Where industries are mature, but complex, and require substantial investments, headquarters units must engage in strategic control. And where complexity is combined with technological advance, headquarters offices must supply entrepreneurially oriented strategic planning.

As in Chandler's other works, many of his conclusions fit easily within an "economizing" institutional economics framework. Thus, for example, the increased need for headquarters strategic planning that characterizes advancing technology can be seen as induced by the costs of haggling and hold-up that would be borne were the divisions to plan on a decentralized basis. However, Chandler's essential contributions go far beyond this static picture. In reaching his conclusions, Chandler uses the methods he has perfected: the historical analysis of challenge and managerial response. In this paper we do not see firms "applying" concepts or somehow driven to the efficient response by selection pressure. Instead, we see managements getting it wrong, suffering consequences, struggling to understand the nature of their dilemmas, and then, perhaps, creating new structures, policies, and methods to cope with, and possibly to transcend, the problem. Chandler's real message is not that one must get the headquarters design just right, but that those firms which dominate their industries are those which have shown the most resilience and insight in responding to the challenges that their own growth and expansion have generated.

The third paper, "Strategizing, Economizing, and Economic Organization," by Oliver Williamson, is a call to arms. The war is against the idea that "strategizing" is a source of competitive advantage, and in favor of stressing the importance of "economizing." He argues that whereas the field of strategy should be concerned with first-order economizing ("rectangles"), it has imported doctrines from industrial organization economics which are focused on second-order economizing ("triangles"). Williamson contends that if strategic management is to unlock the sources of long-run competitive advantage, and if it is going to rely on economic thinking to assist it, then it ought not to rely so uncritically on economic perspectives that appeal to market power (strategies that restrict product competition) as the source of advantage. Rather, the field should develop more of an efficiency perspective—that being good at what you do and avoiding waste is more important than, say, exploiting, switching costs or playing oligopoly games.

Note that Williamson's economizing firm is miles away from Porter's low-cost producer; the economizer is not necessarily efficient at production, but in the broad range of business functions. For example, the economizer may be very efficient at managing the transition from design to production, or at tailoring products to local tastes. Williamson's position on this issue is at variance with the traditional (economic) assumption that firms are "on their cost curves." If firms are assumed to be technically efficient, the problem is simply to determine the level of output. Williamson, by contrast, sees the fundamental challenge as organizing and governing activities so as to eliminate waste.

In this paper Williamson uses a transaction cost (efficiency) perspective to analyze a number of issues in strategic management, giving special attention to the role of the headquarters unit in multibusiness firms. Williamson's central argument is that the senior management of a multibusiness firm is basically engaged in designing and administering incentive systems. These incentives are, he points out, necessarily less intense than pure market incentives, but that lessened intensity may be necessary for bilateral coordination. In addition, the systems of review in a multibusiness firm ameliorate, in part, the agency problems introduced by the separation of ownership and control.

In the fourth paper, "Takeovers in the 1960s and 1980s: Evidence and Implications," Andrei Shleifer and Robert Vishny investigate the wave of unrelated diversification in the 1960s followed by a wave of restructuring and retrenchment in the 1980s. Shleifer and Vishny review the available evidence and conclude that unrelated diversification did not improve economic efficiency. Unrelated diversification was carried too far in the 1960s, they argue, because of antitrust enforcement as well as agency problems connected with multidivisional structures: "The M-form begot the monster of the conglomerate."

What makes Shleifer and Vishny's paper especially interesting is their treatment of the efficient market hypothesis. Since the stock market responded to conglomerate acquisitions in the 1960s, many researchers have concluded that they created value. This paper argues that the stock market was merely reflecting the mistaken beliefs of a majority of investors. Drawing on their research on arbitrage and market fads, Shleifer and Vishny contend that fads persist because it is too costly for the best informed investors to bet against them.

The boom and bust of conglomerates is a convenient vehicle for this argument, but its implications extend well beyond the issue of conglomeration. Event studies, using stock market residuals, have become a standard way of investigating the "value" of various policies and strategies. If these studies do not really measure value, but only what investors think value is, then this whole methodology may be significantly weakened.

As with each of the fundamental questions posed here, we

have no definitive answer to the question of the value or role of the headquarters unit of the multibusiness firm. Collectively, however, these papers do expand our understanding of the role and value of important aspects of complex administrative structure. More important, the papers pose fresh questions, redirect research focus, and suggest different theoretical perspectives than those commonly applied by strategic management to the matter of multibusiness governance. The existence of multiple business units is difficult for traditional economic theory to contemplate and embrace, but new perspectives such as those offered here help us to understand this complex administrative structure.

11

Diversification and Economic Performance: Bringing Structure and Corporate Management Back into the Picture

Charles W. L. Hill

Introduction

The relationship between diversification strategy and economic performance has been the focus of extensive research in the strategic management literature (e.g., Amit and Livnat, 1988; Bettis, 1981; Christensen and Montgomery, 1981; Montgomery, 1985; Rumelt, 1974, 1982; Wernerfelt and Montgomery, 1988). Despite all of this effort, a recent survey concluded that the findings of studies attempting to demonstrate the effects of diversification on performance remain inconclusive (Ramanujam and Varadarajan, 1989). Aside from methodological flaws, there is a plausible explanation for the lack of clear-cut results. Most research on diversification has ignored the importance of organizational structure for the strategy-performance relationship. This is unfortunate; it is now more than 30 years since Chandler (1962) noted that the success of a diversification strategy depends on how it is implemented. Diversification alone will not produce superior performance; the corporate management of the firm must also adopt the appropriate internal organizational arrangements. By ignoring the effect of organizational characteristics on the diversification-performance relationship, many diversification studies may have produced erroneous results.

Acknowledgments: Thanks are due to Paul Collins, Tom Hammond, Mike Hitt, Bob Hoskisson, Dan Schendel, and David Teece for comments on an earlier draft of this paper.

The objective of this paper is to bring organizational structure and corporate management back into the picture. It draws on the economic and management literatures to demonstrate how the organizational choices made by top management influence the relationship between diversification and economic performance. The paper starts with an examination of the economic rationale for diversification. Next, it identifies the organizational arrangements necessary to realize the economic value inherent in different diversification strategies. In a third section, the paper considers the organizational limits to efficient diversification. The final section of the paper outlines the implications of these arguments for academic research and management practice.

The Economic Rationale for the Diversified Firm

Economic theory asks, Why might we expect to observe some diversified firms in competitive equilibrium? It seeks to establish under what conditions diversification is an efficient strategy, and in what circumstances it is only the product of top management attempts to derive psychic satisfaction from "empire building" growth strategies (Marris, 1964; Jensen, 1986). The transaction cost literature contains powerful economic arguments for the existence of the multibusiness firm (Teece, 1980, 1982; Williamson, 1975, 1985). There are two main themes emphasized in this literature. One focuses on the role of economies of scope, while the other stresses the superior governance characteristics of diversified firms organized along multidivisional (M-form) lines. Each theme is considered in some detail below. First, however, it is useful to give a brief overview of transaction cost economics.

An Overview of Transaction Cost Theory

Transaction cost theory argues that an economic rationale for multibusiness firms must be found in an analysis of the relative costs of coordinating exchange via the *invisible* hand of the price system, compared to the costs of coordinating exchange via the *visible* hand of a management hierarchy (Coase, 1937). Under certain conditions coordination via the market mechanism is costly. These costs are referred to as transaction costs. If the transaction costs of market-mediated exchange exceed the bureaucratic costs of coordinating that exchange through a management hierarchy, transaction cost theory predicts that in competitive equilibrium that exchange will be governed by hierarchy.

There are two main branches to the transaction cost literature: the *measurement* branch and the *asset specificity* branch. The measurement branch sees the measurement problems that exist under conditions of uncertainty as being the major factor explaining the evolution of nonmarket institutions (Akerlof, 1970; Alchian and Demsetz, 1972; Barzel, 1982; Ouchi, 1980). For example, Alchian and Demsetz (1972) argue that difficulties associated with measuring the marginal productivity of individual actors when technological nonseparabilities require that they cooperate on team production give rise to the free rider problem. In such circumstances, hierarchical governance is seen as giving a residual claimant (the entrepreneur) the authority structure required to attenuate the free rider problem and realize the full gains of cooperation. More generally, the measurement branch emphasizes that uncertainties as to the true value of the inputs that factors of production bring to an exchange, or uncertainties as to the value of the outcome of an exchange, inevitably give rise to contracting and monitoring problems. The measurement branch also stresses that information asymmetries between the parties to an exchange can exacerbate uncertainties. It is argued that in some circumstances, the problems that arise due to uncertainties and information asymmetries can be solved by adopting a hierarchical governance to manage the exchange.

The asset specificity branch of transaction cost economics focuses explicitly on the role of specific asset investments as a determinant of hierarchical governance (Klein, Crawford, and Alchian, 1978; Williamson, 1975, 1985). According to this branch, investment in specific assets to support an exchange generates quasi-rent. In such cases, the possibility exists that once the investment has been made an opportunistic party might expropriate the quasi-rent by refusing to pay or serve. The adoption of safeguards in the form of contingent claims contracts, monitoring mechanisms, and credible commitments to insure against opportunism gives rise to ex ante transaction costs. In addition, since the uncertain and complex nature of the real world and the bounded rationality of economic actors make it impossible to draft a fully comprehensive contingent claims contract, the probability of some loss occurring due to uninsurable opportunism still remains. This expected loss can be viewed as ex post transaction costs. If the sum of ex ante and ex post costs exceeds the bureaucratic costs of hierarchical governance, the asset specificity branch of transaction cost theory predicts that in competitive equilibrium such an exchange will be governed by hierarchy rather than by the price system. Thus, this branch views hierarchical governance as a means of facilitating cooperation between the parties to an exchange when one, or both, have made specific asset investments.

It must be recognized that the bureaucratic costs of hierarchical governance are nontrivial. These costs arise due to the administrative mechanisms necessary to coordinate exchange within a hierarchy, the incentive problems that arise when transactions are removed from a market setting, and problems of control loss that emerge in complex multibusiness organizations (Jones and Hill, 1988; Milgrom and Roberts, 1990a; Williamson, 1985). Ultimately the existence of bureaucratic costs must imply a fundamental limit to efficient diversification.

Economies of Scope

The potential for realizing economies of scope arises when an imperfectly divisible asset, whether in the form of human or physical capital, can be used to produce two or more end products, and when the asset is currently underutilized. By diversifying into the production of an additional product, the firm can utilize previously idle capacity and so gain cost savings. Both Penrose (1959) and Chandler (1962, 1977) have emphasized how the desire to help ensure the continuing full use of resources underlies much diversification. Penrose goes even further, arguing that successful firms have a perennial tendency to generate excess capacity in human capital—particularly with regard to management, engineering, and research personnel. Excess capacity emerges as the managerial and technical problems involved in establishing a business are solved, and as the task of running a business becomes more and more routine. Penrose sees the need to fully utilize excess capacity in human capital as the engine that drives corporate growth and diversification.

By definition, such diversification must occur in an area that has some commonality with the existing business of the firm, whether in terms of manufacturing, marketing, R&D, or some other area.

Operationally, diversification to realize economies of scope requires the sharing of resources and/or transfer of skills between two or more otherwise distinct businesses. Authors in the management literature typically refer to such diversification as *related diversification*. Moreover, the exploitation of underutilized resources most often involves internal growth, as opposed to acquisitive growth.

The task of transaction cost theory is to explain why the realization of economies of scope necessitates hierarchical governance. After all, in principle it might be possible for a firm to lease out underutilized resources to other enterprises and earn rents on them in that way. Teece (1980, 1982) emphasizes two scenarios where hierarchy is a more efficient mechanism for realizing economies of scope. The first occurs when the underutilized resource is specialized physical capital. According to Teece, any attempt to lease underutilized specialized resources exposes the firm to the risk of opportunism. The resulting contractual problems give rise to transaction cost that can only be economized by hierarchical governance. (The logic underlying this first scenario rests squarely on the asset specificity branch of transaction cost theory.)

In Teece's second scenario the underutilized resource is know-how embodied in human capital. According to Teece, markets do not work well as a mechanism for trading know-how because (1) much know-how is tacit and difficult to separate out for sale; and (2) uncertainties as to the value of know-how make its sale problematic. Arrow (1962) has offered a paradox that explains why it is difficult to contract out know-how in the form of human capital (expertise). According to Arrow's paradox, the buyer needs to know information in order to evaluate its worth to him. However, once this information is given to the buyer for evaluation, there is no reason for the buyer to pay for the information since he already possesses it. Thus, there are considerable impediments associated with selling knowledge through the market mechanism. These arise from *uncertainties* as to the true value of that knowledge in the presence of *information asymmetries*. It follows that if a firm has developed know-how in one line of business, which can now be profitably applied to another line of business, this can best be achieved through hierarchical rather than market governance. The logic underlying this second scenario is much more closely allied to the measurement branch of transaction cost theory (uncertainty about the true value of know-how gives rise to measurement problems that inhibit market exchange).

To Teece's arguments can be added a third scenario. Specifically, by definition, exploiting economies of scope involves the sharing of a resource between two or more businesses. In such circumstances the question arises as to how the costs and revenues associated with the shared resource are to be allocated among cooperating businesses. The issue is complicated because of the significant *measurement problems* involved in assessing relative contribution, given that the joint utilization of a shared resource essentially reduces to a case of team production under conditions of uncertainty as described by Alchian and Demsetz (1972). Accordingly, in a market context contracting problems, haggling, and free riding might give rise to prohibitive transaction costs. Following Alchian and Demsetz, it can be argued that hierarchical governance gives top management the authority structure required to address such problems. Thus, hierarchy might be required to realize economies of scope.

Governance Characteristics

The theory sketched out above is not sufficient to explain the existence of the pure conglomerate firm in which there are no commonalities between business units (an "unrelated" firm) and therefore no potential for realizing scope economies. The lack of association between the business units of conglomerates has led critics to damn such enterprises (Jensen, 1988; Reich, 1983). This negative view is reinforced by empirical evidence in the strategic management literature, which suggests that most firms that grew during the 1960s and early 1970s by making unrelated acquisitions had below-average profitability by the end of that period (Rumelt, 1974, 1982) and spent much of the 1980s pursuing a strategy of de-conglomeration (Williams, Paez, and Sanders, 1988). A study of the long-run effects of conglomerate acquisitions by Ravenscraft and Scherer (1987, 1988) arrived at a similar negative view. Ravenscraft and Scherer (1988: 208) concluded:

Good companies were acquired, and on average, their profits and market shares declined following acquisition. A smaller but substantial subset of these good companies experienced traumatic difficulties triggering sell-off to non-conglomerate organizations that could manage them more effectively. There was considerable distress and wreckage on the road to conglomerate riches.

On the other hand, Ravenscraft and Scherer admit that the stock price evidence shows that those who invested early in the leading conglomerates of the early 1960s prospered. Moreover, it is possible to identify conglomerates that have excelled on all performance measures over a 25-year period. The British firms BTR, GEC, and Hanson Trust all fit this bill (Goold and Campbell, 1987). So what is going on here? Is the strategy of conglomerate diversification a mistake, or do conglomerate firms have efficiency properties that cannot be realized through the market mechanism? Williamson's (1970, 1975, 1985) work suggests that conglomerates have efficiency properties that arise from their governance characteristics.

According to Williamson, the capital market suffers from information and control disadvantages in its relationship with freestanding firms. Significant information asymmetries enable top managers to misrepresent the value of the firm to investors. Consequently, top managers may be able to pursue strategies that maximize their on-the-job consumption, at a nontrivial cost to the wealth of investors (top management may indulge in empire building, maintain a high degree of organizational slack, award themselves high-flying corporate perks, and so forth). Due to measurement problems in the face of uncertainty and information asymmetries, investors may not know that this is occurring. In addition, Williamson maintains that the capital market lacks an ability to fine-tune the operations of a firm. Instead, it is limited to costly discrete adjustments, such as takeovers (costly because of the high premiums over market value that are paid on most takeovers). As a consequence, even if investors do detect on-the-job consumption by top managers, it may not pay to do anything about it unless the problem becomes sufficiently serious.

Against the background of these *alleged* capital market inefficiencies, Williamson maintains that corporate management of the diversified firm is able to establish an internal capital market that overcomes the information and control disadvantages of the external market. This explanation relies heavily on the supposedly superior governance characteristics of the multidivisional (M-form) structure. At this point Williamson draws on Chandler's (1962) description of the M-form firm.

According to Chandler, a principal feature of the M-form is that each conceptually distinct business is placed in its own functionally self-contained division. Responsibility for day-to-day operating decisions is decentralized to the divisions. The divisions are controlled by a distinct and separate head office unit consisting of top corporate management and a specialist staff. Since each division is autonomous with regard to day-to-day operations, divisional management can also be held accountable for divisional profit performance.

Williamson argues that, within the context of such a structure, corporate management can use internal audits to overcome information asymmetries by divisional management and identify on-the-job consumption. Thus, the measurement problems that capital market investors encounter when trying to establish the value of a freestanding firm are attenuated within the M-form. In addition, corporate management can use hire-and-fire policies, reward and incentive schemes, and internal competition for capital resources as mechanisms for fine-tuning divisional operations and creating a culture that focuses the attention of divisional managers on maximizing the efficiency of their divisions. Thus, the M-form also mitigates control problems that capital market investors experience vis-à-vis the freestanding firm. The implications are that *conglomerate M-form firms can achieve a more efficient allocation of capital resources, and police the efficiency of divisions more effectively, than the external capital market could were each division a freestanding firm in its own right.*

It is important to note, however, that Williamson's arguments do contain two critical, and questionable, assumptions. First, Williamson assumes a degree of inefficiency in the external capital market that many would contest (Jensen and Ruback, 1983). Second, Williamson assumes that in the face of significant capital market failures, the top managers of M-form firms are somehow immune to on-the-job consumption. He justifies this assumption by claiming that the separation of divisional and corporate management functions provides top executives with a "psychological commitment" to optimizing the overall performance and profitability of the firm. This is more of an assertion than a carefully argued point of logic in Williamson's work. There is certainly no empirical evidence to this effect. There are also rather strong arguments to counter Williamson's position.

Jensen's Free Cash Flow Theory

Jensen (1986, 1988) is among those who have rejected Williamson's assumption that corporate management is somehow immune to on-the-job consumption. In contrast to Williamson, Jensen suggests that the agency conflict between top management and shareholders is severe in many public corporations, including the conglomerates that Williamson seeks to justify. Jensen depicts the agency conflict as being particularly problematic with regard to the payout of free cash flow. Free cash flow is defined as cash generated by the firm in excess of what is required to fund all projects with a positive NPV. According to Jensen, this cash should be returned to shareholders in the form of higher dividend payments. However, like Marris (1964) before him, Jensen suggests that "empire building" top management prefers to invest free cash flow in funding unprofitable diversification into unrelated industries. The reason for this is that top management derives psychic benefits from such investments, even though the yields are often below the cost of capital.

Jensen's preferred solution to this problem is to keep free cash flow out of the hands of top management by engineering leveraged buyouts of firms that are generating extensive free cash flow. The leveraged buyout, by exchanging debt for equity, forces top management to disgorge free cash flow to bondholders in the form of debt payments. According to Jensen, the need to service high debt payments has the added benefit of forcing top management to divest many of the firm's diversified businesses, and to improve the efficiency of the remaining core businesses. Jensen's position stands in stark contrast to that of Williamson, whose arguments suggest that top management of the M-form firm can invest free cash flow more efficiently than shareholders.

Who is correct? As so often in the social sciences, the empirical evidence is mixed. On the one hand, a number of ex ante (event) studies have found evidence that is consistent with the free cash flow hypothesis (Lang, Stulz, and Walkling, 1989; Lehn and Poulsen, 1989; Mitchell and Lehn, 1990). Similarly, a large-sample ex post study by Kaplan (1989a) presents evidence that highly leveraged management buyouts are associated with increases in operating profits, as Jensen's arguments predict. A recent series of clinical studies published in the *Journal of Financial Economics* have arrived at essentially the same conclusion (Baker and Wruck, 1989; Kaplan, 1989b).

On the other hand, advocates of Williamson's thesis point to the evidence in support of the M-form hypothesis. The M-form hypothesis predicts that because of their superior governance characteristics, firms organized along lines that are consistent with a Williamsonian internal capital market will outperform those that lack such an organizational structure. Those lacking M-form features include (1) functionally organized firms (U-form firms); (2) multidivisionals where top management intervenes in the day-to-day operations of divisions, thereby violating the M-form principles of operating autonomy and profit accountability; and (3) "holding companies" in which divisional cash flows are returned to source, rather than reallocated between competing claims on the basis of relative yield. The bulk of the empirical evidence is consistent with the M-form hypothesis (Armour and Teece, 1978; Harris, 1983; Hill, 1985; Hoskisson and Galbraith, 1985; Steer and Cable, 1978; Teece, 1981a; Thompson, 1981), although there have been at least three studies that have found no evidence of superior M-form performance (Cable and Dirrheimer, 1983; Cable and Yasuki, 1985; Hill, 1988).

Where does this leave us? It would seem that on balance there is evidence to support both theories. This ambiguity may reflect the methodological problems inherent in social science research. Alternatively, it is possible that there might be a valid synthesis of Williamson's thesis and Jensen's antithesis. Consider the following paradox in Jensen's theory. He argues for the breakup of old-style conglomerates, but also for the existence of takeover specialists that perform this function. While some of these takeover specialists are leveraged buyout organizations such as KKR, others are themselves conglomerates such as Hanson PLC. The difference between the "good" conglomerates, like Hanson, and the "bad" ones may involve top management attitudes and the organizational structures that top management puts in place. There is clinical evidence to suggest that high-performing conglomerates such as Hanson and BTR are classic

M-form firms as described by Chandler and Williamson (Goold and Campbell, 1987; Hill, 1984, 1992). Alternatively, many of the now-defunct poorly performing conglomerates such as SCM, the Imperial Group, and Thomas Tilling appear to have suffered from the agency problems of on-the-job consumption and a failure to pay out free cash flow (Hill, 1984, 1992). Consequently, they were eventually acquired and dismembered by M-form conglomerates (Hanson acquired Imperial and SCM, while BTR acquired Tilling).

If this synthesis is correct, it points to the critical role of internal organizational structure and top management philosophy in creating value from efficient internal governance. If the correct management philosophy and organizational structure is in place, the conglomerate firm may function like an internal capital market, with all of the benefits that implies. If the required management philosophy and organizational structure are not in place, the agency problems that Jensen highlights may emerge within the conglomerate.

Strategy and Structure

We have seen how transaction cost theory suggests that diversification may add value as long as it is consistent with (1) the efficient utilization of nonmarketable productive resources to yield economies of scope, and (2) efficient internal governance of the internal capital market variety. However, for a firm to fully realize value from hierarchical governance, the correct internal organizational structure and control systems must be in place. I have already touched on this issue with regard to the M-form structure and the internal capital market. This section draws on the management literature to consider the issue in greater depth.

It has long been argued that the multidivisional (M-form) structure is the appropriate organizational form for diversified firms (Chandler, 1962). Moreover, the empirical evidence indicates that most diversified firms are indeed multidivisionals (Channon, 1973; Hill and Pickering, 1986; Pavan, 1972; Rumelt, 1974; Thanheiser, 1972; Wrigley, 1970). However, M-form structures are not a homogeneous set (Hill and Hoskisson, 1987). Studies have found that superficially similar M-form firms may have substantial differences in internal arrangements with regard to centralization, integration, and internal control (Allen, 1978; Hill and Pickering, 1986; Lorsch and Allen, 1973; Vancil, 1980). Of course, Williamson (1975) recognized the existence of such variation within the M-form framework in his discussion of suboptimal M-form firms. But whereas Williamson argues that anything deviating from the stereotypical M-form is suboptimal, the arguments outlined below suggest otherwise.

The basic thrust of this section is that within the context of a multidivisional structure, the realization of economies of scope requires organizational arrangements that stress *cooperation* between divisions. In contrast, realizing governance economies of the internal capital market variety requires organizational arrangements that emphasize *competition* between divisions. It is suggested that these two sets of arrangements are incompatible with each other.

Cooperative Organizations

Within a diversified M-form firm, cooperation between divisions is necessary to realize economies of scope. There is a need to coordinate the activities of otherwise independent divisions so that skills can be transferred and resources shared. Child (1984) has argued that some *centralization* is necessary to achieve such coordination. Similarly, Mintzberg (1983) noted that interdependencies among divisions in related diversified firms encourage the corporate office to retain some control over the functions common to the divisions to ensure coordination. Consistent with this view, both Berg (1973) and Pitts (1977) found evidence that the interdivisional sharing of technological resources is achieved through centralization of research activities. Also, Sloan (1963) observed that in the case of General Motors, centralized oversight is necessary to ensure that the strategy and investments of cooperating divisions are complementary.[1] Consistent with Sloan's argument, Ackerman (1970) found that the identification of and impetus for major capital investment decisions was more centralized in M-form firms with a high degree of interdivisional integration than in M-form firms with a low degree of interdivisional integration. Therefore,

---

[1] At GM centralized oversight was used to ensure consistency in the pricing and product strategies of different divisions so that, to paraphrase Sloan, Cadillac didn't produce a car in the Chevrolet price range.

some degree of centralized control over the strategic and operating decisions of interdependent divisions in related diversified firms is required to realize economies of scope.

In addition to centralization, coordination between divisions also requires *integrating mechanisms* to achieve lateral communication between divisions. The complexity of these mechanisms will vary, depending on the extent of interdependence, from simple liaison roles and temporary task forces to permanent teams (Child, 1984; Galbraith, 1977; Lawrence and Lorsch, 1967). As Luke, Begun, and Pointer (1989) have noted, in related diversified firms interdependent divisions need to be tightly coupled.

One problem with attempting to achieve coordination between interdependent divisions is that it can create *performance ambiguities* (Govindarajan and Fisher, 1990; Gupta and Govindarajan, 1986; Hill and Pickering, 1986; Lorsch and Allen, 1973; Vancil, 1980). This is essentially the problem of team production as discussed by Alchian and Demsetz (1972) recurring within the firm. Specifically, when divisions lack complete autonomy with regard to operating and strategic decisions, objective rate-of-return criteria, which might be used to assess divisional performance, do not constitute an unambiguous signal of divisional efficiency. Poor financial performance of a certain division might be due to inefficiencies within that division, inefficiencies in another division with which it is tightly coupled, or poor central input into key operating decisions. Without access to more information, it can be difficult to assign accountability.

The firm can overcome performance ambiguity problems by increasing the amount of information it processes (Daft and Lengel, 1986). More precisely, as interdivisional coordination increases, the firm may de-emphasize rate-of-return measures of divisional performance and emphasize more *subjective modes of evaluating performance* (Govindarajan and Fisher, 1990; Hill, 1988; Ouchi, 1980). That is, in cooperative organizations the corporate head office needs to base its assessment of divisional performance on a wide range of criteria. These criteria might include more subjective measures of divisional performance (e.g., ability to innovate) along with objective measures in addition to rate-of-return criteria (e.g., labor productivity, capacity utilization, market share, and growth). Moreover, we would expect corporate management to allocate cash flows between competing claims based on such multiple criteria. In sum, corporate management needs to rely on a wide range of subjective and objective criteria when evaluating divisional performance and allocating cash flows if it is to overcome performance ambiguities arising from interdependent divisions and realize maximum economic benefits. Consistent with this thesis, an empirical study by Gupta and Govindarajan (1986) found that the greater the degree of resource sharing among divisions, the greater the reliance on subjective criteria in assessing the performance of divisional managers.

Finally, coordination may be enhanced if reward and incentive schemes emphasize interdivisional cooperation rather than the performance of each division as an independent unit (Gupta and Govindarajan, 1986; Kerr, 1985; Lorsch and Allen, 1973; Pitts, 1974; Salter, 1973). This can be achieved if profit bonus schemes for divisional managers in related diversified firms are linked to *corporate* rather than divisional profitability. Since corporate profitability will depend upon the success of interdivisional cooperation, such reward schemes will provide divisional managers with an incentive to cooperate. It follows that in related diversified firms there is a need to emphasize incentive schemes based on corporate profitability if the economic benefits associated with economies of scope are to be realized.

Competitive Organizations

Like firms attempting to realize economies of scope, pure conglomerate firms attempting to realize benefits from efficient internal governance may require an M-form structure (Chandler, 1962; Rumelt, 1974). However, there are clear indications that the internal organizational arrangements of conglomerate firms are different from those found in related diversified firms (Hill and Hoskisson, 1987; Mintzberg, 1983; Vancil, 1980).

Williamson (1975) has proposed that for a conglomerate to realize governance economies a number of organizational features must be present. First, each division must have autonomy with regard to operating decisions so that divisional managers can be held accountable for divisional profit performance (operating decisions should be decentralized). Second, to preserve autonomy the relationship between the corporate office and operating divisions should be an arm's-length one. The corporate office should not intervene in divisional affairs except to audit operations, discipline opportunistic or incompetent divisional managers, and correct performance shortfalls. Third, the corporate office should exercise control over divisions by setting rate-of-return targets and monitoring outcomes. Fourth, incentive systems for divisional managers should be linked to divisional returns. And fifth, the corporate office should allocate cash flows among divisions to high-yield uses on a competitive basis, rather than returning them to source divisions.

Within the conglomerate, these features replicate the relationship that exists between investors and freestanding firms in the stock market, while overcoming the limitations associated with the stock market (Williamson, 1985). Each division is evaluated on the basis of its rate of return as a self-contained unit. Divisional managers are responsible for all relevant operating decisions. Consequently, they are accountable for the performance of the divisions under their control, and they have a stronger incentive to maximize the efficiency of divisional operations than they would if accountability were weaker. Also, it is clear to divisional managers that promotional opportunities and job tenure are contingent on the attainment of specific rate-of-return targets. Gearing bonus pay to divisional returns, and allocating capital among divisions on the basis of relative yields, reinforces the incentive to maximize performance.

The system is predicted to produce competition among divisions for capital (Williamson, 1975). Divisional managers may also be compared on the basis of their ability to achieve rate-of-return targets for their respective divisions. Thus, internal promotion opportunities may be determined by competitive criteria. The internal ethos of such organizations is explicitly *competitive* rather than *cooperative*.

Organizational Incompatibilities

The above description suggests that two fundamentally different organizational philosophies are required to realize economies of scope and governance economies of the internal capital market variety. The basic differences between these two structural forms are summarized in Table 11-1. Companies such as IBM, 3M, and Dow Chemical fit the cooperative M-form model quite well. Companies such as BTR PLC, Hanson PLC, and General Electric seem to fit the competitive M-form model.

Table 11-1
Comparing Structural Forms

	Source of Economic Benefit	
	Economies of Scope	*Governance*
Basic Structure	Multidivisional	Multidivisional
Operating- and Business-Level Strategic Decisions	Some Centralization of Critical Functions	Complete Decentralization
Interdivisional Integrating Mechanisms	Moderate to Extensive	Nonexistent
Divisional Performance Appraisal	Mix of Subjective and Objective Criteria	Primary Reliance on Objective Financial Criteria (ROI)
Divisional Incentive Schemes	Linked to Corporate Performance	Linked to Divisional Performance

One conclusion that might be drawn from the radical differences between cooperative and competitive M-form structures is that it may be difficult for diversified firms to simultaneously realize economic benefits from economies of scope and efficient governance of the internal capital market variety. The lack of commonalties between divisions in unrelated conglomerates precludes economies of scope. Related firms may find it difficult to simultaneously realize benefits from economies of scope and an internal capital market because of the performance ambiguities that arise from substantial interdependencies among divisions.

Earlier I argued that because of performance ambiguities, to control the divisions of a related firm, corporate executives must process more information and undertake more subjective performance evaluations than their counterparts in conglomerate firms. Williamson (1975) asserted that subjective evaluations increase the probability that the biases of corporate executives will enter the performance evaluation process. As a consequence, compared to conglomerate firms, there is a greater tendency in related firms for rewards to be determined and capital funds allocated by a political bargaining process, rather than by reference to objective financial criteria. Since, by definition, the realization of economies from an internal capital market requires that rewards be determined and resources allocated on an arm's-length basis according to objective financial criteria, this makes it difficult for the related diversified firm to realize such economies. Thus, a fundamental trade-off is involved here. Related diversified firms organized on a cooperative basis can realize economies of scope, but the resulting performance ambiguities increase the probability that subjective biases will enter the control and resource allocation processes. Hence, it becomes more difficult for the firm to realize economies from an internal capital market. While this partly explains the incompatibility between the two structures, other differences are also evident.

Competitive and cooperative organizations have different internal configurations with regard to centralization, integration, control practices, and incentive schemes. As a result, the internal management philosophies of cooperative and competitive organizations are incompatible. In cooperative organizations, cooperation between divisions is fostered and encouraged. In competitive organizations, competition between divisions is fostered and encouraged. It is exceedingly difficult to simultaneously encourage competition and cooperation between divisions.

The notion that different structures and control systems are needed to implement related and unrelated diversification strategies is supported by the work of several authors. For example, Mintzberg (1983) made a similar distinction between the internal structure of "related-product" and "conglomerate" firms. Pitts's (1977) distinction between the internal structure and incentive systems of internal diversifiers (largely related firms) and acquisitive diversifiers (largely unrelated conglomerates) echoed similar themes. The distinction made by Lorsch and Allen (1973) between conglomerates and vertically integrated firms is similar in many respects to that discussed here for related and unrelated firms. Vancil (1980) also found differences in decentralization and control practices among firms pursuing different diversification strategies. Moreover, several authors have observed that the appropriate incentive systems for divisional managers are a function of the degree of resource sharing (relatedness) among divisions (Gupta and Govindarajan, 1986; Kerr, 1985; Lorsch and Allen, 1973; Pitts, 1974; Salter, 1973).

Limits to Efficient Diversification

Can the appropriately organized diversified firm continue to expand indefinitely, as Penrose (1959) has suggested, or are there organizational limits to growth? In his seminal article Coase (1937) indicated that limits to growth take the form of diminishing returns to management. If this were not the case, all production could conceivably be organized in one big firm. More recently, the transaction cost literature has focused on the factors that determine the bureaucratic costs to internal governance (Williamson, 1985). Bureaucratic costs can be defined as the costs of managing exchange within the firm. They are the internal organizational equivalent of transaction costs. They include not just the costs of hierarchy (which are nontrivial and include factors such as the salaries of upper-level management), but also the inefficiencies that arise within hierarchies due to information-processing problems in complex organizations (Hill and Hoskisson, 1987; Jones and Hill, 1988), incentive distortions (Williamson, 1985), and internal politics (Milgrom and Roberts, 1990a). In this section it is argued that these inefficiencies are an increasing function of (1) the diversified scope of the firm, and (2) the extent of interdependence among business units. If this is true, at some point the bureaucratic costs of hierarchy must outweigh the economic benefits of internalizing one more transaction inside the firm. At this point the firm reaches the limit of profitable expansion. Cooperative M-form organizations reach this limit sooner than competitive M-form firms.

Information-Processing Constraints

An agency theory perspective suggests that the internal incentive and control structure of the firm is of critical importance (Jensen and Meckling, 1976; Fama, 1980). Within the M-form firm we can conceive of top managers as the principals, and all other employees from divisional heads on down as agents. In the absence of adequate monitoring by top management, the agents have a tendency to engage in on-the-job consumption (shirking, free riding, and pursuing subgoals that are at variance with efficiency maximization). Accordingly, one of the basic functions of top management is to monitor the performance of lower-level employees, particularly divisional heads, to ensure that they are performing adequately. However, even in the best-designed organizations the ability of top management to perform the monitoring function depends on (a) their information-processing capabilities, and (b) the amount of information that has to be processed in order to reduce on-the-job consumption to acceptable levels. When (a) < (b) the result will be loss of control, rising levels of on-the-job consumption, and a failure of the firm to perform up to its potential. Put another way, when (a) < (b) the gains from internalizing transactions will be increasingly swamped by a rising tide of bureaucratic costs.

What determines (a) and (b)? With regard to (a), we know that top management's information-processing capability is ultimately limited by bounded rationality. With regard to (b), it has been argued that both the number of divisions and the interdependencies among those divisions determine the amount of information that has to be processed to reduce on-the-job consumption to acceptable levels (Hill and Hoskisson, 1987; Jones and Hill, 1988). The relationship between the number of divisions and information-processing requirements is obvious. On this point, Bettis and Hall (1983) and Haspeslagh (1982) have reported that because of information overload problems, top management in highly diversified firms has an increasing tendency to allocate large sums of money to different divisions with competing claims on the basis of only the most superficial investment analysis. That is, the amount of information that has to be processed in order to make meaningful capital investment decisions exceeds the information-processing capabilities of top management. As a consequence, such firms may reach a point of diminishing returns to diversification. It is highly unlikely that the top management of these firms would have been able to perform the capital allocation function more efficiently than the external capital market. Consequently, these companies would not have been able to benefit from efficient governance of the internal capital market variety.

Interdependencies among divisions are likely to make this type of problem even more severe. Recall that in cooperative M-form firms interdependencies among divisions give rise to performance ambiguities. It was argued earlier that to overcome such performance ambiguities, top management must process more information. This places greater demands on top management. It is one thing to evaluate the performance of 10 divisions when each is a self-contained unit that does not interact with other divisions. It is quite another thing when the 10 divisions are continually interacting with each other to share resources and transfer skills. The implication is that the level of diversification at which (a) < (b) will be reached much sooner in the case of cooperative M-form firms attempting to realize economies of scope than in the case of competitive M-form firms attempting to realize benefits from efficient governance of the internal capital market variety. The organizational limits to the growth of related diversified firms are thus encountered sooner than those of the pure conglomerate, although both kinds of organizations ultimately run into limits.

Internal Politics and Influence Costs

A second source of bureaucratic costs mentioned in the literature relates to the inefficiencies that derive from organizational politics. Milgrom and Roberts (1990a) have coined the term "influence costs" to describe these inefficiencies. They define (1990: 58) influence costs as

> the losses that arise from individuals within an organization seeking to influence its decisions for their private benefit (and from their perhaps succeeding to do so) and from the organization's responding to control this behavior.

From the current perspective, it should be apparent that influence costs are subsumed under bureaucratic costs. According to Milgrom and Roberts, influence costs arise because individuals and groups within the organization (such as divisional managers) expend time and effort attempting to influence the decisions of higher-level management. The objective is to get higher-level management to make decisions that are consistent with the subgoals of lower-level managers. Influence costs also arise because inefficient decisions result from these efforts or, less directly, from attempts to control them. Implicit in this approach is the idea that the subgoals of individuals and groups within the organization are at variance with those of higher-level managers when the latter are acting in shareholders' best interests.

This argument is, of course, an elaboration on the agency

argument. While agency theory stresses subgoal pursuit in the form of on-the-job consumption, Milgrom and Roberts simply widen the notion of subgoal pursuit to include attempts at influencing the decisions of higher-level management. According to Milgrom and Roberts, influence is inevitable because higher-level decision makers must rely on lower-level employees for information—a fact that gives lower-level employees opportunities to distort or withhold information (the "gatekeeper" phenomenon).

That such influence occurs is undoubtedly correct. The phenomenon has been extensively documented in the organizational theory literature (e.g., Pfeffer, 1981), although Milgrom and Roberts seem unaware of this. The critical issue is the extent to which the phenomenon contributes to the limits of organization. There is clearly a relationship between the information-processing constraints discussed above and influence costs. Put simply, as long as the information-processing capabilities of top management exceed the information-processing requirements necessary to control the organization, influence problems, while they may occur, will be limited in extent by top management's ability to cross-check the validity of information provided by divisional managers. Top management can make such a check by using the corporate staff to undertake independent audits of operating divisions that are suspected of withholding or distorting information (Chandler, 1962; Williamson, 1970, 1975). Indeed, the knowledge that such an audit might be performed could be enough to keep divisional management honest and influence costs to a minimum (although the cost of undertaking an audit is itself an influence cost—albeit a relatively minor one). On the other hand, when information-processing requirements exceed the information-processing capabilities of top management, the door may be left wide open for influence.

Incentive Problems

According to Williamson (1985), the incentive problems that arise within a management hierarchy constitute a major source of bureaucratic costs. Williamson sees incentive problems as occurring when top management tries to mimic high-powered market incentives within the firm. For illustration of the problem, consider a single-product enterprise managed by an owner-entrepreneur. The market rewards firms that maximize their efficiency with greater profits. Since the owner-entrepreneur has the title to the profit stream generated by his firm, he has a definite incentive to maximize efficiency. The better run his firm, the richer he becomes.

Now consider what happens if this single-product firm is acquired by an M-form conglomerate. The owner-entrepreneur takes his money and goes off to a tropical island, while a professional manager is appointed to run the new division. If he is like most professional managers, his tenure in the job will probably be limited. Most important, if he can demonstrate good performance he will move on to bigger and better things. The M-form conglomerate tries to mimic high-powered market incentives by giving the manager of the new division a share in the profit stream it produces. There is also the implicit promise of promotion if divisional performance is maximized. However, the divisional manager does not own the title to the profit stream or assets of the division. Consequently, while he has an incentive to increase the current profit stream, thereby increasing both his current income and his promotional prospects, he may actually have an incentive to erode the assets of the division. The possibility arises that he will underinvest in asset upgrades in order to maximize the current profits of the division—at the cost of long-term efficiency and profits.

This is the short-term profit maximization problem, which several authors have argued is endemic in the M-form conglomerate (Baysinger and Hoskisson, 1989; Hayes and Abernathy, 1980; Hill, Hitt, and Hoskisson, 1988; Hoskisson and Hitt, 1988). As long as the top management of the firm has spare information-processing capacity, they can attenuate the problem by auditing the affairs of the new division to make sure that the manager does not opportunistically underinvest in asset upgrades. However, if the scope and complexity of the firm is such that the information-processing capabilities of top management are already stretched to their limit, the problem may become a very real one. Thus, as in the case of influence costs, when information-processing requirements exceed the information-processing capabilities of top management, the door may be left wide open for short-run profit maximization and related phenomena to occur.

Conclusion: Implications of Research and Practice

My argument has three main themes. The first is that there are two different ways in which multibusiness firms can create economic value. One involves the realization of economies of scope by resource sharing across related businesses. The other involves establishing efficient governance of the internal capital market variety.

The second theme is that creating value from the internalization of transactions requires the firm to adopt the appropriate (M-form) organizational arrangements. The realization of economies of scope requires an organization that encourages coopera‐ tion between related divisions. The realization of gains from an internal capital market requires an organization that encourages competition between divisions. These different organizational arrangements may well be incompatible, forcing the firm to choose between them.

The third theme is that *even for the appropriately organized firm* the limited information-processing capabilities of top management give rise to very real barriers to efficient growth. The greater the scope of the firm, and the greater the degree of interdependence among divisions, the greater the amount of information that must be processed in order to limit influence and incentive problems. At some point information-processing requirements will be greater than the information-processing capabilities of even the best top managers. When this occurs the economic benefits realized from internalizing transactions will be outweighed by bureaucratic costs.

Implications for Research

Unless the economy is in a state of competitive equilibrium, which is highly unlikely given the almost continuous stream of Schumpeterian shocks that buffet the economic system, at any one point in time efficient and inefficient diversified firms will exist alongside one another. The efficient multibusiness firms will be those that (1) are attempting to realize value from economies of scope or from an internal capital market, (2) have adopted the appropriate internal (M-form) organizational arrangements, and (3) have not expanded past the point at which the information-processing requirements for controlling the firm exceed the information-processing capabilities of top management. The inefficient firms will be those that (1) do not have a coherent strategy, and/or (2) have adopted inappropriate organizational arrangements, and/or (3) have expanded to such a degree that the information-processing requirements for controlling the firm exceed the information-processing capabilities of top management.

Any empirical research on the relationship between diversification and economic performance that does not take these factors into account is bound to yield biased results. Most of the research on diversification and performance found in the strategic management and economics literature falls into this category. To get around this bias, researchers interested in the diversification-performance relationship need to start collecting data on internal organization. Moreover, the arguments assembled here suggest that it is not enough to identify whether an organization is a multidivisional or not. To effect a reasonably accurate organizational classification, the researcher also needs to collect detailed data on decentralization, internal control practice, integrating mechanisms, and the like. Obviously this cannot be achieved simply by mining publicly available data bases (e.g., Compustat, Trinet, FTC Line of Business Data, and so forth). To perform relatively unambiguous empirical tests that can conceivably refute the hypotheses advanced here, researchers are going to have to conduct surveys, semistructured interviews, and other studies *within* organizations. While this is neither convenient nor easy, there are already enough examples in the literature to suggest that it is possible (e.g., Grinyer, Yasai-Ardekani, and Al-Bazzaz, 1980; Hill, 1985, 1988).

Implications for Practice

The arguments assembled here suggest three essential tasks for corporate management: (1) to select the corporate diversification strategy of the firm, (2) to adopt and maintain an organization that is congruent with that strategy, and (3) to ensure that the firm does not grow beyond the point at which bureaucratic costs outweigh any gains from internalizing transactions. They also suggest that the management philosophy of corporate executives is a crucial element determining the efficiency of the firm. If corporate management is more interested in on-the-job consumption than in discharging their responsibility to share-holders, it is quite likely that they will expand the boundaries of the firm beyond the limits of efficiency.

The only issue that I have not discussed in any depth so far is the criteria that management might use to choose between different strategies. I have discussed two viable alternatives centered around economies of scope and efficient governance of the internal capital market variety, but which of these alternatives, if either, should top management choose? The answer probably depends upon the nature of the firm's resource base. Penrose's (1959) arguments suggest that a firm which has developed excess capacity in nonmarketable fungible productive resources should diversify into related areas to realize economies of scope, preferably by internal growth. On the other hand, if the fungible productive resource is top management, and if top management has skills in acquiring and managing businesses, then diversification to establish an internal capital market becomes a possibility. In such a case the acquisition of unrelated businesses might be entirely consistent with value creation. The job of top management is to identify firms that, because of weak governance, are not operating as efficiently as they might be. Once acquired and exposed to the superior governance of an M-form conglomerate, the efficiency of these firms should increase.

Finally, it needs to be stressed that in many situations not diversifying will be the optimal choice. Not all firms have fungible resources that can be profitably employed outside their core business. And not all firms have top management with the skills necessary to acquire and subsequently manage poorly performing firms so as to realize economic benefits from an internal capital market. When this is the case, it will pay not to diversify. When such firms are generating free cash flow, those monies should be returned to stockholders in the form of higher dividend payments, rather than invested in unproductive diversification.

12

The Functions of the HQ Unit in the Multibusiness Firm

Alfred D. Chandler, Jr.

The functions of the headquarters unit in the multibusiness firm is indeed a basic question for the understanding of the operations of modern business enterprise. As has been pointed out by the editors of this volume, the diversified corporation has become a dominant form of business organization. They rightly said in their organizing conference statement that: "It is no exaggeration to argue that the economies of the industrial world now depend crucially on the performance of large multibusiness, diversified companies." That statement is as true for the past as it is for today. As in the past, the decisions made by the senior executives at their headquarters have been absolutely critical to the performance of multinational and multiproduct companies. For those corporate executives not only monitor the current performance of their several businesses, but also determine and implement the investment in facilities and personnel required for future production and distribution in the different product and geographical markets they serve. On such decisions depend the competitive success or failure of their enterprises and the national industries in which they operate.

I begin this analysis of the functions of the HQ unit by reviewing the evolution of the multibusiness firm and the administrative structures created to operate it. I then examine how corporate headquarters carries out its functions, focusing largely on its entrepreneurial and administrative activities. Throughout this analysis I stress that industries have different characteristics, reflecting different technologies of production and different market demands. I conclude by examining how in implementing these functions senior executives at HQ units came to understand the limits to growth and the boundaries of the firm, and how, in turn, the functions and boundaries were shaped by the different characteristics of the industries in which the firms operated.

The Historical Evolution of the Multibusiness Firm

The modern business enterprise with its hierarchy of lower, middle, and top management appeared in the United States and Europe suddenly in the 1850s to operate the new forms of transportation and communication. By the 1880s railroad and telegraph companies had created organizational structures and internal control systems (including the adoption of the M-form for multiregional systems) as complex as those created a half-century later in industry and commerce. At the same time the unprecedented volume, speed, and above all, regularity of the flow of goods and messages through the economy made possible by the railroad and the telegraph revolutionized the processes of production and distribution. In distribution the modern mass retailer appeared—the department store, the mail-order house, and the chain store. In production, the technological potential created by the new flows precipitated a wave of technological innovations that swept across Western Europe and the United States—a phenomenon that historians have properly termed the Second Industrial Revolution.

The new technologies transformed the processing of tobacco, grains, whiskey, beer, sugar, vegetable oil, and other foods. They revolutionized the refining of oil and the making of metals and materials—steel, nonferrous metals (particularly copper and aluminum), glass, abrasives, and other materials. They created brand-new chemical industries that produced man-made dyes, fibers, fertilizers, and medicines. They brought into being a wide range of machinery—light machines for sewing, agriculture, and office use; heavier standardized machinery such as elevators, refrigerating equipment, and greatly improved printing presses, pumps, and boilers. Most revolutionary of all were the new machines to mass-produce and distribute electric power. That new energy source not only transformed the mechanical process of production within factories and created new forms of urban transportation, but it revolutionized the processing of many metals and chemicals.

These industries that began to drive economic growth and transformation in the late nineteenth century had two basic characteristics that differentiated them from existing labor-intensive industries such as textiles, apparel, furniture, paper, lumber, leather, shipbuilding, and mining. So did the transforming industries of later decades—those based on the internal combustion engine before World War II and those based on electronics, particularly the computer, after that war. First, all the processes of production were far more capital-intensive than in the older industries. That is, the ratio of capital to labor per unit of output was much higher. Second, in these industries large plants had significant cost advantages over smaller ones in producing a single line of products. Up to a minimum efficient size (based on the nature of the technology and the size of the market) the cost per unit dropped more quickly as the volume of output increased than was the case in the labor-intensive industries. Besides such economies of scale, large works often utilized economies of scope—those resulting from making different products in a set of facilities using the same raw and semi-finished materials and the same intermediate processes of production.

In all these capital-intensive industries, however, the new large plants were able to maintain the cost advantages of scale and scope only if the entrepreneurs who built them made two other sets of investments. They had to create a national and then an international marketing and distributing organization. And they had to recruit lower and middle managers to coordinate the flow of products through the processes of production and distribution, and top managers to coordinate and monitor current operations and to plan and allocate resources for future activities. The small number of first movers—those that made the three-pronged set of investments in manufacturing, marketing, and management essential to exploit fully the economies of scale and scope—quickly dominated their industries and usually continued to do so for decades. Challengers did appear, but they were only a few.

The three-pronged investment by the first movers created the modern industrial enterprise administered through functional departments whose heads, with the president, formed the corporate headquarters. (That is, new firms were administered through the U-form of organization.) That investment also transformed the structure of industries. The new capital-intensive industries were quickly dominated by a small number of large managerial enterprises, which competed for market share and profit in a new oligopolistic manner. Price remained a significant competitive weapon. But these firms competed more forcefully through functional and strategic efficiency—that is, by performing more effectively the different processes of production, distribution, marketing, production development, and the like, and by moving more quickly into expanding markets and out of declining ones. The test of such competition was changing market share. In the new oligopolistic industries market share and profits changed constantly.

This oligopolistic competition sharpened the product-specific capabilities of workers and managers. Such capabilities, plus retained earnings from the new and profitable capital-intensive technologies, became the basis for the continuing growth of these managerial enterprises. Firms did grow by combining with competitors (horizontal combination) or by moving backward to control materials and forward to control outlets (vertical integration), but they usually did so in response to specific situations that varied with time and place. For most firms in these capital-intensive industries the continuing long-term strategy of growth was expansion into new markets—either into new geographical areas or into related product markets. The move into geographically distant markets was normally based on competitive advantage of organizational capabilities developed by exploiting economies of scale. Moves into related industries rested more on advantages developed by exploiting economies of scope. Such organizational capabilities honed by oligopolistic competition provided the dynamic for the continuing growth of these firms, of the industries they dominated, and of the national economies in which they operated.

The expansion into new geographical and related product markets by the 200 largest industrial enterprises in the United States, Britain, and Germany from the 1880s to the 1940s is described and documented in my book, *Scale and Scope.* An appendix in that book gives the product lines of these companies (by three-digit SIC categories of the U.S. Census) for 1930 and 1948. A follow-up list for 1973 is given in Chandler and Tedlow (1985). Scott (1973) summarized several studies on the continuing diversification into new markets of the largest 100 firms in the United States, Britain, France, and Italy between 1950 and 1970. By the 1960s the multibusiness enterprise had become the norm in modern capital-intensive, technologically complex industries.

In the interwar years in the United States, but rarely before 1950 in Europe, senior executives rationalized the management of this multimarket growth by adopting some variations of the M-form with its corporate headquarters and integrated product or geographical divisions. (In this chapter the terms "corporate headquarters," "corporate office," and "HQ unit" are synonymous.) The M-form came into being when senior managers operating through existing centralized, functionally departmentalized U-form structures realized they had neither the time nor the necessary information to coordinate and monitor day-to-day operations, or to devise and implement long-term plans for the various product lines. The administrative overload had become simply too great. At DuPont, the innovator in 1921, and then in other new multibusiness enterprises, the solution was to establish divisions to administer the production and distribution of their major product lines or geographical regions and a general or corporate headquarters to administer the enterprise as a whole. The divisional offices coordinated production and distribution (and often product development) using the U-form structure. From the start the function of the corporate headquarters of these new multimarket business enterprises was that of maintaining the long-term health (usually defined as continued profitability) and growth of their firms.

To fulfill this role the executives at the new headquarters had to carry out two closely related functions.[1] One was entrepreneurial or value-creating, that is, to determine strategies for maintaining and utilizing in the long term the firm's organizational skills, facilities, and capital and to allocate resources—capital and product-specific technical and managerial skills—to pursue these strategies. The second was more administrative or loss preventive. It was to monitor the performance of the operating divisions; to check on the use of the resources allocated;

---

[1] The executives at the corporate headquarters carried out an additional and most essential function, that of handling the enterprise's relations with legislatures and other governmental bodies concerning taxes, tariffs, and regulation. In this chapter I concentrate on the two basic functions because they focus on managerial issues arising in matters internal to the firm.

and, when necessary, to redefine the product lines of the divisions so as to continue to use the firm's organizational capabilities effectively.

The administrative tasks of monitoring were, of course, intimately related to the entrepreneurial task of strategic planning and resource allocation. Monitoring provided the essential information about changing technology and markets and about the nature and pace of competition in the different businesses. And it permitted a continuing evaluation of the performance of divisional operating managers. Indeed, management development has long been a critical function of the corporate headquarters. Of all the enterprise's resources, product-specific and firm-specific managerial skills are the most essential to maintaining the capabilities of its existing businesses and to taking the enterprise into new geographical and product markets where such capabilities give it a competitive advantage.

Facilitated by adoption of the M-form, the size and numbers of multibusiness firms—both multinational and multi-industrial—increased rapidly, particularly after World War II. So too did the variety of markets they entered; and, therefore, the number of divisions they operated. Such growth intensified competition. Until the 1960s, however, world events—the two global wars and the massive global depression of the 1930s—held back the full impact of international and interindustry competition. In the 1960s European and Japanese enterprises began to compete with American firms in the United States and abroad, and many more American firms moved overseas. In these same years U.S. enterprises, which had begun to enter closely related markets during the interwar years, began to expand in this manner more aggressively. For example, by the 1960s, agricultural, mining, industrial, construction machinery, and truck and auto companies had moved into each other's markets, and glass, rubber, and food firms expanded their activities in chemicals. Rapidly growing R&D expenditures intensified such interindustry competition.

Continued growth into new markets encouraged structural change, for like the initial diversification, it resulted in a decision-making overload at both the corporate office and division levels. Senior executives at DuPont reviewing the company's organizational structure "saw striking parallels between the company's problems in the 1920s and those of the late 1960s" (Hounshell and Smith, 1988: 586). The solution at DuPont and many other companies was to form integrated business units within the divisions, which coordinated and controlled a single product or very closely related product lines. In others it was to place the divisions under larger "group" offices.

But whatever the names used, by the 1970s most large multibusiness enterprises had three (not just two) levels of autonomous planning and administrative offices. They are referred to in this paper as the business unit, the division, and the corporate HQ or office. The business unit normally operated through the functional U-form structure; the divisions, like the corporate office, operated through a version of the M-form structure with its own staff and senior executives responsible for profit, market share, and other measures of performance.[2]

The corporate office continued to define growth paths and goals for the corporation as a whole and to monitor the performance of the subordinate operating units. In these same years new regulatory legislation forced the headquarters to sharply increase its role as mediator with government agencies and other public bodies. By the 1980s, according to Donaldson and Lorsch's study (1983: 13) of corporate office executives of 12 large American manufacturing companies, several CEOs said that they spend 30–40% of their time in dealing with such matters.

New players from abroad and from related industries gave many U.S. companies the greatest competitive challenge they had faced since their founding decades earlier. Many U.S. managers responded by reinvesting to improve their competitive capabilities in their own and closely related industries. But others began to grow by moving into industries in which their organizational competencies provided little or no competitive advantage. Because they had had little competition from abroad since before World War II—and because they were being told by some academics that management was a generalist skill— many of these executives had come to believe that, if they were

---

[2]   In some companies there were five levels—profit centers, business units, divisions, groups, and the corporate offices. But in nearly all, profit centers were within business units and were usually related to functional activities, and the group usually remained part of the corporate HQ. Here I use the term "business unit" for the lowest-level multifunctional office, and "division" for the highest-level office where senior line executives had profit responsibility.

successful in their own industry, they could be just as successful in others. For many managers, as Donaldson and Lorsch (1983) have documented, the goal of this broad-based diversification was long-term growth. Others simply enjoyed empire building. Moreover, their companies were cash-laden precisely because the postwar years of American hegemony had been so prosperous.

So these managers sought to invest their retained earnings in industries that appeared to show a greater profit potential than their own. And they did so even though those industries were at best only distantly related to their companies' core capabilities. They lacked the knowledge of their target industries' operations, and they lacked, too, the necessary capabilities to build plants and develop personnel through direct internal investment as they had in the past. So these diversifiers grew by acquisition or, occasionally, merger.

In these same years a new form of multibusiness enterprise appeared, the conglomerate. The conglomerate can be defined as a firm that grew almost wholly by making acquisitions in unrelated industries. Such firms were of two types. One was firms in older sectors of the economy whose capabilities failed to give them a base for growth comparable to those of the large industrial diversifiers. They were utilities and transportation firms such as ITT, Tenneco, Illinois Central Industries, Northwest Industries, Ogden, and Greyhound, and industrials such as Textron, U.S. Industries, Walter Kidde, Dart Industries, and Colt Industries. These included 11 of the 15 conglomerates listed among the top 200 in 1973. A few years later similar firms appeared in Britain, including BTR and Hanson Trust. As they diversified, most sold off their original business. The other type was enterprises that entrepreneurs created from scratch. Four of the top 15 U.S. conglomerates in 1973 were such entrepreneurial start-ups—LTV, Litton, Gulf + Western, and Teledyne. Some of these enterprises profited by improving the management and hence the profits of the companies acquired. But others increased the value of their shares through creative, but legal, accounting that recorded on the balance sheets an inflated picture of their assets, revenues, and earnings.

Table 12-1, which was compiled by Norman Berg, documents the differences in the size and personnel of corporate HQ of conglomerates and those of diversified majors. The differences reflect differences in the strategies of diversification. For each the number of general executives was about the same, but the size and activities of the corporate staff varied. Since their unrelated activities offer no synergies, the conglomerates had no need for manufacturing, marketing, purchasing, traffic, and research staffs. Even in finance and control they employed smaller numbers than did the major diversifiers. Only in public, including government, relations were the numbers much the same.

Implementing the Entrepreneurial and Administrative Functions

I have presented this historical review to explain why the multibusiness firm became such a pervasive and powerful institution in modern economies, why the corporate office appeared and how its functions developed. A more precise understanding of these functions and of the mechanisms used to implement them calls for a more detailed analysis based on information from specific enterprises. I rely on Michael Goold and Andrew Campbell's *Strategies and Styles: The Role of the Centre in Managing Diversified Corporations* (1987) for information on 16 carefully selected British diversified and conglomerate firms. For the U.S. conglomerates I examine the historical experience of International Telephone and Telegraph (ITT) with brief references to other conglomerates. For the U.S. multibusiness firms I review the history of two diversified majors, General Electric (GE) and DuPont, with a brief reference to International Business Machines (IBM). As these data come almost wholly from manufacturing enterprises, the analysis here essentially concerns the functions of corporate HQ in industrial multibusiness enterprises.

Because the data are rich and the functions carefully categorized in the Goold and Campbell study, I begin with the British companies. In *Strategies and Styles* the authors describe three major types of management styles used by senior managers at corporate headquarters: strategic planning, strategic control, and financial control. "The three main styles," they write, "lead to different strategies and different results" (Goold and Campbell, 1987: 87). I would argue that these three styles, like the internal organization of the headquarters, result from different paths of growth and, therefore, from different patterns of investment and different sets of organizational capabilities. These capabilities in turn reflect the different characteristics of the

Table 12-1

Differences in Size and Personnel of the Offices of Diversified Majors and Conglomerates

STATISTICAL DATA ON COMPANIES

Statistical Data Companies	Sales (million $)	Fortune Rank	1969 Assets (million $)	Employees (thousands)	Number of Divisions	4-Digit SIC #	Approx. # Acquis. 1959–69	1959 Sales (million $)	Fortune Rank
Diversified Majors:									
Bendix	$1,468	72	$980	63.5	53	30	16	$684	62
Borg-Warner	1,087	108	949	41.6	35	25	3	650	68
Ingersoll-Rand	711	160	690	33.7	27	31	11	162	269
Company 'X'	About 500	—	—	—	—	About 35	n/a	—	—
Average	About 1,000	—	—	—	—	About 30	—	—	—
Company 'Y'	—	—	—	—	—	About 50	n/a	—	—
Conglomerates:									
Gulf + Western	$1,564	64	$2,172	85.0	37	89	45	—	—
Kidde (W. J.)	786	143	775	35.7	55	n/a	74 ('64–'69)	$41	—
Lear-Siegler	587	186	319	26.6	56	40	50	87	431
Litton	2,177	39	1,580	116.0	70	64	80	126	322
Textron	1,682	57	895	70.0	32	85	55	308	146
Average	$1,359	98	$1,148	66.6	50	70	61	—	—

332

ORGANIZATIONAL DATA ON COMPANIES

Companies / Functions	Diversified Majors							Conglomerates							
	Company				Four Cos:		'Y'	Company					Five Cos:	
	A	B	C	X	Total	Avg.		F	G	H	I	J	Total	Avg.
General Executives	5	5	4	2	16	4	23	4	1	4	3	14	26	5
Finance	28	61	101	144	334	84	582	8	22	29	91	106	256	51
(of which Control)	(10)	(36)	(78)	(107)	(231)	(58)	(424)	(6)	(12)	(8)	(38)	(49)	(113)	(23)
Legal-Secretarial	4	10	22	42	78	20	92	1	7	5	6	66	85	17
Personnel Adm.	11	6	20	25	62	16	90	1	2	3	10	20	36	7
Research & Dev.	54	130	139	232	555	139	1,012	0	0	0	0	0	0	0
Marketing	5	0	34	0	39	10	101	0	0	0	0	0	0	0
Manufacturing	5	1	0	5	11	3	190	0	0	0	0	0	0	0
Public Relations	1	6	9	16	32	8	45	5	3	5	6	9	28	6
Purchasing & Traffic	10	1	33	4	48	12	30	0	0	0	2	0	2	0
Corporate Planning	3	3	2	6	14	5	8	5	4	1	7	9	26	5
TOTALS	126	223	364	476	1,189	301	2,173	24	39	47	125	224	459	91

Source: Norman Berg, "Corporate Role in Diversified Companies," Harvard Business School Working Paper #71-2BP2, reprinted in Alfred D. Chandler, Jr., and Richard S. Tedlow, The Coming of Managerial Capitalism: A Casebook on the History of American Economic Institutions (Homewood, Ill.: Richard D. Irwin, 1985), pp. 758–759.

333

Table 12-2

Three Types of Management Styles and Their Organizational Structures:
The 16 Participant Companies

Company	Main activity	Sales 1985 (£m)	Rank in Times 1000
BP	Oil	47,156	1
ICI	Chemicals	10,725	4
GEC	Electricals	5,222	14
Imperial	Tobacco, food, drinks	4,919	15
BTR	Diversified	3,881	18
Hanson Trust	Diversified	2,675	33
Courtaulds	Textiles and chemicals	2,173	45
STC	Electronics	1,997	48
BOC	Gases and health care	1,901	54
Cadbury Schweppes	Confectionary, soft drinks	1,874	56
UB	Foods	1.806	60
Tarmac	Construction	1,536	72
Plessey	Electronics	1,461	76
Lex	Distribution	1,041	110
Vickers	Engineering	611	159
Ferranti	Electronics	568	169

Strategic planning companies: organizational structure (1985)

	Number of divisions	Overlaps between businesses	Number of businesses	Overlaps between businesses within divisions
BOC	4	Low-medium	37	High
BP	11	Medium	11(S)	High
Cadbury Schweppes	4	Low-medium	45(H)	High
Lex	3	Low	9(H)	Medium-high
STC	4	Medium-high	20–25	High
UB	3	Medium	13	Medium

Strategic control companies: organizational structure

	Number of divisions	Overlaps between divisions	Number of businesses	Overlaps between businesses within divisions
Courtaulds	8	Low-medium	30–40	Medium
ICI	20	Generally low	50–60	High
Imperial	3	Low	20–25	Medium
Plessey	3	Medium	20–25	High
Vickers	10	Low	25–30	Medium

Table 12-2 (*Continued*)
Financial control companies: organizational structure

	Number of divisions	Overlaps between divisions	Number of businesses	Overlaps between businesses
BTR	27	Low	150	Low
Ferranti	5	Low	3	Medium
GEC	12	Low	170	Medium
Hanson Trust	9	Low	70	Low
Tarmac	6	Low	6	—

Source: Michael Goold and Andrew Campbell, *Strategies and Styles: The Role of the Centre in Managing Diversified Corporations* (Oxford: Basil Blackwell, 1987), pp. 7, 48, 87, 112.

businesses in which the firms operate. Finally, the success of HQ units in adapting management styles to their industries' characteristics determines the effective size and boundaries of their enterprises.

Table 12-2 suggests the different paths to growth by diversification that the firms in each of these styles may follow. The companies in the strategic planning category are by and large the least diversified, operate the smallest number of businesses, and have the highest linkages between divisions and the highest overlap between business units within divisions. The strategic control companies operate more businesses, have fewer overlaps between the divisions, and on the whole have less synergy between the business units. Three of the five financial control companies are the most diversified in the sample. Of the other two, Ferranti is small in terms of sales and assets, and Tarmac is the only construction company on the list. All five have the lowest linkages between divisions and the lowest overlap between units within divisions.

Implementing Functions in Financial Control Companies

The basic differences in size, personnel, and, therefore, the activities of the corporate office in financial control companies and in companies in the two strategic categories are much the same as the differences between the American conglomerates and major diversifiers indicated in Table 12-1. The financial control companies in Britain grew almost wholly by acquisition, not by direct internal investment. Hanson Trust, BRT, and the smaller Tarmac were true conglomerates. They followed the pattern of most U.S. conglomerates by moving out of their original business after acquiring firms in unrelated industries. General Electric Company (GEC, no relation to the American GE) was a government-sponsored merger of Britain's three leading electrical equipment companies, which, after a modicum of rationalization, continued to operate quite autonomously with relatively little supervision from the corporate office. GEC grew largely through acquisition. Ferranti, too, is a product of British government policy. The government rescued it from bankruptcy in 1974 to permit it to retain its position in data handling systems, instrumentation, and other electronic businesses for which the military was its largest customer.

In all five the corporate office has remained small. Like those of the U.S. conglomerates these offices include a few general line officers and almost no functional staff executives except in finance and public relations. The division managers are considered part of the corporate headquarters. The division managers "play a linking and surveillance role between the units and the centre" (Goold and Campbell, 1987: 115). So while the corporate executives may suggest strategic moves, the business units within the divisions are responsible for defining their strategies.

In these financial control companies the budget is the basic means of control. It thus becomes almost by default the primary instrument of planning. Budgets are prepared by the business units and reviewed and approved by the corporate office with relatively little discussion between executives in the center and the operating units. In approving capital expenditures the corporate office looks for a quick (two- to three-year) payback. Each budget (and each project) is considered on its own merits and not in relation to a larger overall strategic plan. Nor do the budgets of one unit relate their activities to those of another.

The budget is taken very seriously. It is considered a contract between the corporate office and the business unit. The center monitors the performance by comparing monthly and quarterly reports of actual results against the budget (Goold and Campbell, 1987: 129). Current financial performance is the critical measure of achievement. Failure to meet financial targets often means a change in the management of the unit. In drawing up budgets the goal is short-term profit rather than reinvestment for long-term earnings based on a unit's organizational capabilities. Of the 16 companies studied by Goold and Campbell the financial control companies had the best profit performance and the largest growth, but growth was almost wholly through the buying of new operating units and not through direct internal investment in existing operating units (1987: 309–311).

The basic function of the corporate HQ in these financial control companies was then administrative or loss preventive. It was to review the financial performances of the businesses controlled and to adjust the enterprises' portfolio accordingly. Weak performers were sold off and new ones that met the logic of this type of control were purchased. In their acquisitions the British conglomerates avoided buying enterprises in technologically complex, capital-intensive industries where product and process innovations required long-term investment and associated risks. Lord Hanson and the senior executives of BTR have expressed themselves strongly about this strategy (Goold and Campbell, 1987: 135, 252; Feder, 1989). Neither of the two financial control companies that remain in high-technology industries—GEC and Ferranti—have prospered. GEC has moved out of consumer electronics and control systems, and has purchased a shipyard and a weighing machine company. Recently Ferranti sold off its basic data system division, which had accounted for 37% of its business. If they are to succeed, Goold and Campbell predict, "a change to Strategic Control may occur" (1987: 144).

The history of the U.S. conglomerates has been more complex than that of their British counterparts, possibly because the British firms have been more successful in defining their portfolios. The experience has been one of expansive growth through unrelated acquisitions in the 1960s and into the 1970s, then drastic pullbacks in the 1980s.

A brief review of the history of ITT, the pioneering U.S. conglomerate and for a long time the largest, is revealing. Until the 1960s, ITT was a giant global telecommunications enterprise. (Formed in 1920, in 1925 it acquired all the foreign operations of Western Electric, the manufacturing arm of AT&T). In the 1960s under Harold Geneen it began to diversify. As losses of its operating telephone companies in Eastern Europe immediately after World War II and then in Latin America reduced its operations and slowed its growth, the new CEO developed a well-considered strategy of growth at home rather than abroad.

This plan meant growth by acquisition in unrelated industries, for in the United States, AT&T and Western Electric dominated telecommunications. By the mid-1970s ITT had acquired some 300 companies.

Geneen, an accountant by training, required a detailed set of monthly financial reports from every operating unit. These were analyzed at monthly staff meetings attended by Geneen and all operating managers. The CEO also called for annual business plans and detailed five-year plans. In the 1970s Geneen was heralded as a pioneer in a new form of business administration—management by the numbers. It did not work. The overload became staggering. One participant, the president of Avis, estimated that comparing and analyzing the annual business plans represented 13 months' work for the corporate staff (Dinerstein, 1980).

After Geneen reluctantly retired in 1979, his successor R. V. Araskog pulled back and attempted "to transform ITT from a loosely based conglomerate into a rational, broadly based, international electronics corporation with major stress on telecommunications" (Sobel, 1982: 70). He tried, in other words, to return ITT to its core business. But it was much too late. ITT never recovered its foreign markets from its powerful competitors, Siemens and Ericsson. By 1988 it had withdrawn from telecommunications and electronics. By then Araskog had sold off over 100 companies and consolidated the remaining seven businesses, four of which were in services—hotels, insurance, financial lending, and information services. Today these are its major sources of revenue. The other three were industrial businesses: auto parts, pumps and valves, and electric components and systems largely for the U.S. military. By the late 1980s the senior executives at ITT had learned that growth was limited by the corporate HQ's inability to manage its unrelated operating units profitably.

By that time executives in corporate headquarters of other conglomerates had learned much the same lesson. Northwest Industries had been dismembered. LTV and Greyhound were then in bankruptcy proceedings. Gulf + Western had spun off over 100 of its operations to become a movie company—Paramount Communications. Kidde and U.S. Industries had been swallowed up by the Hanson Trust. Those that remained among the 200 largest U.S. industrials had followed ITT's pattern of selling off a major share of their operations and concen-

Table 12-3
Planning and Control Systems for Multidivisional Firms

	Financial Control	Strategic Control	Strategic Planning
Size of HQ	small	large	large
Mechanisms of control:			
(a) budgets	strong	moderate	weak
(b) strategic plans and reports	none	moderate	strong
Responsibility for strategic definition	business units	divisions	corporate HQ
Interbusiness unit interdependencies within divisions	low	moderate	high
Examples	ITT, Hanson Trust	DuPont to 1980 GE in 1980s	IBM to 1980 DuPont in 1980s

trating on industries whose production processes, final products, and markets remained relatively stable. If they stayed with more technologically advanced products, they normally sold them to the Department of Defense. Thus, Tenneco focused on shipbuilding for the U.S. Navy, agricultural equipment, and packaging materials, as well as its original natural gas pipeline business. Litton had narrowed its business to four product lines—marine engines, industrial automation, oil and gas exploration, and defense electronics. By 1989 well over half its business came from defense contracts. Teledyne did much the same, with 35% of its revenues coming from the federal government. In 1985 Textron spun off 22 divisions and acquired Avco, a longtime producer of aircraft parts and equipment, which complements the Bell aircraft unit it purchased in 1960. By 1989 aerospace/defense business accounted for 46% of sales, financial services and insurance 29%, and consumer products 25%.

As the corporate officers of the conglomerates came to realize, the small headquarters depicted in Table 12-3 had only facilities for financial control. That is, the functions of the corporate HQ were primarily administrative or loss preventive. Such controls were effective in service industries and in industries involving relatively inexpensive production facilities and small R&D expenditures. If the conglomerates remained in more technologically complex, capital-intensive industries, they had little choice but to pull back and to concentrate their portfolios in a small number of groups of related product lines about which the senior executives had more than just financial knowledge; to make such product lines work, executives needed experience and close contacts with buyers, particularly government officials. Conglomerates have been challenged to develop strategic and planning capabilities within those industry groups. These firms, like British GEC, appear to be shifting to a style of strategic control.

Implementing Functions in Strategic Planning and Strategic Control Companies

The most successful of the conglomerates, a new phenomenon of the 1960s, were those that acquired and managed companies in industries where financial control alone was sufficient to maintain profitability. On the other hand, nearly all major diversifiers in both Britain and the United States were long-established enterprises whose headquarters from their beginnings carried out both the entrepreneurial, value-creation function and the administrative, loss-prevention one. That is, their relatively large headquarters (Table 12-3) had been involved in strategy planning and control.

All but one of the companies in Goold and Campbell's sample of strategically oriented companies were long-lived. That exception, Lex, began as a distributor for Volvo and then continued to operate as a distributing and leasing firm. Except for three leaders in food, drink, and tobacco—Cadbury Schweppes, United Biscuits, and Imperial Tobacco (Hanson acquired the last in 1986)—these British firms were in industries with relatively technologically complex processes and products. All but the food companies had large research and development departments. All grew much more by direct internal investment than by acquisition. This was also true of the American firms studied—IBM, GE, and DuPont. Each of the three U.S. companies has been for decades the leading firm in a significant transforming industry of the past century. Their experience, particularly the growth and pullback of the second two, helps explain how the finite ability of the corporate office to carry out its basic functions sets limits to growth.

The planning and control functions and the mechanisms that the British companies developed to implement them in the two strategic styles identified by Goold and Campbell—strategic planning and strategic control—had many similarities. In both the strategic definition began in the business units. In both, division headquarters played a significant role in the review process. In both, the officers at the three levels—business unit, division, and corporate office—had extensive staffs. Both types of companies had annual planning cycles with annual reviews of "business plans" and "operating plans." These resulted in budgets that, unlike those in the financial control companies, were linked to long-term strategic plans. In three companies such plans were formally developed on an annual basis, and in one company every two years. For the others, long-term strategic planning was less formalized. The aim of the business plans and operating reviews was "to raise the quality of business thinking, to allow multiple perspectives to be expressed, and to permit corporate views to influence strategy" (Goold and Campbell, 1987: 70).

The difference between strategic planning and strategic control companies was that in the first the corporate office played a more decisive role. The different attributes of these two planning and control systems and also those of financial control are summarized in Table 12-3. Corporate executives in strategic planning companies reviewed strategic themes, relating them to their portfolio mix, and examined the particular thrusts or suggestions of the individual business units. In planning they focused attention on interbusiness and interdivisional opportunities and dependencies. The proposals for new projects requiring large-scale capital allocation and entries into new businesses came from both the business and the corporate offices; but corporate sponsorship was essential for any major new initiative. Long- and short-term goals (both strategic and financial) and budgets emerged from the agreed-upon plans. Such plans did not exist at the financial control companies. Monitoring was carried out through regularly scheduled reports from the business units, which gave details about actual results. But, unlike at the financial control companies, financial targets and budgets were not sacrosanct in terms of incentives (bonuses) or sanctions (management removal). Instead, they were the basis for discussions between the business units and centers concerning progress made toward achieving long-term strategic and financial goals. As a result, in the strategic planning companies administrative controls were employed much more flexibly than in those companies using the financial control style, or even in those firms relying more on strategic controls.

The strategic control companies differed from the strategic

planning ones in that much of the planning devolved upon the divisional headquarters. This difference reflected a greater number of business units within the firms and a wider variety of businesses served by the firms. The divisions often had as large functional staffs, including those for research and development, as had the corporate office. (Where divisions were placed in groups, the group executives had very little staff and were considered members of the corporate office.) The divisions, responsible for coordinating the activities of the business units under their command, integrated the planning process. Corporate executives rarely made or suggested strategic themes or thrusts to guide the strategic planning process. They made little attempt to coordinate synergies or review interdependencies among divisions. Capital projects and proposals for new business entries came from the divisions, not the corporate office, with the corporate office taking the initiative only on closures and divestitures.

The corporate office did make the final allocation of resources to support the agreed-upon strategies and priorities. It set long- and short-term goals and strategic and financial targets more precisely than did its counterpart in strategic planning companies. As in firms in the other categories, business units reported regularly and in detail to corporate management. But, unlike in the strategic planning companies, budgets and financial goals were taken seriously. They were not the basis for discussions. They were targets to be met in terms of both incentives and sanctions.

In these companies the corporate office became a headquarters of headquarters. That is, the divisional headquarters carried out most of the functions of the corporate HQs in the strategic planning companies, but under the guidance of the corporate office. The arrangement had weaknesses. Often in defining and particularly in implementing strategy, long-term gains were sacrificed for short-term ones. Opportunities that might have been explored if closer attention had been paid to planning were lost. Such weaknesses suggest how the capabilities of the corporate HQ can limit the effective size of firms in capital-intensive, technologically complex industries. Does a corporate HQ supervising subcorporate HQs really add value? A brief review of the American leaders in each of the three most transforming industries of the past century—computers, electrical equipment, and chemicals—raises the same question.

American Examples: IBM, GE, and DuPont

Although there are no studies comparable to that of Goold and Campbell on the American experience, an examination of the functions of the corporate headquarters at IBM, GE, and DuPont supplements the British story. In addition, the data available on these companies provide a much longer time span than the single decade of the 1980s, which was the time frame for the British cases. The GE and DuPont stories in particular tell of shifts in planning and control procedures.

In each of the three companies the relationships of the corporate office to the operating units differed widely. The IBM story is one of a highly focused business machinery company that through impressive strategic planning became one of the most powerful first movers in a modern industry. That of GE is one of a relatively unstructured, centralized industrial empire that underwent drastic and dramatic decentralization in the 1950s. In the 1960s and 1970s it probed the boundaries of strategic planning and then in the 1980s moved toward strategic control. The DuPont experience is more one of a coming up against the limits of strategic control in the 1960s and 1970s and then in the 1980s moving closer to strategic planning.

IBM

IBM, a producer since 1911 of a variety of business machines, became the first mover in the computer industry with the introduction in 1965 of its mainframe System 360, the result of five years of intense research and development. As entrepreneurs developed new computer architectures for different markets, IBM quickly moved into these markets, becoming the leading producer at home and abroad of minicomputers in the 1970s and of microcomputers in the 1980s. As it advanced in computers, it shed its typewriter and other business machine products. At the same time, IBM became the major producer of peripherals, consumables, semiconductors, software, and computer services. No other computer company, nor other information processing enterprise, attempted to enter all these activities, let alone become the leader in these different lines of business. During the long period of rapid growth of the computer and other information processing businesses, IBM dominated this industrial sector.

To maintain its dominance, senior managers from the 1950s on were committed to heavy investment in research and development and to the strategic planning and management development necessary to help assure long-term payback on that investment. Although it occasionally made forays outside of computers, it quickly pulled back. Concentrating on its full line of core products, the corporate office continued to play a major role in planning—a process in which large staffs at both the corporate headquarters and the operating divisions participated. As one executive stressed: "We want to integrate as much as possible and maintain control through centralized planning and tracking, but we also want to decentralize implementation and operating decisions. There are no major strategic decisions that are delegated" (Goold and Campbell, 1987: 261).

By the 1980s the planning process of IBM had become elaborate. It had three parts which were closely integrated with its control mechanisms. "Program plans" that usually came from the operating units were meshed with a group plan. The group ("division" in the terminology used here) staff working with the corporate staff then hammered out an "operating plan," which became a two-year rolling budget. As a senior manager explained (Goold and Campbell, 1987: 165):

> The operating plan is the major management vehicle at IBM. It is the point at which all resources are approved—where you get your capital, your head count, your expense dollars, your parts committed to you from other divisions.

The five-year strategic plan was an extension of the operating plan. The literature available does not indicate how tight the financial and strategic targets were set. But given the continuing interaction between the corporate staff and the operating divisions, one can assume that they were flexible; the reasons for differences between actual performance and targets set would have been discussed constantly as forecasted conditions changed. In these ways, then, at IBM the entrepreneurial (strategic) and the administrative (monitoring) functions remained closely intertwined and reinforced one another.

During the 1980s, technologies (particularly in personal computers and chips) were rapidly changing and companies were adopting "open" nonproprietary systems of software conforming to industry standards so that applications were interchangeable and data could be shared among different manufacturers' systems. Both developments intensified competition. IBM's market share in several lines of businesses began to decline both at home and abroad. To remain dominant in nearly all major products in the nation's largest technologically dynamic industry became the overriding challenge to top management. From 1985 on, the Management Committee, the company's senior decision-making body, concentrated on that challenge.

A new CEO, John Akers, and his three associates on the Management Committee began to streamline product lines, reduce capacity, and relocate personnel. In 1988, the committee embarked on a major structural reorganization. Operating decisions were turned over to product and regional groups. Corporate headquarters staff was cut 75%. It became the personal staff of the Management Committee.

The committee's energies were to be even more sharply focused on long-term strategy and the monitoring of operational performance. With the drastically reduced number of line as well as staff participants, the cycle time of the planning process was cut almost in half. What had been essentially a numerical planning system became one of offering and discussing strategic options. In carrying out its entrepreneurial functions, the Management Committee made the final decisions on strategic moves (including the approval of an increasing number of joint ventures and other strategic alliances), on major production and marketing issues, and on the development of human resources. It determined the technological direction and allocation of the R&D expenditures but left the identification of new markets and the development of new technologies to the operating groups. In addition, the committee met twice a year with the senior operating manager at strategic planning conferences to discuss new initiatives, revise priorities, and examine performances and competitive standings.

In carrying out its monitoring function, the committee reviewed operational performance and competitive market share on a regular basis at its twice-weekly meetings. In addition, the committee met monthly with the heads of the largest geographical groups (Europe/Middle East/Africa, Asia/Pacific, and Canada/Latin America). Every three months the committee conferred with the heads of the major "line of business" groups. The monitoring role of corporate headquarters was further enlarged by the creation of three new corporate senior staff vice presidents: one for quality, one for allocation of resources and setting technological priorities, and the third for environmental concerns. At the same time the tasks of the senior vice president for personnel were enlarged.

Yet apparently this restructuring and refocusing was not enough. Decline in market share and profits continued. At the end of 1991 came the announcement of another reorganization. The new plan called for further decentralization of operations—a transition that would ultimately lead to the formation of new, almost freestanding, corporate subsidiaries. These subsidiaries would themselves be corporate multinational giants. Revenues from IBM software would be five times that of Microsoft. The proposed changes would, Akers believed, "permit headquarters to identify the strategic business units with the most potential for growth, and let the units pursue their business opportunities." The monitoring role of the new Management Committee has not been spelled out at the time of this writing (autumn 1992).[3] The corporate office is still in flux. Three of its members recently retired; the relationships between the operating subsidiaries and corporate headquarters have still to be defined.

Possibly, given the extraordinary growth of this global industry, one firm can no longer retain dominance in its several major product lines. Detailed strategic planning by the corporate office has become too difficult. Instead at IBM that task will be carried out for each major line in the new autonomous corporate subsidiaries, with the Management Committee and its knowledgeable staff maintaining control over the overall strategic direction of the several giant enterprises it owns and legally controls.

GE

If IBM was the first mover in the most important transforming and growth industries of the second half of the twentieth century, GE and DuPont were leaders in the two most important such industries at the end of the nineteenth century. Both pioneered in modern research and development. Both were

---

[3]   *Editor's Note:* Since that time John Akers was replaced by Lou Gerstner as CEO and all of these plans are subject to further change. Of interest is that "outside" board members of IBM apparently did not share the same view of the future as did Akers.

among the very first to become multibusiness enterprises on the basis of such R&D.

GE, like the other first movers in the electrical equipment sector—Westinghouse, and two German companies, Siemens and AEG—quickly expanded beyond its original line of electric power, generating and transmission equipment, and urban traction and industrial motors. By World War I its work on wire insulation had already taken it into varnishes, adhesives, and plastics; and its improvement of the light bulb had led it into metal alloys and vacuum tubes. Then came the development of radio and also X rays and other medical equipment. In the 1920s, too, GE began to produce a wide variety of electrical appliances as well as electric locomotives, and in the 1930s it began to make diesel locomotives. The number of its product lines (lines for which operating results were accounted separately) rose from 10 in 1900, to 30 in 1910, 85 in 1920, 193 in 1930, and 281 in 1940 (Chandler, 1990a: 221).

These diversified lines were administered through a hodgepodge of operating units—functional departments, integrated product divisions, subsidiaries, and special ventures. Strategic planning and monitoring was carried out by the corporate office in centralized fashion, at least on paper. By the late 1930s the need to rationalize these lines and to create a structure to manage them was obvious. But World War II delayed reorganization.

Then in 1946 Ralph Cordiner began to restructure. That restructuring became even more sweeping after he took over as president in 1950. In line with the management thinking of the time, Cordiner fashioned a highly decentralized structure. He set up 70 autonomous product departments, each with its own production, marketing, and engineering units. These were organized into divisions which, in turn, were administered by one of five groups (Chandler, 1962: 369). If one department grew large, Cordiner divided it into smaller parts. Thus there were several departments producing much the same consumer appliances. By 1960 the number of departments had reached 106.

By the 1960s GE's corporate office was losing control. Existing departments grew, often by developing new lines. Diversification had moved the company into more distantly related areas—commercial jet engines, nuclear power, and computers, to name a few. In the late 1960s the company had 190 departments ("business units" in the terminology used here), 46 divisions and 10 groups. By then the overload on the corporate office was becoming intolerable. Profits were down, capital appropriations were made without priorities, and new ventures were doing poorly (Aguilar and Hamermesh, 1985: 777–779, 783). The limits of growth appeared to have been reached.

Frederick Borsch, who succeeded Cordiner in 1963, began to restructure. First, he tightened administrative controls over the departments. He did so by strengthening the divisional staffs and by improving the divisional reporting and accounting controls. Next, in 1968, he strengthened the corporate office's planning procedures. He set up two boards: the corporate operations board, responsible for administration; and the corporate policy board, responsible for strategy formulation.

A planning structure was then laid over the existing operational structure. Strategic business units (SBUs) were formed to carry out the planning process. They were aligned as much as possible to discrete businesses. Close to half of the divisions (21) also became SBUs. Sixteen SBUs were departments, four were placed in groups. Each of the operating departments sent its strategic plans to one of 43 such SBUs. After coordinating these plans each SBU forwarded its version to the corporate policy board. Each SBU had a manager in charge supported by a full-time planner. Thus, by 1980 there were approximately 200 senior planners at GE (Aguilar and Hamermesh, 1985: 779–786; Goold and Campbell, 1987: 272).

A new CEO, Reginald Jones, who took office in 1972, put the new planning process into effect. It worked well. The company product lines were pruned, and many of the less profitable were spun off. A total of 76 lines exited during Jones's term. The profit and loss sheets improved after the hemorrhaging computer division was sold off. Similar sales helped to clean up the "venture messes." The corporate office was also impressed by the way the new system improved its ability to carry out the critical task of selection and development of managers.

Nevertheless, the planning overload at the top continued. To reduce that pressure Jones created another planning level—the sector. It represented a macrobusiness or industry area. In the words of one senior planning officer: "Conceptually the SBUs are expected to develop new business opportunities by extending into contiguous product-market areas. Sectors are expected to develop new SBUs by diversifying within their macroindustry scopes. And corporate is expected to develop new sectors by diversifying into unserved macroindustries" (Aguilar and Hamermesh, 1985: 788). The senior sector executive acted as the GE spokesperson for his macroindustry, had oversight for the SBUs in that sector, and was responsible for integrating the SBUs' strategies into a sector strategic plan.

To further stimulate the planning process the corporate office now began that process by sending "strategic challenges" to the sectors and SBUs. The SBUs then worked out plans with their sector office. Once approved these plans were converted into budgets for each of the departments. Their department general managers were expected to meet the budgeted net income and return-on-investment figures. These targets were taken seriously, but with the recognition that short-term considerations should not threaten long-term positions (Goold and Campbell, 1987: 272). In these ways, then, Reginald Jones attempted to carry out both the strategic and administrative functions of the corporate office. But given the size of GE and the diversity of its product lines, planning and capital appropriations procedures became bureaucratized. The company was responsible for simply too many units for the corporate office to play an influential role in shaping their strategies. The limits of HQ planning thus determined the limits to growth of the enterprise.

Under John Welch, who took Jones's place in 1981, the company began to shift away from a strategic-planning style toward one of strategic control. Welch sized down GE's product lines and shifted the company's product mix even more than Jones had done in the early 1970s. The new CEO kept the SBUs but greatly reduced their staff, as he did those at other levels. He preferred to bypass the planning process and to have executives in corporate headquarters talk directly with one or two SBU chiefs at a time. By 1985 Welch had eliminated the sectors and groups. As he reduced the administrative and planning organization, Welch intensified the role of the corporate office in management development. GE, like IBM, had long paid close attention to the training, positioning, and evaluation of its managers.

Earlier in his tenure, Welch grouped GE business units into three categories: core, high technology, and service. The managers of the "core" divisions—the long-established, mature, stable businesses—received relatively little planning or direction from the corporate office. Instead that office controlled core divisions through tight budgets and carefully defined strategic targets. Managers' bonuses, options, and future prospects in the company were closely related to their success in meeting these targets. The same style appears to have been used for the GE services category. On the other hand, in new high-technology endeavors, Welch and the corporate headquarters continued to play a large role in strategic planning.

By the end of the 1980s, the corporate office at GE had more sharply defined its corporate strategy and structure. The strategy was that, as Welch wrote in the 1989 Annual Report (p. 3), "Each business was to be number one or number two in its particular market. For those that were not, we had a very specific prescription—they were to be fixed, sold or closed." By then GE's many lines were integrated into 13 different businesses whose heads reported directly to Welch, the chairman, and two vice chairmen. Of these businesses, three remain in high-technology areas where new product development is critical to continuing competitive success—aerospace, aircraft engines, and medical equipment. The others include electrical distribution and control, industrial power systems, lighting, motors, transportation systems, plastics, appliances, and communication and services. Except for the last, these are all businesses in which GE has successfully operated for at least 70 years. In addition, there are Financial Services and NBC, the latter having come out of the merger with RCA.

Clearly, the new strategy has meant concentration on those products for whose production, distribution, and continuing improvement GE has developed impressive organizational capabilities over the decades. With the dismantling of much of Jones's planning apparatus, the management style at GE moved toward one of strategic control. Strategy became based primarily on the utilization of organizational capabilities that had been honed over the decades. In technologically complex, capital-intensive industries, competitive advantage lies more in constantly improving product and process than in developing new products and processes, and strategic control was the most suitable style to carry out both the entrepreneurial and administrative functions of the corporate office. That is, strategic planning devolved on the businesses (or "divisions"), with the corporate office maintaining overall strategic control.

DuPont

At DuPont underlying changes in the planning and control functions of the corporate office came more slowly than they did at GE. These more evolutionary developments have led the company from relying on a weak strategic control style to relying on a stronger strategic planning one. So at DuPont the story is the reverse of that of GE. But in both the changes in the activities of the HQ unit reflected differences in the characteristics of the industries in which they came to operate.

DuPont, which had a research organization as old as that of General Electric, was a pioneer in creating the multidivisional form as an answer to management overload resulting from a strategy of product diversification. Indeed, its structure became a model for the growing number of multibusiness enterprises that appeared in the United States in the 1920s and 1930s (Chandler, 1962: ch. 2). After DuPont's reorganization in 1921, the senior executives of the corporate office carried out both planning and monitoring by maintaining constant and close contact with the heads of the product divisions. (At DuPont such divisions were termed "departments.") In the 1921 reorganization the division heads were given full authority and responsibility for carrying out all activities in their product line, including the improvement of product and process and the planning for future production and distribution. Although each of the five to seven members of the executive committee of the board were assigned product divisions to oversee, they were explicitly denied direct line authority over division managers. They could advise but not order. And until the very end of the 1970s this distinction remained sacrosanct.

The Executive Committee met every Monday in the chart room with the senior managers of one division (in the 1920s and 1930s the divisions numbered between 7 and 10.) There, with charts that incorporated nearly every aspect of past and present performance, they reviewed operations and performance and related them to earlier plans and targets. They then discussed future operations. On the basis of these meetings and the information provided by both corporate and division staffs, the corporate financial office developed budgets and capital appropriation plans that in turn were discussed and approved by the Executive Committee. In this way the corporate office influenced the direction and pace of growth and exercised control over the performance of the operating divisions.

From the late 1920s on, the corporate department for research began to play a major part in defining the direction of the growth of the enterprise, particularly into markets not yet reached by the divisions. It did so by investing in fundamental research in untapped fields of chemistry. In 1927 the department began research on polymer chemistry that led to the development of man-made fibers (including nylon, dacron, orlon, and lycra), as well as neoprene and other man-made materials. Central Research (initially called Central Chemical Department) was responsible for basic research and for the far more costly initial development of new processes and products. Once commercialized, these were turned over to the product divisions for production and distribution and for further refinement. This structure permitted DuPont to continue its highly profitable strategy of growth through closely related diversification (Hounshell and Smith, 1988: chs. 5, 12).

After World War II the company continued to grow by expanding existing lines and developing new ones. Soon, divisions such as textile fibers became as large as the DuPont Company itself had been in the 1920s. Because of the successful exploitation of fundamental research by Central Research, the Executive Committee now allocated extensive sums to the divisions for comparable research. At the same time other chemical firms both in the United States and Europe were making much larger investments in research and development than they had before World War II. So product lines proliferated and competition intensified.

Yet the basic planning and administrative structure of the company remained unchanged. The Executive Committee no longer had the time or information to influence divisional plans effectively. The divisions, in turn, became increasingly powerful large multibusiness enterprises in their own right. Close working contact between members of the Executive Committee at headquarters and the senior division managers disintegrated. The committee now did little more than approve divisional plans and review actual performance by relating it to the plans. As at General Electric, profits went down, product development in both divisional and corporate research became much more costly, and payback on product development was smaller and required more time. Nor were product developments and other interdependencies coordinated effectively within the company. As at GE, the limits to growth appeared to have been reached.

As these difficulties began to press upon the Executive Committee, it entered into an extended debate over what should be done. The outcome was a decision to expand the Development Department, which since 1903 had carried on planning activities at the corporate office. An energetic young manager, Edwin A. Gee, took charge. Gee's mandate was to appraise each of the division's "diversifying activities in order to detect any inadequacies in technology, markets and organization" (Hounshell and Smith, 1988: ch. 22; Fast, 1977: ch. 5). His department was also to seek out new business opportunities in areas not covered by the divisions. For antitrust reasons Gee and the Executive Committee decided not to grow through acquisition of even small firms and to stay out of defense-oriented industries. Instead, Gee's department was to concentrate on developing new ventures that used some of DuPont's specific organizational capabilities. Some of the new products developed did pay off. But by the mid-1960s the committee and Gee agreed that the "New Venture Program" was not a success. The heavy investment in R&D was not paying off. Too often the company's specific functional capabilities were not enough to achieve a strong competitive advantage in the new product markets. And the necessary complementary facilities and skills were too costly and time-consuming to create.

This outcome and the continuing low rate of return on investment led the Executive Committee for the first time since 1920 to appraise seriously the basic strategy and structure of the company as well as its own role in the company. One committee member, Lester Sinness, attributed the deteriorating earnings to low research productivity and the failure of the Executive Committee to play a guiding and coordinating role. He considered "the research output of the company as a whole to be disgraceful and inexcusably low in proportion to the caliber of the men we employ, the facilities we give them, and the amount of money we allow them to spend" (Hounshell and Smith, 1988: 531). But essentially, he insisted, the Executive Committee had only itself to blame. In the earlier self-examination proposed changes were "submerged in a welter of conflicting opinions within the Executive Committee. . . . Through a distorted preoccupation with the concept of the departmental autonomy . . . the Executive Committee loses sight of its own responsibilities. [It] appears to sit only as a judicial body reviewing the past performances of the Departments [divisions] and weighing whatever projects and proposals on policy and procedures may emanate from the Industrial or Staff departments. The Executive Committee seldom discusses or initiates anything of and by itself." Through its "ritual schedule of charts and reports," Sinness continued, "the Committee no longer had the time needed to examine and discuss periodically the future of the company or determine whether the company policies, organizations and procedures needed altering." Another member urged the committee "to take a more critical role in originating and implementing programs to insure the future health of the company." By the mid-1960s DuPont suffered from ineffective planning mechanisms for the enterprise as a whole and weak controls over the operations and performance of the operating units.

Even so, change came slowly. The president, Charles B. McCoy, and other members of the committee were cautious. In 1967 came the organizational restructuring mentioned earlier, which created the autonomous business units (termed "profit centers") whose managers were responsible for production, distribution, R&D, and profit and loss in the product business they headed. The departmental (divisional) headquarters monitored and helped to plan the activities of the business units under their supervision. They decided, for example, how funds for research would be allocated to their different business units.

The next move came seven years later, when the committee created a small 12-person Corporate Plans Department. It was to have "broad responsibility" for coordinating all strategic business planning activities in the company, specifically by analyzing DuPont's portfolio of businesses (Hounshell and Smith, 1988: 585). The Development Department was folded into Central Research. At the urging of the new planning department the Executive Committee reduced the research budgets in the operating divisions, particularly funds for fundamental research, and put tighter controls on the initiation of research programs not closely related to existing product lines or technologies. The company's long-term, more fundamental research became concentrated in the enlarged corporate research department. The committee agreed that Corporate Plans working with

Central Research should play a critical role in defining the company's broader strategic moves into new lines. To ensure that it carried out this function, in 1979 the committee gave its member designated as research advisor, Edward G. Jefferson, line authority over Central Research. This was the first time since the 1921 reorganization that an Executive Committee member was given such authority. Jefferson's initial strategic move was a commitment to the company's long-term development of the new biogenetic field and other life sciences, particularly in pharmaceuticals and agricultural chemicals (Houshell and Smith, 1988: 505–507).

After Jefferson became CEO in May 1981 he continued to strengthen the role of the corporate office in both its planning and resource allocation and monitoring functions (Hounshell and Smith, 1988: 591). Members of the Executive Committee began to have authority and responsibility for the performance of the divisions under their supervision. During the 1980s, as the company began to move into specialty chemicals, electronics, medical and other high-technology products and to spin off some of its commodity chemicals, they became more deeply involved in strategic planning. But the lines of authority and responsibility were becoming unclear. Moreover, in making strategic and administrative decisions, Executive Committee members tended to see issues in terms of the businesses they knew best and those for which they were becoming increasingly responsible. In addition, the top managers of Conoco, the oil company that was unexpectedly acquired in 1983, had not yet been integrated into the corporate office. The resulting pressures led to a careful analysis of the company's organization. In the fall of 1991 came the announcement of the most far-reaching internal restructuring that the company had undergone in 70 years.

The new organizational structure abolished the Executive Committee and existing departments. An Office of the Chairman and an Operating Group were created. The first consisted of the chairman (the CEO), a vice chairman (whose special area was science and technology), and executive vice president for Conoco. Attached to that office were two senior vice presidents—one for Human Resources and Corporate Planning and the other for Finance. The Operations Group included these five, plus 14 DuPont executives and five Conoco executives. Four of the latter were responsible for the different functional activities in the oil business, and one was in charge of Consolidation Coal, a major enterprise that came with the Conoco acquisition. The Operating Group had oversight of all the company's products, functions, and geographical regions.

As part of the reorganization, the DuPont product lines in its reshaped portfolio of businesses were consolidated in seven "industrial segments." Within the segments closely related product lines were grouped for administrative purposes as profit centers. Four of these segments—Polymers, Agricultural Products, Electronics, and Imaging and Medical Products—are in industries where new product development remains essential for competitive success. Three—Fibers, Chemicals (petrochemicals and pigments) and Automotive Products—are in more mature, stable industries where competition is based more on improving product and process. The remaining six senior vice presidents that make up the corporate office are responsible for the functional activities of the corporation as a whole— Research & Development, Engineering, Information Systems, Logistics (purchasing), External Affairs, and Legal. Because of this reorganization the executives in the corporate office now have far more direct operating and planning responsibilities than they had during the previous 70 years.

The stated objectives of reshaping the corporate office were to break down barriers between operating divisions and to have top management develop a corporate rather than a product or functional perspective. To encourage the latter, most of the senior vice presidents that make up the Operating Group handle more than one activity. For example, a senior vice president for Chemicals also has responsibility for manufacturing for the company as a whole, and a senior vice president for Electronics oversees the Asia/Pacific region. In this way the corporate headquarters is expected to develop a global view, to enhance human capabilities at all levels, and to speed up high-level decision making. At DuPont, where the portfolio includes a number of new and technologically advanced products, the functions of the corporate headquarters have been strengthened; while at GE, where the strategy has concentrated on obtaining dominant positions in more mature and stable industries, the role and size of the corporate office has been reduced.

Summary

The effectiveness of the more focused long-term strategy at DuPont and GE and the resulting structures will be determined in the 1990s. (I see the purchase of Conoco, like GE's acquisition of RCA, not as part of long-term strategy but rather as a response to the more immediate and most complex business situations.) In carrying out and modifying the new strategies and in implementing and tuning the new structures the executives in the corporate offices at DuPont and GE should keep in mind the lessons learned during the 1970s and 1980s about the paths to growth and the limits to the size of the firm.

One lesson of the 1970s and 1980s was that moves into new businesses based on existing capabilities required the development of a set of complementary skills and facilities to supplement existing ones. If the production facilities provided competitive advantage in the new market, in most cases complementary marketing capabilities needed to be developed. Another lesson was that not only were the size and boundaries of enterprises shaped by existing capabilities and by their success in developing complementary ones, they were also determined by the ability of the corporate headquarters to carry out both its basic functions—entrepreneurial and administrative.

Most significant of all, those years showed that the HQ functions varied with the characteristics of the industries in which they operated. Therefore, the production and distribution of different types of products or services required different types of planning and control systems. In industries in which new product development is a critical component of interfirm competition, where R&D expenditures are high, state-of-the-art facilities costly, and marketing requires specialized skills, the corporate office needs to concentrate on the entrepreneurial (value-creating) function. Here it needs to play a strong role in the strategic planning process if it is to utilize fully the company's existing competitive strengths in technologically advanced businesses and to determine paths for new product and process development. Nevertheless, as the IBM story suggests, strategic planning for all lines in a high-technology global industry by a single dominant firm may become too complex for a single office to handle. Strategic planning may then be delegated to the operating subsidiaries, with the corporate head-quarters providing no more than broad strategic direction.

In more mature industries where the nature of the final product remains stable, where R&D expenditures continue to be essential but primarily for improving product and cost-cutting processes, and where facilities are costly and marketing complex but the facilities and skills required have been well established; in such industries the corporate office can more easily delegate strategic planning to the operating divisions and maintain strategic control by setting targets and establishing long-term goals for the corporation as a whole. Finally, as the experience of the conglomerates reinforces, in the service industries and mature manufacturing industries where the products remain much the same, where the technology of production is not complex, where facilities are less costly and where competition lies more in distribution and marketing, particularly advertising, than in production or R&D, financial controls alone have usually been enough to prevent losses and maintain profits in multibusiness enterprises.

Conclusion

The story told here of DuPont, GE, and the U.S. conglomerates is representative of much of American industry. The 1980s were for U.S. industrial firms a decade of reshaping corporate strategies and rebuilding organizational structures. As firms focused on a smaller number of product lines, they often used funds garnered from spin-offs to acquire other enterprises needed to fill out their portfolio of related lines. Most of these rearrangements were carried out through friendly transactions, but at times firms were acquired by hostile takeovers. As Bhagat, Shleifer, and Vishny (1990) report, even firms grabbed by raiders in hostile takeovers ended in the hands of other firms in their sectors, with the raiders profiting (handsomely) as temporary brokers. On the whole, however, the capital markets in the form of raiders and of LBOs and other privatization forms have played only a limited constructive role in the recent restructuring of American industrial enterprises.

The part that the capital markets played in this corporate restructuring reflects, in much the same way as the changes made by senior corporate managers in their strategy and structure, the characteristics of the industries in which the enterprise operates. For example, one major innovation—the privatization of enterprises through LBOs and other techniques—has been insignificant in capital-intensive industries where competitive strength depends on continuing long-term investment in R&D and costly capital facilities; that is, in industries where strategic planning and control has been essential to remain competitive. The great majority of the firms privatized have been in industries where financial controls were sufficient to maintain the competitive capabilities of the operating unit of a multibusiness enterprise.

As Bronwyn Hall's studies of 2,000 manufacturing companies (1990, forthcoming) document, between 1977 and 1987—the period of the LBO boom—224 of the 1,980 public companies had become privatized. (Of these only 76 were LBOs.) The 224 accounted for 5.7% of the total employment of the companies studied but only 1.4% of total R&D expenditures. Of these 224, one hundred and fifty were smaller firms in what Hall defines as low-tech industries (food, textiles, including apparel, and paper and wood products) and stable short-term horizon industries (fabricated metals; stone, glass and clay; rubber and plastics; soap and toiletries). While these industries accounted for 36% of total manufacturing employment in her overall sample, they accounted for 83% of employment in the firms that had gone private. And while R&D investment for the U.S. manufacturing sector as a whole averaged $2,000 per employee, for the firms that went private the average was $500 per employee.

Hall's information shows that after a decade of well-publicized privatization, privatized firms are finding a place in low technology and other industries where R&D is minimal. It also emphasizes that the widely held public company overwhelmingly dominates in the capital-intensive, technologically complex industries on which so much of the nation's industrial growth and competitive success depends—industries that include chemicals, pharmaceuticals, aircraft and aerospace, computers and semiconductors, electrical and electronic equipment, oil, metals, and a wide variety of agricultural, construction, mining, and industrial equipment, as well as engines, motor vehicles, and other transportation equipment.

Hall's data also emphasize that financial entrepreneurs and intermediaries have become aware, as have corporate managers, of differences in industry characteristics. Money managers have learned that, if firms in the more capital-intensive, technologically complex industries are to remain competitive, they will have to make long-term investments in highly product-specific skills. Such long-term investments demand value-creating strategic planning and control by experienced managers as well as a continuing reinvestment of earnings (particularly from established lines) into new and improved products and processes. So in assisting and even promoting LBOs and other privatization transactions, financiers concentrate on firms and industries where capital costs are relatively low, specific skills are not complex, synergies from R&D, production, and distribution are limited, and where cash flows are relatively steady and long-term strategic planning relatively unnecessary. In such industries multibusiness firms have few competitive advantages over single-business ones. Firms in such industries, whether operated through the office of a conglomerate or an LBO association, can be administered through financial control alone. But such industries are not the major source of economic growth and transformation, or of national competitive strengths. In the industries that require long-term investment in R&D and capital facilities the public corporation will continue into the twenty-first century to be, as it was throughout the twentieth century, the engine of industrial strength and transformation.

In the 1980s business and financial managers learned the importance of understanding the differences in industry characteristics in the management of their business and the making of their investments. The time has come for academics to learn to make comparable distinctions in their analyses of business enterprises and their management.

13
Strategizing, Economizing, and Economic Organization

Oliver E. Williamson

Business strategy is a complex subject. It not only spans the functional areas in business—marketing, finance, manufacturing, international business, and so forth—but it is genuinely interdisciplinary, involving, as it does, economics, politics, organization theory, and aspects of the law. Business strategy has become increasingly important with the growth of the multinational enterprise and of international trade and competition.

Although several different approaches to business strategy can be distinguished, the main contestants cluster under two general headings: strategizing and economizing. The first of these appeals to a power perspective; the second is principally concerned with efficiency. Both of these orientations are pertinent to the study of business strategy, but power approaches, at least until recently, have dominated the business strategy literature.

In part that may be because the analysis of efficiency is believed to have reached such an advanced state of development that further work of this kind is unneeded. Economizing is important, but we know all about that. What we don't understand, and need to study, is strategizing. Not only is strategizing where many of the novel practices and new issues reside, but the pressing realities of foreign competition are first and foremost of a strategizing kind.

I take exception to both these arguments. Although it is true

Acknowledgments: The helpful comments of David Levine, Vai-Lam Mui, David Teece, and other participants in the Institutional Analysis Workshop at Berkeley are gratefully acknowledged.

361

that efficiency analysis of the firm-as-production-function genre has reached a high state of refinement, that genre does not exhaust all that is relevant to the assessment of efficiency. Efficiency analysis properly encompasses governance costs as well as production costs, and the analysis of comparative economic organization (governance) is still in early stages of development.

I furthermore aver that economizing is much more fundamental than strategizing. That is because strategizing is relevant principally to firms that possess market power—which are a small fraction of the total (ephemeral market advantages ignored). More important, I maintain that a strategizing effort will rarely prevail if a program is burdened by significant cost excesses in production, distribution, or organization. All the clever ploys and positioning, aye, all the king's horses and all the king's men, will rarely save a project that is seriously flawed in first-order economizing respects.

Accordingly, I advance the argument that economizing is more fundamental than strategizing—or, put differently, that *economy is the best strategy*. That is the central and unchanging message of the transaction cost economics perspective. Among other things, emphasis on economizing restores manufacturing and merchandising to a place of importance within the business firm and on the academic research agenda.[1]

To be sure, economizing and strategizing are not mutually exclusive. Strategic ploys are sometimes used to disguise economizing weaknesses. (Lee Iacocca has tried this.) More often, strategic ploys can be used to promote economizing outcomes. Pricing with reference to learning curve costs is an illustration. "Technostructure" (Galbraith, 1967) and related theories of the firm that hold that the imperatives of strategic planning carrying the day have turned out to be unserviceable. The beguiling language of strategizing—warfare, credible threats, and the

---

[1]   This is broadly consonant with the Robert Hayes and Steven Wheelwright perspective (1984: 27):

> The notion that manufacturing can be a competitive weapon, rather than just a collection of rather ponderous resources and constraints, is not new, although its practice is not very widespread. Even in many well-managed firms, manufacturing plays an essentially neutral role, reflecting the view that marketing, sales and R and D provide better bases for achieving a competitive advantage.

But the argument extends beyond manufacturing to core businesses of every kind. Thus Sears is reported "finally [to be] focusing on [its] biggest problem. Its costs are among the highest in retailing" (Schwadel, 1990: B1).

like—notwithstanding, students of economic organization are better advised to focus on more mundane issues of an economizing kind, of which harmonizing, credible commitments, adaptation, and discriminating alignments are examples. Here as elsewhere, the need is to get and keep the priorities straight.

This paper is organized in five parts. Section 1 sketches what I take to be the principal efficiency approaches to strategy and sets out the rudiments of the transaction cost economics approach. Section 2 addresses a series of organization form issues from the economizing perspective. Applications of transaction cost economics to the governance of contractual relations are treated in Section 3. An economizing interpretation of the Japanese corporation is advanced in Section 4. Concluding remarks follow.

1. Efficiency and Transaction Cost

The leading efficiency approaches to business strategy are the resource-based and the dynamic capabilities approach. These two approaches have been developing very rapidly[2] and, as described by Joseph Mahoney and Rajendran Pandian (1992), blend into each other. Edith Penrose's early work on the growth of the firm (1959) and more recent work by Jay Barney, Cynthia Montgomery, William Ouchi, M. A. Peteraf, David Teece, Birger Wernerfelt, and others have been especially influential to the resource-based perspective. The dynamic capabilities approach takes its inspiration from Joseph Schumpeter (1942) and has been successively elaborated by Giovanni Dosi, Gary Hamel, Richard Nelson, C. K. Prahaled, Richard Rumelt, David Teece, Sidney Winter, and others.

It is not obvious to me how these two literatures will play out, either individually or in combination. Plainly they deal with core issues. Possibly they will be joined. As matters stand at present, these two literatures offer general frameworks and provoke insights for which additional structure is needed.

As I have discussed elsewhere (Williamson, 1975, 1985), transaction cost economics is inspired by the work of John R. Commons (1934), Ronald Coase (1937), Chester Barnard (1938),

---

[2] The recent Joseph Mahoney and Rajendran Pandian (1992) review lists over 100 books and articles of these kinds.

Friedrich Hayek (1945), Herbert Simon (1947, 1962), Alfred Chandler (1962), and Kenneth Arrow (1962, 1969). Whether this approach can help to explicate the strategic issues that the resource-based and dynamic capabilities approaches have raised remains to be seen. In any case, my treatment of efficiency is predominantly informed by the transaction cost economics perspective.[3]

That has both advantages and disadvantages. On the one hand, the efficiency approach to business strategy is sorely in need of a well-focused perspective. On the other hand, business strategy has a broad mandate. A narrow lens cannot be expected to inform all of the relevant strategy issues. I submit, however, that transaction cost economics illuminates a wide range of issues of an economizing kind. If, as I argued at the outset, economy is the best strategy, then this view deserves to be heard.

1.1 First-order Economizing

Although the need to get priorities straight is unarguably important, first-order economizing—effective adaptation and the elimination of waste—has been neglected.

Adaptation.[4] Friedrich Hayek insistently argued that "economic problems arise always and only in consequence of change" and that this truth was obscured by those who held that "technological knowledge" is of foremost importance (1945: 523). He disputed the latter and maintained that "the economic problem of society is mainly one of rapid adaptation in the particular circumstances of time and place" (Hayek, 1945: 524). Of special importance to Hayek was the proposition that the price system is an extraordinarily efficient mechanism for communicating information and inducing change (Hayek, 1945: 524–527).

Interestingly, Chester Barnard (1938) also held that the main concern of organization was adaptation to changing circumstances. But whereas Hayek was concerned with adaptation in markets, Barnard's concern was with the adaptation of internal organization. Confronted with a continuously fluctuating environment, the "survival of an organization depends upon the

---

[3] Pertinent contributions include Williamson (1975, 1985, 1990), Benjamin Klein, Robert Crawford, and Armen Alchian (1978), Alchian (1984), Teece (1982, 1986), Sanford Grossman and Oliver Hart (1986), and Scott Masten, James Meehan, and Edward Snyder (1991).

[4] This subsection is based on my treatment of these issues in "Comparative Economic Organization" (1990a).

maintenance of an equilibrium of complex character. . . . [This] calls for readjustment of processes internal to the organiza- tion. . . , [whence] the center of our interest is the processes by which [adaptation] is accomplished" (Barnard, 1938: 6).

The apparent conflict notwithstanding, I submit that adapt- ability is the central problem of economic organization and that both Hayek and Barnard are correct. The two of them are refer- ring to adaptations of different kinds, both of which are needed in a high-performance system. The adaptations Hayek means are those for which prices serve as sufficient statistics. Changes in the demand or supply of a commodity are reflected in price changes, in response to which "individual participants. . . [are] able to take the right action" (Hayek, 1945: 527). I will refer to adaptations of this kind as adaptation (A), where (A) denotes autonomy. This is the neoclassical ideal, in which consumers and producers respond independently to parametric price changes so as to maximize their utility and profits, respectively.

That explanation would entirely suffice if all disturbances were of this kind. Some disturbances, however, require coordi- nated responses, lest the individual parts operate at cross- purposes or otherwise suboptimize.

Recourse to a different mechanism is suggested as the needs for coordinated investments and for uncontested (or less con- tested) coordinated realignments increase in frequency and con- sequentiality. Adaptations of this coordinated kind will be re- ferred to as adaptation (C), where (C) denotes coordination. The conscious, deliberate, and purposeful efforts to craft adaptive internal coordinating mechanisms were those with which Bar- nard was concerned. Complex contracting and internal organi- zation are required if adaptation through coordination (C) is to occur.

Bureaucracy and waste.   Bureaucracy and waste are irrele- vant if firms can be assumed to be operating continuously on production functions and maximizing profits. Alas, that is an egregious oversimplification.[5] As Hayek remarked (1945: 523):

> [T]he task of keeping cost from rising requires constant struggle, ab- sorbing a great part of the energy of the manager. How easy it is for an

---

[5]   To be sure, the literature on X-efficiency is concerned with many of the salient issues. That literature, however, has never developed a positive research agenda. It operates at a very high level of generality and has never identified the appropriate unit of analysis. Among other things, issues of remediable and irremediable X- inefficiency are never faced. Irremediable flaws—that is, those that cannot be reme- died with net gains (Coase, 1964)—are operationally irrelevant.

inefficient manager to dissipate the differentials on which profitability rests, and that it is possible, with the same technical facilities, to produce at a great variety of costs, are among the commonplaces of business experience which do not seem to be equally familiar in the study of the economist.

Relatedly, Frank Knight expressed concern over the neglect of waste (1941: 252):

> [M]en in general, and within limits, wish to behave economically, to make their activities and their organization "efficient" rather than wasteful. This fact does deserve the utmost emphasis; and an adequate definition of the science of economics . . . might well make it explicit that the main relevance of the discussion is found in its relation to social policy, assumed to be directed toward the end indicated, of increasing economic efficiency, of reducing waste.

Or consider Oskar Lange's argument that *"the real danger of socialism is that of the bureaucratization of economic life,* and not the impossibility of coping with the problem of allocation of resources"* (1938: 109; emphasis in original). Inasmuch, however, as Lange believed that this argument belonged "in the field of sociology" he concluded that it "must be dispensed with here" (1938: 109). Subsequent informed observers of socialism followed this lead. With the benefit of ensuing experience, it is now evident that the preoccupation of socialist economic theory with marginal cost pricing principles and activity analysis missed much of the crucial economic action. More fundamental issues of first-order economizing, with respect to waste and bureaucracy, were disregarded.[6]

One way of interpreting waste, bureaucracy, slack, and the like is to assert that these are sources of managerial utility (Williamson, 1964). I want here, however, to argue a different position: these cost excesses contribute negligibly to utility but are principally due to inferior organization and maladapted operations. That the profits differ in two firms in the same industry using the same technology selling to the same customers is not

---

[6] Instead, the efficacy of socialism was judged in terms of whether the enterprise could be expected to combine factors of production in a least-cost way and set output so that price equals marginal cost (Bergson, 1948: 432–433). Abram Bergson's (1948) sanguine assessment of socialism was based on the application of marginalist principles to the socialist program and carried the day. Abba Lerner was so confident of the theory of efficient resource allocation in the socialist state that he "went to Mexico to see Trotsky to persuade him that all would be well in a communist state if only it reproduced the results of a competitive system and prices were set equal to marginal cost" (Coase, 1988: 8).

because the managers in the one are working harder than managers in the other. Instead, managers in the two firms are working equally hard, but one of them is working smarter—through better organizational form, better internal incentives and controls, and better alignment of the contractual (interfirm and intrafirm) interfaces.

The differences between first- and second-order economizing can be illustrated with a simple partial equilibrium welfare economics setup. Consider an industry that is selling product q_1 at a price p_1 and is just covering its average, but bloated, costs, which are given by $c_0 + b$—where c_0 is the minimum average costs at which product q_1 can be supplied and b represents the bloat (excess bureaucratic costs or waste). Suppose now that the bloat is removed by a reorganization that eliminates unneeded bureaucrats and wasteful bureaucratic practices. But suppose that the price remains at p_1. Substantial social gain nonetheless results from waste elimination—the cost savings being measured by the rectangle $W = bq$ (where W denotes waste) in Figure 13-1. Assume now that price is reduced to the new level of costs, whence $p_2 = c_0$. Added allocative efficiency benefits—given by $L = \frac{1}{2}b\Delta q$ (where $\Delta q = q_2 - q_1$ and L denotes deadweight loss)—thereby result. Albeit important, this price-induced (second-order) efficiency gain is small in relation to the first-order efficiency gain (from waste elimination). Indeed, the ratio of W to L, which is given by $2q_1/\Delta q$, is easily of the order of 10:1.

The message here is plain: the principal action is in the first-order efficiency rectangles (the base and height of which are q_1 and b, respectively) rather than in the second-order efficiency triangles (the base and height of which are Δq and b, respectively). What may have been obvious to Knight and was intuited by Lange did not, however, carry the day: economists have mainly assumed the problem of waste away and have concentrated attention on the triangles. Little wonder that the welfare consequences of monopoly, which focus on second-order price distortions, are held to be negligible (Harberger, 1954).

1.2 Transaction Cost Economics

The main hypothesis out of which transaction cost economics works is this: *align transactions, which differ in their attributes,*

Figure 13-1

An Illustration of First- and Second-Order Economizing

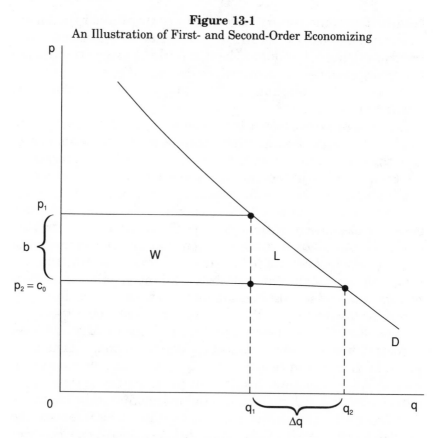

with governance structures, which differ in their costs and competencies, in a discriminating (mainly, transaction cost economizing) way. This economizing orientation notwithstanding, transaction cost economics does not assert, much less insist, that economic organization is relentlessly taut.[7] To the contrary, if economic organization is formidably complex, which it is, and if economic agents are subject to very real cognitive limits, which they are, then failures of alignment will occur routinely. Excesses of waste, bureaucracy, and slack are mainly explained, I submit, by failures of alignment. Transaction cost economics is pertinent to the study of business strategy precisely because

---

[7] One informed student of economic organization has remarked that Alfred P. Sloan, Jr., was relentlessly given to profit maximization. Sloan was also an organizational genius. He is the exception that proves the rule.

first-order economizing alignments are not always obvious and/ or may be at variance with managerial preferences.[8] It is therefore important to examine the microanalytics of organization and show which alignments go where and why.

The transaction cost economics program has been set out elsewhere (for recent summaries, see Alchian and Woodward [1987] and Williamson [1989]). I focus here on four features: (1) the behavioral assumptions, (2) the dimensionalization of transactions, (3) the key features of governance, and (4) the concept of incomplete contracting in its entirety.

Behavioral assumptions. Transaction cost economics aspires to describe "man as he is" (Coase, 1984: 231) in terms of cognition and self-interest. It works out of two key behavioral assumptions: bounded rationality and opportunism. The first of these implies that behavior is "*intendedly* rational, but only *limitedly* so" (Simon, 1947: xxiv). Opportunism refers to the use of guile in the pursuit of self-interest.

The principal ramifications of these behavioral assumptions for economic organization are these: (1) all complex contracts are unavoidably incomplete and many complex incentive alignment processes cannot be implemented (because of bounded rationality); (2) to rely on contract-as-promise is fraught with hazard (because of opportunism); and (3) added value will be realized by organizing in such a way as to economize on bounded rationality and to safeguard transactions against the hazards of opportunism. Hypothetical contracting modes (Arrow-Debreu; mechanism design) and hypothetical reputation effect mechanisms (Fama, 1980) are disallowed by the first of these. Ideal (utopian) forms of organization are disallowed by the second. Transaction cost economizing is implicated by the third.

Unit of analysis. Transaction cost economics regards the transaction as the basic unit of analysis (Commons, 1925, 1934) and maintains that the principal dimensions (in terms of transaction cost economizing) with respect to which transactions differ are frequency, uncertainty, and asset specificity (Williamson, 1975, 1979, 1983); to these dimensions ease of measurement should probably be added (Barzel, 1982; Kenney and Klein,

---

8   The waste consequences of managerial preferences—say, in favor of vertical integration—are assumed greatly to exceed the managerial utility gains (to which salary or other reductions in the managerial compensation package could be ascribed).

1983; Alchian and Woodward, 1987; Holmstrom, 1989). Of these four, asset specificity—which has reference to the ease with which an asset can be redeployed to alternative uses and by alternative users without loss of productive value (Williamson, 1971, 1975, 1979; Klein, Crawford, and Alchian, 1978)—has had the greatest significance for examining the governance of contractual relations.

Governance. Whereas noneconomists have long been persuaded that the "micro-forces within organizations" matter, economists have only recently conceded that proposition. So long as organization form was believed to have only third-order economizing effects, then the firm-as-production-function carried the day.

A rather cautious version of the micro-forces argument is as follows (Kreps and Spence, 1985: 374–375):

> [I]f one wishes to model the behaviour of organizations such as firms, then study of the firm as an organization ought to be high on one's agenda. This study is not strictly speaking, necessary: one can hope to divine the correct "reduced form" for the behaviour of the organization without considering the micro-forces within the organization. But the study of the organization is likely to help in the design of reduced forms that stress the important variables.

Because divination is in short supply, transaction cost economics takes the stronger position that knowledge of the microanalytics of organization, with special reference to their transaction cost economizing properties, is *vital* to the design of reduced forms that stress the important variables. A key step in this exercise is the identification of the performance attributes with respect to which governance structures differ. As described above, adaptations of autonomous and cooperative kinds (types A and C, respectively) are centrally implicated. Autonomous adaptations are those for which prices are sufficient statistics and markets excel (comparatively). Cooperative adaptations are those for which coordinated responses are required and hierarchies excel (comparatively). The argument extends, moreover, to include the hybrid modes—long-term contracts, franchising, joint ventures, and the like—that are located between markets and hierarchies.[9] Mixed adaptation (A/C) obtain for these.

Efficiency and power. Power of two kinds is usefully distin-

---

[9] The aforementioned condition of asset specificity largely determines which type of adaptation is most needed (see Section 3, below). The upshot is that markets align to autonomous adaptation, hierarchies to bilateral adaptation, and hybrids service mixed adaptation (A/B).

guished within the strategic arena: market power and resource dependency. Transaction cost economics cautions against the overuse of power arguments of both kinds.

Temporary market advantages excepted, most firms lack market power of the kind that is routinely assumed by the strategizing literature. It is fatuous to ascribe strategic importance to temporary market advantages. But even significant market advantages of a more durable kind are often undone by Schumpeterian "handing on" (1947: 155), according to which prices fall to the new level of costs wherever rivals are alert to the new opportunities and are not prevented by purposive (especially political) restrictions from responding to them.

Power of a resource dependency kind does not play a larger role in the transaction cost economics scheme of economic organization both because initial endowments are ordinarily taken as given and because the contracting process is examined in its entirety. To be sure, taking endowments as given does not mean that initial conditions are beyond question. But it is necessary to start somewhere.

One possibility is to begin with the initial conditions, ask if they are objectionable, and, if they are, propose a remedy. Objectionable initial conditions, however, are sometimes irremediable—that is, they cannot be corrected in a way that yields expected net gains (Coase, 1964). Assume, arguendo, that the obvious net gain opportunities have been exhausted and consider the ramifications of examining the contracting process in its entirety.

The standard transaction cost economics assumption that parties to a transaction adopt a relatively farsighted approach (or quickly learn from mistakes, including the mistakes of others) has power-mitigating/vitiating effects. Such parties anticipate potential dependency conditions and prepare for them from the outset. Accordingly, dependencies that come as a surprise to unwitting victims under a resource dependency setup are priced out; they elicit safeguards and related organization responses under an approach in which the contracting process is examined in its entirety.[10] The types of power arguments that are featured

---

[10] Repeated application of the discriminating alignment hypothesis to intermediate product markets, labor markets, capital markets, regulation/deregulation, corporate governance, and so forth discloses that a wide range of economic phenomena can be interpreted as variations on the same transaction cost economizing theme. The predicted regularities, moreover, are borne out by the evidence.

by the resource dependency literature are significantly relieved in the process.

More generally, transaction cost economics holds that price, technology, and governance structure are determined simultaneously. Thus consider the supply of a good or service and assume that specialized technologies yield production cost savings but pose contractual hazards (because of asset specificity). Such transactions will carry a hazard-premium (reflected in the price) unless integrity-infusing safeguards are provided (governance structure). Sometimes net gains are realized by shifting a transaction from one mode of organization to another. Sometimes hazards are mitigated by enlarging the transaction. Transaction cost economics addresses both phenomena.

2. The Modern Corporation

I am concerned in this section with the question, What are the functions of the headquarters unit in a multibusiness firm? I address that issue by breaking it down into five subsidiary questions. The focus is on the internal organization of the modern corporation.

2.1 Strategy or Structure

Which is primary, strategy or structure? That is, is the multidivisional form (M-form) the administrative solution to the problems created by product-market diversification and/or the need to internalize transactions, or is it itself the innovation which permits efficiencies from the assembly of various business units in a common hierarchy?

My interpretation of Alfred D. Chandler's classic book, *Strategy and Structure* (1962), is that the multidivisional form was devised as a response to the control problems experienced in large, complex business firms—of which DuPont, General Motors, Standard Oil of New Jersey, and Sears were all examples and leading organizational innovators. Of these firms, the management at General Motors appears to have been most self-conscious in considering the merits of this new organizational structure (Brown, 1924; Sloan, 1964). But Chandler makes clear that the management of all of these firms perceived a need to separate operating and strategic decision making and to provide an organizational structure that would implement that purpose.

The logic of the M-form structure can be and has been interpreted in terms of economizing on bounded rationality and attenuating opportunism (Williamson, 1970, 1975, 1985). The bounded rationality argument is a variant on W. Ross Ashby's analysis of ultrastability (1960) and Herbert Simon's treatment of near-decomposability (1962). In brief, this argument states that hierarchy serves to economize on bounded rationality by grouping the operating parts into separable entities within which interactions are strong and between which they are weak, and by making temporal distinctions whereby frequent, small disturbances are dealt with at the operating level and cumulative or large, infrequent disturbances are assigned to the strategic part.

It is subgoal pursuit that raises concerns about opportunism. Separating the general executives (who are located in the general office or strategic part) from the operating executives (who are engaged in day-to-day decisions) makes it easy and natural for the former to emphasize overall enterprise goals, whereas enterprise goals were frequently crowded out by subgoal pursuit in the earlier unitary form structure (Chandler, 1966: 382–383). Relatedly, the added internal oversight and control apparatus located in the general office—including especially the interdivisional competition for resources that multidivisionalization encouraged—introduced added constraints on and altered incentives with respect to subgoal pursuit.

The upshot is that the large, complex enterprise in which multidivisionalization is feasible and has been effected enjoys advantages over an identical enterprise organized as a U-form structure. Once introduced, moreover, multidivisionalization can be extended—by integrating into activities that were previously too costly to manage internally, and by diversifying. Multidivisionalization spread by imitation (Chandler, 1966) and by both takeover and voluntary divestiture (Williamson, 1988c).

Although at the outset (circa 1920, when the M-form structure was first introduced), structure followed necessity—the imperative was to find a way to control proliferating variety (which may or may not be interpreted as strategy)—the M-form structure can now be regarded as an instrument of strategy. Firms that perceive opportunities profitably to integrate or diversify—through their own investment or, more often, by acquisition—can use the M-form structure to facilitate those purposes if the requisite decomposability conditions obtain. More disciplined internal organization—stronger incentives, better accountability, superior internal resource allocation—prospectively result. (But see the qualifications below.)

2.2 Entrepreneurial or Administrative

Which is primary, the entrepreneurial (value-creating) role of the headquarters unit, or the administrative (loss-preventing) role? Can a headquarters unit simultaneously perform both roles?

A well-functioning headquarters unit is one that simultaneously is alert to market opportunities and hazards, creates an internal operating ethos and rules of the game to which division managers relate and are responsive, and recognizes both its own limitations and those endemic to large firms in general. Such a management is engaged in both entrepreneurial and administrative roles.

Note in this connection that technological innovation is ordinarily thought of as an entrepreneurial activity. The relation of the large M-form enterprise to technological innovation is complex. That is partly because, as compared with small firms, large firms are seriously limited in their capacity credibly to offer, and thereafter to make delivery on, high-powered incentives (Williamson, 1975, ch. 10; 1985, ch. 6). Although it is a condition with which many large firms are loath to come to terms, the incentive limits of firms are real nonetheless. Upon realizing that taking a transaction out of the market and organizing it internally unavoidably degrades incentive intensity, firms should (1) expressly factor the prospective loss of incentive intensity into the decision about whether or not to internalize; and (2) for those transactions that are taken out of the market and organized internally, recognize that internal incentive intensity is an instrument to be set optimally (within the feasible range). Deliberately limiting internal incentives—because high-powered incentives encourage suboptimization and can get in the way of bilateral adaptability—may be a valid choice.[11] The use of salaries and career rewards, rather than claims over net receipts, to compensate executives thus reflects considerations of both feasibility (the impossibility of replicating mar-

---

[11] Bengt Holmstrom and Paul Milgrom (1989) also make this argument.

ket-like incentives within firms) and design (promoting internal cooperation). Whether executive compensation should be made much more heavily contingent on net receipts, as some advise, depends on how these feasibility and design features play out. The distinction between routine and innovation is pertinent.

I submit that high-powered incentives are especially germane to innovation. Net receipt participation will be facilitated by according greater degrees of autonomy to new projects (possibly by creating task forces) and by making managerial rewards contingent on performance. The latter, however, is not easy. For one thing, credible checks against manipulative internal accounting, whereby transfer prices are "adjusted" or net receipts are absorbed as overhead, are difficult to create. And even if the accounting is immune to such manipulation, firms will sometimes flat-out renege (Williamson, 1985: 158–160). The firm being its own court of ultimate appeal on such matters, high-powered internal incentives are discounted very heavily. Also, whereas the firm can offer the carrot of upside participation (albeit, perhaps, with limited credibility), the stick of capital losses which the market provides is beyond replication.

The object of increasing internal incentive intensity is twofold: to elicit the added energies that are often vital to successful innovation, and to discourage project renewals when the expected returns are net negative. Upon realizing that the large firm is seriously limited in incentive intensity respects, the large firm will consciously favor those internal projects for which its disabilities are least and will look to the market to support projects for which strong incentive intensity (of a two-sided kind) is especially crucial. Adopting a systems orientation to innovation suggests the following strategy: eschew early-stage innovation in favor of acquiring successful venture capital supported firms.

To be sure, an interested (large firm) buyer then needs to be matched with an interested (small firm) seller. Inasmuch as the entrepreneurial managers in start-up firms are often poorly suited to manage large-scale production and distribution, the basis for reaching an acceptable agreement in which both parties benefit frequently exists.

Value creation and loss reduction are both realized in the M-form enterprise (as compared with its U-form predecessor). With reference to innovation, the M-form enterprise is better suited than the U-form firm to implement the above-described acquisitions approach (actually, systems approach). The M-form also creates value in that it solves the problem of efficient decomposition more effectively. Disengaging the general management from operating matters can create further value since it may yield more credible internal incentives within the operating divisions. And losses can be reduced by creating a more credible internal competition for funds, which serves as a check on managerial politicking. (Chandler, 1966: 154)

2.3 Amalgamation and Divestment

What, if any, are the limits to the amalgamation of business units in multibusiness firms? Relatedly, how can the value presently being created by the breakup of diversified firms be reconciled with the value created by their creation in the past?

This is a two-part question and requires a two-part answer. Regarding the limits of amalgamation, the basic answer is that increasing size and variety introduces added opportunities for managerial discretion. Selective intervention being impossible, projects that promise only small coordination gains will not be able to support the added bureaucratic costs and related distortions that growth or acquisition would entail.

Suppose, however, that nontrivial coordination gains are in prospect—at least initially. What then? Should acquisitions, once made, be regarded as permanent?

That firms should be expected to engage in once-and-for-all business acquisitions is surely unrealistic. Circumstances— technology, rivalry, supply alternatives, tastes, regulations, and so forth—change. The composition of activities in which a firm is engaged should change responsively. To regard acquisitions favorably and voluntary divestiture unfavorably is simply wrongheaded.

To be sure, new internal projects and/or acquisitions quickly develop a constituency, and hence take on a life of their own. Voluntary divestiture often faces resistance on that account. But voluntary divestiture is valued for precisely that reason. Spin-offs, sell-offs, and, where feasible, management buyouts of divisions ought not, therefore, to be regarded negatively—even where, as is sometimes the case, these amount to an admission that an acquisition ought not to have been made initially. Admitting and correcting what, in the fullness of knowledge, turns out to be an error is better than burying mistakes. Furthermore, there may have been no ex ante error at all: the system simply experienced a bad ex post stochastic outcome.

An alternative to vertical or lateral integration that is sometimes favored is the "strategic alliance," possibly in the form of a joint venture. Viewed in transaction cost economics terms, the joint venture should not be regarded as an effective alternative to integration. Instead, what mainly recommends the joint venture is that it supports quick responsiveness. So regarded, it should be considered a temporary form of organization. Both successful and unsuccessful joint ventures will commonly be terminated when contracts expire. Successful joint ventures will be terminated because success often means that each of the parties, who chose not to merge but instead decided to combine their respective strengths in a selective and timely way, will have learned enough to go it alone. Unsuccessful joint ventures will be terminated because the opportunity to participate will have passed them by. Steady state or continuing supply needs and immediate (real-time responsiveness) needs are different and should be distinguished. Consider the following (*The Economist,* 1991: 71):

> For Mitsubishi, the partnership with Chrysler has long since served its purpose. It has allowed the Japanese firm to export to America without an extensive distribution and servicing network. . . .
> [S]uch an arrangement seriously limits Mitsubishi's long-term prospects in the American market. Lately, the Japanese firm has been spending heavily on building an image of its own, as well as an independent distribution system.

Note that changes in public policy and changes in the instruments for controlling managerial discretion can both influence the efficacy of diversification.[12] During the 1960s and much of the 1970s, when antitrust restraints on even small horizontal and vertical acquisitions were severe, the only option for acquiring a firm, thereby to supplant the incumbent management, was by conglomerate acquisition. If that was less cost-effective than, say, a vertical acquisition, and if merger restraints were later relaxed, a subsequent sale to which further added value could be ascribed might be feasible. The conglomerate could simply

---

[12] For a similar and more expansive discussion, see Andrei Shleifer and Robert Vishny (1990a).

sell the acquired part to the previously prohibited but now permitted vertically related firm.

Also, financial innovations are pertinent. The development of leveraged buyouts and the junk bond market can be interpreted as corporate control innovations that partly supplant earlier forms (the proxy contest). Moreover, bust-up takeovers can be interpreted both in terms of the rationality of debt financing and the reluctance of incumbent managers to self-enforce against the excesses of managerial discretion.

To be sure, there is a need to employ arguments of this kind in a discriminating way, otherwise the exercise is one of unrestrained ex post rationalization. Some of the issues are discussed further in Section 3, below. Suffice it to observe here that a logic of economic organization, informed in part by the application of transaction cost reasoning to corporate finance, is crucial to the exercise.

2.4 Managerial Discretion

Strategic management is normally taken to mean the explicit oversight and review of the strategy formulation process together with systems for allocating resources among businesses. Do firms that impose "strategic management" on portfolios of businesses add value, and if so, what is the mechanism?

Firms can and sometimes do impose "strategic management" on portfolios of businesses. One possible purpose is risk diversification (Adelman, 1961). But that is much less important than the allocation of cash flows to high-yield purposes. Stockholders, after all, are able to diversify their own portfolios through mutual funds or otherwise. But stockholders need assistance in checking the propensity of managers to reinvest earnings in a mature business from which there are large cash flows. M-form divisionalization, in which the firm operates as a miniature capital market and reallocates cash flows to high-yield uses, can add value if the market for corporate control is weak or lacking.

Indeed, the M-form innovation is remarkable in that *internal organization* became a means to squeeze out managerial discretion. That constitutes an unexpected response to the doubts raised by Berle and Means as to whether "those in control of a modern corporation will also choose to operate it in the interests of the stockholders" (1933: 121). Faced with the objective limits of competition in product and capital markets circa 1930, the separation of ownership from control reported by Berle and Means elicited grave concern (Mason, 1959). Some authorities have proposed that strictures be placed on the composition and committee structure of the board of directors. Others have urged that the inculcation of "corporate responsibility" is the answer. The possibility that top management would *reorganize* the firm in such a way as to introduce *self-restraints* long went unremarked and unrecognized. If management was the problem, how could it also be the solution?

Managers are not, however, uniformly given to managerial discretion. Moreover, the exercise of discretion by lower-level managers can limit the latitude, and hence be at variance with the preferences, of their superiors. If, for whatever reason, the M-form innovation gets introduced,[13] follow-on systems consequences of an unanticipated kind obtain. Once the M-form firm gains better control over its immediate mix of activities, the added organizational competence it has gained can be applied to other activities (Penrose, 1959). The merger with and/or takeover of firms that are given to excesses of managerial discretion is one possibility. Were this to obtain, then the M-form innovation would serve to attenuate managerial discretion both within the firms where it was adopted and, directly (by takeover) or indirectly (by inducing potential takeover candidates to adopt preventive measures), throughout the universe of large firms more generally (Williamson, 1983, 1988c; Pelikan, 1989). Those are benefits not to be regarded lightly.

2.5 Lessons of Divisionalization

Are there corollaries to headquarters units in nonbusiness organizations and, if so, what are the comparative lessons to be learned?

The logic of the M-form enterprise—in economizing on bounded rationality and attenuating opportunism—is robust and applies to large, complex organizations of whatever sort. Ashby (1960) was concerned with the most fundamental organizational needs: to design a brain that would be adaptive to alterations both of degree and in kind. Similarly, Simon (1962) was concerned with the rudimentary architecture of complexity in physical, biological, and human organizations.

---

[13] This could be an intentional response and, for some firms, arguably was (Brown, 1924; Sloan, 1964). But it need not be. For a discussion, see Williamson (1990b).

Although the performance of nonprofit and government organizations is usually more difficult to evaluate, I submit that the lessons of bounded rationality and opportunism for economic organization are everywhere the same: use hierarchy to decompose complex tasks into manageable operating units; use hierarchy to adapt effectively to disturbances of a bilateral kind; be alert to subgoal pursuit, where hierarchical incentives and controls can be used to check discretion. It is furthermore important to recognize and come to terms with the incentive limits of internal organization. And where continuity matters, it is everywhere important to give and receive credible commitments.

Interestingly, the organization of the public schools in Tokyo and Los Angeles is being examined along M-form lines by William Ouchi, who observes that the Tokyo system permits much greater autonomy to the local units and is less beset by bureaucratic excesses. Aspects of this resonate with the recent study by John Chubb and Terry Moe (1990), who strongly favor granting greater local autonomy to the public schools in the United States so as to encourage better performance. Chubb and Moe do not expressly call for the use of the M-form, possibly because the M-form is more easily compromised than a "market solution," but neither do they propose full autonomy.

Indeed, one of the potential problems with divisionalization—perhaps especially among nonprofit enterprises—is that it will be used too aggressively. Thus while there is merit in organizing universities according to the principle "each tub on its own bottom," especially if the alternative is the Maoist practice of "everyone eating out of one big pot," a third alternative warrants consideration: divisionalization combined with *limited* cross-subsidization. The hazard is that subsidies can become addictive and virulent, in which event incentive intensity is compromised. The challenge is to use the M-form structure in a nonprofit enterprise in a disciplined way. But that is much easier said than done. More than most forms of organization, the study of nonprofits is shot through with unmeasurable and/or incommensurate values.

3. Comparative Contracting

It is not only possible but customary to study the modern corporation by examining alternative forms of administrative organization. This entails making comparisons *within* a generic form of governance—namely, hierarchy. Transaction cost economics maintains, however, that comparisons *between* alternative generic modes—markets, hybrids, and hierarchies—are at least as important if not more so. Many of the errors of myopic strategic reasoning[14] can be avoided by approaching the problem of economic organization as one of incomplete contracting in its entirety. As discussed in the efficiency and power subsection above, parties to an incomplete contract are assumed to behave perceptively with respect to present and prospective benefits and hazards, which enable them to decide *simultaneously* on (1) the technology to be employed, (2) the price under which a good or service will be transferred, and (3) the governance structure within which a transaction is located.

Transaction cost economics is pertinent to questions of the following kinds:

1. When can forward integration into distribution be used to deter entry, and when will such efforts predictably fail? (The American Sugar Company's attempt to drive out its competitors by buying into wholesale and retail distribution predictably ended as a miserable failure.)
2. When does lateral integration offer added value and when does it represent a misuse of corporate resources? (The acquisition of Reliance Electric by the Exxon Corporation was arguably of the latter kind and could have been so identified at the outset.)
3. Why is the acquisition of one firm by another always attended by the loss of incentive intensity? (The incentive failures of Series E and Series H stock issues by General Motors [following GM's acquisition of EDS and Hughes Electronics, respectively] were the predictable consequences of the "impossibility of selective intervention.")
4. What additional factors need to be considered when contracting under a weak property rights regime? (Both marketing channel and technology transfer decisions are pertinent.)
5. Is there an efficient choice of debt and equity, and how

---

14 See the discussion of resource dependency in the efficiency and power subsection, above.

does this relate to the use of leveraged buyouts and management buyouts?

6. Should membership on the board of directors be shared among interested stakeholders or should it be concentrated on a particular group?

7. What types of businesses are well suited for the partnership form, and what happens if a mismatch occurs? (Booz-Allen's decision to go public is an example of a mismatch that was subsequently reversed.)

8. Given the intertemporal propensities of bureaucratic forms of organization to ratify and renew earlier decisions, what counterbiasing checks should be made? (The obvious check is to require all new projects to cross a very high threshold for approval.)

Uses of transaction cost economics to deal with strategic issues of the above kinds are developed elsewhere. Since explicating all of these strategic uses is beyond the scope of this paper, I merely sketch two: (1) the organization of intermediate product markets (under both strong and weak property rights regimes); and (2) the discriminating use of debt and equity, including assessments of corporate governance and the partnership form of organization. The main purpose is to give an idea of how transaction cost economics reconceptualizes the issues. Interested readers are encouraged to examine the pertinent references for more expansive treatments. Note in this connection that all of the strategic issues I have listed can be recast as variations on the basic transaction cost economizing theme set out in Section 1.2, above. (I also conjecture that further and deeper uses of transaction cost economics to address strategy are in prospect.)

3.1 Intermediate Product-Market Transactions

The mundane issue of make or buy not only goes to the heart of transaction cost economizing but also poses interesting strategic issues. The rudiments are sketched here. Both strong and weak property rights regimes are considered.

Strong property rights. Although there are a variety of factors that bear on vertical and lateral integration—economies of scale, taxes, quotas, and monopoly power included—transaction cost economics focuses on the attributes of the transactions and asks which governance structures are best suited to organize which transactions and why. The issues here have been developed at length elsewhere (Williamson, 1971, 1975, 1979; Klein, Crawford and Alchian, 1978; Riordan and Williamson, 1985; Grossman and Hart, 1986). The basic argument hinges on the condition of asset specificity and the main results are these: (1) market procurement has the advantage over internal organization when the condition of asset specificity is negligible, the reason being that markets have exceptional incentive intensity features (which elicit autonomous adaptation), and each party to a nonspecific transaction can go its own way at little cost to the other; (2) hierarchy is favored as the condition of asset specificity becomes great, the reason being that the high-powered incentives of markets are maladaptive, as compared with unified ownership and the attendant use of fiat, for the purposes of harmonizing an exchange relation where bilateral adaptation needs are ascendant; and (3) hybrid forms (such as long-term contracts or franchising, which include safeguards against defection) are best suited to manage transactions with an intermediate degree of asset specificity, intermediate degrees of incentive intensity and mixed adaptability (A/C) being most cost effective under these circumstances.

More generally, let $M = M(k)$, $X = X(k)$, and $H = H(k)$ be reduced form expressions that denote market, hybrid, and hierarchy governance costs as a function of asset specificity (k). Assuming that each mode is constrained to choose the same level of asset specificity,[15] the following comparative cost relations obtain: $M(0) < X(0) < H(0)$ and $M' > X' > H' > 0$. The first of these two sets of inequalities reflects the fact that bureaucratic costs vary inversely with incentive intensity. The intercept for market governance is thus lower than the intercept for hybrid, which in turn is lower than the intercept for hierarchy. The second inequality reflects the marginal disability of

---

[15] To be sure, this oversimplifies. For one thing, the condition of asset specificity is a design variable rather than a given, from which the value of asset specificity and the type of governance are determined simultaneously rather than sequentially (Riordan and Williamson, 1985; Masten, 1982). Also, there are sometimes advantages in both making and buying, in that each mode disciplines the other. But these remarks merely elaborate transaction cost arguments in transaction cost terms. The underlying logic is unchanged.

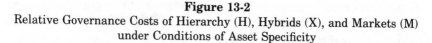

Figure 13-2
Relative Governance Costs of Hierarchy (H), Hybrids (X), and Markets (M)
under Conditions of Asset Specificity

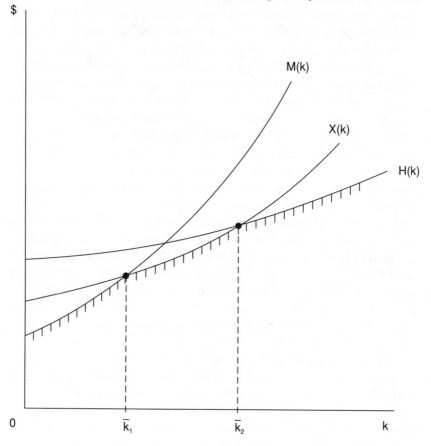

markets as compared with hierarchies in adaptability respects as asset specificity, and hence bilateral dependency, becomes more consequential. As shown in Figure 13-2, these reduced form expressions (for appropriate parameter values) yield a three-part region for efficient supply: I, use markets for $k < \bar{k}_1$; II, use hybrids for $\bar{k}_1 < k < \bar{k}_2$; and III, use hierarchy for $k > \bar{k}_2$.[16]

---

[16] This assumes that X(0) is less than H(0) in nontrivial degree, since otherwise X(k) could intersect H(k) from below at a value of $k < \bar{k}$—in which event the hybrid mode would be dominated throughout by the least cost choice of either market or hierarchy.

Note that the usual strategic approach assesses the private net benefits of integration as positive—because integration is believed to be the source of added power.[17] Accordingly, absent diseconomies of scale or unexplained capital constraints, the orthodox make-or-buy decision is easy: integrate! By contrast, transaction cost economics regards vertical integration that is not attended by transaction cost economies as a source not of power but of weakness.[18] That is because internal organization always experiences a loss of incentive intensity and added bureaucratic costs as compared with markets and hybrids. If, therefore, there are not compensating gains (bilateral or multilateral adaptability advantages), integration is the source of cost without benefit. Firms that mindlessly integrate weaken themselves in relation to nonintegrated rivals.

Indeed, the usual strategic preference for vertical or lateral integration is reversed by the transaction cost economics approach to the issues. Vertical integration is the organization form of last resort, to be adopted when all else fails. Try markets, try long-term contracts and other hybrid modes first, and revert to hierarchy only for compelling reasons. Absent preexisting monopoly power, in the event of which strategic considerations can arise,[19] the logic of transaction cost economizing reserves integration for those transactions for which the condition of bilateral dependency is substantial.

Weak property rights. The foregoing treatment of vertical and lateral integration assumes that property rights are well defined and easy to enforce. "Markets experience problems" because contracts are incomplete and transactions get out of alignment under conditions of bilateral dependency. Therein resides the main incentive to resort to more complex forms of governance under a strong property rights regime.

Added incentives to introduce contractual safeguards to deter loss of intellectual property rights arise under a *weak* property rights regime. David Teece (1986) has advanced the argument

---

[17] For a recent assessment of the market power consequences of integration in a "double duopoly" context, see Oliver Hart and Jean Tirole (1990). Also see Steven Salop and David Scheffman (1983) on "raising rival's costs."

[18] That assumes away the incentives to integrate discussed in note 16, above. It furthermore assumes strong property rights. As discussed in the next subsection, weak property rights can sometimes induce integration as a protective measure.

[19] See, however, Williamson (1985: 100) and note 17, above. See also the weak property rights subsection below.

that innovators may be induced to integrate into related stages (backward, forward, lateral) if such integration serves to mitigate contractual hazards under "weak regimes of appropriability." If contracting with related stages runs the risk that valued know-how will leak out, and if firms operating in related stages possess specialized assets, effective control over innovations may inadvertently pass into the hands of others.

To be sure, integration into related stages can operate in the service of trade secrecy whether the newly integrated assets are specific or not. The denial of know-how to specialized stages is especially important, however, where asset specificity has cost-reducing effects. If de facto control of the innovation accrues to those who *combine* know-how with asset specificity, innovating firms can help prevent the leakage of know-how by integrating into co-specialized stages of production and distribution (Teece, 1986).

It is relevant in this connection to distinguish between the licensing problem and the franchising problem. Both pose leakage hazards, but whereas the franchisee can be deterred from dissipating quality by (1) requiring him to make nonredeployable investments in the franchise and (2) imposing a termination-at-will clause (Klein, 1980), this same strategy will not work for licensing. That is because termination is of no concern to the licensee, once he has acquired the relevant know-how. Accordingly, the licensing agreement needs to be embedded in a larger contractual relation in which penalties other than termination have integrity-infusing properties. Some of the pertinent issues have been addressed by Farok Contractor (1981) in the context of the multinational enterprise. Absent the ability to effect deterrence—by the credible threat of enforcing trademarks more vigorously, using politics to limit foreign market access to domestic markets, restricting access to proprietary technical improvements, and so forth—and assuming that direct foreign investment is prohibitively expensive, transaction cost economics predicts that licensing will take the form of a one-time, lump-sum fee rather than a royalty agreement.[20]

A related, but different, argument has been advanced by Jan Heide and George John (1988), who are concerned with intertemporal hazards that sometimes arise in distributing a good

---

[20] This last is a "node B" transaction cost argument (Williamson, 1985: 32–35).

or service. They consider the situation of a manufacturer that has developed a new product and needs specialized distribution to get it to market. The manufacturer could make these investments himself or could employ manufacturers' agents, who already know the market and can service it more cheaply. These agents will be leery, however, of deepening their investments if the success of their marketing efforts invites the manufacturer to bypass them and sell directly.

In effect, there are three scenarios to be evaluated: (1) the manufacturer sells directly from the outset, its disadvantages in this respect notwithstanding; (2) the manufacturer initially uses an agent to sell to the market and subsequently enters if the agent's efforts are successful but not otherwise;[21] and (3) the manufacturer uses an agent but is deterred from subsequent entry by the use of linking investments made by the agent. Farsighted agents under the last scenario recognize that their market development efforts will be expropriated by the manufacturer unless they are able to develop ties to the customers that preclude the second scenario from materializing. Which scenario is the most cost effective will vary with the circumstances. As Heide and John argue, linking investments are often the most effective way to go.

3.2 Corporate Finance and Corporate Governance

Debt and equity.[22] Debt, equity, leasing, and so forth are more than financial instruments. They are also instruments of governance. Just as there is a rational basis for deciding whether to make or to buy a component, so is there a rational basis upon which to finance an asset. In order of complexity, lease (rent) is the simplest form of governance. Debt finance for self-owned assets comes next. Equity is the most intrusive and complicated form of governance. Since governance is costly, the general rule is to reserve complicated forms of finance for complicated investments. Expressed in terms of asset specificity,

---

[21] There are two variants of the second scenario: the manufacturer could offer to compensate the agent for any specialized investments should the manufacturer decide to integrate, or the manufacturer could refuse to compensate. I assume the latter, there being many problems in establishing value for the former (for a discussion, see Williamson, 1985, ch. 13).

[22] The argument in this subsection is based on Williamson (1988).

fungible assets can be leased, semispecific assets can be debt financed, and equity is the financial form of last resort—to be used for assets of a very nonredeployable kind.

Whereas most earlier treatments of corporate finance work out of an undifferentiated or composite capital framework,[23] transaction cost economics examines the asset attributes of individual investment projects. Thus suppose that a firm wishes to operate a fleet of trucks, build or otherwise have the use of a general purpose factory, acquire inventories, install equipment, procure dies, and the like. Assuming that the trucks are of a general purpose kind, such durable assets on wheels are ones for which leasing is a feasible form of finance. (To be sure, user costs and preventive maintenance are concerns; but rules and standards governing these can often check egregious abuses.) Repossession and redeployment of these assets by a specialized owner (leasor), who buys in quantity and services a broad market, is easy in the event that payments are late or other problems intrude. Assuming that the factory is located in a population center, the factory building is also a highly redeployable asset. Renting extant space is one possibility. Buying the property with debt secured by a mortgage is another. Loans can also be easily arranged for inventories of raw materials that are unspecialized and easily liquidated. Suppose, however, that lenders are now asked to supply funds for assets that are much more highly specialized. Is debt financing equally well suited to these?

Assume, for this purpose, that debt is defined as a rules-governed structure whereby (1) fixed interest payments must be made at regular intervals, (2) the business must continuously meet certain liquidity tests, (3) principal must be repaid at the loan expiration date, and (4) in the event of default, the debtholders will exercise preemptive claims against the assets in question. If everything goes well, interest and principal are paid on schedule. In the event of default, however, debtholders will realize differential recovery in the degree to which the assets in question are redeployable. As the degree of asset specificity deepens, the value of a preemptive claim declines, and the terms of debt financing will be adjusted adversely.

---

[23] For a discussion of composite capital, see Williamson (1988b: 576–579).

Confronted with the prospect that specialized investments will be financed on adverse terms, the firm might respond by sacrificing some of the specialized investment features in favor of greater redeployability. But might it be possible to invent a new governance structure to which suppliers of finance would attach added confidence? Suppose, arguendo, that a financial instrument called equity is invented and assume that equity has the following governance properties: (1) it bears a residual claimant status to the firm in both earnings and asset liquidation respects; (2) it contracts for the duration of the life of the firm; and (3) it is awarded its own board of directors that (a) is elected by the pro rata votes of those who hold tradable shares, (b) has the power to replace the management, (c) decides on management compensation, (d) has access to internal performance measures on a timely basis, (e) can authorize audits in depth for special follow-up purposes, (f) is apprised of important investment and operating proposals before they are implemented, and (g) in other respects bears a decision review and monitoring relation to the firm's management.

An *endogenous response* to the governance needs of suppliers of finance who are asked to invest in nonredeployable projects has thereby resulted. These suppliers bear a residual claimant status to the firm and are awarded "control" over the board of directors in exchange. Note that equity comes in late in this scenario. Because it is a relatively cumbersome form of finance, equity is the financial instrument of *last resort*.

Expressed in terms of markets and hierarchies, debt is the market-like form of organization. That formulation works well as long as assets are redeployable. Markets (rules) give way to administration (discretion; hierarchy) when assets become highly specific, however. The argument tracks this phenomenon in intermediate product markets: equity, like vertical integration, is reserved for transactions that are subject to market breakdowns. That reverses the power orientation, which regards vertical integration and equity as the more muscular and hence favored forms of organization and finance, respectively.

Stakeholder participation on the board of directors. Worker participation can take various forms, many of them productive (Levine, 1990). Participation can yield both direct (private) benefits and indirect (social) benefits. Above some threshold, however, added participation usually comes at a cost. The nature of these costs and benefits varies with the task, the group, and the context.

My concern here is strictly with participation on the board of directors, and I address this matter entirely with respect to the composition of one-tier boards. The modern manufacturing corporation is considered first. The organization of professional firms follows.

Stakeholder approaches to corporate governance in the modern manufacturing corporation take a variety of forms. One variant of "interest group management" would award seats on the boards of directors to "one-third representatives elected by employees, one-third consumer representatives, one-third delegates of federal, state, and local governments" (Dahl, 1970: 20). The view is that it is ungenerous, antidemocratic, and antiproductive to deny workers, consumers, the public, and other interested stakeholders the chance of representation on the board of directors.

Transaction cost economics aspires to assess the contractual relation between each constituency and the enterprise symmetrically. The general argument is that each input will contract with the enterprise in a discriminating way. Specifically, inputs that are exposed to contractual hazards will either devise a contractual safeguard or the input will demand and receive a risk premium. Assuming that corporate governance matters, in that awarding corporate control to the wrong constituencies introduces added risk—which in turn will be reflected in the costs of organization—the first and simplest lesson of transaction cost economics is that corporate governance should be reserved for those who supply or finance specialized assets to the firm. Large numbers of nonspecific groups with which the firm has contracts are thus eliminated from potential stakeholder status immediately.

For those who qualify as stakeholders in asset specificity terms, the key issue is how best to secure that stake. The possibility of using the board of directors as a security instrument for some or all of these constituencies warrants consideration. There are several options: (1) mixed boards, in which all constituencies that make specific investments are awarded a pro rata stake; (2) specialized boards, whereby the contractual relation with all types of stakeholders but one is perfected at the contractual interface, the board being awarded to the stakeholder whose contractual relation to the firm is most difficult to perfect (and who thus has the status of a residual claimant); and (3) specialized boards where one stakeholder group is dominant but where provision for others is made by awarding them observer status, thereby permitting them to give specialized advice and/ or satisfying their informational needs.

These issues are discussed elsewhere (Williamson, 1985, ch. 12; 1989). Suffice it to observe here that constituencies that have a well-defined contractual relation to the firm will benefit by tuning up the contractual interface. Not only is the board of directors a diffuse and cumbersome instrument, but such protective powers as it possesses are compromised by inviting broad participation on the board. Residual claimant status is at best risky and is made all the more so if the claims of many constituencies are subject to ex post bargaining at the board level. In effect, broad participation on the board invites two bites at the apple (get your full entitlement at the contractual interface; get more in the distribution of the residual). Confronted with added risk, those who are the "natural" residual claimants in the nexus of contracts will adjust the terms under which they will contract adversely. If, as is typically the case in manufacturing (declining industries being a possible exception), equity is the natural residual claimant, the cost of equity would increase if the interest group management model of the board (or some variant thereof) were to be adopted.

The contrast between boards of directors in manufacturing firms and professional firms (law firms, accounting firms, and the like) is striking. The boards of directors in professional firms are entirely made up of the employees (managing partners). Why the difference?

Two things are very different. First, the physical assets in these firms are very generic and redeployable—hence can be leased or financed by debt. Outside equity is unneeded—indeed, is contraindicated, since to use equity finance for such assets is to incur costs without benefits. Having financed these assets with debt (or by the membership), the assets at risk, for which added protection is needed, are the human assets and the reputation of the firm. Control and residual claimancy are appropriately assigned to the key employees who have a stake in developing and preserving the value of these assets. Henry Hansmann agrees and observes that "the only important industries in the United States in which worker-owned firms are clearly the dominant form of organization are the service industries, such as law, accounting, investment banking, and management consulting, where partnership and professional corporations (that is, corporations in which shareholding is confined to professionals practicing in the firm) are the typical form of practice" (1986: 54).

Interestingly, the transaction cost logic of economic organization not only supports this general result but also helps explain organizational differences within the partnership form. Thus Ronald Gilson and Robert Mnookin (1985) examine compensation practices in law firms—the leading payment alternatives being equal shares to senior partners versus a marginal productivity payment scheme—and advance a rationale in which differential transaction-specific values (between clients, lawyers, and law firms) figure prominently. Ceteris paribus, sharing arrangements among partners are favored (and high-powered incentives are disfavored) as the relation between clients and law firms deepens.

The central message of this section is that there is a logic to economic organization that (1) turns on a few key transaction cost economizing principles, (2) deals with comparative economic organization at a microanalytic level, (3) has wide application, (4) can be adapted to address anomalies (weak property rights; professional firms), (5) can be communicated to and explicated for managers, and (6) violations of which are the source of avoidable costs (competitive *dis*advantages). Although transaction cost economizing does not exhaust all that is germane to business strategy, it fundamentally implicates and gives predictive content to the proposition that "economy is the best strategy."

4. The Japanese Corporation

One reason for extending the argument to consider the Japanese corporation is that it is impossible to discuss the matter of business strategy long without the issue of Japanese economic organization surfacing, if not dominating the conversation. My main reason, however, is that I argue that the Japanese firm is distinguished not merely by different attributes but by a *syndrome* of attributes. The existence of this syndrome pushes the analyst to address systems considerations that do not arise when contractual relations are examined one at a time.

A variety of explanations have been advanced to explain why Japanese firms have been so successful in international competition. One of the leading explanations is that the Japanese employment relation (lifetime employment; seniority promotions) is different. Another is that Japanese industry has been the beneficiary of planning and targeting by the Ministry of International Trade and Industry. Relatedly, Japanese firms engage in sharp, possibly predatory, business practices in which the home market is protected (and organized as a cartel) while foreign markets are subject to dumping. Cultural differences, including legal differences, purportedly contribute to the success differential. Also, extensive subcontracting is believed to be a contributing factor; Japanese banking, finance, and control are different; and the Japanese have been unusually clever in hiring the marketing expertise and subverting the political process in foreign countries to promote their economic interests.

There plainly is no lack of explanatory factors. The more favored explanations, at least in the popular press, are of a strategizing kind. I submit, however, that the Japanese have long been aware that economy is the best strategy. The main explanation for their success is that first-order economizing has been assiduously pursued.

My arguments rely in significant degree on the recent survey and assessment of the Japanese firm by Masahiko Aoki (1990). The basic argument (which I believe is consistent with but is nevertheless different from Aoki's) is this: (1) three key factors—employment, subcontracting, and banking—are fundamentally responsible for the success of the Japanese firm; (2) the efficacy of each of these rests on distinctive institutional supports; and (3) the three key factors bear a complementary relation to each other.

4.1 The Employment Relation

As Aoki puts it, the "mystifying notion of 'life-time' employment and the 'seniority' system tells only half of the truth," and even that fraction has been declining in recent years (1990: 12). Not only does the Japanese firm use rank hierarchy as an incentive system, but "the existence of a credible threat of discharge when the employee does not meet the criteria for continual promotion" buttresses the rank hierarchy (1990: 12).[24]

What I would like to emphasize here is that the administration of rank hierarchies in the Japanese firm relies on two crucial *institutional* supports. The first of these is the elevation of the personnel department within the firm. The second is the enterprise union.

The personnel department administers the rank hierarchy in the Japanese firm in a much more comprehensive, career-oriented manner than is attempted by the usual U.S. corporation. A dramatically different relation between superiors and subordinates creates added confidence in the rank hierarchy. As compared with most U.S. firms, immediate superiors in Japanese firms have much less control over the destiny of subordinates. If the career tracks of both superiors and subordinates are administered "on the merits" by the same personnel department, then endemic problems of corporate politicking are likely to be relieved.

To be sure, there are trade-offs between current, local knowledge (where immediate superiors have the advantage) and overall career performance (where the personnel department has the advantage). Conceivably, however, the allocation and professionalization of the personnel department in the Japanese firm has had effects not unlike those that Chandler ascribed to the M-form structure: managers at every level relate to their jobs in a more objective way (Chandler, 1966: 382–383; 1977: 460). If so, the Japanese personnel department is an organizational innovation of real importance.

Additionally, as compared with a craft or industry union in the United States, the enterprise union in the Japanese firm both relates to the purposes and needs of the firm in a more nuanced way and serves as a more effective check on (and voice with respect to) the integrity of the personnel department. Being an enterprise union, its purposes are more narrowly focused on the economic needs of the enterprise and its workers. The more general political purposes to which industry unions relate are therefore less apt to intrude; and the needs of distant firms and

---

[24] Note that Aoki expressly takes exception to the prevailing U.S. view that Japanese wages are tied more closely to seniority than are U.S. wages. Contrast Alan Blinder (1990: 21) with Aoki (1988, ch. 3).

workers, which are often very different, do not have to be factored in. To be sure, there is always a hazard that local union leadership will be bought off or will be ineffectual. Here as elsewhere, credible checks against opportunism (Williamson, 1983) are not only vital but will frequently be in the long-term interests of workers and firms alike (indeed, union integrity is one manifestation of "enlightened management"—which is too often an empty slogan under U.S. personnel administration).

Taken together, these twin institutional supports for the employment relation promote the enrichment and more effective deployment of firm-specific human capital.

4.2 Subcontracting

Large Japanese manufacturing firms are much less integrated than their U.S. counterparts. In terms of the intermediate product-market schema described in Section 3, Japanese manufacturers rely much more extensively on hybrid contracting. In effect, the locus $X(k)$ in Figure 13-2 is lower among Japanese than among U.S. firms—whence the value $\bar{k}_2$ is pushed to the right and a larger amount of activity that would be organized under hierarchy in the United States is organized under the hybrid mode in Japan.

The contracting mystique is that the Japanese have a greater propensity to cooperate (Aoki, 1988, ch. 8). Ethnic homogeneity and long experience with the sharing of water rights are believed to be contributing factors. As with the employment relation, however, investments in specialized assets for which bilateral adaptability is needed will be promoted by crafting supporting governance structures and providing added safeguards.

Again, contracting mystique gives way to the logic of economic organization. At a very general level, Japanese and U.S. procurement practices are alike. Thus strategic investments and those of a highly specific kind are undertaken by the prime contractor. Vertical integration is used for these investments. At the other end of the spectrum are generic items. Classical market procurement is observed for these. The question, however, is what supports the broader band of hybrid contracting.

Banri Asanuma (1989) develops a seven-part scale to characterize outside contracting and uses four measures of relation-specific skills to describe Japanese buyer-supplier relations. As Asanuma observes and interprets Japanese contracting practices, contracts vary systematically with (1) the nature of the part to be supplied, (2) the history of the contractual relation, (3) the maturity of the industry, and (4) supplier ratings on each of the relation-specific skills. An economizing orientation informs the entire procurement exercise (Asanuma, 1989: 29). This is done, moreover, in a highly individuated way. "Core plants in the electric machinery industry purchase both [generic] parts . . . and [specialized] parts" from the same supplier but contract differently for parts of each kind (1989: 13).

Suppliers are graded A through D. Suppliers of grades A and B are cultivated, grade D suppliers are eliminated, and grade C suppliers are used to buffer variations in demand (Asanuma, 1989: 17–18). Even grade A and B suppliers are subject to competition at contract renewal intervals (the period of which varies with the nature of the part in question) (1989: 4, 8). Relations of trust notwithstanding, bilateral monopoly conditions are avoided: "Whenever feasible, [core firms] endeavor to correct the situation by developing alternative qualified sources" (1989: 26).

There is nothing romantic or soft-headed about Japanese contracting practices. What seems to distinguish these practices is that they have been raised to a higher level of refinement than is observed elsewhere. In part that may reflect the Japanese understanding that vertical integration is the organization form of last resort. As discussed in Section 4.4, below, systems considerations are pertinent to both the attractions and successes of Japanese subcontracting.

4.3 Banking

Individual banks in Japan are permitted to hold stocks in nonfinancial companies up to a maximum of 5%. But combinations of banks can and do own more: "Financial institutions as a whole (including insurance companies) own about 40 percent of the total stock outstanding of listed companies" (Aoki, 1990: 14). What is also interesting is that banks behave collectively: one "main bank" is assigned to each company. Aoki describes the relation as follows (1990: 14):

> The main bank plays the role of manager of a loan consortium when a group of banks extends major long-term credit to the company, and it is

responsible for closely monitoring the business affairs of the company. If the company suffers a business crisis, the main bank assumes major responsibility for various rescue operations, which include the rescheduling of loan payments, emergency loans, advice for the liquidation of some assets, the facilitation of business opportunities, the supply of management resources, and finally reorganization, to secure the claims of the consortium (Sheard, 1989). In the normal course of events, however, the main bank exercises explicit control neither in the selection of management nor in corporate policy making.

One of the interesting questions is whether the main bank will refuse to discharge its responsibilities during a business crisis. I submit that this is an example of collective organization where reputation effects can be expected to operate with usual reliability. Failure by a main bank to discharge its assigned function virtually guarantees that it will be punished by others in the banking group of which it is a member. Furthermore, other groups will observe and record this behavior, regard it as an unacceptable breach, and will themselves refuse membership. The would-be defector is thus faced with massive reputation effect penalties.

Another interesting feature of this bank ownership system is that the managements of Japanese firms are insulated from takeover raids through the open market (Aoki, 1990: 14). Management displacement, if it occurs, is orchestrated by the main bank (1990: 15).

4.4 Systems Effects

Each of these Japanese practices is interesting in its own right. Moreover, some can be and have been imitated by U.S. corporations—which, for example, are now much more aware of the potential cost-saving merits of hybrid contracting.

What I want to emphasize here, however, is that these three practices are linked. In particular, the efficacy of Japanese employment practices is supported both by extensive subcontracting and by banking control.

As previously remarked, transaction cost economics maintains that all long-term contracts are unavoidably incomplete and pose contractual hazards. Lifetime employment is an especially long-term contract. Such contracts pose hazards of four kinds.

For one thing, firms that assume this obligation may be subject to severe strain if they are beset by economic adversity—caused, say, by periodic drops in demand. Second, workers in core firms may treat the job as a sinecure and shirk their duties. Third, the workers who tailor their productive talents to the needs of a particular firm may find that the agreement is breached—possibly through takeover. Finally, not all workers in the firm may bear an equally important relation to the enterprise, yet demands for equalitarian treatment are hard to resist. Accordingly, lifetime guarantees are awarded to all. I will hereafter refer to these as (1) adversity, (2) shirking, (3) breach, and (4) equalitarianism.

I contend that the institutional matrix within which core firms operate relieves these hazards. For one thing, the Japanese personnel office in combination with enterprise unions significantly relieves shirking and helps to relieve the problem of equalitarianism. If subcontractors are less constrained in lifetime employment respects than core firms, extensive subcontracting helps to relieve adversity. But there are added benefits. Extensive subcontracting simplifies personnel administration and enterprise union operations in the prime contractor by homogenizing the work force. When there is less variety, the task of personnel administration, which is often incredibly demanding, is significantly reduced in scope. Also, wage disparities within the membership of the enterprise union are reduced. In effect, variety is removed to the subcontractors (each of which is relatively homogeneous), which relieves the problem of equalitarianism. The system as a whole supports variety, but each of the parts is relatively homogeneous. But for this simplification, the Japanese employment system would experience much greater strain.[25]

Hazards of breach that arise because incumbent managements have been displaced by new owners (takeover) are arguably reduced by the Japanese main bank ownership scheme. To be sure, the so-called breach of trust that Andrei Shleifer and

---

[25] As Aoki observes, "the differentiation of employment status with a single firm is not easy to administer from the industrial relations point of view. Also, under the institution of enterprise-based unions organized on the union-shop principle, it may become difficult for the union to represent the divergent interests of different groups of employees fairly." These considerations encourage firms to "spin off or subcontract those activities which require qualitatively different working conditions." A "relatively undifferentiated employment structure" results (Aoki, 1984: 27–29).

Figure 13-3
Supports for Lifetime Employment

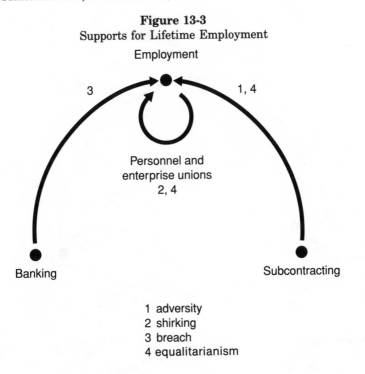

Employment

3   1, 4

Personnel and
enterprise unions
2, 4

Banking   Subcontracting

1 adversity
2 shirking
3 breach
4 equalitarianism

Lawrence Summers (1988) have ascribed to takeover is, I think, exaggerated (Williamson, 1988c). To the extent, however, that lifetime employment arrangements are in place, this hazard is greater and added protection is warranted.

The upshot is that the hazards associated with lifetime employment are mitigated by the combined forces shown in Figure 13-3. More generally, the set of connections that join the Japanese employment relation, banking, and subcontracting go beyond those shown in Figure 13-3 to encompass the wider set of forces shown in Figure 13-4. Arguably, this network of relations has value-infusing consequences—which is to say that the whole is greater (and more difficult to replicate) than the sum of the parts.[26]

---

[26]   Japanese economic organization continues, however, to evolve. The role of banks has been less significant since 1984–1985 than it had been previously. The possibility that the interpretation of the Japanese corporation set out here will soon be obsolete and mainly of historical interest cannot be dismissed (Emmett, 1991: 36–40).

Figure 13-4
Japanese Corporate Connectedness

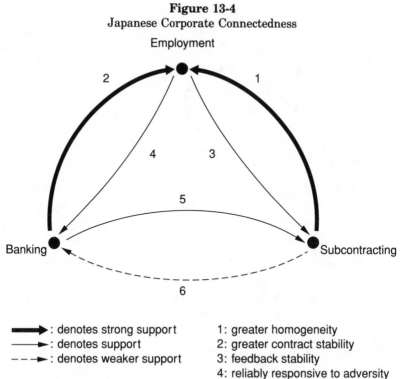

Employment

Banking   Subcontracting

▬▬▶ : denotes strong support   1: greater homogeneity
───▶ : denotes support   2: greater contract stability
─ ─ ▶ : denotes weaker support   3: feedback stability
                                4: reliably responsive to adversity
                                5: financial planning
                                   (convergent expectations)
                                6: no surprises

5. Conclusions

Peter Drucker wrote an important book on *The Concept of the Corporation* in 1946. That book had significant ramifications for the study of the headquarters unit in a multibusiness firm. Alfred Chandler's *Strategy and Structure* was published in 1962 and Alfred P. Sloan's *My Years with General Motors* in 1964. Both of these significantly advanced our knowledge of the purposes served by the headquarters unit of a multibusiness firm. My own understanding of and approach to the modern corporation and the purposes served by organization form was massively influenced by Chandler.

The elemental foundations for the approach to business strategy proposed here go back, however, to a much earlier contribution; Ronald Coase's prescient article on "The Nature of the

Firm" (1937) together with the related literature that I refer to in Section 1 is where I suggest that the study of business strategy should begin. The proposition that economy is the best strategy needs to be related to those foundations.

What is missing in business strategy, but is desperately needed, is a core theory. To be sure, game theory provides the requisite tools for the strategizing branch of strategy.[27] But strategizing is pertinent for only a small subset of transactions, whereas economizing is relevant for all. A core theory to anchor economizing is the pressing need.

My argument is that the microanalytic, comparative institutional, economizing orientation of transaction cost economics deals with many of the key issues with which business strategy is or should be concerned. With effort, moreover, extensions and refinements can be made which extend the reach, sharpen the analysis, and make the approach even more germane. Inquiring into the functions served by the headquarters unit is pertinent to business strategy. Section 2 of this paper outlines some of the reasons why. But these and related questions need to be addressed in the context of a more general economizing setup. As I have observed elsewhere (Williamson, 1990c), the 1990s is the decade when the new science of organization will come of age. The economizing approach to strategy should both contribute to and benefit from these developments.

---

[27] See Carl Shapiro (1989).

14

Takeovers in the 1960s and the 1980s: Evidence and Implications

Andrei Shleifer and Robert W. Vishny

Introduction

The American economy has experienced two large takeover waves in the postwar period: one in the 1960s and one in the 1980s. Both waves had a profound impact on the structure of corporate America. The dominant trend in the 1960s was diversification and conglomeration. The 1980s takeovers, in contrast, reversed this process and brought American corporations back to greater specialization. In many respects, the last 30 years were a round-trip for corporate America.

In this paper, we summarize what is known about these two takeover waves, and interpret this 30-year experience. The major changes that the two takeover waves brought about provide a natural testing ground for theories and ideas about how corporations and financial markets work. We try to use the available evidence to draw lessons for these various theories, as well as for public policies suggested by the theories.

The first section of the paper summarizes the evidence on the two takeover waves. The next section examines alternative interpretations of these experiences and argues that there is only one sensible view. Implications are then drawn from available evidence for Chandler's "strategy and structure" approach to corporate evolution, for agency theory, for market efficiency, and for antitrust policy. A concluding section follows.

Summary of the Evidence

Takeovers in the 1960s

The takeover wave of the 1960s was the largest since the "mergers for monopoly" (Stigler, 1968a) at the turn of the century. A typical 1960s transaction was a friendly acquisition, usually for stock, by a large corporation of a smaller public or private firm outside the acquirer's main line of business. Such unrelated diversification was common among the large companies. Rumelt (1974) reports that the fraction of single business companies in the *Fortune* 500 dropped from 22.8% in 1959 to 14.8% in 1969. The fraction of "unrelated business" companies, which are essentially conglomerates with no dominant businesses, rose from 7.3% to 18.7%. There was also a substantial move toward diversification among companies that retained a dominant business. The critical feature of the 1960s takeovers, then, was unrelated diversification.

There were many reasons why unrelated diversification occurred in the 1960s. To begin, the 1960s wave, like all the others, was in part driven by large corporate cash flows and high valuations of company stocks. Reluctant to pay out the high cash flows as dividends, and able to issue equity at attractive terms, managers naturally turned their attention to acquisitions. The interest of corporate managers in growth and survival of their companies is well understood (Donaldson, 1984). From this point of view, dividends were regarded as a complete waste, and acquisitions as a very attractive way to conserve corporate wealth.

But why did the takeover wave take the form of diversification? By far the most important reason is the aggressive antitrust enforcement in the 1960s and 1970s that simply disallowed mergers of firms in the same industry, regardless of the effects of these mergers on competition. In some cases, antitrust authorities even challenged mergers of two unrelated firms. Faced with this policy, a corporate manager who wanted to make acquisitions basically had to diversify or face a costly antitrust challenge.

There are, of course, some reasons why managers might have wanted to diversify even if they did not have to. They might have believed that they could better manage the targets, perhaps by following internal capital reallocation methods across divisions. Williamson (1975), among others, has argued that central offices can do this better than external capital markets. Scientific management theories that put accounting in the centerfold of growth manuals also had many admirers. Small companies acquired in the process were alleged not to know management. If these theories were correct, acquisitions guided by more informed management would create shareholder value.

In addition, diversification has some benefits for the managers. It may reduce personal risk of the managers, cut the cyclicality of cash flows, and so allow regularization of investment, or simply help managers entrench themselves. Both the belief in the efficiency of diversification and these managerial objectives were probably behind the movement. Nonetheless, it is hard to believe that diversification would have taken the enormous proportions that it did without the prevailing antitrust policy.

Evidence from the stock market suggests that shareholders liked having their firms diversify relative to the alternatives that might have been chosen. Using a data set from the 1960s and early 1970s, Matsusaka (1990) reports that, on the announcement of an unrelated acquisition, the stock price of the bidder rose an average of $8 million, adjusting for market movements. On the announcement of a related acquisition, in contrast, a bidder's stock price fell by $4 million. The difference between the two returns is significant. It seems that investors fully subscribed to the belief that unrelated acquisitions benefited their firms relative to the alternatives, which makes it even less surprising that firms diversified. They just did what the stock market told them to do.

One of the reasons that firms diversified was to get into growing lines of business when their current operations matured. When continued growth could not be sustained from existing operations, firms bought growth in unrelated lines of business. Interestingly, the stock market liked acquisitions of rapidly growing companies more than those of slowly growing ones. Matsusaka (1990) examined bidder stock returns on the announcement of acquisitions in the 1960s and found that firms that bought rapidly growing targets earned higher returns on the announcement. Buying growth was the type of diversification shareholders especially approved of, and not surprisingly, the managers obliged.

Contrary to the expectations of the 1960s, the experience with diversification has been disappointing. As extensively documented by Ravenscraft and Scherer (1987), profitability of acquired companies did not, on average, improve. Moreover, starting in the 1970s, many of the acquisitions were reversed through divestitures. Porter (1987) reports that half of the unrelated acquisitions made by conglomerates were later divested. Ravenscraft and Scherer (1987) estimate that one-third of all (including related) acquisitions made in the 1960s and 1970s were later divested, and their sample stopped before divestitures became really massive. Kaplan and Weisbach (1990) report that 44% of all acquisitions made between 1971 and 1982 were divested by 1989. Kaplan and Weisbach also report that prices obtained in these divestitures were sufficiently attractive to make them a reasonable investment ex ante. Nonetheless, the fact that diversification of the 1960s did not, on average, lead to profitability improvements and was, to a substantial extent, subsequently reversed, is clear evidence of a failure that was not expected in the 1960s.

Takeovers in the 1980s

Takeovers in the 1980s were very different from takeovers in the 1960s. First, the size of the average target has increased enormously from the modest level of the 1960s. Of the 1980 *Fortune* 500 companies, at least 143, or 28%, were acquired by 1989. Second, many transactions, especially the large ones, were hostile—carried out against the will of the target firm's management. Third, the medium of exchange in takeovers became cash rather than stock. In all these respects, the 1980s were very different from the 1960s.

The 1980s were also characterized by some even more radical new forms of control changes. These include "bust-up" takeovers, which were followed by sell-offs of a substantial fraction of the target's assets to other firms. Such bust-up takeovers were only a part of the larger divestiture movement, whereby firms sold their divisions to other firms. Another new organization in the 1980s was the leveraged buyout, the largely debt-financed acquisition of a firm by its own management. Like bust-up takeovers, management buyouts were followed by divestitures of a substantial fraction of the assets (Bhagat, Shleifer, and Vishny, 1990; Kaplan, 1990).

Many of these features of the takover wave of the 1980s can be understood in light of the changed antitrust policy, initiated when the new Reagan administration picked a new set of enforcers. It is fair to characterize the new policy as hands-off. As antitrust authorities stopped challenging mergers of firms in the same industry, the number of such mergers increased sharply.

Most important, there was a sharp increase in the number of friendly related acquisitions, notably in the airline, timber, food, oil, and several other industries. But, in addition, hostile takeovers also turned out to be a response to the antitrust policy. Subsequent to such takeovers, the acquirer typically busted up the target and sold off many of the divisions to other firms that were in the same industry as these divisions, a strategy that would not have been possible in the 1960s. In fact, Bhagat et al. (1990) show that, when one follows through with divestitures, over 70% of the assets acquired in hostile takeovers ended up managed by firms in the same line of business as these assets. In contrast, only 4.5% of the assets ended up managed by unrelated acquirers. This is a stark contrast to the diversification strategies of the 1960s, as Rumelt's (1974) evidence makes clear.

Even leveraged buyouts can, to some extent, be viewed as a reaction to the relaxation of antitrust enforcement. Within three years of such buyouts, about 50% of the assets are typically sold off to buyers in the same industry as those assets (Kaplan, 1990). Bhagat et al. (1990) view LBOs and, to some extent, other hostile takeovers as temporary organizational forms that serve the function of brokering the assets of a diversified company to other firms in the same industry as those assets.

The evidence from the stock market suggests that shareholders, again, liked what was happening. Morck, Shleifer, and Vishny (1990) found that in the 1980s, stock prices of the bidding firms rose when they bought other firms in the same industry, and fell with unrelated diversification. It is clear that the market disfavored unrelated diversification: when Kodak acquired Sterling Drug, its market value fell by $2 billion, the full amount of the premium. Morck et al. (1990) also found that bidding shareholders' returns to buying rapidly growing companies were also negative in the 1980s, in contrast to the experience in the 1960s. It is not at all surprising that, in light of such market reception, firms stopped diversifying and buying growth. In fact, Mitchell and Lehn (1990) show that firms that lost market value when they made acquisitions were themselves likely future takeover targets.

Unlike in the case with takeovers of the 1960s, we do not have much evidence on the ex post performance of the 1980s takeovers. There is some evidence (Kaplan, 1989a) that leveraged buyouts improve profitability, and there is also some evidence (Lichtenberg and Siegel, 1990) that productivity of plants rises after they experience a control change. This may, however, result from reduced investments, and not necessarily from improvements in the present value of profits. One study that has shown increases in profitability, that of Healy, Palepu, and Ruback (1990), may not have adequately corrected for asset sales.

At this point, no satisfactory studies of changes in profitability after takeovers have been made. There are, however, some reasons for optimism. First, there is evidence that takeover targets in the 1980s were poor performers (Morck, Shleifer, and Vishny, 1988; Servaes, 1989), which suggests that they had room for improvement. Second, there is some evidence that divisions of diversified firms do not perform as well as similar businesses that stand alone or are part of undiversified firms (Lichtenberg, 1990). This evidence would suggest that the return to specialization might improve efficiency. It is still probably the case, however, that a large chunk of the shareholder wealth gains in takeovers come from tax savings rather than from operating improvements. The critical evidence on post-takeover performance of companies in the 1980s wave is still to come.

In sum, the evidence strongly indicates that the takeovers of the 1980s were so different from those of the 1960s largely because they undid what the previous wave had created. In the 1960s, conglomerates were created; in the 1980s, many of them were destroyed. The 1960s were a move to unrelated diversification; the 1980s were a move to consolidation and specialization. This round-trip of the American corporation is an intriguing example of corporate evolution in action, which sheds substantial light on how firms behave.

Interpretations

There are two alternative theories of the two takeover waves. The first says that conglomerate mergers of the 1960s were a good idea back then, but were no longer a good idea 10 years later. In this theory, corporations always move toward efficiency, with takeovers helping them along, but just what is efficient changes. Hence, the reason for the round-trip is that what is efficient changed over time.

An alternative interpretation of the experience is that diversification was a mistake from the start, and was undone only gradually. In this theory, corporate America took a 30-year detour away from efficiency. The circumstances are not different in essential respects, but the road to efficiency circled around. In this section, we appraise the two theories. In our opinion, both theory and evidence strongly favor the view that unrelated diversification was a mistake from the start.

Efficient Diversification

According to the optimistic view of the 1960s takeovers, conglomerates during this period were an efficient organizational structure. This view is argued, perhaps most eloquently, by Williamson (1975), generalizing the framework suggested by Chandler (1962). According to Williamson, conglomerates were a product of the M-form of corporate organization, in which the central office allocates investment resources among divisions. Such allocation is more efficient than that obtained when divisions are independent firms, because the central office knows better than the market where the growth opportunities are. In the relatively quiet and uncompetitive 1960s, goes the argument, when aggressive hands-on management was not essential, this advantage in capital allocation exceeded whatever disadvantages might have arisen from the fact that headquarters' management was not intimately familiar with the businesses of the divisions. Because conglomerates had a benefit and relatively small costs, they were an efficient organization at the time.

In the 1980s, in contrast, the business environment became much more competitive. American manufacturing was challenged by high oil prices, an uneducated labor force, and competitors from the Far East. For a variety of reasons, productivity had declined and many manufacturing firms required aggressive hands-on management. In these circumstances, conglomerates were no longer an efficient organization form, as much closer attention was required from the headquarters than conglomerates' central offices could deliver. The market responded to these pressures by breaking up conglomerates and reallocating their assets to more focused and specialized companies that could provide the essential managerial inputs. Luckily, the antitrust policy accommodated this essential move to efficiency.

In some respects, this view of the two takeover waves is very appealing. For one, it is consistent with stock market efficiency, since it says that the market correctly approved of both the diversification in the 1960s and the return to specialization in the 1980s. Moreover, this view offers quite an optimistic appraisal of the takeover market, which effectively enforced efficient organizational changes in both the 1960s and the 1980s. In some respects, this view takes the experience of the last three decades as a further confirmation of the theory that "structure follows strategy" on the road to efficiency.

Inefficient Diversification

An alternative interpretation of the evidence is that a substantial part of diversification of the 1960s was a mistake, which was prompted to a large extent by aggressive antitrust policy. In this theory, it was never efficient for divisions to be run from above by scarcely informed central offices, even in the economically placid 1960s. Although these central offices might have been able to allocate capital across divisions, their advantage over the private market was small at best. Moreover, this advantage did not compensate for the problems of uninformed central management, which simply could not run R&D and investment-intensive divisions. In this view, the M-form was not designed to deal with unrelated diversification.

This theory holds that managers pursued unrelated diversification only because they were committed to personal objectives, such as growth and survival of their firms. If it were not for antitrust policy, they would have pursued these objectives through related acquisitions as they did in the 1920s and 1940s. But even investing in businesses that they knew fairly little about was preferable, from their viewpoint, to returning free cash flow to shareholders. In this theory, then, diversification in the 1960s was a manifestation of agency problems. Managers could get away with diversification because shareholder control mechanisms in this period were fairly weak. It is also possible that shareholders were confused about the benefits of unrelated diversification—recall that the stock market evidence indicates that shareholders approved of unrelated diversification.

Ten years later, it became clear that diversification failed. In addition, the antitrust environment had changed dramatically, so diversification could be effectively reversed. This is indeed what happened in the 1980s, through divestitures, takeovers, and LBOs. When corporate managers were fast to recognize their past mistakes, they divested and managed to preserve the core businesses intact and under their control. When they failed to do so, hostile raiders did the job for them and brokered the unrelated businesses to other firms in the same line of business. The role of such raiders and of LBOs was then to accelerate this process of return to specialization.

This view of the two takeover waves is also, in some respects, appealing. It explains why Ravenscraft and Scherer (1987) failed to find any evidence of improved performance after takeovers in the 1960s. It also explains why such massive divestitures followed. In some respects, it is much more consistent with the Chandlerian view that unrelated diversification into growth businesses that require intensive management could not work. The managers in the 1960s should have known when they acquired growing businesses that passive capital allocation is not sufficient to manage them, and that success would prove elusive. The inefficient view suggests that the world does not always move toward efficiency.

Summary

Which of the two views do we believe? Both have some intuitive appeal, but both have some problems.

Consider first the efficient diversification view. The view has some empirical problems. Most important, there is no evidence we know of that suggests that conglomerates improved the profitability and efficiency of the firms they acquired. Rumelt (1974) was the first to cast doubt on the efficiency of conglomerates, but Ravenscraft and Scherer (1987) provided perhaps the strongest evidence to date of no improvements in profitability. The evidence on massive divestitures is also problematic for the efficiency of conglomerates, but one can question it by saying that the institution of marriage cannot be evaluated in front of a divorce court. The trouble is, there are so few successful marriages from the period of diversification. Without positive evidence on profitability improvements from unrelated acquisitions, it is hard to believe the efficiency theory.

This view also has some theoretical problems. Chandler (1990a) has stated clearly the position that not all companies can be effectively managed by financial controls from central headquarters. Some companies, particularly in growing industries, require everyday intrusive hands-on management that is highly responsive to changing circumstances. Annual or even quarterly financial evaluations do not provide enough flexibility to manage such companies. This theoretical argument seems to be compelling, even as applied to the relatively uncompetitive 1960s.

Yet we know from the evidence that the market approved of conglomerates buying rapidly growing firms, presumably because it thought they could manage them better. The market appeared to believe the opposite of Chandler's theory, which predicts that although conglomerates could manage maturity, they could not manage growth. There appears to be a very serious tension between Chandler's theory and the stock market evidence, although not between Chandler's theory and ex post performance evidence of Ravenscraft and Scherer. In some sense, this tension is the crux of the matter. The inefficient diversification view is consistent with Chandler's theory and the ex post performance evidence, but not with the stock market evidence.

The main difficulty with the inefficient diversification view is that it suggests that the market got it completely wrong in being optimistic about unrelated diversification and buying growth in the 1960s. This, of course, is only one instance of the market's making a mistake, but the mistake is quite major. It represents a problem for those who believe that much can be inferred from stock price reactions. For if one gauged the wisdom of the 1960s conglomerate mergers from bidder stock returns, one would have gotten exactly the wrong idea.

In choosing between the two views, we are inclined to give up on market efficiency. The Chandlerian theoretical arguments seem to us to be compelling, and there is a variety of anecdotal evidence that conglomerates in fact failed to manage technology (Holland, 1989). Moreover, the dearth of evidence of profitability improvements under conglomerates is striking. On the other hand, it is not really surprising that the market's optimism was misplaced, since unrelated diversification was a new experience and no one but careful readers of Chandler could really predict what would happen. The market made only one mistake, but it made it consistently across a large number of transactions. In sum, we conclude that diversification was a mistake from the beginning and was corrected in the 1980s.

Implications

This section attempts to trace the implications of the above analysis for several issues pertinent to the analysis of firms. These are: (1) the strategy and structure approach, (2) agency theory as applied to takeovers, (3) capital market efficiency, and (4) antitrust policy. We believe that the two takeover waves teach us something about each of these issues.

The Strategy and Structure Approach

Chandler's (1962) strategy and structure approach to the internal organization of the firm, extended by Williamson (1975) and others, has proved to be a very successful way of thinking about firms. The main idea of the approach is that a multidivisional structure (M-form) was invented when large corporations began to diversify their lines of business and so needed to reduce the decision-making workload of the central office. The approach has proved successful in explaining the evolution of large corporations around the world (Chandler, 1990b).

One of the themes of Chandler's and Williamson's work—although not a logical consequence of the strategy and structure approach—is the tendency toward greater efficiency in organizational design. Thus, the M-form replaced the U-form (a more vertical structure) because the former was more efficient. When Chandler says that structure follows strategy, he means that structure adapts efficiently to strategic requirements.

The experience of the 1960s presents a serious problem for this optimistic view, although, in one sense, it confirms the underlying model. The multidivisional structure indeed accommodated the strategy of unrelated diversification, but this was not an efficient strategy. Although the internal organization was ideal in terms of efficiency, the fact that it fostered the strategy of unrelated diversification can be seen as an indictment of the organizational structure. The M-form begot the monster of the conglomerate.

Chandler (1990a) quite correctly points out that financial management of conglomerates is only effective in stable environments, where financial controls are an effective management tool. Financial controls are, in many ways, similar to debt, in that as long as the division meets its plan—or debt payments—there is no interference from the headquarters. But when the division fails to meet the plan, headquarters interferes, just as the creditors take control when a firm defaults on its debt. And just as debt is an appropriate financing device for stable firms, and inappropriate in cases of great growth and uncertainty, when creditors would be taking control all the time, so financial controls are inappropriate in such circumstances. Firms then need equity as the means of external financing, and active management as the means of internal monitoring. Because conglomerates failed to deliver such management, they could not effectively run competitive and growing divisions. Chandler's theory thus predicts that conglomerates investing in growth were doomed from the start. The theory is correct in that it could have predicted the failure ex ante. However, the belief that the world is always moving toward efficiency is belied by the conglomerate wave of the 1960s.

Agency Theory

Another extremely useful approach to the analysis of corporate behavior has been agency theory, or the idea that managers pursue their own objectives, which need not serve the interest of shareholders. Students of agency theory discuss the various means by which shareholders attempt to enforce value maximization, including compensation arrangements, boards of directors, debt finance, and, perhaps most important, takeovers. Jensen (1986) interpreted hostile takeovers in the 1980s as mainly the attempt to control nonvalue-maximizing behavior of corporate managers.

In his paper, Jensen focused on excessive investment as the type of nonvalue-maximizing behavior that takeovers stopped. Subsequent research has suggested that excessive investment is not such a big problem. A more empirically accurate view is that the nonvalue-maximizing behavior that hostile takeovers have reversed is unrelated diversification. When managers in the 1960s had their hands on substantial free cash flow, they spent it on unrelated diversification that hurt the shareholders in the long run, the initial favorable stock market reaction notwithstanding. Those managers who failed to divest these acquisitions fast enough in the 1970s and 1980s, perhaps because they wanted to maintain their empire, faced the threat of a hostile takeover and a forced bust-up. The hostile takeovers of the 1980s solved some of the agency problems created by the diversification of the 1960s.

Although this view puts a fairly positive light on the hostile takeovers of the 1980s, it also says clearly that not all acquisitions serve the interest of shareholders. In particular, the diversification of the 1960s was a manifestation of agency problems, not a solution to them. The notion that some takeovers are bad is quite antithetical to at least the early views of takeover enthusiasts. Ravenscraft and Scherer's (1987) negative evidence on diversification was criticized for judging the institution of marriage in front of the divorce court. The criticism was unfair, since when it came to the corporate marriages of the 1960s, divorce was not the exception but the rule. As we pointed out in 1988, in appraising takeovers, it is essential to distinguish those that solve and those that reflect agency problems.

Viewing the diversification of the 1960s as nonvalue-maximizing behavior complements Chandler's strategy and structure perspective, according to which these acquisitions did not make sense. The agency perspective suggests that they made sense from the viewpoint of the managers. In the long run, the Chandlerian inefficiency of these acquisitions became self-evident, and hostile takeovers were the result. On the other hand, the agency perspective explains why Williamson's optimism (and perhaps Chandler's in the 1960s) that corporations always move toward greater efficiency is inappropriate. The experience of the past 30 years has been a detour.

Market Efficiency

Perhaps the thorniest point in the theory that the diversification of the 1960s was a mistake to begin with is the fact that the market value of bidding firms rose on the announcement of such acquisitions (Matsusaka, 1990). To an economist schooled in efficient markets, this enthusiasm of market participants is prima facie evidence that these acquisitions were a good idea from the shareholders' viewpoint. These economists are much more likely to subscribe to the first view of diversification that we described, namely, that ex ante it was a good idea but ex post, as the world changed, specialized firms became more efficient. Hostile takeovers facilitated this move to specialization, again with the approval of the stock market.

The trouble with this view, of course, is that there is no evidence that profitability improved after conglomerate mergers, and there is quite a bit of evidence that it did not, including that of Rumelt (1974) and Ravenscraft and Scherer (1987). The divestiture evidence is no indication of success either. We are, therefore, inclined to believe that the market's expectations about unrelated diversification into growth were wrong.

Of course, one cannot view each acquisition independently as a mistake. It is much more appropriate to think of this strategy as one mistake correlated across transactions. Stock market participants had a model in mind—scientific management or internal capital allocation—that was the source of their optimism about diversification. This was not a model that could have been refuted by prior experience, since unrelated diversification was a new phenomenon, and so there was no evidence to go on. It happened to be the wrong model, and diversification was reversed. The horizon of reversals was far too long for whatever smart money was available to try to take advantage of it. It did not pay to sell stocks of conglomerates short on the expectation that in the long run their stock prices would fall, and with the risk that in the meantime they could rise enormously. As a result, the incorrect "popular model" of scientific management carried the day, and the market incorrectly reacted positively to diversification.

Although inconsistent with the view that the market holds unbiased expectations, this interpretation of the evidence is quite in line with recent research on market inefficiency (Shiller, 1984; Shleifer and Summers, 1990; Shleifer and Vishny, 1990b). According to this research, fads or popular models can influence stock prices for prolonged periods of time. Arbitrage by smart investors will be weak and will not undo these influences, because arbitrage over several-year horizons, as would be required in the case of conglomerates, is very costly and risky. Betting against the conglomerates would have proven to be a mistake for all but the longest horizon investors with access to cheap capital. According to these theories and the evidence that supports them, the mistaken market enthusiasm about particular events such as conglomerate mergers is a commonplace equilibrium occurrence in financial markets. The fact that the market thought that conglomerates were a good idea does not mean that they were.

Antitrust Policy

The first three implications of takeovers we have discussed were for economic analysis; the last is for economic policy. Perhaps the single most important aspect of the environment that shaped the two takeover waves has been antitrust policy. The extremely strict antitrust enforcement of the 1960s made most related acquisitions infeasible, or at least costly, and so forced firms determined to make acquisitions to diversify. This policy might not have been as distortionary if managers were willing to return the excess cash flow to shareholders, but as long as they were not, strict antitrust was largely responsible for diversification.

Similarly, the much looser antitrust policy of the 1980s allowed the divestitures, acquisitions, and bust-up takeovers, which to a crucial extent relied on the ease of resale of divisions. If the antitrust policy remained as it was, we would probably have seen either a restructuring via different means than eventual acquisition of assets by the firms in the same industry, or no restructuring at all. In either case, we would not have had the hostile takeover wave of the 1980s. Whatever one thinks of the changes this wave brought to corporate America, the antitrust policy is, to a large extent, responsible for them.

All things considered, the current antitrust stance is certainly preferable to that of the 1960s. Even if one sees some problems with the takeovers in the 1980s, it is hard to believe that they will turn out as badly as the diversification of the 1960s. In the first best world, aggressive antitrust enforcement may be a good idea. But in the world where corporations are committed to growth through acquisitions, the antitrust policy of the 1960s, like deposit insurance in the 1970s and 1980s, had inadvertent, damaging effects that much outweighed the benefits it created. For this reason, the message of the research on takeovers is clearly in support of lax antitrust enforcement of the sort we have seen in recent years. There is no question that such lax policy has led to some anticompetitive mergers, such as those in the airline industry, but it is better to have a few monopolies than a lot of conglomerates.

Conclusion

Recent research has produced considerable evidence on the takeover waves of the 1960s and 1980s. The most plausible interpretation of the evidence is that the takeover wave of the 1980s served largely to reverse unrelated diversification of the 1960s. Over a 30-year period, corporate America took a detour.

This experience has several implications for economic analysis as well as for policy. It supports the Chandlerian strategy and structure approach, but suggests also that the world does not always move toward greater efficiency. It shows that takeovers can be as much a manifestation of agency problems as a route to correcting them. It also demonstrates that using the stock market as a gauge of profitability of corporate actions can lead one seriously astray; investors can and do make systematic mistakes. Finally, the experience cautions that aggressive government policy, in this case antitrust policy, can have large unintended effects. In part, misguided public policy is to blame for this 30-year corporate detour.

Part IV

What Determines Success or Failure in International Competition?

The question of what determines the success or failure of firms in international competition may be the most fundamental question that strategic management poses. There are two aspects to the question. One deals with the matter of success, and at the extreme, with survival. The other deals with the ultimate in geographic competitive scope: competition on an international, multidomestic scale. These two aspects are related in that competitive survival within a national or regional economy may be possible when it may be impossible on an international scale. In other cases, it may be impossible to be successful or even survive unless activities are undertaken on an international scale. Three papers are included in this section, and each relates to both aspects of this question. Before discussing each paper's relationship to the issue, there are several features of the question worth noting.

Success, for a strategically distinct business, requires that a competitive advantage be created and sustained. Competitive advantage yields an economic rent—in other words, it creates a situation in which economic costs are exceeded by revenues generated. Costs may be less than those of competitors, volume sold may be greater, or price (owing to unduplicated product features) may exceed that of competitors, or any combination of these three elements may be the proximate source of the advantage. However, the underlying sources to the proximate source(s) are the professional manager's real stock-in-trade, and despite their causal importance they are poorly understood.

Survival, in the economist's equilibrium sense, requires that all costs incurred be met over some (longer) time period. In this sense, success is equivalent to survival. If revenues exceed costs, all adjusted for risk and time, then relatively higher returns exist, and success is more than mere survival. Where such "abnormal" returns exist, a competitive advantage exists, and its source is of direct interest to alert managers. Indeed, creating and maintaining such sources is at the very heart of what good managers do. Understanding what managerial work to undertake, and how to do that work, however, is much harder than understanding the mere concept itself.

As skills of competitors have increased, and continue to increase, the underlying sources of abnormal returns become more remote, harder to discern, and much more complicated managerially. As competition moves to a worldwide basis, these sources become even more complex and harder to create and understand. The fundamental aspect of this move to international competition is the much richer set of decision variables open to the discerning manager. The most important strategic decision variable, however, involves understanding just which value-creating activities should be undertaken in which geographic locations. The set of activities (Porter's "value chain") that comprise value creation needs to be maximized for its advantage potential and the returns it yields.

This work, managerial and otherwise, may or may not require multiple political boundaries to be crossed. It is possible to specify sets of value-creating activities that can be "maximized" within a single political environment, while other sets must cross such boundaries. In crossing political boundaries, "sovereignty risk" is created and must be offset by the lower costs or by the higher volume/revenue potential of participation in multiple political jurisdictions.

As Porter's paper, "Toward a Dynamic Theory of Strategy," argues, the source of specific competitive advantage is difficult to identify, although the nature of the advantage is relatively easily seen. Porter develops a causal inquiry into the source of advantage ("the cross-sectional problem") and includes a further inquiry into what he calls the "longitudinal problem," essentially an examination of how advantages are built through the accumulation of decisions and events over time.

A key aspect of Porter's argument is the notion of economic activities as the unit of analysis, from which it is possible to understand how proximate competitive advantage and favorable position arises. Porter sees certain drivers of advantage as key, and the solution to the cross-sectional problem of creating relative advantage, success, and long-run survival. Understanding drivers, which can range widely from environmental features to organizational ones, is of great importance to the manager.

Yet all of this does not solve the whole problem for Porter, and he goes on to ask another crucial question: How does the original, relative position of advantage arise in the first place? He claims understanding the cross-sectional problem is relatively easy. At any moment we can explain why some competitor was successful, but we don't necessarily know the origins of that success. To this longitudinal question he sees two possible answers—luck and initial conditions, or unique managerial (entrepreneurial) decisions. At the end of this causal chain, Porter concludes that entrepreneurial choice may be more fundamental.

Ultimately, this inquiry takes Porter into the realm of international competition and the source of competitive advantage resident in national economies or countries. Here he sees the combination of unique conditions coupled with unique managerial choices as giving rise to competitors with skills and competence that exceed that of their rivals. Only by honing skills through tough competition from producers and through the demands of consumers can competitors arise and remain successful.

Paul Krugman's paper, "Location and Competition: Notes on Economic Geography," outlines conditions under which firms develop competitive advantage rooted in their country or regional geographic base. In this respect his paper's subject is similar to Porter's thesis. What is most interesting about the Porter and Krugman papers in combination is that they show why competitive activity tends to concentrate in certain locations, and why intense competition from skilled competitors is necessary to survival and ultimate success. Contrary to intuition, severe competition around a strong set of input factors yields strong competitors, and in the end strong barriers to others who would compete.

In their paper, "Managing DMNCs: A Search for a New Paradigm," Doz and Prahalad develop a different thesis, yet one related to success and survival on an international basis. They argue that the diversified multinational corporation (DMNC) is an organizational form that creates advantage through the manner in which it organizes and adapts to complex environmental conditions. The strengths of a DMNC cannot be matched by simpler, more conventional organizational forms and processes, and DMNCs create competitive advantages out of the very manner in which they adapt to international competition. Their paper goes on to relate extant theories of organization to the DMNC and to show that no single theory is yet able to explain the phenomena they observe.

This is all something of an old story in that, once again, complex strategies have founded complex organizational forms to permit the advantage potential to be realized. Chandler's paper in Part III of this volume expounds on this idea, and, of course, the seminal work on the subject of strategy and structure was Chandler's over 30 years ago. It is interesting that structure once again appears, this time as an important aspect of this fundamental question of success and survival in a multinational competitive environment. What is part of the new story is that organizational processes and forms are seen as an important and perhaps as the most fundamental source of advantage, and it has taken study of the international level of competition to make a fresh contribution to our understanding of the modes of survival and ultimate success.

15
Toward a Dynamic Theory of Strategy

Michael E. Porter

The question of why firms succeed or fail is perhaps the central question in strategy. It has preoccupied strategy scholars since the inception of the field four decades ago. The issue of firm success or failure has implications for all the other questions that have been raised in this collection of papers. It is inextricably bound up in questions such as why firms differ, how they behave, how they choose strategies, and how they are managed. While much of the work in the field has been implicitly domestic, it has become increasingly apparent that any search for the causes of firm success must confront the reality of international competition, and the striking differences in the performance of firms in the same industry but based in different nations.

Yet the question of why firms succeed or fail raises a still broader question. Any effort to understand success must rest on an underlying theory of the firm and an associated theory of strategy. While there has been considerable progress in developing frameworks that explain differing competitive success at any given point in time, our understanding of the dynamic processes by which firms perceive and ultimately attain superior market positions is far less developed. Worse yet, some recent research has tended to fragment or dichotomize the important parts of the problem rather than integrate them, as I will discuss later.

Acknowledgments: I am grateful to Pankaj Ghemawat, Cynthia Montgomery, and others in the Competition and Strategy group at Harvard for a long series of discussions that have immensely benefited my thinking about these issues, and to Jay Barney, Richard Rumelt, and Garth Saloner for their insights while visiting. David Collis, Cynthia Montgomery, Richard Rumelt, Elizabeth Teisberg, and Dan Schendel provided helpful comments on this manuscript.

My purpose here is to sketch the outlines of a dynamic theory of strategy. Drawing on recent research, some parts of the outline can be filled in. Many unanswered questions remain, however, and I will try to highlight some of the most important of them.

As a starting point for building a dynamic theory of strategy, we must step back from specific hypotheses or models and look broadly at the literature in both strategy and economics. I will begin by describing the traditional rationale for company success that emerged in the early literature on strategy. This rationale reflected the distinctive orientation of the strategy field, which differed in important respects from that of most research in economics, arguably the discipline with the most obvious connection to strategy. The strategy field's traditional answer to why firms succeed or fail was also based on a set of largely implicit, but crucial assumptions about the nature of firms and the environment in which they operate.

Although these assumptions grew out of a deep understanding of practice, they raise profound challenges for a theory of strategy. I will outline some of the most important challenges and the trade-offs they involve in both theory and empirical testing. Taking these challenges as a starting point, I will then describe my own explanation of the causes of superior firm performance, which can be framed as a chain of causality. This problem, which I term the *cross-sectional problem*, is logically prior to a consideration of dynamics and is better understood. A body of theory that links firm characteristics to market outcomes must provide the foundation for any fully dynamic theory of strategy. Otherwise, dynamic processes that result in superior performance cannot be distinguished from those that create market positions or company skills that are worthless.

I will then move to the dynamic process by which positions are created, which I term the *longitudinal problem*. To understand the dynamics of strategy, we must move further back in the causality chain. I will explore three recent streams of research that begin to address it: game-theoretic models, models of commitment under uncertainty, and the so-called resource-based view of the firm. This research illuminates important characteristics of the dynamic processes by which advantage is created and sustained, but it falls short of exposing the true origins of advantage, and I will discuss the reasons why. One important category of these origins, which has emerged from my recent work, is the nature of the "local" environment in which the firm is based. We observe striking concentrations of successful firms in a particular industry in particular locations, which suggests that something about these locations is fundamental to creating and sustaining advantage. I will summarize some of my findings about these issues. Many questions remain unanswered in our search for a dynamic theory of strategy, however, and this paper will conclude with some challenges for future research.

Determinants of Firm Success: The Early Answers

Any discussion of the determinants of firm success must begin with a clear definition of what success means. For purposes of this paper, I will assume that firm success is manifested in attaining a competitive position or series of competitive positions that lead to superior and sustainable financial performance. Competitive position is measured, in this context, relative to the world's best rivals. Financial success derived from government intervention or from the closing of markets is excluded. A successful firm may "spend" some of the fruits of its competitive position on meeting social objectives or enjoying slack. Why a firm might do this, however, is treated as a separate question.

To explain firm success, the early literature on strategy defined three essential conditions.[1] The first is that a company develop and implement an internally consistent set of goals and functional policies that collectively define its position in the market. Strategy is seen as a way of integrating the activities of the diverse functional departments within a firm, including marketing, production, research and development, procurement, finance, and the like. An explicit and mutually reinforcing set of goals and functional policies is needed to counter the centrifugal forces that lead functional departments in separate directions. Strategy, in modern language, is a solution to the agency problem that arises because senior management cannot participate in or monitor all decisions and directly ensure the consistency of the myriad of individual actions and choices that

---

[1]   See Learned, Christensen, Andrews, and Guth (1965). See also Andrews (1971).

make up a firm's ongoing activities.[2] If an overarching strategy is well understood throughout the organization, many actions are obviously ruled out and individuals can devise their own ways of contributing to the strategy that management would be hard pressed to replicate.

The second condition for success is that this internally consistent set of goals and policies align the firm's strengths and weaknesses with the external (industry) opportunities and threats. Strategy is the act of aligning a company and its environment. That environment is subject to change, as are the firm's own capabilities. Thus, the task of strategy is to maintain a dynamic, not a static, balance.

The third condition for success is that a firm's strategy be centrally concerned with the creation and exploitation of its so-called distinctive competences,[3] the unique strengths that make possible its competitive success. Recent work on the notion of firm resources or competences is interesting in light of this heritage.[4] I will return to this stream of work later.

The early strategy literature contained only broad principles governing firm success. It is instructive to consider why these authors, coming as they did from a tradition that stressed the administrative point of view and the study of in-depth cases, chose to approach the question in this way. There were two principal reasons. The first was that their orientation, and that of many in the strategy field, was to inform business practice. A theory that sought to explain part of a phenomenon, but that did not attempt to offer credible guidance for individual companies, was seen as inadequate to the task.

A second reason was the recognition of, indeed the preoccupation with, the fact that competition was complex and highly situation-specific. The early scholars in the strategy field, especially those at Harvard, recognized that firms were composed of numerous functions and subfunctions, and that many diverse aspects of a firm and its environment could be important to success in particular cases. Indeed, they saw the achievement of consistency of action in the many parts of the firm as crucial to competitive success. Scholars like Andrews saw each com-

---

[2] In the absence of a strategy, the narrow motivations and logistics of each functional area will guide behavior.
[3] This notion originated with Selznick (1957).
[4] See, for example, Wernerfelt (1984) and Prahalad and Hamel (1990).

pany as unique, with its own history, personality, capabilities, and current policies. Every industry was also unique, with its own circumstances and critical success factors. Finally, every period of time was unique, because both companies and their environments were in a state of constant change. Yet firms were seen as possessing considerable ability to build on their strengths and overcome their weaknesses, to influence or alter their environment, and to engineer change over time, not merely respond to it. Indeed, the recognition that industry structure and other exogenous conditions affect performance and constrain choices had to await further work.

The Challenges for a Theory of Strategy

The view of the world that guided the early efforts to formulate a theory of strategy raises profound challenges for research. The complexity, situation specificity, and changing nature of the firm and its environment strains conventional approaches to theory building and hypothesis testing. Indeed, the early research offered no theory for examining the firm and its competitive environment at all; instead strategy formulation involved applying the broad principles of consistency and fit to individual case studies.

As one contemplates a theory of strategy, four principal issues emerge from the nature of actual economic competition.

Approach to theory building. First, there is a fundamental question about the approach to theory building that will best advance both knowledge and practice. The broad alternatives are represented in Figure 15-1.

On the one hand, one can approach the task of developing a theory of strategy by creating a wide range of situation-specific but rigorous (read mathematical) models of limited complexity. Each model abstracts the complexity of competition to isolate a

Figure 15-1
Approaches to Theory Building

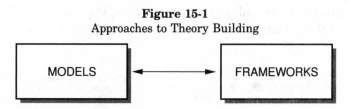

few key variables whose interactions are examined in depth. The normative significance of each model depends on the fit between its assumptions and reality. No one model embodies, or even approaches embodying, all the variables of interest, and hence the applicability of any model's findings is almost inevitably restricted to a small subgroup of firms or industries with characteristics that fit the model's assumptions.

This approach to theory building has been popular among economists in the last few decades.[5] It has spawned a wide array of interesting models in both industrial organization and trade theory. These models provide clear conclusions, but it is well known that they are highly sensitive to the assumptions underlying them and to the concept of equilibrium that is employed. Another problem with this approach is that it is hard to integrate the many models into a general framework for approaching any situation, or even to make the findings of the various models consistent. While few economists would assert that this body of research in and of itself provides detailed advice for companies, these models, at their best, offer insights into complex situations, which can inform the analysis of a particular company's situation.

Given the goal of informing practice, the style of research in the strategy field, including my own, has involved a very different approach.[6] To make progress, it was necessary to go beyond the broad principles outlined in the early work and provide more structured and precise tools for understanding a firm's competitive environment and its relative position. Instead of creating models, the approach was to build frameworks. A framework— such as the competitive forces approach to analyzing industry structure—encompasses many variables and seeks to capture much of the complexity of actual competition. Frameworks identify the relevant variables and the questions that the user must answer in order to develop conclusions tailored to a particular industry and company. In this sense, they can be seen almost as expert systems. The theory embodied in frameworks is contained in the choice of included variables, the way variables are organized, the interactions among the variables, and the way

---

[5]   Interestingly, the earlier work in industrial economics, in the Mason/Bain tradition, was much closer to strategy research in its effort to capture complexity.

[6]   See examples such as Porter (1985) and Ghemawat (1991).

in which alternative patterns of variables and company choices affect outcomes.

In frameworks, the equilibrium concept is imprecise. My own frameworks embody the notion of optimization, but not equilibrium in the normal sense of the word. Instead there is a continually evolving environment in which a perpetual competitive interaction among rivals takes place. In addition, not all the interactions among the many variables in the frameworks can be rigorously drawn.[7] The frameworks, however, help the analyst to think through the problem by illuminating the firm and its environment and defining and selecting among the strategic alternatives available, no matter what the industry and starting position.

These two approaches to theory building are not mutually exclusive. Indeed, the tension between them can be constructive. Models are particularly valuable in ensuring logical consistency and exploring the subtle interactions involving a limited number of variables. Models should challenge the variables included in frameworks and assertions about their link to outcomes. Frameworks, in turn, should challenge models by highlighting omitted variables, the diversity of competitive situations, the range of actual strategy choices, and the extent to which important parameters are not fixed but continually in flux. The need to inform practice has demanded that strategy researchers like me pursue the building of frameworks rather than restrict research only to theories that can be formally modeled. As long as the building of frameworks is based on in-depth empirical research, it has the potential not only to inform practice but to spur the development of more rigorous theory.

Chain of causality. A second fundamental issue in creating a theory of strategy is where to focus in the chain of causality. A generic example will illustrate. We might observe a successful firm and find that its profitability is due to a low relative cost position compared to its rivals. But the firm's cost position is an outcome and not a cause. The question becomes: Why was the firm able to attain this cost position? Some typical answers might be that it is reaping economies of scale, or has moved

---

[7] Frameworks can also be challenged because their complexity makes it difficult to falsify arguments. Yet ascribing this property to models is also problematic if they omit important variables.

aggressively down the learning curve. But again, why? Some possible answers might include entering the industry early, or the firm's ability to organize itself particularly well for cost reduction. Once again, however, the question is why. And we could continue moving along such a chain of causality even further.

Another way of framing the same set of issues is as the problem of drawing the boundary between exogenous and endogenous variables. Should the environment be considered a given? Is the firm's scale an outcome or a cause? And so on. The literature in both strategy and economics addresses many different points in this chain of causality. Indeed, many of the differences between them are less conflicts than theory positioned at different points in the chain, as we will see later.

Any theory of strategy must grapple with how far back in the chain of causality to go. The answer may well be different for different purposes. A theory that aims very early in the chain may be intractable or lack functionality. Also, aspects of the firm that are variable in the long run may be fixed or sticky in the short run. Conversely, a theory oriented later in the chain may be too limiting and miss important possibilities.

Time horizon. A third challenge for theory is the time period over which to measure and analyze competitive success. Should we be building theories for explaining success over two or three years, over decades, or over centuries? Clearly, the likelihood of significant environmental change will differ, as will the exogenous and endogenous variables. A theory that aims at explaining success over 50 years will focus on very different variables, almost inevitably more internal ones, than a theory that addresses success over one or two decades. This is because industry and competitive conditions are likely to be wholly different over a half century, placing greater emphasis on a firm's ability to transform itself. Time period relates closely to position in the chain of causality. Over long periods, theories aimed earlier in the chain will seem more appropriate.

Empirical testing. A final important issue is how to test theories of strategy empirically. Empirical testing is vital both for frameworks and models. Testing of models is difficult given the need to match their assumptions. Given the myriad of relevant variables in frameworks and the complex interactions among them over time, rigorous statistical testing of frameworks is also difficult, to say the least. In my own research, I pursued cross-sectional econometric studies in the 1970s but ultimately gave up as the complexity of the frameworks I was developing ran ahead of the available cross-sectional data. I was forced to turn to in-depth case studies to identify significant variables, explore the relationships among them, and cope with industry and firm specificity in strategy choices.

The need for more and better empirical testing will be a perennial issue in dealing with this subject. Academic journals have traditionally not accepted or encouraged the deep examination of case studies, but the nature of strategy requires it. The greater use of case studies in both books and articles will be necessary for real progress at this stage in the field's development.

Toward a Theory of Strategy

To explain the competitive success of firms, we need a theory of strategy that links environmental circumstances and firm behavior to market outcomes. My own research suggests a chain of causality for doing so, outlined in Figure 15-2.

The basic unit of analysis in a theory of strategy must ultimately be a strategically distinct business or industry. While firms can redeploy or share resources, activities, and skills across different businesses, the competitive value of such actions can only be measured in terms of some set of rivals delivering a discrete product or service to some set of buyers. Meaningful approaches to corporate-level strategy for diversified firms must grow out of a deep understanding of how companies prosper in individual businesses, and the role of the corporate office and other sister business units in the process.

At its broadest level, firm success is a function of two factors: the attractiveness of the industry in which the firm competes and its relative position in that industry. Firm profitability can be decomposed into an industry effect and a positioning effect. Some firm successes come almost wholly from the industry in which they compete; most of their rivals are successful, too! The distinction between industry structure and relative position is important because firms can choose strategies that improve one while harming the other. Firms' actions, by triggering imitation, can positively or negatively influence the structure of an industry without leading to competitive advantage. Ideally,

Figure 15-2
The Determinants of Success in Distinct Businesses

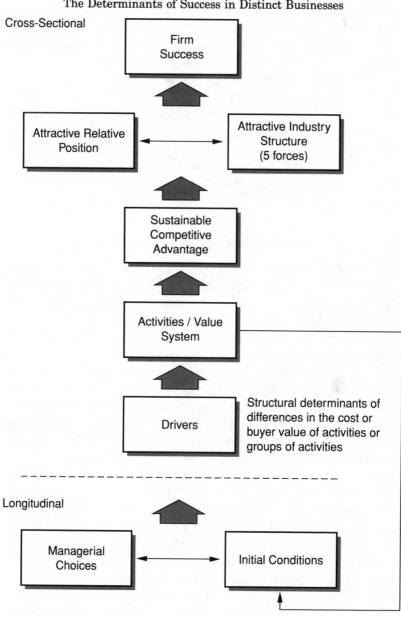

Figure 15-3
Five Forces Summary of Key Drivers

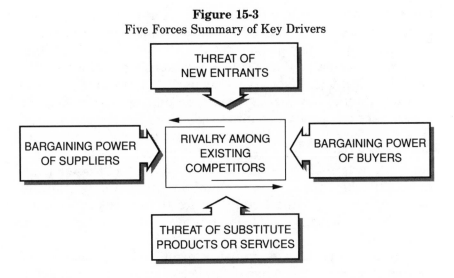

however, a firm's actions trigger responses by rivals which improve industry structure but simultaneously allow the innovating firm to gain competitive advantage (because rivals' ability to imitate the chosen mode of competition is incomplete).

Industry structure. I have presented a framework for diagnosing industry structure, built around five competitive forces that erode long-term industry average profitability (see Figure 15-3). This framework has been explored, contributed to, and tested by many others. The industry structure framework can be applied at the level of the industry, the strategic group (or group of firms with similar strategies), or even the individual firm. Its ultimate function is to explain the *sustainability* of profits against bargaining and against direct and indirect competition. Profit differences vis-à-vis direct rivals, though, depend on positioning.

Industry structure is partly exogenous, and partly subject to influence by firm actions. Hence, structure and firm position ultimately interrelate, although separating them may be a useful simplification for analytical purposes. The firm's ability to influence industry structure, and ways of modeling it, are a fruitful area for research. My focus here, however, is on relative position because this is where many of the most interesting questions for a dynamic theory of strategy lie.

Relative position. If industry structure is held constant, a successful firm is one with an attractive relative position. An attractive position is, of course, an outcome and not a cause. The question is, Why or how did the attractive position arise? The answer must be that the firm possesses a sustainable competitive advantage vis-à-vis its rivals. To understand competitive advantage, however, we must decompose it. Competitive advantages can be divided into two basic types: lower cost than rivals, or the ability to differentiate and command a premium price that exceeds the extra cost of doing so. Any firm with a superior performance has achieved one or both of these advantages. In other words, superior profitability can only logically arise from commanding a higher price than rivals or enjoying lower costs (including, at a lower level in the causality chain, asset costs).[8]

Competitive advantage cannot be examined independently of competitive scope. Scope has a number of dimensions, including the array of product and buyer segments served, the geographic locations in which the firm competes, its degree of vertical integration, and the extent of related businesses in which the firm has a coordinated strategy. Competitive advantage is attained within some scope, and the choice of scope is a central one in strategy. Scope choices can also influence industry structure.

These principles make it clear that the essence of strategy is choice. There is no one best position within an industry, but rather many positions involving choices about the type of advantage sought and the scope of the advantage. Several positions can be attractive in absolute terms, and which is the most attractive to a particular firm may depend on the firm's starting position. It is essential that firms make a choice, however, because there are logical inconsistencies in pursuing several types of advantage or different scopes simultaneously. Also, the firm must stake out a distinct position from its rivals. Imitation almost ensures a lack of competitive advantage and hence mediocre performance.

Activities. If competitive advantage within some scope yields an attractive relative position, the question once again is why. In order to address it, we must decompose cost, differentiation, and scope. This requires a theory that provides an elemental look at what firms do. My own approach to such a theory, and to

---

[8] A firm that can command higher volume at a given price takes its superior profitability in the form of lower costs, provided costs are scale sensitive.

the sources of competitive advantage, centers around *activities* (Porter, 1985). A firm is a collection of discrete but interrelated economic activities such as products being assembled, salespeople making sales visits, and orders being processed. A firm's strategy defines its configuration of activities and how they interrelate. Competitive advantage results from a firm's ability to perform the required activities at a collectively lower cost than rivals, or to perform some activities in unique ways that create buyer value and hence allow the firm to command a premium price. The required mix and configuration of activities, in turn, is altered by competitive scope.

The basic unit of competitive advantage, then, is the discrete activity. The economics of performing discrete activities determines a firm's relative cost, not attributes of the firm as a whole. Similarly, it is discrete activities that create buyer value and hence differentiation.

The activities in a firm can be schematically arrayed in what I term the value chain and the value system (see Figure 15-4). The term value refers to customer value, from which the potential profit ultimately derives. A firm's strategy is manifested in the way in which it configures and links the many activities in its value chain relative to competitors. The value chain distinguishes between activities that directly produce, market, and deliver the product and those that create or source the inputs or factors (including planning and management) required to do so. Support activities, then, are integral to the process by which assets internal to the firm are acquired.

Discrete activities are part of an interdependent system in which the cost or effectiveness of one activity can be affected by the way others are performed. I term these "linkages." The cost of after-sale service, for example, is influenced by the way product design, inspection, and installation are performed. Such linkages can extend outside the firm to encompass the activities of suppliers, channels, and buyers. The concept of linkages begins to operationalize the notion of internal consistency.

Activities involve human resources, purchased inputs, and a "technology" for performing them, broadly defined to include organizational routines. Activities also use and create information.[9] Performing an activity requires tangible and intangible assets that are *internal* to the firm, such as physical and often

---

[9]   See Porter and Millar (1985).

Figure 15-4
Value Chain

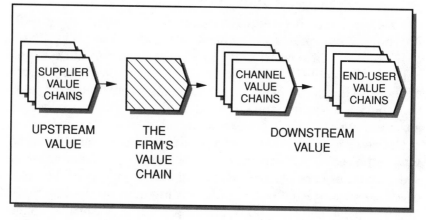

Value System

financial assets (e.g., working capital) as well as intangible assets embodied in human resources and technology. Performing an activity, or a group of linked activities, also creates assets in the form of skills, organizational routines, and knowledge. While the tangible assets normally depreciate, the intangible assets involved in performing activities can cumulate over time (provided the environment remains relatively stable).

These become an important part of corporate balance sheets, as many writers have stressed.[10]

Performing activities can also create assets *external* to the firm. Some are tangible assets such as contracts. Most, however, are intangible assets such as brand images, relationships, and networks. These external assets then feed back to influence the cost or effectiveness of performing activities on an ongoing basis. A strong brand reputation established by past advertising, for example, can lower the cost of current advertising or make a given rate of spending more effective. Without reinvestment, however, both the external and internal intangible assets attached to activities depreciate. Maintaining or enhancing these assets demands reinvestment through performing activities. Neither the external nor internal assets are valuable in and of themselves; instead their value lies in their fit with industry structure and firm strategy. Activities performed poorly, or inconsistently with buyer needs, can create liabilities not assets. At the same time, technological and othe industry changes can nullify assets or turn them into liabilities.

The value chain provides a template for understanding cost position, because activities are the elemental unit of cost behavior.[11] The move to activity-based costing is a manifestation of this perspective.[12] The value chain is also a means to systematically understand the sources of buyer value and hence differentiation. Buyer value is created when a firm lowers its buyer's cost or enhances its buyer's performance. This, in turn, is the result of the ways a firm's product as well as its other activities affect the value chain of the buyer. Firms must not only create value, but "signal" that they will do so, through their sales forces and other activities. Households and individual consumers have value chains, just as do industrial or institutional buyers. By considering how households perform activities related to a product (e.g., procurement, storage, use, and disposal), the sources of differentiation can be better understood. Finally, the value chain provides a tool for analyzing the added costs that differentiating may require. Only when differentiation results in a price premium that exceeds the extra costs of delivering it is the firm's performance superior.

[10]   See, for example, Itami and Roehl (1987) and Baldwin and Clark (1991).
[11]   See Porter (1985, ch. 3).
[12]   See Johnson and Kaplan (1987), Cooper and Kaplan (1988, 1991).

Drivers. If competitive advantage grows out of discrete activities, however, once again we must ask why. Why are some firms able to perform particular activities at lower cost or with more valuable results than others? My answer is the concept of *drivers*. These are structural determinants of differences among competitors in the cost or buyer of activities or groups of activities. The most important drivers of competitive advantage in an activity include its scale, the cumulative learning it involves, its linkages with other activities, its ability to be shared with other business units, its pattern of capacity utilization over the relevant cycle, its location, the timing of investment choices it requires, the extent of vertical integration in its performance, institutional factors (such as government regulation) that affect how it is performed, and the firm's policy choices about how to configure the activity independent of other drivers. The same set of drivers determines both relative cost and differentiation. The mix and significance of individual drivers varies by activity, by firm, and by industry.

Moving to the level of drivers also sheds light on the important question of sustainability. The sustainability of competitive advantage vis-à-vis rivals depends on the number of competitive advantages in the value chain and, especially, the particular drivers underlying each one. The durability of an advantage based on learning, for example, depends on the ability to keep the learning proprietary, while the sustainability of advantages due to timing of factor positions depends on factor market imperfections.

Drivers constitute the underlying sources of competitive advantage, and make competitive advantage operational. For example, brand reputation is a typical competitive advantage identified by managers. But brand reputation may be a source of cost advantage (less need for marketing) in some cases and a source of differentiation (and a premium price) in others. The substantive implications are very different depending on which it is. Yet brand reputation is an outcome, not a cause. The real question is how and why brand reputation is an advantage. To understand this, one must move to the level of drivers. For example, timing may have allowed the firm to begin advertising early and hence to develop a reputation uncluttered by the competing claims of rivals. The reputation from cumulative advertising then allows the firm to spend less on current advertising or to spend at a rate comparable to rivals but command a premium price. Alternatively, greater current company sales volume may lead to efficiencies in advertising that allow the firm to enjoy a superior reputation while spending at a rate comparable to its rivals. Only by moving to the level of underlying drivers can the true sources of competitive advantage be identified. Tying advantage to specific activities/drivers is necessary to operationalize the notion in practice.

The value chain also provides the basic architecture for analyzing international strategy and diversification, both fundamentally questions of competitive scope. The central issue in international strategy involves the spread of activities to other countries (configuration) and the integration of dispersed activities (coordination) (Porter, 1986). In corporate-level strategy for diversified firms, the central issue is how firms can share activities across businesses, or share proprietary skills in particular activities even when the value chains of business units are distinct (Porter, 1987).

The Origins of Competitive Advantage

This set of frameworks aims to build a careful link between market outcomes and the underlying choices a firm makes in terms of its industry, positioning, and configuration of activities. The proper choices depend on a firm's existing position, which can be evaluated systematically via its value chain and drivers. The best strategy also depends on the capabilities and probable behavior of rivals, which can likewise be assessed through their value chains and drivers. Finally, strategy depends on a sophisticated understanding of industry structure.

Firms inherit positions that constrain and shape their choices, but do not determine them. They have considerable latitude in reconfiguring the value chain with which they compete, expanding or contracting their competitive scope, and influencing important dimensions of their industry environment. Strategy is not a race to occupy one desirable position, but a more textured problem in which many positions can be chosen or created. Success requires the choice of a relatively attractive position given industry structure, the firm's circumstances, and the positions of competitors. It also requires making all the firm's activities consistent with the chosen position.

While these frameworks have pushed a considerable distance backward along the chain of causality, the focus thus far has been on what I term the "cross-sectional problem." What makes some industries, and some positions within them, more attractive than others? What makes particular competitors advantaged or disadvantaged? What specific activities and drivers underlie the superior positions?

But in answering these questions, we again confront the question of causality. Why were particular firms able to get into the advantaged positions, and why did they sustain or fail to sustain them? This is what I term the "longitudinal problem," which requires crossing the dotted line on Figure 15-2.[13]

The frameworks for addressing the cross-sectional problem are agnostic as to the process by which the superior positions were attained, and are largely unaffected by it. Whether the strategy was consciously chosen, happenstance, the result of incremental steps, or driven by one major decision does not affect the attractiveness of the position, which is independent of the activities and drivers on which it rests. Similarly, the past process by which firms accumulated their strengths and capabilities is not, in and of itself, decisive. The cross-sectional frameworks address the choice of strategy given whatever array of capabilities the firm and its rivals possess at a point in time and can feasibly develop in the future. The effort by some to dichotomize process and substance is simply mistaken.[14] Both are necessary and important to understand.

The cross-sectional problem is also logically prior. Without a rather specific understanding of what underpins a desirable position, it is virtually impossible to analyze the process of getting there. Strategy becomes an aimless process in which luck determines the winners.

Assuming an understanding of the cross-sectional problem, however, the longitudinal problem takes on prime importance. Why do some firms achieve favorable positions vis-à-vis the drivers in the value chain? Why do some firms gain scale advantages? Why do some firms move early, or late, whichever leads to advantage? Why do some firms conceive of and implement

---

[13] I avoid the terms "static" and "dynamic" intentionally because both the cross-sectional and longitudinal problems have both static and dynamic components.

[14] See, for example, Mintzberg (1990).

superior configurations of activities or spot entirely new and desirable competitive positions?

Logically, there are two answers. The first is *initial conditions*. Firms may have preexisting reputations, skills, and in-place activities as a result of their history. These initial conditions may reside within an individual firm or, as I will discuss later, in its environment. Initial conditions clearly influence feasible choices as well as constrain them.[15]

The second reason that firms might achieve favorable positions is through pure *managerial choices*, or choices independent of initial conditions, putting aside for the moment the process by which the choices were made. These managerial choices, which are made under uncertainty about the future, define the firm's concept for competing (positioning), its configuration of activities, and the supporting investments in assets and skills. Pure managerial choices lead to the assembly or creation of the particular skills and resources required to carry out the new strategy.

Numerous case studies illustrate vividly that highly successful firms often arise out of creative acts in situations where there were few initial strengths. Wal-Mart decided to locate in small and medium-sized towns and configure its logistical system in a particular way because it had a better idea, not because of any compelling preexisting strengths. If anything, its choices were shaped more by what it did not possess than what it did. The same could be said about Federal Express, Apple Computer, Crown Cork and Seal, and many other companies. American Airlines developed its MIS systems almost by accident. Its frequent flyer program was partly a function of the existence of its MIS system, but other airlines had these as well. American's management was simply more creative.

Many strategies reflect some combination of initial conditions and creative choice. The balance between the influence of initial conditions and acts of pure managerial choice varies by company and industry. Yet there may well be a tendency, for a variety of reasons to be discussed later, to overstate the role of initial conditions.

Lying behind all initial conditions internal to the firm were

---

[15] Initial conditions can also be set at different points in time. See below.

earlier managerial choices. The skills and market position a firm possesses today are the result of past choices about how to configure activities and what skills to create or acquire. Some of these choices, as Ghemawat's (1991) work among others has emphasized, involve hard-to-reverse commitments (path dependency). Earlier choices, which have led to the current pool of internal skills and assets, are a reflection of the environment that surrounded the firm at the time. The earlier one goes back in the chain of causality, the more it seems that successive managerial choices and initial conditions *external* to the firm govern outcomes.

The cross-sectional problem also highlights the importance of managerial choice. Whatever configuration of activities and skills a firm has inherited may or may not be competitively valuable. Simply having pools of skills, knowledge, or other resources is not in itself a guarantee of success. They must be the right ones. If managers can understand their competitive environment and the sources of competitive advantages, they will be better able to search creatively for favorable positions that are different from competitors', assemble the needed skills and assets, configure the value chain appropriately, and put in place supportive organizational routines and a culture that reinforces the required internal behavior. The most successful firms are notable in employing imagination to define a *new* position, or to find *new* value in whatever starting position they have.

Toward a Dynamic Theory

How, then, do we make progress toward a truly dynamic theory of strategy? Scholars in strategy, organizational behavior, and economics, sensing this as the frontier question, have made some headway. Three promising lines of inquiry have been explored in recent years. Each addresses important questions, though focusing on a somewhat different aspect of the problem.

Game-theoretic models. The first line of inquiry involves game-theoretic models of competitive interaction, which seek to understand the equilibrium consequences of patterns of choices by competitors over a variety of strategic variables such as capacity and R&D. Since this literature is reviewed elsewhere in this volume,[16] the treatment here can be brief. The central concern of these models is to identify the conditions that lead to mutually consistent equilibria and the nature of these equilibria. Each model is restricted to one or a few variables, and the environment (technology, products, preferences, and so forth) is assumed to be fixed except for the variables examined. Given this structure, timing plays a central role in determining outcomes. With a frame of reference in which these assumptions are plausible, Shapiro (1989) terms this literature a theory of business strategy.

These models have helped us understand better the logical consequences of choices over some important strategy variables. In particular, they highlight the importance of information and beliefs about competitive reaction and the conditions required for a set of internally consistent choices among rivals.

But this line of work stops short of offering a dynamic theory of strategy. By concentrating sequentially on small numbers of variables, the models fail to capture the simultaneous choices over many variables that characterize most industries. The models force a homogeneity of strategies, yet it is the trade-offs and interactions involved in configuring the entire set of activities in the value chain that define distinct competitive positions. Finally, the models hold fixed many variables that we know are changing. Ironically, these models explore the dynamics of a largely static world. (The papers by Saloner and Camerer in this volume raise additional useful questions.)

Commitment and uncertainty.   Another body of work is beginning to emerge on the problem of making irreversible commitments under uncertainty. Ghemawat's recent book (1991) is a notable example. The notion here is that strategy is manifested in a relatively few investment decisions, which are hard to reverse and which tend to define choices in other areas of the firm. These commitments must be made under uncertainty. Ghemawat highlights the importance of such choices and argues that they should consume much of the attention in strategy analyses. He posits that analysis of such decisions must begin with cross-sectional frameworks. In choosing among feasible positions, however, Ghemawat stresses the need to carefully exam-

---

[16]   See Chapters 5, 6, and 7.

ine their sustainability and the influence of uncertainty in the process of choice. He brings a broader perspective to bear on sustainability than is present in the game-theoretic models.

Related to Ghemawat's research is work that seeks to define ways of understanding the uncertainties a firm faces, and the alternative ways it can be addressed in strategy choices. The scenario technique for organizing and bounding uncertainty has received much attention.[17] More recently, taxonomies have begun to emerge that attempt to categorize the ways in which firms can respond to uncertainty.[18] In addition, Teisberg (1991b) has drawn on work in behavioral decision analysis and cognitive psychology to explore the biases and heuristics in decision making in complex and uncertain circumstances that distort strategy choices.

This emerging stream of work emphasizes the lumpiness of strategy choices and the importance of uncertainty in making them. It sheds important light on how to approach discrete investment decisions from a rich strategic perspective. Its insights come at the price, however, of a focus on large, discrete, sequential investments rather than on the simultaneous set of choices throughout the value chain that define a firm's competitive position. Like the game-theoretic models, it considers the environment as relatively stable (though uncertain) so that commitments have long-lived consequences and the possibilities for reconfiguring the value chain are limited. This approach tends to stress the value of flexibility in dealing with change rather than the capacity to rapidly improve and innovate to nullify or overcome it. By focusing on discrete choices, most of these treatments implicitly limit the discretion a firm has to shape its environment, respond to environmental changes, or define entirely new positions.[19]

The resource-based view. A third body of research in search of the origins of competitive advantage is the so-called resource-based view of the firm.[20] Closely related to the resource-based

---

[17]   See Wack (1985a and b) and Schwartz (1991).

[18]   See Wernerfelt and Karnani (1987), Porter (1985, ch. 13), Teisberg (1991a), and Collis (1991a).

[19]   Teisberg's (1991a) essay, which makes influencing industry structure a way of dealing with uncertainty, is an exception.

[20]   Conversations with Cynthia Montgomery have stimulated and informed my interest in this literature. Perhaps the pioneer of this school is Penrose (1959). An early paper was Wernerfelt (1984a). For other references, see the bibliographies in Peteraf (1993) and Collis (1991b). Recent papers include Barney (1991) and Grant (1991).

view is the notion of "core competences" and treatments that stress intangible assets. Since this literature is more prominent and more extensive than that on commitment/uncertainty, it deserves a more detailed treatment.

Of the three literatures, the resource-based view is the most introspective and centered on the firm itself. The argument is that the origins of competitive advantage are valuable resources (or competences) that firms possess, which are often intangible assets such as skills, reputation, and the like. These resources are seen as relatively immobile and are considered strengths to be nurtured, which should guide the choice of strategy. The implicit focus of much of this literature is on the underpinnings of successful diversification. It is, of course, essential when diversifying to understand a firm's distinctive strengths (remember Andrews).

The resource-based view has been proposed as an alternative theory of strategy.[21] What is really unique about a firm, so the argument goes, is its bundle of resources. It is factor market impediments, then, rather than product-market circumstances that define success. The role of internal resources is an important insight for economic modelers, though not as novel a notion for strategy researchers.

The promise of the resource view for the strategy field is its effort to address the longitudinal problem, or the conditions that allow firms to achieve and sustain favorable competitive positions over time. As with the other literatures, however, more work remains to be done. At its worst, the resource-based view is circular. Successful firms are successful because they have unique resources. They should nurture these resources to be successful.[22] But what is a unique resource? What makes it valuable? Why was a firm able to create or acquire it? Why does the original owner or current holder of the resource not bid the value away? What allows a resource to retain its value

---

21 Some writers in the resource school draw stylized comparisons with industrial organization (IO)-based theories that confuse rather than clarify. For example, Peteraf's survey (1993) asserts that IO-based models focus only on the heterogeneity of markets while denying the heterogeneity of firms and the existence of differential competitive positions; it argues that they are based only on monopoly rents, lead only to strategies of collusion, and are restricted to formulating strategy at the business unit level. This view is puzzling unless one is talking about the IO-based models of the 1970s, before research aimed at bridging IO and firm strategy began.

22 In this respect, the paper by Prahalad and Hamel (1990) is perhaps the most inward-looking and the most troubling.

in the future? There is once again a chain of causality, which this literature is just beginning to unravel.

Some authors have begun to deal with these questions by seeking to specify the conditions under which resources are valuable. Valuable resources are those that are superior in use, hard to imitate, difficult to substitute for, and more valuable within the firm than outside. Yet valuable resources, in order to yield profits to the firm, have been acquired for less than their intrinsic value due to imperfections in input markets, which Barney (1986a) argues are usually due to informational asymmetries (read better managerial choices) or luck.

But the resource-based view cannot be an alternative theory of strategy. It cannot be separated from the cross-sectional determinants of competitive advantage or, for that matter, from the conception of a firm as a collection of activities. Stress on resources must complement, not replace, stress on market positions.[23]

Resources are not valuable in themselves, but because they allow firms to perform activities that create advantages in particular markets. Resources are only meaningful in the context of performing certain activities to achieve certain competitive advantages. The competitive value of resources can be enhanced or eliminated by changes in technology, competitor behavior, or buyer needs, which an inward focus on resources will overlook. More reliable Japanese products, for example, degraded the value of Xerox's copier service organization. The immobility of resources, then, is as likely to be a risk as a source of strength. For every firm with resources that convey advantage, there will be another (and perhaps many others) with resources that impede change or prove to be a liability in light of environmental changes.

Competitive advantage derives from more than just resources. Scale, sharing across activities, an optimal degree of integration, and other drivers are independent influences, unless "resources" are defined so broadly as to strain credibility. It is the collective advantage gained from all sources that determines relative performance.

The conditions that make a resource valuable bear a strong

---

[23] Collis's paper (1991b) concludes with this point, which emerges from his detailed case study of ball bearings.

resemblance to industry structure. Bargaining power of suppliers refers to input markets, substitutability to the threat of substitution, and imitability to barriers to entry/mobility. The bargaining power of buyers and the dissipation of resource rents through rivalry via price cutting or competition from alternative resource bundles represent additional threats to the profitability of firms.

The connection between resources and activities is even more fundamental, however. Resources represent an inherently intermediate position in the chain of causality. Resources arise either from performing activities over time, acquiring them from outside, or some combination of the two. Both reflect prior managerial choices. Performing an activity or group of linked activities over time creates internal skills and routines that accumulate. It can also create external assets. A firm's reputation, for example, is a function of the history of its marketing and customer service activities, among other things. Both internal and external assets depreciate, however, unless they are reinvigorated through the renewed performance of activities. The rate of depreciation appears to vary widely across different types of assets, and can be rapid. Firms, then, have accumulated differing resources because of differing strategies and configurations of activities. Resources and activities are, in a sense, duals of each other.[24]

Resources, then, are intermediate between activities and advantage. An explicit link between resources and activities, along with the clear distinction between internal and external resources that was drawn earlier, is necessary to carefully define a resource in the first place. Some firm attributes termed resources involve activities—such as sales forces or R&D organizations. A second and more appropriate category of resources is skills, organizational routines, or other assets attached to particular activities or groups of interrelated activities.

The concept of activity drivers allows more precision in defining how resources were created. Some skills and routines emerge because of learning over time. This learning is a reflection of past strategy choices, which have defined how activities

---

[24] Since the great preponderance of resources are created either by past activities or managerial choices to assemble outside resources in new activity configurations, my own view is that activities are logically prior. Yet it is clear that causality blurs as accumulated resources affect the cost or uniqueness of activities.

are configured. Other resources were obtained through well-timed factor purchases (timing). Still others are the result of the ability to share across units. In turn, the resource view adds an important dimension to the concepts of activities and drivers. Underlying the ability to link activities or share them across business units, for example, are organizational skills and routines that represent important assets.

A final category of resources is external assets such as reputation and relationships.[25] These are normally created through performing activities over time. Recognizing these assets, and their link with the ongoing cost or differentiation of activities, is another valuable contribution of the resource view. The existence of such assets is implicit in the concept of drivers but not well developed.

All this still leaves unanswered the question, however, of the origins of competitive advantage. Why can valuable resources be created and sustained? Interestingly, the requirement of imperfect factor markets points strongly in the direction of managerial choice, and goes against the primacy of prior resources (initial conditions) in determining competitive advantage.

Resources whose value is obvious are bid up in value. Hence the presence within the firm of resources/activities that are rent-yielding is likely to reflect past managerial choices to assemble resources in unique ways, combine particular resources, pursue undiscovered market positions, or create resources internally. This allows resources to be acquired cheaply and avoids the bargaining away of their value to employees. Few resources begin as inherently scarce. Their scarcity is created through choice. Current managerial choices, in turn, allow the innovative assembly of new resources and the rendering obsolete of prior ones.

The resource-based view will have the greatest significance in environments where change is incremental, the number of strategic variables and combinations is limited (so that a few scarce resources can govern outcomes), and the time period is short to intermediate term (so that managerial choices can replicate or offset resource stocks). The greatest value of the re-

---

[25] Defining a market position as a resource is inappropriate, because it confuses the longitudinal problem with the cross-sectional problem and obscures the mechanism by which advantage is created.

source view will be in assessing opportunities for diversification, provided the resource and activity views are integrated.[26] A resource-based view of diversification that defines resources broadly, however, runs the risk of justifying the sort of unrelated diversification that was so disastrous in the 1970s and 1980s.

The Origins of the Origins

We are still left short of a dynamic theory of strategy, though we are beginning to learn about the subprocesses involved. In order to understand why firms choose and successfully implement the right strategies, and why their internal activities and assets are what they are, at least four important issues must be addressed.

First, a theory must deal simultaneously with both the firm itself and the industry and broader environment in which it operates. The environment both constrains and influences outcomes, an effect that the more introspective resource view neglects. Second, a theory must allow centrally for exogenous change in areas such as buyer needs, technology, and input markets. If there is little exogenous change, the choice of strategy can be viewed as a once-and-for-all game and the initial stock of (properly defined) resources can be crucial. In a world where exogenous change is rapid or relatively continuous, however, the analytical problem becomes far more complicated. The value of past resources is continually depreciated or even rendered negative. The choice of strategy is a series of ever-changing games in which the position in one game can influence, but does not determine, the position in the next. Case after case illustrates that the leaders in one generation of products often fail to lead in the next.

Third, a theory must give the firm latitude not only to choose among well-defined options but to create new ones. The firm cannot be seen only as optimizing within tight constraints, but should be represented as having the ability to shift the constraints through creative strategy choices, other innovative activity, and the assembly of skills and other needed capabilities. There are alternative strategies open. The extent to which the

---

[26] See Montgomery and Wernerfelt (1988) and Montgomery and Hariharan (1991).

environment shapes initial conditions and choice, in contrast to the idiosyncratic, creative decision-making process within the firm, is a fundamental question.

A final issue that cuts across the others is the role of historical accident or chance. There is a growing belief that historical accidents influence competitive outcomes. Some of what economists term historical accidents may simply be good strategy choices, or reflect so far unmeasured aspects of the environment. There are often reasons why firms are "lucky," as I will stress below. Be that as it may, the extent of randomness in competition, and the role of true luck, has an important influence on how one develops a theory of strategy.

Origins within the Firm

How then do we explain good strategic choices and the ability to carry them out? One view is that since the number of variables is substantial and environmental change is continuous and unpredictable, the problem is not selecting good strategies but creating a flexible organization that learns and is able to continually redefine its strategy. The resource view, taken to an unhealthy extreme, is sometimes argued to encompass this position. The critical resources are the capacity for learning and adaptation.

The problem with this notion is its collision with empirical reality. Most successful organizations improve strategy, but they do not often change it outright.[27] They gain advantage from new insights into competition and from consistent refinement of their ability to implement a stable overall strategy (e.g., differentiation), though its details are continually evolving and improving.

Another view of the origin of advantage is that it lies in the ability to make good strategy choices and implement them. While this can happen by chance, the odds are elevated by better information and careful analysis. Once a choice is made, the successful organization is one that can make all its activities consistent with the strategy and rapidly accumulate the necessary activities and resources. New choices are made as the environment changes or as accumulating activities and resources

---

[27] See Porter (1990) and Ghemawat (1991).

open up new options. But it must be said that giving a prominent role to choice and capacity for implementation still begs the question of why some firms are better at it than others.

The Environment as the Origin of Advantage

Instead of lying solely within the firm, the true origin of competitive advantage may be found in the firm's proximate or local environment. The proximate environment will define many of the input (factor) markets the firm has to draw on, the information that guides strategic choices, and the incentives and pressures on firms to both innovate and accumulate skills or resources over time. Competitive advantage, then, may reside as much in the environment as in an individual firm. The environment shapes how activities are configured, which resources can be assembled uniquely, and what commitments can be made successfully.

This richer view of the role of the environment has emerged from my study of the causes of international competitive success in a large sample of industries in 10 leading trading nations. This line of work began with a puzzle. After having written about global strategy, and the ability of firms to transcend national markets, I observed that competitive advantage in particular industries tended to be strongly concentrated in one or two countries, often with several if not many successful home-based competitors. These local rivals pursue different strategies and push each other to innovate and improve much more rapidly than foreign rivals, which allows them to penetrate and prosper in foreign markets. The concentration of successful competitors was particularly pronounced if one examined strategically distinct industry segments rather than broad aggregates, and if one excluded cases where firms were not truly successful but merely surviving or sheltered by government intervention. While the focus of the research was on the role of the national environment, it was also clear that successful firms were also geographically concentrated *within* nations. The same theoretical framework can be used to help explain the concentration of success in nations, regions within nations, or even cities. It also seems possible to extend it to help explain why one particular firm outperforms others.

The starting point for the theory is that environmental

change is relentless, and firms, through innovation, have considerable latitude in both influencing their environment and responding to it. Firms create and sustain competitive advantage because of their capacity to continuously improve, innovate, and upgrade their competitive advantages over time. Upgrading is the process of shifting advantages throughout the value chain to more sophisticated types, and employing higher levels of skill and technology. Successful firms are those that improve and innovate in ways that are valued not only at home but elsewhere. Competitive success is enhanced by moving early in each product or process generation, provided that movement is along a path that reflects evolving technology and buyer needs, and that early movers subsequently upgrade their positions rather than rest on them. In this view, firms have considerable discretion in relaxing external and internal constraints.

These imperatives of competitive advantage, however, collide with the organizational tendencies of firms. Firms value stability, and change is difficult and unsettling. Strong external or environmental influences are often essential in overcoming these tendencies.

Environmental Determinants of Innovation and Upgrading

Four broad attributes of the proximate environment of a firm have the greatest influence on its ability to innovate and upgrade, as illustrated in Figure 15-5. These attributes, which I collectively term the "diamond," shape the information that firms have available. Such information allows firms to perceive opportunities, the pool of inputs, skills and knowledge they can draw on, goals that condition investment, and the pressures on firms to act. The environment is thus important in providing the initial insight that underpins competitive advantage, the inputs needed to act on it, the ability to accumulate knowledge and skills over time, and the forces needed to keep progressing.

The most important factors of production are highly specialized factors tailored to the needs of particular industries. Generalized factor pools are either readily available or easy to source through global networks. Specialized local factor pools support the most rapid accumulation of skill and the greatest rate of innovation. Generic technology is readily sourced from distant

Figure 15-5
Determinants of National Competitive Advantage

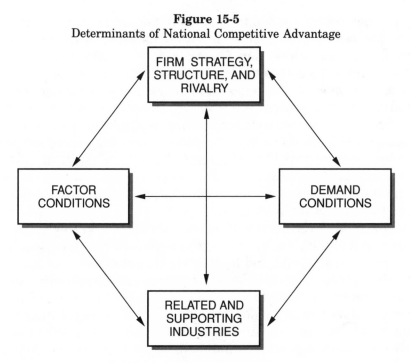

suppliers, but transfer of know-how benefits from proximity. Specialized factors are almost always created through private and social investments. The presence of unique institutional mechanisms for creating them in particular industries is an important determinant of competitive success. Selective disadvantages in the more basic factors (e.g., unskilled labor, natural resources) are, paradoxically, often a source of advantage. They break dependence on factor costs and trigger innovation and upgrading.

Home demand is important more for its character than for its size. Home demand plays a disproportionate role in influencing the perception of buyer needs and the capacity of firms to improve products and services over time. Sophisticated and/or especially demanding home customers often stimulate competitive success, as do home market needs that anticipate those elsewhere.

Competitive advantage is also strongly influenced by the presence of home-based suppliers and related industries in those products, components, machines, or services that are specialized and/or integral to the process of innovation in the industry. Inputs themselves are mobile, but there are local externalities for the process of innovation in interactions between the firm and local input suppliers. Home-based suppliers and related industries provide advantages in terms of information, signaling, access to new technologies, and market pressures. In many industries, the scarce technology is know-how, which can be difficult to transfer without cultural and physical proximity. Companies with home-based suppliers have the opportunity to influence their suppliers' technical efforts, help establish specifications to fit particular needs, serve as test sites for R&D work, and maintain senior management contact. All of these accelerate the pace of innovation.

The final determinant of advantage is firm strategy, structure, and rivalry, or the context for competition in a region or nation. The national and local environments have a strong influence on management practices, forms of organization, and the goals set by individuals and companies. The presence of local rivalry also has a profound influence on the rate of improvement, innovation, and ultimate success in an industry. Local rivals provide a greater stimulus to upgrading than foreign rivals. Proximity speeds information flow and encourages competition. The presence of domestic competitors negates basic factor advantages and forces firms to develop higher-order and more sustainable advantages. Actual rivalry provides a greater stimulus than potential rivalry. Intense local rivalry may hold down profits in the home market but spurs advantages that allow attractive profits (contingent on overall industry structure) in global markets.

Local rivalry also feeds back to improve other parts of the diamond. It overcomes monopsony-based impediments to the development of specialized suppliers, encourages investments in specialized factors such as university programs and specialized infrastructure, helps to stimulate local demand, and so on.

There is a role for true chance events and historical accidents in the process by which competitive advantage is created, an issue that I raised earlier. However, historical accidents are less common than they seem upon first impression. What appear to be accidents are really events driven by conditions in the diamond. Also, the role of accidents cannot be considered independently of more stable aspects of the local or national environment. True accidents rarely result in competitive industries unless other favorable conditions in the diamond are present. Similarly, accidents that simultaneously occur in different locations result in a competitive firm in that location with the most favorable diamond.

There are many cases where a company was founded in one location in an act of pure entrepreneurship, then relocated to another region or even to another country because the new location offered a better setting in which to nurture or reap the rewards of that innovation. The pilgrimage of aspiring actors and actresses to Hollywood is simply one example of how ideas and talent flow to the environment in which they can command the highest returns. The ability to command the highest returns depends on the simultaneous presence of unusual local demand, related industries, active rivals bidding, and other aspects of the diamond.

A final influence on the environment for competitive advantage is government. The role of government policy is best understood by looking at how it influences the diamond. Government at all levels can improve or impede national advantage through its investments in factor creation, through its influence on the goals of individuals and firms, through its role as a buyer or influencer of buyer needs, through its competition policies, and through its role in related and supporting industries. Government plays an important part in shaping the pressures, incentives, and capabilities of the nation's firms.

Government's proper role is as a catalyst and challenger. It should encourage or even push companies to raise their aspirations and move to higher levels of competitive performance, even though this process may be unpleasant and difficult. Government plays a role that is inherently partial and that succeeds only when it works in tandem with favorable underlying conditions in the diamond. Successful government policies are those that create an environment in which companies can gain competitive advantage rather than those that involve government directly in the process. (It is an indirect, rather than direct, role.)

The Diamond as a Dynamic System

These aspects of the local environment constitute a dynamic system. The dynamism of the environment bears centrally on the firm processes that give rise to advantage. The effect of one determinant depends on the state of others. The presence of sophisticated and demanding buyers, for example, will not result in advanced products or production processes unless the quality of human resources enables firms to respond to buyer needs. There must also be a climate that supports sustained investment to fund the development of these products and processes. Similarly, having selective disadvantages in basic factors (e.g., higher labor, energy, or raw material costs) will not spur innovation and upgrading unless there is an environment of vigorous competition among firms. It is this contingent relationship that explains why, for example, a selective factor disadvantage stimulates innovation in one country while hastening decline in another.

The parts of the diamond are also mutually reinforcing. The development of specialized supporting industries, for example, tends to increase the supply of specialized factors. Vigorous domestic rivalry stimulates the development of unique pools of specialized factors. This is particularly likely if the rivals are all located in one city or region. The University of California at Davis, for example, has become the world's leading center for wine-making research, working closely with the California wine industry. Active local rivalry also upgrades home demand by educating buyers and providing choice, and it promotes the formation of related and supporting industries. Japan's world-leading group of semiconductor producers, for example, has spawned world-leading Japanese semiconductor equipment manufacturers.[28]

The effects can work in all directions, and causality can become blurred over time. Sometimes world-class suppliers become new entrants in the industry they have been supplying. Or highly sophisticated buyers may enter a supplier industry,

---

[28] The mutual reinforcement of the determinants suggests a particularly important role for local rivalry, healthy new business formation, and the responsiveness of local institutions to signals from industry. Local rivalry stimulates improvements in all the other determinants. New business formation, whether through start-up or internal development, is a sine qua non of developing related and supporting industries as well as healthy rivalry. Competitive advantage also depends on the capacity of the local education system, infrastructure providers, and government institutions to respond to the specialized needs of particular industries. Institutional responsiveness allows the proper types of skills, resources, and infrastructure to be created.

particularly when they have relevant skills and view the upstream industry as strategic. In the case of the Japanese robotics industry, for example, Matsushita and Kawasaki originally designed robots for internal use before selling them to others.

The diamond also bears centrally on a nation's ability to *attract* factors of production, rather than merely serve as a location for them. This represents a final form of mutual reinforcement. Mobile factors, particularly ideas and highly skilled individuals, are becoming increasingly important to international competitiveness. Mobile factors tend to be drawn to the location where they can achieve the greatest productivity, because that is where they can obtain the highest returns. The theory outlined above, because if focuses on the determinants of productivity, also explains the attraction of mobile factors. The same features that make a nation an appealing home base also help it attract mobile factors.

The national and local environment for competing in a particular industry itself evolves in a dynamic process. The environment is created over time through the mutual reinforcement of the determinants. It begins with an inheritance drawn from other industries and history, and exists amid a set of local institutions, values, and attitudes. The mutual reinforcement of the determinants, which reflects in part the actions of firms themselves, builds up the environment over time. As this process goes on, causality becomes blurred.

In industries with modest levels of skill and technology, firms can gain advantage solely on the basis of factor advantages such as cheap labor or abundant raw materials. (Such advantages are notoriously unstable, however, in a world of globalization, technological change, and rapid substitution.) Competitive advantage in more sophisticated industries and industry segments, on the other hand, rarely stems from strength in a single determinant. Sustained success in these industries and segments usually requires the interaction of favorable conditions in several of the determinants and at least parity in the others. This is because advantages in various parts of the diamond are self-reinforcing.

It is thus the juxtaposition of advantages in one location that leads to competitive success, and not simply the presence of any single advantage no matter how strategic. The firm's home base, which consists of that group of activities most centrally involved in the process of innovation and learning, must be located in the same place to allow the internal coordination and contact with the local environment that is necessary for rapid progress. A firm's ability to progress rapidly and appropriately by integrating research and production spread widely among several locations, machines sourced from many disparate and distant suppliers, and so on, is limited. The firm that concentrates its core activities at a favorable home base, while competing nationally and globally, will normally progress more rapidly. Activities outside the home base are focused on sourcing low-cost basic factors and securing market access.

These same arguments explain why we observe *clusters* of competitive industries in one location. Clusters involve supplier industries, customer industries, and related industries that are all competitive. Such clusters are characteristic of every advanced economy—American entertainment, German chemicals, Japanese electronics, Danish foods. Clusters grow and transform themselves through spin-offs and diversification of firms into upstream, downstream, and related industries and activities. The fields where several clusters overlap are often fertile grounds for new business formation. In Japan, for example, the common ground between electronics and new materials is spawning new competitive strengths in fields as diverse as robotics and displays.

Another implication of this theory is the importance of successful firms and clusters being concentrated in particular cities or regions. National clusters are often themselves geographically concentrated. Geographic concentration elevates and magnifies the interaction of the four determinants, improves information flow and signaling, makes innovation-enhancing interactions with customers and specialized suppliers less costly, and provides a check on opportunistic behavior, among other benefits.[29]

Firms lose competitive advantage either because of emerging weaknesses in their local environment or because of rigidities or other internal problems that external circumstances cannot overcome.[30] For example, a major shift in technology may require an entirely new set of specialized suppliers that are not

[29] For a detailed treatment and empirical tests, see Enright (1990). See, also, Krugman (1991a).
[30] I discuss these issues more fully elsewhere. See Porter (1990).

present, or local demand characteristics may evolve in ways that distract from instead of anticipating international needs. However, firms sometimes fail not because their environment is unfavorable but because of organizational or managerial rigidities that block improvement and change. The environment can provide important pressures to advance, but firms differ in their responsiveness to them.

Environmental Influences on the Dynamics of Strategy

The environment, via the diamond, affects both a firm's initial conditions and its managerial choices. The diamond, through its influence on information and incentives, shapes the content of strategies. It influences the ability of firms to carry out particular types of strategies, hence limiting choice. Choices that may look accidental or internally driven are often partly or wholly derived from the local diamond. Over time, through its stress on markets for difficult-to-trade inputs, the state of the diamond conditions the rate of accumulation of resources. It also puts the pressure on firms to improve and upgrade. The diamond, then, begins to address a dynamic theory of strategy early in the chain of causality.

Yet firms retain a central role. Firms must understand and exploit their local environment in order to achieve competitive advantage. There are often sharp differences in the performance of firms based in the same region or nation. These differences are partly a function of managerial choices, differential rates of resource accumulation, or chance. The differences also appear, however, to be partly a function of the subenvironment of each particular firm—its early customers, supplier relationships, factor market access, and so forth.

An important role for the local environment in competitive success does not eliminate the role of strategy nor the need for competitive analysis. Industry structure, positioning, activities, resources, and commitments remain important. Rather, the diamond highlights new issues for strategy that are normally ignored, such as the need to develop and nurture home-based suppliers, the utility of local specialized factor markets, and the balance between home-based activities and those dispersed to other locations as part of a national or global strategy.

The local environment creates potential for competitive success, but firms must sense and respond to it. Firms also have a considerable ability to influence their environment in ways that reinforce or detract from their capacity to accumulate skills and resources and to innovate—there is a feedback loop between firm actions and the local diamond. Many if not most firms, even in favorable environments, do *not* achieve competitive advantage. Firms based in an unattractive environment, however, face profound challenges in achieving competitive success. More and more firms are relocating their home bases accordingly.

Issues for Further Research

Recent research has begun to shed some light on the chain of causality that constitutes a dynamic theory of strategy, but many unanswered questions remain. Of these, four deserve special attention. First, we need to better understand the balance between environmental determinism and company/leader choice in shaping competitive outcomes. What is emerging is the beginnings of a more sophisticated way of understanding how the environment surrounding a firm influences both firm choices and outcomes, and of the internal processes of choice and of skill and asset (resource) accumulation that underpin competitive advantage. It is clear that company actions still matter, and that firms in a given environment achieve widely different levels of success. Can we, by looking across different firms in a given nation or city, isolate unique subenvironments that explain these differing levels of performance? Or, can we identify patterns of commitments to activities and resource accumulation that characterize superior performers?

Second, we need to better understand the degree of stickiness or inertia in competitive positions once a firm stops progressing, or, to put it another way, the durability of early mover advantages. How important is a burst of innovation versus the capacity to improve and innovate continually? How important are pure rents from scarce factors versus advantages that result from innovation or that raise the value of factors? My research suggests the latter is characteristic of successful firms that have sustained their competitive positions, but much more investigation is necessary.

Third, we need to know how necessary or helpful it is to push even further back in the chain of causality. I have argued that resources are an intermediate step in the chain, from which we can learn much. Yet an important theoretical issue is where in the chain of causality we can best cut into the problem. An example will illustrate that even focusing on the local environment of the firm does not trace advantage to its ultimate origin. The presence of a specialized skill in a region or nation is often the result of skill pools inherited from other industries as well as human resources trained at preexisting institutions. These institutions, however, often draw to some extent on the general education system, which itself is affected by social values and history. Just how far back does one need to go to reach the ultimate source and to examine these questions most effectively? I chose in my own research to model the phenomena at the level of the diamond, while noting that each of its components is the result of history and other local conditions. The appropriateness of this choice is a subject for research. It should be said that understanding the ultimate origins of advantage may not always be necessary for thinking about how to improve future advantage.

Finally, there is the important challenge of crafting empirical research to make further progress in understanding these questions. Some argue that models that exceed a certain level of complexity can never be tested. Yet it is clear that there are many aspects of both firms and their environments which determine competitive success. How can we collect and analyze data to help us discriminate among explanations and weigh the various factors? I concluded in my most recent research that detailed longitudinal case studies covering long periods of time were necessary to study these phenomena. Moreover, these case studies had to encompass a large number and wide range of industries and national contexts in order to develop confidence about the appropriate variables and their influence on outcomes. This style of research nudges strategy research, and indeed industrial economics, into the world of the historian. It also involves enormous fixed costs. I am convinced that more research of this type will be needed to address the dynamics of strategy. It also raises the question of whether there are other approaches to empirical testing that can be used to address these issues, or whether we must wait until theories have been much better developed before we can highlight the relatively few variables that can be measured and rigorously examined statistically.

16

Location and Competition: Notes on Economic Geography

Paul Krugman

Introduction

Whether the home base of a firm affects its competitive advantage depends on several factors. One is whether there are external economies associated with particular geographic locations; a second is whether the clustering of production activities creates networks that are open to firms of different national origins. In this paper, only the first of these two issues is examined. The conclusion is that geography matters, and that the borderless economy has not yet arrived; although borders may be defined in ways that do not coincide with nation-states. Indeed, the removal of trade barriers is likely to lead to greater industrial clustering around existing centers of concentration. Accordingly, firms will need to be global in the scope of their activities to access the economies associated with collocation in such clusters.

International Integration

It is apparent to everyone that the world economy has become increasingly integrated over the past generation. International trade has grown much more rapidly than world output; the international distribution of investment has diverged increasingly from that of saving, as capital has begun to flow more freely; the volume of financial transactions on international markets has exploded even faster than on domestic markets. It is tempting to conclude that this represents a qualitative change in the nature of economics, that we are on the brink of becoming a "borderless" world in which firms are truly global, even anational.

Yet this millenialism—what I think of as the "gee-whiz" view of international integration (or perhaps, if the disappearance of borders is asserted, the "oh my" view)—is misleading. For one thing, it shows a lack of historical sense. International integration is nothing new: it only seems new because the quite remarkably integrated economy that existed in 1913 was fragmented by wars and protectionism (as our own in some ways less integrated economy could be again). The United States today is far less dependent on international trade than the economy that celebrated Queen Victoria's Diamond Jubilee; and Japan has never, even in a single year, invested as large a fraction of its savings abroad as Britain invested in an average year over the 40 years before World War I.

More important, the gee-whiz view overlooks the continuing importance of national and even local advantages in determining the course of international competition. Although transportation costs have fallen and the ability to transmit information has risen, many global industries remain highly concentrated in a few countries, and often in a few narrow localities within these countries. Perhaps the greatest service performed by Michael Porter in his important book on international competition (1990) has been his willingness to swim against the tide, to assert that, in spite of the shrinking of the world, location still matters.

Now to some extent location matters because of comparative advantage. That is, mining companies must dig where there is ore, agribusiness plant where there is suitable land, and sweatshops cluster where there is cheap labor. Such garden variety resource-driven specialization has always been a large part of international trade, and remains so today. For the competition among advanced nations, however, much more important are the locational factors that do not arise because of exogenously given resources, but instead are created advantages. Even a casual examination of interregional specialization within the United States reveals the striking tendency of industries to form local clusters, often on the basis of seemingly trivial historical accidents. The same is true, in a harder to measure way, of international specialization; and arguably the clustering of industry will increase rather than decline as the world becomes more integrated.

Why do such geographical clusters form? Porter has provided a clever didactic device in his "competitive diamond"; but his framework is difficult for an economist to work with, because the logic of the linkages is somewhat unclear. What I want to do here is to go over the same ground from a more traditional economist's standpoint, providing somewhat more specific examples and some additional evidence on the role of the locational factor in competition.

This paper is in four parts. The first offers an explanation of how large-scale clustering of industry—like the "manufacturing belt" of late nineteenth-century America or the clustering of service industries in the Northeast—takes place. This question is, I hope, of some interest in its own right. The answer is also relatively easy to illustrate with simple examples, and thereby offers a guide to the more complex, but related, forces that lead to clustering on a smaller scale.

The second part turns to localization, the clustering of individual industries in particular districts; it uses some historical illustrations and U.S. evidence to demonstrate both the pervasiveness of the phenomenon and some of its characteristic modes.

The third part contrasts localization within the United States and within Europe; this comparison is, I would argue, useful not only as a way of thinking about the future of Europe but as a way of assessing the impact of growing international integration on the geography of competition.

The final part of the paper draws the threads together and suggests some conclusions.

Large-Scale Clustering

The geographic concentration of production is clear evidence of the pervasive influence of increasing returns. Precisely for this reason, of course, equilibrium-minded economists have usually been uncomfortable with economic geography.

Increasing returns affect economic geography at many levels. At the bottom of the scale, the location of particular industries— autos in Detroit, chips in Silicon Valley—often reflects the "locking in" of transitory advantages. At an intermediate level, the existence of cities themselves is evidently an increasing returns phenomenon. At the grand level, the uneven development of whole regions (which in the United States may well be bigger than European nations) can be driven by cumulative processes that have increasing returns at their root.

Here I will pass over the question of urbanization. It has been better studied than the other issues I will consider (urban economics is a more accepted field than economic geography), and it is also less relevant than the other aspects to international competition, which is the subject of this paper. So I will focus on the small and the large: the localization of particular industries, and the differential development of huge regions. First we look at the large, then at the small.

A Model of Geographic Concentration

The story of geographic concentration[1] that I will outline here relies on the forward and backward linkages that arise from the interaction of increasing returns and transportation costs. Given sufficiently strong economies of scale, each producer wants to serve a geographically extensive market from a single location. To minimize transportation costs, she chooses a location with large local demand and readily available inputs. But local demand will be large, and inputs readily available, precisely where other producers choose to locate. Thus there is a circularity that tends to keep a geographic cluster in existence once it is established.

Perhaps the simplest example is one in which we ignore the question of input supply and focus entirely on the backward linkage that runs through demand.

Imagine a country in which there are only two possible locations of production, East and West, and two kinds of production. Agricultural goods are produced using a location-specific factor (land), and as a result the agricultural population is exogenously divided between the locations; for the moment we assume that the division is 50–50.

Manufactured goods (of which there are many symmetric varieties) can be produced in either or both locations. If a given manufactured good is produced in only one location, transportation costs must be incurred to service the other market. On the other hand, if the good is to be produced in both locations, an additional fixed set-up cost is incurred. The manufacturing labor

---

[1]   This paper presents only a sketch of a model. It will be apparent that this sketch is sloppy about a number of issues, including: what is the market structure in manufacturing; what happens to profits, if any exist; and what resources are used in both fixed costs and transportation. It is possible to derive similar results in a fully specified general equilibrium monopolistic competition model; such a model is presented in Krugman (1991a).

Table 16-1

A Manufacturing Location Story

Distribution of manufacturing employment		Costs of typical firm if it produces in:		
		East	West	Both
East only	Fixed	4	4	8
	Transportation	3	7	0
	Total	7	11	8
West only	Fixed	4	4	8
	Transportation	7	3	0
	Total	11	7	8
50-50 split	Fixed	4	4	8
	Transportation	5	5	0
	Total	9	9	8

force in each location is proportional to manufacturing production in that location.

Finally, assume that the *demand* for each manufactured good in each location is strictly proportional to that location's population.

The basic idea can then be illustrated with a numerical example. Suppose that 60% of a country's labor force are farmers, divided equally between East and West. Suppose also that the total demand for a typical manufactured good is 10 units. Then if all manufacturing is concentrated in one location, that location will demand 7 units (3 demanded by the local farmers, 4 by the manufacturing workers), while the other demands 3; if manufacturing is evenly divided between the locations, each location will offer a local demand of 5.

To figure out what happens, we need to specify the fixed costs and transportation costs; suppose that the fixed cost of opening a plant is 4, and that the transportation cost per unit is 1. Then we have the situation shown in Table 16-1. The table shows the costs to a typical firm for each of three locational strategies, contingent on the locational strategies of all other firms. Thus suppose that all other manufacturing is concentrated in East. Then our firm will have a local demand in East of 7 units, and a local demand in West of only 3 units. If it serves the national market from a single plant in East, it will incur a fixed cost of 4 and a transport cost of 3. This is obviously less than serving the national market from a plant in West, which will have the same fixed cost plus a transport cost of 7; it is also less than building a plant to serve each local market, which saves the transport cost but incurs a double fixed cost of 8. In this case, then, the typical firm will choose to produce in East for a national market.

If each firm concentrates its production in East, however, then manufacturing production as a whole will be concentrated in East—which is what is assumed. So concentration of production in East is an equilibrium.

But it is not the only possible equilibrium. As the rest of the table shows, if manufacturing is concentrated in West, each firm will also want to concentrate its production in West. And if production is split between East and West, each firm will want to split its production, too. So in fact all three distributions of production—all in East, all in West, and a 50–50 split—are equilibria in this example.

This example demonstrates several points. First, it shows how a circular relationship—production follows demand, and demand follows production—can lead to geographical clustering. Second, it shows that where the concentration takes place may be to some extent arbitrary: either East or West may get it, presumably depending on which gets a head start. And third, the example sheds some light on the necessary conditions for geographical clustering.

To see this last point, notice that concentration of production is not an equilibrium for all parameters. Suppose, for example, that the fixed cost of establishing a second production unit were only 2 instead of 4. Then we would have the situation illustrated in Table 16-2.

Clearly, in this case the only equilibrium is one in which production is evenly split between East and West.

It is straightforward to show that concentration of production, geographical clustering, depends on three parameters: large fixed costs, i.e., strong economies of scale; a high share of "footloose" production not tied down by natural resources; and low transportation costs.[2]

---

[2] In Krugman (1991b) I argue that there was actually a qualitative change in the geography of the U.S. economy in the mid-nineteenth century. In the early United States, with its primarily agricultural population, where manufacturing was marked by few scale economies, and where transportation was costly, no strong geographical concentration could occur. As the country began its industrial transition, manufacturing arose in areas that contained most of the agricultural population outside the South—and the South was, for reasons having to do with its

Table 16-2
An Alternative Manufacturing Location Story

Distribution of manufacturing employment		Costs of typical firm if it produces in:		
		East	West	Both
East only	Fixed	2	2	4
	Transportation	3	7	0
	Total	5	9	4
West only	Fixed	2	2	4
	Transportation	7	3	0
	Total	9	5	4
50-50 split	Fixed	2	2	4
	Transportation	5	5	0
	Total	7	7	4

This last point may seem surprising. One might have expected that the importance of geographical concentration would decline as transportation costs fall, i.e., as an economy becomes more integrated. What this analysis suggests, however, is that increased integration actually fosters the concentration of production. As I will argue below, a comparison of the United States with Europe seems to confirm this insight.

Localization

In 1895 a teenaged girl named Catherine Evans, living in the small Georgia city of Dalton, made a bedspread as a wedding gift. It was an unusual bedspread for the time, in that it was tufted; the craft of tufting or candlewicking had been common in the eighteenth and early nineteenth centuries, but had fallen into disuse by that time. As a direct consequence of that wedding gift, Dalton emerged after World War II as the preeminent carpet manufacturing center of the United States. Six of the top twenty carpet-manufacturing firms in the United States are located in Dalton; all but one of the rest are located nearby, and

---

uniquely awful institutions, unsuited for manufacturing. During the second half of the nineteenth century, however, manufacturing economies of scale increased, transportation costs fell, and the share of the population in nonagricultural occupations rose. The result was that the initial advantage of the already established manufacturing areas was locked in. Even though new land and new resources were exploited to the west, and even though slavery ended, for three-quarters of a century the pull of the established manufacturing areas was strong enough to keep the manufacturing core virtually intact.

the carpet industry in Dalton and vicinity employs 19,000 workers.

I'll come back to Catherine Evans and her story shortly. For now let me simply assert that aside from being particularly charming, the carpet story is a fairly typical one. To a remarkable extent, manufacturing industries within the United States are highly localized; and when one tries to understand the reasons for that localization, one finds that it can be traced back to some seemingly trivial historical accident.

Before telling stories, however, let us consider an analytical structure.

Sources of Industry Localization

The observation of high localization of industries is, of course, not a new one. Indeed, it was such a striking feature of the process of industrialization that it attracted a great deal of attention in the late nineteenth century, and the 1900 U.S. Census contained a fascinating monograph on the subject. It was Alfred Marshall (1890), however, who presented the classic economic analysis of the phenomenon. (Actually, it was the observation of industry localization that underlay Marshall's concept of external economies, which makes the modern neglect of the subject even more surprising.)

Marshall identified three distinct reasons for localization. First, by concentrating a number of firms in an industry in the same place, an industrial center allows a pooled market for workers with specialized skills; this pooled market benefits both workers and firms. Second, an industrial center allows provision of nontraded inputs specific to an industry in greater variety and at lower cost. Finally, because information flows locally more easily than over greater distances, an industrial center generates what we would now call technological spillovers:

> The mysteries of the trade become no mystery; but are as it were in the air. . . . Good work is rightly appreciated, inventions and improvements in machinery, in processes and the general organization of the business have their merits promptly discussed: if one man starts a new idea, it is taken up by others and combined with suggestions of their own; and thus it becomes the source of further new ideas.

On the whole, I like Marshall's turn of phrase better than the modern one. Cut through the archaism of his language and his lack of formalism, and you will see that he had a pretty sophisticated model in mind. He missed a few tricks that I will try to point out, but on the whole the task for the contemporary analyst is to rephrase Marshall in a drier, less felicitous style, and thereby bring it up to date.

Let us therefore consider each of the Marshallian reasons for localization in turn.

Labor Market Pooling

Imagine for a moment that there is some industry that consists of just two firms, each of which can produce in either of only two locations. These firms both use the same distinctive kind of skilled labor. However, the firms' demands for labor are not perfectly correlated. For example, they may produce differentiated products that face uncertain demand; or they may be subject to firm-specific production shocks. Whatever the reason, the labor demand of the firms is both uncertain and imperfectly correlated.

To make the example more concrete, suppose that each firm may experience either "good times," in which it would like to hire 125 specialized workers at the going wage, or "bad times," in which it would like to hire only 75. We also suppose that there are 200 of these workers in total, so that *average* demand for labor equals supply. (In this example I take the wage rate for the specialized labor as given, so that there may be either excess demand for labor or excess supply. If you like, imagine a wage-bargaining process that sets the wage at an expected market-clearing level before the shocks to labor demand are revealed—not too unrealistic an assumption. This assumption is not essential, however. Even if the wage rate is completely flexible and the labor market clears, the basic story remains the same.)

Now we may ask: Will firms and workers be better off if the two firms choose different locations—each thus forming a company town with a local labor force of 100—or if the two firms choose the same location, with a pooled labor force of 200 that can work at either firm?

You may immediately ask about the possibility of exploitation: Wouldn't each firm prefer to have a captive local labor force? I'll come back to that soon, and show that it doesn't work the way you may think. For now, just put the possibility aside and assume that the wage is set at an expected market-clearing level. It should then be immediately apparent that it is in the interest of both firms and workers for everyone to be in the same place.

First, consider the situation from the firms' point of view. If each has its own town, with a labor force of 100, it will be unable to take advantage of its good fortune when labor demand is high: during good times, there will be an unfillable excess demand of 25 workers. If the two firms are in the same place, however, then at least occasionally one firm's good times will coincide with the other firm's bad times, and there will be additional workers available.

Next consider the situation from the workers' point of view. If they live in a company town, then the firm's bad times are their bad times too: whenever the firm has low labor demand, 25 workers will be laid off. If the firms are in the same place, at least sometimes one firm's bad times will be offset by the other firm's good times, and the average rate of unemployment will be correspondingly lower.

This is a pretty trivial example. Yet it is useful as a way to clear up some points that are often misunderstood.

First, the example clarifies the nature of the gains from labor market pooling. The use of the word "pooling" has led many economists, including labor economists, to assume that the incentive to create a pooled labor market is something like portfolio diversification, i.e., that it has something to do with risk aversion on the part of workers. No doubt minimizing risk is also an issue, but it played no role in the example. Even if workers were entirely risk neutral there would be an efficiency gain from creating a localized industry with a pooled labor market.

Second, the example shows that uncertainty alone won't generate localization; increasing returns are also crucial. The key point is that in order to make a pooled labor market advantageous the model assumes that each firm had to choose one location or the other, not both. If each firm could produce in both locations, or for that matter if each firm could be split into two identical firms, one in each place, the full "portfolio" of firms and workers could be replicated in each location, and the motivation for localization would be gone. But the most natural justification for the assumption that firms do not locate in both places is that there are sufficient economies of scale to militate for a single production site.

So it is the *interaction* of increasing returns and uncertainty that makes sense of Marshall's labor-pooling argument for localization.

What about monopsony power? Won't firms prefer to have a captive labor force that they can exploit? Yes, other things equal. But other things won't be equal—and in fact the monopsony issue acts as a further reason for localization.[3]

One way to think about this is the following: there is a tug-of-war between firms, which prefer a less competitive labor market and hence production in both locations, and workers, who prefer a more competitive market and hence concentration in one location. Workers will win this tug-of-war because a more competitive labor market is also more efficient; given noncollusive choice of location by firms, this efficiency gain decisively tips the scales toward the concentrated solution.

An alternative, and perhaps deeper, way to view the issue is in terms of credibility. Firms would like to convince workers that they will *not* try to exploit their monopsony power, so that they can attract workers to their production location.[4] But the only credible way to do this is to have enough firms in the location that competition for workers is assured. The commonsense idea that firms would like to have a company town in which workers could be exploited is right; but the point is that workers will shun such towns if they can, so that firms will end up finding it more profitable to locate in agglomerated centers that are *not* company towns.[5]

Intermediate Inputs

Marshall's second reason for agglomeration, the availability of specialized inputs and services, seems straightforward enough. A localized industry can support more specialized local

---

3   This point was first made by Julio Rotemberg and Garth Saloner. The style of their model is very different from the one I present here, but essentially I am just offering a variant of their analysis.

4   In Rotemberg and Saloner's formulation workers are not mobile, but immobile workers must decide whether to invest in industry-specific human capital. The basic principle is the same.

5   Of course, company towns do exist. Impressionistically, they seem to happen for one of two reasons. First, there may be specific natural advantages that cause individual factories to be located on scattered sites, as was the case for water-driven New England textile towns. Second, the economies of scale in an industry may be so large that a single firm dominates the industry and agglomerates its plants in order to achieve pooling, like Eastman Kodak in Rochester or Boeing in Seattle.

suppliers, which in turn makes that industry more efficient and reinforces the localization.

There are two points, however, that could perhaps use some clarification; many economists are confused about them.

First, the intermediate inputs story, like the labor pooling story, depends crucially on at least some degree of economies of scale. If there were no economies of scale in the production of intermediate inputs, even a small-scale center of production could replicate a large one in miniature and still achieve the same level of efficiency. It is only the presence of increasing returns that makes a large center of production able to have more efficient and more diverse suppliers than a small one.

Second, the intermediate inputs story does not depend on asymmetry in transportation costs between intermediate and final goods. It is often suggested that in order to justify the formation of localized industrial complexes it is somehow necessary to suppose that it is more costly to transport intermediate inputs than final goods. This is a misleading impression. In fact, localization will tend to occur unless the costs of transporting intermediates are particularly *low* compared with those of transporting final goods. And a general reduction in transport costs, of both intermediates and final goods, will ordinarily tend to encourage localization rather than discourage it.

To see why, it is useful to consider a tricky sort of model in which intermediates and final goods are the same thing. Imagine a group of products each of which is demanded both as a final good and as an input into all of the others. For example, suppose that the typical product in the group has total sales of 10, but that 4 of these sales are to manufacturers of other products in the group. And correspondingly we must suppose that to produce these 10 units requires 4 units of intermediate inputs, which again are drawn from the same industry. Notice that by making each good both final and intermediate, we have a fortiori imposed symmetry among intermediates and final goods in terms of their tradeability.

Now suppose that there are two possible locations of production, each of which is also the location of half the final demand, i.e., 3 units of each product. Where will a firm want to locate? The answer obviously depends on the decisions of other firms. If everyone else is in East, then 7 of the 10 units of total demand will be in East (3 final plus 4 intermediate); this will provide a firm with an incentive to locate its own production in East as well. The incentive will be reinforced by the fact that all of the firm's supplies of intermediate goods will come from East, and will therefore be cheaper there. Thus there will be both backward and forward linkages that provide an incentive to concentrate production. Of course there will also be an incentive to move closer to final demand that will pull the other way.

This should be sounding familiar: it sounds a lot like the model of large-scale clustering sketched out earlier. And indeed it is possible to construct a model of intermediate goods and industry localization that is formally exactly analogous to that model. This is helpful, because we already know something about that model. In particular, we know that the prospects for formation of a core-periphery pattern depend negatively on transportation costs, positively on the share of "footloose" demand, and positively on the importance of economies of scale. The same should be true here, if these variables are suitably reinterpreted. In particular, the role played in the core-periphery model by the share of manufactures is here taken instead by the share of the industry's output that is used as an intermediate good rather than directly for final demand. Given this, we see that lower transport costs make industrial localization more likely, even if the cost of transporting intermediates falls along with that of transporting final goods.

Technological Spillovers

I have saved for last the reason for localization that many economists would put first—namely, the more or less pure externality that results from knowledge spillovers between nearby firms. The emphasis on high technology in much policy discussion, and the fame of such clusters as California's Silicon Valley and Boston's Route 128 have made technological externalities the most obvious thing to mention. Furthermore, economists with a conventional background still have a hankering to preserve perfect competition in their models; purely technological externalities do this.

I have chosen to put pure technological external economies last, not first, for several reasons.

First, it is an empirical fact that many of the industries that are highly localized within the United States now or were highly localized in the past are nothing like high-technology sectors. Silicon Valley is famous; but equally remarkable concentrations may be found of carpet producers around Dalton; of jewelry producers around Providence, Rhode Island; of financial services in New York; and historically, of such industries as shoes in Massachusetts or rubber in Akron. Evidently forces for localization other than those involving high technology are quite strong.

Second, as a matter of principle I think we should try to focus first on the kinds of external economies that can be modeled other than by assumption. Labor pooling or intermediate goods supply are things that in principle one could examine directly and predict given a knowledge of the technology of the industry. And on the other side, the concreteness of these forces places constraints on what we can assume. Knowledge flows, by contrast, are invisible; they leave no paper trail by which they may be measured and tracked, and there is nothing to prevent the theorist from assuming anything about them that she likes. A sociologist might be able to help with survey methods; but I would like to get as far as possible with drab, down-to-earth economic analysis before turning to the other social sciences.

Finally, high technology is fashionable, and I think we are all obliged to make a deliberate effort to fight against fashionable ideas. It is all too easy to fall into a facile "megatrends" style of thought in which the wonders of the new are cited, and easy assumptions are made that everything is different now. Of course the world has changed—but it was a pretty remarkable place even before the coming of very large-scale integrated circuits, and even high-technology industries respond to old-fashioned economic forces.

So while I am sure that true technological spillovers play an important role in the localization of some industries, one should not assume that this is the typical reason—even in the high-technology industries themselves.

Some Empirical Evidence

I have alluded to some facts about the degree of localization of industry within the United States. But what sort of facts do we actually have?

One kind of evidence, which I regard as very important in spite of its lack of rigor, consists of case studies. Nothing is better at suggesting the kind of model that we ought to use than a collection of examples, particularly with some historical depth, of how particular industries come to be in particular places. Before turning to stories, however, I want to discuss some very preliminary statistical work that I have undertaken.

The objective of this work was to answer two questions. First, how localized is the "typical" U.S. industry? Are familiar examples like those of cars around Detroit and computer chips in Silicon Valley normal, or are they outliers?

Second, what sorts of industry are highly localized? Are localized industries typically high-technology sectors (which would lend support to a technological spillover model), or are they more prosaic? Are they industries that use highly skilled labor, or more general-purpose workers?

The technique I have tried to get at these questions is to construct "locational Gini coefficients" for as many U.S. manufacturing industries as possible. A locational Gini curve for an industry is constructed as follows. First, for each state we calculate both the share of total national manufacturing employment and the share of national employment in the industry. Then we rank the states by the ratio of these two numbers. Finally, we run down the ranking, keeping a cumulative total of both the sum of total employment share and the sum of employment share in the industry. The results are given in an appendix to this paper.

What do we learn from this exercise? The first impression that emerges from the results is that many industries are indeed highly concentrated geographically. Twenty-two industries have Ginis that exceed 0.4, which is remarkable given the problems of aggregation across both industry and geography. The automotive industry offers a useful benchmark. It is a famously localized industry. Although there has been some dispersal since the heyday of Motown, half of the employment is still in the traditional automotive district of southern Michigan and neighboring regions of Indiana and Ohio. So we might expect the motor vehicle industry to be exceptional, but it isn't. It is just slightly above the median. The point is not that automotive production is not highly localized—it is. But so are a lot of other industries.

The other notable feature of the data is that the most highly concentrated industries by this admittedly crude calculation are not cutting-edge, high-technology sectors. Indeed, the thing that leaps out from the table is not the localization of high-technology industries but the cluster of textile-related industries, all of them in more or less the same place: the Piedmont area of the Carolinas and Georgia. Half of the top 20 industries according to my Gini ranking are Piedmont textile sectors.

There is probably a bias in this evidence against finding the localization of high-tech industries. For one thing, two high-tech industries that are famously localized geographically had to be excluded from the table because of withheld data: aircraft, dominated by Boeing's huge Seattle facilities, and photographic equipment, with Kodak's Rochester complex. These are, of course, industries that are concentrated in ownership as well as in geography.

More important, the fact that the classification scheme is so antiquated means that quite small traditional industries still rate their own three-digit codes, while advanced sectors are buried in meaningless aggregates. Silicon Valley and Route 128 are real enough, but you just can't find them in the statistics.

So the evidence does not show that high-technology industries are not localized. What it shows is simply that low-technology industries are also localized. Whatever drives industries to concentrate in one place, it is not solely a matter of technological spillovers.

One of the Piedmont textile industries that is highly concentrated geographically is the carpet industry. It is a classic case of the role of historical accident and cumulative processes in generating localization.

As mentioned above, in 1895 the teenaged Catherine Evans made a bedspread as a gift. The recipients and their neighbors were delighted with the gift, and over the next few years Miss Evans made a number of tufted items, discovering in 1900 a trick of locking the tufts into the backing. She began to sell the bedspreads, and she and her friends and neighbors launched a local handicraft industry that was soon selling items well beyond the immediate vicinity.

The handicraft industry became a semimechanized one in the 1920s, as tufting was used to satisfy the surging demand for chenille sweaters; but production continued to be done by individual households.

Immediately after World War II, however, a machine was developed for producing tufted carpets. Until that time, machine-made carpets had been woven. Tufting proved to be far cheaper. And guess where one could find people who knew about tufting, and were quick to see the potential of this innovation? In the late 1940s and early 1950s, many small carpet firms sprang up in and around Dalton; a cluster of supporting firms providing backings, dyeing, and so forth. Existing carpet manufacturers initially clung to weaving; they eventually either went out of business, driven out by the upstarts from Dalton, or moved their own operations from traditional sites in the Northeast to Dalton. And so the little Georgia city emerged as America's carpet capital.

It's a lovely story; it's also a very typical one. The whole process of industrialization within the United States was marked by similar stories of small accidents leading to the establishment of one or two persistent centers of production. Anyone who thinks that Silicon Valley is a distinctly modern creation should look at the fascinating monograph, "The Localization of Industries," contained in the 1900 U.S. Census. The monograph identifies 15 highly localized industries in 1900, including collars and cuffs, localized in Troy, New York; leather gloves, localized in the two neighboring New York towns of Gloversville (sic) and Johnstown; shoes, in several cities in the northeastern part of Massachusetts; silk goods, in Paterson, New Jersey; jewelry, in and around Providence, Rhode Island; and agricultural machinery, in Chicago.

In each of these cases there is a story similar to, if not quite as charming as, that of Catherine Evans. An accident led to the establishment of the industry in a particular location, and thereafter cumulative processes took over. The Massachusetts shoe industry owed its start to the Welsh cobbler John Adams Dagyr, who set up shop in 1750; the dominance of the Providence jewelry industry (which still makes it into our list of highly localized industries) began when a local man invented "filled" gold in 1794; the reign of Troy as the detachable collar and cuff center (ah, fashion!) was inaugurated by a Methodist minister in the 1820s.

What is important to the economist here is, of course, not the initial accident but the nature of the cumulative process that allows such accidents to have large and long-lasting effects. What the historical record shows us are two things. First, such cumulative processes are pervasive; Silicon Valley is not at all unique either in time or space, but is simply a glitzy version of a traditional phenomenon. And second, Marshall's first two reasons for localization, labor pooling and the supply of specialized inputs, play a large role even when pure technological externalities seem unlikely to be important.

Europe versus America

How does increasing economic integration affect the importance of geographical concentration? Does location cease to matter in an integrated economy, as many suppose, or do low transportation and transaction costs actually foster geographic concentration, as the discussion above suggests?

A comparison of the United States with Europe offers an interesting test. The Western European economy is roughly comparable in population and output to that of the United States; but until recently it has been considerably less integrated. How has this affected the importance of local advantages?

Here as in the previous section I have tried some first-pass quantification in an effort to get an empirical feel for the issues. Again the approach is crude but suggestive; because I now need to deal with international data, the results are even cruder than those for U.S. industries. But they are, I think, interesting.

The starting point of this piece of work is the observation that the "Great Regions" of the United States—the Northeast (New England plus Middle Atlantic), the Midwest (East North Central and West North Central), the South, and the West—are comparable in population and economic size to the European Big Four. So one might expect the degree of economic differentiation among U.S. regions and among European nations to be roughly similar. In fact, one might expect localization to have proceeded further in Europe, if only because the distances involved in the United States are so much larger.

To make the comparison, one needs comparable data. This is a problem. The best I have been able to come up with is a set of employment statistics by (more or less) two-digit industries for European nations, which can be compared with regional employment statistics for (more or less) the same industries for U.S. regions. It's a crude comparison, but the best that I could do.

Using this data, I construct indices of regional/national divergence, which are as follows. Let s_i be the share of industry i in total manufacturing employment in some region/country; and let a "star" indicate that we are referring to some other region/country. The index then is

$$\sum_i |s_i - s_i^*|$$

Table 16-3
Indices of Industrial Specialization

A: U.S. regions, 1977	NE	MW	S	W
NE	—	.224	.247	.242
MW	—	—	.336	.182
S	—	—	—	.271

B: EC countries, 1985	FR	FRG	IT	UK
FR	—	.200	.197	.083
FRG	—	—	.175	.184
IT	—	—	—	.184

Suppose that two regions had identical industrial structures, i.e., that industry shares of employment were the same for all i. Then the index would of course be zero. A little less obviously, if two regions had completely disjointed industry structures, the index would be 2 (because each share in each region would be counted in full). So the index is a rough way of quantifying differences in structures, and hence regional specialization.

What I have done is to calculate this index for twelve pairs of regions/nations: for U.S. regions compared with one another, and for Europe's Big Four compared with one another. (I don't trust the comparability of the data enough to try the direct U.S.-Europe indices). The results are shown in Table 16-3.

The result does not come through as strongly as I would have liked, probably because the data is grossly overaggregated, but it is there: European nations are *less* specialized than U.S. regions. You might have the impression that the United States is a great homogeneous society in which regional differences have faded away; and culturally you would be right. But in terms of the economic roles they play, U.S. regions are more distinct than European nations.

A somewhat clearer picture emerges if I cheat a little and focus on what I think is the most revealing case. Compare the specializations of the Midwest and the South, on one hand, and of Germany and Italy, on the other. In both cases we are in effect comparing a traditional heavy industrial producer with a traditional light, labor-intensive producer. And as we see in Table 16-4, which compares employment shares in selected sectors, the patterns of revealed comparative advantage in key industries are similar.

Table 16-4
Industrial Specialization
(share of manufacturing employment)

	Germany	Italy	U.S. Midwest	U.S. South
Textiles	3.7	9.1	0.3	11.7
Apparel	2.6	5.6	2.4	10.6
Machinery	15.8	12.9	15.0	7.1
Trans. equip.	13.2	10.4	12.8	5.9
Sum of share differences		35.2		62.6

But the degree of specialization linked to this revealed comparative advantage is very different. At one extreme, the Midwest has essentially no textile industry, compared with Germany's still substantial one. At the other, the South produces far less machinery than Italy.

Let me offer another illustrative comparison, this one involving the automotive industry. Table 16-5 compares the regional distribution of the U.S. auto industry with the national distribution of the European industry. What it shows is that the U.S. industry is far more localized. In essence, the U.S. industry is a Midwestern phenomenon, with only a scattering of assembly plants in other parts of the country. The European equivalent would be a concentration of half the industry within 150 kilometers of Wolfsburg.

So although the data are spotty, the conclusion seems clear: localization has gone much further in America than in Europe.

Why? Obviously the reason is the existence of barriers to trade. It may be helpful to return to one of the localization stories from the previous section, the one that focused on interdiate goods. There I pointed out the strong analogy between

Table 16-5
Distribution of Auto Production

U.S.		EC	
Midwest	66.3	Germany	38.5
South	25.4	France	31.1
West	5.1	Italy	17.6
Northeast	3.2	UK	12.9

the core-periphery model and a simplified model in which each manufactured good within an industry is both a final and an intermediate good. In both cases concentration tends to take place when transportation costs fall and economies of scale increase. (The difference is that the share of manufacturing in demand in the core-periphery model corresponds, in the case of the intermediate goods model, to the share of output that is used as an input.)

Consider what happened during the nineteenth century: in both Europe and America, transportation costs fell and economies of scale became more important. Thus the logic of localization grew stronger. But in Europe the fall of transport costs was opposed by tariffs, often rising ones. And of course for 45 years after 1913 Europe was fragmented by exchange controls and, alas, worse things. Even since the formation of the EC, borders have remained significant nuisance barriers to trade, supplemented by differences in regulation and more subtle government policies that discriminate in favor of national products. The end result is that European economic localization is still far short of U.S. levels.

Implications

This paper has tried to accomplish three things. First, I have tried to suggest a framework for thinking about the forces that lead to geographical clustering of industries. This framework identifies three factors, in particular, that foster clustering: strong economies of scale, strong forward and backward linkages, and—perhaps surprisingly—low transportation costs. This last point suggests that as the world becomes more closely integrated, production will often become more, not less, geographically clustered.

Second, I have offered a rough look at U.S. data, which suggests both the pervasiveness of geographical clustering—often based on seemingly trivial historical accidents—and that such clustering is not exclusively or even especially characteristic of high-technology industries.

Third, I have presented some rough data suggesting that European industries are *less* localized than their U.S. counterparts; this supports the view that as the world economy becomes more integrated, location will matter more, not less, for competitive advantage.

Appendix

	SIC	SIC INDUSTRY	GINI	EMPLOYEES ('000s)	CUMULATIVE EMPLOYEES
1	303	RECLAIMED RUBBER	0.5	0.7	0.7
2	313	BOOT AND SHOE CUT STOCK AND FINDINGS	0.482845	6.8	7.5
3	315	LEATHER, GLOVES, AND MITTENS	0.48233	3.9	11.4
4	222	WEAVING MILLS, SYNTHETICS	0.476676	140.8	152.2
5	237	FUR GOODS	0.468169	3.4	155.6
6	223	WEAVING AND FINISHING MILLS, WOOL	0.451512	13.1	168.7
7	221	WEAVING MILLS, COTTON	0.443084	76.9	245.6
8	319	LEATHER GOODS, N.E.C.	0.442542	7	252.6
9	227	FLOOR COVERING MILLS	0.432963	41.9	294.5
10	228	YARN AND THREAD MILLS	0.428421	108.6	403.1
11	386	PHOTOGRAPHIC EQUIPMENT AND SUPPLIES	0.428276	119.3	522.4
12	277	GREETING CARD PUBLISHING	0.427133	20.8	543.2
13	224	NARROW FABRIC MILLS	0.423601	17.5	560.7
14	385	OPHTHALMIC GOODS	0.414319	25.8	586.5
15	376	GUIDED MISSILES, SPACE VEHICLES, PARTS	0.411017	146.3	732.8
16	374	RAILROAD EQUIPMENT	0.410767	34.5	767.3
17	226	TEXTILE FINISHING, EXCEPT WOOL	0.410014	58.1	825.4
18	304	RUBBER AND PLASTICS HOSE AND BELTING	0.408587	24.9	850.3
19	235	HATS, CAPS, AND MILLINERY	0.407575	15.7	866
20	316	LUGGAGE	0.404685	16	882
21	302	RUBBER AND PLASTICS FOOTWEAR	0.402163	17.6	899.6

STATE WITH HIGHEST # EMPLOYEES			STATE WITH HIGHEST RATIO OF SIC/TOTAL		
1ST	2ND	3RD	1ST	2ND	3RD
ALABAMA	ALASKA	ARIZONA	WYOMING	WISCONSIN	WEST VIRGINIA
2 MASSACHUSETTS	1.6 MISSOURI	0.75 MAINE	MAINE 0.17980161	MISSOURI 0.11200893	MASSACHUSETTS 0.08791508
1 NEW YORK	0.5 WISCONSIN	ALABAMA	WISCONSIN 0.04880094	NEW YORK 0.03553783	WYOMING
52.4 SOUTH CAROLINA	34.6 NORTH CAROLINA	14.2 VIRGINIA	GEORGIA 0.72945278	SOUTH CAROLINA 0.72789988	NORTH CAROLINA 0.24502494
3 NEW YORK	ALABAMA	ALASKA	NEW YORK 0.12229195	WYOMING	WISCONSIN
3.5 GEORGIA	2.1 MAINE	1.75 PENNSYLVANIA	MAINE 0.26132998	RHODE ISLAND 0.21233546	NEW HAMPSHIRE 0.12941582
26.6 NORTH CAROLINA	17.1 GEORGIA	16.8 SOUTH CAROLINA	SOUTH CAROLINA 0.10955927	GEORGIA 0.08251046	NORTH CAROLINA 0.0807355
1.2 CALIFORNIA	1.1 TEXAS	0.7 NEW YORK	TEXAS 0.02793562	MASSACHUSETTS 0.0213508	CALIFORNIA 0.01602335
23.9 GEORGIA	3.7 CALIFORNIA	2.7 PENNSYLVANIA	GEORGIA 0.21165236	SOUTH CAROLINA 0.02872522	VIRGINIA 0.01960466
54.4 NORTH CAROLINA	17.1 GEORGIA	9.4 SOUTH CAROLINA	NORTH CAROLINA 0.11691717	GEORGIA 0.05842591	SOUTH CAROLINA 0.04340744
5.6 ILLINOIS	5.2 CALIFORNIA	5 NEW JERSEY	COLORADO 0.02941722	MINNESOTA 0.01689541	OKLAHOMA 0.01520488
3.5 ARKANSAS	3.5 MISSOURI	1.75 KANSAS	ARKANSAS 0.16110897	KANSAS 0.0907457	MISSOURI 0.08010254
3.5 NORTH CAROLINA	2.6 RHODE ISLAND	2 PENNSYLVANIA	RHODE ISLAND 0.2361517	NEW HAMPSHIRE 0.08718929	NORTH CAROLINA 0.0466809
3.5 MASSACHUSETTS	3.5 NEW YORK	3.1 CALIFORNIA	ARIZONA 0.08289383	RHODE ISLAND 0.06160785	MASSACHUSETTS 0.04054998
85 CALIFORNIA	3.5 ARIZONA	3.5 COLORADO	CALIFORNIA 0.05430562	UTAH 0.05192087	ARIZONA 0.02923665
13.3 PENNSYLVANIA	10.1 ILLINOIS	1.75 INDIANA	PENNSYLVANIA 0.06344917	ILLINOIS 0.05340753	WEST VIRGINIA 0.04251921
16 SOUTH CAROLINA	10.9 NORTH CAROLINA	5.5 GEORGIA	SOUTH CAROLINA 0.1381052	NORTH CAROLINA 0.04378845	RHODE ISLAND 0.04377233
6.5 OHIO	2.7 NORTH CAROLINA	1.75 COLORADO	NEBRASKA 0.14214258	COLORADO 0.07047136	OHIO 0.04665307
3.5 NEW YORK	2.7 MISSOURI	1.75 IOWA	IOWA 0.09498297	MISSOURI 0.0818664	NEW YORK 0.03089754
3.6 NEW YORK	2.8 TENNESSEE	1.75 COLORADO	RHODE ISLAND 0.17384966	COLORADO 0.10967106	TENNESSEE 0.06924645
3.5 FLORIDA	3.5 MAINE	1.75 CALIFORNIA	MAINE 0.32418775	NEW HAMPSHIRE 0.16857146	MARYLAND 0.08093586

Appendix (*continued*)

	SIC	SIC INDUSTRY	GINI	EMPLOYEES ('000s)	CUMULATIVE EMPLOYEES
22	396	COSTUME JEWELRY AND NOTIONS	0.400823	41.9	941.5
23	391	JEWELRY, SILVERWARE, AND PLATED WARE	0.397361	50.2	991.7
24	375	MOTORCYCLES, BICYCLES, AND PARTS	0.396409	13	1004.7
25	387	WATCHES, CLOCKS, AND WATCHCASES	0.388946	16.8	1021.5
26	311	LEATHER AND LEATHER PRODUCTS	0.387232	19.5	1041
27	317	HANDBAGS AND OTHER PERSONAL LEATHER GOODS	0.379857	25.3	1066.3
28	333	PRIMARY NONFERROUS METALS	0.366064	43.9	1110.2
29	225	KNITTING MILLS	0.365623	204.8	1315
30	373	SHIP AND BOAT BUILDING AND REPAIRING	0.363088	205	1520
31	372	AIRCRAFT AND PARTS	0.352313	538.6	2058.6
32	393	MUSICAL INSTRUMENTS	0.345101	17.8	2076.4
33	253	PUBLIC BUILDING AND RELATED FURNITURE	0.344445	18.8	2095.2
34	379	MISCELLANEOUS TRANSPORTATION EQUIPMENT	0.326485	42.9	2138.1
35	352	FARM AND GARDEN MACHINERY	0.324905	113.8	2251.9
36	272	PERIODICALS	0.324702	94	2345.9
37	287	AGRICULTURAL CHEMICALS	0.324638	50.9	2396.8
38	383	OPTICAL INSTRUMENTS AND LENSES	0.323826	50	2446.8
39	301	TIRES AND INNER TUBES	0.320952	70.3	2517.1
40	365	RADIO AND TV RECEIVING EQUIPMENT	0.320622	65.6	2582.7
41	282	PLASTICS MATERIALS AND SYNTHETICS	0.319335	141	2723.7
42	348	ORDNANCE AND ACCESSORIES, N.E.C.	0.316472	79.4	2803.1

STATE WITH HIGHEST # EMPLOYEES			STATE WITH HIGHEST RATIO OF SIC/TOTAL		
1ST	2ND	3RD	1ST	2ND	3RD
12.4 RHODE ISLAND	6.1 NEW YORK	3.8 CONNECTICUT	RHODE ISLAND 0.47039581	CONNECTICUT 0.04240255	NEBRASKA 0.03620201
15.3 NEW YORK	9.2 RHODE ISLAND	6.7 MASSACHUSETTS	RHODE ISLAND 0.2912996	UTAH 0.0756576	NEW MEXICO 0.05477504
3.5 TENNESSEE	1.75 OHIO	1.75 PENNSYLVANIA	NEBRASKA 0.11668187	TENNESSEE 0.106533	OKLAHOMA 0.05980031
2.8 NEW YORK	1.75 ARKANSAS	1.75 CONNECTICUT	ARKANSAS 0.09973413	CONNECTICUT 0.04870240	MISSISSIPPI 0.03983229
2.7 NEW YORK	2.6 WISCONSIN	2.5 MASSACHUSETTS	MAINE 0.15804012	NEW HAMPSHIRE 0.06085802	WISCONSIN 0.05075297
8.9 NEW YORK	2.5 MASSACHUSETTS	1.9 CALIFORNIA	NEW YORK 0.04875566	RHODE ISLAND 0.04711905	MASSACHUSETTS 0.02953669
6.4 WASHINGTON	5.5 TEXAS	2.7 ARIZONA	MONTANA 0.35162808	NEW MEXICO 0.09395353	WASHINGTON 0.09384492
80.5 NORTH CAROLINA	22.5 PENNSYLVANIA	18.6 NEW YORK	NORTH CAROLINA 0.09174347	TENNESSEE 0.02434445	VIRGINIA 0.02269031
21.5 CALIFORNIA	16.4 MISSISSIPPI	14.9 FLORIDA	MISSISSIPPI 0.07137947	FLORIDA 0.02943345	MAINE 0.0278327
112.4 CALIFORNIA	61.3 CONNECTICUT	43.2 TEXAS	KANSAS 0.06568389	CONNECTICUT 0.05321286	NEVADA 0.02866037
2.3 ILLINOIS	2.2 INDIANA	1.9 CALIFORNIA	MISSISSIPPI 0.08772056	ARKANSAS 0.04034189	INDIANA 0.03861541
1.9 MICHIGAN	1.8 TEXAS	1.75 CONNECTICUT	ARKANSAS 0.0814849	CONNECTICUT 0.04352138	MISSISSIPPI 0.03559482
8.8 CALIFORNIA	6.8 INDIANA	5.1 PENNSYLVANIA	INDIANA 0.04952331	NEBRASKA 0.03535814	MICHIGAN 0.02161823
20.5 ILLINOIS	19.2 IOWA	11.1 WISCONSIN	NORTH DAKOTA 0.2130256	IOWA 0.14376936	NEBRASKA 0.11374261
34.8 NEW YORK	10.7 ILLINOIS	7.4 CALIFORNIA	DC 0.40170438	NEW YORK 0.05131058	ILLINOIS 0.02076616
8 FLORIDA	4.7 LOUISIANA	3.8 TEXAS	IDAHO 0.13643799	LOUISIANA 0.08322136	FLORIDA 0.06364744
11 CALIFORNIA	8.3 MASSACHUSETTS	4.5 NEW YORK	NEW HAMPSHIRE 0.11867431	MASSACHUSETTS 0.04961927	CONNECTICUT 0.03272808
9.6 ALABAMA	7.2 OKLAHOMA	6.3 NORTH CAROLINA	OKLAHOMA 0.10616043	ALABAMA 0.07495986	IOWA 0.03757628
8.9 CALIFORNIA	5.2 TENNESSEE	4.4 ILLINOIS	TENNESSEE 0.03136599	ARKANSAS 0.02554167	MISSOURI 0.02539837
17.9 SOUTH CAROLINA	17.4 TENNESSEE	15.9 VIRGINIA	DELAWARE 0.10963564	SOUTH CAROLINA 0.06366491	VIRGINIA 0.05293138
9.6 MINNESOTA	7.7 CALIFORNIA	5.7 CONNECTICUT	VERMONT 0.08391374	NEVADA 0.08332029	MINNESOTA 0.06962927

Appendix (*continued*)

	SIC	SIC INDUSTRY	GINI	EMPLOYEES ('000s)	CUMULATIVE EMPLOYEES
43	334	SECONDARY NONFERROUS METALS	0.310073	19.2	2822.3
44	286	INDUSTRIAL ORGANIC CHEMICALS	0.309039	143.6	2965.9
45	314	FOOTWEAR, EXCEPT RUBBER	0.308738	121.4	3087.3
46	351	ENGINES AND TURBINES	0.305607	112	3199.3
47	331	BLAST FURNACE AND BASIC STEEL PRODUCTS	0.303562	365.7	3565
48	229	MISCELLANEOUS TEXTILE GOODS	0.303407	55.8	3620.8
49	371	MOTOR VEHICLES AND EQUIPMENT	0.302518	615.6	4236.4
50	395	PENS, PENCILS, AND OFFICE AND ART SUPPLIES	0.30166	32.2	4268.6
51	236	CHILDREN'S OUTERWEAR	0.296566	71.3	4339.9
52	339	MISCELLANEOUS PRIMARY METAL PRODUCTS	0.293852	25.9	4365.8
53	234	WOMEN'S AND CHILDREN'S UNDERGARMENTS	0.292174	81.6	4447.4
54	232	MEN'S AND BOYS' FURNISHINGS	0.289464	298.9	4746.3
55	357	OFFICE AND COMPUTING MACHINES	0.283499	404	5150.3
56	231	MEN'S AND BOYS' SUITS AND COATS	0.281515	75.2	5225.5
57	281	INDUSTRIAL INORGANIC CHEMICALS	0.278271	107.7	5333.2
58	363	HOUSEHOLD APPLIANCES	0.27411	129.4	5462.6
59	381	ENGINEERING AND SCIENTIFIC INSTRUMENTS	0.266791	42.8	5505.4
60	238	MISCELLANEOUS APPAREL AND ACCESSORIES	0.259691	50	5555.4
61	251	HOUSEHOLD FURNITURE	0.255488	263	5818.4
62	259	MISCELLANEOUS FURNITURE AND FIXTURES	0.255273	35.8	5854.2
63	346	METAL FORGINGS AND STAMPINGS	0.254278	236.3	6090.5

STATE WITH HIGHEST # EMPLOYEES			STATE WITH HIGHEST RATIO OF SIC/TOTAL		
1ST	2ND	3RD	1ST	2ND	3RD
2.4 CALIFORNIA	2 ILLINOIS	1.75 SOUTH CAROLINA	SOUTH CAROLINA 0.04570914	ALABAMA 0.03144882	INDIANA 0.02115437
32.9 TEXAS	15.7 LOUISIANA	14.4 NEW JERSEY	WEST VIRGINIA 0.13484156	LOUISIANA 0.09853714	TEXAS 0.04072913
15.5 MAINE	13.6 MISSOURI	11.2 PENNSYLVANIA	MAINE 0.20813937	NEW HAMPSHIRE 0.08658281	MISSOURI 0.0533288
19.6 WISCONSIN	11.8 ILLINOIS	11 NEW YORK	WISCONSIN 0.06661328	MARYLAND 0.02543699	MICHIGAN 0.01966632
85.3 PENNSYLVANIA	56.4 INDIANA	53.1 OHIO	WEST VIRGINIA 0.05990128	INDIANA 0.04818503	PENNSYLVANIA 0.03838994
6.4 NORTH CAROLINA	5.5 GEORGIA	5.1 SOUTH CAROLINA	RHODE ISLAND 0.05412217	SOUTH CAROLINA 0.04583552	MAINE 0.04090111
203.4 MICHIGAN	81.5 OHIO	38.3 INDIANA	MICHIGAN 0.07660725	OHIO 0.02366057	DELAWARE 0.02312899
4.1 NEW JERSEY	4 CALIFORNIA	3.7 NEW YORK	RHODE ISLAND 0.08638492	IOWA 0.03704926	NEW JERSEY 0.03483975
9 NEW YORK	8.8 PENNSYLVANIA	7.5 NORTH CAROLINA	SOUTH CAROLINA 0.04642165	MAINE 0.04001195	RHODE ISLAND 0.03901255
3.3 MICHIGAN	2.8 PENNSYLVANIA	2.5 CALIFORNIA	MICHIGAN 0.02954144	CONNECTICUT 0.02166227	INDIANA 0.02111039
9.9 NORTH CAROLINA	9.8 NEW YORK	9 PENNSYLVANIA	ALABAMA 0.05448886	MISSISSIPPI 0.0492046	GEORGIA 0.03001187
32.9 GEORGIA	30.7 TENNESSEE	28.1 ALABAMA	MISSISSIPPI 0.05910478	ALABAMA 0.05160518	GEORGIA 0.04084221
112.7 CALIFORNIA	36.6 MASSACHUSETTS	33.6 MINNESOTA	MINNESOTA 0.04789597	ARIZONA 0.04688719	COLORADO 0.04293769
16.1 PENNSYLVANIA	9.3 NEW YORK	6.3 MASSACHUSETTS	PENNSYLVANIA 0.0352372	MARYLAND 0.03355517	GEORGIA 0.02861867
16.4 TENNESSEE	8.8 OHIO	6.3 WASHINGTON	HAWAII 0.12642945	TENNESSEE 0.06025424	NEVADA 0.05733138
16.1 OHIO	14.4 ILLINOIS	11.6 TENNESSEE	SOUTH DAKOTA 0.04232515	TENNESSEE 0.03547179	IOWA 0.03160926
5.7 CALIFORNIA	4.3 MICHIGAN	3.9 NEW JERSEY	DELAWARE 0.1663342	ARIZONA 0.04996871	WASHINGTON 0.02632022
10.7 NEW YORK	3.7 CALIFORNIA	3.5 NORTH CAROLINA	MARYLAND 0.04232714	MISSISSIPPI 0.03568973	NEW YORK 0.02965987
67.4 NORTH CAROLINA	30.3 CALIFORNIA	20.1 VIRGINIA	NORTH CAROLINA 0.05981545	MISSISSIPPI 0.04037147	VIRGINIA 0.03587364
4.8 CALIFORNIA	3.4 ILLINOIS	3.2 NEW YORK	UTAH 0.04546702	RHODE ISLAND 0.03329922	MARYLAND 0.02728436
44.5 MICHIGAN	39.1 OHIO	24.6 ILLINOIS	MICHIGAN 0.04366302	OHIO 0.0295719	WISCONSIN 0.02029689

Appendix (*continued*)

	SIC	SIC INDUSTRY	GINI	EMPLOYEES ('000s)	CUMULATIVE EMPLOYEES
64	353	CONSTRUCTION AND RELATED MACHINERY	0.25105	325.8	6416.3
65	274	MISCELLANEOUS PUBLISHING	0.244823	45.3	6461.6
66	345	SCREW MACHINE PRODUCTS, BOLTS, ETC.	0.239701	94	6555.6
67	271	NEWSPAPERS	0.237544	401.5	6957.1
68	273	BOOKS	0.237544	111.7	7068.8
69	279	PRINTING TRADE SERVICES	0.235163	56	7124.8
70	283	DRUGS	0.234789	165.7	7290.5
71	278	BLANKBOOKS AND BOOKBINDING	0.232561	61.2	7351.7
72	341	METAL CANS AND SHIPPING CONTAINERS	0.232013	58.9	7410.6
73	233	WOMEN'S AND MISSES' OUTERWEAR	0.231918	418.9	7829.5
74	354	METALWORKING MACHINERY	0.231087	283.2	8112.7
75	252	OFFICE FURNITURE	0.230208	58.7	8171.4
76	382	MEASURING AND CONTROLLING DEVICES	0.224846	227.7	8399.1
77	366	COMMUNICATION EQUIPMENT	0.224418	600.6	8999.7
78	332	IRON AND STEEL FOUNDRIES	0.22053	157.4	9157.1
79	306	FABRICATED RUBBER PRODUCTS, N.E.C.	0.217496	89.4	9246.5
80	367	ELECTRONIC COMPONENTS AND ACCESSORIES	0.218259	515.8	9762.3
81	336	NONFERROUS FOUNDRIES	0.215594	75.4	9837.7
82	284	SOAPS, CLEANERS, AND TOILET GOODS	0.210857	127.3	9965
83	343	PLUMBING AND HEATING, EXCEPT ELECTRIC	0.201985	47.9	10012.9
84	285	PAINTS AND ALLIED PRODUCTS	0.201037	54.1	10067
85	361	ELECTRIC DISTRIBUTING EQUIPMENT	0.197298	105.3	10172.3

STATE WITH HIGHEST # EMPLOYEES			STATE WITH HIGHEST RATIO OF SIC/TOTAL		
1ST	2ND	3RD	1ST	2ND	3RD
TEXAS 73.3	ILLINOIS 39.2	OHIO 23.1	OKLAHOMA 0.04835908	WYOMING 0.04363588	IOWA 0.0410635
NEW YORK 9.6	CALIFORNIA 5.4	ILLINOIS 2.7	DC 0.2344384	COLORADO 0.03984265	KANSAS 0.03571449
ILLINOIS 14.4	CALIFORNIA 12.8	MICHIGAN 9.4	RHODE ISLAND 0.02959143	CONNECTICUT 0.02884846	ILLINOIS 0.02794698
CALIFORNIA 46.1	NEW YORK 31.2	TEXAS 25.7	NEW YORK 0.03263308	VERMONT 0.03067643	MINNESOTA 0.02062281
NEW YORK 26.3	ILLINOIS 7.9	MASSACHUSETTS 7.5	NEW YORK 0.03263308	VERMONT 0.03067643	MINNESOTA 0.02062281
NEW YORK 9.7	CALIFORNIA 5.7	ILLINOIS 5.6	DC 0.14750083	MARYLAND 0.02543699	NEW YORK 0.02400707
NEW JERSEY 31.6	NEW YORK 16.7	INDIANA 16.2	NEW JERSEY 0.0521809	INDIANA 0.03054573	DELAWARE 0.01841306
NEW YORK 8.3	ILLINOIS 6.5	CALIFORNIA 6.2	MASSACHUSETTS 0.02393244	NEW JERSEY 0.02146035	MISSOURI 0.02100167
CALIFORNIA 9.3	ILLINOIS 6.9	OHIO 4.7	COLORADO 0.0297918	MARYLAND 0.02487556	ILLINOIS 0.02137145
NEW YORK 87	CALIFORNIA 63	PENNSYLVANIA 54.4	HAWAII 0.03157653	NEW YORK 0.02878488	PENNSYLVANIA 0.02137381
MICHIGAN 48.6	OHIO 43.2	ILLINOIS 27.3	VERMONT 0.04570895	MICHIGAN 0.03978877	OHIO 0.02726194
MICHIGAN 11.7	CALIFORNIA 8.7	NORTH CAROLINA 5.7	MICHIGAN 0.04621312	IOWA 0.0254043	NORTH CAROLINA 0.02266449
CALIFORNIA 43.2	MASSACHUSETTS 19.4	PENNSYLVANIA 18.9	NEVADA 0.06779303	VERMONT 0.02926109	NEW HAMPSHIRE 0.02680391
CALIFORNIA 137.3	NEW YORK 51.1	TEXAS 45.6	MARYLAND 0.0429625	NEW MEXICO 0.03204786	FLORIDA 0.02582392
OHIO 21.9	MICHIGAN 14	PENNSYLVANIA 13.7	ALABAMA 0.03138706	WISCONSIN 0.0309548	OHIO 0.02486598
OHIO 18.1	CALIFORNIA 7.3	MASSACHUSETTS 5.4	OHIO 0.03618323	NEW HAMPSHIRE 0.03318633	ARKANSAS 0.02945160
CALIFORNIA 135.1	NEW YORK 57.1	TEXAS 33.2	ARIZONA 0.05808066	VERMONT 0.02503463	CALIFORNIA 0.02448165
OHIO 9.9	CALIFORNIA 8.5	MICHIGAN 7.6	OHIO 0.02346551	MICHIGAN 0.02337006	WISCONSIN 0.02322251
NEW JERSEY 25	ILLINOIS 11.7	NEW YORK 11.7	NEW JERSEY 0.05373517	MISSOURI 0.02131513	MARYLAND 0.01982207
CALIFORNIA 6.2	ILLINOIS 3.5	PENNSYLVANIA 3.3	VERMONT 0.05961304	WEST VIRGINIA 0.03062448	KENTUCKY 0.02803507
CALIFORNIA 6.5	ILLINOIS 5.9	OHIO 5	NEW JERSEY 0.02174794	ILLINOIS 0.0198955	KENTUCKY 0.01985775
PENNSYLVANIA 13.9	ILLINOIS 9.4	CALIFORNIA 7.7	MISSISSIPPI 0.02626737	KENTUCKY 0.02550579	PENNSYLVANIA 0.021726

Appendix (*continued*)

	SIC	SIC INDUSTRY	GINI	EMPLOYEES ('000s)	CUMULATIVE EMPLOYEES
86	335	NONFERROUS ROLLING AND DRAWING	0.194648	166.7	10339
87	364	ELECTRIC LIGHTING AND WIRING EQUIPMENT	0.186535	159.4	10498.4
88	254	PARTITIONS AND FIXTURES	0.182132	59.7	10558.1
89	239	MISCELLANEOUS FABRICATED TEXTILE PRODUCTS	0.180902	173.8	10731.9
90	362	ELECTRICAL INDUSTRIAL APPARATUS	0.180583	191.4	10923.3
91	347	METAL SERVICES, N.E.C.	0.180022	96.9	11020.2
92	342	CUTLERY, HAND TOOLS, AND HARDWARE	0.17853	140.9	11161.1
93	289	MISCELLANEOUS CHEMICAL PRODUCTS	0.173693	82.3	11243.4
94	384	MEDICAL INSTRUMENTS AND SUPPLIES	0.170018	141.3	11384.7
95	358	REFRIGERATION AND SERVICE MACHINERY	0.163089	171.7	11556.4
96	394	TOYS AND SPORTING GOODS	0.160812	98.9	11655.3
97	276	MANIFOLD BUSINESS FORMS	0.155267	49.5	11704.8
98	356	GENERAL INDUSTRIAL MACHINERY	0.153676	313.6	12018.4
99	355	SPECIAL INDUSTRY MACHINERY	0.148829	182.5	12200.9
100	349	MISCELLANEOUS FABRICATED METAL PRODUCTS	0.140874	283.6	12484.5
101	369	MISCELLANEOUS ELECTRICAL EQUIPMENT AND SUPPLIES	0.137169	147.1	12631.6
102	399	MISCELLANEOUS MANUFACTURES	0.128871	141.7	12773.3
103	344	FABRICATED STRUCTURAL METAL PRODUCTS	0.119871	421.9	13195.2
104	359	MISCELLANEOUS MACHINERY, EXCEPT ELECTRICAL	0.109036	282.1	13477.3
105	275	COMMERCIAL PRINTING	0.101342	451.7	13929
106	307	MISCELLANEOUS PLASTICS PRODUCTS	0.096105	478.9	14407.9

STATE WITH HIGHEST # EMPLOYEES			STATE WITH HIGHEST RATIO OF SIC/TOTAL		
1ST	2ND	3RD	1ST	2ND	3RD
13.8 INDIANA	12.1 NEW YORK	11 ILLINOIS	WEST VIRGINIA 0.0527983	RHODE ISLAND 0.05053544	NEVADA 0.03968585
18.7 NEW YORK	17.5 ILLINOIS	16.2 OHIO	RHODE ISLAND 0.03490081	WEST VIRGINIA 0.02454057	ILLINOIS 0.02002857
7.5 CALIFORNIA	6.7 NEW YORK	5.9 ILLINOIS	NEBRASKA 0.0592856	ARKANSAS 0.02806588	ILLINOIS 0.01802926
25.4 NEW YORK	18.1 CALIFORNIA	15.2 NORTH CAROLINA	NORTH DAKOTA 0.05230649	HAWAII 0.02686132	SOUTH CAROLINA 0.02423794
20.6 OHIO	19.8 WISCONSIN	15.5 NEW YORK	WISCONSIN 0.03937731	ARKANSAS 0.03351567	OHIO 0.01923497
17.2 CALIFORNIA	8.7 ILLINOIS	7.9 OHIO	RHODE ISLAND 0.04100832	MICHIGAN 0.01842402	CALIFORNIA 0.01659109
13 CALIFORNIA	13 ILLINOIS	11.7 MICHIGAN	CONNECTICUT 0.03616912	MICHIGAN 0.01925273	WEST VIRGINIA 0.01804577
7.9 CALIFORNIA	7.7 OHIO	6.8 NEW JERSEY	NEW MEXICO 0.03341078	KANSAS 0.02621087	NEW JERSEY 0.02260768
23.1 CALIFORNIA	12.2 NEW YORK	10.3 PENNSYLVANIA	SOUTH DAKOTA 0.09044144	UTAH 0.06450975	NEBRASKA 0.05009696
16.5 OHIO	14.7 NEW YORK	11.8 TEXAS	KENTUCKY 0.03307201	MINNESOTA 0.02213679	TENNESSEE 0.02004972
13.1 NEW YORK	12.2 CALIFORNIA	7.1 NEW JERSEY	RHODE ISLAND 0.02812532	NEW JERSEY 0.01964306	VERMONT 0.01924816
5.2 CALIFORNIA	4.5 OHIO	3.9 TEXAS	VERMONT 0.05768616	UTAH 0.02630657	KANSAS 0.02614733
32.7 OHIO	26 ILLINOIS	25.5 PENNSYLVANIA	OKLAHOMA 0.0274339	NEW HAMPSHIRE 0.02324615	CONNECTICUT 0.02206521
16.5 OHIO	16.2 CALIFORNIA	15.1 MASSACHUSETTS	NEW HAMPSHIRE 0.02786872	MASSACHUSETTS 0.02473184	WISCONSIN 0.02398599
27.5 TEXAS	25.2 OHIO	23.9 CALIFORNIA	OKLAHOMA 0.0215641	RHODE ISLAND 0.02129772	IOWA 0.0210329
13.8 CALIFORNIA	13.6 INDIANA	12.2 OHIO	VERMONT 0.04529402	INDIANA 0.02888579	COLORADO 0.02181279
16.9 NEW YORK	15.2 ILLINOIS	14.7 CALIFORNIA	NEVADA 0.08092515	ILLINOIS 0.01956924	NEW YORK 0.01652998
46.6 TEXAS	35.1 CALIFORNIA	30.8 PENNSYLVANIA	OKLAHOMA 0.03144749	LOUISIANA 0.02349838	RHODE ISLAND 0.02222789
40.6 CALIFORNIA	23.2 TEXAS	19.1 NEW YORK	NEW MEXICO 0.01949455	OKLAHOMA 0.01653465	LOUISIANA 0.01597420
47.6 CALIFORNIA	44.6 NEW YORK	44.4 ILLINOIS	DC 0.06008446	MINNESOTA 0.02129156	ILLINOIS 0.01793218
55.4 CALIFORNIA	38.3 OHIO	34.3 ILLINOIS	NEVADA 0.03223319	NEW HAMPSHIRE 0.0205325	NEW JERSEY 0.01662628

17
Managing DMNCs: A Search for a New Paradigm

Y. L. Doz and C. K. Prahalad

The increasing intensity of global competition (Porter, 1986), the development of multinational companies (Dunning and Pearce, 1985; Stopford, Dunning, and Haberich, 1980) and the attendant academic and managerial interest in the role of the diversified multinational firm (DMNC) (Bartlett and Ghoshal, 1989; Ghoshal, 1987; Prahalad and Doz, 1987) is too well documented in the literature to merit repetition. While there has been a lot of debate on the nature of global competition and that of the DMNC, very little attention has been paid to the conceptual and theoretical frameworks used to analyze DMNCs and their management. Many attempts have been made to analyze aspects of the MNC starting from an established theoretical base. For example, Buckley and Casson (1986) and Hennart (1982) have attempted to seek a rationale for the MNC using a transaction cost perspective. Others (e.g., Dunning, 1973, 1980, 1981) have emphasized the need for an "eclectic" theory explaining the DMNCs. We will argue, in this article, that on the whole, scholarly research in the area of the functioning of the MNC has suffered from a desire, among some scholars, to persist with existing paradigms, and among others from the ignorance of what existing theories could bring them. Since existing paradigms, by the very nature of their underlying simplifying assumptions, are not fully adequate to capture the complexity and richness of the DMNC, and since discipline-based researchers have seldom taken the DMNC as an object of research, this discrepancy is not surprising.

The development of a "process school" of research on the DMNC over the past 15 years has led to the emergence of a new

495

paradigm. This article positions this new paradigm and existing "streams" of organization theory research vis-à-vis each other, in an attempt to resolve the observed discrepancy between organization theorists and scholars of the DMNC. The argument is developed in three main steps. First, we will describe the nature of the DMNC—its complexity and scope. We will derive some basic requirements that a paradigm used in the study of DMNCs must satisfy. Second, we will analyze the dominant paradigms that have been used by researchers studying organizations (not necessarily DMNCs) and evaluate the adequacy as well as the adaptability of specific paradigms to the study of DMNCs. Finally, we will outline the search for a new paradigm, and the contributions of a process school of research on multinational management.

The Nature of the DMNC and the "Specification" of a Paradigm for Research

In this section, based on the empirical and inductive analysis of management processes in DMNCs, we attempt to establish how the complexity of the DMNC, as an organizational form, sets some distinctive requirements for any theory to be useful in analyzing, conceptualizing and explaining management tasks in the DMNC.[1]

We see the essential difference between DMNCs and simpler organizations as stemming from the combined consequences of multidimensionality and heterogeneity.

Multidimensionality results from the very nature of DMNCs: they cover multiple geographical markets, with multiple product lines, in typically multifunction activities, such as sales, manufacturing, service, R&D, etc. DMNCs therefore face the problem of structuring the interfaces between these multiple dimensions that are intrinsic to their activities. In turn, multidimensionality means that no simple unidimensional hierarchical "solution" to the issue of structuring the DMNC exists (Beer

---

[1]   Our purpose here is not to explain why the DMNC exists, as an organizational form. Various researchers, starting with Hymer (1960) and culminating in Dunning's "eclectic theory," have explained the logic for "internalization" of transactions and firm-specific assets in the DMNC. Our purpose in this article is to analyze management processes in DMNCs, not to set the boundaries of DMNCs against other forms of organization of international investment and trade.

and Davis, 1976; Davis and Lawrence, 1977; Doz, 1976, 1979; Prahalad, 1975; Stopford and Wells, 1972). Beyond the *structural indeterminacy of DMNCs* lies the need to handle multiple stakeholders, externally, and by reflection internally, and multiple perspectives on choices and decisions. Simple concepts of centralized versus decentralized organizations break down in the face of strategic, structural, and political multidimensionality, calling for more complex "multifocal" approaches which constantly reach trade-offs between priorities expressed in different dimensions (Doz, 1979, 1986) and embodied in different management subgroups.

Heterogeneity results from the differences between the optimal trade-offs for different businesses, countries, functions, and tasks as the function of a whole range of economic and political characteristics which differ between countries and affect individual businesses and tasks in quite varied ways. DMNCs are therefore very heterogeneous organizations. Any theory of organization that one sets out to apply to DMNCs has to be able to incorporate this heterogeneity. In particular, some businesses and functions may be much more "global" than others, which are more "local." The advantages of globalization versus the needs for local responsiveness and adaptations are quite varied across businesses, countries, and functions. To be applied to DMNC an organizational theory must therefore incorporate a *differentiated approach to businesses, countries, and functions,* and provide enough flexibility for different trade-offs between multiple dimensions to be made.

The need for differentiation makes a structural theory of DMNCs relatively difficult to develop. In fact, except in advocating a matrix organization, which is another way to acknowledge structural indeterminacy, a structural theory of DMNCs would have little to offer. One needs a theory that transcends the structural dimensions to focus on underlying processes. Issues of information and control become essential. More than the formal structure, the informal flow of information matters (Egelhoff, 1982). So do the processes of influence and power, of *how* the trade-offs between multiple stakeholders and multiple perspectives are made.

If one considers the evolution of sources of advantage in global competition, the perception of the importance of information flows is reinforced. As competitors increasingly achieve parity in access to resources (including technology) between various parts of the world, sources of competitiveness shift from location-specific factors to firm-specific factors, and to overall organizational capabilities to coordinate the use of resources to respond to short-lived opportunities that may arise in many different parts of the world. The traditional stable international oligopolies, with a handful of "friendly" competitors are replaced by a quick succession of potential shorter-term monopolies, which only the more agile and discerning firms identify and exploit. While this shift takes place unevenly across global industries (with financial services and electronics leading the way, and more stable traditional products such as tires being less affected) it does suggest that researchers need to shift their emphasis from the physical infrastructure and the resource deployment of DMNCs to their information-processing networks and to resource mobilization (Doz and Prahalad, 1988; Martinez and Jarillo, 1989).

Adopting an information network and organizational capability perspective, however, is not enough. The size and complexity of the typical DMNCs, often with hundreds of business units active in scores of countries, means that linkages and interdependencies cannot be planned, or centrally managed.

Which linkages are going to be useful at a particular point in time for a specific task between two or more subunits is unpredictable, and probably needs to be self-adjusting. Management in the DMNC thus calls for providing decentralized delegated decision contexts within which opportunities for linkages between subunits will arise at various points, levels in organization, and times. In that sense an interorganizational relation perspective may well be necessary to account for the polycentric MNCs (Ghoshal and Bartlett, 1990).

This raises an issue of "fuzzy boundaries," in which relational contracting within the DMNC and with external partners, customers, and suppliers is no longer always clear-cut and well delineated. A theory of DMNC management has to take this fuzziness of firm boundaries into consideration as well. Here again an interorganizational network perspective is appropriate.

The nature of this decentralized network management process creates a trade-off between repeatability and learning. For the DMNC organization to survive and keep its value to subunits, it must allow repeatability at a low cost, i.e., provide for routines and organizational memory that allow interaction patterns to be repeated. Yet at the same time it has to invent, select, and retain new interaction patterns when external conditions require an innovative response. This involves a delicate balance between institutional continuity and change capability.

In summary, considering the multidimensionality and the heterogeneity of the DMNC has led us to specify particular demands on the DMNC organization and on its management task that an organizational theory of the DMNC has to take into account.

1. *Structural indeterminacy:* no single stable unidimensional structure or simple concepts of structure like centralization and decentralization are likely to be useful.

2. *Internal differentiation:* management processes need to differentiate among various countries, products, and functions in the management process.

3. *Integrative optimization:* i.e., the need for management processes to foster varied decision trade-offs between multiple priorities expressed along different dimensions, and represented by diverse groups of managers.

4. *Information intensity:* the importance of information flows, both formal and informal, in DMNCs is such, as a source of competitive advantage and as an implicit structure, that managing information becomes a central task of management.

5. *Latent linkages:* the fact that in a complex DMNC it is not possible to prespecify linkages and interdependencies, but only to facilitate the emergence of appropriate linkages as the need for them arises, in a decentralized self-structuring process.

6. *Networked organization and "fuzzy boundaries":* this creates a need to explicitly incorporate partners, customers, and suppliers' relationships, as well as networked relationships in the management tasks.

7. *Learning and continuity:* the tension between the need for repeatability of interactions at a low cost and that for innovation and change.

These seven demands on DMNC organization and management derived from the multidimensionality, complexity, and heterogeneity of the DMNC provide a grid against which to review various strands of organizational theory, and to assess how, and to what extent, they may contribute to an understanding of DMNC management.

The Applicability of Organization Theory to the Study of DMNCs

In the first section we have summarized the distinctive demands facing the management of DMNCs, from a phenomenological perspective, and outlined the conditions a theoretical paradigm of the management of DMNCs would have to meet. In this section we review what the major streams of organization theory contribute to the development of such a paradigm.

Organizational theorists have very seldom taken the DMNC as their focus of investigation. They have, however, dealt with many of the issues that are germane to the DMNC, and some that are conceptually similar. We will examine the contributions that theorists can make to the study of DMNCs from two standpoints: Do contributions meet the seven criteria established above, and how useful are they to help conceptualize DMNC management processes?

The study of complex organizations has had a long intellectual history. Illustrious scholars have contributed to this effort. Any attempt to summarize this field must therefore be approached with caution and humility. By its very nature such an effort is likely to cluster different streams of intellectual effort, attempt to distill the basic premises behind the lines of inquiry, and make generalizations. Also, the focus of our effort is *not* to review exhaustively many different theoretical and empirical streams of research, but merely to highlight how a few key contributions to these streams contribute to research on DMNCs, as key steps in the evolution of these research streams. Further, our brief review is made from a very particular perspective: we want to determine to what extent these theories contribute to an understanding of the tasks involved in meeting the specific demands of DMNC management, as outlined in the first section of this paper. We recognize the risks; but this attempt, with all its limitations, is an important part of building a new paradigm.

An implicit recognition of the complexity of the phenomenon under scrutiny—complex organizations—is the fact that there is no dominant paradigm that is used to study it. However, over the last 10 years, several streams have gained currency in the academic literature. We will examine them below.

Economic Theories of Organization

The application of institutional economics theories to DMNCs has grown from two distinct but increasingly intertwined theories: transaction cost analysis and principal-agent theory (Arrow, 1985; Williamson, 1975, 1985; Williamson and Ouchi, 1981). The former focuses on transaction costs in markets, and explains organizations as a consequence of market failure. The latter focuses on transaction costs within hierarchies and focuses on the cost of control and compliance in organizations (Fama and Jensen, 1983; Jensen and Meckling, 1976).

Transaction cost analysis provides a powerful departure point to analyze choices between institutional forms, and thus can be used to establish the efficient boundaries of a DMNC (Buckley and Casson, 1986; Dunning, 1980; Hennart, 1982; Teece, 1985). The usefulness of transaction cost analysis for research on management processes is limited by the simplifying assumptions inherent in the "hierarchy" category, and by its primary focus on single transactions as units of analysis. Thus, although transaction cost analysis does not formally violate the seven criteria we have established, it is of limited usefulness for our purpose unless one adds to it reputational (Kreps, 1984) and relational contracting (Dore, 1983) dimensions.

Transaction cost analysis has proven useful in analyzing specific types of interorganizational relationships in a North American context such as relationships between U.S. firms and their suppliers, vertical integration (Monteverde and Teece, 1982; Stockey, 1983), and joint ventures with rigorous constraints on the nature of the joint venture (Hennart, 1982). Transaction cost analysis, however, does not explain relationships between Japanese firms and their suppliers, a relationship built on mutual trust and on a belief that the joint benefits (in contrast to self-interest) are worth pursuing in a "win-win" framework, over the long term (Dore, 1983).

In fact one of the most challenging management tasks in the DMNC is to make the assumptions of transaction cost analysis "untrue"; hence the emphasis on organizational culture, clan behavior and control (Ouchi, 1980), and normative integration of managers in MNCs (Hedlund, 1981). Transaction cost analysis, by its very assumptions about human beings and organizations, prohibits itself from addressing managerial issues.

Agency theory, on the other hand, aims itself at analyzing management control issues in various forms of contractual relationships between principals and agents, and makes a useful contribution to the study of DMNC management. Agency theory does raise relevant managerial issues by casting issues of control in "outcome" or "behavioral" terms (Eisenhardt, 1989a). For example, the outcome-based model of control provides an interesting perspective in which to cast the problem of controlling subsidiaries; especially nationally responsive subsidiaries about which the headquarters may have very little information, whose behavior cannot be monitored easily and whose managers may not fully share headquarters goals. Conversely, control over globally integrated subsidiaries may be seen as a problem in behavior-based control, as the relationship between specialized and interdependent subsidiaries can be based on substantive understanding at the headquarters of the tasks to be performed. In fact, headquarters may provide the skills needed at the subsidiaries. The task is one of creating greater goal convergence between headquarters and subsidiaries, which is often fostered by international mobility of managers, multidimensional measurement systems, and a desire to create a shared sense of purpose. In that sense agency theory provides but a departure point for the study of DMNC management issues. In fact the dichotomy between outcome-based and behavior-based control is not new, remains quite simplistic, and certainly underemphasizes the noneconomic dimensions of control. The simplicity of the binary choice it posits prevents it from exploring the more subtle blends of control and management approaches used in companies (Lawrence and Dyers, 1983).

By emphasizing these noneconomic dimensions the literature on organizational culture that stresses "clan" behavior and control (Ouchi, 1980) and normative integration of MNCs (Hedlund, 1981) challenges the simplifying assumptions of the agency theory approach in a much-needed direction to include psychological affiliation models of control and goal congruence often ignored by the economic theories of organization—somewhat relaxing the assumptions of economic self-interest and rationality.

Further, agency theory implies a hierarchical relationship between principal and agent, and assumes implicitly the centrality of headquarters. By treating the organization as a series of contracts, agency theory may not include the multitude of contingencies that arise in the management of DMNCs. As one tries to extend the agency theory framework to include a complex web of networked relationships, the researcher's task becomes extremely complex and difficult as the one-to-one nature of relationships, the simplicity of contracts, and the clear identities of principals and agents tend to fade.

The increasingly related theories of transaction costs and principal-agent relationships both suffer from too restrictive, and culturally bound, assumptions to allow them to do more than raise managerial issues. While they provide useful starting points to consider firm boundaries and control issues, their formulation of the working of an organization is too simplified to be useful for management research purposes.

Environmental Adaptation Theories

The issue of whether, and how, organizations adapt to their environment to succeed—or at least survive within it—has been central to organization theory for decades. Out of the very rich and diverse literature on organizational adaptation, which we cannot review in whole, stand out the themes of proactive versus reactive or even random adaptation, and that of the modes and processes of adaptation, which are studied at various levels of aggregation populations of organization, organizational fields, and individual organizations and their subunits. Since each of these levels is relevant to DMNC management research, as is the polarity between active and passive adaptation, we concentrate our analysis on three main streams of environmental adaptation theories: population ecology, institutional theory, and differentiation-integration models.

Population Ecology

Population ecology provides the "null hypothesis" to strategic management of the DMNC: population ecology assumes that environmental resources are unequally distributed between "niches" in the environment, and either an organization finds itself in a resource niche it can use or it does not, and succeeds or falters accordingly (Hannan and Freeman, 1977). Population ecology normally assumes strategic choices on the part of organizations to be unfeasible (Aldrich, 1979), although some more recent developments now distinguish "core" unchanging features of organizations, and "peripheral" ones which can be changed, creating the possibility of proactive adaptation (Singh and Lumsden, 1990). From the standpoint of research on the management of DMNCs, population ecology is most useful when it stresses the difficulties that limit the feasibility of successful strategic redirection in MNCs (Hannan and Freeman, 1989). Population ecology reaches findings similar to those of some researchers of DMNC management processes when it stresses how over-adaptation to specific environmental conditions makes reaction to changes in the environment particularly difficult (Aldrich, 1979; Doz, 1979; Prahalad and Doz, 1987). However, the level of aggregation of the theory of population ecology— populations of organizations—tells us little about why or how companies fail to adapt, as compared to the management process literature (Bartlett and Ghoshal, 1989; Doz, 1979; Doz and Prahalad, 1984).

The very fact that population ecology does not consider managerial issues, but questions their relevance, makes it a little unfair to apply our seven criteria of appropriateness to management issues to population ecology: population ecology fails on nearly all criteria (see Table 17-1), but population ecology never set out to analyze managerial behavior!

Perhaps, however, the population ecology theory can be made useful by shifting the level of aggregation at which it is applied to the inside of large complex firms, where it can provide a logic to selection and adaptation of subunits within the DMNC network, the network itself being considered as the population (Hannan and Freeman, 1989; Delacroix and Freeman, 1993). Focusing on selection processes within the firm and on the relative success of various geographical affiliates and product lines in different environments, and over time under specified management processes and management system settings, can open an interesting avenue for research and use population ecology reasoning to study the adaptation of subunits to different environments under different management conditions.

Institutional Theory

Considering subunit adaptations to differentiated "local" environments and to corporate management systems is roughly where institutional theory is most useful for research on DMNCs. The concept of organizational field (DiMaggio and Powell, 1983) allows us to consider interactions, mutual awareness, information and patterns of competitive and coalitional behavior between organizations as determinants of their adaptation. This is clearly consistent, in spirit, with the early categorization work on MNC structures (Fayerweather, 1960; Perlmutter, 1969) and the more recent clinical studies of organizational adaptation to diverse types of multinational environments (Bartlett and Ghoshal, 1989; Doz, 1976, 1979; Prahalad, 1975). By showing that some of the most interesting institutionalization processes may occur in organizations that straddle several fields (Zucker, 1987), institutional theory is also consistent with the observation on the part of DMNC scholars that "multifocal" (Doz 1979, 1986) or "transnational" (Bartlett and Ghoshal, 1989) management processes both hold the most strategic promises and raise the most difficult managerial issues in the context of DMNCs.

At a second level of analysis, that of adaptation within firms rather than between institutions, institutional theory is also interesting. Both Meyer and Rowan (1977) and Zucker (1983) stress that organizations are powerful entities providing meaning and encouraging conformity in individual behavior. The fact that MNC managers are subject both to corporate and external influences (Westney, 1993) makes them a particularly rich territory to apply institutionalization theory.

Although the current development of institutional theory is not specific enough—in its analysis and conceptualization of institutionalization mechanisms—to make it directly applicable in the management of MNCs, it provides a most helpful theoretical base to researchers. For example, it allows formulation of problems of headquarters-subsidiaries relationships, and of the possible organizational implications of addressing national responsiveness and global integration demands at multiple levels of aggregation from the individual to the interorganizational level (Scott, 1987b).

In summary, institutional theory is very consistent in its

Table 17-1
The Relevance of Organization Theories to DMNC Management Research

Criteria of relevance to DMNC management	Major streams of organization theory						
	Transaction cost	Agency	Population ecology	Institutional theory	Contingency theory	Power relationships and adaptation	Organizational learning
1. Structural indeterminacy	Yes	Implicitly hierarchical	No	Yes	No, structure fits the environment, except for matrix management	Yes, self-adjusting network of power relationships	Yes
2. Internal differentiation	Yes	Simplistic: outcome vs. behavior control	No	Yes, depending on influences	Yes	Yes, depending on external uncertainties	Yes
3. Decision trade-offs between multiple priorities	Narrowly defined self-interest not compatible, extension needed to include relational contracting	No, mainly dyadic principal-agent relationships	No	Not explicitly, but encompassed in multiple fields	Yes, at least on the part of some researchers (Lawrence and Lorsch, 1967)	Yes, power games embody multiple priorities	Yes, part of learning processes

4. Importance of information flows	Yes, but limited to uncertainty and asymmetry issues	Yes, but focused mainly on observability of behavior and measurability of results	No	Yes	Yes	Yes, information is a key determinant of influence	Yes
5. Emergent rather than prescribed linkages	Transaction patterns are not specified a priori. Hierarchies, however, are useful for interorganizational analysis	Yes, series of contracts but not encompassing multiplicity of linkages	No	Yes	Possible, but not specified clearly, although consistent with theory	Yes	Yes, result of learning processes
6. Fuzzy boundaries	Yes, well suited to the analysis of boundaries, but needs to be complemented to incorporate rational contracting	Yes	No	Yes isomorphic pressures to conform	Not explicitly	Yet, network of relationship in and out of the organization	Not explicitly, but not excluded
7. Repeatability vs. change			Change capabilities are very limited	Yes	No	Yes, depends on network structure	Yes, central to theory

approach to organizational phenomena with the criteria established earlier. The dearth of explicit use of institutional theory in the study of DMNCs may reflect more the "youth" of the theory, the lack of discipline base for many MNC scholars (more on that later), and the methodological and epistemological differences between institutional theory researchers and the clinical researchers working on the management of DMNCs. However, it seems that the further development of institutional theory holds many promises for the study of DMNC management issues and processes.

Contingency Theory

Contingency theories of organization developed mainly in the 1960s (Lawrence and Lorsch, 1967; Thompson, 1967; Woodward, 1965). Contingency theory clearly influenced research on MNCs. The early models of structural adaptation of MNCs to geographic and product diversity (Fouraker and Stopford, 1968; Stopford and Wells, 1972) are clearly examples of structural functionalist contingency theory applied to MNC organizational forms. Research on patterns and modes of headquarters control over affiliates (Doz and Prahalad, 1984; Ghoshal and Nohria, 1989; Hedlund, 1981; Negandhi and Baliga, 1981; Negandhi et al., 1980a,b) has also been clearly cast in a contingency model, although it has considered both the adjustment and subsidiaries to their environment and to the culture and style of the parent company, thus raising issues of institutional isomorphism which are closer to the institutional school of organization theory. Researchers who focused on information flows and information-processing capabilities of MNCs also clearly adopted a contingency framework (e.g., Egelhoff, 1988), drawing largely on the work of Lawrence and Lorsch (1967) and on that of Galbraith (1973). Subsequent research by Bartlett and Ghoshal (1986, 1989) also clearly draws on the contingency framework, although the interpretation of their detailed analysis of nine MNCs draws on many strands of theory, and remains phenomenological in focus.

Although the contingency theory of organization, and its emphasis on differentiated responses to diverse environments and integration of action across environments, has had the most direct impact of all strands of organization theory on MNC management research, it leaves the issues of change and adaptation to new environmental demands, and thus part of the challenge to management research from population ecology, unanswered. Empirical research on contingency theory has been mostly static, seldom researching change process. The most notable exceptions are Doz (1976, 1979), Doz and Prahalad (1981, 1987) and Prahalad (1975). The primarily static and functionalist views taken by most contingency theory research do not easily allow the incorporation of change processes in their theory, except at the broadest level of assuming that system dynamics applies to organizational change processes. Issues of empowerment, decentralization, deliberate mismatch between organization and environment to create a state of tension that facilitates adaptation are all recent additions, and often challenges, to contingency theory (e.g., Hamel and Prahalad, 1989; Normann, 1976). A functionalist top management–driven perspective, in which adaptation is primarily organization design and development, begs the question of how top management perceives the need for adjusting the "fit" or for responding to new environmental conditions.

Further, an explicit use of contingency theory may lead to simplistic dichotomous thinking in considering the management of DMNCs, in particular to polarizing one's understanding of MNC management into an opposition between responsiveness and integration categories when, in fact, a fusion is needed: i.e., managers must consider how to achieve integration and responsiveness together, and build on the dualities that result (Evans and Doz, 1989).

Despite the possible criticisms that contingency theory is static and encourages dichotomous thinking, it does meet most of our criteria, at least to an extent. While contingency theory does not encompass structural indeterminacy (except in its extension to matrix organizations by Davis and Lawrence, 1977), it does provide for internal differentiation and multiple perspectives. It also stresses the importance of information flows (e.g., the interfunctional integration in Lawrence and Lorsch, 1967) and the possibility of new emergent linkages, in the management of interdependencies, rather than the presumption of linkages a priori.

Beyond the obvious applicability of a differentiation-integration framework to the managerial dilemmas of the DMNC, argued above, the language in which contingency theory was developed provided the intermediate levels/conceptual constructs that allowed us to bridge theory and the phenomenological approach to MNC management. The analysis of management processes and systems done by Lawrence and Lorsch (1967) provides a rich basis to study integration within complex organizations, and can be readily applied to DMNCs. In sum, contrary to the other more abstract streams of organization theory described above, which seldom develop intermediate-level constructs, contingency theory went a good part of the way toward process research and provided a relatively firmer and easier framework for scholars of the DMNC. In fact, one wonders whether contingency theory has not had an excessive influence on subsequent research and thus limited progress in research on the DMNC.

Power Relationships and Organizational Adaptation

Among other analyses of power in organizations, the work of Crozier (1964) and Crozier and Friedberg (1980) provides an insightful analysis of organizations as networks of relationships in which "actors" play self-interested and individually rational strategies in collective "games" mediated by collectively accepted "rules" and driven by the resources and constraints of the individual actors. In particular, control over uncertainties affecting the performance of other members of the organization was seen by Crozier as a critical resource.

The network of relationships is thus never totally integrated or disintegrated. Organizations maintain a degree of cohesion, and consistency vis-à-vis their environment through the regulation of internal antagonism (Astley and Van de Ven, 1983). The "game" in the system of relationships balances tensions between integration and fragmentation. Its rules must be followed for the mutually beneficial association to continue, but players follow different personal strategies in the game depending on their own objectives and the resources they control.

In this perspective, adaptation to the environment takes place through the players most directly able to mediate dependencies with the environment for other players becoming more influential in the network of power relationships. Uncertainty—brought by control over information—is a key dependency, but other sources of dependence are also important; for example, the ability to influence environment's munificence. Structural inertia does exist, as in the population ecology view, but adaptation to changes in the environment may take place through an evolution in the game that reflects the changing relative criticality of various dependencies with the environment and brings more power to players best able to face these dependencies successfully. The adaptive capability of the organization depends on the density of the network of relationships. Very hierarchical organizations, with star-and-spoke patterns of communication and dependence, are not adaptive because the games they allow comprise relatively few strategies and cannot be changed easily. Organizations with more diverse linkages in their networks, in particular more lateral and diagonal rather than vertical linkages, are more adaptive. The network of relationships can reconfigure itself as new environmental contingencies become important. A system of relationships is, therefore, more or less "blocked" or adaptive, depending on whether its structure is narrowly hierarchical or not (Crozier, 1964). This is congruent with earlier studies of the innovativeness and adaptativeness of organizations (e.g., Burns and Stalker's (1961) contrast of "mechanistic" and "organic" organizations).

In this approach power flows to players who control resources, irrespective of their hierarchical positions; the model thus posits no hierarchical system or collective goals, and thus escapes the criticisms levelled by population ecologists at the strategic choice and deliberate environment-organization adaptation models. Adaptation takes place, or not, as a function of the structure of the network of relationships, and of the external constraints in the environment (and presumably of how fast they change). While individual rationality is usually assumed, organizational rationality does not necessarily follow. Information asymmetry, misunderstanding of the strategies of other actors, and differences in goals among individuals allow for the "loose coupling" and unstructured decision-making processes. Action can emerge, and generate random variation in the system, which in turn helps its adaptation. Events can thus unfold and be incorporated into the relational system that responds to them (March and Olsen, 1976; Weick, 1979).

By providing a very rich, yet simple, analytical theory of intraorganizational influence processes the power dependence school addresses, albeit often implicitly, the seven criteria in this paper for a relevant theory of the management of DMNCs. Beyond these criteria the power and dependence model is clearly seductive to MNC management scholars, who usually originated from a phenomenological rather than disciplinary perspective, and had an applied rather than theoretical focus.

First, its assumptions about human beings and the nature of organizations seem more realistic than those of other models, including the strategic choice model. The assumptions about human beings as purposively rational and self-interested, but with differentiated personal goals and operating in a boundedly rational fashion, is realistic enough to those familiar with organizational life. The assumption of an organization as a network of relationships between members of the organization, where uncertainty-reducing information is a resource and a source of influence, is also useful. In particular, it makes it possible to incorporate information-processing theories of MNCs (Egelhoff, 1988) into a broader theory. The fact that the network of relationships may extend outside the organization, to key players in its environment is also realistic.[2]

Second, the power and dependence model is seductive to MNC management scholars because it clearly holds application potential. It is both a theoretical and an applied model, i.e., it can easily drive action. Analyzing and understanding the network of relationships that constitute the organization, and discovering the strategies followed by participants in the games played along these relationships allow the researcher to start considering how the stakes and perceptions of the players can be modified, and to simulate how changes in the rules of the game, and in the active relationships in the network would affect outcomes, i.e., the overall behavior of the system of rela-

---

[2]   For example, researchers on MNC management have observed that headquarters-subsidiary relationships in the MNC could not necessarily be understood without an explicit analysis of the relationship with major customers and the governmental authorities of countries in which the subsidiaries operate. Country managers may use their privileged relationships with the local subsidiary environment to limit the influence headquarters, or other affiliates, may exert on their operations. Since the relationship is not transparent, such opportunities to leverage external relationships internally lead managers to "seek out" their environment in ways that increase their own influence in the organization. In so doing, they contribute to making the organization more responsive to the constraints and opportunities in the environment. Strategic choice is not central, it results from individual strategic choices made by individual players in selecting and adapting to their relevant environment.

tionships. This is clearly a powerful set of tools for implementing actions in MNCs, in line with an applied perspective.

However, gains in realism and applicability offered by the power and dependence theory, as compared to the other strands of organization theory applied to MNCs, come at a loss of simplicity and theoretical power. The detailed analysis of internal relationships, and the careful categorization of players (which do not easily match organizational lines) require clinical research of a very detailed variety, not easily carried out by most organization researchers. Simpler models of power relationships in and between organizations (Dahl, 1957; Pfeffer, 1981), provide a less grounded argument than Crozier's, but make its integration with other theories easier and more explicit. Pfeffer's work, for instance, introduces explicit contingency dimensions and can be seen as a detailed analytical approach to the solution of agency problems.

The influence of the resource dependence and power approach on scholars of MNC management is rather obvious. Early work on the responsiveness-integration dilemma in MNCs conceptualized the issue as one of relative power (Prahalad, 1975) and discussed adaptation to contradictions in the environment as achieving a "power balance" between geographic and product-line executives (Doz, 1976, 1979). Work on matrix organizations in DMNCs used a rather similar set of premises (Davis, 1984; Davis and Lawrence, 1977). Thus, the research on MNC management process has drawn extensively on the power and dependence literature. Similarly, studies of strategic control of affiliates have used the power and dependency model extensively (Doz and Prahalad, 1981; Negandhi et al., 1980a,b).

Although less explicitly connected to process research on DMNCs, the research on external power and dependence (in particular Pfeffer and Salancik, 1978) is also quite relevant to research on DMNCs. Models of external control and dependence were used, for example, by Prahalad and Doz (1980) in their study of different relational modes between headquarters and subsidiaries in DMNCs.

Organizational Learning and the DMNC

Of the various major strands of organization theory, the organizational learning literature is the only one to focus primarily on change and development. Although they all discuss environment-organization adaptation, other strands of the literature usually start from a static perspective and do not empirically address learning, change, and development processes, with the exception of some recent institutionalization theorists (Scott, 1987b).

This may be partly because most scholars of organization learning take the view that learning and development are essentially individual, but in the context of an organization, while other theories have a more aggregate view of learning, and ignore the issue altogether. More recent work stresses that learning involves adaptive processes at all levels of the organization (Levitt and March, 1988) and that the institutionalization of learning takes place through organizational routines in which inferences about past successes and failures are embedded (Nelson and Winter, 1982). Organizational routines then guide behavior.

Levitt and March (1988) also point out why and how the concept of organizational learning itself is fraught with problems. Learning along a wrong trajectory leads to "competency traps." Inductive learning from experience by individuals is far from always being accurate, largely because real causality linkages may be much more complex and interdependent than those inferred by observers and participants in an organization. Satisfying behavior leads to superstitious learning, i.e., the first plausible explanation of successful outcome is taken for true. Further, the assessment of outcomes as "successful" or "unsuccessful" may be very idiosyncratic and personal. Finally, the diffusion of results from learning in organizations is far from perfect, and learning results decay if they are not frequently used. Further, the process of "deepening" the knowledge of an organization (from information to understanding) often conflicts with the process of sharing such knowledge within the organization (Chakravarthy and Kwun, 1989).

Although the organizational learning literature, as opposed to the individual learning literature, is still in its infancy, it holds tantalizing promises for the MNC management scholars. It has been loosely argued (e.g., Ghoshal, 1987) that a key asset of MNCs is their opportunity to learn from multiple markets and multiple environments, in particular as they build differentiated networks to achieve such learning (Ghoshal and Nohria,

1989); our limit of the applicability of the organizational learning literature is its content-free nature, i.e., what the object of learning is remains unspecified. In the context of the MNC the extent and process of learning may be quite different according to content. A lot of local autonomous learning may be vital to marketing success, while local experimentation and learning on safety of operations may be lethal if technical operations are invariant between countries. The blend of responsiveness and integration in various tasks drives the need for autonomous localized learning and for sharing such learning in those tasks. Processes for learning may need to be different for geography-based learning, for learning about management systems and processes, which need to reflect both integration and responsiveness needs, and for rather invariant disciplines, such as safety procedures. More research is needed on both organizational learning processes in general and their application to MNCs.

Overview

In the first section of this paper we set out to specify the MNC-specific issues that organization theory needs to address to be relevant to strategic management in DMNCs. We then briefly discussed what we see as the major streams of research in organizational theory from the perspective of strategic management in DMNCs. A summary of that discussion is provided in Table 17-1, using the seven categories we have established.

With the exception of population ecology, where level of analysis makes our criteria less applicable unless one applies the theory to subunits within a DMNC (which was assumed in our treatment of population ecology in Table 17-1), most other streams of research do not contradict the criteria established earlier in this article. However, the managerial usefulness of these theories varies greatly.[3]

Although they differ deeply in their premises, as well as in the levels of analysis they cover (Figure 17-1, on the vertical axis), most streams of organization theory share a few key char-

---

[3] Obviously, most organization theorists would not consider managerial usefulness as relevant, since they did not set out to analyze, enlighten, or improve managerial behavior, but rather to analyze the behavior of organizations.

Figure 17-1
Levels of Aggregation and Theory Development

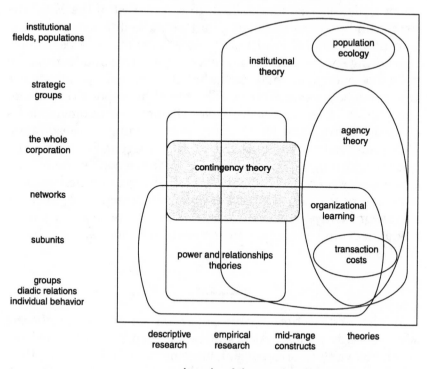

Levels of theory development

acteristics that make their application to the study of management in MNCs somewhat difficult.

First, with the exception of contingency theory and of some recent developments of institutional theory, these theories fail to operationalize the theories into a model, or a framework, in terms other than statistical. As a result they are relatively weak at the operational construct level, i.e., the linkage between theory and empirical analysis, the horizontal axis on Figure 17-1. When the object of study is homogeneous groups of organizations that are relatively similar (e.g., local administrative units and agencies in public administration) and not excessively complex, it is indeed quite feasible to move between variable specification and measurement and theory directly, using simple statistical tests. This is clearly less feasible when dealing with heterogeneous groups of complex organizations, or when focusing on their management. Mid-range constructs are needed to conceptualize and model the behavior (both strategic and organizational) of complex organizations and to be managerially relevant (Bourgeois, 1979). In summary, studying large numbers of relatively similar, relatively simple organizations leads one to very generalizable theories, but theories that treat the organizations as a "black box" and do not develop detailed knowledge of how organizations work. What is needed from a managerial research standpoint is a robust conceptual model of how the DMNC works, a model researchers and managers can play with to simulate reality.

Although we did not review it here, much of the literature on multinational management suffers from an opposite, but almost symmetrical, problem. While it is long on descriptive analysis, it is short on theories, and even shorter on mid-range constructs. As a result, many clinical studies of MNCs amount to little more than compendia of descriptive case studies, and the few large-sample studies focusing on the management of MNCs often suffer from lack of conceptual and theoretical integrity (e.g., Negandhi et al., 1980a,b). What is required is a mid-range theory that bridges the gap between descriptive analysis and theories and can span various levels of aggregation, from individuals and small groups within MNCs to clusters of MNCs following conceptually similar strategies.

Second, the streams of organization theory, while all conceptually relevant, need a more detailed way to address process variables and process issues. Key managerial processes, such as resource allocation (both financial and human) or conflict resolution processes within organizations need to be captured by the theory. With the exception of the models based on power and relationship analysis, organization theories usually operate at too high a level of abstraction to capture such processes. Further, they do not, for the most part, focus on processes, with the exception of institutional, power, and learning theories.

Third, change and adaptation processes need more explicit attention. Organization theories are mostly static, geared to cross-sectional analysis rather than to longitudinal processes of change. While it is possible to use these theories to analyze and conceptualize change processes, such use requires many intermediate steps of conceptualization, with the exception of the organization learning and power/relationship streams.

Fourth, most theories of organization do not accommodate

substantive variables, i.e., do not overcome the false dichotomy between context and process observed in the strategy literature. Context variables are captured, if at all, by abstract proxies.

Lastly, although the tests have seldom been made systematically, some aspects of organization theory may well be culture-bound. For example, the assumption of self-interest and opportunism, key to transaction cost theory, may be deeply rooted in an economic and legal tradition quite specific to the professions in the United States.

In summary, the review of the main strands of the organization theory literature suggests the need for a mid-range theory of the working of DMNCs, emphasizing constructs and frameworks and linking a potentially very useful set of theories with the often insufficiently conceptual and theoretical descriptive analyses performed by the observers and analysts of DMNC. An effort at developing such a mid-range theory is summarized in the next section.

The Search for a Paradigm

The Development of MNC Management Research: Toward a New Paradigm

While early scholars of the MNC phenomenon (e.g., Fayerweather, 1960; Perlmutter, 1969; Wilkins, 1970) had developed organizational process categories and identified the essential tension between fragmentation and unity in managing MNCs, the bulk of researchers' attention was then focused on economic and competitive models of the MNC, building on the seminal works of Hymer (1960) and Vernon (1966). Only Stopford and Wells (1972) and Franko (1976) devoted their main attention to structural and managerial issues in the research stream originated by Vernon. It was only later, following the development of contingency theory and the emergence of a process school of policy research (e.g., Bower, 1970), that empirical research on the organization and management processes of MNCs started in earnest.

The line of research starting with the work of Prahalad (1975) is united on the common theme of organizational processes and organizational capabilities in DMNCs, but focuses on various aspects of the general management task in DMNCs (Bartlett and Ghoshal, 1989; Doz and Prahalad, 1988; Prahalad and Doz,

1987). While a full summary of the findings of this research is not the purpose of this article, a few words putting the various contributions to that line of research in perspective may be useful. In particular, understanding the stream of process research on the management of DMNCs is complicated by the lack of discipline among researchers in the choice of labels to describe the concepts and in the language systems used. Further, the language system used by individual researchers also evolved over time as their understanding progressed. This can give the impression to a casual reader of a lack of conceptual unity to the whole line of research.

Prahalad's research (1975) focused on the processes by which the management of a single business, not subject to intense host government constraints, perceived changing environmental demands and responded to these by redirecting the attention of managers, refocusing the strategic direction, and realigning power and influence processes, consistent with the new environmental conditions.

The work of Doz (1976, 1979) analyzed, on a comparative basis, the management processes used in several companies, and in several businesses in each company, to manage the tension between economic and technological pressure for globalization and integration, and host government demands for responsiveness to national industrial policies. Doz (1979, 1980) then analyzed how differences in competitive positions between firms in the same industry affected their response to the tension outlined above.

Bartlett (1979) compared the management systems and processes used in a sample of companies in industries differently affected by global integration and national responsiveness demands, analyzed how different functions were affected by these pressures, and further extended the understanding of redirection processes initiated by Prahalad (1975) and Doz (1978). Mathias (1978) compared redirection processes initiated by top management, with processes emerging from tensions among middle managers in the organization without top management playing an active role in the initiation of change processes. Bartlett then considered how what he called the "institutional heritage" of a firm constrains the development of new capabilities, and constitutes a form of "organizational inertia" that top management has to take into consideration (Bartlett, 1981).

Ghoshal (1986) added a detailed analysis of innovation processes, stressing the existence of different patterns of interactions between affiliates and headquarters, and among affiliates in the innovation process. This led to a more general analysis of DMNCs as differentiated networks (Ghoshal and Nohria, 1989) and to the discussion of network theory applied to DMNCs (Ghoshal and Bartlett, 1990).

Finally, the research of Prahalad and Hamel (1990) led to reconceptualization of the basis for global competitiveness away from resource deployment to skill development and leverage; both their work and that of Doz and Prahalad (1988) stress the importance of organizational capabilities in this process.

Simultaneously, but largely independently, a rather similar line of process research developed in Sweden, based on the clinical analysis of the internationalization of major Swedish companies. Initially much of this work was concentrated on empirical tests of the validity of various propositions stemming from previous research (e.g., that a subsidiary's managerial autonomy would be inversely correlated to cross shipments of goods between that subsidiary and other parts of the organization) or of grounded propositions stemming from detailed case studies of Swedish MNCs (e.g., Hedlund, 1981). However, interesting theoretical developments followed from the empirical research, in particular the concept of "heterarchic" DMNC (Hedlund, 1986; Hedlund and Rolander, 1990) emphasizing the geographic diffusion of corporate functions, a wide range of "between market and hierarchy" governance modes and an emphasis on action learning and on variation selection and retention processes in organizational adaptation.

Although this enumeration of issues, authors, and research work may look somewhat disjointed, it is important to understand its cumulative nature and underlying logic. The process of research has been to start initially with relatively discrete, researchable "building blocks," bounding both the territory researched and the complexity of the concepts and constructs developed. Each step then constitutes an attempt to challenge, extend, and enrich the preceding steps by taking their findings to a broader, more complex set of issues and adding to the existing concepts based on a richer understanding of their applicability.

While each research piece illuminates only an aspect of the

managerial task in DMNC, taken together the work of Prahalad, Doz, Bartlett, Ghoshal, Hedlund, Hamel, and others following the same research approach provides us with a rich organizational theory of the DMNC, and with a detailed understanding of managerial tasks in DMNCs.

The emerging paradigm that results from this cumulative work has a few key characteristics.

1. Substance and process in a DMNC are captured using the same underlying framework. The underlying business characteristics can be mapped using the *global integration–local responsiveness (I–R) framework* (for a summary, see Prahalad and Doz, 1987). All the elements that contribute to the pressures for global integration (I) needs, such as economies of scale, universal products, privileged access to raw materials, global customers, technology intensity, and presence of global competitors, are supported directly in the literature on competitive dynamics and strategy. The framework considers all factors that contribute to the pressure for global integration simultaneously, rather than one element at a time, as is common in the literature. Similarly, pressures for local responsiveness needs such as distribution differences, local customs, differences in customer needs, market structure, and host government demands also find support in the literature, and are considered simultaneously. Further, the relative importance of the integration and responsiveness pressures can be used to *map industry characteristics*. The critical difference between this approach and traditional research approaches is that it explicitly recognizes the need for integrative optimization between multiple and often conflicting pressures in a business. Studying the process of balance across apparently conflicting demands is seen as more important than studying the management demands created by one element of the business (e.g., technology intensity) at a time.

2. The same framework can be used to chart the changing nature of a business—by evaluating the shifts in the relative balance between the forces that contribute to the integration and responsiveness needs, and their impact on various key functions within a business—such as R&D, manufacturing, or marketing.

Furthermore, one can analyze management systems in a DMNC, and in its various countries of operation, functions, and businesses, and assess whether these management systems form a context consistent with the external demands, given business conditions and competitive positions.

The causes of enduring mismatches between external demands, strategic choices, and management systems, and the refocusing and realignment processes used to adapt to, or to anticipate, new environmental demands have been part of the emerging paradigm (Doz, 1978; Doz and Prahalad, 1981; Doz, Bartlett, and Prahalad, 1981; Prahalad, 1976). In that sense the emerging paradigm can be used both cross-sectionally, to compare industries, business strategies, and management systems and processes at one point in time, and longitudinally to map out, analyze, and understand change and adaptation processes.

3. *The basic unit of analysis of the paradigm is the individual manager, rather than an abstraction at a higher level of aggregation.* Thus, the primary purpose of organizational processes— formal structure, administrative tools, decision-making culture—can be conceptualized as (1) influencing the mindsets or the *cognitive orientations of managers,* (2) legitimating a currently dominant *coalition* of managers representing a certain strategy that is pursued, and (3) representing the authority structure and *power* to allocate resources. Organization can then be conceptualized as consisting of these three subprocesses. We can make the following generalizations.

(a) Formal structure in an organization is nothing more than a shorthand way of capturing the underlying subprocesses— managers' mindsets (and the attendant information infrastructure in the firm), a consensus on strategy, and power to allocate resources consistent with strategy. As a result, managers consistently desire to have "pure organizations"— be it worldwide business or area organization—because they describe the three orientations of managers unambiguously (Prahalad and Doz, 1987).

(b) Managers believe that a matrix organization is complex, because in a matrix the three subprocesses—cognitive orientations, strategic consensus, and power—are not aligned with the lines in an organization chart. Managers must understand the subprocesses in the matrix, independent of the formal structure. Irrespective of the formal structure, as shown in the organization chart, these three subprocesses go on, and must be explicitly managed. Top managers must deal with the subprocesses and individual managers. This need to deal at the level of subprocesses in the organization makes a matrix complicated for managers who are not skilled at operating at the level of subtlety and detail.

(c) Strategic change requires that managers change the cognitive orientations of a constellation of managers, gain a new consensus on strategy, and realign the relative power balance among the various groups involved in the interaction in the business.

(d) The subprocesses in the organization can be effectively managed by the use of administrative tools such as planning, budgeting, MIS, rewards and punishments, training, career management, and socialization (Doz and Prahalad, 1984). The implication is that major strategic redirection can take place without a formal structural change.

(e) The nature of interaction and the intensity of information flow between subsidiary and head office and across subsidiaries is a reflection of the strategic missions assigned to various units (Ghoshal and Nohria, 1989). Even within a single business, all country organizations need not have the same strategic mission, and the differences will be manifest in the pattern and intensity of information flow. Patterns of information flow are a predictor of the cognitive orientation of managers (which depend on the information infrastructure that they have access to), the strategic consensus process (where the sources of tension are and who is involved in resolving the tensions), and the relative power balance to allocate resources.

4. The whole paradigm is focused on mid-range constructs. It does not pretend to develop a universally applicable all-encompassing theory of organization, but much more modestly to provide a set of integrative constructs allowing the observation, analysis, understanding, and normative assessment of interaction processes between managers in DMNCs. As such it provides a starting point toward the development of a mid-range theory, useful to link strategic issues with theoretical bases (Bourgeois, 1979).

5. It is not possible to ensure a theory is not culture-bound. It may be culture-bound in its observations or in its observers. Scholars of DMNC management belong to a wide range of nationalities and cultures and have researched MNCs with a variety of home countries. Several research contributions (e.g., Bartlett and Ghoshal, 1989) have built cultural variety into their research design by systematically comparing U.S.-, Europe- and Japan-based MNCs. While this does not offer a full guarantee against cultural bias, at the very least it decreases the odds of cultural boundaries.

Finally, this line of research cumulatively addresses the seven specific demands on DMNC organization defined in this article. For example, Prahalad and Doz's early work clearly focuses on structural indeterminacy, the need for internal differentiation and the mechanisms and preconditions for integrative optimization. Most researchers have clearly recognized the high information intensity required of the DMNC network and discussed how to provide for it, while Egelhoff (1982, 1988) adopts explicitly an information-processing view. Bartlett and Ghoshal's research, as summarized in their 1989 book, clearly focuses on latent linkages, while their more recent work explicitly advocates the use of interinstitutional models for the study of relationships within DMNCs. Finally, while many authors identify the trade-off between learning and continuity, Hedlund's analysis of the DMNC as a "heterarchy" represents a clear attempt at identifying how the trade-off may be managed in practice.

Conclusion

MNC Management Research and Organization Theory: A Missed Opportunity for Cross-fertilization?

We stressed above that most organization theories were compatible with the characteristics that make the DMNC different from simpler organizations. We argued that it was not so much the features of the theories as the perspective adopted by the proponents of these theories which made their application to MNCs difficult. We also showed that researchers studying the management processes of MNCs had borrowed more from organization theories than they, or for that matter organization theorists, are likely to acknowledge. Why such a surreptitious rather than explicit convergence?

Theoretical Dogma versus Atheoretical Phenomenology

We believe that organization theorists have remained too involved with the development of their theories, while many, if not all, scholars of MNC management have underexploited the theories available to them. The former have typically studied much simpler organizations than DMNCs, while the latter have often been engrossed in the complexity of what they studied, and failed to develop, or borrow, a sufficiently powerful conceptual framework to shed light on the observed phenomenon. As a result the bridge between the MNC phenomenon and organization theory was not built.

Managerial versus Institutional Concerns

The difference in perspective between organizational theorists and scholars of the MNC also extends to the purpose of their theories: MNC scholars have usually undertaken to "educate" practice, i.e., have put managerial relevance before theoretical elegance. The converse is true of most organizational theorists. This made the dialogue more difficult.

Theory Building versus Theory Testing

By and large, scholars of MNC management have used data to develop their understanding of the phenomenon and then to illustrate their concepts to facilitate their presentation. There was essentially no attempt to test propositions and hypotheses. Theory development progressed by attempts at refutation, and by tentative extensions. Some researchers were not concerned with testing hypotheses (their priority being to provide an insightful perspective on the MNC phenomenon rather than to delimit its exact contours or specify all its characteristics). Most deemed the testing of hypotheses premature, or too complex given the complexity of MNCs and the large number of control variables. As a result, the line of research lacks rigor in measurement techniques. The work of Ghoshal (1987) constitutes a useful shift of emphasis toward measuring and testing. Overall, it is only very recently that researchers have undertaken to test systematically some of the key propositions from process research on DMNCs (Kim and Mauborgne, 1991). More of this work can be done now as the conceptual structure exists to understand the management processes in DMNCs.

Research Complexity versus Simplicity

Process research on the DMNC is complex and costly, not always consistent with the funding and reward processes in place at many academic institutions. It is also demanding for the researcher, involving numerous interviews and process observations in many parts of the world that only skilled field researchers can carry out effectively. As a result, management process research on MNCs has taken place only at a relatively few academic institutions with a tradition of field research, abundant funding, and a specific institutional interest in MNCs. The dearth of researchers has slowed down research progress.

A State or an Elusive Phenomenon?

Observers have noticed that both managerial cognitive maps and management tools in MNCs, and the focus of attention of MNC scholars, have shifted over time, without much clarity as to which one influenced the other (or maybe they influenced each other over time). The underlying difficulty is the evolutionary nature of the MNC phenomenon itself. For example, the shift in MNCs from relatively long-term positions rooted in access to resources, or in economies of scale, to a succession of shorter-term positions built on intangible assets, puts very different demands on management. Or the evolution of communication and information technologies may, in turn, allow very different responses to existing problems, and change management approaches. It is therefore not even clear that the search for a stable organization theory of the MNC is warranted. Perhaps researchers ought to satisfy themselves with addressing an evolving agenda of managerial issues created by changes in success conditions for MNCs and in enabling technologies for their management.

Afterword

Richard P. Rumelt, Dan E. Schendel, and David J. Teece

Other Fundamental Questions

The four fundamental questions treated in this volume do not
exhaust the set that researchers should consider when framing
their work. One question concerning the "policy process" was
asked at the conference, but was dropped from this volume; in
this section we discuss why, and what we can learn from the
experience. In addition there were three "also ran" questions
that were strongly considered, but that were not used. They
deserve and receive some mention here. Finally, there was a
question we now wish we had asked when designing the conference; here we state it and explain its interest.

Policy Process

When the editors designed the conference that led to this volume, five fundamental questions were posed. One of them was,
How does the policy process matter? Note that the question was
not, as some seemed to feel, Does the policy process matter?
Rather, we sought to direct attention to the fact that studies of
the policy process rarely, if ever, connect attributes of the process with quality of outcome. The full text of the question as
originally posed follows.

How Does the Policy Process Matter?

In organizations of any size, policy or strategy is not the choice of a
single individual, but is the outcome of organizational processes and procedures. Whatever policy process an organization uses must cope with the
two basic facts of organizational decision making: the information and
knowledge organizations gain through size and scope cannot be simply
pooled (if one person could know it all there would be no gains to specialization in the first place), and each member of the organization has (per-

haps unannounced) goals and values which may conflict with those of others. Given these constraints, how should the firm organize to generate and execute policy?

One stream of research in this general area has concentrated on empirical description of the policy process. Thus, for example, we have valuable insights into how organizations sometimes structure decision processes (Mintzberg, Raisinghani, and Théorêt 1976), the resource allocation process (Bower, 1970), "Muddling Through" (Lindblom, 1968), "Logical Incrementalism" (Quinn, 1980), and "loose-coupling" (March and Olsen, 1976). Another research stream, centered in political science, concerns the ways in which various individuals or interest groups affect outcomes in different political arrangements (i.e., how agendas are set, how voting is structured, etc.).

Despite the inherent value of these research traditions, neither cuts to the heart of the fundamental issue in strategy—the link between the policy process and the quality of decision, defined in competitive terms. That is, the organizational stream has not focused on producing a normative calculus and the political science tradition views outcomes in distributive rather than competitive terms. The subquestions which may help further define and deepen our understanding of this fundamental issue are:

> What are the basic modes of policy formulation? Can a succinct taxonomy of policy modes be set out?
>
> In what ways, if any, should the nature of the problem, the nature of the organization, and other situational factors influence the choice of a policy formulation process? In other words, what are the basic contingencies to be considered in designing a policy process?
>
> Should (or can) the same subunits in an organization be responsible for both strategy formulation and strategy execution?
>
> Diversity in cognitive frameworks may stimulate fresh approaches to strategy formulation but impede implementation. How may this tension be managed?

Thomas Hammond's paper (Chapter 4) was originally written as a response to this question, although it is also responsive to the question we have placed it with in this volume. Hammond's paper indicates that the process question we posed lies at the forefront of current research in political science. Nevertheless, and despite our best intentions, this question, How does the policy process matter? proved to be too removed from most current research activities and interests in strategic management to generate a fruitful dialogue *on the issues posed*. The current state of the field is such that the term "process" is most often used to refer to "management," as opposed to "strategy." Process is viewed as being influenced by structure, by culture, by history, by leadership and vision, and by the challenges that the firm faces. Current thinking sees policy decisions as largely emergent, whereas our question suggests that policy processes can be designed or chosen. Hence, there was a gap (a gulf?) between our question and the current state of process research.

Among those unhappy with the question as posed, the general reaction was that it reflected unwarranted presumptions of rationality and reductionism. Real processes in real corporations, we were told, are very complex, are subtly nuanced, deal with ambiguities so great that no objective appraisal is possible, and frame, rather than solve, problems. Additionally, many process researchers envision a world in which the strategic decisions are already taken and have lasting effect—they are contained in a vision or intent that guides the firm over decades. In such a case, process is about motivating people and mobilizing resources to accomplish the vision.

We are sympathetic to this reaction. In particular, we fully understand the criticism that the "policy decision" literature sees decisions as mandated by the top, whereas process researchers increasingly see significant innovations as flowing from the coordinated insights and actions of many actors, each possessing specialized information and competences. Nevertheless, we are also disappointed. We believe there are times when firms (or nation-states!) do face critical choices and that their leaderships also face choices about how to choose. How should the management of Northrop react to the end of the cold war and how should it choose its future path? Is the use of consultants advisable? Should it first reorganize and then choose, or vice versa? Who should be involved in the policy process? It may be that policy at most companies emerges out of complex political, interpersonal, cognitive, and structured interactions, but is this always desirable? Might not the "garbage can" mode of policy making in most organizations simply reflect the lack of a superior, proven alternative?

Irving Janis, a social psychologist, is perhaps the only scholar who is currently addressing this question head-on. He writes (1989: 11):

> If we had a valid theory describing linkages between procedures for arriving at policy decisions and good versus poor outcomes, we could extract valuable prescriptions for improving the quality of policy-making in government, business, and public welfare organizations. Do we have anything approaching such a theory at present? Unfortunately, not. What we do have are numerous unintegrated hypotheses supported to varying degrees by empirical evidence, much of which is subject to debate and disagreements among social scientists.

Janis goes on to suggest that we already know what good process is—it is "vigilant problem solving." That is, good process involves a cycle of energetic problem formulation, information gathering and analysis, and evaluation. The problem with process, according to Janis, is that this is rarely done. Instead, policy makers use unconscious decision rules to act. For example, one psychological rule is "bolstering": grabbing the first minimally acceptable alternative and pressing for early closure by mentally stressing the positives and by acting to commit oneself and others. Another such rule is the affiliative "groupthink" rule: go along with whatever consensus seems to be emerging. Janis describes 18 other such dysfunctional shortcuts.

Whether Janis is right or wrong, at least he is attacking the issue. We believe that the time is long past when management research can depend on the method of describing and prescribing the practices of the "best firms." It is precisely because the causes of excellent performance are so difficult to discern that we need good theory. Without theory, management schools will continue in the long-standing tradition of teaching the practices of the large and profitable. In 1972 students learned the planning methods of Xerox and the structure of General Motors; in 1978 they feasted on Texas Instruments' planning system; in 1988 Canon and Komatsu's visions provided the icons. Today's (1993) heroes are the new slimmed-down GE and Ford, companies in which large bureaucracies have been significantly transformed. Yet history shows that success stories are transient. We need to remember Frederick Taylor's insight that naturally emerging practices can be dramatically improved through careful analysis.

"Also Ran" Questions

In arriving at the fundamental questions structuring the conference and this book, we consulted many of our colleagues. Over several months, we presented various lists of questions to individuals and small groups and sought their reactions. The five questions that structured the conference, and the four that structure this book, were derived from this process. To complete the record, we should briefly discuss some of the "fundamental questions" that were investigated in some depth but eventually set aside. There were three:

Are there strategies?
How do industries evolve?
How is organizational competence generated and sustained?

Are there strategies? Do firms really have internally consistent sets of antecedent decisions and actions that create functional policies aimed at competing in a certain way or targeted at particular product-market goals? If so, how are these decisions and actions made? Clearly fundamental, this question cuts to the center of the strategic management field. Chandler (1962), of course, invented the term "strategy" to help him understand organization structures. He was less concerned about how strategies arose than he was with their existence. Most writers in strategic management presume the existence of strategies, at least in successful firms, and go on to stress the incremental or incoherent nature of most policy-making processes. Appearing under the labels "muddling through," "logical incrementalism," "emergent strategies," and the "garbage-can" model of choice, there is a substantial literature arguing that coherent, carefully thought-out strategies are extremely rare. Nevertheless, this question was thought too skeptical in tone and content, almost insulting. In the end, we did not use the question because there did not appear to be enough systematic empirical research on the subject to generate any light.

How do industries evolve? Are there predictable patterns in the evolution of competitive structures? Understanding the environment is critical to good strategy, and the two main frameworks used to apprehend a firm's environment are: (1) industrial organization economics, and (2) life-cycle or stages views of product-market development. The second group includes, for example, product-life-cycle models and the "dominant design" model. Product-life-cycle models predict that the form of competition will change as the rate of growth and age of the market change; strategic wisdom, in this framework, consists of anticipating maturity while still in the growth phase, and anticipating decline during maturity. The "dominant design" framework posits that technological competition over the basic form of the product or service culminates in the arrival of a dominant design, after which competition is based on added features, quality, and price. We suggest that the fundamental question here is whether or not there actually are predictable patterns or epochs in the evolution of industries. It is always possible to find examples to support a hypothesized pattern, but do any of these models actually have predictive power? Furthermore, are there other aspects of industry evolution that may have predictable elements?

How is organizational competence generated and sustained? The idea that firms have, or should have, special "distinctive competences" goes back to Selznick (1957) and is as old as the strategy field. Recently, there has been a resurgence of interest in this issue sparked by the evolving "resource-based viewpoint" and the writings of Prahalad and Hamel (1990). While it has always been clear that organizations must have competences to perform their tasks, strategy's incorporation of equilibrium thinking has generated a new focus on those competences—call them "strategic" competences—that resist imitation and diffusion. It is fairly easy to enumerate conditions that made competencies immobile (e.g., tacitness, product specificity, team embodiment), but such description leaves a crucial question unanswered: How do strategic competences arise? Is it chiefly through learning by doing, by investment in competence building, serendipity, or other mechanisms? What are the principal impediments to the imitation and diffusion of competences? Where do strategic competences reside? Are they chiefly held within specialized groups performing functional tasks (e.g., diesel engine assembly), or are they expressed through integration and coordination (e.g., product design)? The traditional experience curve, for example, points to product efficiency competences gained through learning by doing. By contrast, the work of Clark and Fujimoto (1991) suggests that strategic competences reside in activities directed at coordinating across functions and across pools of specialized knowledge.

Though we were tempted by these "also ran" questions, in the end we set them aside. They are easy to pose, but they do not compel further inquiry with the motivation and clarity we feel are necessary to drive our inquiry into fundamental issues in strategy.

A Question We Missed: Inertia in Organization

Since the conference, it has become even clearer that the research frontier in strategic management deals with the efficiency and effectiveness of organizations. Research to date has helped clarify the nature of product-market competition and develop tools for describing and analyzing strategic moves. But the enduring sources of competitive advantage seem to have more to do with organization than with product-market moves. Yet, if organization is a critical source of advantage, one must ask why organizations differ so in quality. The most evident answer is that organizations are very hard to change; even when challenges are almost overwhelming, organizations resist the adoption of fairly obvious improvements. For example, General Motors has had a joint venture with the world's most efficient car maker for a decade, yet is the least improved and now the most inefficient of the "Big Three." We suggest that the fundamental question that needs to be asked here is, Why are organizations so resistant to change?

One line of reasoning is that organizational inertia is unavoidable, and even necessary. Organizing, it can be argued, involves specialization, commitment, investments of specialized human and physical capital, and the development of social bonds of loyalty and trust. Organizations are inefficient without these attributes, but they also act to inhibit change. However, other lines of reasoning suggest that inertia is due to agency problems, or problems of collective action (Who moves first? Who sacrifices for the gain of the many?), or operating methods that have the force of habit behind them.[1] The question then becomes, How much of inertia is the unavoidable concomitant of organizing, and how much is waste and abuse?

Organizational inertia is interesting to the strategist because it suggests that the returns to innovation are larger than naive economic analysis suggests. Because economic models portray competitors as vigilant and energetic, they foresee rapid imitation and much competition. But if potential competitors are gripped by inertia, competitive response is dulled. Thus, inertia is a critical ingredient in competitive modeling. Game-theoretic models that posit rational, flexible opponents are incorrect: it is not rational to assume your opponent is rational and flexible if you really believe he isn't.

---

[1] Kuran (1988) provides a concise summary of many sources of inertia. Postrel and Rumelt (1992) discuss both the functionality and inertial properties of habit and routine.

Organizational inertia is interesting to those who study process because it is the factor that prevents the adoption of good practice. Teaching "best practice" is pointless unless there are ways of moving organizations to adopt it.

Economics and Strategy

One of the themes that recurred throughout the conference was the impact of economics on strategic management. After all, economics is the social science most relevant to managing firms. No one doubts the size of the impact, but many question the wisdom or correctness of using economic reasoning in connection with questions of managing organizations. In this section we deal with this issue and provide the editors' views on the present and future role of economics in our field.

Why Economics in Strategic Management?

Why has the "content" side of strategic management recently come to draw so heavily on economics?[2] The trend cannot have been driven by practice; very few, if any, of the unregulated firms in the United States employ microeconomists to analyze strategies or help chart strategic direction. It cannot have been driven by teaching; most strategic management courses continue to rely on cases that are more integrative than analytic. We contend that the infusion of economic thinking has been driven by five forces or events, all connected with the research program of strategic management. They are (1) the changing nature of economics (this force has been discussed in the editors' introduction), (2) the need to interpret performance data, (3) the experience curve, (4) the problem of persistent profit, and (5) the changing climate within business schools. Each of the forces or events has shaped the connection between economics and strategic management and each continues to pose practical and intellectual challenges that will shape future developments.

---

[2] Much of the material that follows in this section appears in Richard Rumelt, Dan Schendel, and David Teece (1991), "Strategic Management and Economics" in *Fundamental Issues in Strategy and Economics*, 12, pp. 5–31, and is reproduced here with the permission of John Wiley and Sons.

The Need to Interpret Performance Data

In the early 1970s strategy researchers began to look systematically at corporate performance data, particularly return on investment, in attempts to link results to managerial action. Fruhan's (1972) study of the airline industry, Rumelt's (1974) study of diversification strategy, Hatten, Schendel, and Cooper's (1978) brewing industry study, Biggadike's (1979) study of entry and diversification, and the PIMS studies were the early examples of this new style of research. The problem implicit in each of these studies was that of interpreting the observed performance differentials. What meaning should be ascribed to performance differences between groups, or to variables that correlate with performance? The need to find an adequate answer to these questions was one of the forces engendering economic thinking among strategy researchers.

The story of the market-share effect provides a good illustration of this dynamic. The empirical association between market share and profitability was first discerned in IO economics research[3] where the relationship was interpreted as evidence of "market power." Why? Because using the structure-conduct-performance paradigm as the driver, market share represented "structure" ("conduct" was implicit) and supernormal returns were interpreted as poor social "performance." Within the strategic management community, the market-share issue was raised by The Boston Consulting Group and sharpened by the PIMS studies, carried out on the first business-level data base available for economic research. The leading role both BCG and PIMS gave to market share helped shape thought about strategic management in the late 1970s. The viewpoint they espoused saw market share as an asset that could be bought and sold for strategic purposes.[4] BCG advised its clients to "invest" in share in growing industries (where competitive reaction was either absent or dulled) and "harvest" share in declining industries.

---

[3] Imel and Helmberger (1971), Shepherd (1972), and Gale (1972) all address this phenomenon. In the marketing literature models were also proposed and studied that linked market share to profitability, but without much attention being paid to the underlying theoretical issues involved.

[4] Their views were also echoed by some economists. Shepherd (1979: 185) claimed that "present market share . . . will yield a given profit rate. . . . The firm can maintain that profit rate. Or it can raise it now, while yielding up some of its market share to other firms. Or it can 'invest' present profits in building up a higher future market share."

PIMS researchers and consultants went further and told managers they could increase share, and thus profit, by redefining their markets (i.e., redefining their competitors and presumably their share position).

In 1979, Rumelt and Wensley (1980) began an empirical study using PIMS data that was designed to estimate the "cost" of gaining market share. Their motivation was discomfort with the consultants' advice to gain share in growing markets (or new industries, and so forth). The advice seemed to be too much of a "free lunch." Were there really simple rules of strategy that could always be expected to pay off? Expecting to find the cost of share gains to be at least equal to their worth in each context, they were quite surprised to find no cost to share gains. Changes in share and changes in profitability were positively related in every context examined. *It was not possible to interpret this result without extensive forays into economic theory and advanced econometrics.* In the end, they adopted the assumption that share changes were properly "priced" and interpreted their results as implying that the share-profit association was causally spurious. Instead, an unobserved stochastic process (i.e., luck, good management) was jointly driving both share and profitability. Subsequent empirical research has generally supported their view.[5] The market-share issue also stimulated efforts to model competitive equilibria in which share and profitability are associated. Note that most of this work has been carried out within strategic management rather than by economists.[6]

The market-share story exemplifies an argument over data analysis and equilibrium which continues in new forms today. Simply stated, equilibrium means that all actors have exploited the opportunities they face. Thus, competitive equilibrium rules out (by assumption) the possibility that differences in firm wealth can be attributed to differences in freely variable strategy choices, or easily reversible decisions. Instead, observed differences in wealth must be attributed to phenomena that are uncontrollable or unpredictable, e.g., order of entry, nonimitable

---

[5]   See Jacobson (1990). For an intermediate view, see Boulding and Staelin (1990). As part of the Purdue brewing studies, Schendel and Patton (1978) provided a simultaneous view of the search for market share, profitability, and growth.

[6]   Lippman and Rumelt's (1982) theory of uncertain imitability generates this sort of equilibrium, as does the differentiated oligopoly modeled by Karnani (1985). Elegant models in which market share "matters" have been developed by Wernerfelt (1984, 1991).

differences in quality or efficiency, and of course, luck. By making this assumption, the widely used study of performance versus some parameter or other loses much of its value. For example, if the world is in equilibrium, the fact that growing industries are more profitable does not mean that one should invest in growing industries. Instead, the assumption of equilibrium leads the researcher to presume that the observed profitability is balanced by the expectation of future losses and by risk, or is sustained by impediments to entry, or is a reputation-based premium, or is otherwise balanced by unseen scarcity and cost.

Equilibrium assumptions are the cornerstone of most economic thinking and are the most straightforward way of modeling competition. Researchers who eschew equilibrium assumptions risk gross errors in the causal interpretation of data. On the other hand, the risk in adopting an equilibrium assumption is that it may be unwarranted. Observed differences in performance may actually reflect widespread ignorance about the phenomena being studied. Which risk is undertaken is not just a matter of preference, but more likely one of conditions, especially the presence of innovation and change. The general approach to making this judgment is to rule in favor of equilibrium when the underlying assets or positions are frequently traded or contested, when the level of aggregation and the type of data is familiar to actors in the industry, when the data are widely available and frequently reviewed, and when the connections between the data and profits are widely understood.

While equilibrium assumptions often drive out consideration of innovation, change, and heterogeneity, this is not invariably the case. In the neoclassical world, equilibrium meant that profits were everywhere zero, or more generally, that all opportunities had been exploited. But more sophisticated views now permit more sophisticated equilibria. The basic idea of Nash equilibrium—wherein each actor does the best he or she can with what he or she individually knows and controls—especially when coupled with uncertainty, asymmetric information, and unequal resource endowments, permits a broad range of intriguing outcomes. For example, one could model the gradual imitation of an innovation as a process in which competitors observe its operation and market results, and then gradually learn what the leader already knows. In such a model large profits would be earned, firms might enter and then exit, and competition would gradually increase. Although the product market would not be in neoclassical equilibrium, the behavior described is still equilibrium behavior in that none of the actors have passed up any opportunities for profit that are *known to them*. Thus, it is possible to describe many aspects of innovation and the profit-creating transient responses they induce with "equilibrium" models, although a plethora of nonneoclassical assumptions will be required.

An example of an equilibrium assumption of use in strategic management is that of "no rule for riches"—that there can be no general rules for generating wealth. There is no substitute for judgment in deciding whether or not this exclusion should be applied to a particular context (that is, deciding how general is "general"). Interestingly, this equilibrium assumption rationalizes the traditional case-based situational analysis that has been the hallmark of strategic management instruction. If there are no general rules for riches, then a strategy based on generally available information and unspecialized resources should be rejected. Opportunities worth undertaking must be rooted in the particulars of the situation. They must flow from special information possessed by the firm or its managers, from the special resources, skills, and market positions that the firm possesses. Viewed in this light, traditional case analysis is a legitimate search for opportunity. What is worth recognizing is that the acceptance of this level of economic equilibrium does not nullify strategic management, nor does it imply that one should teach economic theorems rather than management. It does imply that professional educators are right in their focus on developing skills in the analysis of the particular rather than the general. In addition, it suggests a framework for where to look for opportunities and, once identified, a basis for judging their relative merits. Theory alone is insufficient absent intimate, unique knowledge of technical conditions and the ability to position assets and skills to create favorable competitive positions.

The Experience Curve

During the 1970s the experience curve doctrine, developed by The Boston Consulting Group,[7] was a powerful force within

---

[7]   See The Boston Consulting Group, *Perspectives in Experience,* 1970.

strategic management. Although the idea that some costs followed a learning-by-doing pattern had been around since the 1920s, it was largely ignored by economists because it was a theoretical nuisance; it destroyed the ability of standard models to reach equilibrium. BCG added four critical ingredients: (1) They argued that the pattern applied not just to direct labor, but to all deflated cost elements of value added; this expanded version of the learning curve was called the *experience curve;* (2) they provided convincing data showing experience effects in a broad variety of industries; (3) they argued that experience-based cost reduction was not restricted to the early stages of production, but continued indefinitely;[8] and (4) they explored the competitive implications of the experience effect. An example of the latter is BCG's (1970: 29) suggestion that "there is no naturally stable relationship with competitors on any product until some one competitor has a commanding market share of the normal market for that product and until the product's growth slows. Furthermore, under stable conditions, the profitability of each competitor should be a function of his accumulated experience with that product."

The idea that cumulative production experience, not scale, could be a primary driver of unit costs implied a value in doing business apart from the immediate profits earned. In the second half of the 1970s, virtually every article, book, and presentation on strategy referred in some way to the experience curve. The idea's power was that it provided an explanation for the sustained dominance of leaders and for heterogeneity, despite competition. There was also the simple fact that it supported many managers' tastes for pursuing dominance and growth at the expense of current profit.

The impact of the experience curve on the strategic management community extended beyond the overt content or correctness of the doctrine. The experience curve was the first wedge in the widening split between the study of management process and the study of competitive action and market outcomes. In a

---

[8] This was a critical issue. Scherer's (1970: 74) contemporaneous industrial organization text dismissed the importance of learning by doing in mass production industries because "the rate of cost reduction evidently declines as cumulative output rises beyond several thousand units." Interestingly, the second, revised edition, published in 1980, abandoned the disclaimer and treated learning by doing as an important phenomenon, citing BCG, among others.

field that had traditionally seen the firm as embedded within an "environment," the experience curve focused attention on the actions of alert rivals. Most important, the logic of the experience curve engendered a taste for a microeconomic style of explanation: for the first time there was a simple, parsimonious account of what competitive advantage was, how it was gained, and where it should be sought. Adding piquancy was the fact that the logic of experience-based competition was not imported from economics, but was instead developed within strategic management and then exported to economics. Finally, among those who sought more precision, there was the need to clarify assumptions about competitive behavior, to more exactly characterize the resulting equilibria,[9] and to empirically estimate the relative importance of scale, industry experience, and firm-experience effects.[10] Thus, the very act of developing and grappling with the logic of experience-based competition encouraged economic thinking within strategic management.

The Problem of Persistent Profit

One of the key empirical observations made by traditional strategy case research was that firms within the same industry differ from one another, and that there seems to be an inertia associated with these differences. Some firms simply do better than others, and they do so consistently. Indeed, the existence of these differences was the origin of the strategy concept. In standard neoclassical economics, competition should erode the extra profits earned by successful firms, leaving each firm just enough to pay factor costs. Yet empirical studies show that if you do well today, you tend to do well tomorrow; good results persist.

One of the factors in the 1970s that drove strategy researchers to search for theoretical explanations of persistent performance differences was the enormous success and legitimacy of the capital asset pricing model (CAPM). Developed by financial economists, the CAPM not only had practical usefulness, it gave great

---

[9] Experience-based equilibria are analytically intractable. Spence's (1981) remains the best analysis, accomplished by ignoring discounting.

[10] Lieberman (1984), studying 37 chemical products, found learning effects much larger than scale economies and showed that they were associated with cumulative output rather than calendar time.

strength to the idea that markets were *efficient*. Consequently, an intellectual climate developed in the academy which tended to presume efficiency in all markets, even product markets, and aggressively challenged assertions to the contrary. The experience curve doctrine provided a partial response to this challenge, but it clearly was not the whole story.

In searching for explanations for enduring success it was natural to reach for relevant economic theory. The most obvious theory was that of industrial organization economics and its various explanations for abnormal returns. Traditional entry-barrier theory yielded the concepts of scale economies and sunk costs; mobility barrier theory stressed the importance of learning and first-mover advantages in making specialized investments in positions within industries. The Chicago tradition supported the notion that high profits were returns to specialized, high-quality resources. Game theory provided models of firms that use preemption, brand crowding, dynamic limit-pricing, signaling, and reputations for toughness to strategically protect market positions. The economics of innovation brought a focus on Schumpeterian competition, intellectual property, and the costs of technology transfer. And evolutionary economics yielded the idea that skills, embedded in organizational routines, resisted imitation and had to be developed anew by each firm.

Within strategic management there has been a great deal of work aimed at synthesizing these ideas into coherent frameworks. The most prominent effort is Porter's (1980, 1985). Taking the basic ideas of the Mason/Bain structure-conduct-performance paradigm, Porter changed the perspective from that of the industry to that of the firm, and formulated what had been learned from this perspective into a theory of competitive strategy. Porter catalogued, described, and discussed a wide range of phenomena that interfered with free competition, thus allowing abnormal returns, and suggested how their interaction and relative importance varied across contexts. Porter's (1985) later approach, delineated in *Competitive Advantage*, extended the earlier analysis of competitive strategy to encompass positioning within an industry (or strategic group) so as to achieve sustained competitive advantage. Positing two basic types of firm-specific advantage (cost based or differentiation based), Porter argued that advantage could be sustained from a product-market position and a configuration of internal activities that were mutually reinforcing (i.e., strong complementarities among activities and the conditions of demand).[11]

A second effort at synthesis is the resource-based view of strategy. This view shifts attention away from product-market barriers to competition and toward factor-market impediments to resource flows. Identifying abnormal returns as rents to unique resource combinations, rather than market power, this perspective emphasizes the importance of specialized, difficult-to-imitate resources. The creation of such resources is seen as entrepreneurship: strategic management consists of properly identifying the existence and quality of resources, and in building product-market positions and contractual arrangements that most effectively utilize, maintain, and extend these resources. This perspective finds its greatest use in examining heterogeneity within industries and in the discussion of "relatedness" among diversified businesses. Nelson (Chapter 9) discusses a recent version of this viewpoint, which incorporates learning and is called the "dynamic capabilities" approach. Prahalad and Hamel's (1990) recent discussion of core competencies is an expression of the resource-based view.

Ghemawat (1991) provides a new attempt at synthesis around the idea of *commitment*. His view is that the persistence of strategies and of performance both stem from mechanisms that link and bind actions over time. He identifies lock-in, lock-out, lags, and inertia as the key irreversibilities at work and reinterprets a great deal of strategic doctrine in terms of the selection and management of commitments.

In summary, the single most significant impact of economics in strategic management has been to radically alter explanations of success. Where the traditional frameworks had success follow leadership, clarity of purpose, and a general notion of "fit" between the enterprise and its environment, the new framework focused on the impediments to the elimination of abnormal returns. Depending upon the framework employed, success is now seen as sustained by mobility barriers, entry barriers, market preemption, asset specificity, learning, ambiguity, tacit knowledge, nonimitable resources and skills, the sharing of core competencies, and commitment. That fit is correlated with success

---

[11] This argument can be couched in strict equilibrium terms by introducing strategy-specific assets or other sources of first-mover advantage.

can be argued, but that it is causal cannot be. The fit argument lies in the long line of work that Porter (Chapter 15) describes as a continuing search for causal explanation. Teaching frameworks that suggest the importance of fit are correct as far as they go, but it is the new economic frameworks that establish the causal linkages. That has been learned from the pressure of asking questions from an economics perspective.

The Changing Climate within Business Schools

Business schools have transformed themselves profoundly over the past 30 years. This transformation has moved business schools and their faculty from collecting and transmitting the best current practice to developing and transmitting theoretical understanding of pervasive phenomena and issues surrounding the practice of management, principally the management of complex business firms. This transformation has influenced the strategy field and its connection to economics in important ways. There are several reasons why it occurred: the impetus of the Ford Foundation and Carnegie Foundation, university hiring and promotion practices, the rise of consulting firms as repositories of best practice, and the relative proximity of economics departments. Without these collective changes, the field as we know it would be different, and the involvement of economics in strategy would have been less.

In the late 1950s, the Gordon and Howell (1959) and Pierson (1959) reports were published, both of which critiqued the business schools of their day. The criticisms were many and the changes they prompted were extensive, but one of the most far-reaching recommendations was that business schools needed to be infused with rigor, methods, and content of basic disciplines: mathematics, economics, sociology, and psychology. This recommendation was avidly followed, with the result that a good many economists, psychologists, and others trained solely in the basic social science disciplines found employment in business schools alongside traditional, professionally oriented faculty members. The traditional faculty found its scholarship in studying business firms, identifying the best practice they could find, and transmitting what they learned in the classroom, typically through cases and the occasional published article. Along the way such faculty were frequently cast in the role of consultants to practicing business managers, and many found greater financial reward in such work than they did from their scholarship alone. The new, discipline-based faculty, on the other hand, found their scholarship inside the academy, in the writings of others similarly placed, and in advancing the theory of their field, often without resort to practice and application of what they learned. Their minds and rewards were concentrated on what they produced inside the academy. A process that retired practice-based scholars in favor of discipline-based ones was set in motion.

After a time, probably longer than anticipated, the discipline-based preference in hiring and promotion led to a stronger and stronger presence of discipline-based scholars, including economists. Indeed, some newer business schools, and some older ones as well, were organized with the economics departments as part of their faculty. As business schools became more discipline based, their standards for hiring and promotion came into alignment with the social sciences. The primary measure of excellence became publication in discipline-based journals and acceptance by the community of discipline-based scholars, rather than relevance to practice or contributions to professional education. Discipline-based scholars not only earned internal rewards more easily, they also typically lacked the cushion of consultation that would otherwise allow a greater adaptation to the special circumstances of professional schools. This self-reinforcing cycle is still present today.

Throughout most of this period very high growth rates characterized business schools, as they moved from granting about 12,000 to over 70,000 MBA degrees per year, and to many more schools offering the MBA. Well-trained faculty in specialty areas such as marketing, finance, accounting, and other functions were in short supply, especially in the earlier years of greatest growth. To fuel expansion it was a short step to hiring discipline-based faculty directly and worrying about their adaptation to applications in business firms later. Some made the transition, some did not, but many who did retained an allegiance to their base disciplines that included seeking publication reputations, not in the field in which they were to teach, but in the basic discipline in which they had been trained.

In the world of business, more and more large firms began to create their own management development programs, aimed at filling the gap between the increasingly theoretical MBA education and the needs of practice. In addition, consulting firms grew in scope and sophistication. In many functional areas, including management and strategy, specialist consulting firms replaced business schools as repositories of best practice.

These factors led to an increased proportion of business school faculty either trained in economics directly, or importantly influenced by the standards common to discipline-based scholars. Unforeseen by Gordon, Howell, and Pierson was the changing character of economics and other social sciences. Less and less concerned with empiricism, economics became increasingly concerned with working out the internal logic of its theoretical structure and less and less concerned with describing real institutions. This trend continues today, with "advanced" departments of economics offering Ph.D. programs in which price theory is considered applied and not even covered during the first year of study.

These changes in business schools forced those interested in strategic management to "take sides" and adopt a discipline. Early on, the typical faculty member in strategic management (then called business policy) was recruited from those with experience and high rank in a functional area (e.g., marketing). The switch required was to that of the total enterprise and its general management function. The increased discipline base of business schools made this switch more difficult, and many schools began to hire young faculty and expect them to move up through the ranks on the merit of work done in strategy. To move through the system in this "new" field was especially difficult, as it tended to lack the infrastructure peculiar to promotion needs: patrons, senior faculty who had been through the system; and journals, venues for exchange of views. It also had a case-based tradition of research increasingly shunned by the academy. Consequently, groups interested in general management and strategy began to take either organization theory or economics as their base discipline.

Throughout the 1970s it appeared that organization theory was the discipline of choice for strategy groups. However, this balance was reversed in the 1980s, largely owing to the success of Porter's approach to strategy. While some schools and their strategy faculty retained an essentially behaviorally focused group, many others moved to economics-based views. Like economics itself, economic-based strategy groups now also differentiate themselves on their commitment to mathematical modeling versus verbal reasoning and their interest in theory versus empiricism. Within the behavioral groups, the split is chiefly between those following organization theory and those taking a managerial process view of strategic management.

Which group has the better idea? Who will dominate? That remains to be seen, but if what the top research-oriented (for example, Stanford, Northwestern, Chicago, Berkeley) schools are doing now is any guide, you have to bet on those emphasizing the contribution of economics, if not relying totally on economists. If, on the other hand, the top European schools or practice is your guide, and if what managers listen to makes a difference, those who combine a modicum of economics with a focus on managerial process are clear winners. No matter what you believe will be the outcome of this contest, economics has clearly infused and informed strategic management, not only through its power to yield insights, but through the transformation of the business school and the evolution of strategic management as a field.

From the viewpoint of strategic management we see a danger in these trends. We have advocated a balanced view of the field, perhaps tipped slightly in favor of tests of theoretical constructs by practice and application. If the balance, as it has at some schools, goes too far toward theory or toward a single discipline base such as economics, there is no counterweight from practice and application likely in either research or teaching. Similarly, if the balance tips too far toward managerial process or even best practice, as it has at other schools, there are no theoretical constructions to accumulate and build for the good of the field. Either unbalanced outcome is bad. In our view, balance requires both theory and application, in their fullest and finest representations, in our research, in our teaching, and in our faculty. That such balanced views represented by portfolios of scholars, some at the discipline end, others at the practice end, do not exist, especially at our best schools, is a sad comment on the lack of administrative leadership and faculty understanding that exists about strategic management, its content, and its challenges. Simon's (1967: 16) description of the problem of running a professional school has special relevance to strategic management: "Organizing a professional school . . . is very much like mixing oil with water.... Left to themselves, oil and water will separate again." He also noted (1967: 12) that

> a professional school administration—the dean and senior faculty—have an unceasing task of fighting the natural increase of entropy, of preventing the system from moving toward the equilibrium it would otherwise seek. When the school is no longer able, by continual activity, to maintain the gradients that differentiate it from the environment, it reaches that equilibrium with the world which is death. In the professional school, "death" means mediocrity and inability to fulfill its special functions.

Unfortunately, strategic management is too often inhibited by those who see no need for, and who may even fear, the balance we advocate.

Will Competitive Strategy Become Applied Microeconomics?

We believe that strategic management has clearly profited from the infusion of economic thinking. There is no question that the presumption of equilibrium and the specification of alert rivals, rather than an amorphous "environment," has generated valuable new frameworks, new insights, and greatly sharpened thinking among strategy scholars. Nevertheless, it is vital also to recognize that this infusion has come only after the weakening of orthodoxy within economics. For decades economics impeded research into strategy by committing its intellectual capital and influence to static analysis, an almost exclusive focus on price competition, the suppression of entrepreneurship, a too stylized treatment of markets, hyper-rationality assumptions, and the cavalier treatment of know-how. Had orthodoxy weakened sooner, strategy would have had the benefits from useful economic thinking earlier. That orthodoxy weakened was perhaps partially a result of research in strategic management.

Economics has been chiefly concerned with the performance of markets in the allocation and coordination of resources. By contrast, strategic management is about coordination and resource allocation *inside the firm*. This distinction is crucial and explains why so much of economics is not readily applicable to the study of strategy, and why strategy can inform economics as much as economics can inform strategy. Twenty-five years ago, economists, asked how a firm should be managed, would have (and did) argue that subunits should be measured on profit, they should transfer products, services, and capital to one another at marginal cost, and the more internal competition the better.

Today, we know that advising managers to run a firm as if it were a set of markets, is ill-founded. Firms replace markets when *nonmarket* means of coordination and commitment are superior. Splendid progress has been made in defining the efficient boundaries of firms—where markets fail and hierarchies are superior—but there are limits to building a theory of management and strategy around market failures. It is up to strategy scholars to flesh out the inverse approach, supplying a coherent theory of effective internal coordination and resource allocation, of entrepreneurship and technical progress, so that markets can be identified as beginning where organizations fail.

The most interesting issue regards the future of the competitive strategy portion of strategic management. It is this subfield that has turned most wholeheartedly toward the use of economic reasoning and models. If the trend continues, does the competitive strategy subject matter have an independent future, or will it become just a branch of applied economics? There are two reasons for concern about this issue. The first is parochial: the field's most elementary wisdom suggests that competing head-on with economics departments in their own domain is a losing strategy. The second has to do with the internal integrity of the field. To split off part of a problem for separate inquiry is to presume its independence from other elements of the problem. Yet the sources of success and failure in firms, and therefore the proper concerns of general management, remain an issue of debate (see, for example, Williamson's argument in Chapter 13). It would be a great loss if the study of competitive strategy became divorced from the other elements of strategic management.

We believe that competitive strategy will remain an integral part of strategic management and that its connection with economics will evolve and take on new forms in the future. We believe that fears of "absorption" will not be realized for these reasons: (1) strategy is not "applied" economics; (2) economists will not learn about business; (3) microeconomics is a collage and apparently cannot provide a coherent integrated theory of the firm or of management; (4) what is strategically critical changes over time; and (5) organizational capability, not market exchange, may increasingly assume center stage in strategic management research.

Strategy Is Not Applied Microeconomics

We assert this because it is patently clear that skilled practitioners do not develop or implement business or corporate strategies by "applying" economics or any other discipline. There are economists who argue that this only proves that practitioners are not very skilled after all, but such a response is neither social science, which studies natural order, nor good professionalism, which seeks to solve, rather than ignore, the problems of practitioners. We do not deny that economic analysis may be useful to a strategist, but so may demography, law, social psychology, and an understanding of political trends, as well as an appreciation for product design, process technology, and the physical sciences underlying the business. Part of any competitive strategy can be tested against known economic theory and models of competitive reaction; but most business strategies also contain implicit hypotheses concerning organizational behavior, political behavior, technological relationships and trends, and rely on judgments about the perceptions, feelings, and beliefs of customers, suppliers, employees, and competitors. Competitive strategy is integrative—not just because it integrates business functions and helps create patterns of consistent, reinforcing decisions, but also because creating and evaluating business strategies requires insights and judgments based on a broad variety of knowledge bases.

Economists Will Not Learn about Business

Economics has a strong doctrinal component that resists displacement. Strategic management, by its nature and audience, is pragmatic. If certain approaches don't shed light on business practices, or if practitioners deny their validity, the proclivity of the strategy field will be, and should be, to reject them. In addition, we believe that economics will not delve very deeply into business practices to generate new theory. This belief is based on judgments about long-term trends in academia. As Simon (1969: 56) commented on academic tastes, "Why would anyone in a university stoop to teach or learn about designing machines or planning market strategies when he could concern himself with solid-state physics? The answer has been clear: he usually wouldn't." Having become as mathematical as physics, and more axiomatic, mainstream economics will not learn enough about business and management to challenge strategic management in its domain. Thus, for example, as industrial organization increasingly becomes infatuated with formal modeling (it didn't until the mid-1970s), it may lose the rich empirical base that made it possible for the Mason/Bain tradition to undergird Porter's work. In other words, industrial organization may have already made its important contributions to strategy.

An example may help illustrate the very real gap between theory, economic or otherwise, and the need to internalize a vast amount of information pertaining to business practice. A case instructor used to ask, What are this company's strengths? Economic reasoning has now helped us understand that what we may mean to ask is, What firm-specific, nonimitable resources or sustainable market positions are presently underutilized? The restatement helps: it is more precise, it provides a definition of "strength," and it defends against critics who insist on a discipline base behind university education. But are economists better equipped to answer the question? We suspect not. It is probably much easier to teach these economic concepts to a generalist than it is to teach economists about business.

Microeconomics Is a Collage

The upshot of all the ferment in economics is that with regard to issues of most concern to strategic management, the neoclassical theory of the firm is no longer a contender. However, there is no new "theory of the firm" to replace it. Instead, there are areas of inquiry characterized by the assumptions that are acceptable in building models and by the phenomena to be explained. There is excitement and vitality in the new economics because the range of phenomena that can be explained has been dramatically enlarged. However, there is also confusion over the loss of the old determinism. With the old theory of the firm, everyone knew how to price—you just set marginal revenue equal to marginal cost. But now price can signal quality to customers and price may tell a potential entrant something about the profits to be made. With the old theory of the firm, a topic like "corporate culture" was outside the realm of consideration, classified with faith healing and voodoo. But now it is clear that there can be many types of social equilibria among the actors within a firm, with the equilibria depending upon sets of beliefs and history, and that these equilibria have radically different efficiency properties. More generally, it used to be that given a technology, the neoclassical theory delivered a prediction about the allocation of resources. But now one has to specify the technology, the information sets of the actors, including their beliefs, and the order of play, and one still usually obtains many possible equilibria. The descriptive power of the new economics has been paid for by the loss of determinism.

The limitation of the new microeconomics is that it *explains* rather than *predicts*. That is, it tends to consist of a series of models, each of which has been purposefully engineered to capture and illustrate a particular phenomenon. Models have been constructed to examine markets with consumer loyalty, experience effects, producer reputations, complex signaling games, the strategic use of debt, multimarket deterrence, and causal ambiguity. In addition, models have been used to explore joint ventures, venture capital, vertical integration, the appropriability of intellectual capital, governance structures, and many other phenomena. All of this has been informative and provides strategic management with a panoply of useful insights. However, these phenomena have not been *deduced* from these models or from some general theory. Rather, each of these many models has been carefully engineered to deliver the phenomena being studied. The contribution of a good modeler is in finding the least aggressive assumptions that enable the phenomena in question. Consequently, the new microeconomics is essentially a formal language for expressing knowledge elsewhere obtained. Camerer (Chapter 6) calls this the "collage problem."

The "collage problem" is simply that formal theorizing has collapsed to examples. Consequently, part of the intellectual structure of the new microeconomics is evolving to look more like strategic management. Any scholar working in strategic management must be aware of the traditional economist's normal reaction to most of the work in our field: "The subject is interesting, but there is no tight theory—it looks like a bunch of lists." But the new economics, taken as a whole, is a "bunch of lists." More precisely, it delivers a large number of tightly reasoned submodels, but no strong guidance as to which will be important in a particular situation.

The new microeconomics is still a developing field and in the future we will see further elaboration of existing frameworks. But we can also confidently expect to hear the clangs of new monkey wrenches being thrown. One already in the air is the strong evidence for persistent biases in human judgment and decision making. Another that can be anticipated is the observation that managers not only have different information sets, they also differ in their beliefs[12] and in their understandings of the causal mechanisms they face. A third, emphasized by Nelson (Chapter 9), is that firms do not apprehend complete sets of alternatives, but grope forward with only a limited understanding of their own capabilities and the opportunities they face.

The implications of this research style for strategic management are several. First, it should be clear that knowledge about what phenomena need be studied is outside its scope. Hence, there remains a central and important role for scholars who identify phenomena worth studying. For example, it is up to strategy and management scholars to convince financial economists that most firms really do budget as if they were equity constrained—only then will useful models of this phenomenon appear. Similarly, it is up to strategy researchers to reveal the patterns of global interdependence and competition—economic modeling will come after the fact. Second, the economist's approach to these phenomena is to show their existence; yet this is rarely sufficient to help in practical strategy work. Yes, it is useful to know that reputational equilibria are enabled when product quality cannot be determined by inspection and warranties are unavailable, but this is of little help to a firm that wants to know whether its reputation in the United States for workshirts will help it in Eastern Europe. It is up to strategy (or marketing or other functional fields) to develop the measures, tools, and methods to help in specific situations. Third, each of the economist's models tends to be minimal and independent of the others—they do not integrate into any cohesive theory of the firm. For example, game theorists can model entry deterrence as based on reputations for toughness, as flowing from asset specificity, as responsive to uncertainty about post-

---

[12] A belief is a prior probability assignment to an unobservable variable. Interesting beliefs are those that affect decisions yet that are not significantly updated by events.

entry performance, and find that entry is encouraged by opportunities for learning, by the presence of technology options, and
by economies of scope involving related products. However,
these separate models provide little or no information about
which of these phenomena, if any, will predominate in a specific
situation, nor do they help much in determining even the rough
magnitudes of the wealth impacts each of these phenomena can
induce. This lack of specificity not only hinders empirical testing, it renders the professional utility of these concepts dramatically smaller than model builders imagine.

What Is Strategic Changes Over Time

What is strategic changes as time and discovery alter the
basis of competition. These changes arise, in part, because of
technological, legal, social, and political changes. They also
arise because education and research disseminate knowledge,
reducing the degree to which a particular issue can be a source
of advantage. The rise of Japanese competition, for example,
has substantially altered the research agenda for strategy scholars. By contrast, little or no accommodation to such changes is
seen in microeconomics. Business school deans like to argue
that their research programs, though abstract, constitute the
practices of tomorrow. The opposite is closer to the truth. Yesterday's business strategies are the subject of today's research in
strategic management (e.g., takeovers and LBOs, kaizen), and
economics is just beginning to theorize about phenomena that
developed half a century ago (e.g., separation of ownership and
control, the diversified firm, national advantages). Today's strategic issues (e.g., the growth of new "network" empires in Europe and Asia, time-based competition) are only dimly perceived
by anyone within the academy.

Advantage May Be Internal

Both theoretical and empirical research into the sources of
advantage has begun to point to organizational capabilities,
rather than product-market positions or tactics, as the enduring
sources of advantage. If this is so, our investigations will increasingly take us into domains where economics is presently
at its weakest—inside the firm. Transaction cost economics and
agency theory have made bids to become "organization science,"
and we can expect new and important insights from these fields.

However, their comparative advantage is the analysis of individual responses to incentives. If behavior turns on interacting expectations, beliefs and routines, and if diagnosis, problem solving, and the coordination of knowledge rather than effort are central, then economic views of organization will continue to be useful, but also will be only one part of the story.

Research Agenda

We believe that the four fundamental questions we posed in this book help define the field of strategic management and have important implications for its broad, current research agenda. The central interest is the firm, what we might call a strategically unique business, or combinations of strategically unique businesses. Beyond the firm, the perspective is the firm's management team, which must choose and execute strategic directions for the business(es) and the firm. The context is one of extensive competition among firms, and complex, interactive technical, social, and competitive environments.

Research needs to pursue answers to the fundamental questions we pose. The approach taken to answers should not be one of noting exemplars, describing best practice, or extending such observed practice in the classroom or in the boardroom. All experience suggests such answers lack durability and power to yield advantage. Descriptions of emerging phenomena are, of course, another matter. Such rich descriptions have served the field well, and have given it a broad menu of items to engage attention.

The approach we believe is needed is one that searches for theory capable of explaining phenomena well enough that causality can be attributed to the explanation. It would be naive to think that such causal explanations will be anything more than richly stochastic in nature; they are unlikely to be deterministic, single point answers to issues. Without the care and logic that is necessary to find, test, and apply such theoretical explanations, the field is unlikely to advance beyond the latest fad or fanciful explanation for action and success.

Disciplines develop through rigorous search for truth and causality. The value of allied disciplines to strategic management is the ideas and rigor they offer. Their complementary interest in the fundamental questions offers differing approaches to answering the questions. Their application to study of the questions helps us gain insight into important organizational phenomena.

You will note that we are not giving a menu of research projects here, we are stating something of a research philosophy. We believe strategic management should be phenomena driven. We believe theoretical development to explain the phenomena are necessary, not so much because causality will be found, but because the rigor and logic it generates will characterize the search as well as the answers. The outcome will be testable, tested and/or replicable, and will have a chance at prediction, at saying something about causality. Whether the fundamental questions we pose capture all of the interesting phenomena of the day is less important than that they show the power of fundamental questions, and that their answers demonstrate the methods of a scientist.

What of the practicing manager? The manager pleads for help—problems exist, answers are needed, and isn't the promise of an answer worth a try? The same logic is used today in terminal illness like AIDS or cancer. Shouldn't every avenue be tried by those in trouble? What's the harm? The harm is not so much for the dying patient, but for the living, who hang on the result and pay in side effects for the attempt. The harm is to those who fall prey to the easy answer when they might be spared by a harder one. The harm is in the "noise" put in the knowledge stream. Because results are often ambiguous, confusing, and unclear in impact, the rigor of method and the sieve of skepticism is needed for truth to be found. Our plea is for rigor of method, skeptical inquiry, and careful application. There are no easy answers!

Appendix A
Fundamental Issues in Strategy:
A Research Agenda for the 1990s

Richard P. Rumelt, Dan E. Schendel, and David J. Teece

Policy, today often termed strategy or strategic management, is a required MBA-level course and has a rich tradition and long history as a teaching area in business schools, a history virtually as long as that of business schools themselves. The research activity undergirding policy is much more recent, and scholars are just beginning to confront the core issues and problems defining it as a field of inquiry. Some history, briefly examined, will place these core issues in perspective and will help define the major research challenges and needs for further development of the field. In passing, something will be said about the definition and boundaries of strategic management as a field of serious study.

Some History

Prior to the 1960s, the underlying teaching metaphor of the field was simply one of functional integration. The backbone of business school curricula was, and continues to be, a matrix of specialized courses split into two streams. One stream of courses parallels the basic units of a functional organization (marketing, production, finance, international business, labor relations, and so forth) and the other stream presents a series of academic disciplines which provide managers with useful tools and theories (statistics, mathematical programming, social psychology, economics, organization theory, and so forth). The educational, if not the managerial, task was seen as integrating these business functions and discipline bases. Under this metaphor, the value added by "policy" came from the integration of pockets of specialized knowledge within broader perspectives. The perspectives were dual: that of the firm as a whole, including its performance, and that of the role of the general manager. Together with an intellectual style that stresses pragmatic realism over abstraction, these perspectives remain at the center of the field, and act to distinguish it from other fields with interests in the same core issues.

The 1960s. A new metaphor was introduced in the 1960s, that of "strategy." Strategy was seen as more than just coordination or integration—it included the selection of the product-market arenas in which the firm would compete and the key policies defining how it would compete. Strategy was not necessarily a single decision or a primal action, but was a collection of related, reinforcing, resource-allocating decisions and implementing actions. Depending on whether one read Philip Selznick's *Leadership in Administration* (1957), Alfred Chandler's *Strategy and Structure* (1962), Kenneth Andrews' material in *Business Policy: Text and Cases* (1965), or Igor Ansoff's *Corporate Strategy* (1965), a company's mission or strategy somehow led to or built on "objectives," "distinctive competence," or "competitive advantage." Since the 1960s, the strategy metaphor has survived, even without the careful definition necessary for research purposes. That it came to the fore and now maintains its primacy speaks well for its appeal, both to practice and teaching. However, questions remain as to the use and value of the concept in a research setting.

During this same period the practice of management began to include formal recognition of strategy as something that mattered, and, therefore, as something to be managed. Top management began to include the responsibility for long-range planning; and later, strategic planning, something that meant more than the mere extrapolation of extant trends implied by long-range planning. For some, the strategy metaphor was equivalent to an organizational process for thinking about, and perhaps deciding, the future of the firm. For most, strategic-planning processes were seen as the organizational mechanisms for causing, collecting, and coordinating decisions and actions that positioned the firm in its environment.

The 1970s. The 1970s was a time of great growth in the acceptance and application of the strategy metaphor. Using the construct, executives gained insights that proved of value to management. The decade was marked by the rise and rapid expansion of consulting firms specializing in strategy, the establishment of professional societies, and the advent of journals offering material on strategy. In academia, for the first time, positions in strategy were offered that could lead to tenure. The "market demand" for strategy was high, even if the quality of the construct was not yet well developed or of unequivocally proven worth.

Three forces helped strategy flourish in the 1970s. First, the hostility and instability of the environment of the decade led to a disenchantment with "planning" and the search for methods of adapting to and taking advantage of the unexpected. The energy crisis, rapid inflation, deregulation, the globalization of many industries, and, for Americans and Europeans, the rise of Japanese competition, taught managements the futility of either counting on the status quo or attempting to forecast the future. The strategy doctrines of the 1970s offered an alternative—building and protecting specialized strengths that weather change, and expressing those strengths in new products and services as markets shift.

The second important force was the development of strategy consulting practices based on analytic tools and concepts. The Boston Consulting Group pioneered in this regard, creating the "experience curve" and the "growth-share matrix." Other firms offered related tools and some managements came to look on strategy work as the application of specialized tools—segmentation analysis, activity-cost studies, PIMS studies, national experience curve analysis, and so forth.

The third key force at work was the maturation of the diversified firm. During the 1960s and early 1970s, diversification was the dominant form of growth among large firms. Top managements began to see their corporations as portfolios of business units and their primary responsibility as capital allocation; but traditional capital budgeting systems proved woefully inadequate when senior managements were not familiar with the details of a business's situation. The new systems that evolved, dubbed "strategic management," forced business managers to define their plans and goals in competitive terms and generated a brisk demand for strategic tools and strategy analysis.

Up until the 1970s, academic strategy research consisted chiefly of clinical case studies of actual situations, with generalizations obtained through induction. Although this style of research continues to play an important role, the 1970s saw the rise of a new research style, one based upon statistical and econometric methods. At Purdue University, Schendel, Hatten, Patton, and others explored the links between organizational resource choices, policies, and performance; their work was the first to clearly measure and demonstrate the structural heterogeneity within industry. At the Harvard Business School, Wrigley and Rumelt inaugurated a stream of research linking diversification strategy and corporate performance. And at the Harvard Department of Economics, Hunt, Newman, Caves, and Porter modified the traditional structure-conduct-performance paradigm to include the strategic positions occupied by firms within industries, inaugurating the study of "strategic groups."

Another watershed came in the late 1970s when a conference of policy scholars was organized at the University of Pittsburgh by Dan Schendel and Charles Hofer. This conference served three key purposes: (1) it announced and helped develop the new "strategic management" paradigm; (2) it initiated organized interchange among policy scholars around the world; and (3) it helped raise the shared expectations concerning the quality of the research in the field and importance of critical thinking.

The 1980s. The newer focus and wider acceptance of the strategy metaphor was helped in the early 1980s by the establishment of new outlets for publishing and communicating research, such as the *Strategic Management Journal,* which began publication in 1980, and an international professional association, the Strategic Management Society. The development of an improved infrastructure for the field was an important milestone in improving the dissemination of work and the spread of critical thinking.

Whereas work in the 1970s introduced new methods and paid careful attention to the protocols of the scientific method, there was a relative lack of critical attention to basic theory. In particular, strategy researchers tended to pay scant attention to the concept of competitive equilibrium. However, in the 1980s attention turned to theoretical developments in related disciplines which emphasized the centrality of competition, selection, and efficiency in explaining the strategies and structures of firms. Michael Porter's *Competitive Strategy* (1980) and *Competitive Advantage* (1985) led this change, and, in a remarkably short time, Porter's concepts of mobility barriers, generic strategies, and the value chain came to occupy the center stage in teaching, consultation, and many research projects.

Porter's approach to strategy relied heavily on industrial organization economics. Other disciplines also offered perspectives that were found useful by strategy researchers. Organizational economics offered efficiency, rather than "power" explanations for the elements of organizational form and pattern of institutional arrangements; Teece, for example, coupled Williamson's transaction cost analysis with a rent-seeking view of innovation to produce a new view of technology-based strategy. Another example was the population ecology approach to organizational form which coupled the economist's assumption of competition with the sociologist's assumption that organizations are largely unable to alter their resource positions or policies. Modern game theory not only offered insights as to the logic of preemption and the economics of first-mover advantages, it also shed light on the whole question of what is meant by "rational" behavior. Political science, social psychology, behavioral decision theory, and other associated disciplines each had concepts and frameworks that bear on the problem of strategy.

One of the consequences of the field's increased interest in the disciplines has been a blurring of the boundary that demarks the strategy field. In the 1970s there was no doubt about what "policy" or "strategy" research was, and certainly there was no difficulty in separating it from work in economics or other disciplines. Today those distinctions are less clear. Yet, despite the growing overlap between strategy research and work in related disciplines, there is little dialogue between these groups. For example, in a recent article in the *RAND Journal of Economics,* Carl Shapiro equated business strategy with game theory without any reference to the extensive literature of the strategy field. Similar examples could be drawn around questions of organization structure and strategy, as organization theorists explore issues of central interest to strategy researchers. Unfortunately, as illustrated by Shapiro's article, researchers in the base disciplines are not taking advantage of the strategy field's research and empirical base, forfeiting thereby an important opportunity to advance not only their own work, but that of the policy field as well.

The Present Challenge

Given these trends, it is well to ask what are the interrelationships between economics, organization theory, indeed all of the social sciences, and strategy? Does strategy have an independent research future, or should it merely wait for research developments to occur and then give attention to their application? As the strategy field begins to adopt the language and tools of agency theory, population ecology, behavioral decision theory, social psychology, political science, and so on, and as scholars in those fields realize there are really important and significant policy questions and issues to be addressed, how should the relationship between the fields be viewed, and in particular, what does it mean for a research agenda for strategy? Indeed, what does it mean for a definition of the strategic management field itself? Is the metaphor of strategy coupled with the perspective of the firm, attention to performance, and the role of the manager substantially different from the metaphor of the market and the perspective of public welfare of economic theory, or the metaphor of the mind and the perspective of the individual that characterizes psychology? We believe the answer is affirmative.

We also believe that the appropriate response to these questions and challenges is an affirmation and deepening of strategy's intellectual roots. We believe that the time is ripe for strategy scholars to redefine the field in terms of fundamental problems or questions rather than in terms of techniques, empirical methods, "conceptual schemes," or even the perspective of discipline-based theories. We believe that by centering on the right substantive questions we can build a place to stand that will allow a strategy scholar to borrow the power of underlying base disciplines without being defined as being in that discipline, or vice versa. We hope these questions, perspectives, and viewpoints are of sufficient appeal to discipline-based scholars, especially those who have become uncomfortable with their discipline's blinders and conventional wisdom, to cross over and see themselves as members of the strategy field.

As was done a dozen years ago to foster redirection of the

field, we propose to use the mechanism of commissioned papers and a conference to attract both scholars from basic social science disciplines as well as strategy researchers, and together, address a set of fundamental questions that shape the core of the field. In particular the conference should:

- Encourage a focus on the fundamental intellectual questions that lie at the center of the strategy field.
- Call for another significant increase in the sophistication, rigor, and scholarly quality of policy research.
- Demonstrate a fruitful interaction between policy researchers and discipline-based scholars.
- Show the potential of the intersection of basic discipline theory and strategy for improving management practice and organization performance.

The Fundamental Questions

A fundamental question acts to define a field of inquiry and to orient the efforts of researchers who work in that domain. Ronald Coase, for example, defined the field of institutional economics by asking "Why are there firms?" Despite its apparent simplicity, this question was a subtle critique of neoclassical microeconomics when it was posed, it still is, and it has proven to be an extremely fruitful impetus to new thinking. Note that the value of the question is undiminished by the fact that it has not yet been answered satisfactorily.

Fundamental questions are not necessarily the most often stated or the most fashionable; nevertheless, they serve to highlight the issues and presumptions which differentiate a field of inquiry, making its axioms, methods, or phenomena of interest different from those of other related fields. Thus, one of the fundamental questions for policy is, Why are firms different?—a question that echoes Coase's, but directs attention away from common properties of all firms and focuses instead on the phenomena which produce and sustain continuing heterogeneity among firms.

The Fundamental Issues in Strategy Conference will bring together a group of researchers and scholars active in strategy and in associated disciplines to jointly assess the progress made in answering the fundamental questions and issues posed here.

Although there are limits to what any conference can address, we believe there are at least five fundamental questions worth close attention and which can serve to advance the field. They are:

1. Why do firms differ?
2. How do firms behave?
3. How are policy outcomes affected by the policy process?
4. What are the functions of the headquarters unit in a multi-business firm?
5. What determines the international success or failure of firms?

Note that the perspective is that of the firm, meaning the corporate form, and which may contain multiple businesses and may compete in multiple markets and in more than one national economy. The management of the firm at the highest level of responsibility is another dimension of the perspective that is assumed throughout. The responsibility of management for the survival and performance of the firm is of central concern and is the measure of performance used here.

1. Why Do Firms Differ?

One of the key empirical observations made by strategy researchers, an observation as well as a perspective that sets the strategy field apart from industrial organization economics, is that firms within the same industry differ from one another, often dramatically. The source of this heterogeneity lies at the root of competitive advantage, and understanding *why* it arises and translating that into *how* it can be achieved is of central concern to the field.

For those who do not accept the idea of equilibrium, there is, of course, no puzzle in heterogeneity—people differ and so must firms. But, competition, it is normally thought, should eliminate differences among competitors; good practices and successful techniques will be imitated and firms that cannot or will not adopt good practices will be driven from the field. Therefore, the challenge is to retain the power of equilibrium thinking and still correctly explain the observed differences among competitors.

Differences among firms may arise from intention, or stochastically, and they may be created and sustained through property rights, active prevention of imitation, or through natural impediments of imitation and resource flows. In addition, these differences may also arise and be sustained through differing conceptual views, theories or causal maps, from differing organizational processes within firms, different levels of organizational learning and team skills, and/or through the action of ambiguity.

There are many different theories that can be used to deal with this question. To suggest the range of these theories, these subsidiary questions expand the scope of this fundamental question and suggest the underlying disciplines that may have something to offer:

- To what extent are the differences among firms the results of purposeful differentiation rather than unavoidable heterogeneity in resources and their combinations? That is, should strategy be thought of as the exploitation of existing asymmetry or the search for and creation of unique resources or market positions?
- Are the most important impediments to equilibration rooted in market phenomena (e.g., first-mover advantages), or are they chiefly rooted in internal organizational phenomena (e.g., cultural differences or learning)?
- Is the search for rents based on resource heterogeneity contrary to public welfare or does it act in the public's welfare?

2. How Do Firms Behave?

Strategy is about the choice of direction for the firm. But what assumptions should the strategist entertain about the choices made by other firms, choices that inevitably are interdependent? Is it even reasonable to think of the behavior of a firm as reflecting "choices," or should a much less rational model be used? Thus, the question of how firms behave has two components— the empirical issue of the actual patterns of behavior observed among firms and the more abstract question as to what modeling assumptions are most fruitful in explaining observed patterns or guiding competitive strategy.

The dominant assumption used by economists is that the firm behaves like a rational individual. Therefore, the question, How do firms behave? directs attention toward situations in which such an assumption is unwise. Since there is good empirical evidence that individual behavior does not meet strict norms of rationality, even when it is intendedly rational, and since most firm behavior reflects organizational outcomes rather than individual action, it is a reasonable conjecture that the standard rational model of firm behavior is rarely accurate.

The subquestions that appear appropriate to this fundamental question are these:

- What are the foundation assumptions that differentiate among various models of firm behavior (e.g., resource dependence, "garbage-can" models, Nelson and Winter's routines, population ecology models, and so forth)?
- According to behavioral decision scientists, there are predictable biases in human decision making. Are there predictable "biases" in firm or organizational behavior? What do we know about the relationships between organizational size (or other stable characteristics) and behavior?
- "Rational" models of competitive interaction posit players who engage in very subtle and complex reasoning. Yet our common experience is that decision makers are far less analytic and perform far less comprehensive analyses than these models posit. If one is a player, is it really "rational" to posit such complex behavior in others?
- Can game theorists deal with biased behavior or with the nonrational aspects of firm behavior? Can analytic models of nonrational or extra-rational behavior move beyond their present ad hoc status?

3. How Are Policy Outcomes Affected by the Policy Process?

In organizations of any size, policy or strategy is not the choice of a single individual, but is the outcome of organizational processes and procedures. Whatever policy process an organization uses must cope with the two basic facts of organizational decision making: the information and knowledge organizations gain through size and scope cannot be simply pooled (if one person could know it all there would be no gains to specialization in the first place), and each member of the organization has (perhaps unannounced) goals and values which may conflict with those of others. Given these constraints, how should the firm organize to generate and execute policy?

One stream of research in this general area has concentrated on empirical description of the policy process. Thus, for example, we have valuable insights into how organizations sometimes structure decision processes (Mintzberg, Raisinghani and Théorêt 1976), the resource allocation process (Bower, 1970), "muddling through" (Lindblom, 1986), "logical incrementalism" (Quinn, 1980), and "loose-coupling" (March and Olsen, 1976). Another research stream, centered in political science, concerns the ways in which various individuals or interest groups affect outcomes in different political arrangements (i.e., how agendas are set, how voting is structured, and so forth).

Despite the inherent value of these research traditions, neither cuts to the heart of the fundamental issue in strategy—the link between the policy process and the quality of decision, defined in competitive terms. That is, the organizational stream has not focused on producing a normative calculus and the political science tradition views outcomes in distributive rather than competitive terms. The subquestions which may help further define and deepen our understanding of this fundamental issue are:

- What are the basic modes of policy formulation? Can a succinct taxonomy of policy modes be set out?
- In what ways, if any, should the nature of the problem, the nature of the organization, and other situational factors influence the choice of a policy formulation process? In other words, what are the basic contingencies to be considered in designing a policy process?
- Should (or can) the same subunits in an organization be responsible for both strategy formulation and strategy execution?
- Diversity in cognitive frameworks may stimulate fresh approaches to strategy formulation but impede implementation. How may this tension be managed?

4. What Are the Functions of the Headquarters Unit in the Multibusiness Firm?

The diversified corporation is the dominant form of business firm in the industrialized world. The study of the creation and management of these enterprises has been heavily researched by strategy scholars. Nevertheless, the relative strengths and weaknesses of this organizational form remain poorly understood. In particular, the question of what is, or should be, the value added by the headquarters unit of such firms is of central concern to the strategy field.

There appear to be two general points of view with regard to the role of the headquarters unit in multibusiness firms: the first emphasizes value creation and the second emphasizes loss prevention. According to the first viewpoint, the headquarters unit formulates the overall strategy for the corporation, including its degree of diversification and organizational form. Also, it manages the process of resource allocation among constituent businesses, apparently better than would the unaided capital markets. Finally, the headquarters unit maintains the existence of key shared resources and manages the processes by which business units share these resources.

By contrast, the loss prevention school of thought sees management as reviewing the strategies of the business units (strategic management), apparently to make sure that egregious logical errors are not made. Second, the headquarters unit monitors the operations of the subunits, providing surer supervision of the agents operating the businesses than would independent boards of directors or the competitive marketplace. Finally, the headquarters unit can extract free cash flow from a mature business unit at much lower cost than can the unaided capital markets or the market for corporate control.

There are, of course, perspectives beyond these two. Financial economics suggests gains from corporate diversification if bankruptcy is costly, and transaction cost economics suggests gains from internalizing businesses sharing co-specialized assets. Finally, there is a skeptical perspective which sees these complex firms as the result of agency problems—as long as managers prefer to invest excess cash rather than pay it back to stockholders, and as long as they can do so, maturing profitable businesses will spawn diversified firms.

The persistence of multibusiness firms cannot be ignored. However, it is no trivial task to isolate the forces that generate and sustain these firms. The subsidiary questions which may aid inquiry into these considerations include:

- Which is primary, strategy or structure? That is, is the multidivisional form (M-form) the administrative solution to the problems created by product-market diversification and/or the need to internalize transactions, or is it itself the innovation which permits efficiencies from the assembly of various business units in a common hierarchy?
- Which is primary, the entrepreneurial (value-creating) role of the headquarters unit, or the administrative (loss-preventing) role? Can a headquarters unit simultaneously perform both roles?
- What, if any, are the limits to the amalgamation of business units in multibusiness firms? Relatedly, how can the value presently being created by the breakup of diversified firms be reconciled with the value created by their formation in the past?
- Strategic management is normally taken to mean the explicit oversight and review of the strategy formulation process together with systems for allocating resources among businesses. Do firms which impose "strategic management" on portfolios of businesses add value, and if so, what is the mechanism?
- Are there corollaries to headquarters units in nonbusiness organizations and, if so, what are the comparative lessons to be learned?

5. What Determines the International Success or Failure of Firms?

This question has two parts of interest. One part is the more fundamental issue of why some firms enjoy more success than others. Further, what is the dynamic competitive process that gives rise to firms, their relative success and what causes some to decline, some to fail (or, more commonly, for some to be sold to other firms who more efficiently employ their assets)? This issue is at the heart of competitive dynamics and the workings of capitalism and needs to be understood better in its own right.

Another part of the question deals with international competition and the competitiveness of firms, and indeed, of nations and cultures. At stake is not just firm survival or success, but the level of the quality of life for economies and their respective cultures.

There are a number of disciplines that can shed light on these fundamental issues, including international trade theory, political science, and organizational theory. Subsidiary questions that need to be addressed include these:

- To what extent do firms from different countries (cultures) possess inherent competitive advantages in certain arenas? The issue at stake is not simply the economists' comparative advantage, which would not operate when a domestic firm invests abroad, but a subtler set of management skills, technologies, and norms of work.
- Are there "strategic" industries and, if so, what makes them strategic? That is, are there significant positive externalities associated with the presence of a particular industry within a nation? Note that the often postulated efficacy of Japan's MITI or an "industrial policy" in the United States rests on the presumption that there are strategic industries.
- Are there rules for global competition that are not simply the extension of rules for competition within a large nation-state or continent?

Summary

These five questions represent some of the most fundamental puzzles in the strategy field. While other questions could be posed, all relate in one way or another to the five developed here. By addressing these questions in terms of fundamental disciplines, with a view to their application to managerial problems in competing firms, the intellectual "food" chain will be completed in a way that has not been characteristic of the strategy field thus far in its short research history. We hope that these questions bridge the region between pure theory and management practice in a way that sets an agenda for research in the 1990s and that challenges workers to build an even richer and more exciting field as we move into the next century.

Conference Structure

The conference agenda will be focused on the five fundamental questions identified in this document. The conference administrators and general editors of the two publications proposed as the archival product of the conference will be Richard Rumelt, Dan Schendel, and David Teece (hereafter referred to as RST). One half-day conference session will be devoted to each question. Three scholars will be invited to prepare papers on each question, and the papers will be presented at the conference. One of these scholars, the Question Leader, will be a person who has worked and taught in the strategy field; the other two scholars, the Question Analysts, will be persons whose work and base discipline lies outside the strategy field. In addition, for each question, two Question Commentators have been invited to comment on the questions and on the papers prepared by the Question Leaders and Question Analysts.

Publications

Two publications are planned from the papers and materials prepared for the conference. One of these will be the inaugural issue of an invited paper series for the *Strategic Management Journal*. This first issue will be produced in 1991 and will be edited by RST. This issue will carry only selected material and minimal editorial content.

The second publication will be a major book, to be published by the Harvard Business School Press. It will contain the entire set of materials produced by the Question Leaders, Question Analysts, and Question Commentators. In addition it will contain major editorial material prepared by RST to link, compare, contrast, and critique the material of the book. In addition, RST will offer their own opinions and original work in ways that will integrate the material of the book so that it will not merely be a collection of proceedings, but an integrated whole.

This book is expected to find usage by any scholar in the field and it is hoped that it will be required reading in doctoral seminars in this field around the world. Moreover, it should represent a coherent statement of the status and future of the field.

Conference Schedule

The conference is scheduled for November 29 through December 1, 1990. The layout for the conference itself is given below:

	Thursday Nov 29	Friday Nov 30	Saturday Dec 1
AM	Arrive	Q2	Q4
PM	Q1	Q3	Q5
Evening	Disc.	Disc.	

The conference closes officially at 5 p.m. Saturday, December 1st.

Each half-day will see one question presented and discussed. A typical half-day layout will be scheduled like this:

8:30 a.m.   Introduction by Question Leader
8:50 a.m.   View of First Question Analyst
9:30 a.m.   View of Second Question Analyst
10:10 a.m. Break
10:30 a.m. Question Commentator Panel Led by Question Leader
11:00 a.m. General Discussion
12:00 p.m. Luncheon

Conference Speakers

The conference program Questions Leaders, Analysts and Commentators:

Question 1:

Question Leader:	Jeff Williams—Carnegie-Mellon
Question Analysts:	Richard Nelson—Columbia
	Glenn Carroll—Berkeley
Question Commentators:	Armen Alchian—UCLA
	Birger Wernerfelt—MIT

Question 2:

Question Leader:	Jay Barney—Texas A&M
Question Analysts:	Garth Saloner—Stanford
	Daniel Kahneman—Berkeley
Question Commentators:	Colin Camerer—Wharton
	Richard Cyert—Carnegie-Mellon

Question 3:

Question Leader:	Ian Mitroff—USC
Question Analysts:	Andrew Marshall—DOD, Pentagon
	Thomas Hammond—Michigan State
Question Commentators:	Joseph Bower—Harvard
	C. K. Prahalad—Michigan

Question 4:

Question Leader:	Charles Hill—Washington
Question Analysts:	Oliver Williamson—Berkeley
	Alfred Chandler—Harvard
Question Commentators:	Andrei Shleifer—Harvard

Question 5:

Question Leader:	Michael Porter—Harvard
Question Analysts:	Keith Pavitt—Sussex, UK
	Paul Krugman—MIT
Question Commentators:	James Utterback—MIT
	Giovanni Dosi—Rome

Conference Attendance

In order to keep the conference small, so that productive discussion is facilitated, attendance is by invitation only and is restricted to about 60 persons. The breakdown by role is as follows:

Conference Organizers	3
Question Leaders	5
Question Analysts	10
Discussants	10
Invited Participants	32
TOTAL	60

Conference Site

The site for the conference is the Silverado Country Club and Resort in Napa, California. This site was selected for the opportunities it provides for quiet discussion, for its distance from urban distraction, and for its amenities. The Silverado is located in Napa Valley, 50 miles northeast of San Francisco. A special bus runs from San Francisco Airport to the Silverado approximately every two hours, making the trip in 1 hour and 45 minutes. Rental automobiles are also available at the San Francisco Airport.

The Silverado is a 1,200 acre resort that has developed around the 1870 mansion of Maj. Gen. John Franklin Miller. It features a beautiful natural setting, an 18-hole golf course, a number of swimming pools, and a fine tennis complex. Racquetball, hot-air ballooning, glider flying, riding, and wine tasting are nearby recreational activities. Napa is famous as the wine-growing capital of the United States. Its climate is mild, with a typical December daytime temperature of 55°F. The region is known for its beauty, its opportunities for wine tasting, and for its excellent cuisine.

Conference participants will be housed in three-room (bedroom, bath, sitting room) condominium units, each having a small kitchen area and fireplace. Spouses can be accommodated at no additional lodging expense.

Appendix B
List of Participants

Armen Alchian	UCLA
Raphael Amit	University of British Columbia
Elizabeth Bailey	Yale
Jay Barney	Texas A&M
Edward Bowman	University of Pennsylvania
Joseph Bower	Harvard
Philip Bromiley	Minnesota
Robert Burgelman	Stanford
Colin Camerer	University of Pennsylvania
Glenn Carroll	UC-Berkeley
Kathleen Conner	University of Pennsylvania
Alfred Chandler	Harvard
Karel Cool	INSEAD
Richard Cyert	Carnegie-Mellon
José de la Torre	UCLA
Giovanni Dosi	University of Rome
Carol Franco	Harvard
Sumantra Ghoshal	INSEAD
Richard Gilbert	UC-Berkeley
John Grant	University of Pittsburgh
William Guth	New York University
Thomas Hammond	Michigan State University
Connie Helfat	Northwestern
Charles Hill	University of Washington
Daniel Kahneman	UC-Berkeley
Bruce Kogut	University of Pennsylvania
Paul Krugman	MIT
Daniel Levinthal	University of Pennsylvania
Marvin Leiberman	UCLA
Kenneth MacCrimmon	University of British Columbia

Andrew Marshall	Department of Defense
Scott Masten	Yale
Henry Mintzberg	McGill
Ian Mitroff	University of Southern California
Richard Nelson	Columbia
Sharon Oster	Yale
Keith Pavitt	University of Sussex
Andrew Pettigrew	University of Warwick
Michael Porter	Harvard
Steven Postrel	UCLA
C. K. Prahalad	Michigan
Richard Rosenbloom	Harvard
Richard Rumelt	UCLA
Garth Saloner	Stanford
Dan Schendel	Purdue
Paul Shoemaker	Chicago
Carl Shapiro	UC-Berkeley
Andrei Shleifer	Harvard
J.-C. Spender	Stevens Institute
David Teece	UC-Berkeley
Howard Thomas	Illinois
James Utterback	MIT
James Walsh	Dartmouth
Birger Wernerfelt	MIT
Robin Wensley	University of Warwick
Jeffrey Williams	Carnegie-Mellon
Oliver Williamson	UC-Berkeley
Carolyn Woo	Purdue
Sidney Winter	U.S. General Accounting Office
Edward Zajac	Northwestern

References

Aaker, D. A. (1989). "Managing Assets and Skills: The Key to a Sustainable Competitive Advantage." *California Management Review* 31, pp. 91–106.

—— (1990). "Brand Extensions: The Good, the Bad, and the Ugly." *Sloan Management Review* 31, pp. 47–56.

Ackerman, R. W. (1970). "Influence of Integration and Diversity on the Investment Process." *Administrative Science Quarterly* 15, pp. 341–351.

Adams, J. S. (1963). "Toward an Understanding of Inequity." *Journal of Abnormal and Social Psychology*, pp. 422–436.

Adelman, M. A. (1961). "The Antimerger Act, 1950–1960." *American Economic Review* 51, May, pp. 236–244.

Aguilar, F. J., and R. Hamermesh (1985). "General Electric, Strategic Position—1981." In A. D. Chandler, Jr., and R. S. Tedlow (eds.), *The Coming of Managerial Capitalism*. Homewood, Ill.: Richard D. Irwin, pp. 776–804.

Akerlof, G. A. (1970). "The Market for 'Lemons': Quality, Uncertainty, and the Market Mechanism." *Quarterly Journal of Economics* 84, pp. 488–500.

Alchian, A. (1950). "Uncertainty, Evolution and Economic Theory." *Journal of Political Economy* 58, pp. 211–222.

—— (1982). "Property Rights, Specialization and the Firm." In J. F. Weston and M. Granfield (eds.), *Corporate Enterprise in a New Environment*. New York: KCG Productions, pp. 11–34.

—— (1984). "Specificity, Specialization, and Coalitions." *Journal of Economic Theory and Institutions* 140, March, pp. 34–59.

Alchian, A., and H. Demsetz (1972). "Production, Information Costs, and Economic Organization." *American Economic Review* 62, pp. 777–795.

Alchian, A., and S. Woodward (1987). "Reflections on the Theory of the Firm." *Journal of Institutional and Theoretical Economics* 143, March, pp. 110–136.

—— (1988). "The Firm Is Dead: Long Live the Firm—A Review of Oliver E. Williamson's *The Economic Institutions of Capitalism*." *American Economic Review* 26, pp. 65–79.

Aldrich, H. E. (1979). *Organizations and Environments*. Englewood Cliffs, N.J.: Prentice-Hall.

Aldrich, H. E., and P. V. Marsden (1988). "Environments and Organizations." In N. J. Smelser (ed.), *Handbook of Sociology*. Beverly Hills: Sage, pp. 361–392.

Allen, S. A. (1978). "Organizational Choices and General Management Influence Networks in Divisionalized Companies." *Academy of Management Journal* 16, pp. 341–365.

Allison, G. (1971). *Essence of Decision*. Boston: Little, Brown.

577

Amburgey, T., D. Kelley, and W. Barnett (1990). "Resetting the Clock: The Dynamics of Organizational Change and Failure." Unpublished manuscript, University of Wisconsin.

Amit, R., and J. Livnat (1988). "Diversification Strategies, Business Cycles and Economic Performance." *Strategic Management Journal* 9, pp. 99–110.

Anderson, E., and D. C. Schmittlein (1984). "Integration of the Sales Force: An Empirical Examination." *Rand Journal of Economics* 15, pp. 385–395.

Andreoni, J., and J. Miller (1991). "Rational Cooperation in the Finitely Repeated Prisoner's Dilemma: Experimental Evidence." Working Paper #9102, University of Wisconsin Social Science Research Institute, March.

Andrews, K. R. (1971). *The Concept of Corporate Strategy.* Homewood, Ill.: Dow-Jones Irwin.

Andrews, K., E. Learned, C. R. Christensen, and W. Guth (1965). *Business Policy: Text and Cases.* Homewood, Ill.: Richard D. Irwin.

Ansoff, H. I. (1965). *Corporate Strategy: An Analytical Approach to Business Policy for Growth and Expansion.* New York: McGraw-Hill.

Ansoff, H. I., and R. I. Brandenburg (1971). "A Language for Organization Design: Part II." *Management Science* 17, pp. 705–731.

Aoki, M. (1984). *The Economic Analysis of the Japanese Firm.* New York: North Holland.

—— (1988). *Information, Incentives and Bargaining in the Japanese Economy.* New York: Cambridge University Press.

—— (1990). "Toward an Economic Model of the Japanese Firm." *Journal of Economic Literature* 23, March, pp. 1–27.

Araskog, R. V. (1989). *The ITT Wars.* New York: Henry Holt.

Argote, L., S. L. Beckman, and D. Epple (1990). "The Persistence and Transfer of Learning in Industrial Settings." *Management Science* 36, pp. 140–154.

Armour, H. O., and D. J. Teece (1978). "Organizational Structure and Economic Performance: A Test of the Multidivisional Hypothesis." *Bell Journal of Economics* 9, pp. 106–122.

Arnold, J., III (1986). "Assessing Capital Risk: You Can't Be Too Conservative." *Harvard Business Review* 64(5), pp. 113–121.

Arrow, K. J. (1951). *Social Choice and Individual Values.* New York: John Wiley.

—— (1962). "Economic Welfare and the Allocation of Resources of Invention." In National Bureau of Economic Research (ed.), *The Rate and Direction of Inventive Activity: Economic and Social Factors.* Princeton, N.J.: Princeton University Press, pp. 353–358.

—— (1963). *Social Choice and Individual Values.* New Haven, Conn.: Yale University Press.

—— (1969). "The Organization of Economic Activity: Issues Pertinent to the Choice of Market vs. Nonmarket Allocation." In *The Analysis and Evaluation of Public Expenditures: The PPB System.* 1, U.S. Joint Economic Committee, 91st Session. Washington, D.C.: U.S. Government Printing Office, pp. 59–73.

—— (1974). *The Limits of Organization.* New York: W. W. Norton.

—— (1985). "The Economics of Agency." In J. W. Pratt and R. J. Zeckhauser (eds.), *Principals and Agents: The Structure of Business.* Boston: Harvard Business School Press, pp. 37–51.

Asanuma, B. (1989). "Manufacturer-Supplier Relationships in Japan and the

Concept of Relation-Specific Skills." *Journal of Japanese and International Economics* 3, March, pp. 1–30.

Ashby, W. R. (1960). *Design for a Brain.* New York: John Wiley.

Astley, W. G., and A. H. Van de Ven (1983). "Central Perspectives and Debates in Organization Theory." *Administrative Science Quarterly* 28, pp. 265–273.

Aumann, R. J. (1985). "What Is Game Theory Trying to Accomplish?" in K. J. Arrow and S. Honkapohja (eds.), *Frontiers of Economics.* Oxford: Blackwell, pp. 37–63.

—— (1989). *Lectures on Game Theory.* Boulder, Colo.: Westview.

—— (1991). "Irrationality in Game Theory." In D. Gale and O. Hart (eds.), *Economic Analysis of Markets and Games.* Cambridge, Mass.: MIT Press, pp. 51–70.

Axelrod, R. M. (1984). *The Evolution of Cooperation.* New York: Basic Books.

Axelrod, R. M., and Hamilton, W. D. (1981). "The Evolution of Cooperation." *Science* 211, March, pp. 1390–1396.

Ayres, I. (1990). "Playing Games with the Law." *Stanford Law Review* 42, May, pp. 1291–1317.

Bagwell, K., and G. Ramey (1989). "Oligopoly Limit Pricing." Northwestern University. Photocopy.

Bailey, E. E., and J. R. Williams (1988). "Sources of Economic Rent in the Deregulated Airline Industry." *Journal of Law and Economics* 31, pp. 173–202.

Bain, J. S. (1956). *Barriers to New Competition.* Cambridge, Mass.: Harvard University Press.

—— (1968). *Industrial Organization,* 2d ed. New York: John Wiley.

Baker, G. P., and K. H. Wruck (1989). "Organizational Changes and Value Creation in Leveraged Buyouts: The Case of O. M. Scott & Sons Company." *Journal of Financial Economics* 25 (2), pp. 162–190.

Baldwin, C. Y., and K. B. Clark (Rev. 1991). "Capabilities and Capital Investment: New Perspectives on Capital Budgeting." Working Paper #92-004, Harvard Business School.

Barnard, C. (1938). *The Functions of the Executive,* fifteenth printing, 1962. Cambridge, Mass.: Harvard University Press.

Barnett, W. P. (1990a) "The Organizational Ecology of a Technological System." *Administrative Science Quarterly* 35, pp. 31–60.

—— (1990b). "Strategic Deterrence Among Multipoint Competitors." Working Paper #2-90-3, University of Wisconsin.

Barnett, W. P., and G. R. Carroll (1987). "Competition and Mutualism Among Early Telephone Companies." *Administrative Science Quarterly* 30, pp. 400–421.

Barney, J. B. (1986a). "Strategic Factor Markets: Expectations, Luck and Business Strategy." *Management Science* 5, October, pp. 1231–1241.

—— (1986b). "Organizational Culture: Can It Be a Source of Sustained Competitive Advantage?" *Academy of Management Review* 11, pp. 656–665.

—— (1991). "Firm Resources and Sustained Competitive Advantage." *Journal of Management* 17(1), pp. 99–120.

—— (1992). "Integrating Organizational Behavior and Strategy Formulation Research: A Resource Based Analysis." In P. Shrivastiva, A. Huff, and J. Dutton (eds.), *Advances in Strategic Management,* Vol. 8. Greenwich, Conn.: JAI Press, pp. 39–62.

Bartlett, C. A. (1979). "Multinational Structural Evolution: The Changing Decision Environment in International Divisions." Unpublished dissertation, Harvard Business School.

——— (1981). "Multinational Structural Change: Evolution versus Reorganization." In L. Otterbeck (ed.), *The Management of Headquarters-Subsidiary Relationships in Multinational Corporations.* Aldershot, England: Gower, pp. 121–145.

Bartlett, C. A., and S. Ghoshal (1986). "Tap Your Subsidiaries for Global Reach." *Harvard Business Review* 64(6), pp. 87–94.

——— (1989). *Managing Across Borders.* Boston: Harvard Business School Press.

Barzel, Y. (1982). "Measurement Cost and the Organization of Markets." *Journal of Law and Economics* 25, April, pp. 27–48.

——— (1985). "Transaction Costs: Are They Just Costs?" *Journal of Institutional and Theoretical Economics* 141, pp. 4–16.

Bateman, T. S., and C. T. Zeithaml (1989). "The Psychological Context of Strategic Decision: A Model and Convergent Experimental Findings." *Strategic Management Journal* 10, pp. 59–74.

Baumol, W., S. Blackman, and E. Wolff (1989). *Productivity and American Leadership: The Long View.* Cambridge, Mass.: MIT Press.

Baysinger, B., and R. E. Hoskisson (1989). "Diversification Strategy and R&D Intensity in Multiproduct Firms." *Academy of Management Journal* 32, pp. 310–332.

Bazerman, M. H., and W. F. Samuelson (1983). "I Won the Auction but Don't Want the Price." *Journal of Financial Economics* 27, pp. 618–634.

Beard, T. R., and R. O. Beil (1990). "Do People Rely on the Utility Maximization of Others? An Experimental Test." Working paper, Auburn University Department of Economics, April.

Beer, M., and S. M. Davis (1976). "Creating a Global Organization: Failures Along the Way." *Columbia Journal of World Business,* Summer, pp. 72–84.

Berg, N. A. (1969). "What's Different About Conglomerate Management?" *Harvard Business Review* 46(6), pp. 112–120.

——— (1973). "Corporate Role in Diversified Companies." In B. Taylor and K. Macmillan (eds.), *Business Policy: Teaching and Research.* New York: John Wiley.

Bergson, A. (1948). "Socialist Economics." In H. Ellis (ed.), *Survey of Contemporary Economics.* Philadelphia: Blakiston, pp. 430–458.

Berle, A. A., and G. C. Means, Jr. (1968, 1933). *The Modern Corporation and Private Property.* New York: Macmillan.

Bettis, R. A. (1981). "Performance Differences in Related and Unrelated Diversified Firms." *Strategic Management Journal* 2, pp. 379–394.

Bettis, R. A., and W. K. Hall (1983). "The Business Portfolio Approach: Where It Falls Down in Practice." *Long Range Planning* 16, pp. 95–104.

Bhagat, S., A. Shleifer, and R. W. Vishny (1990). "Hostile Takeovers in the 1980s: A Return to Corporate Specialization." In *Brookings Papers on Economic Activity: Microeconomics,* pp. 1–72.

Biggadike, E. R. (1979). *Corporate Diversification: Entry, Strategy, and Performance.* Division of Research, Harvard Business School.

Binmore, K. (1987). "Modeling Rational Players? I." *Economics and Philosophy* 3, pp. 179–214.

——— (1988). "Modeling Rational Players? II." *Economics and Philosophy* 4, pp. 9–55.

——— (1990). *Essays on the Foundations of Game Theory.* Cambridge, Mass.: Basil Blackwell.

——— (1992). *Fun and Games: An Introduction to Game Theory.* Lexington, Mass.: D. C. Heath.

Bjurulf, B. H., and R. G. Niemi (1982). "Order-of-Voting Effects." In M. J. Holler (ed.), *Power, Voting, and Voting Power*. Wurzburg: Physica-Verlag.

Black, D. (1958). *The Theory of Committees and Elections*. Cambridge, England: Cambridge University Press.

Blau, P. M. (1970). "A Formal Theory of Differentiation in Organizations." *American Sociological Review* 35, pp. 201–218.

Blau, P. M., and W. R. Scott (1962). *Formal Organizations*. San Francisco: Chandler.

Blinder, A. (1990). "There Are Capitalists, Then There Are the Japanese." *Business Week*, October 8, p. 21.

Boeker, W. P. (1988). "Organizational Origins: Entrepreneurial and Environmental Imprinting at the Time of Founding." In G. R. Carroll (ed.), *Ecological Models of Organizations*. Cambridge, Mass.: Ballinger, pp. 33–52.

Bolton, P., and M. D. Whinston (1989). "Incomplete Contracts, Vertical Integration, and Supply Assurance." Harvard University. Photocopy.

Bonanno, G., and J. Vickers (1988). "Vertical Separation." *Journal of Industrial Economics* 36, March, pp. 257–266.

Borjas, G. (1986). "The Self-Employment of Immigrants." *Journal of Human Resources* 21, pp. 485–506.

Boston Consulting Group, The (1970). *Perspectives in Experience*. Boston.

Boulding, K. (1956). "General Systems Theory: The Skeleton of Science." *Management Science* 2, pp. 197–208.

——— (1964). "A Pure Theory of Conflict Applied to Organizations." In G. Fisk (ed.), *The Frontiers of Management Psychology*. New York: Harper & Row.

Boulding, W., and R. Staelin (1990). "Environment, Market Share, and Market Power." *Management Science* 10, pp. 1160–1177.

Bourgeois, J. (1979). "Toward a Method of Middle-Range Theorizing." *Academy of Management Review* 4(3), pp. 443–447.

Bourgeois, L. J., III, and W. G. Astley (1979). "A Strategic Model of Organizational Conduct and Performance." *International Studies of Management and Organization* 9, pp. 40–66.

Bourgeois, L. J., III, and K. M. Eisenhardt (1988). "Strategic Decision Processes in High Velocity Environments: Four Cases in the Microcomputer Industry." *Management Science* 34, pp. 816–885.

Bowen, M. G. (1987). "The Escalation Phenomena Reconsidered: Decision Dilemmas or Decision Errors?" *Academy of Management Review* 12, pp. 52–66.

Bower, J. L. (1970). *Managing the Resource Allocation Process: A Study of Corporate Planning and Investment*. Boston: Division of Research, Harvard Business School.

——— (1974). "Planning and Control: Bottom-Up or Top-Down?" *Journal of General Management* 1, pp. 20–31.

Bower, J. L., and Y. Doz (1979). "Strategy Formulation: A Social and Political Process." In D. E. Schendel and C. W. Hofer (eds.), *Strategic Management: A New View of Business and Planning*. Boston: Little, Brown.

Bower, J. L., and T. M. Hout (1988). "Fast-Cycle Capability for Competitive Power." *Harvard Business Review* 66(6), pp. 110–118.

Bowman, E. (1974). "Epistemology, Corporate Strategy, and Academe." *Sloan Management Review* 15(2), pp. 35–50.

——— (1982). "Risk Seeking by Troubled Firms." *Sloan Management Review* 23(4), pp. 33–42.

Brandenburger, A. (1991). "Knowledge and Equilibrium in Games." Working Paper #91-032, Harvard Business School.

Bresnahan, T. F. (1987). "Competition and Collusion in the American Automobile Industry: The 1955 Price War." *Journal of Industrial Economics,* June, pp. 457–482.

————— (1989). "Empirical Studies of Structure and Performance." In R. Schmalensee and R. Willig (eds.). *Handbook of Industrial Organization.* New York: North Holland.

Bresnahan, T. F., and R. Schmalensee (1987). "The Empirical Renaissance in Industrial Economics: An Overview." *Journal of Industrial Economics* 35, pp. 371–377.

Brittain, J., and J. Freeman (1986). "Entrepreneurship in the Semiconductor Industry." Academy of Management Paper.

Bromiley, P. (1986). *Corporate Capital Investment: A Behavioral Approach.* New York: Cambridge University Press.

Brown, D. (1924). "Pricing Policy in Relation to Financial Control." *Management and Administration* 1, February, pp. 195–258.

Brown, G. W. (1951). "Iterative Solution of Games by Fictitious Play." In Cowles Commission for Research in Economics, monograph #13, *Activity Analysis of Production and Allocation.* New York: John Wiley.

Buchanan, J. M. (1986). "Rights, Efficiency, and Exchange: The Irrelevance of Transaction Costs." In J. M. Buchanan (ed.), *Liberty, Market and State: Political Economy in the 1980s.* Brighton, England: Harvester Press.

Buchanan, J. M., and G. Tullock (1962). *The Calculus of Consent.* Ann Arbor: University of Michigan Press.

Buckley, P. J., and M. C. Casson (1976). *The Future of the Multinational Enterprise.* New York: Macmillan.

————— (1986). *The Economic Theory of the Multinational Enterprise.* London: Macmillan.

Burgelman, R. A. (1983). "A Model of the Interaction of Strategic Behavior, Corporate Context, and the Concept of Strategy." *Academy of Management Review* 8, pp. 61–70.

—————. (1990). "Strategy-Making and Organizational Ecology: A Conceptual Integration." In J. V. Singh (ed.), *Organizational Evolution: New Directions.* Newbury Park, Cal.: Sage, pp. 164–181.

Burgelman, R. A., and R. Rosenbloom (1989). "Technology Strategy: An Evolutionary Process Perspective." In R. Burgelman and R. Rosenbloom (eds.), *Research on Technological Innovation, Management, and Policy* Vol. 4. Greenwich, Conn.: JAI Press.

Burns, M. (1986). "Predatory Pricing and Acquisition Cost of Competition." *Journal of Political Economy* 94, pp. 286–296.

Burns, T., and E. Stalker (1961). *The Management of Innovation.* London: Tavistock.

Burt, R. S. (1983). *Corporate Profits and Cooptation.* New York: Academic Press.

Burton, R. M., and A. J. Kuhn (1979). "Strategy Follows Structure: The Missing Link of Their Intertwined Relation." Fuqua School of Business, Duke University, May.

Burton, R. M., and B. Obel (1984). *Designing Efficient Organizations: Modelling and Experimentation.* Amsterdam: North Holland.

Busentiz, L. (1992). *How Are Entrepreneurs Different from Managers in Large Organizations? Applications of Prospect Theory.* Unpublished dissertation, Department of Management, Texas A&M University.

Cable, J. R., and M. J. Dirrheimer (1983). "Hierarchies and Markets: An Empirical Test of the Multidivisional Hypothesis in West Germany." *International Journal of Industrial Organization* 1, pp. 43–62.

Cable, J. R., and H. Yasuki (1985). "Internal Organization, Business Groups, and Corporate Performance." *International Journal of Industrial Organization* 3, pp. 401–420.

Cachon, G., C. F. Camerer, and E. Johnson (1991). "Cognition and Behavior in Forward Induction Games." Working paper, University of Pennsylvania Department of Decision Sciences.

Camerer, C. F. (1991). "How Much Game Theory Is Good For Strategy Research?" Wharton School. Photocopy.

Camerer, C. F., and A. Vepsalainen (1988). "The Economic Efficiency of Corporate Culture." *Strategic Management Journal* 9, Summer, pp. 115–126.

Camerer, C. F., and Keith Weigelt (1988). "Experimental Tests of a Sequential Equilibrium Reputation Model." *Econometrica* 35, January, pp. 1–36.

Cantwell, J. (1989). *Technological Innovation and Multinational Corporations*. London: Basil Blackwell.

———— (1990). "The Technological Competence Theory of International Production and Its Implications." University of Reading Discussion Paper #149.

Capen, E. C., R. V. Clapp, and W. M. Campbell (1971). "Competitive Bidding in High-Risk Situations." *Journal of Petroleum Technology* 23, pp. 641–653.

Carroll, G. R. (1984). "Organizational Ecology." *Annual Review of Sociology,* 10, pp. 71–93.

———— (1985). "Concentration and Specialization: Dynamics of Niche Width in Populations of Organizations." *American Journal of Sociology* 90, pp. 71–93.

———— (1988). *Ecological Models of Organizations*. Cambridge, Mass.: Ballinger.

Carroll, G. R., J. Delacroix, and J. Goodstein (1988). "The Political Environments of Organizations: An Ecological View." In B. Staw and L. Cummings (eds.), *Research in Organizational Behavior,* Vol. 10. Greenwich, Conn.: JAI Press, pp. 359–392.

Carroll, G. R., J. Goodstein, and A. Geynes (1990). "Managing the Institutional Environment: Evidence from Hungarian Agricultural Cooperatives." *European Sociological Review* 6, pp. 73–86.

Carroll, G. R., and E. Mosakowski (1987). "Career Dynamics of Self-Employment." *Administrative Science Quarterly* 32, pp. 570–589.

Carroll, G. R., and A. Swaminathan (1991). "The Organizational Ecology of Strategic Groups in the American Brewing Industry from 1975 to 1990." *Industrial and Corporate Change* 1, pp. 12–29.

Caves, R. E. (1980). "Industrial Organization, Corporate Structure and Strategy." *Journal of Economic Literature* 18, pp. 64–92.

Caves, R. E., and D. Barton (1990). *Efficiency in U.S. Manufacturing Industries*. Cambridge, Mass.: MIT Press.

Caves, R. E., and M. E. Porter (1977). "From Entry Barriers to Mobility Barriers: Conjectural Decisions and Contrived Deterrence to New Competition." *Quarterly Journal of Economics* 91, pp. 241–261.

Chakravarthy, B. S., and S. Kwun (1989). "The Strategy-Making Process: An Organizational Learning Perspective." Working paper, Strategic Management Research Center, University of Minnesota.

Chamberlin, E. H. (1933). *The Theory of Monopolistic Competition*. Cambridge, Mass.: Harvard University Press.

Chandler, A. D., Jr. (1962). *Strategy and Structure: Chapters in the History of the Industrial Enterprise*, Cambridge, Mass.: MIT Press.

—— (1966). *Strategy and Structure*. Garden City, N.Y.: Doubleday.

—— (1977). *The Visible Hand: The Managerial Revolution in American Business*. Cambridge, Mass.: Belknap Press.

—— (1990a). *Scale and Scope: The Dynamics of Industrial Capitalism*. Cambridge, Mass.: Belknap/Harvard University Press.

—— (1990b). "The Enduring Logic of Industrial Success." *Harvard Business Review* 68(2), pp. 130–140.

—— (1991). What Are the Functions of the HQ Unit in a Multibusiness Firm?" *Strategic Management Journal* 12, Winter, pp. 31–50.

Chandler, A. D., Jr., and S. Salsbury (1971). *Pierre S. du Pont and the Making of the Modern Corporation*. New York: Harper & Row.

Chandler, A. D., Jr., and R. S. Tedlow (1985). *The Coming of Managerial Capitalism: A Casebook on the History of American Economic Institutions*. Homewood, Ill.: Richard D. Irwin.

Channon, D. F. (1973). *The Strategy and Structure of British Enterprise*. London: Macmillan.

Child, J. (1984). *Organization: A Guide to Problems and Practice*, 2d ed. London: Harper & Row.

Christensen, C. R., K. R. Andrews, and J. L. Bower (1973). *Business Policy: Text and Cases*. Homewood, Ill.: Richard D. Irwin.

Christensen, C. R., K. R. Andrews, J. L. Bower, R. G. Hamermesh, and M. E. Porter (1987). *Business Policy: Text and Cases*, 6th ed. Homewood, Ill.: Irwin.

Christensen, H. K., and C. A. Montgomery (1981). "Corporate Economic Performance: Diversification Strategy versus Market Structure." *Strategic Management Journal* 2, pp. 327–343.

Chubb, J., and T. Moe (1990). *Schools, Politics, and Markets*. Washington, D.C.: Brookings Institution.

Clark, K., and T. Fujimoto (1991). *Product Development Performance: Strategy Management and Organization in the World Auto Industry*. Boston: Harvard Business School Press.

Coase, R. H. (1937). "The Nature of the Firm." *Economica* 4, pp. 386–405.

—— (1964). "The Regulated Industries: Discussion." *American Economic Review* 54, May, pp. 194–197.

—— (1972). "Industrial Organization: A Proposal for Research." In V. R. Fuchs (ed.), *Policy Issues and Research Opportunities in Industrial Organization*. New York: National Bureau of Economic Research, pp. 59–73.

—— (1988). "The Nature of the Firm: Influence." *Journal of Law, Economics, and Organization* 4, Spring, pp. 33–47.

Cohen, W., and R. Levin (1989). "Empirical Studies of Innovation and Market Structure." In R. Schmalensee and R. Willig (eds.), *Handbook of Industrial Organization*. New York: North Holland, pp. 1059–1107.

Cohen, W., and D. Levinthal (1989). "Innovation and Learning: The Two Faces of R&D." *Economic Journal*, September, pp. 11–27.

—— (1990). "Absorptive Capacity: A New Perspective on Learning and Innovation." *Administrative Science* 35, pp. 128–152.

Colburn, F. D. (1986). *Post-Revolutionary Nicaragua*. Berkeley: University of California Press.

Collis, D. J. (1991a). "The Strategic Management of Uncertainty." Working Paper #89-019, Harvard Business School.

—— (1991b). "A Resource-Based Analysis of Global Competition: The Case of the Bearings Industry." *Strategic Management Journal* 12, pp. 49–68.

Commons, J. R. (1925). "Law and Economics." *Yale Law Journal* 34, pp. 371–382.

—— (1934). *Institutional Economic Behavior.* Madison: University of Wisconsin Press.

Conner, K. (1991). "A Historical Comparison of Resource-Based Theory and Five Schools of Thought Within Industrial Organization Economics: Do We Have a New Theory of the Firm?" *Journal of Management* 17, pp. 121–154.

Contractor, F. (1981). "The Role of Licensing in International Strategy." *Columbia Journal of World Business,* Winter, pp. 73–83.

Cool, K. O., and D. Schendel (1987). "Strategic Group Formation and Performance: The Case of the U.S. Pharmaceutical Industry, 1963–1982." *Management Science* 33, pp. 1102–1124.

Cooper, A. C. (1971). "Spin-Offs and Technical Entrepreneurship." *IEEE Transactions on Engineering Management* 18, pp. 21–34.

Cooper, A. C., W. Dunkelberg, and C. Woo (1988). "Entrepreneur's Perceived Chances for Success." *Journal of Business Venturing* 3, pp. 97–108.

Cooper, R., and R. S. Kaplan (1988). "Measure Costs Right: Make the Right Decision." *Harvard Business Review* 66(5), pp. 96–103.

—— (1991). *The Design of Cost Management Systems.* Englewood Cliffs, N.J.: Prentice-Hall.

Cooper, R., D. V. DeJong, R. Forsythe, and T. W. Ross (1989). "Communication in the Battle of the Sexes Games: Some Experimental Results." *Rand Journal of Economics* 20, Winter, pp. 568–587.

—— (1992). "Communication in Coordination Games." *Quarterly Journal of Economics* 107, May, pp. 739–771.

Coughlin, A., and B. Wernerfelt (1988). "Competition and Cooperation in Marketing Channel Choice: Theory and Application. *Marketing Science* 4, Spring, pp. 110–129.

Crozier, M., and E. Friedberg (1980). *Actors and Systems: The Politics of Collective Action.* Chicago: University of Chicago Press.

Curley, S. P., F. J. Yates, and R. A. Abrams (1986). "Psychological Sources of Ambiguity Avoidance." *Organizational Behavior and Human Decision Processes* 38, pp. 230–256.

Cyert, R., and J. March (1963). *A Behavioral Theory of the Firm.* Englewood Cliffs, N.J.: Prentice-Hall.

Cyert, R., and H. A. Simon (1983). "The Behavioralist Approach: With Emphasis on Economics." *Behavioral Science* 28, pp. 220–238.

Daft, R. L., and R. H. Lengel (1986). "Organization Information Requirements: Media Richness and Structural Design." *Management Science* 32, pp. 554–571.

Dahl, R. (1957). "The Concept of Power." *Behavioral Science* 2, pp. 201–215.

—— (1970). "Power to the Worker." *New York Times Book Review,* November 19, pp. 20–24.

Dalton, M. (1959). *Men Who Manage.* New York: John Wiley.

Davis, D. (1985). "New Projects: Beware of False Economies." *Harvard Business Review* 64(2), pp. 95–101.

Davis, S. (1984). "Two Models of Organization: Unity of Command vs. Balance of Power." *Sloan Management Review,* Fall, pp. 29–40.

Davis, S., and P. R. Lawrence (1977). *Matrix*. Reading, Mass.: Addison-Wesley.

Dawes, R. M. (1988). *Rational Choice in an Uncertain World*. Orlando: Harcourt Brace Jovanovich.

Dawes, R. M., and R. H. Thaler (1988). "Anomalies: Cooperation." *Journal of Economic Perspectives* 2, pp. 187–197.

Delacroix, J., and G. R. Carroll (1983). "Organizational Foundings: An Ecological Study of the Newspaper Industries of Argentina and Ireland." *Administrative Science Quarterly* 28, pp. 274–291.

Delacroix, J., and J. Freeman (1993). "The Organizational Ecology of European Subsidiaries of American Multinational Companies: An Empirical Exploration." In S. Ghoshal and E. Westney (eds.), *Organization Theory and the Multinational Corporation*. New York: St. Martin's Press, pp. 297–332.

Demsetz, H. (1973). "Industry Structure, Market Rivalry, and Public Policy." *Journal of Law and Economics*, April, pp. 1–9.

Demsetz, H., and K. Lehn (1985). "The Structure of Corporate Ownership: Causes and Consequences." *Journal of Political Economy* 93, pp. 1155–1177.

Dertouzos, M., R. Lester, and R. Solow (1989). *Made in America*. Cambridge, Mass.: MIT Press.

Dierickx, I., and K. Cool (1989). "Asset Stock Accumulation and Sustainability of Competitive Advantage: Reply." *Management Science* 35, p. 1514.

DiMaggio, J., and W. Powell (1983). "The Iron Cage Revisited: Institutional Isomorphism and Collective Rationality in Organizational Fields." *American Sociological Review* 48, pp. 147–160.

——— (1988). "Interest and Agency in Institutional Theory." In L. G. Zucker (ed.), *Industrial Patterns and Organization*. Cambridge, Mass.: Ballinger, pp. 3–22.

Dinerstein, F. (1980). "ITT: Adaptation to Change in a Conglomerate Corporation." Unpublished paper, Columbia University, February 12.

Dixit, A. (1980). "The Role of Investment in Entry Deterrence." *Economic Journal* 90, pp. 95–106.

Domowitz, I., R. G. Hubbard, and B. C. Petersen (1987). "Oligopoly Supergames: Some Empirical Evidence on Prices and Margins." *Journal of Industrial Economics* 35, June, pp. 379–398.

Donaldson, G. (1984). *Managing Corporate Wealth*. New York: Praeger.

Donaldson, G., and J. Lorsch (1983). *Decision Making at the Top: Shaping of Strategic Direction*. New York: Basic Books.

Dore, R. P. (1983). "Goodwill and the Spirit of Market Capitalism." *British Journal of Sociology* 34(4), pp. 459–482.

Dosi, G. (1982). "Technological Paradigms and Technological Trajectories." *Research Policy* 11, pp. 147–162.

Dosi, G., D. J. Teece, and S. Winter (1990). "Towards a Theory of Corporate Governance: Preliminary Remarks." Unpublished paper, Center for Research in Management, University of California, Berkeley.

Dow, G. K. (1987). "The Function of Authority in Transaction Cost Economics." *Journal of Economic Behavior and Organization* 8, pp. 13–38.

Downs, A. (1957). *An Economic Theory of Democracy*. New York: Harper & Row.

——— (1967). *Inside Bureaucracy*. Boston: Little, Brown.

Doz, Y. (1976). "National Policies and Multinational Management." Unpublished doctoral dissertation, Harvard Business School.

——— (1978). "Managing Manufacturing Rationalization Within Multinational Companies." *Columbia Journal of World Business* 13(3), pp. 82–94.

—— (1979). *Government Control and Multinational Strategic Management.* New York: Praeger.

—— (1980). "Strategic Management in Multinational Companies." *Sloan Management Review* 21(2), pp. 27–46.

—— (1986). *Strategic Management in Multinational Companies.* Oxford: Pergamon Press.

Doz, Y., and C. K. Prahalad (1981). "Headquarter Influence and Strategic Control in MNCs." *Sloan Management Review* 23(1), pp. 15–29.

—— (1984). "Patterns of Strategic Control in Multinational Corporations." *Journal of International Business Studies,* Fall, pp. 55–72.

—— (1987). "A Process Model Strategic Redirection in Large Complex Firms: The Case of Multinational Corporations." In A. Pettigrew (ed.), *The Management of Strategic Change.* Oxford: Basil Blackwell, pp. 63–83.

—— (1988). "Quality of Management: An Emerging Source of Global Competitive Advantage?" In N. Hood and J. E. Vahlne (eds.), *Strategies in Global Competition.* London: Croom-Helm, pp. 345–369.

Doz, Y., C. A. Bartlett, and C. K. Prahalad (1981). "Global Competitive Pressures vs. Host Country Demands: Managing Tensions in Multinational Corporations." *California Management Review* 23(3), pp. 63–74.

Drucker, P. (1946). *The Concept of the Corporation.* New York: John Day.

Duhaime, I., and C. Schwenk (1985). "Conjectures on Cognitive Simplification in Acquisition and Divestment Decision Making." *Academy of Management Review* 10, pp. 287–295.

Dun & Bradstreet (1967). *Patterns of Success in Managing a Business.* New York: Dun & Bradstreet.

Dunning, J. H. (1973). "The Determinants of International Production." *Oxford Economic Papers,* November, pp. 289–336.

—— (1980). "Toward An Eclectic Theory of International Production: Some Empirical Tests." *Journal of International Business Studies,* Spring/Summer, pp. 9–30.

—— (1981). *The Eclectic Theory of the MNC.* London: Allen & Unwin, ch. 4.

Dunning, J. H., and R. A. Pearce (1985). *Profitability and Performance of the World's Largest Industrial Companies.* London: The Financial Times.

Durkheim, E. (1984, originally published in 1893). *The Division of Labor in Society.* New York: Free Press.

Eccles, R. G., and H. C. White (1988). "Price and Authority in Inter-Profit Center Transactions." *American Journal of Sociology* 94, pp. S17–S51.

The Economist (1991). "Chrysler and Mitsubishi Motors." April 20, p. 71.

Egelhoff, W. G. (1982). "Strategy and Structure in Multinational Corporations: An Information-Processing Approach." *Administrative Science Quarterly* 27, pp. 435–458.

—— (1988). "Strategy and Structure in Multinational Corporations: A Revision of the Stopford and Wells Model." *Strategic Management Journal* 9(1), pp. 1–14.

Eisenhardt, K. M. (1989a). "Agency Theory: An Assessment and Review." *Academy of Management Review* 14, pp. 57–74.

—— (1989b). "Making Fast Strategic Decisions in High-Velocity Environments." *Academy of Management Journal,* 32, pp. 543–576.

—— (1990). "Speed and Strategic Choice: How Managers Accelerate Decision Making." *California Management Review* 32, pp. 39–54.

Elster, J. (1989). *The Cement of Society.* Cambridge: Cambridge University Press.

Emery, F. E., and E. L. Trist (1965). "The Causal Texture of Organizational Environments." *Human Relations* 18, pp. 21–32.

Emmett, W. (1991). "International Finance: Gamblers, Masters, and Slaves." *The Economist,* April 27, pp. 5–52.

Enright, M. J. (1990). "Geographic Concentration and Industrial Organization." Unpublished doctoral dissertation, Harvard University.

Evans, M. D. R. (1989). "Immigrant Entrepreneurship: Effects of Ethnic Market Size and Isolated Labor Pools." *American Sociological Review* 54, pp. 950–962.

Evans, P. E., and Y. Doz (1989). "The Dualistic Organization." In P. Evans, Y. Doz, and A. Laurent (eds.), *Human Resource Management in International Firms.* London: Macmillan, pp. 219–242.

Fahey, L. (1981). "On Strategic Management Decision Processes." *Strategic Management Journal* 2, pp. 43–60.

Fama, E. F. (1980). "Agency Problems and the Theory of the Firm." *Journal of Political Economy* 88, pp. 288–307.

Fama, E. F., and M. C. Jensen (1983). "Separation of Ownership and Control." *Journal of Law and Economics* 26(2), pp. 301–325.

Farrell, J. (1987). "Cheap Talk, Coordination, and Entry." *Rand Journal of Economics* 18, pp. 34–39.

Fast, N. D. (1977). *The Rise and Fall of Corporate New Venture Divisions.* Ann Arbor: University of Michigan Research Press.

Fayerweather, J. (1960). *Management of International Operations: Text and Cases.* New York: McGraw-Hill.

Feder, B. F. (1989). "Hanson's Meteoric Rise." *New York Times,* March 5, F38.

Fershtman, C., and K. Judd (1987). "Equilibrium Incentives in Oligopoly." *American Economic Review* 77, December, pp. 927–940.

Fiegenbaum, A. (1990). "Prospect Theory and the Risk-Return Association." *Journal of Economic Behavior and Organization* 14, pp. 187–203.

Fiegenbaum, A., and H. Thomas (1988). "Attitudes Toward Risk and the Risk Return Paradox: Prospect Theory Explanations." *Academy of Management Journal* 31, pp. 85–106.

―――― (1990). "Strategic Groups and Performance: The U.S. Insurance Industry, 1970–1984." *Strategic Management Journal* 11, pp. 197–215.

Fishburn, P. C., and G. A. Kochenberger (1979). "Two-Piece von Neumann-Morgenstern Utility Functions." *Decision Sciences* 10, pp. 503–518.

Fisher, F. (1989). "Games Economists Play: A Noncooperative View." *Rand Journal of Economics* 19, pp. 113–124.

Florida, R., and M. Kenney (1991). "Transplanted Organizations: The Transfer of Japanese Industrial Organization to the United States." *American Sociological Review,* June, pp. 381–398.

Fouraker, L. E., and J. Stopford (1968). "Organization Structure and Multinational Strategy." *Administrative Science Quarterly* 13(1), pp. 47–64.

Franko, L. G. (1976). *The European Multinationals: A Renewed Challenge to American and British Big Business.* Stamford, Conn.: Greylock.

Fredrickson, J. W. (1986). "The Strategic Decision Process and Organizational Structure." *Academy of Management Review* 11, pp. 280–297.

Freeman, C. (1989). "The Nature of Innovation and the Evolution of the Production System." Paris: OECD. Photocopy.

Freeman, J., and M. T. Hannan (1990). "Technical Change, Inertia and Organizational Failure." Unpublished manuscript, Cornell University.

Freud, S. (1953). *The Complete Psychological Works of Sigmund Freud.* London: Hogarth Press.

Friedman, M. (1953). *Essays in Positive Economics.* Chicago: University of Chicago Press.

Fruhan, W. E., Jr. (1972). *The Fight for Competitive Advantage.* Division of Research, Harvard Business School.

Fuchs, V. (1982). "Self-Employment and Labor Force Participation of Older Males." *Journal of Human Resources* 18, pp. 339–357.

Fudenberg, D., and J. Tirole (1986). "A 'Signal Jamming' Theory of Predation." *Rand Journal of Economics* 17, pp. 366–376.

Fudenberg, D., and D. Kreps (1988). "A Theory of Learning, Experimentation and Equilibrium in Games." Working paper, Stanford University.

Galbraith, J. K. (1967). *The New Industrial State.* Boston: Houghton Mifflin.

Galbraith, J. R. (1973). *Designing Complex Organizations.* Reading, Mass.: Addison-Wesley.

——— (1977). *Organizational Design.* Reading, Mass.: Addison-Wesley.

Galbraith, J. R., and D. A. Nathanson (1979). "The Role of Organizational Structure and Process in Strategy Implementation." In D. E. Schendel and C. W. Hofer (eds.), *Strategic Management: A New View of Business Policy and Planning.* Boston: Little, Brown, pp. 249–283.

Gale, B. T. (1972). "Market Share and Rate of Return." *Review of Economics and Statistics* 54(4), pp. 412–423.

Gerlach, M. (1987). "Business Alliances and the Structure of the Japanese Firm." *California Management Review* 30, pp. 126–142.

Ghemawat, P. (1991). *Commitment: The Dynamic of Strategy.* New York: Free Press.

Ghoshal, S. (1986). "The Innovative Multinational: A Differentiated Network of Organizational Roles and Management Processes." Unpublished doctoral dissertation, Harvard Business School.

——— (1987). "Global Strategy: An Organizational Framework." *Strategic Management Journal* 8, pp. 425–440.

Ghoshal, S., and C. A. Bartlett (1990). "The Multinational Corporation as an Interorganizational Network." *Academy of Management Review* 15(4), pp. 603–625.

Ghoshal, S., and N. Nohria (1989). "Internal Differentiation Within Multinational Corporations." *Strategic Management Journal* 10(4), pp. 323–338.

Gibbard, A. (1973). "Manipulation of Voting Schemes: A General Result." *Econometrica* 41, pp. 587–601.

Gigerenzer, G. U., W. Hell, and H. Blank (1988). "Presentation and Content." *Journal of Experimental Psychology: Human Perception and Performance* 14, pp. 513–525.

Gigerenzer, G., U. Hoffrage, and H. Kleinbolting (1991). "Probabilistic Mental Models: A Brunswikian Theory of Confidence." *Psychological Review* 98, pp. 506–528.

Gilbert, R. (1989). "Mobility Barriers and the Value of Incumbency." In R. Schmalensee and R. Willig (eds.), *Handbook of Industrial Organization.* New York: North Holland, pp. 475–535.

Gilboa, I., E. Kalai, and E. Zemel. (1989a). "Nash and Correlated Equilibria: Some Complexity Considerations?" *Games and Economic Behavior* 1, pp. 80–93.

——— (1989b). "The Complexity of Eliminating Dominated Strategies." MEDS Department working paper, Northwestern University, September.

Gilson, R., and R. Mnookin (1985). "Sharing Among the Human Capitalists: An Economic Inquiry into the Corporate Law Firm and How Partners Split Profits." *Stanford Law Review* 37, January, pp. 313–397.

Gioia, D. A., and K. Chittipeddi (1991). "Sensemaking and Sensegiving in Strategic Change Initiation." *Strategic Management Journal* 12, pp. 433–448.

Goold, M., and A. Campbell (1987). *Strategies and Styles: The Role of the Centre in Diversified Corporations*. Oxford: Basil Blackwell.

Gordon, R., and J. Howell (1959). *Higher Education for Business*. New York: Columbia University Press.

Govindarajan, V. (1988). "A Contingency Approach to Strategy Implementation at the Business Unit Level." *Academy of Management Journal* 31, pp. 828–853.

Govindarajan, V., and J. Fisher (1990). "Strategy, Control Systems, and Resource Sharing: Effects on Business Unit Performance." *Academy of Management Journal* 33, pp. 259–285.

Grant, R. M. (1988). "On Dominant Logic, Relatedness, and the Link Between Diversity and Performance." *Strategic Management Journal* 9, pp. 639–642.

——— (1991). "The Resource-Based Theory of Competitive Advantage: Implications for Strategy Formulation." *California Management Review,* Spring, pp. 119–135.

Green, E. J., and R. H. Porter (1984). "Noncooperative Collusion Under Imperfect Information." *Econometrica* 52, January, pp. 87–100.

Griffin, D., and H. Tversky (1992). "The Weighting of Evidence and Determinants of Confidence." *Cognitive Psychology* 24, pp. 411–435.

Grinyer, P. H., M. Yasai-Ardekani, and S. Al-Bazzaz (1980). "Strategy, Structure, the Environment, and Financial Performance in 48 United Kingdom Companies." *Academy of Management Journal* 23, pp. 193–220.

Grossman, S. J. (1981). "The Informational Role of Warranties and Private Disclosure about Product Quality." *Journal of Law and Economics* 24, pp. 461–483.

Grossman, S. J., and O. D. Hart (1982). "Corporate Financial Structure and Managerial Incentives." In J. J. McCall (ed.), *The Economics of Information*. Chicago: The University of Chicago Press, pp. 107–140.

——— (1986). "The Costs and Benefits of Ownership: A Theory of Vertical and Lateral Integration." *Journal of Political Economy* 94, August, pp. 691–719.

Groves, T. (1985). "The Impossibility of Incentive-Compatible and Efficient Full-Cost Allocation Schemes." In H. Peyton Young (ed.), *Cost Allocation: Methods, Principles, Applications*. Amsterdam: North Holland.

Gupta, A. K. (1987). "SBU Strategies, Corporate-SBU Relations, and SBU Effectiveness in Strategy Implementation." *Academy of Management Journal* 30, pp. 477–500.

Gupta, A. K., and V. Govindarajan (1986). "Resource Sharing Among SBUs: Strategic Antecedents and Administrative Implications." *Academy of Management Journal* 29, pp. 695–714.

Guth, W. D., and A. Ginsberg (1990). *Corporate Entrepreneurship*. Special Issue of the *Strategic Management Journal* 11, Summer, pp. 5–15.

Hall, B. W. (1990). "The Impact of Corporate Restructuring on Industrial Research and Development." Washington, D.C.: Brookings Papers on Economic Activity.

——— (forthcoming). "Corporate Restructuring and Investment Horizons." In

M. Porter (ed.), *Time Horizons in American Industry*. Boston: Harvard Business School Press.

Hall, D. J., and M. A. Saias (1980). "Strategy Follows Structure." *Strategic Management Journal* 1, pp. 149–163.

Hambrick, D. C. (1987). "Top Management Team: Key to Strategic Success." *California Management Review* 30, pp. 126–142.

——— (1989). *Strategic Leaders and Leadership*. Special Issue of the *Strategic Management Journal* 10, Summer, pp. 5–16.

Hamel, G., and C. K. Prahalad (1989). "Strategic Intent." *Harvard Business Review* 67(3), pp. 63–76.

Hammond, T. H. (1986). "Agenda Control, Organizational Structure, and Bureaucratic Politics." *American Journal of Political Science* 30, pp. 379–420.

——— (1993). "Toward a General Theory of Hierarchy: Books, Bureaucrats, Basketball Tournaments, and the Administrative Structure of the Nation-State." *Journal of Public Administration Research and Theory* 3, pp. 120–145.

Hammond, T. H., and J. H. Horn (1983). "Delegating Authority to Sophisticated Subordinates: Implications for Managerial Choice." Unpublished manuscript, Michigan State University.

——— (1985). "Putting One Over on the Boss: The Political Economy of Strategic Behavior in Organizations." *Public Choice* 45, pp. 49–71.

Hammond, T. H., and G. J. Miller (1985). "A Social Choice Perspective on Expertise and Authority in Bureaucracy." *American Journal of Political Science* 29, pp. 611–638.

Hammond, T. H., and P. A. Thomas (1989). "The Impossibility of a Neutral Hierarchy." *Journal of Law, Economics, and Organization* 5, pp. 155–184.

——— (1990). "Invisible Decisive Coalitions in Large Hierarchies." *Public Choice* 66, pp. 101–116.

Hannan, M. T. (1986). "Competitive and Institutional Processes in Organizational Ecology." Technical Report 86-13, Department of Sociology, Cornell University.

Hannan, M. T., and G. R. Carroll (1992). *Dynamics of Organizational Populations: Density, Legitimation and Competition*. New York: Oxford University Press.

Hannan, M. T., and J. Freeman (1977). "The Population Ecology of Organizations." *American Journal of Sociology* 82, pp. 929–964.

——— (1984). "Structural Inertia and Organizational Change." *American Sociological Review* 49, pp. 149–164.

——— (1989). *Organizational Ecology*. Cambridge, Mass.: Harvard University Press.

Hansen, G. S., and B. Wernerfelt (1989). "Determinants of Firm Performance: The Relative Importance of Economic and Organizational Factors." *Strategic Management Journal* 10, pp. 399–411.

Hansmann, H. (1986). "A General Theory of Ownership." Unpublished manuscript.

Harberger, A. (1954). "Monopoly and Resource Allocation." *American Economic Review* 44, May, pp. 77–87.

Harre, R. (1985). *The Philosophies of Science*. Oxford: Oxford University Press.

Harrington, J., Jr. (1986). "Limit Pricing When a Potential Entrant Is Uncertain of Its Cost Function." *Econometrica* 54, March, pp. 426–437.

Harris, B. C. (1983). *Organizations: The Effect of Large Corporations*. Ann Arbor: University of Michigan Research Press.

Harrison, J. R., and G. R. Carroll (1991). "Keeping the Faith: A Model of Cultural Transmission in Formal Organizations." *Administrative Science Quarterly* 36, pp. 552–582.

Harrison, J. R., and J. G. March (1984). "Decision Making and Post-Decision Surprises." *Administrative Science Quarterly* 29, pp. 26–42.

Harsanyi, J. (1967). "Games with Incomplete Information Played by 'Bayesian' Players. I: The Basic Model." *Management Science* 14, pp. 159–182.

—— (1975). "The Tracing Procedure: A Bayesian Approach to Defining a Solution for N-Person Noncooperative Games." *International Journal of Game Theory* 4, pp. 61–94.

Hart, O., and J. Tirole (1990). "Vertical Integration and Market Foreclosure." In M. N. Baily and C. Winston (eds.), *Brookings Papers on Economic Activity: Microeconomics.* Washington, D.C.: Brookings Institution, pp. 205–276.

Haspeslagh, P. (1982). "Portfolio Planning: Uses and Limits." *Harvard Business Review* 60(1), pp. 58–73.

Hatten, K. J., and D. E. Schendel (1977). "Heterogeneity Within an Industry: Firm Conduct in the U.S. Brewing Industry, 1952–1971." *Journal of Industrial Economics* 26, pp. 97–113.

Hatten, K. J., D. E. Schendel, and Arnold C. Cooper (1978). "A Strategic Model of the U.S. Brewing Industry: 1952–1971." *Academy of Management Journal* 21(4), pp. 592–610.

Haveman, H. (1990). "Diversification, Performance and Mortality: The Case of the Savings and Loan Industry." Unpublished manuscript, Duke University.

Hayek, F. A. (1945). "The Use of Knowledge in Society." *American Economic Review* 35, September, pp. 519–530.

—— (1978). *New Studies in Philosophy, Politics, Economics and the History of Ideas.* London: Routledge & Kegan Paul.

Hayes, R. H. (1985). "Strategic Planning—Forward in Reverse?" *Harvard Business Review* 63(6), pp. 111–119.

Hayes, R. H., and W. J. Abernathy (1980). "Managing Our Way to Economic Decline." *Harvard Business Review* 59(4), pp. 67–77.

Hayes, R. H., and S. Wheelwright (1984). *Restoring Our Competitive Edge: Competing Through Manufacturing.* New York: John Wiley.

Healy, P., K. Palepu, and R. S. Ruback (1990). "Do Mergers Improve Corporate Performance?" Harvard Business School. Photocopy.

Heckman, J. J. (1979). "Sample Selection Bias as Specification Error." *Econometrica* 45, pp. 153–161.

Hedlund, G. (1981). "Autonomy of Subsidiaries and Formalization of Headquarters-Subsidiary Relations in Swedish MNCs." In L. Otterbeck (ed.), *The Management of Headquarters-Subsidiary Relations in Multinational Corporations.* Aldershot: Gower, pp. 25–78.

—— (1986). "The Hypermodern MNC: A Hetarchy?" *Human Resource Management,* Spring, pp. 9–35.

Hedlund, G., and D. Rolander (1990). "Action in Hetarchies: New Approaches to Managing the MNC." In C. Bartlett, Y. Doz, and G. Hedlund (eds.), *Managing the Global Firm.* London: Routledge, pp. 15–46.

Heide, J., and G. John (1988). "The Role of Dependence Balancing in Safeguarding Transaction-Specific Assets in Conventional Channels." *Journal of Marketing* 52, January, pp. 20–35.

Henderson, B. D. (1979). *Henderson on Corporate Strategy.* Cambridge, Mass.: Abt Books.

——— (1984). *The Logic of Business Strategy.* Cambridge, Mass.: Ballinger.

——— (1989). "The Origin of Strategy." *Harvard Business Review* 67(6), pp. 139–143.

Henderson, R. (1990). "Underinvestment and Incompetence as Responses to Radical Innovation: Evidence from the Photolithographic Alignment Equipment Industry." Discussion paper, MIT.

Hennart, J. F. (1982). *A Theory of Multinational Enterprise.* Ann Arbor: University of Michigan Press.

——— (1988). "A Transactions Cost Theory of Equity Joint Ventures." *Strategic Management Journal* 9, pp. 361–374.

——— (1989). "A Model of the Choice Between Firms and Markets." Working paper, Wharton School.

Hidding, G. J. (1992). *Strategy Decision Making: A Systems Approach.* Doctoral dissertation, Carnegie-Mellon University Graduate School of Industrial Administration, January.

Hill, C. W. L. (1984). "Profile of a Conglomerate Takeover: BTR and Thomas Tilling." *Journal of General Management* 10, pp. 34–50.

——— (1985). "Internal Organization and Enterprise Performance: Some U.K. Evidence." *Managerial and Decision Economics* 6, pp. 210–216.

——— (1988). "Internal Capital Market Controls and Financial Performance in Multidivisional Firms." *Journal of Industrial Economics* 37, pp. 67–83.

Hill, C. W. L., M. A. Hitt, and R. E. Hoskisson (1988). "Declining U.S. Competitiveness: Reflections on a Crisis." *Academy of Management Executive* 1, pp. 51–60.

Hill, C. W. L., and R. E. Hoskisson (1987). "Strategy and Structure in the Multiproduct Firm." *Academy of Management Review* 2, pp. 331–341.

Hill, C. W. L., and J. F. Pickering (1986). "Divisionalization, Decentralization, and Performance of Large United Kingdom Companies." *Journal of Management Studies* 23, pp. 26–50.

Hirshliefer, J. (1988). *Price Theory and Applications.* Englewood Cliffs, N.J.: Prentice-Hall.

Ho, T. (1991). "An Evolutionary Analysis of the Centipede Game Using Classifier Systems with Genetic-Algorithm Reproduction." Working paper, University of Pennsylvania, Department of Decision Sciences.

Hogarth, R. M., and H. J. Einhorn (1990). "Venture Theory: A Model of Decision Weights." *Management Science* 36, pp. 780–803.

Holland, M. (1989). *When the Machine Stopped.* Boston: Harvard Business School Press.

Holmstrom, B. (1988). "Agency Costs and Innovation." *Journal of Economic Behavior and Organization* 12, December, pp. 305–327.

Holmstrom, B., and P. Milgrom (1989). "Regulating Trade Among Agents." *Journal of Institutional and Theoretical Economics* 146, March, pp. 85–105.

Holmstrom, B., and J. Tirole (1989). "The Theory of the Firm." In R. Schmalensee and R. Willig (eds.), *Handbook of Industrial Organization.* New York: North Holland, pp. 61–133.

Holt, C. A. (1985). "An Experimental Test of the Consistent-Conjectures Hypothesis." *American Economic Review* 75, June, pp. 314–325.

Homans, G. C. (1950). *The Human Group.* New York: Harcourt.

Hoskisson, R. E., and C. G. Galbraith (1985). "The Effect of Quantum vs. M-Form Reorganization on Performance: A Time Series Exploration of Organizational Dynamics." *Journal of Management* 11, pp. 55–70.

Hoskisson, R. E., and M. A. Hitt (1988). "Strategic Control Systems and Relative R&D Investment in Large Multiproduct Firms." *Strategic Management Journal* 9, pp. 605–621.

Hounshell, D. A., and J. K. Smith (1988). *Science and Corporate Strategy: DuPont R&D, 1902–1980.* New York: Cambridge University Press.

Howard, R. A. (1989). "Knowledge Maps." *Management Science* 35, pp. 903–922.

Huff, A. S. (1982). "Industry Influence on Strategy Reformulation." *Strategic Management Journal* 3, pp. 119–131.

Hughes, T. (1983). *Networks of Power: Electrical Supply Systems in the U.S., England, and Germany.* Baltimore: Johns Hopkins Press.

Hymer, S. H. (1960). *The International Operations of National Firms: A Study of Direct Foreign Investment.* Doctoral dissertation, MIT. Published by MIT Press in 1976.

Ijiri, Y. (1989). "Momentum Accounting and Triple-Entry Bookkeeping: Exploring the Dynamic Structure of Accounting Measurements." *Studies in Accounting Research,* Sarasota, Fla.: American Accounting Association.

Imel, B., and P. Helmberger (1971). "Estimation of Structure-Profit Relationships with Application to the Food Processing Sector." *American Economic Review* 62, pp. 614–627.

Isard, W. (1956). *Location and Space-Economy.* New York: John Wiley.

Itami, J., and T. W. Roehl (1987). *Mobilizing Invisible Assets.* Cambridge, Mass.: Harvard University Press.

Jacobson, R. (1988). "The Persistence of Abnormal Returns." *Strategic Management Journal* 9, pp. 415–430.

——— (1990). "What Really Determines Business Performance? Unobservable Effects—The Key to Profitability." *Management Science* 9, pp. 74–85.

Jacobson, R., and D. A. Aaker (1985). "Is Market Share All That It's Cracked Up to Be?" *Journal of Marketing* 49, pp. 11–22.

Jacquemin, A. (1987). *The New Industrial Organization: Market Forces and Strategic Behavior.* Cambridge, Mass.: MIT Press.

Janis, I. L. (1982). *Groupthink.* Boston: Houghton Mifflin.

——— (1989). *Crucial Decisions: Leadership in Policymaking and Crisis Management.* New York: Free Press.

Jennergren, L. P. (1981). "Decentralization in Organizations." In P. C. Nystrom and W. H. Starbuck (eds.), *Handbook of Organizational Design, Vol. II: Remodeling Organizations and Their Environment.* New York: Oxford University Press.

Jensen, M. C. (1986). "Agency Cost of Free Cash Flow, Corporate Finance, and Takeovers." *American Economic Review Papers and Proceedings* 76, pp. 323–329.

——— (1988). "The Takeover Controversy: Analysis and Evidence." In John C. Coffee et al., (eds.), *Knights, Raiders, and Targets.* Oxford: Oxford University Press.

——— (1989). "The Eclipse of the Public Corporation." *Harvard Business Review* 67(5), pp. 61–74.

Jensen, M. C., and W. Meckling (1976). "The Theory of the Firm: Managerial Behavior, Agency Costs, and Capital Structure." *Journal of Financial Economics* 3, pp. 305–360.

Jensen, M. C., and R. Ruback (1983). "The Market for Corporate Control: The Scientific Evidence." *Journal of Financial Economics* 11, pp. 5–50.

Johnson, E., C. F. Camerer, S. Sen, and T. Rymon (1991). "Cognition and

Behavior in Sequential Bargaining Experiments." Working paper, University of Pennsylvania, Department of Marketing.

Johnson, H. T., and R. S. Kaplan (1987). *Relevance Lost: The Rise and Fall of Management Accounting.* Boston: Harvard Business School Press.

Jones, G. R., and C. W. L. Hill (1988). "Transaction Cost Analysis of Strategy-Structure Choice." *Strategic Management Journal* 9, pp. 159–172.

Joskow, P. L. (1988). "Price Adjustment in Long-Term Contracts: The Case of Coal." *Journal of Law and Economics* 31, pp. 47–83.

Judd, K. (1985). "Credible Spatial Competition." *Rand Journal of Economics* 16, Summer, pp. 153–166.

Kagel, J. H., and D. Levin (1986). "The Winner's Curse and Public Information in Common Value Auctions." *American Economic Review* 76, pp. 894–920.

Kahneman, D., J. L. Knetsch, and R. H. Thaler (1991). "The Endowment Effect, Loss Aversion, and Status Quo Bias." *Journal of Economic Perspectives* 5, pp. 193–206.

Kahneman, D., P. Slovic, and A. Tversky (1987). *Judgement Under Uncertainty: Heuristics and Biases.* New York: Cambridge University Press.

Kahneman, D., and A. Tversky (1973). "On the Psychology of Prediction." *Psychological Review* 80, pp. 237–251.

——— (1979a). "Prospect Theory: An Analysis of Decision Under Risk." *Econometrica* 37, pp. 263–290.

——— (1979b). "Intuitive Prediction: Biases and Corrective Procedures." *Management Science* 12, pp. 313–327.

Kalai, E., and E. Lehrer (1990). "Rational Learning Leads to Nash Equilibrium." Discussion Paper #895, Northwestern University Center for Mathematical Studies in Economics and Management Science, March.

Kaplan, R. S. (1986). "Must CIM Be Justified by Faith Alone?" *Harvard Business Review* 64(2), pp. 87–95.

Kaplan, S. N. (1989a). "The Effects of Management Buyouts on Operating Performance and Value." *Journal of Financial Economics* 24(2), pp. 217–254.

——— (1989b). "Campeau's Acquisition of Federated: Value Destroyed or Value Added?" *Journal of Financial Economics* 25(2), pp. 191–222.

——— (1990). "The Staying Power of Leveraged Buyouts." Working paper, University of Chicago.

Kaplan, S. N., and M. S. Weisbach (1990). "The Success of Acquisitions." Cambridge, Mass.: National Bureau of Economic Research, Working Paper #3484.

Karnami, A. (1984). "Generic Competitive Strategies." *Strategic Management Journal* 5, pp. 119–131.

Kaufman, H. (1960). *The Forest Ranger: A Study in Administrative Behavior.* Baltimore: Johns Hopkins Press.

Keeney, R., and A. Raiffa. (1976). *Decisions with Multiple Objectives: Preference and Value Tradeoffs.* New York: John Wiley.

Kennen, J., and R. Wilson (1990). "Can Strategic Bargaining Models Explain Collective Bargaining Data?" *American Economic Review Papers and Proceedings* 80, May, pp. 405–415.

Kenney, R., and B. Klein (1983). "The Economics of Block Booking." *Journal of Law and Economics* 26, October, pp. 497–540.

Kerr, J. L. (1985). "Diversification Strategies and Managerial Rewards: An Empirical Study." *Academy of Management Journal* 28, pp. 297–326.

Kim, C. W., and R. A. Mauborgne (1991). "Implementing Global Strategies:

The Role of Procedural Justice." *Strategic Management Journal,* special issue, Summer, pp. 125–143.

Kim, S. (1992). "The Processing and Aggregation of Information within Organizational Structures." Unpublished dissertation, Michigan State University.

Kimberly, J. (1975). "Environmental Constraints and Organizational Structure: A Comparative Analysis of Rehabilitation Organizations." *Administrative Science Quarterly* 20, pp. 1–9.

Klein, B. (1980). "Transaction Cost Determinants of 'Unfair' Contractual Arrangements." *American Economic Review* 70, pp. 356–362.

Klein, B., R. A. Crawford, and A. A. Alchian (1978). "Vertical Integration, Appropriable Rents, and the Competitive Contracting Process." *Journal of Law and Economics* 21, October, pp. 297–326.

Klein, B., and K. B. Leffler (1981). "The Role of Market Forces in Assuring Contractual Performance." *Journal of Political Economy* 89, pp. 615–641.

Kluft, R. P. (1987). "First-Rank Symptoms as a Diagnostic Clue to Multiple Personality Disorder." *American Journal of Psychiatry* 144, pp. 293–298.

Knight, F. H. (1941). "Review of Melville J. Herskovits' 'Economic Anthology'." *Journal of Political Economy* 49, April, pp. 297–326.

———— (1965). *Risk, Uncertainty, and Profit.* New York: Harper & Row.

Kogut, B. (1987). "Country Patterns in International Competition: Appropriability and Oligopolistic Agreement." In N. Hood and J. Vahlne (eds.), *Strategies in Global Competition.* London: Croom-Helm, pp. 315–340.

———— (1988). "Joint Ventures: Theoretical and Empirical Predictions." *Strategic Management Journal* 9, pp. 319–332.

———— (1991). "Joint Ventures and the Option to Expand and Acquire." *Management Science* 37, pp. 19–33.

Kornai, J. (1986). "The Hungarian Reform Process." *Journal of Economic Literature* 24, pp. 1687–1737.

Kreps, D. M. (1984). "Corporate Culture and Economic Theory." Unpublished manuscript, Stanford University, Graduate School of Business.

———— (1988). "Static Choice in the Presence of Unforeseen Contingencies." Working paper, Stanford University, Graduate School of Business.

———— (1990a). *A Course in Microeconomic Theory.* Princeton, N.J.: Princeton University Press.

———— (1990b). "Corporate Culture and Economic Theory." In J. Alt and K. Shepsle (eds.), *Perspectives on Positive Political Economy.* Cambridge, England: Cambridge University Press, pp. 90–143.

Kreps, D., P. Milgrom, J. Roberts, and R. Wilson (1982). "Rational Cooperation in the Finitely Repeated Prisoner's Dilemma." *Journal of Economic Theory* 27, pp. 245–252.

Kreps, D. M., and J. A. Scheinkman (1983). "Quantity Precommitment Bertrand Competition Yield Cournot Outcomes." *Bell Journal of Economics* 14, Autumn, pp. 326–337.

Kreps, D. M., and A. M. Spence (1985). "Modeling the Role of History in Industrial Organization and Competition." In G. Feiwel (ed.), *Issues in Contemporary Microeconomics and Welfare.* London: Macmillan, pp. 340–379.

Kreps, D. M., and R. Wilson (1982). "Reputation and Imperfect Information." *Journal of Economic Theory* 27, pp. 253–279.

Krugman, P. R. (1991a). *Geography and Trade.* Cambridge, Mass.: MIT Press.

——— (1991b). "History and Industry Location: The Case of the U.S. Manufacturing Belt." *American Economic Review* 81, May, pp. 80–83.

——— (1991c). "Increasing Returns and Economic Geography." *Journal of Political Economy* 99(3), pp. 483–499.

Kuhn, A. J. (1986). *GM Passes Ford, 1918–1938*. University Park: Pennsylvania State University Press.

Kuhn, T. S. (1962). *The Structure of Scientific Revolutions*. Chicago: University of Chicago Press.

Kuran, T. (1988). "The Tenacious Past: Theories of Personal and Collective Conservatism." *Journal of Economic Behavior and Organization* 10, pp. 143–171.

Lambert, R., D. Larcker, and K. Weigelt (1990). "Tournaments and the Structure of Organizational Incentives." Working paper, Wharton School, University of Pennsylvania.

Landau, M., and D. Chisholm (1990). "Fault Analysis, Professional Football and the Arrogance of Optimism: An Essay on the Methodology of Administration." Working paper, University of California.

Lang, L., R. Stultz, and R. Walkling (1989). "Managerial Performance, Tobin's Q, and the Gains from Successful Tender Offers." *Journal of Financial Economics* 24(1), pp. 137–154.

Lange, O. (1938). "On the Theory of Economic Socialism." In B. Lippincott (ed.), *On the Economic Theory of Socialism*. Minneapolis: University of Minnesota Press, pp. 55–143.

Langlois, R. (1991). "Transaction Cost Economics in Real Time." *Industrial Corporate Change*, June, pp. 99–127.

Larkey, P., and R. Smith (eds.) (1984). "Misrepresentation in Government Budgeting." In *Advances in Information Processing in Organizations*. Greenwich, Conn.: JAI Press, pp. 68–92.

Laughhunn, D., J. Payne, and R. Crum (1980). "Managerial Risk Preferences for Below-Target Return." *Management Science* 26, pp. 1238–1249.

Lawler, E. (1986). "Control Systems in Organizations." In *Handbook of Industrial and Organizational Psychology*. Chicago: Rand-McNally, pp. 1247–1291.

Lawler, E., and J. Rhode (1976). *Information and Control in Organizations*. Pacific Palisades, Cal.: Goodyear.

Lawrence, P. R., and D. Dyer (1983). *Renewing American Industry*. New York: Free Press.

Lawrence, P. R., and J. W. Lorsch (1967). *Organization and Environment: Managing Differentiation and Integration*. Boston: Division of Research, Harvard Business School.

Lazear, E., and S. Rosen (1981). "Rank Order Tournaments as Optimum Labor Contracts." *Journal of Political Economy* 89, pp. 841–864.

Lazonick, W. (1990). *Competitive Advantage on the Shop Floor*. Cambridge, Mass.: Harvard University Press.

Learned, E. P., C. R. Christensen, K. R. Andrews, and W. D. Guth (1965). *Business Policy: Text and Cases*. Homewood, Ill.: Richard D. Irwin.

Lehn, K., and A. Poulsen (1989). "Free Cash Flow and Stockholder Gains in Going Private Transactions." *Journal of Finance* 64, pp. 771–781.

Leibenstein, H. (1979). "A Branch of Economics Is Missing: Micro-Micro Theory." *Journal of Economic Literature* 17, pp. 477–502.

Leiberman, M. B. (1984). "The Learning Curve and Pricing in the Chemical Processing Industries." *Rand Journal of Economics* 15, pp. 213–228.

Leiberman, M., and D. Montgomery (1988). "First-Mover Advantages." *Strategic Management Journal* 9, pp. 41–58.

Levine, D. (1990). "Employee Involvement Efforts." Unpublished manuscript.

Levinthal, D. (1988). "A Survey of Agency Models of Organization." *Journal of Economic Behavior and Organization* 9, pp. 153–185.

Levitt, B., and J. G. March (1988). "Organizational Learning." *Annual Review of Sociology* 14, pp. 319–340.

Lichtenberg, F. (1990). "Industrial De-Diversification and Its Consequences for Productivity." Cambridge, Mass.: National Bureau of Economic Research Working Paper #3484.

Lichtenberg, F., and D. Siegel (1990). "Productivity and Changes in Ownership of Manufacturing Plants." *Brookings Papers on Economic Activity: Microeconomics*. Washington, D.C.: Brookings Institution, pp. 643–673.

Lichtenstein, S., B. Fischhoff, and L. D. Phillips (1982). "Calibration of Probabilities: The State of the Art to 1980." In D. Kahneman, T. Slovic, and A. Tversky (eds.), *Judgement under Uncertainty: Heuristics and Biases*. New York: Cambridge University Press, pp. 306–334.

Liebeskind, J. (1988). "Economies of Scope Versus Economies of Control: Towards a Contingency Theory of Organization and Strategy in Diversified Firms." Unpublished doctoral dissertation, UCLA Business School.

Lindblom, C. E. (1959). "The Science of 'Muddling Through'." *Public Administration Review* 19, pp. 79–88.

——— (1968). *The Policy Making Process*. Englewood Cliffs, N. J.: Prentice-Hall.

Lippman, S. A., and R. P. Rumelt (1982). "Uncertain Imitability: An Analysis of Interfirm Differences in Efficiency Under Competition." *Bell Journal of Economics* 13, pp. 418–438.

Lopes, L. (1981). "Decision Making in the Short Run." *Journal of Experimental Psychology: Human Learning and Memory* 7, pp. 377–385.

Lorsch, J. W., and S. A. Allen (1973). *Managing Diversity and Inter-Dependence: An Organizational Study of Multidivisional Firms*. Boston: Division of Research, Harvard Business School.

Lowe, E., and R. Shaw (1968). "An Analysis of Managerial Biasing: Evidence from a Company's Budgeting Process." *Journal of Management Studies* 5, pp. 304–315.

Luke, R. D., J. W. Begun, and D. D. Pointer (1989). "Quasi Firms: Strategic Interorganizational Forms in the Health Care Industry." *Academy of Management Review* 14, pp. 9–19.

Lynch, J. G., and C. Ofir (1989). "Effects of Cue Consistency and Value on Base-Rate Utilization." *Journal of Personality and Social Psychology* 56, pp. 170–181.

McClelland, D. C. (1961). *The Achieving Society*. Princeton, N. J.: Van Nostrand.

MacCrimmon, R. R., and D. A. Wehrung (1986). *Taking Risks*. New York: Free Press.

——— (1990). "Characteristics of Risk Taking Executives." *Management Science* 36, pp. 422–435.

MacDuffie, J. (1989). *Worldwide Trends in Product System Management: Work Systems, Factory Practice, and Human Resource Management*. Working paper, International Motor Vehicle Program, MIT.

MacDuffie, J., and J. Krafcik (1990). *Integrating Technology and Human Resources for High Performance Manufacturing: Evidence from the International Auto Industry*. Working paper, International Motor Vehicle Program, MIT.

McGee, J., and H. Thomas (1986). "Strategic Groups: Theory, Research and Taxonomy." *Strategic Management Journal* 7, March–April, pp. 141–160.

——— (1989). "Research Notes and Communications on Strategic Groups: A Further Comment." *Strategic Management Journal* 10, pp. 105–107.

McKelvey, R. (1976). "Intransitivities in Multidimensional Voting Models and Some Implications for Agenda Control." *Journal of Economic Theory* 16, pp. 472–482.

——— (1979). "General Conditions for Global Intransitivities in Formal Voting Models and Some Implications for Agenda Control." *Journal of Economic Theory* 12, pp. 472–482.

——— (1981). "A Theory of Optimal Agenda Design." *Management Science* 27, pp. 300–321.

McKelvey, R., and T. Palfrey (1990). "An Experimental Study of the Centipede Game." Working paper, California Institute of Technology, Division of Social Sciences.

McKinsey, J. O. (1932). "Adjusting Policies to Meet Changing Conditions." New York: American Management Association General Management Series, AM116.

MacMillan, I., M. L. McCaffrey, and G. Van Wijk (1985). "Competitors' Responses to Easily Imitated New Products—Exploring Commercial Banking Product Introductions." *Strategic Management Journal* 6, pp. 75–86.

McMillan, J. (1992). *Games, Strategies, and Managers.* New York: Oxford University Press.

Mahoney, J. T. (1991). "Organizational Economics Within the Conversation of Strategic Management." Bureau of Economic and Business Research, College of Commerce and Business Administration, University of Illinois at Champaign-Urbana, 91-0144, June.

Mahoney, J. T., and J. R. Pandian (1992). "The Resource-Based View of the Firm Within the Conversation of Strategic Management." *Strategic Management Journal* 13, pp. 363–380.

March, J. G. (1962). "The Business Firm as a Political Coalition." *Journal of Politics* 24, pp. 662–678.

——— (1978). "Bounded Rationality, Ambiguity and the Engineering of Choice." *Bell Journal of Economics* 9, pp. 587–608.

——— (1982). "Footnotes to Organizational Change." *Administrative Science Quarterly* 26, pp. 563–597.

March, J. G., and J. P. Olsen (1976). *Ambiguity and Choice in Organizations.* Bergen: Universitetsforlaget.

March, J. G., and Z. Shapira (1987). "Managerial Perspectives on Risk and Risk Taking." *Management Science* 33, pp. 1404–1418.

March, J. G., and H. A. Simon (1958). *Organizations.* New York: John Wiley.

Marglin, S. A. (1974). "What Do Bosses Do?: The Origins and Functions of Hierarchy in Capitalist Production." *Review of Radical Political Economics* 6, pp. 33–60.

Marris, R. (1964). *The Economic Theory of Managerial Capitalism.* London: Macmillan.

Marris, R., and D. C. Mueller (1980). "The Corporation, Competition, and the Invisible Hand." *Journal of Economic Literature* 18, pp. 32–63.

Marshall, A. (1890). *Principles of Economics.* London: Macmillan (1979 ed.).

Martinez, J. I., and J. C. Jarillo (1989). "The Evolution of Research on Coordination Mechanisms in Multinational Corporations." *Journal of International Business Studies* 20(3), pp. 489–514.

Mason, E. S. (1939). "Price and Production Policies of Large Scale Enterprises." *American Economic Review* 29, pp. 61–74.

—— (1959). "Preface." In C. Kaysen and D. Turner (eds.), *Antitrust Policy.* Cambridge, Mass.: Harvard University Press, pp. xi–xxiii.

Masten, S. (1982). *Transaction Costs, Institutional Choice, and The Theory of the Firm.* Unpublished dissertation, Wharton School, University of Pennsylvania.

—— (1988). "The Organization of Production: Evidence from the Aerospace Industry." *Journal of Law, Economics, and Organization* 4, pp. 403–418.

Masten, S., J. Meehan, and E. Snyder (1991). "The Cost of Organization." *Journal of Law, Economics, and Organization* 7, Spring, pp. 13–29.

Mathias, P. (1978). *The Role of the Logistics System in Strategic Change.* Unpublished doctoral dissertation, Harvard Business School.

Matsusaka, J. G. (1990). "Takeover Motives during the Conglomerate Merger Wave." University of Chicago. Photocopy.

Matthews, S., and L. Mirman (1983). "Equilibrium Limit Pricing: The Effects of Private Information and Stochastic Demand." *Econometrica* 51, pp. 981–995.

Mercer, D. (1988). *The Global IBM: Leadership in Multinational Management.* New York: Dodd, Mead.

Merrow, E., K. Phillips, and C. Meyers (1981). *Understanding Cost Growth and Performance Shortfalls in Pioneer Process Plants.* Santa Barbara, Cal.: Rand Corporation.

Merton, R. K. (1940). "Bureaucratic Structure and Personality." *Social Forces* 18, pp. 16–19.

Meyer, J. W., and B. Rowan (1977). "Institutionalized Organizations: Formal Structure as Myth and Ceremony." *American Journal of Sociology* 83, pp. 340–363.

Meyer, J. W., and W. R. Scott (1983). *Organizational Environments: Ritual and Rationality.* Beverly Hills, Cal.: Sage.

Miles, R. E., and C. C. Snow (1978). *Organizational Strategy, Structure and Process.* New York: McGraw-Hill.

—— (1984). "Fit, Failure and the Hall of Fame." *California Management Review* 26, pp. 10–28.

Milgrom, P., D. North, and B. Weingast (1989). "The Role of Institutions in the Revival of Trade." *Economics and Politics* 2, March, pp. 1–24.

Milgrom, P., and J. Roberts (1982a). "Limit Pricing and Entry Under Incomplete Information: An Equilibrium Analysis." *Econometrica* 50, pp. 443–460.

—— (1982b). "Predation, Reputation, and Entry Deterrence." *Journal of Economic Theory* 27, pp. 280–312.

—— (1986). "Prices and Advertising Signals of Product Quality." *Journal of Political Economy* 94, pp. 796–821.

—— (1990a). "Bargaining Costs, Influence Costs, and the Organization of Economic Activity." In J. M. Alt and K. A. Shepsle (eds.), *Perspectives on Positive Political Economy.* Cambridge: Cambridge University Press, pp. 57–89.

—— (1990b). "Rationalizability, Learning, and Equilibrium in Games with Strategic Complementarities." *Econometrica* 58, November, pp. 1255–1277.

—— (1991). "Adaptive and Sophisticated Learning in Repeated Normal Form Games." *Games and Economic Behavior* 3, pp. 82–100.

—— (1992). *Economics, Organization, and Management.* Englewood Cliffs, N.J.: Prentice-Hall.

Miller, D., and C. Dröge (1986). "Psychological and Traditional Determinants of Structure." *Administrative Science Quarterly* 31, pp. 539–560.

Miller, G. J. (1992). *Managerial Dilemmas: The Political Economy of Hierarchy.* New York: Cambridge University Press.

Miller, N. R. (1980). "A New Solution Set for Tournaments and Majority Voting: Further Graph Theoretical Approaches to the Theory of Voting." *American Journal of Political Science* 24, pp. 68–96.

Miner, J. B., N. Smith, and J. Bracker (1989). "The Role of Entrepreneurial Task Motivation in the Growth of Technologically Innovative Firms." *Journal of Applied Psychology* 74, pp. 554–560.

Mintzberg, H. (1972). "Research on Strategy-Making." *Proceedings of the 32nd Annual Meeting of the Academy of Management.* Minneapolis.

——— (1975). "The Manager's Job: Folklore and Fact." *Harvard Business Review* 53(4), pp. 49–61.

——— (1979). *The Structuring of Organizations.* Englewood Cliffs, N.J.: Prentice-Hall.

——— (1981). "Patterns in Strategy Formulation." *Management Science* 24, pp. 935–948.

——— (1983). *Structure in Fives: Designing Effective Organizations.* Englewood Cliffs, N.J.: Prentice-Hall.

——— (1987a). "Crafting Strategy." *Harvard Business Review* 65(4), pp. 66–75.

——— (1987b). "The Strategy Concept II: Another Look at Why Organizations Need Strategies." In G. R. Carroll and D. Vogel (eds.), *Organizational Approaches to Strategy.* Cambridge, Mass.: Ballinger.

——— (1990). "The Design School: Reconsidering the Basic Premises of Strategic Management." *Strategic Management Journal* 11(3), pp. 121–195.

Mintzberg, H., D. Raisinghani, and A. Théorêt (1976). "The Structure of 'Unstructured' Decision Processes." *Administrative Science Quarterly,* June, pp. 246–274.

Mintzberg, H., and J. A. Waters (1978). "Patterns in Strategy Formation." *Management Science* 24, pp. 934–948.

——— (1985). "Of Strategies, Deliberate and Emergent." *Strategic Management Journal* 6, pp. 934–948.

Mitchell, M., and K. Lehn (1990). "Do Bad Bidders Become Good Targets?" *Journal of Political Economy* 98, pp. 372–398.

Monsen, R. J., Jr., and A. Downs (1965). "A Theory of Large Managerial Firms." *Journal of Political Economy* 73, pp. 221–236.

Monteverde, K., and D. J. Teece (1982). "Supplier Switching Costs and Vertical Integration in the Automobile Industry." *Bell Journal of Economics* 13, pp. 206–213.

Montgomery, C. A. (1985). "Product Market Diversification and Market Power." *Academy of Management Journal* 27, pp. 789–798.

Montgomery, C. A., and S. Hariharan (1991). "Diversified Expansion by Large Established Firms." *Journal of Economic Behavior and Organization* 15, pp. 71–89.

Montgomery, C. A., and B. Wernerfelt (1988). "Diversification, Ricardian Rents, and Tobin's q." *Rand Journal of Economics* 19(4), pp. 623–632.

Montgomery, C. A., B. Wernerfelt, and S. Balakrishnan (1989). "Strategy Content and the Research Process: A Critique and Summary." *Strategic Management Journal* 10, pp. 189–197.

Moorthy, K. S. (1985). "Using Game Theory to Model Competition." *Journal of Marketing Research* 22, pp. 262–282.

———— (forthcoming). "Strategic Decentralization in Channels." *Marketing Science.*

Morck, R., A. Shleifer, and R. W. Vishny (1988). "Characteristics of Hostile and Friendly Takeover Targets." In A. J. Auerbach (ed.), *Takeovers: Causes and Consequences.* Chicago: University of Chicago Press, pp. 242–271.

———— (1990). "Do Managerial Objectives Drive Bad Acquisitions?" *Journal of Finance* 45, pp. 31–48.

Morgan, G. (1986a). "Paradigms, Metaphors, and Puzzle Solving in Organizational Theory." *Administrative Science Quarterly* 25, pp. 605–622.

———— (1986b). *Images of Organization.* Beverly Hills, Cal.: Sage.

Morone, J., and A. Paulson (1991). "Cost of Capital: The Managerial Perspective." *California Management Review* 33, pp. 9–32.

Myers, S. C., and N. S. Majluf (1984). "Corporate Financing and Investment Decisions When Firms Have Information That Investors Do Not Have." *Journal of Financial Economics* 13, pp. 187–221.

Nash, J. (1950). "The Bargaining Problem." *Econometrica* 18, pp. 155–162.

Neale, M., and M. Bazerman (1983). "The Effects of Perspective-Taking Ability under Alternate Forms of Arbitration on the Negotiation Process." *Industrial and Labor Relations Review* 36, pp. 378–388.

Negandhi, A. R. (1980a). "Multinationals in Industrially Developed Countries: A Comparative Study of American, European and Japanese Multinationals." In A. R. Negandhi and B. R. Baliga (eds.), *Functioning of the Multinational Corporations.* Oxford: Pergamon, pp. 117–135.

———— (1980b). "Adaptability of American, European and Japanese Multinational Corporations in Developing Countries." In A. R. Negandhi and B. R. Baliga (eds.), *Functioning of the Multinational Corporations.* Oxford: Pergamon, pp. 136–164.

Negandhi, A. R., and R. Baliga (1981). "Internal Functioning of American, German and Japanese Multinational Corporations." In L. Otterbeck (ed.), *The Management of Headquarter Subsidiary Relationships in Multinational Corporations.* Aldershot: Gower, pp. 107–120.

Nelson, P. (1974). "Advertising as Information." *Journal of Political Economy* 81, pp. 729–754.

Nelson, R., and S. Winter (1982). *An Evolutionary Theory of Economic Change.* Cambridge, Mass.: Harvard University Press.

Newman, W. H. (1951). *Administrative Action: The Techniques of Organization and Management.* Englewood Cliffs, N.J.: Prentice-Hall.

Normann, R. (1976). *Management and Statesmanship.* Stockholm: SIAR.

North, D. C. (1986). "The New Institutional Economics." *Journal of Institutional and Theoretical Economics* 142, pp. 230–327.

Nyarko, Y. (1990). "Learning in Mis-Specified Models and the Possibility of Cycles." C. V. Starr Center for Applied Economics, New York University Department of Economics Paper, January.

Olson, M. (1965). *The Logic of Collective Action: Public Goods and the Theory of Groups.* Cambridge, Mass.: Harvard University Press.

Olzak, S., and E. West (1991). "Ethnic Conflict and the Rise and Fall of Ethnic Newspapers." *American Sociological Review* 56, pp. 458–474.

Ordeshook, P. C. (1986). *Game Theory and Political Theory.* Cambridge: Cambridge University Press.

Ordeshook, P. C., and T. Schwartz (1987). "Agendas and the Control of Political Outcomes." *American Political Science Review* 81, pp. 179–199.

Ordover, J., and G. Saloner (1989). "Predation, Monopolization, and Antitrust." In R. Schmalensee and R. Willig (eds.), *Handbook of Industrial Organization.* New York: North Holland, pp. 537–596.

Ordover, J. A., G. Saloner, and S. C. Salop (1990). "Equilibrium Vertical Foreclosure." *American Economic Review* 80, March, pp. 127–142.

O'Reilly, C. (1989). "Corporations, Culture and Commitment: Motivation and Social Control in Organizations." *California Management Review* 31, pp. 9–25.

Ouchi, W. G. (1980). "Markets, Bureaucracies, and Clans." *Administrative Science Quarterly* 25, pp. 120–142.

Ouchi, W. G., and A. L. Wilkins (1985). "Organizational Culture." *Annual Review of Sociology* 11, pp. 457–483.

Park, R. E. (1922). *The Immigrant Press and Its Control*. New York: Harper.

Parsons, T. (1937). *The Structure of Social Action*. New York: McGraw-Hill.

Pavan, R. J. (1972). *Strategy and Structure of Italian Enterprise*. Unpublished doctoral dissertation, Harvard Business School.

Pavitt, K. (1987). "On the Nature of Technology." Inaugural lecture given at the University of Sussex, June 23.

—— (1990). "The Stature and Determinants of Innovation: A Major Factor in Firms' (and Countries') Competitiveness." Paper prepared for the conference on Fundamental Issues in Strategy: A Research Agenda for the 1990s.

Pelikan, P. (1989). "Evolution, Economic Competence, and the Market for Corporate Control." *Journal of Economic Behavior and Organization* 12, December, pp. 279–304.

Penrose, E. T. (1959). *The Theory of Growth of the Firm*. New York: John Wiley.

Pepper, S. C. (1942). *World Hypotheses*. Berkeley: University of California Press.

Perlmutter, H. V. (1969). "The Tortuous Evolution of the Multinational Corporation." *Columbia Journal of World Business* 4, pp. 9–18.

Perrow, C. (1986). *Complex Organizations: A Critical Essay*. 3d. ed. New York: Random House.

Petaraf, M. A. (1993). "The Cornerstones of Competitive Advantage: A Resource-Based View." *Strategic Management Journal* 14, pp. 179–192.

Peters, T. (1987). *Thriving on Chaos*. New York: Alfred A. Knopf.

Pfeffer, J. (1981). *Power in Organizations*. Marshfield, Mass.: Pitman.

—— (1982). *Organizations and Organization Theory*. Marshfield, Mass.: Pitman.

—— (1987). "Bringing the Environment Back In: The Social Context of Business Strategy." In D. Teece (ed.), *The Competitive Challenge*. Cambridge, Mass.: Ballinger, pp. 119–135.

Pfeffer, J., and G. R. Salancik (1978). *The External Control of Organizations: A Resource Dependence Perspective*. New York: Harper & Row.

Philadelphia Inquirer (1990). "Fare War By Airlines Is Feared." November 27, p. 5-B.

Pierson, F. (1959). *The Education of American Businessmen: A Study of University College Programs in Business Administration*. New York: McGraw-Hill.

Pisano, G. (1990)."The R&D Boundaries of the Firm." *Administrative Science Quarterly* 34, pp. 153–176.

Pitts, R. A. (1974). "Incentive Compensation and Organizational Design." *Personnel Journal* 53, pp. 338–344.

—— (1976). "Diversification Strategies and Organizational Policies of Large Diversified Firms." *Journal of Economics and Business* 28, pp. 181–188.

—— (1977). "Strategies and Structures for Diversification." *Academy of Management Journal* 6, pp. 239–255.

Plott, C. R. (1989). "An Updated Review of Industrial Organization: Applications of Experimental Methods." In R. Schmalensee and R. Willig (eds.), *Handbook of Industrial Organization*. Vol. 2. New York: North Holland, pp. 1109–1176.

Plott, C. R., and Michael Levine (1978). "A Model of Agenda Influence on Committee Decisions." *American Economic Review* 68, pp. 146–160.

Polanyi, M. (1962). *Personal Knowledge: Towards a Post Critical Philosophy.* London: Routledge & Kegan Paul.

Pooley-Dias, G. (1972). *Strategy and Structure of French Enterprise.* Doctoral dissertation, Harvard University.

Porac, J. F., and H. Thomas (1991). "The Subjective Organization of Local Rivalry." Working paper, University of Illinois, Department of Management, March.

Porter, M. E. (1979). "The Structure Within Industries and Companies' Performance." *Review of Economics and Statistics* 61, pp. 214–227.

——— (1980). *Competitive Strategy: Techniques for Analyzing Industries and Competitors.* New York: Free Press.

——— (1981). "The Contributions of Industrial Organization to Strategic Management. *Academy of Management Review* 6, pp. 609–620.

——— (1983). *Cases in Competitive Strategy.* New York: Free Press.

——— (1985). *Competitive Advantage: Creating and Sustaining Superior Performance.* New York: Free Press.

——— ed. (1986). *Competition in Global Industries.* Boston: Harvard Business School Press.

——— (1987). "From Competitive Advantage to Corporate Strategy." *Harvard Business Review* 65(3), pp. 43–59.

——— (1990). *The Competitive Advantage of Nations.* New York: Free Press.

Porter, M. E., and V. A. Millar (1985). "How Information Gives You Competitive Advantage." *Harvard Business Review* 63(4), pp. 149–160.

Porter, M. E., and A. M. Spence (1979). "The Capacity Expansion Process in a Growing Oligopoly: The Case of Corn Wet Milling." In J. J. McCall (ed.), *The Economics of Information and Uncertainty.* Chicago: University of Chicago Press, pp. 259–316.

Porter, R. H. (1983). "A Study of Cartel Stability: The Joint Executive Committee, 1980–1986." *Bell Journal of Economics* 14, Autumn, pp. 301–314.

Postrel, Steven, and Richard P. Rumelt (1992). "Incentives, Routines, and Self-Command." *Industrial and Corporate Change* 1, pp. 397–425.

Powell, W. W., and P. J. DiMaggio (1991). *The New Institutionalism in Organizational Analysis.* Chicago: University of Chicago Press.

Prahalad, C. K. (1975). *The Strategic Process in a Multinational Corporation.* Unpublished doctoral dissertation, Harvard Business School.

——— (1976). "Strategic Choices in Diversified MNCs." *Harvard Business Review* 54(4), pp. 67–78.

Prahalad, C. K., and R. Bettis (1986). "The Dominant Logic: A New Linkage between Diversity and Performance." *Strategic Management Journal* 7, pp. 485–501.

Prahalad, C. K., and Y. Doz (1980). "Strategic Management of Diversified Multinational Companies." In A. Negandhi (ed.), *Functioning of the Multinational Corporation.* Oxford: Pergamon, pp. 77–116.

——— (1987). *The Multinational Mission.* New York: Free Press.

Prahalad, C. K., and G. Hamel (1990). "The Core Competence of the Corporation." *Harvard Business Review* 68(3), pp. 79–91.

Preisendoerfer, P., and T. Voss (1990). "Organizational Mortality of Small Firms." *Organization Studies* 11, pp. 107–129.

Prescott, E., and M. Visscher (1980). "Organizational Capital." *Journal of Political Economy* 88, pp. 446–461.

Pugh, Derek S. (1976). *Organizational Structure in Its Context: The Aston Programme I.* Farnborough, England.

Quinn, J. B. (1980). *Strategies for Change: Logical Incrementalism.* Homewood, Ill.: Dow Jones-Irwin.

Raiffa, H. (1982). *The Art and Science of Negotiation.* Cambridge, Mass.: Belknap/Harvard University Press.

Ramanujam, V., and P. Varadarajan (1989). "Research on Corporate Diversification: A Synthesis." *Strategic Management Journal* 10, pp. 523–551.

Rappaport, A. (1986). *Creating Shareholder Value.* New York: Free Press.

Rasmusen, E. (1989). *Games and Information: An Introduction to Game Theory.* New York: Basil Blackwell.

Ravenscraft, D. J., and F. M. Scherer (1987). *Mergers, Selloffs, and Economic Efficiency.* Washington, D.C.: Brookings Institution.

—— (1988). "Mergers and Managerial Performance." In J. C. Coffee, L. Lowenstein, and S. Rose-Ackerman (eds.), *Knights, Raiders, and Targets.* Oxford: Oxford University Press, pp. 194–210.

Ravenscraft, D. J., and C. L. Wagner (1991). "The Role of the FTC's Line of Business Data in Testing and Expanding the Theory of the Firm." *Journal of Law and Economics* 34, pp. 703–739.

Redelmeier, D. A., and A. Tversky (1992). "On the Framing of Multiple Prospects." *Psychological Science* 3, pp. 191–193.

Reed, R., and R. J. DeFillippi (1990). "Causal Ambiguity, Barriers to Imitation, and Sustainable Competitive Advantage." *Academy of Management Review* 15, pp. 88–102.

Reich, L. (1985). *The Making of American Industrial Research: Science and Business at G.E. and Bell.* New York: Cambridge University Press.

Reich, R. B. (1983). "Paper Entrepreneurialism." In Reich, *The Next American Frontier.* New York: Times Books, pp. 140–172.

Reinganum, J. (1989). "The Timing of Innovation: Research, Development and Diffusion." In R. Schmalansee and R. Willig (eds.), *Handbook of Industrial Organization.* Vol. 2. New York: North Holland, pp. 849–908.

Riker, W. H. (1962). *The Theory of Political Coalitions.* New Haven, Conn.: Yale University Press.

—— (1980). "Implications from the Disequilibrium of Majority Rule for the Study of Institutions." *American Political Science Review* 74, pp. 432–446.

—— (1982a). *The Theory of Political Coalitions,* reprint. New Haven, Conn.: Yale University Press.

—— (1982b). *Liberalism Against Populism.* San Francisco: W. H. Freeman.

Riordan, M., and O. Williamson (1985). "Asset Specificity and Economic Organization." *International Journal of Industrial Organization* 3, pp. 365–378.

Robinson, J. (1951). "An Iterative Method of Solving a Game." *Annals of Mathematics* 54, pp. 296–301.

—— (1959). *The Economics of Imperfect Competition.* New York: St. Martin's Press. Originally published in 1933.

Roll, L. (1986). "The Hubris Hypothesis of Corporate Takeovers." *Journal of Business* 59, pp. 197–218.

Rosenthal, R. W. (1981). "Games of Perfect Information, Predatory Pricing, and the Chain-Store Paradox." *Journal of Economic Theory* 25, pp. 92–100.

Ross, C. A., and P. Gahan (1988). "Cognitive Analysis of Multiple Personality Disorder." *American Journal of Psychotherapy* 42, pp. 229–239.

Rotemberg, J. (1991). "A Theory of Inefficient Intrafirm Transactions." *American Economic Review* 81, pp. 191–209.

Rotemberg, J., and G. Saloner (1986). "A Supergame-Theoretic Model of Price-Wars During Booms." *American Economic Review* 76, June, pp. 390–407.

——— (1990a). "Collusive Price Leadership." *Journal of Industrial Economics* 34, September, pp. 93–111.

——— (1990b). "Benefits of Narrow Business Strategies." MIT. Photocopy.

——— (1991). "Leadership Style and Incentives." Working Paper #1153, Stanford Graduate School of Business.

Rotemberg, J., and M. Woodford (1989). "Oligopolistic Pricing and the Effects of Aggregate Demand on Economic Activity." National Bureau of Economic Research Working Paper #3206. Cambridge, Mass., December.

——— (1991). "Markups and the Business Cycle." MIT. Photocopy.

Rowan, B. (1982). "Organizational Structure and the Institutional Environment: The Case of Public Schools." *Administrative Science Quarterly* 27, pp. 259–279.

Rubinstein, A. (1991). "Comments on the Interpretation of Game Theory." *Econometrica* 59, pp. 909–924.

Ruefli, T. W. (1990). "Mean-Variance Approaches to Risk-Return Relationships in Strategy: Paradox Lost." *Management Science* 36, pp. 368–380.

Rumelt, R. P. (1974). *Strategy, Structure and Economic Performance.* Boston: Division of Research, Harvard Business School.

——— (1982). "Diversification Strategy and Profitability." *Strategic Management Journal* 3, pp. 359–369.

——— (1984). "Towards a Strategic Theory of the Firm." In R. B. Lamb (ed.), *Competitive Strategic Management.* Englewood Cliffs, N.J.: Prentice-Hall, pp. 556–570.

——— (1987). "Theory, Strategy, and Entrepreneurship." In D. Teece (ed.), *The Competitive Challenge.* New York: Harper & Row, pp. 137–158.

——— (1991). "How Much Does Industry Matter?" *Strategic Management Journal* 12(3), pp. 167–185.

Rumelt, R. P., D. Schendel, and D. Teece (1990). "Fundamental Issues in Strategy: A Research Agenda for the 1990s." Photocopy.

Rumelt, R. P., and R. Wensley (1981). "In Search of the Market Share Effect." Working Paper MQL-61, University of California, Los Angeles.

Russell, R., and R. Hanneman (1991). "Births and Deaths of Israeli Cooperatives 1948–1989." Paper presented at the Annual Meeting of the American Sociological Association, Cincinnati, Oh.

Salancik, G. R., and J. R. Meindl (1984). "Corporate Attributions as Strategic Illusions of Management Control." *Administrative Science Quarterly* 29, pp. 238–254.

Saloner, G. (1982). *Essays on Information Transmission Under Uncertainty.* Unpublished dissertation, Stanford University.

——— (1987). "Predation, Mergers, and Incomplete Information." *Rand Journal of Economics* 18, Summer, pp. 165–186.

Salop, S., and D. Scheffman (1983). "Raising Rivals' Costs." *American Economic Review* 73, May, pp. 267–271.

Salter, M. S. (1973). "Tailor Incentive Compensation to Strategy." *Harvard Business Review* 51(3), pp. 94–102.

Samuelson, P. A. (1963). "Risk and Uncertainty: A Fallacy of Large Numbers." *Scientia* 98, pp. 108–113.

Samuelson, W., and R. Zeckhauser (1988). "Status Quo Bias in Decision Making." *Journal of Risk and Uncertainty* 1, pp. 7–59.

Satterthwaite, M. A. (1975). "Strategy-Proofness and Arrow's Conditions: Existence and Correspondence Theorems for Voting Procedures and Social Welfare Function." *Journal of Economic Theory* 10, pp. 187–217.

Scharfstein, D. S., and J. C. Stein (1990). "Herd Behavior and Investment." *American Economic Review* 80, June, pp. 465–479.

Schendel, D. E., and C. W. Hofer (1979). *Strategic Management: A New View of Business Policy and Planning.* Boston: Little, Brown.

Schendel, D. E., and G. R. Patton (1976). "A Simultaneous Equation Model of Corporate Strategy." *Management Science* 24, November, pp. 1611–1621.

Scherer, F. M. (1970). *Industrial Market Structure and Economic Performance.* Chicago: Rand McNally.

Schmalensee, R. (1978a). "Entry Deterrence in the Ready-to-Eat Breakfast Cereal Industry." *Bell Journal of Economics* 9, Autumn, pp. 305–327.

——— (1978b). "A Model of Advertising and Product Quality." *Journal of Political Economy* 86, pp. 485–503.

——— (1982). "Product Differentiation Advantages of Pioneering Brands." *American Economic Review* 72, June, pp. 349–365.

——— (1985). "Do Markets Differ Much?" *American Economic Review* 75, pp. 341–351.

Schmalensee, R., and R. Willig, eds. (1989). *Handbook of Industrial Organization.* New York: North Holland.

Schumpeter, J. A. (1911/1934). *The Theory of Economic Development.* Cambridge, Mass.: Harvard University Press.

——— (1942). *Capitalism, Socialism, and Democracy.* New York: Harper.

——— (1947). "The Creative Response in Economic History." *Journal of Economic History* 7, November, pp. 149–159.

Schwadel, F. (1990). "Sears' Brennan Faces Facts About Costs." *The Wall Street Journal,* August 10, p. 81.

Schwartz, P. (1991). *The Art of the Long View.* New York: Doubleday.

Scitovsky, Tibor (1990). "The Benefits of Asymmetric Markets." *Journal of Economic Perspectives* 4, pp. 135–148.

Scott, B. R. (1973). "The Industrial State: Old Myths and New Realities." *Harvard Business Review* 51(2), pp. 133–145.

Scott, W. R. (1987a). *Organizations: Rational, Natural and Open Systems.* Englewood Cliffs, N.J.: Prentice-Hall.

——— (1987b). "The Adolescence of Institutional Theory." *Administrative Science Quarterly* 3, pp. 493–511.

Seligman, M. E. (1991). *Learned Optimism.* New York: Alfred A. Knopf.

Selten, R. (1965). "Spieltheoretische Behandlung eines Oligopolmodells mit Nachfrageträgheit." *Zeitschrift für die gesamte Staatswissenschaft* 12, pp. 301–324.

——— (1978). "The Chain-Store Paradox." *Theory and Decision* 9, pp. 127–159.

——— (1991). "Evolution, Learning, and Economic Behavior." *Games and Economic Behavior* 3, pp. 3–24.

Selznick, P. (1949). *TVA and the Grass Roots.* Berkeley: University of California Press.

———— (1957). *Leadership in Administration: A Sociological Interpretation.* New York: Harper & Row.

Servaes, H. (1989). "Tobin's Q, Agency Costs, and Corporate Control." Center for Research in Security Prices, University of Chicago.

Shapira, Z. (1986). "Risk in Managerial Decision Making." Working paper, Hebrew University, School of Business Administration.

Shapiro, C. (1989). "The Theory of Business Strategy." *Rand Journal of Economics* 20, Spring, pp. 125–137.

Shapley, L. (1964). "Some Topics in Two-Person Games." *Annals of Mathematical Studies* 5, pp. 1–28.

Shepherd, W. G. (1972). "The Elements of Market Structure." *Review of Economics and Statistics* 54, pp. 25–37.

———— (1979). *The Economics of Industrial Organization.* Englewood Cliffs, N.J.: Prentice-Hall.

Shepsle, K. A. (1978). *The Giant Jigsaw Puzzle: Democratic Committee Assignments in the Modern House.* Chicago: University of Chicago Press.

———— (1979). "Institutional Arrangements and Equilibrium in Multidimensional Voting Models." *American Journal of Political Science* 23, pp. 27–59.

Shepsle, K. A., and B. R. Weingast (1981). "Structure-Induced Equilibrium and Legislative Choice." *Public Choice* 37, pp. 503–519.

———— (1984). "Uncovered Sets and Sophisticated Voting Outcomes with Implications for Agenda Institutions." *American Journal of Political Science* 28, pp. 49–74.

Sherman, H. (1966). *It All Depends: A Pragmatic Approach to Organization.* Tuscaloosa, Ala.: University of Alabama Press.

Shiller, R. J. (1984). "Stock Prices and Social Dynamics." *Brookings Papers on Economic Activity.* Washington, D.C.: Brookings Institution, pp. 457–498.

Shleifer, A., and L. Summers (1988). "Breach of Trust in Hostile Takeovers." In A. Auerbach (ed.), *Corporate Takeovers: Causes and Consequences.* Chicago: University of Chicago Press, pp. 33–56.

———— (1990). "The Noise Trader Approach to Finance." *Journal of Economic Perspectives* 4, pp. 19–33.

Shleifer, A., and R. W. Vishny (1988). "Value Maximization and the Acquisition Process." *Journal of Economic Perspectives* 2, pp. 7–20.

———— (1990a). "The Takeover Wave of the 1980s." *Science* 249, pp. 745–749.

———— (1990b). "Equilibrium Short Horizons of Investors and Firms." *American Economic Review Papers and Proceedings* 80, pp. 148–153.

Shoemaker, P. J. H. (1990). "Strategy, Complexity, and Economic Rent." *Management Science* 36, pp. 1178–1192.

Simon, H. A. (1947). *Administrative Behavior.* New York: Macmillan.

———— (1962). "The Architecture of Complexity." *Proceedings of the American Philosophical Society* 106, December, pp. 467–482.

———— (1967). "The Business School: A Problem in Organizational Design." *Journal of Management Studies* 4, pp. 1–16.

———— (1969). *The Sciences of the Artificial.* Cambridge, Mass.: MIT Press.

———— (1978). "Rationality as Process and as Product of Thought." *American Economic Review* 68, pp. 1–16.

———— (1991). "Organizations and Markets." *Journal of Economic Perspectives* 5, pp. 25–44.

Singh, J., and C. J. Lumsden (1990). "Theory and Research in Organizational Ecology." *Annual Review of Sociology* 16, pp. 161–195.

Singh, J., D. J. Tucker, and R. J. House (1986a). "Organizational Legitimacy and the Liability of Newness." *Administrative Science Quarterly* 31, pp. 171–193.

——— (1986b). "Organizational Change and Organizational Mortality." *Administrative Science Quarterly* 31, pp. 587–611.

Sipple, E. W. (1989). "When Change and Continuity Collide: Capitalizing on Strategic Gridlock in Financial Services." *California Management Review* 31, pp. 51–74.

Skinner, B. F. (1953). *Science and Human Behavior*. New York: Macmillan.

Sloan, A. P., Jr. (1964). *My Years with General Motors*. Garden City, N.Y.: Doubleday.

Smith, J. M. (1982). *Evolution and the Theory of Games*. Cambridge: Cambridge University Press.

Sobel, R. (1982). *ITT: The Management of Opportunity*. New York: Times Books.

Spanos, N. P., J. R. Weekes, and L. D. Bertrand (1985). "Multiple Personality: A Social Psychological Perspective." *Journal of Abnormal Psychology* 94, pp. 362–376.

Spence, A. M. (1974). *Market Signaling*. Cambridge, Mass.: Harvard University Press.

——— (1977). "Entry, Capacity, Investment, and Oligopolistic Pricing." *Bell Journal of Economics* 8, pp. 534–544.

——— (1979). "Investment Strategy and Growth in a New Market." *Bell Journal of Economics* 10, pp. 1–19.

——— (1981). "The Learning Curve and Competition." *Bell Journal of Economics* 12, pp. 49–70.

Spence, M., and R. Zeckhauser (1972). "The Effect of the Timing of Consumption Decisions and the Resolution of Lotteries on the Choice of Lotteries." *Econometrica* 40, pp. 401–403.

Spender, J. C. (1989). *Industry Recipes*. Oxford: Basil Blackwell.

Starbuck, W., and F. Milliken (1988). "Challenger: Fine-Tuning the Odds Until Something Breaks." *Journal of Management Studies* 25, pp. 319–340.

Staw, B., and J. Ross (1988). "Good Money After Bad." *Psychology Today* 22, pp. 30–33.

——— (1989). "Understanding Behavior in Escalation Situations." *Science* 246, pp. 216–220.

Steer, P. O., and J. Cable (1978). "Internal Organization and Profit: An Empirical Analysis of Large U.K. Companies." *Journal of Industrial Economics* 27, pp. 13–29.

Stein, J. C. (1989). "Efficient Capital Markets, Inefficient Firms: A Model of Myopic Corporate Behavior." *Quarterly Journal of Economics* 104, November, pp. 655–669.

Steiner, G. A. (1969). *Strategic Factors in Business Success*. New York: Financial Executives Research Foundation.

——— (1972). *Pitfalls in Comprehensive Long Range Planning*. Oxford, O.: Planning Executives Institute.

Sterman, J. D. (1989). "Modeling Managerial Behavior: Misperceptions of Feedback in a Dynamic Decision Making Experiment." *Management Science* 35, pp. 321–339.

Stevens, S. S. (1975). *Psychophysics*. New York: John Wiley.

Stigler, G. J. (1968a). "Monopoly and Oligopoly by Mergers." In G. J. Stigler (ed.), *The Organization of Industry*. Chicago: University of Chicago Press, pp. 95–107.

———— (1968b). *The Organization of Industry.* Chicago: University of Chicago Press.

Stinchcombe, A. L. (1965). "Organizations and Social Structure." In J. G. March (ed.), *Handbook of Organizations.* Chicago: Rand-McNally, pp. 153–193.

———— (1990). *Information and Organizations.* Berkeley: University of California Press.

Stockey, J. (1983). *Vertical Integration and Joint Ventures in the Aluminum Industry.* Cambridge, Mass.: Harvard University Press.

Stopford, J., J. Dunning, and K. O. Haberich (1980). *The World Directory of Multinational Enterprises.* New York: Facts on File.

Stopford, J., and L. T. Wells, Jr. (1972). *Managing the Multinational Enterprise.* New York: Basic Books.

Swalm, R. O. (1966). "Utility Theory: Insights into Risk Taking." *Harvard Business Review* 44(6), pp. 123–136.

Taylor, F. W. (1947). *Scientific Management.* New York: Harper.

Taylor, S. E., and J. D. Brown (1988). "Illusion and Well-Being: A Social Psychological Perspective on Mental Health." *Psychological Bulletin* 103, pp. 193–210.

Teece, D. J. (1980). "Economies of Scope and the Scope of the Enterprise." *Journal of Economic Behavior and Organization* 1, pp. 223–245.

———— (1981a). "Internal Organization and Economic Performance: An Empirical Analysis of the Profitability of Principal Firms." *Journal of Industrial Economics* 30, pp. 173–199.

———— (1981b). "The Market for Know-How and the Efficient Transfer of Technology." *The Annals of the Academy of Political and Social Science,* pp. 81–96.

———— (1982). "Towards an Economic Theory of the Multiproduct Firm." *Journal of Economic Behavior and Organization* 3, March, pp. 39–64.

———— (1985). "Multinational Enterprise, Internal Governance and Economic Organization." *American Economic Review* 75, pp. 233–238.

———— (1986). "Profiting from Technological Innovation." *Research Policy* 15, December, pp. 285–305.

———— (1987). "Profiting from Technological Innovation: Implications for Integration, Collaboration, Licensing, and Public Policy." In D. J. Teece (ed.), *The Competitive Challenge: Strategies for Industrial Innovation and Renewal.* Cambridge, Mass.: Ballinger, pp. 185–221.

———— (1988). "Contributions and Impediments of Economic Analysis to the Study of Strategic Management." Technical Report #EAP-29, Center for Research in Management, University of California, Berkeley.

———— (1989). "Innovation and the Organization of Industry." Working Paper #EQP-34, Center for Research in Management, University of California, Berkeley.

———— (1990). "Contributions and Impediments of Economic Analysis to the Study of Strategic Management." In J. W. Frederickson (ed.), *Perspectives on Strategic Management.* New York: Harper & Row, pp. 39–79.

Teece, D. J., G. Pisano, and A. Shuen (1990). "Dynamic Capabilities and Strategic Management." Consortium on Competition and Cooperation Working Paper #90-8, Center for Research in Management, University of California, Berkeley.

Teece, D. J., and S. G. Winter (1984). "The Limits of Neoclassical Theory in Management Education." *American Economic Review* 74, pp. 116–121.

Teisberg, E. O. (1991a). "Strategic Response to Uncertainty." Harvard Business School Case #N9-391-192.

—— (1991b). "Why Do Good Managers Choose Poor Strategies?" Harvard Business School Case #N9-391-172, rev.

Tetlock, P. E., and R. Boettger (1992). "Accountability Amplifies the Status Quo Effect When Change Creates Victims." Working paper, University of California, Berkeley.

Thanheiser, H. (1972). *Strategy and Structure of German Enterprise.* Unpublished doctoral dissertation, Harvard Business School.

Thomas, A. L. (1969). "The Allocation Problem in Financial Accounting Theory." *Studies in Accounting Research #3,* Sarasota, Fla.: American Accounting Association.

—— (1974). "The Allocation Problem: Part Two." *Studies in Accounting Research #9.* American Accounting Association.

—— (1977). "A Behavioural Analysis of Joint-Cost Allocation and Transfer Pricing." International Centre for Research in Accounting, University of Lancaster, England.

—— (1980). "Joint-Cost Allocation Revisited." ICRA Occasional Paper #20, International Centre for Research in Accounting, University of Lancaster, England.

Thomas, L. G., III (1986). "The Economics of Strategic Planning: A Survey of the Issues." In L. G. Thomas (ed.), *The Economics of Strategic Planning.* New York: Free Press, pp. 1–27.

Thompson, J. D. (1967). *Organizations in Action.* New York: McGraw-Hill.

Thompson, R. S. (1981). "Internal Organization and Profit: A Note." *Journal of Industrial Economics* 30, pp. 201–211.

Tiger, L. (1979). *Optimism: The Biology of Hope.* New York: Simon & Schuster.

Tirole, J. (1988). *The Theory of Industrial Organization.* Cambridge, Mass.: MIT Press.

Tushman, M. L., and P. Anderson (1986). "Technological Discontinuities and Organizational Environments." *Administrative Science Quarterly* 31, pp. 439–465.

Tushman, M. L., and D. A. Nadler (1978). "Information Processing as an Integrating Concept in Organizational Design." *Academy of Management Review* 3, pp. 613–624.

Tushman, M. L., W. H. Newman, and E. Romanelli (1986). "Convergence and Upheaval: Managing the Unsteady Pace of Organizational Evolution." *California Management Review* 28, pp. 29–44.

Tversky, A., and M. Bar-Hillel (1983). "Risk: The Long and the Short." *Journal of Experimental Psychology: Learning, Memory, and Cognition* 9, pp. 713–717.

Tversky, A., and D. Kahneman (1981). "The Framing of Decisions and the Psychology of Choice." *Science* 211, pp. 453–458.

—— (1983). "Extensional Versus Intuitive Reasoning: The Conjunction Fallacy in Probability Judgement." *Psychological Review* 90, pp. 293–315.

—— (1986). "Rational Choice and the Framing of Decisions." *Journal of Business* 59, pp. S251–S278.

—— (1991). "Reference Theory of Choice and Exchange." *Quarterly Journal of Economics* 106, pp. 1039–1061.

—— (1992). "Advances in Prospect Theory: Cumulative Representation of Uncertainty." *Journal of Risk and Uncertainty* 5, pp. 297–310.

Utterback, J. M., and W. Abernathy (1975). "A Dynamic Model of Process and Product Innovation." *OMEGA* 3, pp. 639–655.

Vancil, R. F. (1980). *Decentralization: Managerial Ambiguity by Design.* Homewood, Ill.: Dow Jones–Irwin.

Van Huyck, J., R. Battalio, and R. Beil (1991). "The Evolution of Convention in Experimental Coordination Games." Working paper, Texas A&M, Department of Economics.

Vernon, R. (1966). "International Investment and International Trade in the Product Cycle." *Quarterly Journal of Economics* 80(2), pp. 190–207.

Viscusi, K., W. Magat, and J. Huber (1987). "An Investigation of the Rationality of Consumer Valuations of Multiple Health Risks." *Rand Journal of Economics* 18, pp. 465–479.

von Neumann, J., and O. Morgenstern (1944). *The Theory of Games and Economic Behavior.* New York: John Wiley.

Vroom, V. (1964). *Work and Motivation.* New York: John Wiley.

Wack, P. (1985a). "Scenarios: Uncharted Waters Ahead." *Harvard Business Review* 63(5), pp. 73–89.

———— (1985b). "Scenarios: Shooting the Rapids." *Harvard Business Review* 63(6), pp. 139–150.

Walker, A. H., and J. W. Lorsch (1970). "Organizational Choice: Product versus Function." In J. W. Lorsch (ed.), *Studies in Organization Design.* Homewood, Ill.: Richard D. Irwin.

Walker, M. (1980). "On the Nonexistence of a Dominant Strategy Mechanism for Making Optimal Public Decisions." *Econometrica* 48, pp. 1521–1540.

Weber, M. (1947). "The Theory of Social and Economic Organization." In A. H. Henderson and T. Parsons (trans.), Glencoe, Ill.: Free Press (originally published in 1924).

Wehrung, D. A. (1989). "Risk Taking Over Gains and Losses: A Study of Oil Executives." *Annual Operation Research* 19, pp. 115–139.

Weick, K. E. (1979). *The Social Psychology of Organizing.* Reading, Mass.: Addison-Wesley.

———— (1987). "Substitutes for Strategy." In D. J. Teece (ed.), *The Competitive Challenge: Strategies for Industrial Innovation and Renewal.* Cambridge, Mass.: Ballinger, pp. 22–33.

Weigelt, K., and C. Camerer (1988). "Reputation and Corporate Strategy: Review of Recent Theory and Applications." *Strategic Management Journal* 9, pp. 443–454.

Weigelt, K., C. F. Camerer, and M. Hanna (forthcoming). "The Use of Experimental Economics in Strategy Research." In P. Shrivastava, J. Dutton, and A. Huff (eds.), *Advances in Strategic Management.* Vol. 8. Greenwich, Conn.: JAI Press.

Weingast, B. R. (1989). "Floor Behavior in the U.S. Congress: Committee Power under the Open Rule." *American Political Science Review* 83, September, pp. 795–815.

Wernerfelt, B. (1984a). "A Resource-Based View of the Firm." *Strategic Management Journal* 5(2), pp. 171–180.

———— (1984b). "Consumers with Differing Reaction Speeds, Scale Advantages, and Industry Structure." *European Economic Review* 24, pp. 246–251.

———— (1991). "Brand Loyalty and Market Equilibrium." *Marketing Science* 10, pp. 229–246.

Wernerfelt, B., and A. Karnani (1987). "Competitive Strategy Under Uncertainty." *Strategic Management Journal* 8(2), pp. 187–194.

Wernerfelt, B., and C. A. Montgomery (1988). "Tobin's q and the Importance of Focus in Firm Performance." *American Economic Review* 78, pp. 246–250.

Westney, E. (1993). "Institutionalization Theory and the Multinational Enterprise." In S. Ghoshal and E. Westney (eds.), *Organization Theory and the Multinational Corporation*. New York: St. Martin's Press.

White, H. C. (1981). "Where Do Markets Come From?" *American Journal of Sociology* 87, pp. 517–547.

—— (1988). "Varieties of Markets." In B. Wellman and S. D. Berkowitz (eds.), *Social Structures: A Network Approach*. Cambridge, England: Cambridge University Press, pp. 226–260.

Wildavsky, S. (1988). *Searching for Safety*. New Brunswick, N.J.: Transaction Books.

Wilkins, M. (1970). *The Emergence of the Multinational Enterprise: American Business Abroad from the Colonial Era to 1914*. Cambridge, Mass.: Harvard University Press.

Williams, J. R. (1983). "Technological Evolution and Competitive Response." *Strategic Management Journal* 4, pp. 56–66.

—— (1992). "How Sustainable Is Your Competitive Advantage?" *California Management Review* 34, pp. 29–51.

Williams, J. R., B. L. Paez, and L. Sanders (1988). "Conglomerates Revisited." *Strategic Management Journal* 9, pp. 403–414.

Williamson, O. E. (1964). *The Economics of Discretionary Behavior: Managerial Objectives in a Theory of the Firm*. Englewood Cliffs, N.J.: Prentice-Hall.

—— (1970). *Corporate Control and Business Behavior*. Englewood Cliffs, N.J.: Prentice-Hall.

—— (1971). "The Vertical Integration of Production: Market Failure Considerations." *American Economic Review* 61, May, pp. 112–123.

—— (1975). *Markets and Hierarchies: Analysis and Antitrust Implications*. New York: Free Press.

—— (1979). "Transaction-Cost Economics: The Governance of Contractual Relations." *Journal of Law and Economics* 22, October, pp. 233–261.

—— (1981a). "The Modern Corporation: Origins, Evolution, Attributes." *Journal of Economic Literature* 19, pp. 1537–1568.

—— (1981b). "The Economics of Organization: The Transaction Cost Approach." *American Journal of Sociology* 87, pp. 548–577.

—— (1983). "Credible Commitments: Using Hostages to Support Exchange." *American Economic Review* 73, September, pp. 519–540.

—— (1985). *The Economic Institutions of Capitalism*. New York: Free Press.

—— (1988a). "The Economics and Sociology of Organization: Promoting a Dialogue." In G. Farkas and P. England (eds.), *Industries, Firms, and Jobs*. New York: Plenum, pp. 159–185.

—— (1988b). "Corporate Finance and Corporate Governance." *Journal of Finance* 43, July, pp. 567–591.

—— (1988c). "Breach of Trust in Hostile Takeovers: Comment." In A. Auerbach (ed.), *Corporate Takeovers*. Chicago: University of Chicago Press, pp. 61–67.

—— (1989). "Transaction Cost Economics." In R. Schmalensee and R. Willig (eds.), *Handbook of Industrial Organization*. Vol. 1. Amsterdam: North Holland, pp. 135–182.

—— (1990a). "Comparative Economic Organization: The Analysis of Discrete Structural Alternatives." Unpublished manuscript.

—— (1990b). "Markets, Hierarchies, and the Modern Corporation: An Unfolding Perspective." Unpublished manuscript.

—— (1990c). "Chester Barnard and the Incipient Science of Organization." In O. Williamson, (ed.), *Organization Theory: From Chester Barnard to the Present and Beyond.* New York: Oxford University Press, pp. 172–206.

———— (1991). "Comparative Economic Organization: Analysis of Discrete Structural Alternatives." *Administrative Science Quarterly* 36, pp. 269–296.

Williamson, O. E., and W. G. Ouchi (1981). "The Markets and Hierarchies Program of Research: Origins, Implications, Prospects." In W. Joyce and A. Van de Ven (eds.), *Perspectives on Organizational Design and Behavior.* New York: John Wiley, pp. 347–370.

Wilson, J. Q. (1989). *Bureaucracy.* New York: Basic Books.

Wilson, R. (1983). "Auditing: Perspectives from Multiperson Decision Theory." *Accounting Review* 58, pp. 305–318.

Winter, S. G. (1987). "Knowledge and Competence as Strategic Assets." In D. J. Teece (ed.), *The Competitive Challenge: Strategies for Industrial Innovation and Renewal.* Cambridge, Mass.: Ballinger, pp. 159–184.

Wolfson, M. (1985). "Empirical Evidence of Incentive Problems and Their Mitigation in Oil and Gas Tax Shelter Programs." In J. Pratt and R. Zeckhauser (eds.), *Principals and Agents: The Structure of Business.* Boston: Harvard Business School Press, pp. 101–126.

Womsack, J., D. Jones, and D. Roos (1991). *The Machine That Changed the World.* Cambridge, Mass.: MIT Press.

Woodman, R., and L. Schoenfeldt (1990). "An Interactionist Model of Creative Behavior." *Journal of Creative Behavior* 24, pp. 10–20.

Woodward, J. (1965). *Industrial Organization: Theory and Practice.* New York: Oxford University Press.

Wrigley, L. (1970). *Divisional Autonomy and Diversification.* Unpublished doctoral dissertation, Harvard Business School.

Yao, D. A. (1988). "Beyond the Reach of the Invisible Hand: Impediments to Economic Activity, Market Failures, and Profitability." *Strategic Management Journal* 9, Special Issue, Summer, pp. 59–70.

Zajac, E. J., and M. Bazerman (1991). "Blind Spots in Industry and Competitor Analysis: Implications of Interfirm (Mis)perceptions for Strategic Decisions." *Academy of Management Review* 16, pp. 37–56.

Zucker, L. G. (1983). "Organizations as Institutions." In S. Bacharach (ed.), *Advances in Organizational Theory,* Vol. 2. Greenwich, Conn.: JAI Press, pp. 1–43.

———— (1987). "Institutional Theories of Organization." *Annual Review of Sociology* 13, pp. 443–464.

About the Contributors

Jay B. Barney is Associate Professor of Management at Texas A&M University. His research focuses on the relationship between idiosyncratic firm skills and capabilities and sustained competitive advantage. He is currently on the editorial boards of the *Academy of Management Review,* the *Strategic Management Journal,* and is associate editor at the *Journal of Management* and senior editor of *Organization Science.* He has written many articles and coauthored two books: *Organizational Economics* (with William G. Ouchi) and *Managing Organizations: Strategy, Structure, and Behavior* (with Ricky Griffin).

Colin Camerer is Professor of Strategy and Behavioral Science at the University of Chicago Graduate School of Business. His research includes experimental studies of behavior in risky decision making, competitive situations, and markets; and the incorporation of psychological principles into economic analysis.

Glenn R. Carroll is the Paul J. Cortese Professor of Management at the Haas School of Business, University of California at Berkeley. His most recent books include *Organizations in Industry* (forthcoming), coedited with Michael T. Hannan, and *Dynamics of Organizational Populations* (1992), also coauthored with Michael T. Hannan.

Alfred D. Chandler, Jr. is Straus Professor of Business History, Emeritus, at the Harvard Business School. He is the author of *Strategy and Structure* (1962), *The Visible Hand* (1977), awarded the Pulitzer and Bancroft prizes, and *Scale and Scope* (1990).

Yves L. Doz is the John H. Loudon Professor of International Management, and Associate Dean for Research and Development at INSEAD. His research on the strategy of multinational companies, with an emphasis on high-technology industries, has led to numerous publications, including three books: *The Multinational Mission: Balancing Local Demands and Global Vision* (1987, with C. K. Prahalad), *Strategic Management in Multinational Companies* (1986), and *Government Control and Multinational Management* (1979). Professor Doz is also the recipient of the A. T. Kearney Academy of Management Award.

Thomas H. Hammond is Associate Professor of Political Science at Michigan State University. His current research focuses on the development of formal models of bureaucratic structure and of legislature-bureaucracy interactions. His recent articles include "Toward a General Theory of Hierarchy: Books, Bureaucrats, Basketball Tournaments, and the Administrative Structure of the Nation-State" in the *Journal of Public Administration Research and Theory* (1993) and "Rethinking Allison's Models" in the *American Political Science Review* (1992).

Charles W. L. Hill is Professor of Strategic Management at the University of Washington School of Business. He is the author of many scholarly publications and serves on the board of five academic journals, including the *Academy of Management Review,* for which he is also a consulting editor. His research interests center on applying economic theory to problems of business and corporate strategy.

Daniel Kahneman is Eugene Higgins Professor of Psychology and Professor of Public Affairs at the Woodrow Wilson School, Princeton University. He has been a visiting professor at many universities, including Stanford and Harvard. He is the recipient of numerous awards, including the Distinguished Scientific Contribution Award, presented to him in 1992 by the Society of Consumer Psychology. Professor Kahneman is also the author of many articles.

Paul Krugman is Class of 1941 Professor of Economics at MIT. He has served on the U.S. Council of Economic Advisers. Currently he is also a research associate at the National Bureau of Economic Research and a member of the board of economists for the *Los Angeles Times*. His most recent publications include *The Age of Diminished Expectations* (1990), *Geography and Trade* (1991), and *Currencies and Crises* (1992).

Dan Lovallo is a doctoral student at the Haas School of Business at the University of California, Berkeley. His research interests include strategy formulation, behavioral decision research, and organizational decision making. Mr. Lovallo's dissertation is entitled, "Post-Entry Performance Differentials: A Psychological Perspective."

Richard R. Nelson is Professor of International and Public Affairs, Business, and Law at Columbia University. He is the former director of the Institute for Social and Policy Studies at Yale University. His research focuses largely on the process of long-run economic change, with an emphasis on technological advances and the evolution of economic institutions. In addition, Professor Nelson is the author of *National Innovation Systems: A Comparative Study* (1993) and numerous articles.

Michael E. Porter is the C. Roland Christensen Professor of Business Administration at the Harvard Business School and a leading authority on competitive strategy. He also lectures in Harvard Business School's programs for senior executives and speaks widely on competitive strategy to business and government audiences throughout the world. He is the author of many articles and fourteen books. In 1993, Professor Porter was named the Irwin Outstanding Educator in Business Policy and Strategy by the Academy of Management.

Steven Postrel is an Assistant Professor in the Policy and Organization area of the UCLA Anderson Graduate School of Management. His work has appeared in the *Journal of Industrial Economics, Industrial and Corporate Change,* and *Strategic Management Journal.* His research is currently focused on the economic properties of organizational procedures and work processes.

C. K. Prahalad is Professor of Corporate Strategy and International Business at the University of Michigan School of Business Administration. He has also taught at INSEAD and the Indian Institute of Management, Ahmedabad. His current research focuses on the strategic management of large diversified corporations and the role of top management. He has written several articles, including "Strategy as Stretch and Leverage" (1993), "The Core Competence of the Corporation" (1990), and "Do You Really Have a Global Strategy?" (1985), all coauthored with Gary Hamel.

Richard P. Rumelt is Professor of Business Policy at INSEAD. He is on long-term leave from UCLA's Anderson Graduate School of Management, where he holds the Elsa and Harry Kunin Chair in Business and Society.

Garth Saloner is the Robert A. Magowan Professor of Strategic Management and Economics at the Stanford University Graduate School of Business, where he heads the Strategic Management group. He has published numerous papers in refereed journals and books. His research focuses primarily on issues of strategic management, competitive strategy, industrial economics, and antitrust economics; he is currently one of the principal researchers on a major study of the worldwide computer industry funded by the Sloan Foundation.

Dan E. Schendel is Professor of Management at the Krannert Graduate School of Management at Purdue University. He is the founder and editor of the *Strategic Management Journal,* published by John Wiley. The journal is the first to focus on issues of strategic management. Professor Schendel is also the founding president and member of the executive committee and board of the Strategic Management Society (SMS). He is the coauthor of *Divided Loyalties: Whistle Blowing at BART, Strategy Formulation: Analytical Concepts,* and *Strategic Management: A New View of Business Policy and Planning* and author of numerous papers on strategic planning systems, marketing, and strategy formulation.

Andrei Shleifer is a professor of economics at Harvard University and editor of the *Quarterly Journal of Economics.* He has published numerous articles in the areas of financial economics, economic growth, and problems of transition from socialism. In addition, he serves as a senior foreign adviser to the Russian privatization effort. Professor Shleifer received the 1989 Presidential Young Investigator Award in Economics.

David J. Teece is Mitsubishi Bank Professor at the Haas School of Business, University of California, Berkeley. He is associate editor of *California Management Review* and editor of *Journal of Industrial and Corporate Change*. He is the author of numerous articles and has served as a consultant to many corporations, including ARCO, AT&T, Chevron, and McDonnell Douglas.

Robert W. Vishny is Eric J. Gleacher Professor of Finance at the University of Chicago. He is associate editor of the *Journal of Financial Economics* and the *Journal of Finance*. In collaboration with Andrei Shleifer, he has written several articles on privatization in Russia.

Jeffrey R. Williams is Professor of Strategy at the Graduate School of Industrial Administration at Carnegie-Mellon University. He has written many papers, including works in *The Journal of Law and Economics, The Journal of Economic Behavior and Organization,* and studies for the Federal Trade Commission, the Sloan Foundation, and the National Science Foundation. He is also on the editorial board of the *Strategic Management Journal*. Professor Williams received the 1992 *California Management Review* Pacific Telesis Award for his article, "How Sustainable Is Your Competitive Advantage?"

Oliver E. Williamson is the Transamerica Professor of Business, Economics, and Law at the University of California, Berkeley. His recent research focuses on the logic of organization, especially as viewed from the transaction cost economizing perspective. He is currently applying his research to a side-by-side comparison of public and private bureaus.

Index